GOVERNMENT FOR EVERYBODY

To the memory of my mother, Elizabeth Lauckhardt Jantzen, from whom I learned the pleasure of reading widely and the importance of writing well.

ABOUT THE AUTHOR. Steven L. Jantzen began his career in education and publishing as a high school teacher of history and government. Since 1971, when he published his first book, he has been writing and editing educational materials. Previous books by Mr. Jantzen include a history of World War I and textbooks in citizenship, American history, and world history.

GOVERNMENT FOR EVERYBODY

Revised

Steven L. Jantzen

AMSCO SCHOOL PUBLICATIONS, INC.
315 Hudson Street / New York, N.Y. 10013

Reviewers

Joel Fischer
Social Studies Consultant
Lake Oswego, Oregon

Karen E. Hoppes
Social Studies Teacher
Rex Putnam High School
North Clackamas, Oregon

Jane Wang Moy
Social Studies Teacher
Chicago, Illinois

Romeo Randolph
Chairman, Social Studies Department
Miami Senior High School
Miami, Florida

Edwin Selzer
Assistant Principal, Social Studies
Eastern District High School
Brooklyn, New York

Gloria Sesso
Supervisor of Social Studies
Half Hollow Hills Central School District
Dix Hills, New York

When ordering this book, please specify:
R 512 S or GOVERNMENT FOR EVERYBODY, SOFTBOUND
or
R 512 H or GOVERNMENT FOR EVERYBODY, HARDBOUND

ISBN 0-87720-864-6 (Softbound)
ISBN 0-87720-862-X (Hardbound)

Printed in the United States of America

A Textbook as Travel Guide

A trip across country to Washington, D.C., could begin anywhere. From San Francisco, a tour bus would cross the Rocky Mountains on Interstate 80 and complete the 2,843-mile trip in three days and nights of hard driving. Leaving for Washington on the same day, a car heading north from Florida and another car heading south from Maine might eventually meet in bumper-to-bumper traffic at the Washington Monument.

We can also conceive of a different kind of trip—one that takes place in the mind and the imagination. Instead of following an interstate highway to the White House and the Capitol, this book invites you to travel *mentally* over paths that lead to an understanding of our system of government. The route to that understanding can be mapped as follows:

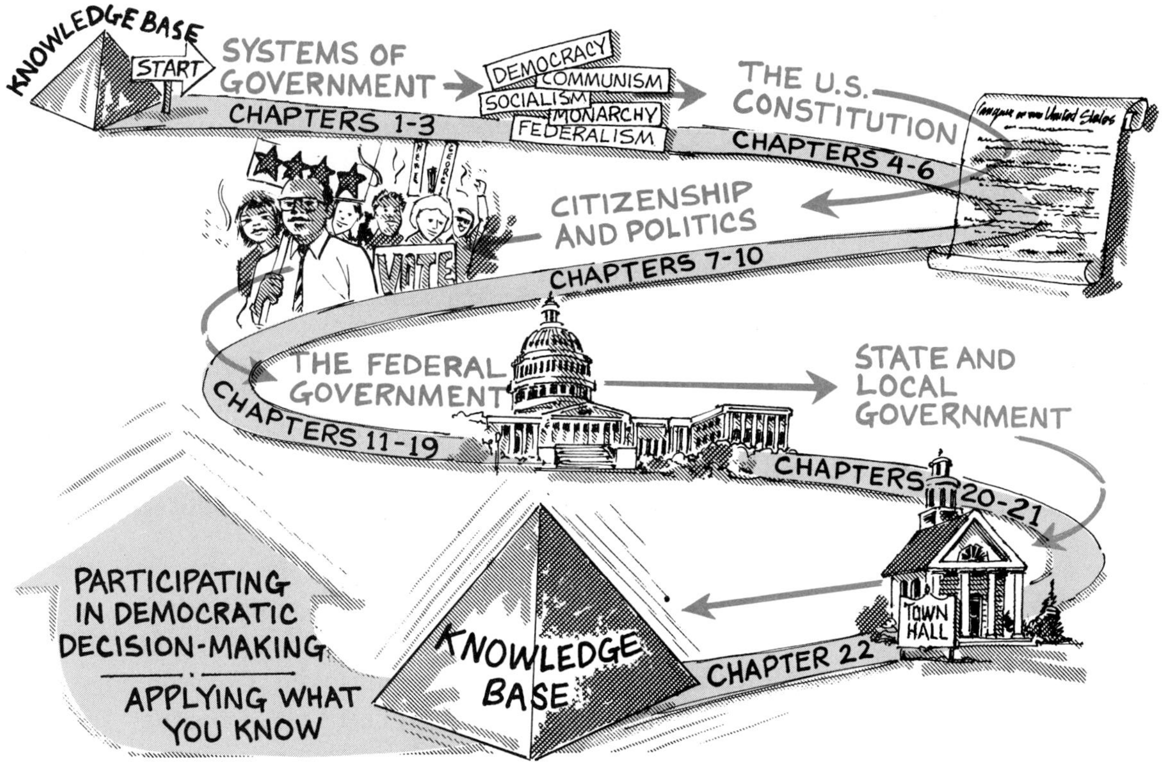

The route leads out from your base of knowledge and continues through 22 chapters to an expanded knowledge of your country's government.

By following the above route, you can expect to learn: (*a*) how the U.S. system of government differs from other governments, (*b*) how and why the U.S. Constitution divides powers among three branches of government, (*c*) how a citizen can influence government decisions at every level, (*d*) how decisions are made in the nation's capital, (*e*) how decisions are made in the state capital, and (*f*) how decisions are made at city hall.

Along the way, you will acquire an ability that is essential to your becoming an effective citizen in a democracy. That is the ability to *apply* your expanding knowledge of American government to current issues and to social and economic problems that directly affect you. Of course, the most important application of your knowledge will be your participation in the democratic process as a voter and a citizen.

To help make your educational trip through this text both interesting and worthwhile, we have included the following special features:

- ***chapter objectives.*** Every chapter begins with a list of learning objectives so that you know in advance to focus your study of the chapter on certain topics and skills. Tests for *Government for Everybody* (provided separately in an *Activities and Tests* book) are tied to these objectives.
- ***skills checks.*** Included in every chapter is a feature that develops your ability to make comparisons, distinguish facts and opinions, conduct research, think critically about political issues, and analyze the information in charts, maps, graphs, and political cartoons.
- ***cartoon corners.*** Included in every chapter is at least one cartoon that presents a major principle of U.S. government. (See, for example, pages 7, 72, and 109.)
- ***case studies.*** The closer you come to seeing government at work the more interesting and understandable the subject becomes. That is why this book gives detailed accounts of such topics as a candidate's campaign (pages 241–245), a senator's workday (pages 284–285), and a court's decision (pages 348–350).
- ***vocabulary builders.*** Vocabulary-building exercises in every chapter enable you to master hundreds of key terms from politics and government.
- ***chapter summaries.*** Every chapter ends with a summary in which *you* supply the missing terms.
- ***picture previews.*** Every unit begins with a picture quiz. (See, for example, pages 2–3.) Your answers to quiz questions might be only guesses at the start of the unit but known facts at the end.

The millions of tourists who annually visit Washington's gleaming white buildings may think of government as some awesome and distant marble structure. This view of government is common—but mistaken. Government consists, instead, of human beings dealing with significant problems that affect all of us. You will begin to see the human side of government as you read the first unit of this text.

The trip to political knowledge and understanding begins now. As a citizen and former teacher, I have made the trip many times—each time discovering something new about the American political process. As the author of this "travel guide" to political knowledge, I wish you a pleasant and successful journey.

Steven L. Jantzen

CONTENTS

Skills Checks

GOVERNMENT FOR EVERYBODY

a.

b.

a. Thomas Jefferson
b. Inca woman
c. Patrick Henry
d. factory worker in China
e. Frederick Douglass

c.

d.

e.

f. Abraham Lincoln
g. American shop owner
h. Prime Minister John Major
i. Swedish doctor

f.

g.

h.

i.

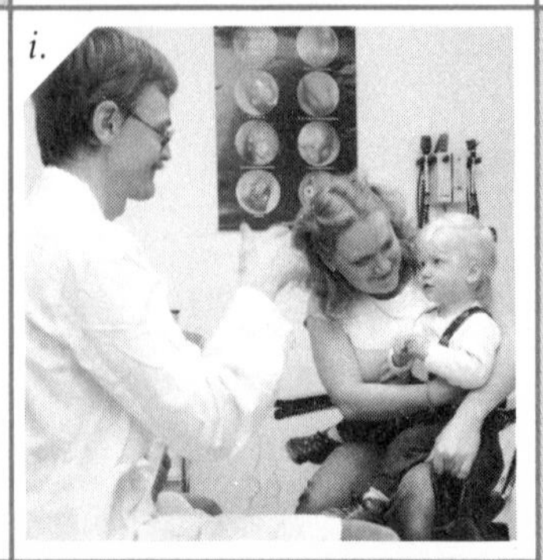

UNIT ONE

Government of the People

PICTURE PREVIEW

Pictured on the opposite page are nine people—some famous, some not. All are related in some way either to the U.S. government or the government of a foreign country. Each person represents one of the topics and ideas that you will be studying in this unit.

How much do you already know about governments of the United States and the world? Quiz yourself by trying to match the people described below with their pictures. (NOTE: Some pictures may match more than one description of a person.)

1. These *two* people were leaders of the American Revolution against British rule.
2. This person is allowed to vote only for the candidates of one political party.
3. This person wrote the Declaration of Independence.
4. Though American-born, this person was not protected by the U.S. Bill of Rights.
5. This person lived in a South American empire ruled by a powerful monarch.
6. These *three* Americans risked their lives for the sake of liberty.
7. Because of the capitalist system, this person is free to seek profits and to succeed or fail in a private enterprise, or business.
8. These *two* people are not elected officials and yet they are employed by the governments of their countries.
9. These *three* people were elected to be leaders of their democratically governed countries.
10. This person is the leader of a parliamentary form of government.

The answers, given below, will be fully explained in the chapters that follow. Each chapter points out ways that our own government compares with other governments of the world. At the end of the unit, you will understand why Abraham Lincoln said that the United States has a "government of the people, by the people, for the people."

Answers

1. *a, c* 3. *a* 5. *b* 7. *g* 9. *a, f, h*
2. *d* 4. *e* 6. *a, c, e* 8. *d, i* 10. *h*

THE JOHNSTOWN FLOOD. The city of Johnstown, Pennsylvania, was almost completely destroyed in 1889 when a heavy rain and broken dam caused one of the worst disasters in U.S. history. Immediately after the flood, why did survivors form a new government?

CHAPTER 1

The Goals of Government

OBJECTIVES

After reading this chapter, you will know

1. the meaning of key words: **government, politics,** and **nation.**
2. reasons why governments are organized.
3. goals of the U.S. government.
4. how the U.S. government is both like and unlike another government (the Inca Empire of Peru).
5. how to tell the difference between facts and opinions.

It had rained hard all day. By midafternoon, the streets of Johnstown, Pennsylvania, were already flooded. Then, from the hills to the east, came a strange and terrifying sound. At first, there was a deep rumble and then a thundering roar. To one person, it sounded like ten freight trains hurtling into town at full speed.

Tumbling down the hillside into the Pennsylvania town was a mass of water—an entire lake. For many years, this lake had been a nice quiet spot for fishing. But the heavy rains that day had brought the level of the lake up to the top of a poorly built dam. The pressure was too much, and the dam gave way. So, from high in the hills, the lake came spilling down into the valley—right into Johnstown.

The center of the oncoming wave was more than 30 feet high. It swept everything before it—railroad cars, barns, trees, and the bodies of drowned horses. Like a gigantic bulldozer, it slammed into houses and stores. In a matter of minutes, hundreds of people drowned. Those who survived clung to rooftops that bobbed on the raging waters like rafts.

The next day, Sunday, the town was a muddy wreck. Stunned, shivering survivors of the flood wandered about, looking for lost relatives. Who was dead? Who was alive? Nobody knew. The city's leaders were missing. Someone had the idea of holding a public meeting in the one schoolhouse that was still standing. At this meeting, people agreed right away that some kind of *government* was needed. A leader was quickly elected and given power to make laws and appoint deputies.

This leader organized small groups to work on different tasks. One group was to form a police force to keep order. Another group was to start the heavy labor of clearing away the wreckage and rebuilding. A third group was to establish temporary hospitals to care for all the injured. A fourth group was to bring dead bodies to a central spot so that relatives might identify them.

Slowly, under their temporary government, the survivors of the flood rebuilt their town. They hauled away the rubbish and buried the dead. As they did so, they counted more than 2,000 people who had perished in the disaster.

The Johnstown flood occurred over 100 years ago—in 1889. Why is the story of that

AFTER THE FLOOD. A historian wrote of the Johnstown wreckage: "Houses were dumped every which way, crushed, broken, split clean in half, or lying belly up in the mire." If the survivors had chosen you to lead Johnstown's government in this emergency, what would have been some of your commands? If a disaster like this occurred today, would you expect government to provide help?

flood included in a book about government? Consider the very first thing that the survivors decided to do after the disaster. They formed a government. Why do you think they did this before anything else?

In this chapter, you will find out what governments are. After reading the chapter, you will know the answers to these questions:

1. Why are governments organized?
2. What are the goals of government?

1. WHY ARE GOVERNMENTS ORGANIZED?

On television news shows, we hear reporters talking constantly about three things: governments, politics, and nations. The words are familiar, but what exactly do they mean? Let us start with GOVERNMENT. How shall we define it?

What is government? Here are two possible definitions of government. Which do you think is the right one?

A. Government is a system—or orderly plan—for managing a group of people.

B. Government is the leader (or leaders) who make laws for society and see that people obey the laws.

Did you choose Definition A? Correct! Every government in the world is a system for managing a group, or community, of people. The size of the governed group could be as small as a family or as large as a nation. Each has a system of some kind for keeping order. Take the community of Johnstown, Pennsylvania, as an example. After the flood, the system set up by the people was a simple one. One person was told by the others: "You take over. Tell us what to do." In the emergency, Johnstown's system of government could be described like this: One leader makes all the laws for the good of the community.

Did you choose Definition B instead? It too is correct. Government is also the people who are put in charge of running the system. We expect these government leaders and officials to take responsibility for the welfare of the entire community.

Since both definitions are correct, let us combine them into one:

GOVERNMENT: a system for managing a community or nation and the leaders or lawmakers who control that system.

What is politics? A second term, POLITICS, has two meanings. First it means anything that involves government. If people argue about government, we say that their differences of opinion are of a political kind. If governments draw boundaries on a map, we say they are political boundaries.

The second meaning of politics is illustrated by the cartoon below. In the cartoon, notice that the van stands for a NATION (any nation of the world). In the back seats are passengers who disagree about what the driver should do. ("Slow down!" . . . "Faster!" . . . "Let me drive!") The attempt of these *citizens* to influence government represents POLITICS.

The people of a nation often disagree about where government should be taking them. One group of people may want changes in the laws, while others are satisfied and oppose any change. Different groups compete for the right to be in the "driver's seat," governing the nation. To settle their argument, one group may even use force against the other. More often, the argument is settled by some peaceful means—such as holding an election.

The second meaning of politics may be stated this way:

> POLITICS: the process of deciding who gets to run the government and make its laws.

What is a nation? A *nation* may be as large as the United States, Canada, or China. It may also be as small as the island nations of Cyprus, Fiji, or Grenada. These places on the map are rightly called "nations" because they have these four characteristics:

CARTOON CORNER

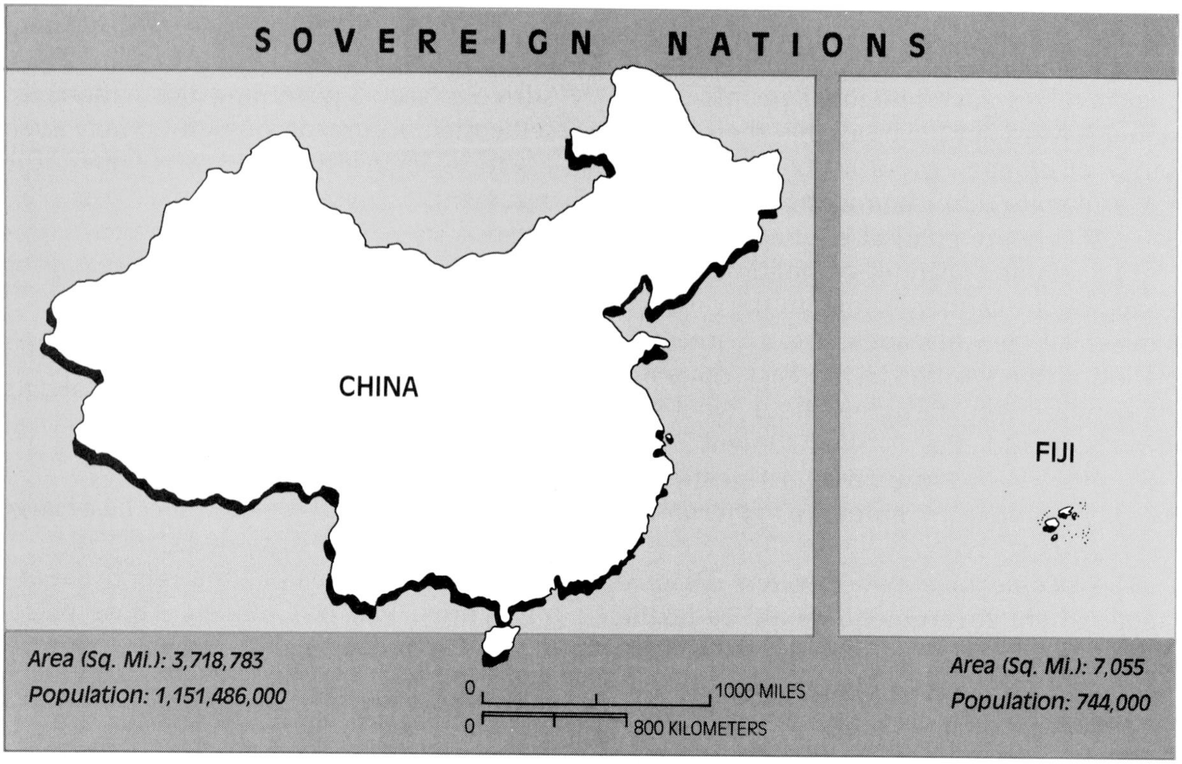

1. Land with definite boundaries
2. People living on the land who have much in common. (Most speak the same language and celebrate the same public holidays.)
3. A system of government
4. Sovereignty. To be *sovereign* means to be completely independent from outside control. The United States is sovereign because its government is free to make laws for the American people. No foreign government can interfere.

Thus, a nation may be defined like this:

> NATION: a people with common customs whose government has sovereign control over a certain territory.

Why are governments organized? So far, we have answered three questions beginning with WHAT? (What is government? What is politics? What is a nation?) Now comes a harder type of question: WHY? Why do all groups (such as the survivors of the Johnstown flood) need to be governed? Why do nations in particular have governments?

Let us start with a list of three reasons for organizing governments. Other reasons will be added later in the chapter.

1. For giving order to a group. Have you ever been in a group where nobody knew what was happening? If so, you may have felt uneasy, even lost. It is a natural feeling. People generally feel insecure without some system of order. They badly want to know what the rules are for living and working in a group. Such rules (or laws) are provided by government.

2. For protection against danger. The flood that wrecked Johnstown in 1889 is just one example of the dangers faced by everyone at all times. Besides floods, there are dangers from storms, fires, accidents, thefts, diseases, and wars. Government is expected to help ward off such disasters. If it fails (as in the case of Johnstown), people expect government to lead them out of trouble.

3. *For the public good (or welfare).* What is the "public good"? It could be providing hospitals for the sick. It could be providing schools for the young. In fact, it could be anything at all that people think is good for their society. Read again, on page 5, about the decisions of Johnstown's government after the flood. How did it decide to serve the public good (or welfare) in that emergency?

In the next section of this chapter, you will read about two governments: one in Peru, the other in the United States. As you will see, each used different methods for achieving much the same goals.

REVIEW

A. Building Your Political Vocabulary

Quoted below are definitions from *Webster's Ninth New Collegiate Dictionary.* Which do you think is the definition for: (*a*) **nation;** (*b*) **government;** (*c*) **politics;** and (*d*) **sovereignty?** On a separate sheet of paper, write the letter of the correct choice next to each number.

1. "The art or science concerned with winning and holding control over a government."
2. "The organization, machinery, or agency through which a political unit exercises authority."
3. "Freedom from external control."
4. "A territorial division containing a body of people of one or more nationalities and possessing a more or less defined territory and government."

B. Applying What You Know

Think of the community (city, town, or county) in which you live. Answer the following questions about this community by applying what you have learned so far about government.

1. Why does your community have a government?
2. Would you call it a sovereign community? Why or why not?
3. What groups can you think of that are probably involved in the politics of the community?
4. What examples can you give of how the community's government maintains order?
5. What examples can you give of how the community's government protects people from danger?
6. What examples can you give of how your community's government tries to serve "the public good"?

C. Agree or Disagree

Say whether you **agree** or **disagree** with each statement and tell why.

1. Everyone has political opinions.
2. Government's decisions and laws affect everybody.
3. The most important thing that government can do for people is to protect them from dangers.

D. Project

Watch a half-hour TV news program. Take notes on any news story that involves politics, either in the United States or in a foreign nation. (You should find **at least five** examples of current politics.)

2. WHAT ARE THE GOALS OF GOVERNMENT?

As you know, governments everywhere share certain goals in common. They maintain order, protect against dangers, and provide for the general welfare. Do not suppose, however, that all governments are alike. Some are strong, while others are weak. Some governments use their power for the good of all, while others use power in harsh and cruel ways.

We can better appreciate our own U.S. government if we compare it with a different government. For this purpose, let us examine the goals of a government that was once one of the strongest in the world. This was the Inca government, which, 500 years ago, ruled a vast empire in South America. Then we shall compare the Incas' goals with those of the U.S. government.

CASE STUDY: Goals of the Inca Government

The lands ruled by the Incas formed what we call an empire. An *empire* consists of formerly independent peoples who have been brought under the rule of one government.

The shape of the Inca Empire was both very narrow and very long. It stretched along the Pacific Coast of South America for about 2,500 miles. On the one hand, the Inca Empire was a spectacular achievement. The king who ruled this *monarchy* created a strong system for maintaining order. On the other hand, 6,000,000 Indians under Inca control were treated almost as slaves. They were allowed very little personal freedom.

Total power of the Inca monarch. Governments have three kinds of power. They have *legislative power* when they make laws for the nation. They have *executive power* when they direct officials, such as the police, to see that laws are obeyed. They have *judicial power* when they judge the guilt or innocence of accused lawbreakers. The Inca monarch possessed all three kinds of power.

In his legislative role, the monarch was the empire's only lawmaker. One of his laws, for example, was a *regulation* (rule) for marriage. Indian men who remained single after their twentieth birthday were

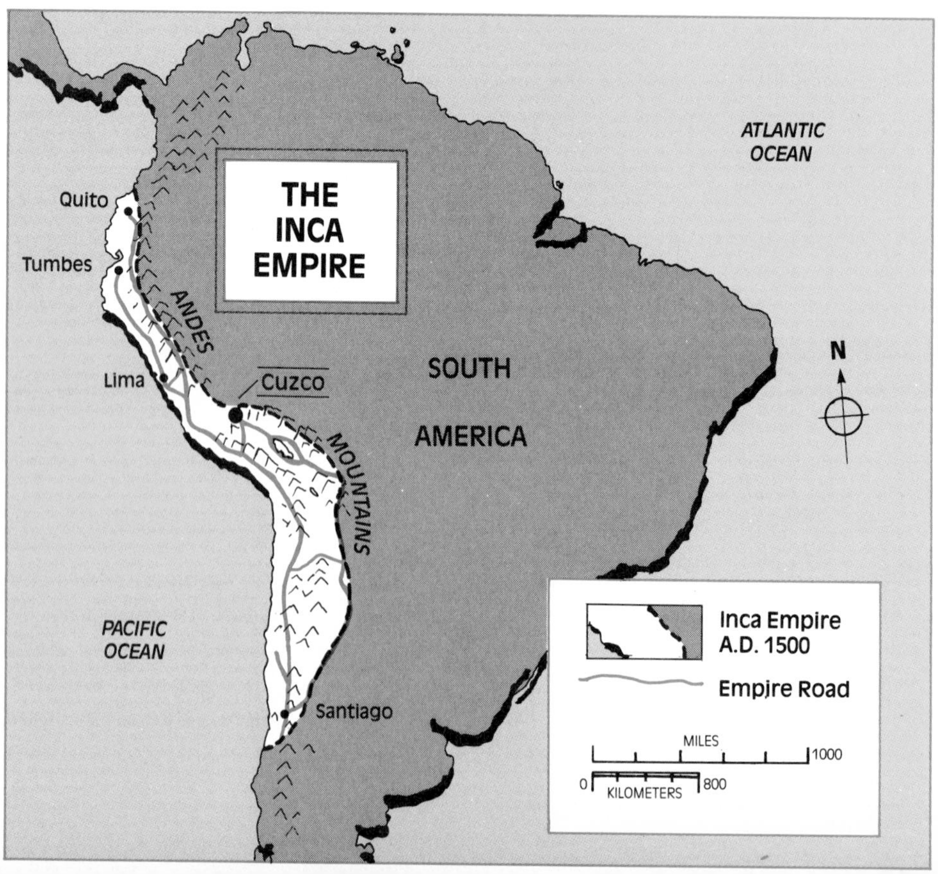

forced to marry. An Inca official would come into a village and order single women to line up against a wall. Single men older than 20 lined up opposite them. Then the official would point out which man was to marry which woman.

In his executive role, the Inca monarch commanded an army that put down rebellions and arrested lawbreakers. He also ordered officials to see that his royal highways were kept in good repair.

In his judicial role, the Inca monarch was the supreme judge of the empire. Political enemies were brought before him for trial. If found guilty, they were fed to beasts or snakes in the royal dungeon.

Punishments for breaking Inca laws. Establishing order, as you know, is a major goal of government. Laws are so important to keeping order that we often speak of "law and order" as if they were one thing.

To keep order, Inca rulers made laws about such crimes as killing, stealing, and destroying property. The penalties for breaking some of these laws may seem cruel. A common Inca punishment was to break a criminal's back by dropping a heavy stone on it.

Inca men and women were not equal under the law. A husband could kill his wife without penalty if she was unfaithful to him. But if a wife was found guilty of killing her husband for the same reason, she was hung up by her heels in view of her neighbors. Dangling upside down, she would suffer agony for days until death finally came.

GREAT WALL OF INCA PERU. Huge stones carved expertly by Indian laborers formed the wall of an Inca fortress near Cuzco. What purpose of government was probably served by the creation of a walled fortress?

SKILLS CHECK: Telling facts from opinions

Think for a minute about the information you have just read. To be a skillful reader, you need to know when a certain sentence is giving a *fact* and when it is giving an *opinion.* A fact is something that can be proved to be true. For example, it is a fact that Incas punished criminals by breaking their backs. An opinion is something that is felt or believed to be true, but cannot be proved. It is an opinion, for example, that the Inca forms of punishment were cruel.

The statements below present either a fact or an opinion. For each statement, write either **F** (fact) or **O** (opinion). If the statement is an opinion, tell whether you **agree** or **disagree** with it and explain why.

1. The Inca Empire was a spectacular achievement.
2. In the Inca system of government, only the monarch had the power to make laws.
3. We should admire the Inca government because of the way it maintained law and order.
4. Political enemies were tried in the presence of the Inca monarch.
5. Any laws that treat women differently from men are unfair.
6. In the Inca Empire, marriage choices were sometimes dictated by the government.

Inca roads and road runners. The Inca Empire was most powerful during the 15th century (from 1401–1500). Of course it had no telegraphs or telephones. How then could the monarch keep in touch with what was happening in remote towns 1,000 miles from his palace in the capital of Cuzco?

The monarch relied for information upon four gigantic roads that led out from Cuzco to the empire's farthest borders. An Inca law forced many thousands of Indians to build and maintain the government's highways. In addition, hundreds of Indians were made to travel the roads as runners and messengers.

The Incas had no horses, no wheeled vehicles, and no form of writing. All government messages had to be passed along by word of mouth from one human runner to the next. Hundreds of huts, spaced about a mile apart, were built along the two highways. One message, for example, might be a command from the Inca monarch in Cuzco to one of his army chiefs. A runner would sprint down the road from Cuzco for about a mile to the next relay station. Panting for breath, he would shout the message to the next runner, who memorized it as he ran the next leg of the relay. Thus, the monarch's messages were sent the length of the empire at the rate of 150 miles a day.

This system of roads and relay runners was vital. It speeded up the movement not only of information but also of conquering Inca armies. Without its long royal highways, the Inca Empire could not have held together. The Inca roads are an example of government's role in unifying and defending a nation.

Inca welfare system. Another marvel of the Inca Empire was its system of storing supplies of food. Along the royal roads at regular distances were storehouses owned by the government. Indians were required to fill up these buildings with baskets of food—corn, beans, and dried llama meat.

A portion of this food supply was sent to feed the king and his huge staff of palace servants. Other portions of it were fed to Inca armies as they marched through a region. There was still enough food left over for local emergencies. In times of bad weather and poor harvests, the Inca government opened its storehouses to keep the people from starving.

BRIDGE TO THE INCA PAST. Though rebuilt, this bridge in Peru is nearly identical to the one that Inca messengers would have used. What goal of *every* government is served by the building of bridges?

In this Inca system, we see an example of the *welfare* function of government.

End of the Inca Empire. While it lasted, the power of the Inca monarch was total. But in 1533, he was captured and killed by a small army of invading Spaniards. After the great monarch's death, the Inca Empire could not continue because it had depended so completely on the rule of one man.

REVIEW

A. Building Your Political Vocabulary

Write an original sentence about the Inca Empire using each of the following terms:

judicial
legislative
executive
regulate
law and order

B. Applying What You Know

In the previous section (pages 9–13), you learned that governments perform three functions:

1. giving order to a group
2. protecting the group from various dangers
3. serving the public good—or welfare

For each function, say whether you think the Inca government did a **good job** or a **poor job** in carrying it out. Give specific facts from the reading to support your opinion.

▶ CASE STUDY: Goals of the U.S. Government

The American people have a form of government that is nearly the opposite of the Inca government. Our government is the original invention of a group of talented men, including George Washington, James Madison, Thomas Jefferson, and Benjamin Franklin. The system of government that they created in 1787 has lasted for more than 200 years.

The document that describes our national government is the United States Constitution. The Constitution begins with three famous words: "We the people. . . ." In one powerful sentence, known as its *Preamble,* the Constitution presents the six purposes of the "people's" government:

GOVERNMENT FOR EVERYBODY. What political goals are served by the laws made in the U.S. Capitol?

We the people of the United States, in order to form a more perfect union, establish justice, insure domestic tranquillity, provide for the common defense, promote the general welfare, and secure the blessings of liberty to ourselves and our posterity, do ordain and establish this Constitution for the United States of America.

The first five purposes in the Preamble are similar to what *all* governments are supposed to do. Inca monarchs as well as U.S. presidents were concerned about these five. Let's see what each means.

1. "To form a more perfect union." In 1787, states such as New York and Virginia were nearly sovereign. They could not be forced to obey the laws passed by a weak U.S. Congress. Therefore, a stronger plan of government, the Constitution, was thought to be needed. Greater unity among the states—"a more perfect *union*"—was the new government's first important goal.

Recall that Inca monarchs were also concerned about unity. Why did they order roads to be built from one end of the empire to the other? It was a means of bringing all parts of the empire under control as a united whole.

2. To "establish justice" Justice is an ancient goal of government. It refers to the government's methods for deciding whether a person has or has not broken a law, and, if so, what the punishment shall be. Justice also refers to the way government settles disputes between people in a fair way. Such disputes may be about property (who owns it?) or an accidental injury (who caused it?).

Different societies have different ideas about what is just (fair) and unjust. The Incas believed it was just to hang a lawbreaker upside down until he or she died. That is not our idea of justice, which will be described in later chapters of this book.

3. To "insure domestic tranquillity." Domestic tranquillity is just another way of saying law and order. It means that rioting and armed rebellion will not occur. If they do occur, the government will be strong enough to bring the riots to an end.

In the Inca Empire, "domestic tranquillity" depended on the ability of the monarch's armies to crush rebellions.

4. To "provide for the common defense." In George Washington's time, this goal involved training soldiers to shoot muskets and cannon. In our own time, it includes training pilots to fly air force jets. But the goal remains the same: defending our nation's borders from possible attack.

Could any government *not* care about "the common defense"? After all, the very survival of the nation depends upon it. The Inca government devoted much care to strengthening its armies. But in the end, the armies failed to stop invasion by foreign enemies. The Inca Empire ceased to exist.

5. To "promote the general welfare." The welfare of the American people is daily promoted by government roads, post offices, parks, and Social Security checks.

PARKS AND PLANES. What purposes of the U.S. Constitution are illustrated by the U.S. national forest (left) and the U.S. fighter plane (right)?

How did the Incas promote the general welfare of their empire?

6. To "secure the blessings of liberty." Despite some similarities to other governments, the U.S. government is also unique, or unlike any other government. One quality, among many, that makes it unique is the sixth goal of the Constitution—*liberty*. Liberty means that government respects everyone's basic right to think, speak, and act freely and without fear.

The Inca monarchs did not know the meaning of the word "liberty." The only purpose of their laws was to keep people firmly under their control. The Inca rulers decided what woman was to be married to what man. They decided where people could and could not make their homes. They even dictated the style of dress of their subjects. In other words, individuals were not allowed free choice.

Not all governments controlled people's lives as much as this. English kings, for example, did not usually interfere with marriage choices. But most kings in England and other parts of Europe had no interest in protecting a citizen's liberty. Until 1787, no government had made liberty into a positive goal—a goal equal in importance to defense and law and order. By mentioning liberty among the purposes of government, the U.S. Constitution did something daring and original.

How do "We the people" and our government "secure the blessings of liberty"? How can we have both liberty *and* law and order at the same time? You will be seeking answers to these important questions in later chapters.

REVIEW

A. Applying What You Know

This section has identified six goals of the U.S. government. It has also given examples of each goal. Other examples exist in your own community. Located close to your home are these offices of the national (U.S.) government or your local government:

1. post office for delivering mail (U.S. government)
2. Social Security office for aiding the elderly and the disabled (U.S. government)
3. courthouse for conducting trials (local government)
4. police department for maintaining law and order (local government)
5. recreation department for maintaining parks and playgrounds (local government)
6. recruiting office for enlisting men and women in the armed forces (U.S. government)

For each of the six examples of government at work, tell which of the six goals of the

U.S. Constitution is served by it. Explain your answers.

B. Making Comparisons

The skill of making comparisons involves two steps. The first step is to tell how the things being compared are **alike.** The second step is to tell how they are **different.** Write two paragraphs about the U.S. government as it compares with the Inca government. In your first paragraph, mention similarities. In your second, differences.

CHAPTER REVIEW

A. Completing the Summary

Select terms from the list below to fill in the blanks in the summary. Write your answers on a separate piece of paper.

Constitution	monarch
executive	nation
government	politics
judicial	sovereign
leaders	tranquillity
legislative	welfare
liberty	

After the flood wiped out much of Johnstown, Pennsylvania, the survivors' first thought was to organize a __(1)__. This event is an example of how important government is to everybody.

Government may be defined as a system of managing a community or nation as well as the __(2)__ who control that system. A __(3)__ is any group of people whose government controls a certain territory. A nation's government is completely independent, or __(4)__.

People often disagree about how the government of a nation or a state should be run. How they choose leaders and policies is one meaning of the word __(5)__.

The ancient government of the Incas was compared with our own U.S. government. The Inca __(6)__ had total political power over the empire he ruled. In making all the laws for the empire, he had __(7)__ power. In seeing that his laws were enforced, he had __(8)__ power. By acting as the supreme judge of individual cases, he had __(9)__ power.

The Inca ruler relied upon his armies to prevent rebellions and thus to preserve "domestic __(10)__." He relied upon storehouses of food on royal highways to serve the public __(11)__.

The Preamble of the United States __(12)__ lists six goals of our own national government. Five of these goals are common to most governments. But a sixth goal was unusual: to "secure the blessings of __(13)__."

B. Making Comparisons

Tell which government is described by each of the phrases, 1–15, below. Does the phrase describe:

A. the Inca government only?
B. the U.S. government only?
C. both governments?
D. neither government?

Write the **letter** of each answer on a separate sheet of paper.

1. punished those who broke the laws
2. contained many states within its borders
3. built and maintained roads
4. fed the people in times of emergency
5. used large numbers of officials to enforce the laws
6. provided protection against foreign enemies
7. relied totally upon the decisions of one leader
8. exercised legislative powers
9. conducted trials to determine a person's guilt or innocence
10. directed the movement of armies
11. was based upon a written constitution
12. controlled marriage choices
13. encouraged individual liberty
14. attempted to unify the nation
15. attempted to maintain domestic tranquillity

C. Word Pyramid

Words defined in this chapter are arranged in the pyramid below. For each word or word group, carry out the instructions directly beneath it. Write your answers on a piece of paper.

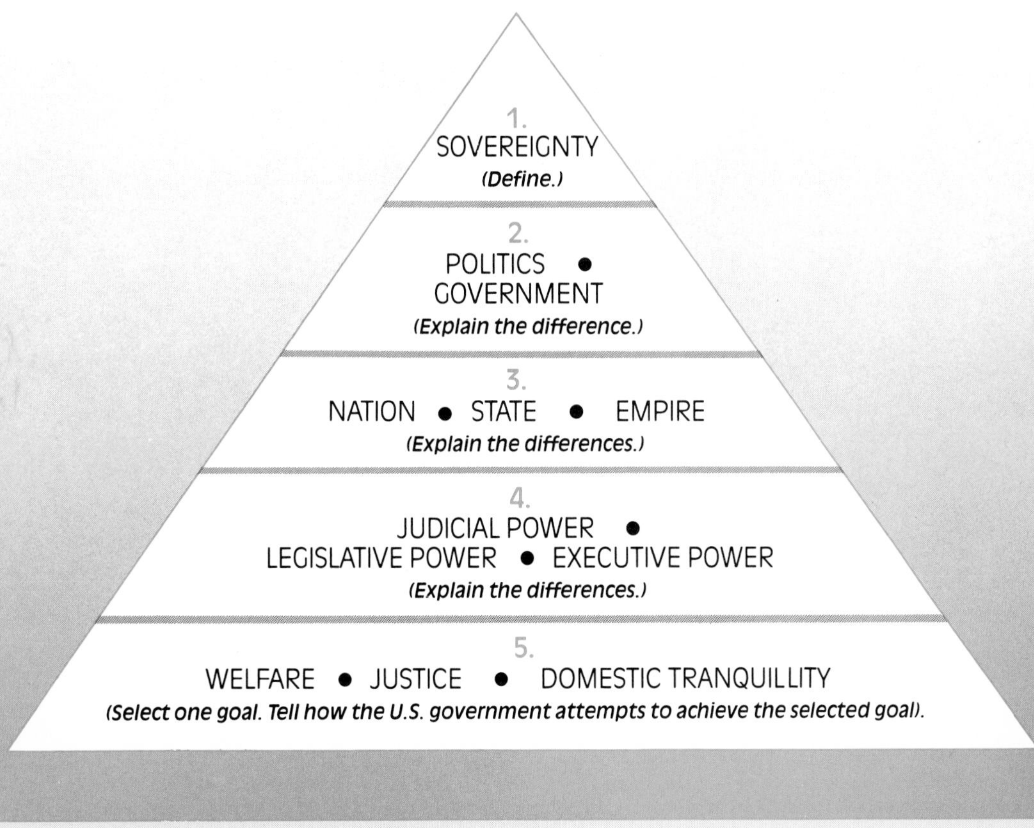

1.
SOVEREIGNTY
(Define.)
2.
POLITICS • GOVERNMENT
(Explain the difference.)
3.
NATION • STATE • EMPIRE
(Explain the differences.)
4.
JUDICIAL POWER • LEGISLATIVE POWER • EXECUTIVE POWER
(Explain the differences.)
5.
WELFARE • JUSTICE • DOMESTIC TRANQUILLITY
(Select one goal. Tell how the U.S. government attempts to achieve the selected goal).

BASEBALL CROWD, HOUSTON. One part of our national heritage is baseball. Another part is political liberty. How would you define "liberty"? (Compare your idea of it with the definition, page 15.)

CHAPTER 2

Our Heritage of Liberty

OBJECTIVES

After reading this chapter, you will know

1. how different groups of Americans contributed to our country's freedom.
2. how the American colonies became self-governing.
3. how the power of England's kings came to be limited by law.
4. why the American colonies revolted against British rule.
5. what the Declaration of Independence says about liberty.
6. how to identify the main idea in a reading.
7. how to interpret a time line.

Before a game of professional baseball, people in the crowd face toward an American flag and sing:

> Oh! say, does that star-spangled banner yet wave
> O'er the land of the free and the home of the brave?

"Free" strikes the highest note in our national anthem. The anthem may be sung with much spirit. But then, as people sit down to watch the game, they may not think again about their heritage of freedom.

Many Americans are so used to freedom that they rarely think about it. Do they wonder how their nation became "the land of the free"? Probably not at a baseball game—and perhaps not even at Fourth of July fireworks.

Americans, however, *do* care about their political freedom. In a general way, they know how rare it is in the world for a government to respect people's rights. Unfortunately, not many people in any crowd can explain what freedom is or trace its history.

After reading this chapter, you will be one citizen who understands how the United States became a "land of the free." Use these questions to guide your study:

1. What risks have Americans taken for the sake of liberty?
2. What unusual conditions helped the United States to become a "land of the free"?
3. How can a government's power be limited to protect citizens' rights?
4. What does the Declaration of Independence say about liberty?

1. WHAT RISKS HAVE AMERICANS TAKEN FOR THE SAKE OF LIBERTY?

To know the meaning of a word, it sometimes helps to know its opposite. The opposite of freedom is slavery. You are a slave—and not free—if some person or government has the authority to control all aspects of your life.

Individuals who control the labor of slaves are known as masters. Government leaders who compel people to obey harsh laws are known as *tyrants*. Those who have been enslaved either by masters or by tyrants know what it means to lose their freedom.

They have thirsted for freedom as a wanderer in a desert thirsts for water.

Two famous Americans were among many who valued freedom more than life. One was a lawyer from Virginia named Patrick Henry. The other was a runaway slave from Maryland who adopted the name Frederick Douglass. Let us see how their lifelong quests for freedom contributed to our own lives and liberties today.

Patrick Henry's Virginia. No American nation existed when Patrick Henry was born in a backwoods farmhouse in Virginia in 1736. Virginia was then just one of 13 separate colonies belonging to England. The colonists were expected to give loyal obedience to England's king—and also to a colonial governor named by the king.

But neither the king nor his governor had complete power to make Virginia's laws. In fact, lawmaking power in the colony belonged chiefly to a group of native Virginians elected to office by their neighbors. This colonial *assembly* was known in Virginia as the House of Burgesses.

Protesting the stamp tax. Patrick Henry, a clever and spirited young lawyer, was first elected to the House of Burgesses in 1765. In the same year, the king's government in London decided to collect a *tax* from the American colonists. It was known as the stamp tax because lawyers, merchants, and printers were required to attach a stamp to all contracts, newspapers, and other documents. The stamp could be bought only from agents of the British government.

No colonial assembly had been asked to approve the stamp tax. This fact angered American colonists. They complained bitterly that they were being taxed without the consent of their elected representatives. "Tyranny!" declared Patrick Henry in a fiery speech that made him a hero among Virginia's citizens.

Between 1765 and 1775, the British government tried to collect different taxes from the colonies. But the colonists refused to pay them, arguing that to do so would be to surrender their liberties.

Patrick Henry and others argued that it was a citizen's duty to defy tyrannical acts. True, the penalty for defiance could be terrible. Anyone accused of rebellion against the British king could be imprisoned and hanged as a traitor. But it was far worse, said Henry, to allow British laws and armies to take away American liberties.

Patrick Henry's greatest speech. In March 1775, Patrick Henry rose to his feet in an emergency meeting of Virginia's assembly. His words were bold and revolutionary. Concluding his speech, Henry urged his

". . . OR GIVE ME DEATH!" In 1775, Patrick Henry delivered his most famous speech for liberty. What did the British do to stir his anger?

more cautious friends to join him in challenging the British army. Of course it was risky, said Henry, *but*:

> Is life so dear, or peace so sweet as to be purchased at the price of chains and slavery? Forbid it, Almighty God! I know not what course others may take; but as for me, give me liberty or give me death!

Less than one month later, shots were fired on a village green in Lexington, Massachusetts. They were the first shots of an American war for freedom known as the American Revolution.

A slave named Frederick. A free man all his life, Patrick Henry spoke up for freedom when he feared it might be taken from him. A young black named Frederick Augustus Bailey cherished freedom as much as Patrick Henry—but for a very different reason. He was born into slavery on a farm in Maryland about the year 1817. He remained a slave for the first 21 years of his life. Ownership of him passed from one master to another.

Unlike most slaves, Frederick managed to teach himself to read and write. The few books that he read, in secret, gave him the idea that slavery was unnatural and wrong. The idea grew. By the time Frederick was 12 years old, he had acquired a lifelong passion for liberty. He would rather die, he thought, than to continue through life in a condition of slavery. This is what he later wrote about his youthful torments:

> I often found myself regretting my own existence, and wishing myself dead; and but for the hope of being free, I have no doubt that I should have killed myself, or done something for which I should have been killed.

SPEAKERS AGAINST SLAVERY. Frederick Douglass (left) and Sojourner Truth (right) were ex-slaves who, in the 1840s, became famous for their rousing speeches against slavery. Do you think their view of liberty differed from that of Patrick Henry?

Escape to freedom. Luckily for Frederick, he was sold to a master in Baltimore and allowed to work for wages in a shipyard. He had to turn over most of his earnings to his master. But he kept just enough for himself to buy a railroad ticket. Disguised in the clothing of a sailor, he boarded a train and anxiously rode into free territory in the North. In New York City, he adopted a new name: Frederick Douglass. At last he was free.

From his escape in 1838 until his death in 1895, Frederick Douglass devoted himself to the task of winning freedom for other blacks. Joining with white reformers of the North, he delivered speeches and wrote books about his former life as a slave. He became famous as a champion for the anti-slavery cause known as *abolition.* (He and other reformers were called abolitionists because they wanted slavery abolished.) In 1845, he began publishing his own independent newspaper. It was called the *North Star* after the star that guided runaway slaves northward. Owned and operated completely by free blacks, Douglass's newspaper was the first of its kind to succeed.

During the Civil War, Douglass helped to persuade Abraham Lincoln to take a strong stand against slavery. Northern victory in that war in 1865 resulted in a law that freed all slaves in the South and abolished the practice of slavery in the United States.

Other champions of American liberty. Patrick Henry and Frederick Douglass both valued liberty more than life itself. Joining them in their quest for freedom were thousands of other Americans—both the famous and the little known. Among these champions of liberty we can list the following:

- The group of American leaders who defied the "tyrannical" laws of Britain and signed the Declaration of Independence in 1776. (See pages 32–34.)
- The soldiers who fought with George Washington against the British army in the American War for Independence.
- The thousands of American women (including Abigail Adams, Sojourner Truth, and Susan B. Anthony) who championed the idea of equal citizenship and political rights for women.
- Leaders of the South (particularly Thomas Jefferson of Virginia and John C. Calhoun of South Carolina) who wanted to preserve the political freedoms of the separate states.
- The millions of immigrants from Europe, Asia, Africa, and Latin America who hoped to find a life of freedom in their adopted country, the United States.
- Members of many ethnic minorities (blacks, Hispanics, Asians, Jews, Irish,

IMMIGRANT CONTRIBUTIONS. Immigrants benefited from the opportunities they found here. In what ways did the United States benefit?

Italians, and many others) who stood up to prejudice and pushed beyond it to assert their dignity.

- The pioneers who settled the American West, founded new states from Tennessee to Hawaii, and made the nation more democratic.
- The many presidents (such as Abraham Lincoln, Theodore Roosevelt, and John F. Kennedy) whose actions and speeches gave new meaning to the idea of liberty.
- The inventive, risk-taking men and women who started new business enterprises and proved the amazing strength of a free economy.
- The young Americans in this century who risked their lives in war (two world wars, the Korean War, the Vietnam War, and the Persian Gulf War). Tens of thousands died in these wars to defend not only their country but also the freedom of other nations.

SOLDIERS' CONTRIBUTIONS. Moments after this picture was taken in June 1965, one of these Marines was killed by a Vietnamese sniper. (For pictures of U.S. wars, see pages 448–449.) For what ideals have Americans risked their lives?

- All citizens who, between 1776 and today, cared enough to think about their government and volunteered their time to public causes.

REVIEW

A. Building Your Political Vocabulary

Define **tyranny** and explain how it is different from **liberty.**

B. Making Inferences

Tell whether you think each statement was probably made by (*a*) a **tyrant** or (*b*) a **lover of freedom**.

1. "Absolute obedience to the government is every citizen's duty."
2. "Be all that you can be."
3. "The president always knows best what's good for the country."
4. "Either submit or pay the terrible penalty."
5. "All revolutionaries should be shot."

C. Agree or Disagree

Tell whether you **agree** or **disagree** with each statement, and give your reason.

1. Tyranny is still common in the world today.
2. The stamp tax of the 1760s was worse than any tax that Americans pay today.
3. Patrick Henry's speech for liberty and Frederick Douglass's writings on slavery were about equally important in the history of liberty.
4. Patrick Henry and Frederick Douglass would define liberty very differently.
5. The greatest contribution to American liberty was made by thousands of soldiers and sailors who fought under the American flag.

2. WHAT UNUSUAL CONDITIONS HELPED THE UNITED STATES TO BECOME A "LAND OF THE FREE"?

Long before Patrick Henry and George Washington were born, American colonists had developed certain habits of thinking and acting. Their political habits made them ready in 1776 to create a different kind of government—one that was committed to freedom.

1. **Habit of self-government.** Before 1776, Americans had more than 150 years of experience in making laws for their own towns and colonies.

2. **Habit of religious toleration.** In the American colonies, Protestants and Catholics learned to tolerate each other's religious differences. Religious liberty for almost all groups was well established by 1776.

3. **Habit of limited government.** Colonists in 1776 believed that they had fundamental rights that no government could take away. As we shall see, this idea of rights combined with limited government was rooted in almost 600 years of English history.

Each habit is important enough to be looked at closely.

First laws of the first colonial assembly. On a May day in 1607, a band of English adventurers decided to explore for gold along the banks of the James River in Virginia. They called their town of crude huts Jamestown. It became the first permanent English settlement in North America. It was also the beginning of the colony (and later the state) of Virginia.

At first, the laws of Jamestown were dictated by just one man. This governor

CONTRIBUTIONS OF THE FIRST SETTLERS. The ships pictured here brought settlers to Jamestown. What method for governing Jamestown was a first step toward achieving political freedom?

took orders from a business firm in London, the Virginia Company, which had put up the money for colonizing Virginia.

In 1619, the company's directors decided to try out an entirely different plan of government. They appointed a new governor and six men to assist him as his council. They also set up a lawmaking group, or assembly, called the House of Burgesses. The colonists themselves could decide who would represent them in this assembly. Each tobacco plantation outside Jamestown was entitled to choose two property owners and vote upon new laws for the colony.

For six days in the summer of 1619, 22 men from 11 plantations met with the governor in a church in Jamestown. They passed laws prohibiting such disorderly acts as:

- getting drunk
- stealing canoes from Indians
- gambling at dice and cards
- selling hounds or "any English dog of quality" to the Indians.

These were among the first laws of the first representative assembly in North America.

After this first session, the House of Burgesses met regularly for many generations before Patrick Henry was first elected to it in 1765. By that time, electing representatives was a firmly established habit.

The Mayflower Compact. On November 21, 1620, after a hard voyage across the storm-tossed Atlantic, Pilgrim families were still living on their crowded ship, the *Mayflower*. Quarrels broke out among the weary travelers. In order to settle their quarrels, they decided to draw up a compact, or written agreement, aboard ship; 41 passengers signed a document that was later called the *Mayflower Compact*. They pledged "in the presence of God and one another" to join together "for our better ordering and preservation." Furthermore, they agreed to make "just and equal laws . . . for the general good of the colony."

The second English colony in America started with the Pilgrims' town of Plymouth in Massachusetts. The Pilgrims had found out right away that they could not rely upon the laws of far-off England. In the American wilderness, settlers had to make their own laws for their own protection.

The Mayflower Compact was another sign that Americans would be a self-governing people. Even before they settled into houses, the Pilgrims had recognized that government was crucial to them—a government of their own making.

"The consent of the governed." The Plymouth colony eventually became part of a larger colony called Massachusetts Bay (or just Massachusetts). Other English colonies were also founded on the Atlantic coast. By 1735, there were 13 colonies in all, each with its own government.

There were differences among the colonial governments. The governors for some of them were appointed (or named) by the English king. These royal colonies included Georgia, Massachusetts, New Hampshire, New Jersey, New York, North Carolina, and South Carolina. The governors for so-called proprietary colonies, Pennsylvania, Maryland, and Delaware, were appointed by individual owners, or proprietors. For example, Pennsylvania's proprietor was William Penn. The governors for two corporate colonies, Rhode Island and Connecticut, were elected by the people.

But the colonies were alike in more ways than they were different. All 13 colonies had assemblies like Virginia's House of Burgesses. Members of the assemblies were elected by farmers, tavern keepers, blacksmiths, and other property-owning citizens. In effect, they represented and spoke for their neighbors. If a proposed law threatened to injure the voters who elected them, assembly members would refuse to give their consent to it. In this way, they prevented governors from acting as tyrants.

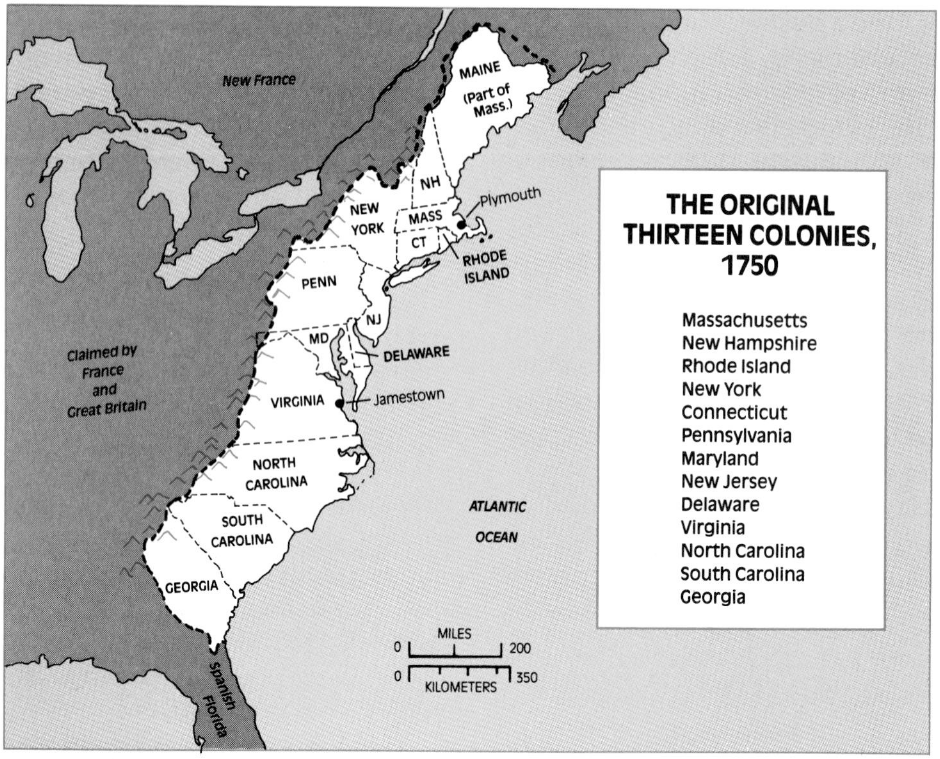

Power of the purse. No government can function without taxes. At the same time, taxes are a burden for the people who must pay them.

In the 1700s, most governments of the world forced people to pay taxes without asking their consent. This was not true, however, in England. English citizens elected representatives to sit in a lawmaking body called *Parliament*. Members of Parliament could vote either for or against the taxes requested by the king.

In the English colonies in America, a similar practice was adopted. Each colonial assembly claimed the *"power of the purse,"* as it called its power to vote on taxes. The royal governor could not tax the people of a colony unless the assembly first consented to it. The power of the purse gave the people's elected representatives more real power than the king's agent—the governor.

Thus, long before they rebelled against British rule in 1776, Americans were used to running their own affairs. For them, self-government had become a habit.

SKILLS CHECK: Identifying the main idea

You have read about several events from history. But none of the events is the **main idea** of the reading. The main idea is what the author is trying to show or demonstrate. For example, this was one of the main ideas in Chapter One.

> MAIN IDEA: One of the goals of all governments is to promote the general welfare.

To support this idea, the chapter presented several facts or details.

> DETAIL (page 12): In times of poor harvests, the Inca government opened its storehouses to keep people from starving.

DETAIL (page 14): The welfare of the American people is daily promoted by government roads, post offices, parks, and Social Security checks.

Notice that the main idea is more general than the specific details that illustrate it.

1. Of the following sentences, which would you say is the **main idea** presented so far in Section 2 of this chapter (pages 24–26)?
   a. The first representative assembly in America met in Jamestown in 1619.
   b. Aboard the *Mayflower* in 1620, English colonists signed a compact, or agreement, about how they intended to govern themselves.
   c. By 1735, there were 13 English colonies on the Atlantic coast, each with its own government.
   d. Colonial assemblies jealously guarded their power of the purse.
   e. Long before the United States was founded, settlers of the English colonies were used to being self-governing.
2. Select any of the above statements (*a–e*) that you thought to be a **detail.** Explain how it helps to prove, or demonstrate, the main idea of the reading.

Habit of religious toleration. The saying "To live and let live" is a way of defining the word *toleration.* In the 1600s and 1700s, the peoples of Europe generally did *not* tolerate one another's religions. French Catholics persecuted (jailed and mistreated) French Protestants. Spanish Catholics persecuted anyone suspected of being Jewish or Protestant. English Protestants banned the Catholic religion. In fact, religious freedom was not common in any European country except Holland.

But in the American colonies, it was different. One reason that settlers came to the New World was to escape religious persecution in the Old World. Pennsylvania, for example, was a haven for Quakers whose religion was not tolerated in England.

Also, as a practical matter, it made no sense to require all settlers to worship in the same way. The colonists were a mixed group, coming from all parts of Europe. There were English Puritans, English Quakers, German Baptists, German Jews, Dutch Reformed Protestants, Scottish Presbyterians, and many others. The energy and labor of every group were needed to settle the American wilderness. Religious faith gave many colonists the courage to face risks and hardships.

The founder of the Maryland colony, George Calvert, was Catholic. But he quickly realized that religious differences should not get in the way of settlement. So his government allowed both Protestant settlers and Catholic settlers to worship as they pleased.

The founder of Rhode Island, Roger Williams, went even further. His colonial government tolerated everyone: Christians, Jews, Moslems, and nonbelievers.

BELIEVERS IN RELIGIOUS TOLERATION. Roger Williams (seated) opposed the government-backed church in Massachusetts. Even more tolerant of religious differences were the Indians who helped him. Why is religious toleration important to liberty?

Not all the colonies were as tolerant as Maryland and Rhode Island. For many years, the laws of colonial Massachusetts required people to attend only Puritan churches. Over time, however, Massachusetts too granted religious freedom to its citizens.

By the year 1750, toleration of many religious groups had become a habit throughout the colonies. Toleration was important in making America a "land of the free."

In the next section, you will learn about a third condition for freedom to grow: the habit of limited government combined with citizens' rights.

REVIEW

A. Building Your Political Vocabulary

From the word list, select the name or term defined by each of the phrases (1–8) below.

assembly	proprietary
Compact	royal
House of Burgesses	taxes
Parliament	toleration

1. a group of elected representatives in England
2. a group of elected representatives in each English colony
3. the agreement signed by Pilgrims on the *Mayflower*
4. practice of allowing different religious groups to worship freely
5. kind of colony whose governor was chosen by the English king
6. kind of colony whose governor was chosen by an individual owner of that colony
7. money that no government can do without
8. the lawmaking group in colonial Virginia that exercised the power of the purse

B. Agree or Disagree

Tell whether you **agree** or **disagree** with each statement below. Give reasons for your answer.

1. The people of a nation can be free only if they tolerate many religions.
2. The people of a nation can be free only if they have the power to influence the government's laws.
3. *In colonial times,* the most important laws were those concerning taxes.
4. *In our own times,* the most important laws are those concerning taxes.

C. Project

In the library, look up information about **one** of these: Anne Hutchinson, Roger Williams, or George Calvert. Take notes and report to the class on the following:

1. when and where the person lived
2. major events in the person's life
3. how the person contributed to the making of a free and tolerant society.

Recommended sources: (*a*) an encyclopedia; (*b*) *Dictionary of American Biography*.

3. HOW CAN A GOVERNMENT'S POWER BE LIMITED TO PROTECT CITIZENS' RIGHTS?

Three habits arose in colonial times that fostered freedom. You have read about two of them: self-government and religious toleration. The third is the colonial habit of thinking that government should be strictly limited and should respect people's *rights*. In this section, we will explore the idea of rights. What are they? Where do they come from?

Rights and privileges. A right is an opportunity that must be granted equally to all citizens. For example, it is every American's right to attend high school. It is also every citizen's right to be treated fairly in a court of law.

Rights are not the same thing as privileges. A privilege is an opportunity that some people may attain, while others do not. For example, it is a privilege to graduate from college, since not every one is entitled to a college degree.

In the past, different groups in society enjoyed special privileges. Nobles were more privileged than peasants. Masters were more privileged than slaves. But the idea of rights—something possessed equally by all—was rare. Among Europeans, people's rights were respected only in England. And they were respected there only after centuries of bitter struggle between the common people and their kings.

The defeat of three English kings. The first king who was forced to grant rights to his people was England's King John. In the year 1215, John's acts of tyranny caused an army of nobles to revolt against him. They finally forced him to agree to their demands. On an English field, they presented the king with a document later named the *Magna Carta* (or great charter). It listed certain unfair acts that he agreed never to commit again. The king promised, for example, that no noble would be arrested and imprisoned "unless by the lawful judgment" of a jury.

LIMITS ON A KING'S POWERS. The document being signed by England's King John is the Magna Carta. Why is this document considered so important to the history of both British liberty and American liberty?

The Magna Carta was important because it established a new principle. It made plain that the written law was more powerful than a monarch. After 1215, the king's power could not be absolute. It was limited.

A later king, Charles I, was also forced to recognize the rights of his subjects. To fight a costly war against the French, he needed to raise taxes. But his Parliament would not agree to raise a penny unless Charles consented to their *Petition of Right* of 1628. The petition listed these rights of English citizens:

- no taxes without the consent of Parliament
- no housing of soldiers in private homes without the consent of Parliament.

The king defied this petition and tried to rule without Parliament. But his enemies revolted against him, took him prisoner, and finally beheaded him in 1635.

The third king whose tyranny provoked revolt was James II. In 1688, leaders of Parliament raised an army against him, forcing him to flee from England. The next year, 1689, they drew up a *Bill of Rights*. These were some of the rights it listed:

- no maintaining an army without the consent of Parliament
- no raising taxes without the consent of Parliament
- no "cruel and unusual punishments" for those accused of crime
- no punishment for crime unless found guilty by a jury.

The revolt against James II affected the American colonies as well as England. It was celebrated as the Glorious Revolution because people's rights had prevailed against a king's pretended power. The rights won by the English prepared the way for many of the rights now claimed by Americans.

Ideas of John Locke. A great writer can have more influence than a dozen weak kings. One such writer was an Englishman named John Locke.

Locke was one of the many lovers of liberty who cheered the Glorious Revolution of 1688. Still thinking about this event, he published *Two Treatises on Government* in 1690. These were his main ideas:

- The first human beings on earth lived in a "state of nature" without any government. In this original state, they had natural rights that belonged equally to all. They were completely free.
- In time, people decided to live in groups and to surrender some of their freedom to a ruler or monarch. They gained security from the government's laws.
- *But* only some freedoms were given up. Others were as much a part of human life as breathing. They could *never* be surrendered. Such "unalienable rights"—or natural rights—included the right to life and to the enjoyment of private property.
- Sometimes monarchs tried to violate a citizen's natural rights. It was then *every citizen's duty* to disobey the tyrant's laws and rise up in revolt.

Locke's ideas about liberty were talked about not only in London, but in the towns of colonial America. The ideas were used by the colonists to justify their 1776 revolt against British rule.

Government limited by a supreme law. From Magna Carta to Locke's essays, one idea was stated again and again. All government officials—even kings—must obey a higher law. The name most commonly given to this highest, or supreme, law was *constitution.* The English people thought of their constitution as a set of political customs and long established rights. It set limits on what kings could and could not do. Certain actions of the government were allowed by the English constitution. But tyrannical acts—anything that threatened basic rights—were not allowed. Why? Because such acts were not constitutional. They were *unconstitutional.*

A nation's constitution (plan of government) can be either written or unwritten. Britain's is the unwritten kind. No single document says that Britain shall be ruled, within strict limits, by a monarch and a parliament. Its plan of government developed slowly over many centuries.

The United States has a written Constitution created in 1787. The people who wrote it had been born as colonists under the British system. They cherished the idea of citizens' rights and a limited government. That is why the Constitution that they wrote listed things that the U.S. government both could do and could not do. Their written Constitution was the "supreme law" that government officials would have to obey, serve, and protect.

✔✔ SKILLS CHECK: Interpreting time lines

How far apart in time are the events mentioned so far? For example, how many years passed between the writing of the Magna Carta and the settling of Jamestown? An excellent way to *see* events in relation to time is to place them on a time line.

We see from the time line (A, page 31) that more than 275 years passed between the Magna Carta and Columbus's most famous voyage of discovery. More than 100 years passed between Columbus's voyage and the settling of Jamestown.

In the previous section (pages 24–28), you read about events on the *American* side of the Atlantic Ocean. In this section (pages 28–31), you read about events on the *English* side. The two time lines below (B) show that these events on either side of the Atlantic took place in about the same time period, 1600 to 1750. Check your skill at reading time lines by answering the questions.

1. What great American document was signed shortly before the English Petition of Right?
2. What two American colonies were founded between 1650 and 1700? In this same period, what was happening in England?
3. How many years after the Pilgrims sailed on the *Mayflower* was Pennsylvania founded?
4. In 1750, who was older: Patrick Henry or George III?
5. Name three English documents that probably influenced Patrick Henry's idea of liberty. Explain how they might have influenced him.

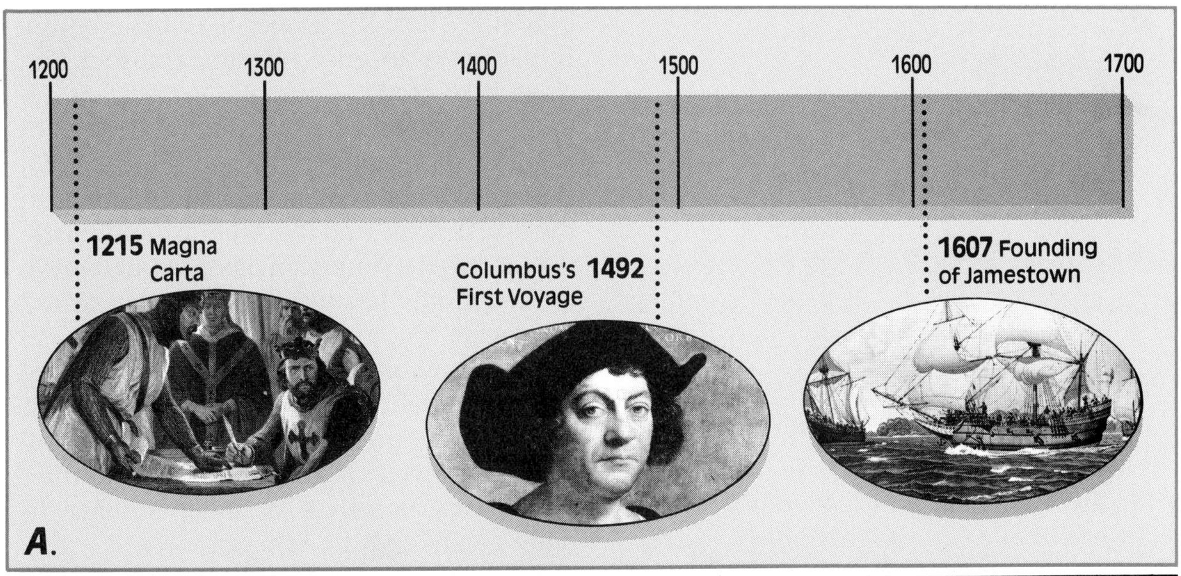

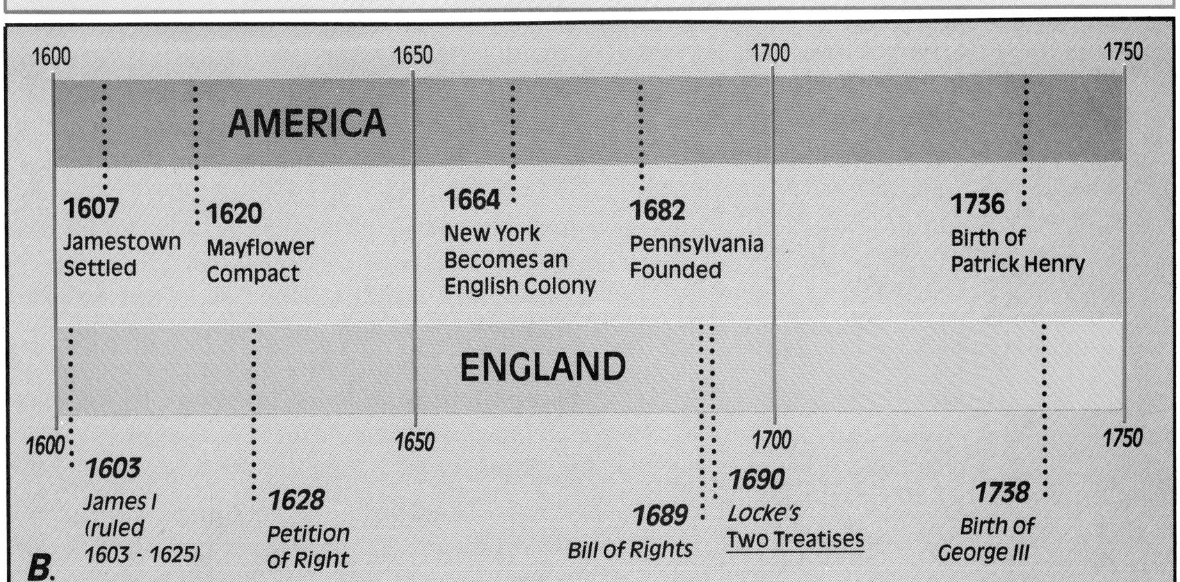

REVIEW

A. Building Your Political Vocabulary

In your notebook, **write** a definition for each of these terms:

constitution
limited government rights

B. Making Comparisons

Explain how the terms or ideas in each pair are **different**:

1. Your rights—your privileges
2. King John's idea of a king's powers—John Locke's idea of a king's powers
3. A constitutional action by a king—an unconstitutional action by a king

C. Applying What You Know

By answering the questions below, you will see how past events influence the present.

1. What rights do we Americans have that can be traced back to English history in the 1600s?
2. Of the following, which would you call a right of all U.S. citizens today?
   a. No punishment without a fair trial
   b. No cruel punishments (such as torture or burning at the stake)
   c. No enslavement of one person by another
   d. No taxes unless they are approved by elected representatives
   e. Guaranteed opportunity to be employed at a fair wage
   f. Guaranteed opportunity to attend school for 12 years

4. WHAT DOES THE DECLARATION OF INDEPENDENCE SAY ABOUT LIBERTY?

How and why did 13 English colonies become 13 independent states? What caused them to form a new nation—the United States—in 1776?

We have already read part of the explanation. Recall Patrick Henry's angry speech attacking the stamp tax of 1765. He feared that Americans' rights to self-government were under attack.

Events leading to revolution. Between 1765 and 1775, Americans became even more alarmed. They resented the British troops that marched and drilled in the center of Boston. Growing resentment and fear led to acts of violence. Angered by rebellious acts in Boston, King George III ordered the British navy to guard Boston's harbor and close it to trade. Outraged Americans regarded the king's harsh measures as acts of tyranny and war. By the summer of 1776, there had been two major battles between the British army and the American colonists.

How were American liberties to be defended from the menace of British arms? To decide this question, *delegates* from 13 colonies traveled to Philadelphia to meet together as a Continental Congress. At first, only a few of the delegates wanted to break away completely from British rule. But their arguments on behalf of independence finally persuaded the others.

Who would write the document announcing to England and the world Congress's decision? The delegate chosen for the task was a young, redheaded Virginian named Thomas Jefferson. In an upstairs room of a Philadelphia boarding house, Jefferson wrote four pages of arguments for independence. He showed his work to an older writer, Benjamin Franklin, who made only a few changes in it. On the evening of July 4, 1776, the Continental Congress voted to accept Jefferson's document as its official declaration to the world. The document was entitled:

THE UNANIMOUS DECLARATION OF THE THIRTEEN UNITED STATES OF AMERICA

We celebrate it today as the Declaration of Independence. It has much to say to us,

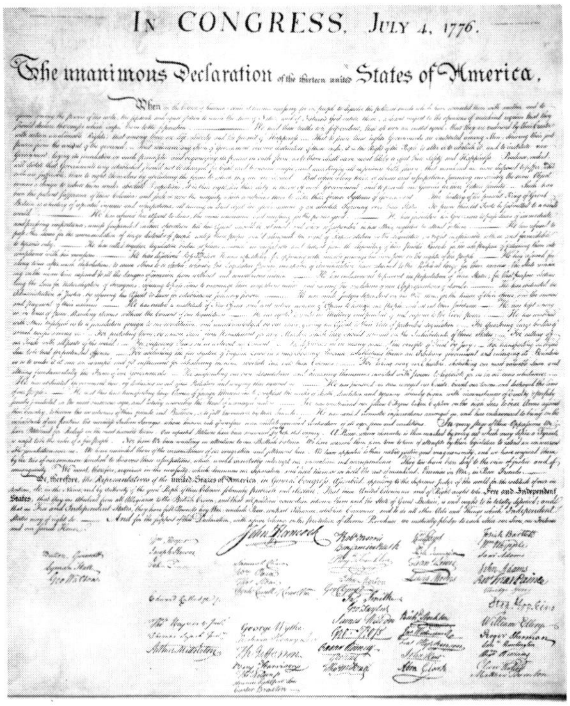

IN CONGRESS. JULY 4, 1776.

The unanimous Declaration of the thirteen united States of America.

FIGHTING BRITISH "TYRANNY." On an April morning in 1775, British troops fired on American militia men at Lexington (above). What other grievances against British rule are listed in the Declaration of Independence (left)?

even today, more than 200 years after it was written. Let us look at the famous Declaration, one paragraph at a time.

First paragraph. Jefferson began by announcing that the time had come for the American colonies to become a separate nation. The purpose of the Declaration was to "declare the causes" for wanting to be independent from English rule.

Second paragraph. This paragraph is the most famous. It presents a theory about government and people's rights. Government's one function, said Jefferson, is to protect people's rights to "life, liberty, and the pursuit of happiness." Government's power to make laws comes from the *consent of the governed* themselves. If any government forgets this fact, then people have a right and a duty to rebel against it. As Jefferson wrote:

> We hold these truths to be self-evident, that all men are created equal, that they are endowed by their Creator with certain unalienable rights, that among these are life, liberty, and the pursuit of happiness. That to secure these rights, governments are instituted among men, deriving their just powers from the consent of the governed. That whenever any form of government becomes destructive of these ends, it is the right of the people to alter or to abolish it. . . .

Why did the American people think it right to revolt against British rule? Jefferson explained:

> The history of the present King of Great Britain is a history of repeated injuries and usurpations [seizing power by illegal means], all having in direct object the establishment of an absolute tyranny over these States.

So ends one of the most famous paragraphs ever written. To this day, it challenges every government on earth to respect people's rights.

TWO GREAT DOCUMENTS. Just below this inscription, in the National Archives in Washington, D.C., are two documents that define American freedom. (See pages 541–544 for the text of the Declaration of Independence and pages 116–130 for that of the U.S. Constitution.)

List of grievances against the king. The longest section of the Declaration of Independent lists grievances against the British king, George III. A *grievance* is an accusation made against a government that is thought to be acting in unjust and harmful ways.

Quoted below are just six of the Declaration's list of 27 grievances. (Each is explained in parentheses.)

- "He has dissolved representative houses repeatedly. . . ." (When colonial assemblies defied the wishes of the royal governors, they were ordered to stop meeting.)
- "He has kept among us, in times of peace, standing armies without the consent of our legislatures." (It was feared that the British troops in Boston could be used to crush liberty.)
- "For quartering large bodies of armed troops among us . . . ." (To add insult to injury, Britain required colonists to use their homes for lodging soldiers.)
- "For imposing taxes on us without our consent . . . ." (One such tax was the stamp tax. Other taxes were placed on tea and other goods imported from England. Colonists defied these taxes by refusing to purchase British goods and by dumping British tea into Boston Harbor.)
- "For cutting off our trade with all parts of the world . . . ." (To punish Boston for destroying British tea, the British navy closed the city to trade.)
- "He has abdicated government here, by declaring us out of his protection and waging war against us." (In April 1775, a British army marched from Boston to the town of Lexington. Here they opened fire on a small troop of armed farmers—"minute men." Marching on to Concord, the British were attacked by other farmers in the first battle of the American Revolution.)

Conclusion. The last paragraph declared the United States to be a new nation.

> We, therefore . . . solemnly publish and declare that these united colonies are, and of right ought to be, free and independent states . . . . And for the support of this Declaration, with a firm reliance on the protection of divine Providence, we mutually pledge to each other our lives, our fortunes, and our sacred honor.

The 56 signers of the Declaration did indeed risk their lives and fortunes. If their side had lost the war, they might have been hanged as traitors. Instead, George Washington's army endured through eight hard years of war, 1775–1783, and finally prevailed.

CARTOON CORNER

George III is like the Bible character Goliath. What Bible character does Jefferson represent?

REVIEW

A. Building Your Political Vocabulary

The words in Column A are found in the Declaration of Independence. Match each **word** with its **definition** in Column B. You can guess the meaning by looking for the word in the Declaration and seeing how it is used. Or you may refer to a dictionary.

COLUMN A	COLUMN B
1. usurpation	*a.* break up
2. abdicate	*b.* give up; let go
3. unalienable	*c.* give
4. secure	*d.* an unlawful seizure of power
5. endow	*e.* put into effect
6. institute	*f.* make safe
7. legislature	*g.* assembly of lawmakers
8. dissolve	*h.* not separable

B. Locating Key Ideas

Where in the Declaration of Independence do we find each of the following arguments? Answer either: **first paragraph, second paragraph, list of grievances,** or **conclusion.**

1. Assemblies were often dissolved.
2. The purpose of the Declaration was to make known the causes for America's break with England.
3. Certain rights belong to all people and cannot be taken away.
4. A government's laws must have the consent of the people.
5. All human beings have equal rights.
6. The former colonies of England are now independent states.

C. Project

Choose **one** paragraph of the Declaration of Independence to memorize. It could be either (*a*) the second paragraph (as shortened on page 33) or (*b*) the concluding paragraph (as shortened on page 34). Know it well enough to recite in class.

CHAPTER REVIEW

A. Completing the Summary

Select terms from the word list to fill in the blanks in the summary below.

abolition	Magna
Burgesses	natural
consent	Petition
Declaration	purse
Douglass	representatives
governors	rights
grievances	toleration
Henry	truths
liberty	tyranny
limited	unalienable
Locke	

Americans should know how their country became a "land of the free." Among thousands who risked their lives for liberty were two famous Americans—one white, the other black. In 1765, Patrick __(1)__ insisted that all taxes had to have the __(2)__ of the governed. Otherwise, they must be opposed as acts of __(3)__. In 1838, a Maryland man escaped from slavery and took the name Frederick __(4)__. He worked for the __(5)__ of slavery, which was achieved in 1865.

Conditions must be right for the growth of liberty. In colonial times, Americans had developed habits of (*a*) self-government, (*b*) __(6)__ government, and (*c*) religious __(7)__.

Though the British king appointed royal __(8)__, new laws could be rejected by assemblies of elected __(9)__. An assembly's power to approve or reject taxes was known as its "power of the __(10)__." Other examples of colonial self-government were the Mayflower Compact and the first meeting of Virginia's House of __(11)__.

Americans' belief in limited government owes much to events in English history. It can be traced back to the __(12)__ Carta of 1215 and the __(13)__ of Right of 1628. The English people were said to have certain __(14)__ that no king could take away. According to the writer, John __(15)__, inborn rights were __(16)__ rights.

Political habits of the English and American people explain the phrases that we read in the __(17)__ of Independence of 1776. This great document declared the United States to be an independent nation. It listed the __(18)__ of the former colonies against Britain's king, George III. Most important, it stated: "We hold these __(19)__ to be self-evident, that all men are created equal, that they are endowed by their Creator with certain __(20)__ rights, that among these are life, __(21)__, and the pursuit of happiness."

B. Making Comparisons

To make an **analogy** is to explain one idea by comparing it to something else. Tell why each of the following terms is like the object pictured.

1. Why is **limited government** like a large dog on a tight leash?

2. Why is **tyranny** like a cage for innocent people?

3. Why is **representation** like an All-Star Baseball Game?

4. Why is the **Declaration of Independence** like a birth certificate?

5. Why is **liberty** like . . . . . . (Invent your own analogy. Explain it and then illustrate it.)

C. Telling Fact from Opinion

Some of the statements below express an **opinion** that cannot be proved either true or false. Others are statements of **fact** that can be proved true. Say whether each statement is a fact or an opinion. Tell why.

1. Frederick Douglass began life as a slave.
2. Patrick Henry was probably the greatest speaker of all time.
3. Thomas Jefferson and Patrick Henry were both born in the British colony of Virginia.
4. Until 1865, some Americans were slaves while others were free citizens.
5. It is everyone's natural right to be employed for wages.
6. The Glorious Revolution of 1688 was less important than the American Revolution of 1776.
7. By 1750, all 13 American colonies had representative assemblies.

D. Classifying Information

Divide a piece of paper into three vertical columns. Write these headings at the top: A. **Documents,** B. **Principles of Liberty,** C. **Events**. Copy the names or terms below onto the appropriate column of your paper.

consent of the governed
settlement of Jamestown
Declaration of Independence
letters of Frederick Douglass
equal rights for all
limited government
meeting of the House of Burgesses
Mayflower Compact
Magna Carta
essays of John Locke
revolt against King John
beheading of Charles I

In your "Documents" column, put a star (*) next to documents written in England. Put two stars (**) next to documents written in America.

NAPOLEON I, FRENCH EMPEROR (1805–1815). How does the government of an autocrat like Napoleon differ from the democratic government led by a U.S. president?

CHAPTER 3

Our Government Compared to Others

OBJECTIVES

After reading this chapter, you will know

1. the differences between an autocracy, an oligarchy, and a democracy.
2. why democracy in the United States is said to be "indirect."
3. why some modern republics are "free" while others are "unfree."
4. how the federalist form of government compares with the unitary and confederate forms.
5. how U.S. capitalism compares with communism and socialism.
6. how to use a chart to make comparisons.

Think for a minute about the great variety of shoes that people wear. There are rugged hiking shoes; glossy, high-heeled shoes; tennis shoes with rubber soles; and slippers that flop off the heel.

How are governments of the world like shoes? They too come in many varieties, shapes, and sizes. Some kinds of governments fit a society well, while others pinch and hurt.

This chapter describes the major kinds of governments found in the world. Some governments, as you know, are commanded by just one person—an all-powerful monarch or *dictator*. Others allow ordinary citizens to vote and hold office. Some governments permit free elections among many competing groups (or political parties). Others allow people to join only one party and prevent any real competition.

You know that the United States calls itself a "democracy." China is known as a "Communist" nation. What is meant by these words? After reading this chapter, you will know. The chapter's five sections answer these questions:

1. How does a democracy differ from an autocracy?
2. How do "free" republics differ from "unfree" republics?
3. What kind of republic is the United States?
4. What is a federalist system of government?
5. How does U.S. capitalism differ from communism and socialism?

1. HOW DOES A DEMOCRACY DIFFER FROM AN AUTOCRACY?

From Chapter One, recall the Inca monarchs who ruled a great empire for 200 years. The greatest of them was named Topa Inca. Compare this all-powerful ruler of a South American empire with one of the greatest U.S. presidents, Abraham Lincoln.

EMPEROR AND PRESIDENT. Compare the picture of the Inca emperor (left) with that of Lincoln, shown here with his son, Tad. How do the pictures reveal the autocratic nature of one leader and the democratic nature of the other?

A comparison of two leaders. Note these similarities between the Inca emperor and the American president:

Similarity 1. Both Topa Inca and Abraham Lincoln commanded the armies of their states.

Similarity 2. Both men were the leaders of their governments. In other words, each was his government's head of state. Different countries refer to their heads of state by different titles. President and emperor are two such titles. Other titles are or have been: king, queen, generalissimo, prime minister, sultan, czar, and kaiser.

Similarity 3. Both Topa Inca and Lincoln determined what policies their governments should follow. A *public policy* is a general direction or course of action that is deliberately chosen. For example, it was Lincoln's policy to proclaim the freedom of Southern slaves. A different policy would have been to let slavery continue to exist.

Though alike in some ways, the Inca ruler and American president approached their jobs in very different ways.

Difference 1. In 1860, Abraham Lincoln was elected to his powerful position by a vote of millions of American citizens. Just as important, there were other millions who voted for rival candidates. On the other hand, the monarch Topa Inca was born to rule. In Peru in the 1400s, power belonged only to one family. It was passed down as a family possession from father to son. Nobody outside this royal Inca family had any hope of becoming head of state.

Difference 2. In his time, President Lincoln was not the only important leader in the U.S. government. Other politicians in Congress and in state governments criticized the president's policies. Lincoln accepted this opposition as normal. He did not try to silence rival politicians by having them executed or thrown into jail.

Contrast Lincoln's attitude toward rivals with the attitude in Peru. Almost no one dared to oppose Topa Inca. The penalty for opposition was known to be torture and death. Living in the royal palace, relatives of the Topa Inca might give him information and advice. But when the head of state decided something, they could not criticize or protest. They either obeyed or died.

Defining autocracy and democracy. Topa Inca was the leader of a political system called an *autocracy*. President Lincoln was the leader of a nearly opposite system called a *democracy*. To define these terms, it helps to break them into parts: AUTO - CRACY and DEMO - CRACY. The prefix *auto-* means one, while *demo-* means people. The suffix *-cracy* comes from a Greek word meaning rule. Therefore:

- AUTOCRACY means rule by one person.
- DEMOCRACY means rule by all the people.

Despots and dictators. In the history of the world, most governments have been autocratic—not democratic. One such government was the autocracy of the Inca monarch. A second example was the autocracy of the ancient Roman Empire. A third example in our own times is the autocracy of the Cuban dictator, Fidel Castro.

What is the difference between an old-fashioned monarch like Topa Inca and a modern dictator like Castro?

Monarchs of old (kings, queens, emperors, sultans) usually claimed that their power came from heaven. In their view, this gave them the "divine right" to rule—a right symbolized by the crowns they wore. The monarchs of ancient Egypt (known as pharaohs) carried their claim to divine power even further. They said that they were actual gods, walking on earth in human bodies.

Modern dictators do *not* wear crowns. Nor do they base their power on some heavenly connections. Instead, they may have used force to seize control of government. They may wear either business suits or military uniforms. Usually they claim that their power comes from the people.

The dictionary gives many words as synonyms for autocrat. Among them are: despot, dictator, tyrant, and absolute monarch. These words describe autocrats who control all the powers of a nation's or empire's government. They rule without any lawful limits on their power.

Totalitarian systems. To maintain their power, dictators often try to establish total control of a nation. They use their power over the government, the armed forces, and the police to force all other institutions in society to support their rule. A political system that establishes total control of a society is known as a *totalitarian system*.

FIDEL CASTRO. Since coming to power in 1959, Castro has been the dictator of a one-party government in Cuba. Can you infer from this fact that Cuba is *(a)* a monarchy, *(b)* a "free" republic, or *(c)* an "unfree" republic? Explain.

The Incas had attempted to rule every aspect of life in their empire. Therefore, their system was an early example of totalitarianism. In our own century, the best-known examples of such systems were the governments of Adolf Hitler in Germany and Joseph Stalin in the Soviet Union. These two dictators used the same methods in the 1930s and 1940s for ruling their countries. Each gained control of all channels of communication. The German people would awake each morning to radio broadcasts praising Hitler and urging loyalty to the nation. Government messages filled the newspapers and radio broadcasts. Schools taught children to regard the dictator as a superhuman national hero.

Another means of control in a totalitarian system is the police force, which investigates and arrests anyone suspected of opposing the government. Therefore, nations ruled by totalitarian dictators like Hitler and Stalin are known as "police states."

✔✔ SKILLS CHECK: Using a chart to make comparisons

A chart like the one below helps us to compare systems of government. In this case, we are comparing how an autocrat is both **like** and **unlike** a democrat.

Two of the boxes in the chart, labeled A and B, need to be completed by you. On a piece of paper, write what could be put in each box to complete the comparison. Then answer the questions below the chart.

COMPARING AN AUTOCRAT WITH A DEMOCRAT

	Powers and Duties	How Chosen	Limits on Leader's Power
 *Autocratic* leader (Topa Inca)	1. head of state 2. commander of armed forces 3. maker of national policies	(A) ?	None
 *Democratic* leader (Lincoln)	1. head of state 2. commander of armed forces 3. maker of national policies	elected by vote of the people	(B) ?

1. What column of the chart shows similarities between autocratic and democratic leaders?

2. How would you summarize the major differences between an autocratic leader and a democratic leader?

REVIEW

A. Agree or Disagree

Tell whether you **agree** or **disagree** with each statement. Give evidence from the chapter (pages 39-42) to support your answer.

1. Abraham Lincoln recognized no limits on his power.
2. There is no difference between a modern dictator and an old-fashioned despot.
3. In a democracy, people may criticize their political leaders without fear.
4. Most dictators of the 20th century inherited their power from a royal parent.

B. Applying What You Know

Tell whether each phrase describes (*a*) **an autocrat of ancient times** (*b*) **a democratic head of state of modern times** (*c*) **a dictator of modern times.** Some phrases describe more than one kind of leader.

1. elected to office by a vote of the people
2. tolerates opposition by rival politicians
3. commands the armies of the nation
4. makes the most important policies of government
5. inherits power from his or her family
6. has despotic power
7. may be removed from power in a national election
8. wears a military uniform

C. Project

In history, some autocrats made life better for the people they governed. Other autocrats were tyrants.

SOME OF THE BEST	SOME OF THE WORST
Elizabeth I, queen of England	John, king of England
Wu Ti, emperor of China	Ivan "the Terrible," czar of Russia
Asoka, emperor of India	Caligula, emperor of Rome
Mansa Musa, king of Mali	Adolf Hitler, dictator of Germany

Select one autocrat from either column, and find out what made his or her rule either **good** or **bad**. Use an encyclopedia article and one other source. Take notes and report to the class about your autocrat.

ENGLISH MONARCH AND GERMAN DICTATOR. An encyclopedia article on Elizabeth I (left) calls her "a strong and clever ruler." Another article on Adolf Hitler (right, without hat) says he "spread death as no person had ever done before." To find out more about one or the other, see the project above.

2. HOW DO "FREE" REPUBLICS DIFFER FROM "UNFREE" REPUBLICS?

Until our own century, most nations of the world were ruled by absolute monarchs. As late as 1900, an empress ruled China. Another monarch, the czar, ruled the vast empire of Russia. A sultan made the laws for the people of Turkey. A kaiser (emperor) ruled Germany. These rulers inherited power from the royal families into which they were born.

But after 1900, there was a great upheaval throughout the world. History's most destructive wars—World War I and World War II—gave many peoples an opportunity to rebel against old systems of government. One by one, the old monarchies were overthrown. Peoples in Asia and Africa demanded independent governments and nations of their own. They would not tolerate the idea of being ruled either by one royal family or by a foreign government. Instead of kingdoms and empires, new nations came into being with names like these:

- *Republic* of Uganda (Africa)
- *Republic* of Tunisia (Africa)
- Syrian Arab *Republic* (the Middle East)
- People's *Republic* of China (Asia)
- *Republic* of Iraq (the Middle East)

These nations are among many that use the word *republic* in their names. Do not suppose, however, that all republics have the same kind of government. One kind of republic protects the rights of its citizens to speak freely and without fear on public issues. Examples of such "free" republics are the United States, Canada, and France. Another kind of republic does not allow its citizens much freedom. Examples of such "unfree" republics are Iraq, Vietnam, and China.

Characteristics of a "free" republic. A republic is a nation in which the common people are represented in government. Only a "free" republic, however, is truly democratic. In every "free" republic, including our own, the people have the right to:

1. vote in an election
2. join any political party or group
3. criticize government leaders and policies.

Let us see why all three rights are necessary in any republic committed to democracy and personal freedom.

The right to vote. Voting is an American habit. It is so much a part of our culture that we do not always appreciate it. In school, as early as the first grade, children are encouraged to vote for team captains. In the sixth grade, they may vote for members of a student council. After reaching the age of 18, they may vote for government officials.

Again and again, you have learned this key principle of democracy: the *majority* rules. In other words, any candidate who receives more than half the total votes is automatically declared the winner. A *plurality* of votes may also decide an election. This occurs whenever several candidates are competing for the same office. The successful candidate may receive less than half the votes. But he or she still wins as the person with a plurality—a greater number of votes than anyone else.

The right to join a political party of one's choice. *A political party* is any group whose members help one another to get elected to office. We will be studying political parties in detail later in this book. For now, we simply need to observe one fact. In almost all "free" republics, there are several political parties competing for votes.

Why is this important? Why isn't it enough for a nation to have just one political party?

The reason is that one party does not allow voters much choice. How can people choose freely if they are presented at election time with candidates who support the same laws and policies? Voting in such one-party elections usually has little meaning.

The right to criticize and oppose government policies. Is our current U.S. president doing a good job or a bad job of governing America? Speak up. Because you live in a "free" republic, you can criticize the president or any other official without fear of being arrested and jailed. If you say "bad job," nothing terrible will happen to you—except that some of your classmates may disagree.

Many governments of the world are tempted to stop people from expressing criticism. After all, once elected to power, officials would prefer to stay there. They may therefore cause political opponents and critics to be arrested as "enemies of the state." But if they do this, their state has ceased to be a "free" republic.

Politics in a "free" republic is much like a game of basketball or other sport. Opposing teams (parties) must always be willing to play fairly and obey the same set of rules. The champion team (party in power) must allow the challenging teams (parties out of power) a fair chance to win. That happens regularly in a "free" republic whenever an election is held.

Three systems for electing leaders. Elections are crucial in a democracy. However, simply because a nation holds elections does not always mean that its government is democratic. It could also be either a dictatorship or an *oligarchy* (rule by a specially privileged group). How do democratic elections differ from the other kinds?

To illustrate the different kinds of elections, let us imagine three summer camps on three islands in a lake. It is the custom in each camp for one person to act as the "Chief." Methods for choosing a Chief differ from one island to another. CARTOON CORNER illustrates the three political systems in use at Camps A, B, and C.

CARTOON CORNER

Camp A: Dictatorship. The camp's owner declares himself to be the Chief. As the dictator he has total power to make policy and give orders. There is an election, but campers and counselors can only vote for the camp owner since there are no other candidates.

Camp B: Oligarchy. At this camp, the counselors form the ruling group—or oligarchy. An oligarchy is a system in which political power is held by a specially privileged group. The counselors at Camp B are the only ones who may vote in the election for Chief. Naturally, the Chief that they elect is always a counselor, never a camper.

Camp C: Democracy. In this society, campers as well as counselors are entitled to vote in the election for Chief. No vote counts any more or less than any other vote. The winning candidate could be anyone in the society (camper or counselor).

Here is an idea that may surprise you. The United States was not always a democracy. In George Washington's time, this nation was an oligarchy because only a small percentage of citizens (white males who owned property) could vote. The United States became fully democratic only after the right to vote was extended to all mature citizens.

Politics in an "unfree" republic. You saw how an old-fashioned autocrat, Topa Inca, compared with an elected leader, Abraham Lincoln. Now let us see how a *modern* autocrat—or dictator—rules a republic of the "unfree" kind.

Imagine a nation that we shall call the Republic of Vakia. It is imaginary in name only. Many republics like it exist in the Middle East, Africa, Asia, Europe, and South America.

In some ways, Vakia's government appears to be truly democratic. Its top officials are elected by a vote of the people. Its laws are written and voted upon in the National Assembly—a lawmaking body similar to our U.S. Congress. However, though people vote in Vakia, they do not vote freely.

Vakia's elections and government are controlled by a dictator whom we shall call Potar Ruhlski. He is the head of the nation's only important political party—the Vakia Nationalist party. He commands the other members of the party, telling them what to think and how to act. Ruhlski decides what members of the Nationalist party shall have their names placed on the election ballot. Those elected to the National Assembly can be counted upon to vote for any law desired by their leader, Ruhlski.

The citizens of Vakia know that it is dangerous to criticize Ruhlski's government. Everywhere there are government spies—members of a secret police force—who pretend to be your friend or just a casual bystander. They are rewarded for reporting Vakian men and women who, in a careless moment, grumble about the government. Those arrested for political "crimes" are taken to prison. Some are executed.

After spending several years in Vakia's capital, one foreigner commented: "This is a bloody, brutal regime. There is a fear here that deadens the senses. People don't talk." A taxi driver explained the situation differently. Speaking to a tourist, he patted the dashboard of his taxi. "This is a car," he said. "But if Potar Ruhlski says this is a bicycle, then it is a bicycle." The driver looked around anxiously and then added: "He could kill me for saying this."

REVIEW

A. Making Comparisons

For each pair of terms, explain how **A** differs from **B.**

1. A—Majority; B—Plurality
2. A—Democracy; B—Oligarchy
3. A—"Free" republic;
   B—"Unfree" republic

B. Making Inferences

You know that the Republic of Vakia is imaginary because the chapter states that it is. (See page 46.) Is Potar Ruhlski a real or imaginary dictator? You can reasonably **infer** that he is imaginary because he rules an imaginary country. An **inference** is an idea that you can suppose to be true, even though it is not directly stated in the reading. Here is another example:

STATEMENT: In a democracy, no vote counts more than any other vote.

INFERENCE: *Your* vote in a democratic election counts the same as the vote of a famous person.

The chapter states that the Republic of Vakia is much like "unfree republics" that really exist. Vietnam is one of these unfree republics. Given this fact, what inferences can you make about the government of Vietnam?

1. Do you think most people in Vietnam would be allowed to vote in elections? Explain.
2. Do you think several political parties would be allowed to compete for votes? Explain.
3. In what ways would you suppose that the people of Vietnam are "unfree"?

3. HOW DOES THE UNITED STATES COMPARE WITH OTHER "FREE" REPUBLICS?

A branching diagram (much like a tree) helps us to review the types of governments studied so far:

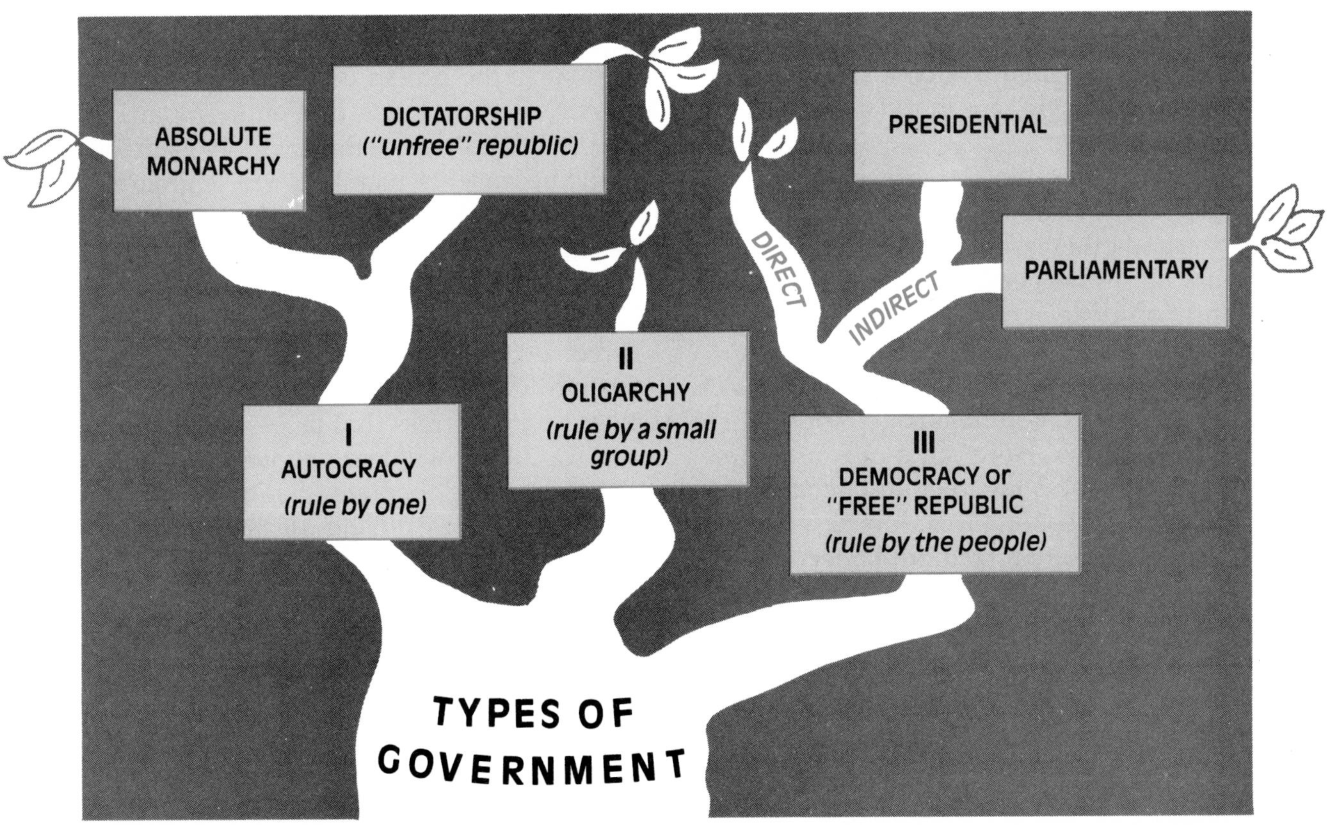

In this section, we will consider only the democratic branch of the government "tree." Notice that the branch DEMOCRACY forks into *direct* and *indirect* forms. Further, the indirect form divides into *presidential* and *parliamentary* forms. In this section, you will learn why the United States has chosen the presidential form.

Direct democracy. In one form of democracy, citizens themselves make the laws of the state by direct vote. At a certain time of the year, they may assemble in one large meeting place. Anyone in the gathering may propose a new law. Then a vote is taken on the proposal. If a majority votes yes, it is passed. If not, it is rejected. Another change in the law is suggested and voted upon . . . and another . . . and another. Finally, someone proposes that the assembly be adjourned, or dismissed.

The great advantage of this system is that government is clearly in the hands of the people. In fact, government *is* the people meeting in assembly. Such a system, however, is extremely rare in today's world for two reasons.

First, the issues of our times are complicated. What to do about pollution, nuclear arms, and other issues requires months and years of study. People cannot vote intelligently on dozens of complex issues if they meet for only a week or two.

A second problem is that most nations of the world have populations of more than a million citizens. How can a million people conduct business together and debate laws in the same meeting place? Just to seat them all would require a stadium larger than 15 Astrodomes.

One famous example of direct democracy was the ancient Greek city-state of Athens. Between the years 500 and 400 B.C., about 10,000 citizens of Athens had the right to sit in an outdoor arena and raise their voices for or against proposed laws.

Indirect (representative) democracy. In a modern democracy like ours, the most practical way to make laws is to elect a small number of representatives who meet as a lawmaking body. The voters then do not make laws directly. But they still have indirect control over the republic's laws. After all, if a majority of voters disagree with their representatives' decisions, they can turn them out of office and elect others.

Take Great Britain as one example of an indirect democracy. British laws are made by a group of 650 officials who represent 650 local areas—or voting districts—that make up the British nation. In a general election, the voters of a district choose between the candidates of different political parties. The winning candidates go to London to make laws in a large meeting room called the House of Commons.

Meeting in another room are lawmakers who represent the noble families of Britain. The House of Lords, as their assembly is called, has much less power than the House of Commons. The two houses together are known as the British Parliament.

Why is the House of Commons an example of indirect democracy? It is democratic because its members are responsible to the people who elected them. It is indirect because elected officials make the laws instead of the people themselves.

In certain ways, the U.S. system of indirect democracy is similar to the British system. American voters elect representatives to a Congress that meets in Washington, D.C. You will learn about Congress in detail in later chapters. For now, simply note these characteristics of the Congress:

- Two separate groups of lawmakers are elected. One is the Senate. The other is the House of Representatives.
- Senators are elected from the different states.
- Representatives are elected from special districts (sections within each state).

GREAT BRITAIN'S HOUSE OF COMMONS. In this British lawmaking body, members of the majority party and the opposition party face each other from two sets of benches. Why does the prime minister always belong to the majority party?

The leadership question. Whether a democracy is direct or indirect depends on who makes the laws. Whether it is "presidential" or "parliamentary" depends on who is elected to enforce the laws. As you might guess, a presidential republic calls its leader a president. A second main type of indirect democracy has a prime minister leading a lawmaking group called parliament.

Prime ministers and parliaments. Many governments of the modern world, including Japan and Israel, have a parliament similar to the British Parliament. All parliamentary republics have a top official known as the prime minister. He or she has the duty of giving leadership to parliament (the legislature) and to the nation as a whole. But the prime minister is *not* elected by popular vote. Instead, members of the country's parliament decide which of them shall be the prime minister. After an election, the political party that wins the most seats in the parliament gets to make this choice.

Presidents. Those who created the U.S. Constitution rejected the parliamentary system for choosing top officials. In our system and others like it, the head of state has the title of president. Instead of being chosen by lawmakers, the president is elected by popular vote, followed by a special vote of "electors" from every state. (See Chapter 11.) Unlike the prime minister, a president has no seat and therefore no vote in the lawmaking body.

Why is this an important difference? The practical effect is that an elected president has *less* power to influence laws than a

THE PRESIDENT AND THE PRIME MINISTER. In 1993, the British Prime Minister John Major came to Washington, D.C., to confer with U.S. President Bill Clinton. How does the British parliamentary system differ from our presidential system?

prime minister. The laws proposed by U.S. presidents are often rejected or changed by the separately elected lawmakers in Congress. But in the British Parliament, all the prime minister's ideas for major laws are expected to pass. If just one law fails to pass, that means that the majority party has turned against its own leader. It is taken as a sign that the British people have lost confidence in their representatives and their prime minister. At that point, an election is held to give people a chance to elect different representatives. The newly elected House of Commons chooses a new prime minister to lead a new government.

REVIEW

A. Two of a Kind

Select the answer that best completes each statement.

1. Israel's Knesset (parliament) and the U.S. Congress are two examples of a(n) (*a*) legislature, (*b*) "unfree" republic, (*c*) direct democracy, (*d*) autocracy.
2. Two nations with a parliamentary system are (*a*) the United States and Canada, (*b*) Great Britain and Israel, (*c*) the United States and Greece, (*d*) Great Britain and the United States.
3. The U.S. president and the British prime minister are (*a*) judges, (*b*) legislators, (*c*) dictators, (*d*) heads of government.

B. Agree or Disagree

Tell whether you **agree** or **disagree** with each statement. Explain why.

1. A presidential system is more democratic than a parliamentary system.
2. In the modern world, direct democracy is not possible.
3. Laws should be made by experts, not by ordinary citizens.

C. Making Comparisons

Tell whether each sentence describes a **parliamentary republic** or a **presidential republic.**

1. The British government is an example.
2. Members of the legislature decide who shall head the government.
3. Voters elect the chief executive.
4. The head of government has a seat in the legislature and may vote with fellow lawmakers.
5. The top official can expect some of his or her ideas for major laws to be rejected.
6. The top official resigns if he or she loses an important vote in the legislature.
7. A prime minister heads the government.
8. The United States government is an example.

4. SHOULD THE NATIONAL GOVERNMENT CONTROL LOCAL GOVERNMENTS?

So far, we have classified governments by seeing how they answered two questions.

First question: Does the government control the people, or do the people control their government? Governments of the first kind are either old-fashioned monarchies or modern dictatorships. Governments of the second kind are either direct or indirect democracies.

Second question: Do lawmakers elect the head of government? If they do, the government is classified as parliamentary. If they do not, it is called presidential.

Defining the relationship between governments. Here is a third important question about governments: **What shall be the relationship between the national government and local governments?** A nation of any size may be divided into many regions that are known by different names: provinces, states, territories, counties, districts, townships, and municipalities. Should each local unit have the power to make its own laws? Or should the lawmaking power belong only to the national government?

There are three possible answers to this question:

1. The *unitary government* answer. A strong national government has tight control over all local areas.
2. The *confederate government* answer. Local governments have far more power than the weak national government.
3. The *federalist government* answer. Both the national government and local governments have power to make important laws.

The unitary state of Bangladesh. An Asian nation, Bangladesh, provides an interesting example of a unitary government. Bangladesh is located on India's eastern border. In area, it is a small country crowded with more than 100 million people—most of them terribly poor. A dictator rules the nation from the capital city of Dacca.

One of this dictator's problems is how to control Bangladesh's 68,385 villages. He decided in 1980 that all villages should be supervised by a group of officials called a Gram Sarkar. Thousands of Gram Sarkars were created, one for every five or six villages. Each consisted of 12 people whose loyalty to the dictator could be relied on. The main duty of each Gram Sarkar was to maintain law and order and to arrest "disloyal" villagers.

A VILLAGE IN BANGLADESH. Do the citizens of this village have much local autonomy?

CARTOON CORNER

Which cartoon represents a federalist system?

Bangladesh is a unitary state because all local regions take orders from the nation's capital. The Gram Sarkars enforce the policies and laws of the dictator. They are not free to make important decisions of their own.

Do not suppose that all or even most unitary governments are dictatorships. France is a democracy, or "free," republic. It is also a unitary state whose local districts take orders from the French capital, Paris.

The Confederate government of the South. For an example of the confederate form—or confederacy—we can look at the states of the American South in the mid-1800s. In 1860 and 1861, South Carolina, Florida, Texas, and eight other states decided to withdraw (or secede) from the United States. They said that they had created a new nation called the Confederate States of America. Elected representatives from each state met in the Confederacy's capital, Richmond, Virginia.

But this national government had few powers compared to the powers of each of the 11 Confederate states. It had great difficulty collecting taxes and resorted to issuing paper money that became nearly worthless. Lawmakers elected by Georgia's citizens met in the state capital of Milledgeville. Their laws were more important to Georgians than the national laws passed in the Confederate capital. The same was true of Louisiana's state government in Baton Rouge, of Texas's government in Austin, and of Florida's government in Tallahassee.

For about four years (1861–1865), each of

the Southern states had something called *autonomy*. Autonomy means a great deal of freedom from outside control. Soon, however, Southerners lost their autonomy in the American Civil War. By 1865, Northern armies had defeated the South and brought the Confederate experiment to an end.

The federalist system in the United States. A third system for dividing power is the one used in the United States. Fifty states are included within our nation. Each state makes laws for the citizens within its borders. At the same time, the national government in Washington, D.C., makes laws for all the people of the United States.

To see how the federalist system works in our country, study the map below. It features two of the 50 states, Arizona and Ohio. Note the state capitals where state laws are made by elected representatives. Note also the national capital, Washington, D.C., where senators and representatives in Congress make U.S. laws.

Finally, look at the map key, which gives the meaning of the gray and lined areas on the map. Draw your own conclusions about our federalist system by answering the SKILLS CHECK questions.

SKILLS CHECK: Interpreting a map

1. If you lived in Ohio, which laws would you be required to obey? (*a*) only those made in Columbus, (*b*) only those made in Phoenix, (*c*) only those made in Washington, D.C., (*d*) those made in Columbus and Washington, D.C.
2. If you lived in Arizona, which laws would apply to you? (*a*) only those made in Columbus, (*b*) only those made in Phoenix, (*c*) only those made in Washington, D.C., (*d*) laws made in Phoenix and Washington, D.C.
3. Name a state not labeled on the map. What laws would apply to that state?

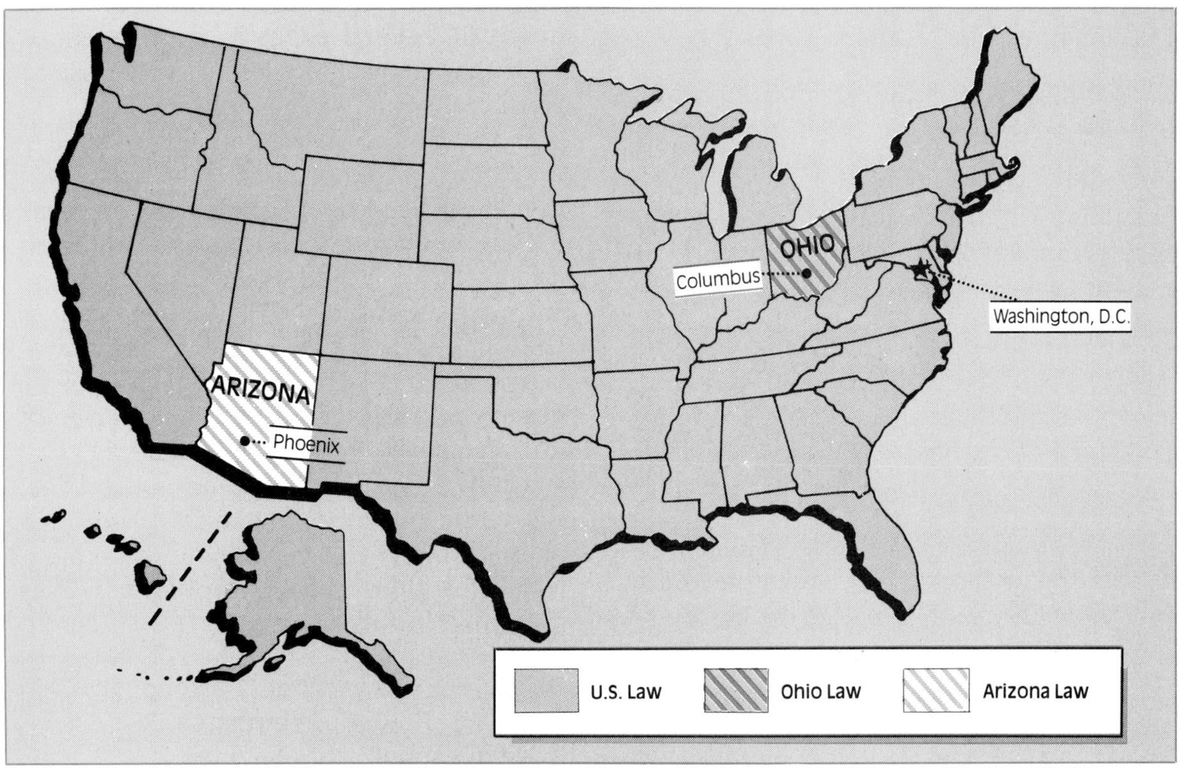

4. How would you explain to someone the meaning of the word "federalism"?

From Chapter One, recall what makes a state different from a nation. Though it has a government of its own, a state is not fully sovereign. Its laws may be overruled if a U.S. court finds them to be in conflict with U.S. laws.

The difference between "federal" and "federalist." Listening to radio or TV news, you often hear reporters speak of the "federal" government. Federal is just another name for the U.S. government, or national government. Do not confuse it with the words "federalism" and "federalist," which refer to the entire system of state and national government.

The *federal government* is just one part of our federalist system. The other major parts are the 50 state governments.

REVIEW

A. Building Your Political Vocabulary

In this section, you learned the meaning of: **autonomy, unitary, federal, federalist, confederate.** Use these terms to complete the sentences below. Write your answers on a separate sheet of paper.

- In a(n) ______ system, the national government is weaker than local units of government.
- In a(n) ______ system, the national government is the only one that makes laws.
- In the years 1861–1865, the states of the South had more ______ than they have today.
- In the United States, the capital of the ______ government is Washington, D.C.
- In a(n) ______ system, citizens are subject to both state laws and national laws.

B. Cartoon Corner

The three systems for dividing power are presented in cartoon form. Tell which system *you* think is shown by each of the three cartoons on page 52. Give reasons for your answers.

5. HOW DOES U.S. CAPITALISM DIFFER FROM COMMUNISM AND SOCIALISM?

Governments of the world differ not only in terms of their organization. They also differ in terms of how much—or how little—they direct the economic life of the nation. Think of the immense variety of products sold to American consumers at supermarkets, suburban shopping malls, and city department stores. For example, stacked from floor to ceiling in a typical supermarket are canned vegetables, frozen foods, laundry soaps, breads, juices, and so on. Just to list the different kinds of cereals on sale might fill several pages of your notebook. To list the titles of movies on videocassettes would take many pages more.

In the United States, consumers have an easy time finding products that satisfy both their basic needs and their desires for pleasure and entertainment. In the Soviet Union, on the other hand, shortages of food occurred frequently. Small luxuries such as chocolates and videocassettes were scarce. Why was this? The chief reason was the difference between the economic and political systems of the two countries.

The U.S. system is an example of *capitalism,* while the Soviet system was an example of *communism.* These economic systems, as well as a third system, *socialism,* will be explained in this section.

Three economic questions. Economics is the study of how different societies answer three questions:

1. *What kinds of goods and services should be produced, and how much of each is needed?* For example, how many perfumes, refrigerators, cereal boxes, and chocolate bars should be produced? How many auto repair centers, fast-food stores, and doctor's offices should be opened?

2. *How shall the needed goods and services be produced?* What kind of production methods will do the best job of turning out the desired amounts of goods and services of each type?

3. *Once produced, how will the various goods and services be distributed to people?* Should some people get more of the goods and services than others? If so, who?

Capitalism, communism, and socialism answer these questions in three different ways.

BRIGHT IDEA FOR A BETTER BULB. In a free enterprise system, who decides whether money should be spent to invent a better and cheaper light bulb?

The capitalist's answer: free enterprise. A capitalist is someone who believes that all important economic decisions should be made by private businesses—not by government. One of the most famous capitalists of all time was the American inventor Thomas Edison. In the 1870s and 1880s, Edison invested his money (or "capital") in a New Jersey laboratory where new products could be created. No government encouraged him to open the laboratory. Neither did anyone in government tell him to work on an electric light bulb or phonograph.

It was Edison's own decision to risk his money on new products, thinking that people would want to buy them. In fact, they did buy Edison's inventions and he became rich as a result. But his success was not guaranteed. Other capitalists of the time lost their money in failing businesses because they could not sell enough of their products to make the venture pay.

Consider how Edison, as a capitalist, answered the three economic questions. *What* was to be produced at his laboratory? Light bulbs, phonographs, and other inventions. *How* were they to be produced? With machinery, raw materials, and labor paid for by Edison's privately owned company. *Who* received the products made at Edison's factory? Any consumers who were able and willing to pay the prices charged by the Edison company (or by privately owned retail stores).

Capitalism is a system of *free enterprise.* Anyone who wishes may start a business firm by selling goods or services to the public. The owner of the business is free to decide what shall be sold and at what prices. The owner strives to take in more money from customers than he or she pays out in wages and other costs. If the business succeeds, it makes a profit (the sum left over after costs are subtracted from sales). A businessperson's desire for profits is the fuel—the moving force—that drives every capitalist economy.

The Communist answer: public ownership. The system called communism answers the three economic questions in an entirely different way. In its pure form, communism does not allow private businesses to exist. Instead, it gives the national government total ownership and control of all industries.

The most famous Communist thinker and writer was a German named Karl Marx. In 1848, Marx published a pamphlet called *The Communist Manifesto.* It describes a "class struggle" between capitalists (business owners) and wage-earners, or workers. He predicted a time when millions of poorly paid workers would join in revolt against the capitalist system. They would seize the factories and farms of a nation and govern them for everyone's benefit. Marx said that nations would disappear as workers all over the world joined in revolution. His *Manifesto* concluded: "Workers of the world, unite. You have nothing to lose but your chains."

In Russia, Marx's writings were admired by a group of students and workers who hated the autocratic rule of the Russian czar. In 1917, one of their leaders—Vladimir Lenin—seized control of the Russian government. Lenin and his Communist followers gave Russia a new name: the Union of Soviet Socialist Republics.

THE KREMLIN. Soviet leaders in Moscow had their offices in the Kremlin (building at the left). How did decisions made in the Kremlin affect the production of all Soviet goods and services?

The Soviet government tried to abolish capitalist ways of making goods. Profits were outlawed. Workers in farms and factories were employed by the government at tasks assigned by Communist party bosses. They were told to work hard, not for their own sake, but so that Soviet society would grow stronger.

Communist nations answer the three economic questions like this: (*a*) What shall be produced? Whatever the government decides that society needs the most. (*b*) How shall different things be produced? Again, the government dictates the methods for getting work done. (*c*) For whose benefit shall production be carried on? For the benefit of society as a whole, as determined by the government. Most Communist governments decide to produce only a few luxury items and to concentrate on basic goods such as bricks, steel, oil, and foods.

The failure of Communist economies. For many years, leaders of Communist nations argued that their economic system was superior to capitalism. They expected such a system to produce the right amount of goods and services to meet the basic needs of all citizens. In recent years, however, the Communist economies have not fulfilled the needs of consumers. In the Soviet Union, for example, stores operated by the government often ran out of meats, vegetables, shoes, soaps, and other essential consumer items. As part of their daily routine, Soviet citizens would spend hours waiting in long lines to obtain a loaf of bread or a box of laundry detergent. Compared to the quality of products made in the United States, Japan, and Western Europe, the quality of Soviet-made goods was usually poor.

As an economic system, what was wrong with communism? In every Communist country, why did the system fail to produce a decent standard of living for the average person? These three reasons are among the most important:

1. Communist decision-makers consider the needs of the state to be more important than the needs of the individual. In telling factories what to produce, the government places much greater emphasis on heavy industry than on consumer goods.

2. A planned economy (or "command economy") cannot adjust to consumer tastes and needs. In order to work well, a master plan for national production must anticipate *all* the needs of *every* member of society on *every* day of the year. It would be like trying to predict what the weather will be like 100 days, 200 days, and even a whole year into the future. It cannot be done.

3. Workers in a Communist economy have no incentives (or motivation) for working hard. If they slack off, they will not lose their jobs, because the government guarantees them employment. On the other hand, if they try to excel, they will probably not be rewarded with extra pay.

In 1989 and 1990, partly because their economies worked so badly, the countries of Eastern Europe voted to get rid of communism and try another system. In 1991, Russia and its neighboring republics broke free from the control of the Communist party and declared an end to the Soviet empire. Today, these republics are struggling to overcome the severe economic troubles caused by communism.

The socialist answer: a mixed economy. Several countries in Western Europe have economies where private businesses and public ownership exist side by side. Sweden is an example. Its Volvo automobiles are made by a privately owned business firm and sold to consumers for profits. Many other companies and shops compete in Sweden as free enterprises.

At the same time, the Swedish government owns and operates radio and television stations, electric power plants, airports, railroads, and a few banks. It also provides medical care for the people.

Unlike capitalist governments, Sweden's government takes care of people "from the cradle to the grave." When a woman gives birth to a baby, the government pays the doctor's fees and hospital costs. It pays for most of a student's education through college as well as high school. It pays for the retraining of workers who need to learn new skills. It pays a person's medical and dental bills throughout life.

Sweden's economic and political system is known by two names: (1) democratic socialism or (2) mixed economy. It is democratic because political freedoms are guaranteed. Also, several Swedish parties compete for votes in free elections. (This is *not* true of Communist countries where all candidates must belong to the Communist party.)

Democratic socialism gives a mixed answer to the three questions of what to produce, how to produce, and for whom to produce. Economic decisions are made partly by private companies and individuals, partly by government agencies.

No system is pure. No nation on earth is either purely capitalistic or purely communistic. The U.S. government owns and operates certain economic enterprises such as the post office and some electric power plants. The Soviet government allowed some individuals opportunities to sell goods for profit. The mix of private and public ownership differs from country to country.

✔✔ SKILLS CHECK: Interpreting a continuum

A **continuum** is a line with opposite values or ideas at either end of it. Reality falls somewhere between the extreme ends. It may be closer to one end or the other, depending on the thing being analyzed. For example, note the continuum on page 58.

NATIONAL ECONOMIES OF THE WORLD

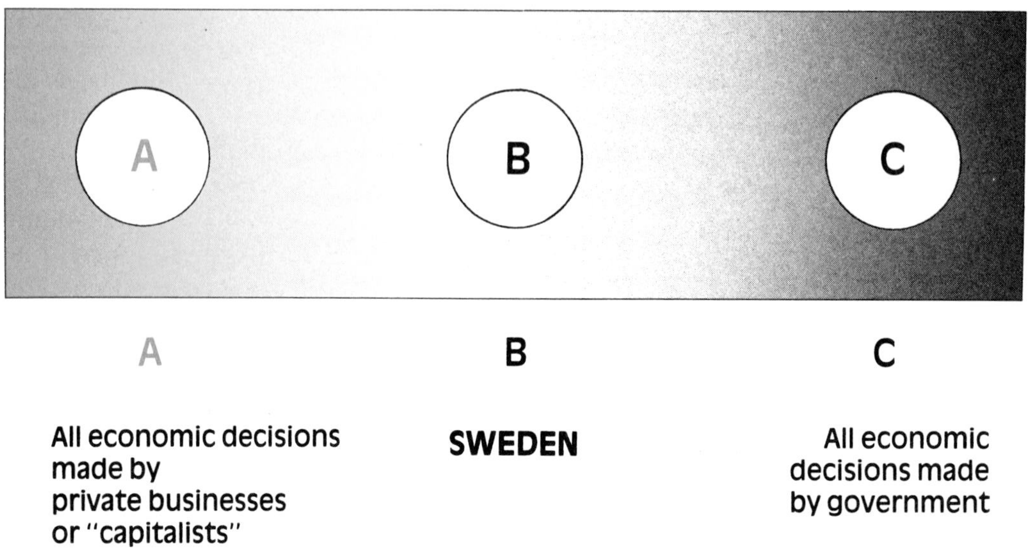

1. Would the U.S. economy be placed nearer to A or to C? Why?
2. Would the economy of the former Soviet Union be placed nearer to A or to C? Why?

REVIEW

A. Fact or Opinion

Tell whether each sentence is a **fact** or an **opinion**. Then, if you think a sentence is an opinion, tell whether or not you agree with it and explain.

1. Karl Marx predicted a world revolution of the working class.
2. Thomas Edison's inventions prove that capitalism is superior to other systems.
3. The Soviet government decided how much candy was to be produced for Soviet consumers.
4. Making a profit is a goal of U.S. candy manufacturers.
5. The United States should adopt some of the welfare programs of Sweden.

B. Applying What You Know

Identify an object that you own—a watch, a sweater, anything at all. Then answer these questions about it:

1. Do you think the object was made in a capitalist nation? Can you prove it?
2. Do you think the Soviet Union would have manufactured as many of the items as the United States? Why or why not?
3. In a nation practicing democratic socialism, who would probably produce the object: (*a*) government or (*b*) a private business? Why do you think so?

CHAPTER REVIEW

A. Completing the Summary

Select terms from the word list to fill in the blanks in the summary below. Write your answers on a piece of paper.

autonomy	oligarchy
capitalism	parliamentary
communism	political parties
democracy	president
dictators	representatives
enterprise	rights
federalist	socialism
indirect	unitary
monarchs	vote

Like types of shoes, governments of the world are many and varied. In the past, most governments were headed by __(1)__ with absolute power. The autocrats of modern times are more commonly called __(2)__. They wear either civilian clothes or military uniforms instead of kingly robes and crowns.

When power belongs to a privileged group, the government is called a(n) __(3)__. When power is shared by all the people, the government is a(n) __(4)__. In a democratic nation, these qualities are most important:

(*a*) the right of adult citizens to __(5)__.

(*b*) the free competition of two or more __(6)__.

(*c*) limits on the power of government and the guarantee of individual __(7)__.

Many modern nations called themselves "republics" because their leaders are not monarchs and the people vote in elections. Some of these nations, however, are "unfree" republics governed by dictators.

The United States and other modern republics practice a form of __(8)__ democracy. Instead of voting on laws directly, the voters elect __(9)__ to make laws for them. Lawmakers in a __(10)__ republic elect a prime minister. The United States has a different system headed by a __(11)__. This official does *not* vote in the national legislature.

Governments differ in the amount of power that they allow to states, provinces, and other local units. Under a confederate form of government, the states have a great deal of __(12)__. Under a __(13)__ form, they have none at all. The __(14)__ system of the United States gives lawmaking power to both the national government and state governments.

Governments of the world give different answers to economic questions. A system called __(15)__ relies upon the efforts of privately owned businesses. The U.S. government regulates businesses but does not tell them what to produce.

An opposite system is __(16)__. Based on the ideas of Karl Marx, this system gives government the power to make all major economic decisions for the nation. A prime example was the planned economy of the Soviet Union.

A third system, practiced in Sweden and elsewhere, is known as democratic __(17)__. Welfare services are provided by the government, while the making of most consumer goods is left to free __(18)__.

B. Making Inferences

There can be no such thing as a centipede with only two legs. This is impossible because a centipede, by definition, is a 100-legged creature. Some of the phrases below are political impossibilities. For each phrase, say whether it is (*a*) **possible** or (*b*) **impossible.** Explain.

1. a presidential republic headed by a prime minister
2. a dictator who rules a unitary state
3. a confederation whose states have very little autonomy
4. a unitary republic that is divided into autonomous states
5. a "free" republic that puts the government's critics in jail
6. a dictatorship with an elected legislature
7. a monarchy that lacks a head of state
8. a federal government with a two-house legislature and a president as head of state
9. a direct democracy whose laws are made by a despot
10. a "free" republic in which a parliament is elected every eight years
11. an indirect democracy in which only 500 people make the nation's laws
12. a direct democracy in which 90 percent of the citizens cannot vote

C. Create Your Own Republic

Imagine that you live on an island in the Somewhere Sea. Named Boomerang because of its shape, it has a population of 100,080. You and the other Boomerangers have just won your independence from the king of a neighboring island. You are now meeting at the Boomerang Beach Hotel with other political leaders of your island nation. Create a plan—or constitution—for the Republic of Boomerang by answering the following questions. (Before answering, study the map.)

1. What should be the republic's capital city? Why?
   (*a*) The oldest city, Rango
   (*b*) The fastest-growing seaport, Boomville
   (*c*) The most centrally located city, Middletown.
2. What should be the requirements for voting in a Boomerang national election?
3. Describe your system for electing representatives to Boomerang's legislature.
4. Should the provinces (states) of Rango Beach, Lorna, and Dune be given power to make their own laws? Explain your answer.
5. Depending on your answer to question 4, tell whether the new Republic of Boomerang is unitary, confederate, or federal.

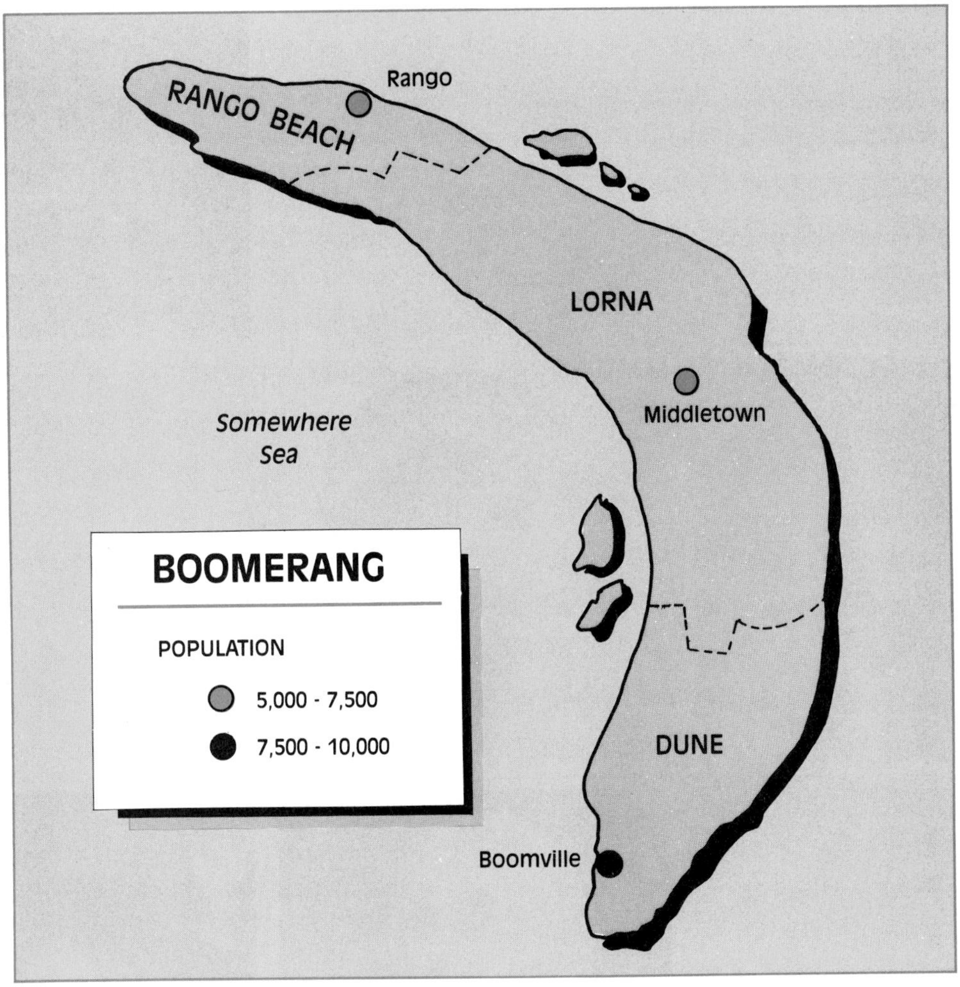
Rango
RANGO BEACH
LORNA
Middletown
Somewhere
Sea
BOOMERANG
POPULATION
5,000 - 7,500
7,500 - 10,000
DUNE
Boomville

a.

b.

c.

d.

e.

f.

g.

a. George Washington
b. Sandra Day O'Connor
c. Susan B. Anthony
d. James Madison
e. Dwight Eisenhower and Richard Nixon
f. College students in the 1970s
g. Harriet Tubman

UNIT TWO

The Amazing U.S. Constitution

The U.S. Constitution is thought by many to be one of the wonders of the modern world. A British prime minister, William Gladstone, once praised it as "the most wonderful work ever struck off at a given time by the brain and purpose of man." Why is the Constitution so greatly admired? You will know why after reading the three chapters that make up this unit.

PICTURE PREVIEW

To start thinking about the Constitution, try to match the people pictured on the opposite page with the statements below. (Answers may be used more than once.) Right now, you probably know enough to guess a few of the answers—but not all. After finishing the unit, return to this page and take the quiz again.

1. These *two* people were among the delegates who drafted and signed the Constitution in 1787.
2. By working to amend the Constitution, this leader helped to win voting rights for millions of Americans.
3. Article III of the Constitution describes the judicial powers of this person.
4. The offices held by these *two* people are the only ones specifically mentioned in Article II of the Constitution.
5. This person made sure that a Bill of Rights was added to the Constitution.
6. These *four* people acted as president under the Constitution.
7. These *four* people never had to pay a federal income tax.
8. During their lifetime, these *two* people were never allowed to vote in a federal or state election.
9. A late amendment to the Constitution gave these *two* people the right to vote.

Answers

1. *a, d*
2. *c*
3. *b*
4. *e*
5. *d*
6. *a, d, e*
7. *a, c, d, g*
8. *c, g*
9. *f*

PHILADELPHIA, 1787. The 55 delegates who met inside this building in 1787 created the U.S. Constitution. Can you name five of them?

CHAPTER 4

How the Constitution Was Made

OBJECTIVES

After reading this chapter, you will know

1. why a new constitution for the United States was written in 1787.
2. in what ways the new constitution differed from the old one.
3. why a Bill of Rights was added to the Constitution.
4. how to interpret a political map of the original 13 states.

It was a warm afternoon in the middle of May 1787. Seated in his Philadelphia garden, Benjamin Franklin heard the city's church bells chime and clang. The bells were announcing the arrival in Philadelphia of a famous visitor from Virginia, George Washington. A few hours later, Washington appeared at Franklin's door. At the age of 81, Franklin was hobbled with age and could hardly walk. But he could still impress anyone with his sparkling intelligence. He greeted the Virginian warmly and chatted with him for the rest of a pleasant afternoon.

In 1787, Washington was no longer a military leader. Four years before, in 1783, he had said farewell to the army that he had led to victory against the British. He had hoped to be permanently retired from the cares of public life. But he recognized that his country was again in crisis. The United States was a new republic struggling to hold its own in a hostile world governed by kings. The original plan of government that had been created for the American nation was not working. Something had to be done to strengthen it.

So Washington and other able Virginians traveled north to Philadelphia to attend a political *convention* there. Franklin too would be attending the convention as a delegate from Pennsylvania. The early arrivals had to wait almost two weeks before the slow-moving stage coaches and sailing ships brought to Philadelphia the delegates from the other states.

On May 25, 1787, the delegates held their first official meeting. The discussions and arguments continued all through the spring and summer. Finally, after four months of work, the weary delegates emerged from their meetings with a printed document. It bore the title: The Constitution of the United States.

Today, this document is admired by millions—not just by Americans but by people of many nations. The Constitution created by Washington, Franklin, and others has stood the test of time. It seems to work just as well today as it did over 200 years ago.

Were Washington and Franklin as confident as we are about the document they produced? No, they were much less certain of final success. All 55 delegates at Philadelphia had grave doubts about certain clauses in the Constitution. In this chapter, you will read about their doubts. You will

BENJAMIN FRANKLIN. Franklin was famous for his inventions: a lightning rod, a stove, and bifocal glasses. His final achievement was working with other delegates to create a new form of government. Do you think a constitution should be created *(a)* by a group of people, or *(b)* by a single talented individual like Franklin?

also read about the decisions they made that produced a strong and enduring plan of government.

Let these questions guide your study:

1. In what ways was the first U.S. government weak?
2. What issues were debated at Philadelphia?
3. How did the delegates settle their differences?
4. How was the Constitution debated and ratified?

1. IN WHAT WAYS WAS THE FIRST U.S. GOVERNMENT WEAK?

We need to understand why Washington, Franklin, and others met in Philadelphia in 1787 to design a new government. Let us look back to points made earlier about the history of American government.

Looking back: points to remember. Recall these important facts and ideas from Chapters 2 and 3:

1. A constitution is another word for a system of government. It answers questions like these: Who shall have power to make the laws? Are there any limits to the government's lawmaking power? Should elections be held and if so, how often?
2. Thirteen American states from New Hampshire to Georgia had originally been colonies of England. In the early 1700s, each colony had its own elected legislature. The colonists jealously guarded their rights to participate in government. Thus, Americans were self-governing long before they won their independence as a nation.
3. Beginning in 1765, Americans like Patrick Henry feared that Britain intended to deprive them of their rights, or liberties. They protested taxes imposed upon them without their consent. Fighting broke out between British troops and American farmers.
4. Meeting in Philadelphia in 1776, delegates from the 13 colonies decided to form a new nation, the United States of America. One delegate, Thomas Jefferson, drafted one of the most influential documents in world history: the Declaration of Independence. It stated this revolutionary idea: "We hold these truths to be self-evident, that all men are created equal."
5. From the day of its founding, the United States was unique among the nations of the world. Its government was a republic, not a monarchy. Preserving liberty was a major goal.
6. Those who write a new constitution must make difficult choices. At one extreme is

the choice of a unitary form of government in which all power belongs to the national government. A second choice is the confederate form in which member states are nearly independent, and the national government cannot control them. Between these two extremes is a third choice known as federalism (national and state governments sharing power).

So ends our review of six points you already know. They are the foundation for understanding the story that follows.

Loyalty to state governments. The first constitution of the United States provided for a government of the confederate type. Adopted in 1781, this constitution was known as the Articles of Confederation.

In the 1780s, the United States of America was a brand-new idea. By comparison, the colonial governments of Massachusetts and Virginia had existed for more than 150 years. Most other colonies were at least 100 years old. People were used to being citizens of New Hampshire or Pennsylvania or North Carolina. They were not at all used to being citizens of the United States. Also, they feared that a strong central government might eventually crush their liberties. Therefore, in 1781, most Americans wanted their familiar state governments to be stronger than an untried national government.

The Articles of Confederation. Let us look at the document that created the first government of the United States. The Articles of Confederation stated the following:

1. Each state was to keep its "sovereignty, freedom, and independence."
2. All states pledged to "enter into a firm league of friendship" and to assist each other when threatened by foreign armies.
3. Delegates from each state would meet together as a United States Congress.
4. A state could send as many as seven delegates to Congress. But the state delegation (group of delegates) had to vote as a single unit. (Example: the seven delegates from Pennsylvania could cast only one vote for or against a proposed law.)
5. No state could go to war unless Congress consented to it.

NASSAU HALL, THE U.S. CAPITOL IN 1783. This building (center) at Princeton College in New Jersey was one of the places where Congress met during the American Revolution. What document defined the powers of Congress in 1783?

6. States were to pay what taxes they could into a "common treasury." Money collected in this way would be used to pay Congress's expenses.
7. A committee of Congress could elect a president for a term of one year. But this president had no executive power.
8. Any change in the Articles of Confederation had to be approved by all 13 state legislatures.

Weaknesses of the Articles. The Congress created by the Articles lacked many things:

It lacked money because most states failed to pay enough taxes into the "common treasury." It lacked steady leadership because the president of Congress had little real authority. Congress lacked the means for enforcing its own laws. It lacked the respect of foreign governments because it could not pay its debts. Often it lacked the number of delegates necessary to conduct business. Because it lacked these things, Congress lacked any real ability to govern.

Shays's Rebellion. A violent event caused many Americans to wonder whether their new nation could long survive under a weak government. The event occurred in western Massachusetts in the fall of 1786. Farmers there had almost no money and could not pay the taxes demanded by the state government. Many of them had fought as patriots in the American Revolution. And yet, for failing to pay taxes, a Massachusetts court tried to take away their property. The farmers resisted violently, taking up arms and marching together as a rebel army. The rioting farmers and their leader, Daniel Shays, were finally brought under control.

2,000 "REBELS." The followers of the Massachusetts farmer, Daniel Shays, were fired upon by the state militia to prevent them from attacking an arsenal. Three of the 2,000 "rebels" were killed. Why did Washington and others worry about the incident?

News of Shays's Rebellion shocked Washington and other American leaders. They feared for the future of their young country. They understood that one cause of the rebellion was money—or the lack of it. The farmers had rebelled because they had no gold or silver coins to pay their debts. Only a strong national government could issue such coins and rescue the country from financial ruin.

Call for a convention. Another important event occurred in the fall of 1786. Meeting in New York City, members of Congress received a written proposal from Annapolis, Maryland. Earlier in the year, leaders from five states had met in Annapolis to discuss certain problems, including the problem of weak government. Their proposal urged Congress to call a special convention of delegates from all 13 states. This convention's purpose would be to decide how the Articles of Confederation should be strengthened.

Congress voted to act on the Annapolis proposal. It invited the *legislatures* of every state to send delegates to Philadelphia in May 1787. Twelve states heeded the call and elected delegates. One state, Rhode Island, failed to send anyone.

REVIEW

A. Correcting the Statements

The underlined word in each sentence makes the sentence incorrect. On a separate piece of paper, write the word that would make the sentence correct.

1. The first constitution of the United States was unitary in form.
2. In 1781, most Americans thought the national government should have greater power than state governments.
3. Before the American Revolution, the king of England had unlimited power to make laws for the colonies.
4. The Articles of Confederation gave each state the right to cast seven votes on any proposed law.
5. Changing the Articles of Confederation required the approval of a majority of states.
6. Daniel Shays, a Massachusetts farmer, rebelled in 1786 against taxes imposed by the U.S. Congress.
7. Rhode Island was the only state not represented at the Annapolis Convention.
8. In 1787, Washington was one of many Americans who thought Congress was too strong.

B. Double Match

Find **two phrases** that describe each term. Use letters to identify them.

1. Congress _____ _____
2. Articles of Confederation _____ _____
3. Declaration of Independence _____ _____
4. Annapolis Convention _____ _____
5. Philadelphia Convention _____ _____

a. served as the legislature of the United States
b. meeting of delegates from five states
c. stated that "all men are created equal"
d. described the union of states as a "firm league of friendship"
e. was written and signed in 1776
f. went into effect in 1781
g. urged that a constitutional convention make changes in the Articles
h. had trouble collecting taxes from the states
i. Washington and Franklin were two of its delegates
j. its meetings began in May 1787

C. Project

Create a **time line** for the period 1765–1787. Place the following events on the time line, indicating the date of each.

1. Patrick Henry protests the stamp tax.
2. United States declares independence from Britain.
3. Articles of Confederation go into effect.
4. Shays's Rebellion arouses fear of disorder.
5. Constitutional Convention meets at Philadelphia.

2. WHAT ISSUES WERE DEBATED AT PHILADELPHIA?

Eventually 55 men from 12 states attended the Philadelphia Convention of 1787. From Monday through Saturday, week after week, they would meet together in a square, high-ceilinged room inside a brick building. In 1787, the building was known as the State House. Today it is better known as Independence Hall.

One of the first decisions of the delegates was to hold their meetings in secret. Until they finished their work, the press and the public would be told nothing. They wanted the work on the constitution they were writing to be free of outside pressures. This goal would have been impossible if newspapers stirred up people's fears.

The delegates' view of politics. The constitution makers at Philadelphia were all experienced in the art of politics. Most of them had served a year or two in the United States Congress under the Articles of Confederation. They had seen at first hand that Congress could not enforce its own laws.

Because they understood politics, the delegates realized that people tended to be self-interested. In any political assembly, individuals will try to get for themselves all that they can. For this reason, laws can never be completely neutral. They may favor either one *interest group* in society or another. In Philadelphia, each delegate expected to speak up for the interests of his own state.

And yet the delegates were also American patriots. They wanted the United States to hold together and to function successfully as a nation. For this larger purpose, they were willing to give up some of their more local goals.

The most influential delegates. In any assembly, some people play only minor roles, while others stand out as leaders. In the Philadelphia Convention, a most influential delegate proved to be a young Virginian, James Madison. Scholars would later refer

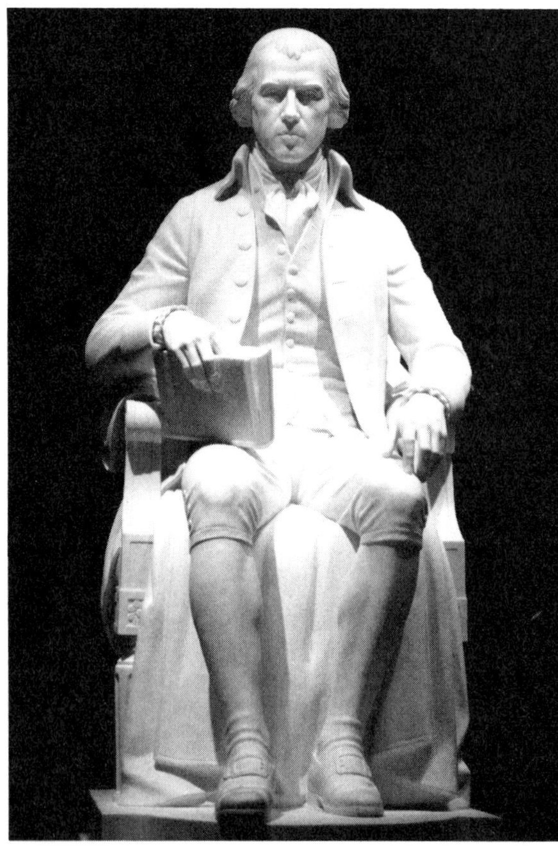

GENIUS FROM VIRGINIA. This statue of James Madison is in the Library of Congress in Washington, D.C. What were Madison's contributions to the making of the Constitution?

to Madison as the "Father of the Constitution." As we shall see, his so-called Virginia Plan sketched the major parts of a federal plan of government. Furthermore, through the long hot summer of argument, Madison kept detailed notes of what the other delegates said. Because of the patient labors of James Madison, we have a wonderful record of the thinking that went into the Constitution.

Among those who helped Madison to frame (organize) the great document were four other leaders:

George Washington of Virginia: The retired general was 56 years old in the summer of 1787. He was chosen unanimously by the other delegates to be the convention's president. His chief contributions were: (1) managing the daily business of the convention with fairness and dignity, (2) giving the American people confidence in the delegates' decisions.

Gouverneur Morris of Pennsylvania: Morris was a witty and able debater. He had lost one leg in a carriage accident, but this did not lessen his tremendous energy. His contributions included: (1) arguing successfully for many of the provisions of the Constitution, (2) turning delegates' ideas into written form. (The drafting of the Constitution was Morris's work.)

James Wilson of Pennsylvania: This scholarly lawyer exerted a powerful influence on other delegates. Listening to Wilson talk, one delegate thought he understood "all the political institutions of the world." Wilson's contributions: (1) proposing a plan for electing the president, (2) arguing that all power should rest finally with the American people (instead of with the states).

Roger Sherman of Connecticut: "Awkward . . . strange in his manner, the oddest-shaped character I ever remember to have met with." That was the way this Connecticut Yankee impressed a Southern delegate. But Sherman came up with key ideas when they were most needed. His idea for a Great Compromise, described below, saved the convention.

The Virginia Plan. How could the national government be strengthened without crushing the independence of the states? To this central question, James Madison proposed a bold solution. Backed by fellow Virginians, the proposal came to be known as the

THREE LEADERS. In drafting the Constitution, Gouverneur Morris (left) included the ideas of James Wilson (center) and Roger Sherman (right). What was Sherman's plan for organizing Congress?

Virginia Plan. These were its major ideas for establishing a stronger government:

- A legislature consisting of two parts, or houses
- Members of one of the legislative houses to be elected by the people
- Members of the second house to be elected by the first house
- An executive (or president) with real power to enforce the laws
- A system of courts for interpreting Congress's laws.

In effect, the Virginians proposed that a new government take the place of the old one. They did not openly say that the Articles of Confederation should be scrapped, but that is what they intended.

How did the Virginia Plan differ from the government created by the Articles of Confederation? CARTOON CORNER below gives the answer. It shows that government in 1787 consisted of just one body, Congress. Madison and other Virginians thought that the "horse" (Congress) would do better if two wheels (a president and a Supreme Court) were attached to the national cart.

The New Jersey Plan. Although many favored the Virginia Plan, others feared it. Among the latter group was a small man from a small state. William Paterson of New Jersey was less than five feet tall. He was a fighter who, when challenged, could stubbornly hold his ground.

In the Philadelphia Convention, Paterson stood up to make a speech. He objected to the Virginians' idea for representing the different states in the new government. Under the Virginia Plan, he said, *both* houses of the new Congress would be controlled by representatives from states with the most people: Virginia, Pennsylvania, and Massachusetts. The states with fewer people, including New Jersey, would have much less power to make the laws of Congress.

The reason was obvious. According to the Virginia Plan, each state could send representatives in proportion to the size of its population. Virginia, being several times more populous than New Jersey, would then be able to outvote Paterson's "little" state.

Paterson therefore presented a plan of his own: the New Jersey Plan. It proposed keeping the one-house Congress of the

CARTOON CORNER

"I THINK IT WOULD WORK BETTER IF WE PUT WHEELS ON IT."
SUPREME COURT
PRESIDENT
JAMES MADISON
CONGRESS
THE NATION

WILLIAM PATERSON OF NEW JERSEY. As a delegate from a "little" state, why did Paterson and his allies oppose the Virginia Plan?

Articles of Confederation. Paterson said *amendments* (written changes) could be added to the Articles to make Congress much stronger. But the system for representing the 13 states would be the same as before. Each state, whether large or small, would be entitled to just one vote.

On June 19, after almost a month of argument, the state delegations voted between the two plans. A majority favored the Virginia Plan. But Paterson and his allies from states with smaller populations would not yield. They threatened to walk out of the convention unless their states were given equal representation.

REVIEW

A. Who Was Who?

Each **phrase** in the righthand column describes a **delegate** in the lefthand column. For each phrase, tell who is meant.

James Madison
William Paterson
George Washington
Roger Sherman
James Wilson
Gouverneur Morris

1. Connecticut compromiser
2. New Jersey delegate
3. convention president
4. one-legged politician
5. champion of the small states
6. "awkward" character
7. scholarly, all-knowing Pennsylvanian
8. "Father of the Constitution"
9. writer of the clauses of the Constitution
10. author of the Virginia Plan

B. Making Comparisons

For each question, point out at least **two differences** between the items named.

1. How did the Virginia Plan differ from the Articles of Confederation?
2. How did the New Jersey Plan differ from the Virginia Plan?
3. How did James Madison's contribution to the Constitution differ from James Wilson's contribution?

C. Agree or Disagree

Tell whether you **agree** or **disagree** with each statement on page 74. Explain.

1. Delegates from New Jersey and Virginia were both acting selfishly in favoring their different plans.
2. By holding their meetings in secret, the delegates showed that they distrusted the American public.
3. Madison's ideas for changing the government were better than Paterson's ideas.

3. HOW DID THE DELEGATES SETTLE THEIR DIFFERENCES?

As it happened, New Jersey's delegates did not leave Philadelphia in anger. The "awkward" fellow from Connecticut, Roger Sherman, suggested a means of satisfying both big states and small ones. He proposed what came to be known as the Great Compromise.

The Great Compromise. A *compromise* is a means of settling an argument between opposing sides. Each side agrees to accept less than what it originally asked for. The trick in arranging a compromise is to give a little to one side and a little to the other side.

Sherman's idea for compromise was to represent the states differently in two houses of Congress. The larger house—the House of Representatives—would be designed to favor the larger states. Representation in the House would be proportional to the size of a state's population. But the second house of Congress—the Senate—would be more to the liking of smaller states. Each state, no matter what its population, would elect two senators. Thus, in the Senate, the states would have equal power. But in the House, the states' power would be unequal.

THREE PLANS COMPARED

	VIRGINIA PLAN	NEW JERSEY PLAN	GREAT COMPROMISE
How many houses in Congress ?	2	1	2
How to represent the states ?	In both houses, states represented according to the size of their populations.	All states represented equally.	*House of Representatives:* States represented according to size of their populations. *Senate:* All states represented equally.

A legislature with two houses instead of one is called a *bicameral legislature.* Its chief advantage over a *unicameral,* or one-house, plan is in giving representation to both the people and the states. On the other hand, a bicameral plan has the disadvantage of slowing down the lawmaking process. Both houses must agree to the same law and, as we shall see, this is often hard to achieve.

Few delegates loved Roger Sherman's compromise plan. James Madison liked it least of all. Many recognized, however, that compromise was needed to save the convention from breaking up. On a hot July afternoon, five states voted for the compromise while four states voted against it. A bare majority carried the day for the Great Compromise.

SKILLS CHECK: Interpreting maps

The map (right) shows the original 13 states as they looked in 1787. It also shows, in parentheses, the number of representatives that each state could send to the House of Representatives. For example, in writing the Constitution, the delegates agreed that New Hampshire would have three representatives while Massachusetts would have eight.

From the map, we can see the relative size of the states in 1787. Look at it carefully. Then answer the questions below.

1. Massachusetts was about equal in population to what other state?
2. Which state had the largest population?
3. Which two states were the smallest both in area and population?
4. The boundaries of several states in 1787 were not the same as their current boundaries. Name two. (See the map of the United States on pages 564–565.)
5. Do you think that New York today still sends six representatives to the U.S. House of Representatives? Why or why not?
6. The map gives only the number of *representatives* for each state. Select any two states, and tell how many *senators* each was entitled to.

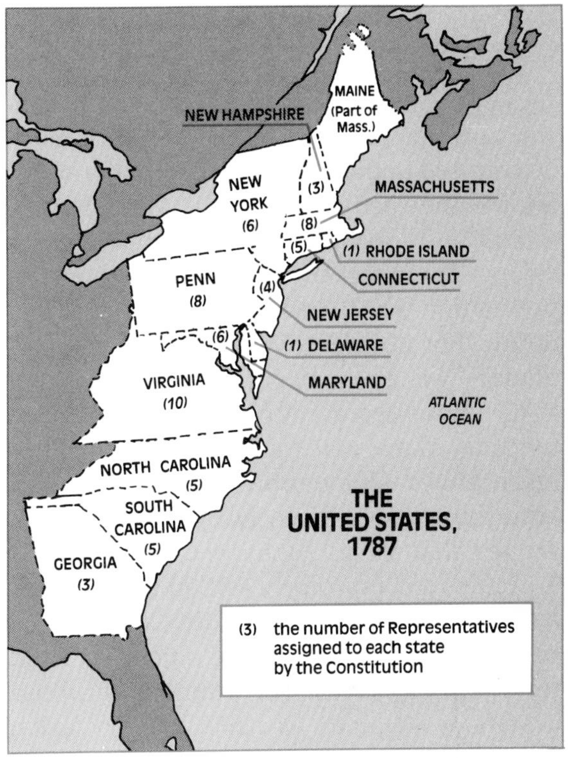

Compromise on the slave trade. After the Great Compromise, another conflict flared up. This one pitted delegates from the North against delegates from the South. The conflict concerned slavery.

In 1787, enslaved blacks were found in Northern towns as well as on Southern plantations. But slavery was much more common and important to trade in the states south of Maryland. Certain Northerners said the practice of importing Africans as slaves should be abolished (stopped). Such opinions worried many Southerners who depended on slave labor.

A delegate from South Carolina wanted a special clause about slavery to be inserted in the new constitution. It would prohibit

Congress from ever interfering with the slave trade. But many Northern delegates protested. Such a clause, they said, would be totally unacceptable.

A compromise was at last worked out. Northern and Southern delegates agreed that no law of Congress could touch the slave trade before 1808. After that date, Congress could do as it wished.

The Three-fifths Compromise. There was still another problem. How were slaves to be counted in the total population of a state? Should they be counted at all? Again Southerners and Northerners gave opposite answers. The effect of counting slaves in the population was to increase the power of the South. For example, South Carolina's population was about half slave and half free. If its slaves were counted, it would have twice as many votes in the House of Representatives. Not wanting the South to outvote their own region, Northern delegates argued that slaves should *not* be counted.

Again, a compromise settled the conflict. It was known as the Three-fifths Compromise because three-fifths was the ratio to be used for counting slaves. For example, suppose a state was found to have 10,000 slaves. Then three-fifths of the total (6,000) would be added to the state's population of free citizens. The total of these two figures would be the basis for representing the state in the House of Representatives. (The three-fifths rule went into effect for the first time after 1790 when the population was officially counted.)

Signing the Constitution. At last, the long summer in Philadelphia came to an end. On September 17, 1787, George Washington held in his hand the final product of the convention's work. Written in a fine script on four large pages was *The Constitution of the United States of America.* Every phrase of it had been debated and voted upon. Now it was time for the delegates to step forward and add their signatures to the document.

Of the 55 delegates, only 42 still remained in Philadelphia. Some of those who left early were disgusted because they did not get their way. Three of the final participants had misgivings about the Constitution and refused to sign it. Even the 39 who came forward to sign had doubts about some of the clauses and compromises. But they believed that the new Constitution would at least be stronger than the Articles of Confederation.

REVIEW

A. Solving Problems

Explain how each of the following disputes was settled by compromise.

1. the dispute between large states (more populous) and small states over representation in Congress
2. the dispute between Northern states and Southern states about the future of the slave trade
3. the dispute between Northern states and Southern states over the counting of slaves

B. Applying What You Know

Study the free and slave populations of States A, B, and C. Then **apply the three-fifths rule** to answer the questions below.

STATE A: free citizens, 100,000; slaves, 50,000

STATE B: free citizens, 150,000; slaves, 1,000

STATE C: free citizens, 90,000; slaves 70,000

1. Which state would be entitled to send the greatest number of representatives to Congress?
2. Which state would be entitled to send the fewest number of representatives to Congress?

3. Suppose that there were no three-fifths rule and that *all* slaves were counted. Which state would then be entitled to the largest representation?

4. HOW WAS THE CONSTITUTION DEBATED AND RATIFIED?

The Constitution was created in secret behind closed doors. Before leaving Philadelphia for home, however, the creators (delegates) gave printed copies of their work to the newspapers. Before long, American citizens everywhere were reading and talking about the proposed plan of government. Many were pleased with the Constitution and said it was better than the Articles of Confederation. But others argued that it was worse.

Rules for ratifying the Constitution. Whether the Constitution was better or worse was left to the American people to *debate* and decide. The seventh and final section of the document stated:

> The ratification of the conventions of nine states shall be sufficient for the establishment of this Constitution between the states so ratifying the same.

To *ratify* means to approve. The creators wanted to give voters the chance of either ratifying or rejecting the proposed Constitution. They decided that, in every state, there should be special conventions of delegates elected by the people of that state. If nine such conventions voted to ratify, the Constitution would be the new national government. The Articles of Confederation could then be ignored and put aside as a "dead letter" (discarded law).

The Federalists. For many months, American newspapers carried weighty arguments both for and against the Constitution. Supporters of the new plan called themselves Federalists. Their leaders included such great popular heroes as Benjamin Franklin and George Washington. Their arguments in defense of the Constitution were forcefully presented in a series of 85 essays. When collected and published in book form, the essays were called *The Federalist Papers*.

Originally they were printed in a New York newspaper under an invented name, Publius. Three authors cooperated with one another to keep the series running. One was the brillant Virginian, James Madison. The two others were New York lawyers, John Jay and Alexander Hamilton. Hamilton's pen was by far the busiest, turning out about 50 essays in just five months.

As 1787 ended, the Federalists had won victories in three states. Delegates to Delaware's convention voted unanimously to ratify the Constitution. Pennsylvania and New Jersey followed quickly with approving votes.

ALEXANDER HAMILTON OF NEW YORK. What did Hamilton do to help the Federalist cause?

The Antifederalists. In the new year, 1788, opponents of the Constitution rallied to beat back the Federalist campaign. They were known as Antifederalists. They too had famous leaders to influence public feeling. In Virginia, they cheered the Antifederalist speeches of Patrick Henry. In New York, they hoped their strong-willed governor, George Clinton, could overcome the youthful genius of Alexander Hamilton.

Antifederalist writers and speakers distrusted the Constitution. They said it gave too much power to the national government. They warned that the independence of the states would soon be lost. Even worse, said the Antifederalists, there were no guarantees in the Federalist document about the rights of citizens. Why, they asked, had the creators failed to include a list of citizens' rights? Was it because they were careless about liberty—or even hostile to it?

Ratification. Once again, a compromise saved the Constitution from defeat. In the ratifying convention in Massachusetts, Federalist delegates promised to add a bill of rights. They would do it, they said, as soon as the Constitution was adopted. The Federalist promise removed some of the fears of the Antifederalists. In February 1788, Massachusetts voted for ratification by a thin majority: 187 to 168.

After this key victory, Federalists in other states had an easier time. Maryland ratified in April, South Carolina in May, and New Hampshire and Virginia in June. By the Fourth of July, 1788, 10 of the 13 states had ratified—more than enough to establish the Constitution as the supreme law. In Philadelphia, happy Federalists shot off cannon and organized a colorful parade to celebrate their triumph.

Adding a bill of rights. The old, one-house Congress continued to meet for a few more months. But in January and February of 1789, Americans elected new leaders according to rules laid down by the Constitution. George Washington was every elector's choice for president. James Madison was one of 10 Virginians to sit in the new House of Representatives.

CELEBRATING THE 200TH ANNIVERSARY. In Philadelphia in 1988, people rang bells and exploded fireworks to commemorate the ratification of the Constitution in 1788. Why does the Constitution deserve to be celebrated?

The Federalists remembered to keep their promise. One of their first actions was to draw up a *Bill of Rights* in the form of 10 amendments (changes) to the Constitution. Again, the states had to ratify these changes. The Bill of Rights was ratified in 1791. Although other amendments would be added later, the basic plan of government under which we live today was complete.

REVIEW

A. Who Is Speaking?

The arguments below were made by different speakers in 1787 or 1788. Tell whether each speaker is probably a **Federalist** or an **Antifederalist.**

1. "On my tomb, write: 'Here lies the man that opposed the Constitution, because it was ruinous to the liberty of America.' "
2. "There is a time to sow and a time to reap. We sowed [planted] our seed when we sent men to the federal convention. Now is the harvest. Now is the time to reap [collect] the fruit of our labor. And if we won't do it now, I am afraid we never shall have another opportunity."
3. "There are some parts of this Constitution which I cannot digest. And, sir, shall we swallow a large bone for the sake of a little meat?"

B. Cause and Effect

Tell how each of the following helped to win ratification of the Constitution:

1. the essays by "Publius"
2. the reputation of George Washington and Benjamin Franklin
3. the vote of the Massachusetts ratifying convention
4. the Federalists' promise concerning a bill of rights

CHAPTER REVIEW

A. Completing the Summary

Select terms from the word list to fill in the blanks in the summary below. Write your answers on a separate piece of paper.

Antifederalists	ratification
bill of rights	Rebellion
compromise	Representatives
Confederation	Rhode Island
Congress	Senate
courts	slavery
Federalists	states
New Jersey	Virginia
Philadelphia	

The first government of the United States was weaker than the separate governments of the __(1)__. The Articles of __(2)__ were adopted in 1781 when the American Revolution was still being fought. It gave certain powers to a one-house __(3)__. Among the powers *not* given to this government was the power to collect a tax directly from the people.

American leaders like George Washington and Benjamin Franklin were alarmed by news of Shays's __(4)__ in Massachusetts. They feared that the nation might fall apart unless changes were made in the U.S. government. In the summer of 1787, delegates from 12 states met in __(5)__. (Not represented was the state of __(6)__.) James Madison, a delegate from __(7)__, proposed strengthening the U.S. government by creating a two-house Congress, the office of president, and a national system of __(8)__. William Paterson from __(9)__ objected to Madison's plan because it gave more power to the more populous states than to the less populous ones.

The dispute was finally settled by means of a __(10)__. In the House of __(11)__, the more populous states would have more votes than the other states. But in the __(12)__, all states would be represented equally.

Two other disputes threatened to break up the convention. Both involved __(13)__. First was the question of whether to allow Congress to end the slave trade. Second was the question of how to count slaves as part of a state's population. Both disputes were finally resolved by compromise.

The delegates signed the Constitution in 1787 and then submitted it to the states for __(14)__. People who supported the Constitution were known as __(15)__. Opponents were called __(16)__. By July 4, 1788, the Constitution had been approved by the required number of states. One of the first acts of the new Congress was to propose a __(17)__, which was added to the Constitution in 1791.

B. How Many?

Complete each sentence by giving the number (to replace the question mark).

1. The Virginia Plan said that Congress should consist of (?) house(s).
2. A total of (?) delegates attended the Philadelphia Convention of 1787.
3. The Constitution went into effect after (?) states ratified it.
4. The U.S. Bill of Rights consisted of (?) amendments to the Constitution.
5. For purposes of representation, (?) of a state's slave population would be counted.

C. Making Comparisons

Explain the difference between each pair of terms or phrases.

1. Articles of Confederation—Constitution
2. Virginia Plan—New Jersey Plan
3. House of Representatives—Senate
4. How Southern delegates wanted slaves to be counted—The Three-fifths Compromise
5. Federalists—Antifederalists

D. Applying What You Know

The statements below are very similar to ones in the original documents of 1781 (the Articles) and 1787 (the Constitution). Tell whether you think each sentence comes from the **Articles of Confederation** or from the **Constitution.** Give reasons for your answers. Relate your answers to the photos and caption questions on page 81.

1. Voters of the different states shall elect the members of a House of Representatives.
2. Each state shall be free and independent.
3. There shall be a U.S. Supreme Court as well as other courts that Congress may establish.
4. The states agree to assist each other

whenever any of them is attacked by a foreign nation.

5. A president shall command the army and navy of the United States.

6. Expenses of the national government shall be paid by the states out of a common treasury, or fund.

EARLY CAPITOLS: PRINCETON, NEW YORK. Top: Still in use on the campus of Princeton University in New Jersey is Nassau Hall, which served in 1783 as the U.S. capitol under the Articles of Confederation. Bottom: The first capitol under the Constitution was in New York City. Here Congress met from 1789–1790, and George Washington took the oath of office as the first president. Today, Federal Hall with its statue of Washington marks the site of the old capitol.

(a) What was similar about the U.S. governments that met in Princeton and New York? *(b)* What was different about these governments?

AERIAL VIEW OF WASHINGTON, D.C. The Constitution gives certain powers to Congress (meeting in the Capitol, domed building, center), while giving other powers to the Supreme Court (meeting in the Supreme Court Building, lower right). Who heads a third branch of government from a building not shown in this picture?

CHAPTER 5

Understanding the Constitution

OBJECTIVES

After reading this chapter, you will know

1. how to look up and identify different articles and sections of the Constitution.
2. the powers that are delegated to the federal government and the powers that are reserved to the state governments.
3. how the principle of checks and balances is carried out in the Constitution.
4. how to create an outline.

To whom shall we, the people, entrust the power of governing the United States? In the U.S. Constitution, we find the answer. It says the leading roles in American government will go to the following:

The people . . . American citizens and voters
Representatives . . . lawmakers in the larger house of Congress (the House of Representatives)
Senators . . . lawmakers in the smaller house of Congress (the Senate)
President . . . chief executive responsible for enforcing federal laws
Vice President . . . official who presides over the Senate and may become president under special circumstances
Supreme Court Justices . . . judges who decide cases of law
The states . . . smaller, self-governing parts of the American nation

That is the entire list. The Constitution gives power and authority to nobody else. Not once does it mention the Republican party or the Democratic party. It says nothing about army generals, FBI agents, Cabinet members, or IRS tax collectors. In fact, there are thousands of government officials whose jobs are not mentioned in the Constitution.

The Constitution is a brief set of rules for governing America. It says no more than needs to be said. That is one of the reasons that it has worked so well for over 200 years.

In this chapter, you will see how the Constitution is organized. You will also see how the political leaders listed above are supposed to carry out their different functions. The chapter's three sections answer these questions:

1. How is the Constitution organized?
2. How are powers divided among the legislative, executive, and judicial branches?
3. What procedures for governing are spelled out in the Constitution?

1. HOW IS THE CONSTITUTION ORGANIZED?

The Constitution begins with its most famous phrase: "We the people." These three words carry tremendous meaning. They suggest that the people—you and your neighbors—are in control. Back in the 1780s, "We the people" established a federal plan of government. Today, "We the people" strongly influence the U.S. government and make it respond to our wishes.

The Preamble. You have already read the Constitution's first paragraph in Chapter 1. After "We the people," it states the six purposes of the national government. They are worth repeating. The purposes are to:

THE PREAMBLE AND ARTICLE I. . . . Which paragraph is the Preamble? What is the subject of Article I?

We the People

Article I

- "form a more perfect union"
- "establish justice"
- "insure domestic tranquillity"
- "provide for the common defense"
- "promote the general welfare"
- "secure the blessings of liberty."

The paragraph presenting these political purposes is known as the Preamble.

Seven Articles. After the Preamble come the rules created during the debates of the summer of 1787. The Constitution's rules for governing America are grouped together in seven main divisions known as **articles**. Here is what they contain in brief:

ARTICLE I describes the two houses of Congress—the House of Representatives and the Senate.

ARTICLE II presents the powers of the president and describes the unusual system for electing the president.

ARTICLE III tells about the Supreme Court, other federal courts, and the cases of law that they may judge.

ARTICLE IV discusses the relations among the states. It guarantees to each state a republican form of government. It also describes the process for admitting new states into the Union.

ARTICLE V tells how the Constitution may be amended, or changed.

ARTICLE VI, only three paragraphs long, declares that the Constitution shall be "the supreme law of the land."

ARTICLE VII, only one sentence, says that 9 states of the original 13 states must ratify the Constitution before it can take effect as "the supreme law."

That is all that the creators wrote in 1787. After they finished the seventh article, they signed their names and went home. They left us with a document that is logically organized and clearly stated.

Sections and clauses. Looking up a rule in the Constitution is almost as easy as looking up a word in the dictionary. That is because the longer articles (I, II, III, and IV) are divided into smaller sections. And each section is identified by number. For example, Article I is organized as follows:

Section 1 (introducing the lawmaking power of Congress)
Section 2 (on the House of Representatives)
Section 3 (on the Senate)
Section 4 (stating the times when Congress shall meet).

A few of the sections are large enough to be subdivided into paragraphs—or clauses. These too are numbered. Thus, finding any rule in the Constitution is a simple matter of reading numbers. For example, on pages 116–127, find the following:

- Article I, Section 2, clause 3
- Article II, Section 1, clause 6
- Article III, Section 2, clause 2.

Note that the section headings in bold type are *not* part of the original Constitution. They have been added as a guide.

Twenty-seven amendments. The making of the Constitution did not end in Philadelphia in 1787. It has continued to our own times through a process called amendment. On page 131, notice what follows the portrait of the creators. There are 27 amendments (added changes) that were added to the 1787 document at a later time.

For example, an amendment of 1865 ended the practice of slavery. Another amendment, adopted in 1920, guaranteed women the right to vote. We will study these and other amendments in later chapters.

✔✔ SKILLS CHECK: Making an outline

By looking at the bold headings and numbers of the Constitution, you can see its major parts (articles) and subparts (sections and clauses). An outline makes its organization even clearer. Below is a partial outline of the Constitution. Only Article II, Section 1 is presented with all its clauses. To indicate what each clause is about, a phrase from the Constitution has been quoted.

Here is the beginning of an outline, to which you will be adding other topics.

OUTLINE OF THE CONSTITUTION

I. The Congress
II. The President
  A. (Section 1) Electing the President
    clause 1. "term of four years"
    clause 2. "number of Electors equal to whole number of Senators and Representatives"
    clause 3. "Electors shall meet in their respective states"
    clause 4. "time of choosing Electors"
    clause 5. "no person except a natural-born citizen . . . shall be eligible"
    clause 6. "removal of the President from office"
    clause 7. "compensation"
    clause 8. "oath of affirmation"

Continue the outline yourself to the beginning of Article III. On a separate piece of paper, copy everything below—*except* the question marks—indenting as shown.

  B. (Section 2) ?
    clause 1. ?
    clause 2. ?
    clause 3. ?
  C. (Section 3) ?
  D. (Section 4) ?
III. ?

Replace the question marks for B, C, and D with a phrase identifying what each section is about. To do this, you should turn to appropriate parts of the Constitution (pages 124–126). Then, under B. (Section 2), quote a phrase to identify what each of the three clauses is about. Finally, give the heading for the next part of the outline, III.

REVIEW

Making Inferences

Where in the Constitution would you find the clauses below? Match each clause to one of these:

Preamble Article I Article II Article III Article IV Articles V-VII amendments

1. a clause outlawing slavery
2. a clause stating that one purpose of the federal government is to "establish justice"
3. any clause debated and written after 1800
4. a clause about one of the powers of the president
5. a clause about the method for electing a U.S. senator
6. a clause giving Congress the power "to regulate commerce"
7. a clause beginning "We the people"
8. a clause describing the process for enacting a law of Congress
9. a clause that names the U.S. Constitution as the "supreme law of the land"
10. a clause about the term of office of a justice of the Supreme Court
11. a clause that reads: "No new state shall be formed or erected within the jurisdiction of any other state"
12. all clauses in the Bill of Rights

2. HOW ARE POWERS DIVIDED AMONG THE LEGISLATIVE, EXECUTIVE, AND JUDICIAL BRANCHES?

Three words summarize the main contents of the Constitution. In this document we find:

- The **purposes** of government (given in the Preamble)
- The **powers** of government
- The **procedures** for making laws and electing officials.

The second topic—powers—is the one that is given the most attention.

Remember the officials listed at the beginning of this chapter (representatives, president, judges, etc.). The Constitution gives these officials the power to take certain actions. It also tells what power they shall *not* be permitted to have.

Separation of powers. The creators of the Constitution feared a national government that might use its powers to crush liberty. To avoid this danger, they divided power among three parts, or branches, of government. Their system for dividing power is called *separation of powers*.

Recall from Chapter One that legislative power is the power to make the laws. Executive power is the power to enforce the laws. Judicial power is the power to interpret the laws. The Constitution gives *most* of the legislative power to a two-house Congress—the *Legislative Branch*. It gives *most* of the executive power to the president—the head of the *Executive Branch*. It gives *most* of the judicial power to the Supreme Court and other federal courts—the *Judicial Branch*.

Checks and balances. The CARTOON CORNER on page 87 shows the three branches: executive, legislative, and judicial. Hanging from them are balance scales equally weighted with powers. Notice the weight cubes (powers) on each tray. Notice that the Executive Branch (president, vice president) has most of the executive powers. But it also has both legislative and judicial power to influence the actions of the other two branches. At the same time, the Legislative and Judicial Branches have powers that enable them to check each other and the Executive Branch.

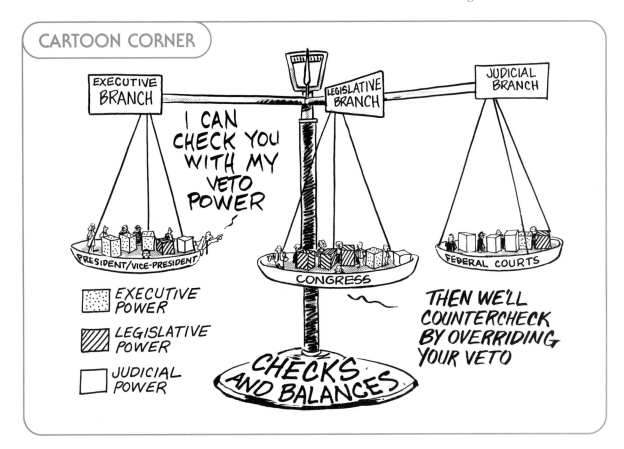

CARTOON CORNER

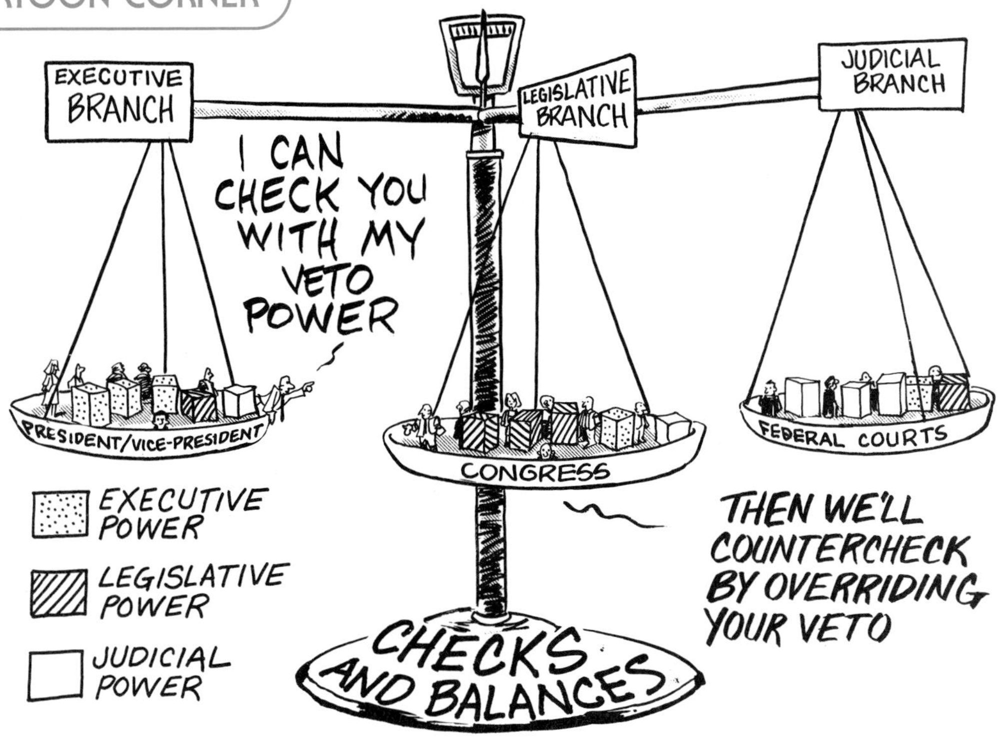

We can illustrate with three examples.

(a) **Appointing judges.** Because they decide cases of law, judges have judicial power. But the Constitution gives the president, as chief executive, the power to name, or appoint, federal judges to their jobs. Congress too gets in the act because the president's appointments must be approved by a vote of the Senate. Congress may also remove judges from office by a process called *impeachment*. Thus, judges in the Judicial Branch are hired and sometimes fired by the other two branches.

(b) **Enacting laws.** Congress passes, or enacts, laws, but the president also participates in the lawmaking process. After a proposal for a law is passed by Congress, the president must decide whether or not to sign it. If he or she does not sign, then the president is said to *veto* Congress's action. This means that Congress's idea for a law is blocked, or checked, by the president. However, the Constitution gives Congress the opportunity to counter the president's move by *overriding* the veto. This will be explained in a later chapter.

(c) **Impeaching the president.** In the wrong hands, the executive power of the president may be used dishonestly. In 1972, for example, a crime was committed by high-level officials in the Executive Branch and then covered up with the approval of President Richard Nixon. In situations like this, Congress may decide to impeach, or accuse, the president of misusing power. Rather than face impeachment, President Nixon decided to resign from office in 1974. Congress's power of impeachment is an example of a legislative check on the Executive Branch.

As these examples show, the creators of the Constitution wanted each branch to be

THE PRESIDENT'S CHOICE. David Souter (left) had served as a judge in a New Hampshire state court. In July, 1990, President Bush (right) announced that Judge Souter was his nominee to fill an empty seat on the U.S. Supreme Court. Judge Souter was then confirmed (approved for the position) by the Senate. How do these facts illustrate the idea of checks and balances?

able to check the actions of the other branches. They also wanted powers to be well balanced (distributed evenly) so that no branch would gain control or mastery of the others. Their carefully constructed plan is known as a system of *checks and balances*.

Why did the creators create a system like this? Once again, protecting liberty was their main concern. They recognized that government officials might misuse their powers. If the three branches could watch and check one another, there would be less danger of government power getting out of hand.

Delegated powers. So far, we have spoken of political power in general. But there are many specific powers that the Constitution gives to the federal government and to the state governments. All powers granted to the federal government are known as *delegated powers*.

The longest list of such powers is found in the 18 clauses of Article I, Section 8. Look at this section on page 119 and notice how the list begins:

"The Congress shall have power:

1. To lay and collect taxes . . .
2. To borrow money . . .
3. To regulate commerce [trade] with foreign nations, and among the several states, and with the Indian tribes."

The list continues with the power to coin and print money and to punish counterfeiters. Congress may establish post offices and post roads. It may raise an army and provide for a navy. It may declare war. It may set aside a piece of land "not exceeding ten miles square," which shall be developed into the nation's capital city. (Congress later used this power to create the District of Columbia—Washington, D.C.)

The list ends with the most important power of all. In Clause 18 (of Article I, Section 8), Congress is given power "to

THE TWO HOUSES OF CONGRESS. The Capitol dome is under construction in this 1862 painting. If the Senate meets in the wing to the right, who meets in the wing to the left?

make all laws which shall be necessary and proper for carrying into execution the foregoing powers." In other words, because of Clause 18, Congress may carry out its 17 other delegated powers in any way that it decides is necessary. It could supply the U.S. Army with a thousand tanks and a million uniforms—or none at all. It could order coins to be made from gold or silver, copper or tin, wood or plastic.

Clause 18, commonly known as the "necessary and proper" clause, is also known as the *elastic clause*. For 200 years, it has given Congress the ability to adapt to changing times. Remember it. It will be mentioned often in this text.

Powers reserved to the states. There are many political powers *not* mentioned in the Constitution. For example, Congress will not pass a law to operate your school. Nor will it hire officials to see that city streets are built.

That is because, in the federal system, there are other governments besides the national one. Governments of the separate states have powers of their own to make and enforce laws. They build roads and bridges, schools and firehouses, courthouses and jails. They provide hundreds of public services for a state's residents. The power to do these things is reserved (set aside) for state governments by one important clause in the Constitution. According to this *reserved powers* clause:

> The powers not delegated to the United States by the Constitution, nor prohibited by it to the States, are reserved to the States respectively . . . .
>
> —Amendment X

Does the Constitution say anything about the president or Congress operating schools and firehouses? No. Does it say that states are prohibited from operating schools and firehouses? No. Then, it can be assumed that the states have this power and *not* the national government.

Powers that are prohibited or denied. To all questions that follow, the answer is **no**.

- Can Congress pass a law declaring someone to be guilty of a crime before any trial takes place?
  No. Such a law, known as a *bill of attainder*, is prohibited by the Constitution (Article I, Section 9, Clause 3).
- Can the U.S. government collect a tax on oranges exported from Florida?
  No. It is prohibited. (See I, 9, 5.)
- Can the state government of Illinois coin money or print dollar bills?
  No. (See I, 10, 1.)
- Can the state government of Texas pass a bill of attainder?
  No. (See I, 10, 2.)
- Can the state of California go to war against some South American nation?
  No. (See I, 10, 3.)
- Can the U.S. Congress pass a law declaring a certain religion to be illegal?
  No. (See Amendment I.)
- Can a U.S. court sentence a prisoner to be tortured?
  No. (See Amendment VIII.)

A BUDDHIST GOD WORSHIPPED IN TIBET. Can the U.S. Congress pass a law that would prohibit the worship of "foreign gods"?

Two kinds of prohibitions. Notice that prohibitions in the Constitution are of two kinds. First, there are powers that the *U.S. government* may not exercise. Second, there are powers that *state governments* may not exercise. In some cases, the NO is really a double NO. The bill of attainder is an example. It is mentioned twice in the Constitution as a power that neither the national government nor the state governments may exercise.

In Article I, look at Section 9, Clause 3. Then compare it with Section 10, Clause 1. In these clauses, you will find something else that is prohibited. Neither Congress nor a state legislature is allowed to make an *ex post facto law.* An ex post facto law would declare a *past* action to be unlawful and subject to punishment. Take the case, for example, of an Idaho bus driver who mistreats her pet cat. The cat dies of its injuries. Six months later, the Idaho legislature declares it to be a crime to mistreat a cat. Can the Idaho bus driver be arrested for what she did to her pet? No, she cannot. Idaho's law was passed *after* the deed was committed. It was ex post facto—after the fact. The Constitution does not allow it.

Can you think of the reason why ex post facto laws are prohibited?

REVIEW

A. Making Comparisons

For each pair of terms, tell how **A** differs from **B**.

1. (A) delegated powers — (B) reserved powers
2. (A) legislative power — (B) executive power
3. (A) ex post facto law — (B) bill of attainder

B. Applying What You Know

For each phrase, tell whether it describes (*a*) a **delegated** power, (*b*) a **reserved** power, or (*c*) a power that is **denied** (or prohibited). The power to:

1. regulate trade with foreign nations
2. build and operate schools
3. hire a local police force
4. mint coins and other money
5. distribute the mail
6. pass ex post facto laws
7. declare war
8. make "necessary and proper" laws
9. pass a bill of attainder
10. repave a state highway
11. torture prisoners

C. Explaining Key Ideas

Answer each question in a sentence or phrase.

1. What is one way that Congress may stop or check a dishonest president?
2. Name the three government branches that are given power by the Constitution.
3. Name the system that gives to all three branches the power to check one another's actions.

4. What is the "necessary and proper" clause? Why is it important?

D. Referring to the Constitution

Answer each question by looking at the Constitution itself (pages 119–125).

1. In Article I, Section 10, find two examples of powers denied to the states.
2. In Article I, Section 8, identify the clause that gives Congress (*a*) the power to maintain a navy, (*b*) the power to punish counterfeiters, (*c*) the power to encourage the work of authors and scientists.
3. In Article II, Section 2, find one example of a power delegated to the president.
4. In Article I, Section 10, find two taxes that states may *not* collect.

3. WHAT PROCEDURES FOR GOVERNING ARE SPELLED OUT IN THE CONSTITUTION?

Besides spelling out the purposes and powers of government, the Constitution also describes basic procedures. It answers, for example, certain questions about procedures for choosing leaders.

How U.S. leaders are chosen. Are the leaders in the national government chosen by the voters?

Answer: Some are, some are not.

Do all officials serve for the same *term* (or length of time)?

Answer: No. The term of office for some is only two years. For others, it is for as long as the person lives.

Must candidates for the different offices meet the same set of requirements?

Answer: No, requirements differ. For example, a president must be at least 35 years old, a senator at least 30, and a representative at least 25. Justices of the Supreme Court can be any age.

Complete answers to the above questions are given in different parts of the Constitution. Look at the chart on this page. Notice that no two offices are filled in the same way. Writers of the Constitution planned it that way. They wanted different officials to be selected at different times by different groups. Their purpose was to divide political power so that no one group could control it all.

	CONGRESS		PRESIDENT	SUPREME COURT
	House	Senate		
How chosen	Elected	Elected	Elected	Appointed by president
Term of office	2 years	6 years	4 years	Until judge dies or retires
Age requirement	At least 25	At least 30	At least 35	None

Special role of the electors. The longest paragraph in the Constitution describes the procedures for electing the president and vice president. This paragraph (II, 1, 3) tells how a small group of citizens from the different states shall cast ballots for president. The citizens are referred to as *electors.*

Electors vote for a president *after* the general public has voted in November. The electors' ballots, when counted in Congress, officially determine the winner of the election.

In a later chapter, you will learn more about the electors. For now, it is enough to know that they exist and that the Constitution describes their special role.

How laws are made. How does Congress carry out its assigned task of making the nation's laws? We find the answer in another unusually long paragraph (I, 7, 2). First, it talks of bills passing the Senate and the House of Representative. A *bill* is a written proposal for a law. If the two houses of Congress approve (or pass) a bill, it goes to the president. The president may decide to sign the bill. In that case, the bill becomes law.

THE WHITE HOUSE. Article II states: "The executive power shall be vested in a president of the United States." Does the president today have any more constitutional powers than the earliest presidents?

On the other hand, the president may decide not to sign the bill. In that case, the bill is vetoed. It is then stopped from becoming law *unless* the Congress attempts to pass it again. The second time around, however, Congress must pass a bill by a vote of *at least two-thirds* of the senators and *at least two-thirds* of the representatives.

The Constitution's longest paragraph also says how votes shall be counted. "In all such cases the votes of both Houses shall be determined by yeas and nays." For 200 years, members of Congress have voted "yea" if they are for a bill, "nay" if they are against it. It is more than just a custom. It is a requirement of the Constitution.

The "supreme law." All procedures described in the Constitution must be carried out exactly as written. That is because the Constitution is "the supreme law of the land." It is higher than any law of Congress and higher than any state law. Government leaders must do no more and no less than the Constitution allows.

Otherwise, the national government would tend to become unlimited in its power. And then the constitutional government that "We the people" created would be lost.

Strict or loose construction? Our national government is built upon the words of the Constitution. Partly because these words are so important, they have been the subject of much argument.

For example, the Constitution gives Congress the power to collect taxes and to borrow money. That is perfectly clear because Article I, Section 8, mentions taxing and borrowing. Not clear, however, is what shall be done with the money that government collects. Of course the money could be put in a bank—perhaps a bank that Congress creates. But banks are not mentioned anywhere in the Constitution. Does that mean that Congress has no power to create a bank for the government's convenience?

INTERPRETING THE "SUPREME LAW." The Supreme Court interprets the meaning of the "supreme law" (the Constitution). Of the people shown in this 1888 engraving, which do you think were members of the highest court?

A much broader question was this: Could the U.S. government do only those things specifically mentioned in the Constitution? Yes, said one group, No, said another group. Those who wanted the words of the Constitution to be strictly interpreted were known as strict constructionists. Those who wanted the same words to be loosely interpreted were known as loose constructionists.

The loose constructionists based their arguments on the 18th power delegated to Congress by the Constitution. This was the "necessary and proper" clause (or elastic clause).

Victory of the loose constructionists. In 1819, the Supreme Court applied the "necessary and proper" clause to a case of law involving a bank. The case was called *McCulloch* v. *Maryland*. Lawyers for Maryland argued that a national bank created by Congress in 1816 should not be allowed, since the Constitution said nothing about banks. But the Supreme Court ruled that such a bank *was* allowed because it was a "necessary and proper" means of carrying out Congress's other powers to tax and to borrow.

The loose constructionists won the argument. As a result of *McCulloch* v. *Maryland* (and other court cases), thousands of laws made by Congress are allowed by the "necessary and proper" clause. Postage stamps, for example, are not mentioned in the Constitution—but post offices are mentioned. Because of the "necessary and proper" clause, nobody questions the post office's right to issue postage stamps.

Every day, lawyers question the meaning of different words and clauses of the Constitution. It is the Supreme Court's job to settle these questions.

REVIEW

A. Building Your Political Vocabulary

Tell what each term means and why it is important.

1. elector
2. bill
3. limited government
4. "supreme law of the land"
5. veto

B. Follow the Arrows

Tell what constitutional procedure is represented by each set of arrows. (Refer to the chart on page 91 as well as the text.)

1. VOTERS → ELECTORS → PRESIDENT/VICE PRESIDENT
2. BILL → HOUSE → SENATE → PRESIDENT → U.S. LAW
3. PEOPLE → 27-YEAR-OLD CANDIDATE → NEW MEMBER OF CONGRESS

CHAPTER REVIEW

A. Completing the Summary

Select terms from the word list to fill in the blanks in the summary below. Write your answers on a piece of paper.

amendments	ex post facto
articles	powers
attainder	Preamble
Bill of Rights	president
checks and balances	reserved
Congress	Senate
delegated	Supreme Court
electors	veto

The Constitution presents the purposes, the powers, and the procedures of the U.S. government. Its most famous paragraph, the __(1)__, begins by declaring that "We, the people" established the Constitution. Then it lists the six purposes of government that you studied in Chapter One.

The main parts of the Constitution are known as __(2)__. Each part may be subdivided into sections and clauses. Added to the Constitution of 1787 are 27 __(3)__ . The first ten of these are known as the __(4)__ .

The term "separation of __(5)__" refers to the organization of government into three divisions, or branches. Legislative power to make the nation's laws belongs to __(6)__. Executive power to enforce the laws belongs to the __(7)__. Judicial power to interpret the laws in specific cases belongs to the __(8)__.

But the legislative, executive, and judicial branches are not free to do whatever they wish. A system of __(9)__ allows the Congress, the president, and the Supreme Court to block one another's actions. An example is the president's power to __(10)__ the acts of Congress.

Under our federalist system, some powers are __(11)__ to the U.S. government, while others are left to the states. A state's powers are sometimes called its __(12)__ powers because of a phrase in the Tenth Amendment to the Constitution.

You know that the United States has a limited government. In other words, certain powers are specifically denied to the state and federal governments. For example, you cannot be punished for some past action that was not illegal at the time it was committed. The Constitution protects you from such __(13)__ laws. It also protects you from bills of __(14)__.

The procedures spelled out in the Constitution concern both elections amd lawmaking. A president is chosen by a small group of citizens from each state, called __(15)__. Every law passed by Congress must be voted upon by both the House of Representatives and the __(16)__.

B. Who Does What?

In this chapter, you learned about the governing powers given to certain people and institutions by the Constitution. Match the **officials** (or institutions) in List I with the **powers and duties** in List II. In some cases, more than one answer is required, as indicated by the symbol.*

I. OFFICIALS

representatives	Supreme Court justices
senators	electors
presidents	state lawmakers

II. POWERS

1. May decide to sign a bill passed by Congress.
2. Cast ballots for president.
3. May debate bills about coining money.*
4. May decide *not* to sign a bill passed by Congress.
5. May pass laws about local schools.
6. Leads the Executive Branch of the U.S. government.
7. Have powers described in Article III.
8. Serve a four-year term.
9. May serve to the end of their lives.
10. May check Congress by their power of judicial review.
11. May vote yea or nay on whether the United States should declare war.*
12. May vote to build local hospitals, roads, and jails.
13. May exercise powers *not* delegated to the national government.
14. Serve six-year terms.
15. May enact whatever they think is "necessary and proper" for carrying out Congress's delegated powers.*

C. The Articles of the Constitution

Carry out the instruction printed in *italics.*

1. The first paragraph of the Constitution presents six purposes of government. *Give three of them.*
2. The next part of the Constitution (Article I) gives legislative power to Congress. *List four powers delegated to Congress.*
3. Presented in Article I are powers that Congress may not exercise. *Copy two clauses from Article I that present examples of powers denied.*
4. Also described in Article I are restrictions on the powers of the states. *List one of these restrictions.*
5. Next we come to Article II, which tells about the executive power of the president and the procedures for electing him or her. *Identify by number the longest paragraph in Article II and summarize what it says.*
6. Article III describes the judicial powers of the U.S. government. *What institution of government is named in Article III?*
7. The last four articles of the original Constitution describe various powers and procedures. *Give the headings for all four articles.*
8. All parts of the Constitution form "the supreme law of the land." *Explain this phrase.*

TRYING TO CHANGE THE CONSTITUTION. These women could not vote in 1912 when they marched in a parade in New York City in hopes of changing the Constitution. What voting rights are currently guaranteed by the Constitution?

CHAPTER 6

Changing the Constitution

OBJECTIVES

After reading this chapter, you will know

1. the process for amending the Constitution.
2. the amendments that guaranteed the right to vote for women, blacks, and young people.
3. how the Constitution was amended to make government work better.
4. the informal ways that the U.S. government may change.
5. how to use a flow chart to illustrate a political process.

More than two hundred years have passed since the Constitution was written. In that time, the United States has grown from 13 states to 50 states. It has changed from a nation of farmers to a nation of factory and office workers. Ben Franklin would be amazed to see the mechanical and electronic wonders owned by today's Americans: our computers, cars, cameras, cassette recorders, and television sets.

Despite changes in much that we do, Americans still recognize as our "supreme law" a document that was drafted in 1787. That document, the Constitution, still gives us a stable and practical form of government. How could one form of government last all these years?

One reason is that the Constitution gives the government enough power to preserve order but also sets strict limits on that power. In other words, it is based on solid principles of good, effective government. A second reason for the Constitution's long life is its flexibility. Those who wrote it expected their young country to grow and change. They made it possible for the Constitution to change as the nation changed.

Only once in 200 years did people's trust in the Constitution break down. In 1861, a conflict over slavery and states' rights caused the two sections of the country, North and South, to fight a civil war. But that terrible constitutional crisis has not been repeated.

Today, we Americans probably believe in the Constitution even more strongly than those who wrote it. We trust it because it has worked so well for so many years. It has been tested in many situations without failing. It has also become stronger since 1787 because of the amendments (changes) made in it.

Let these questions focus your study of the chapter.

1. How can the Constitution be amended?
2. What amendments made our government more democratic?
3. What amendments made our government more efficient?
4. How may the Constitution be changed in informal ways?

1. HOW CAN THE CONSTITUTION BE AMENDED?

Amending—or formally changing—the Constitution is not easy. To be adopted, a proposed amendment must be voted upon again and again by different groups of lawmakers. The lengthy process is described in Article V of the Constitution.

The amendment process. An amendment may be first proposed by the U.S. Congress and then submitted to state legislatures for their approval, or ratification. Article V requires at least *two-thirds* of the members of both houses of Congress to vote for an amendment. Once proposed in this manner, *three-fourths* of the state legislatures must ratify it.

Consider all the politicians whose approval must be obtained in this process. Today, the arithmetic for adopting an amendment to the U.S. Constitution looks like this:

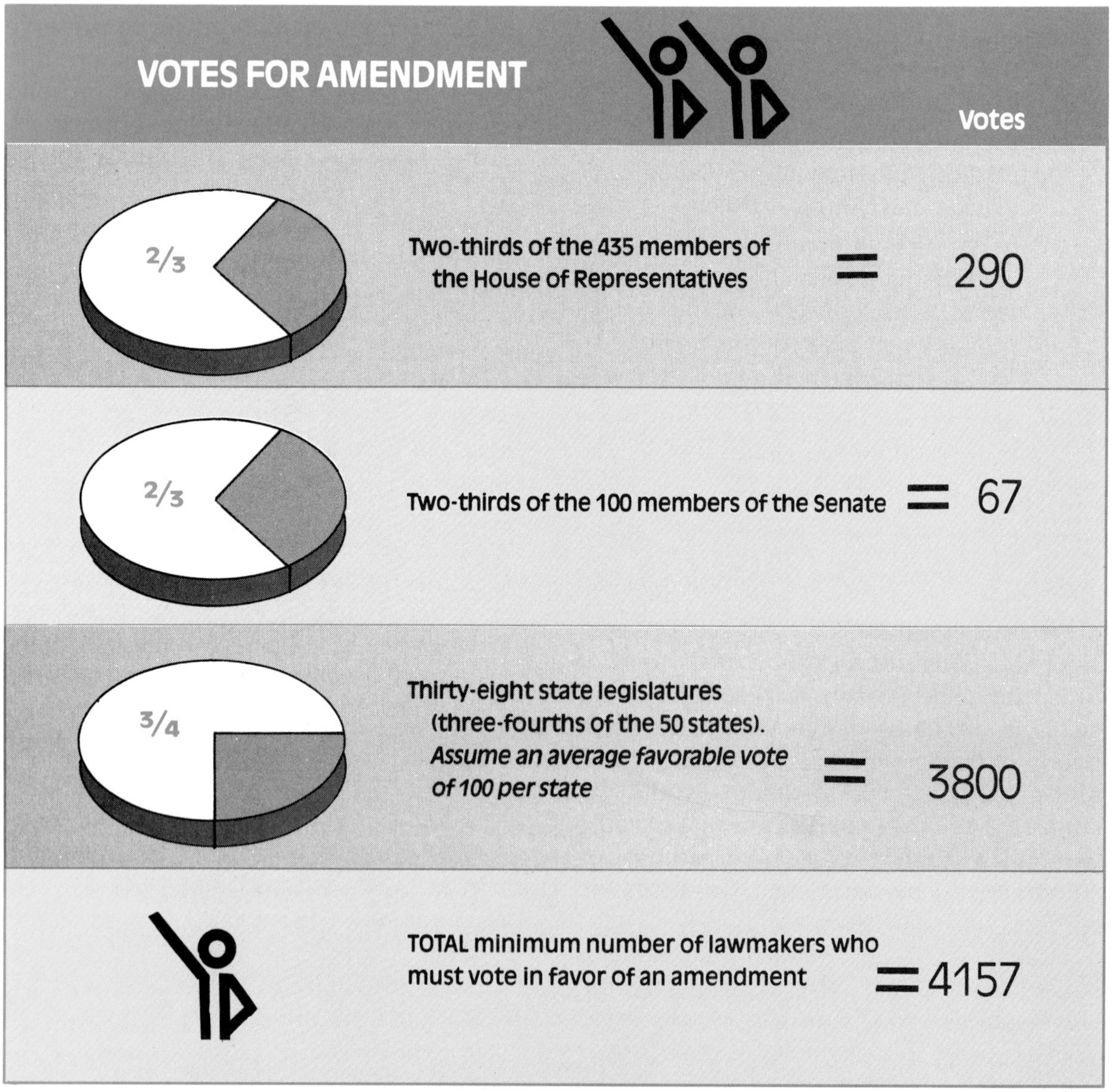

VOTES FOR AMENDMENT
Votes
2/3
Two-thirds of the 435 members of the House of Representatives
= 290
2/3
Two-thirds of the 100 members of the Senate
= 67
3/4
Thirty-eight state legislatures (three-fourths of the 50 states).
Assume an average favorable vote of 100 per state
= 3800
TOTAL minimum number of lawmakers who must vote in favor of an amendment
= 4157

That is a lot of votes to collect. Most amendments fail to get the votes they need. They are thus rejected either at the proposal stage or the ratification stage.

Article V offers other ways of amending the Constitution. But they are even more difficult than the standard method. One alternative method goes like this: (1) Two-thirds of the state legislatures vote for Congress to call a national convention. (2) At this special convention, delegates from all the states propose an amendment. (3) Finally, three-fourths of the state legislatures ratify the amendment. *Never* has this complicated method been used.

Another alternative is for Congress to propose an amendment, but instead of going to state legislatures to be ratified, it is considered by specially called state conventions. A convention consists of delegates elected from different districts (parts) of the state. If three-fourths of the conventions vote in favor of the amendment, it is adopted. *Only once* has an amendment been ratified by state conventions. In 1933, the Twenty-first Amendment was adopted by this route. (It allowed alcoholic beverages to be sold in the United States after they had briefly been prohibited.)

✔✔ SKILLS CHECK: Working with flow charts

No matter what method is used, amending the Constitution involves passing an idea from one group of decision makers to another. A process like this can be complicated and hard to understand. We can more easily understand any process or movement if we can create a picture of it in our minds.

A **flow chart** is a device for picturing a complicated, step-by-step process. It may consist of labeled boxes, circles, diamonds, and arrows. Each diamond stands for a point at which a yes-or-no decision is made. If the decision is yes, the idea moves on to the next stage. If the decision is no, the process either stops or goes back to the beginning and starts over. The arrows in a flow chart point the way to the next step.

The flow chart on page 100 represents three methods of amending the Constitution. Only Method A is completely labeled. Methods B and C are to be completed by you.

1. On a piece of paper, write a label for:

- Box B-1
- Box C-1
- Diamond C-2

Refer to the descriptions of all three methods on pages 98–99.

2. There is a fourth method of amending the Constitution, which, like Method C, has never been used. It consists of three steps: (*a*) Two-thirds of the state legislatures ask Congress to call a national convention. (*b*) The national convention proposes an amendment. (*c*) Special conventions in three-fourths of the states ratify the amendment.

On your piece of paper, **create a flow chart for this fourth method.** Identify it as Method D.

The first ten amendments (Bill of Rights). During the presidency of George Washington, ten amendments were proposed and ratified at the same time. They are popularly known as the Bill of Rights. More than any other part of the Constitution, the Bill of Rights protects the basic freedoms of Americans.

Among those responsible for persuading Congress to propose a Bill of Rights was the same youthful genius from Virginia who had worked so hard for the original Constitution. James Madison was elected in 1789 to sit in the newly created House of Representatives. He realized that the Constitution, as written in Philadelphia, was not complete. Many Americans complained that

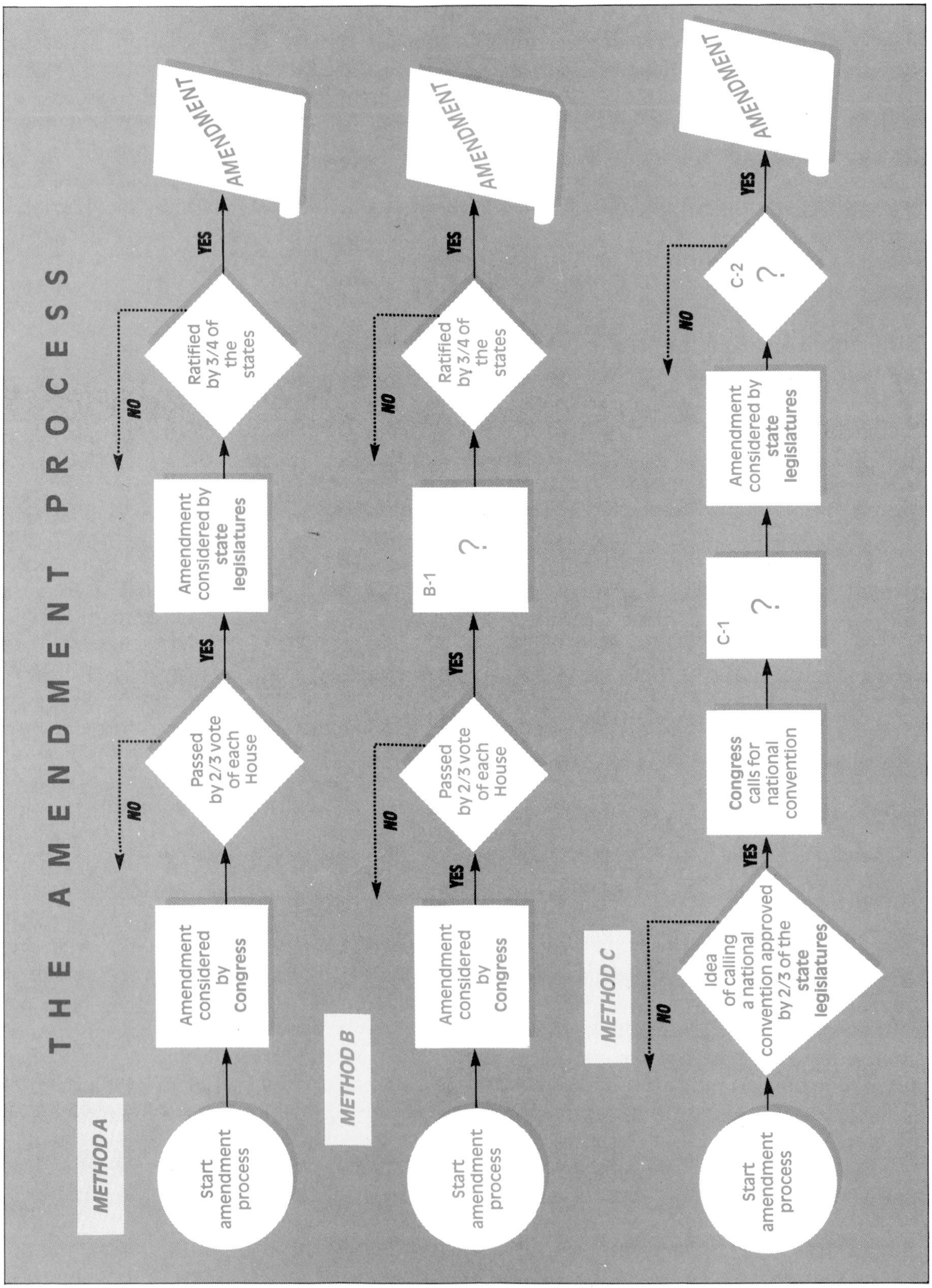
THE AMENDMENT PROCESS
METHOD A
Start amendment process
Amendment considered by Congress
Passed by 2/3 vote of each House
NO
YES
Amendment considered by state legislatures
Ratified by 3/4 of the states
NO
YES
AMENDMENT
METHOD B
Start amendment process
Amendment considered by Congress
YES
Passed by 2/3 vote of each House
NO
YES
B-1 ?
Ratified by 3/4 of the states
NO
YES
AMENDMENT
METHOD C
Start amendment process
Idea of calling a national convention approved by 2/3 of the state legislatures
NO
YES
Congress calls for national convention
C-1 ?
Amendment considered by state legislatures
C-2 ?
NO
YES
AMENDMENT

it lacked specific guarantees concerning such things as freedom of speech and religion. Madison was determined to satisfy them.

By the summer of 1789, Madison had persuaded the House to propose 17 amendments. The Senate accepted only 14 of them. Committees of the two houses finally agreed that 12 amendments should be submitted to the states for ratification. Two years passed as state after state considered Congress's proposal. By 1791, 10 of the 12 amendments were at last ratified by the required number of states. Thus, the Bill of Rights was added to the Constitution as Amendments 1–10.

In a later chapter, you will read about the many freedoms guaranteed by the Bill of Rights. For now, simply note the most famous of them:

- freedom to practice the religion of your choice
- freedom to criticize the government without fear of being arrested
- freedom to join almost any political organization and party
- freedom from unfair police methods
- right of an accused person to receive a fair trial.

REVIEW

A. Completing the Sentence

Use the word list to write the missing word or words on a piece of paper.

Article	legislatures
Bill of Rights	proposed
Congress	ratified
conventions	

1. Methods for amending the Constitution are described in ______ V.
2. Almost all of the 27 amendments to the Constitution have been ______ by Congress and then ratified by the states.
3. Every amendment except one has been ratified by state ______.
4. The Twenty-first Amendment was ratified by state ______.
5. For a national convention to meet, both ______ and two-thirds of the states must call for one.
6. The first amendments to be proposed by Congress were those we call the ______.
7. Of the 12 amendments submitted to the states in 1789, 10 were finally ______ in 1791.

B. Applying What You Know

For each amendment below, determine how many states had to ratify it. Use your knowledge both of math and the amendment process.

1. The *First Amendment,* adopted in 1791 when there were 14 states. How many states had to ratify?
2. The *Fifteenth Amendment,* adopted in 1870 when there were 37 states. How many states had to ratify?
3. The *Twenty-first Amendment,* adopted in 1933 when there were 48 states. How many had to ratify?
4. The *Twenty-sixth Amendment,* adopted in 1971 when there were 50 states. How many had to ratify?

2. WHAT AMENDMENTS MADE OUR GOVERNMENT MORE DEMOCRATIC?

As you learned in Chapter 3, the United States was at first an oligarchy (rule by a minority group) rather than a democracy (rule by all the people). In the 1790s, the only voters were property-owning citizens who were both white and male. That meant that only a minority of people had a voice in government. The United States became increasingly democratic after a series of amendments was added to the Constitution. One amendment abolished slavery. Others guaranteed the right to vote to different groups.

In this section you will learn (*a*) how these amendments were passed and (*b*) how they brought about a fully democratic government that included *all* the people.

Reformers before the Civil War. In the 1850s, the majority of adult Americans could not vote. About half the population were nonvoting women. About 10 percent were blacks, both men and women, most of whom lived in the South as slaves.

In the Northern states, many citizens—including Frederick Douglass—hoped to set blacks free by abolishing slavery. The same reformers championed the idea of *suffrage* (voting rights) for women. These two causes—abolition and women's suffrage—were linked together for a good reason. Reformers argued that the United States should fully live up to its ideals of liberty and equal rights for all.

But many white Southerners were outraged by the anti-slavery ideas of Northern abolitionists. Conflict between North and South finally led to war. In 1861, eleven states of the South declared that they had withdrawn from the Union and set up an independent government. Through four hard years, Southern troops fought Northern troops in a war that took the lives of about 620,000 people. The South surrendered in 1865. The U.S. Congress was then controlled by Northerners who wanted to set free—or emancipate—all slaves and to guarantee their rights as citizens.

The Civil War amendments. To accomplish this purpose, Congress proposed three amendments. Between 1865 and 1870, all three were ratified by the necessary number of states. These were the main provisions of each:

TURNING POINT. The Battle of Gettysburg (July 1–3, 1863) was won by the Union. How did Union victory in the war lead to changes in the Constitution?

- The **Thirteenth Amendment** abolished slavery everywhere in the United States.
- The **Fourteenth Amendment** guaranteed that all persons born in the United States are "citizens of the United States and of the State wherein they reside." In other words, full citizenship was given to freed blacks. They were now entitled to the same political rights as whites. The Fourteenth Amendment also said that all citizens (both blacks and whites) had to be granted *"equal protection of the laws"* by their state government.
- The **Fifteenth Amendment** guaranteed to blacks the right to vote in any federal or state election. No government could deny this right because of a person's "race, color, or previous condition of servitude [the fact of having once been a slave]."

Thus, as a result of the Civil War, the United States took three huge steps toward becoming a truly democratic nation.

"THE FIRST VOTE." This picture was on the cover of *Harper's Weekly*, in 1867. What evidence do you find about the role of the Civil War in changing the Constitution?

CASE STUDY: Campaign for Woman's Suffrage

A lawyer who could not vote. In 1887, Americans celebrated the 100th anniversary of the signing of the Constitution. There was much to celebrate and honor in the 100-year-old document. Yet some citizens thought the Constitution had at least one very serious flaw. It did not guarantee women the right to vote. State governments, which made the voting laws, said that only adult males could vote. To many, this fact seemed both undemocratic and unfair.

Among those who wanted to change the Constitution was a young woman from Kansas named Lilla Day Monroe. In 1895, Monroe passed an examination to practice law in the state. She became the first woman lawyer to argue cases before Kansas's highest court. Because of her profession, she knew more about government and the law than most men. And yet, like other women of her time, Monroe was prevented from voting because politics was thought to be strictly "man's business."

LILLA DAY MONROE

Early campaign for woman's suffrage. Born in 1858, Monroe lived during a period of great changes in American society—changes brought about by human ambitions as well as by new machines. Many women devoted much of their adult lives to the task of winning the right to vote. The first major drive to win the vote for American women took place in Kansas in 1867, when Monroe was only nine years old. Being on the frontier of settlement, Kansas at that time was a rough and lawless country to travel through. Even so, many young *suffragists* spent months on dusty roads and trails making speeches for their cause.

This first campaign for woman's suffrage in Kansas ended in defeat. Many other campaigns ended the same way. The final effort, begun in 1901, was an 11-year campaign in which Lilla Day Monroe—now a mature woman—played a leading role. Why did she take time from a busy career and family life to work for woman's suffrage? This was her explanation:

> It has always been my belief that everyone, whether man or woman, should

render public service to his or her community commensurate with [according to] ability. I did not feel that I was neglecting my family in working for the public good, *their* good.

In 1912, volunteers for the Kansas State Suffrage Association persuaded a majority of male voters to change the state constitution and permit women in the state to vote. As the association's president, Lilla Day Monroe led the successful drive.

Campaign for the Nineteenth Amendment. But Kansas was just one state of the Union. In most of the other states, particularly those in the East, women were still barred from voting by state laws. Many women thought the best way to gain the vote was to work for a *national* amendment to the U.S. Constitution. Leading them was a determined New Yorker named Susan B. Anthony.

In 1878, Congress considered Anthony's proposed amendment. It read:

> The right of citizens of the United States to vote shall not be denied or abridged by the United States or by any state on account of sex.

Congress voted against it in that year . . . and the next year . . . and the next year. For 41 consecutive years, the Anthony Amendment, as it was called, was introduced and voted down. Finally in 1919, it passed. It took only one more year for state legislatures to ratify it. In 1920, the Anthony Amendment became the **Nineteenth Amendment** to the Constitution. Lilla Day Monroe joined thousands of other suffragists in celebrating their victory.

Direct election of U.S. senators. In the election of 1920, every man and woman in the country had an opportunity to vote not only for president but also for U.S. senators. Before 1913, even male voters could not vote for senators. The Constitution, as originally written in 1787, provided that senators were to be chosen by state legislatures. The **Seventeenth Amendment,** adopted in 1913, changed this rule by saying that the voters of a state were to choose U.S. senators by direct election. This was another important step toward making U.S. government more democratic.

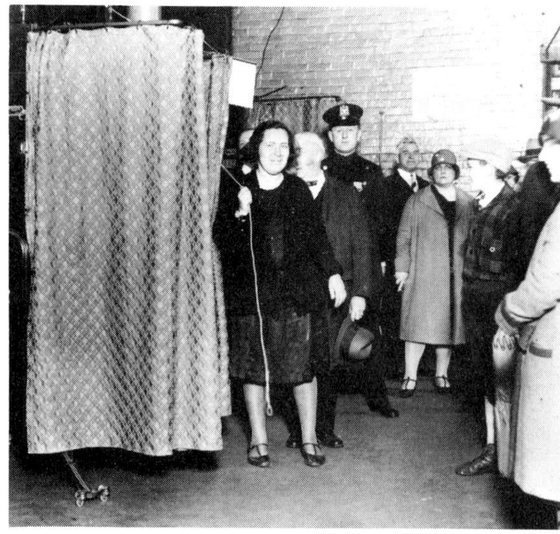

VOTING AT LAST. This woman was one of millions of New Yorkers who voted for the first time in 1920 because of the Nineteenth Amendment. What other amendments made the U.S. Constitution more democratic?

Adding electors, subtracting a poll tax. To remove other obstacles to voting, two more amendments were added in the 1960s.

The **Twenty-third Amendment** (1961) gave to adult residents of Washington, D.C., a means for voting for president and vice president. Under the original Constitution, only states were assigned electors to cast ballots for president. The city of Washington was not part of any state, so it was left out of presidential elections. The Twenty-third Amendment gave three electors to the nation's capital. (The role of electors is explained in Chapter 11).

The **Twenty-fourth Amendment** (1964) concerned a poll tax that some states once collected from voters. (A poll is a place where votes are cast in an election.) Holding elections is an expense of state government. To pay for election costs, some states required voters to pay a small tax as a kind of fee for being issued a ballot. But poorer citizens could ill afford to pay the tax. The Twenty-fourth Amendment abolished the poll tax. Democracy advanced one more step.

Suffrage for 18-year-olds. As shown by the "citizens" time line on page 106, Lilla Day Monroe died in 1929. Her great-granddaughter, Joanna Stratton (born in 1954), took it for granted that she would vote after her 21st birthday. At that time, anyone under 21 could not vote.

But in the 1960s, thousands of young men in Stratton's age group were drafted into the armed forces to fight in Vietnam. Most of them were between the ages of 18 and 21. If they were old enough to risk their lives in war, why weren't they old enough to vote? That was the reasoning behind an amendment proposed by Congress and ratified by the states in 1971. The **Twenty-sixth Amendment** guaranteed everyone 18 years old and older the right to vote.

Joanna Stratton turned 18 in December 1972—just one month too late to participate in the presidential election that year. It was frustrating for her because she had been interested in politics from an early age. She envied her slightly older classmates who in 1972 were among the first 18-year-olds to vote in an American election.

How do we know about the lives and politics of Joanna Stratton and Lilla Day Monroe? Shortly after graduating from college, Stratton published a book about women who settled Kansas when it was still nearly a wilderness. The book, *Pioneer Women: Voices from the Kansas Frontier*, was one that her great-grandmother had wanted to write. Monroe had started the research and writing that Joanna Stratton finally finished more than 50 years later.

YOUNG VOTER, 1972. This college student, aged 18, was allowed to vote in the 1972 election because of which amendment?

JOANNA STRATTON

TWO CITIZENS

1858 LILLA DAY (MONROE) is born in rural Indiana.

1884 She moves to Kansas, where she marries Lee Monroe, a lawyer.

1895 She earns a state license to practice law.

1901 She becomes active in a campaign for women suffrage.

1912 The laws of Kansas allow her to vote for the first time.

1921 She founds a newspaper for the women voters of Kansas and begins work on a book.

1929 She dies before she can finish the book.

1954 Lilla Day Monroe's great-granddaughter, JOANNA STRATTON, is born.

1972 The 26th Amendment allows her to vote for the first time.

1981 She publishes the book begun by Mrs. Monroe.

1840 · 1850 · 1860 · 1870 · 1880 · 1890 · 1900 · 1910 · 1920 · 1930 · 1940 · 1950 · 1960 · 1970 · 1980 · 1990 · 2000

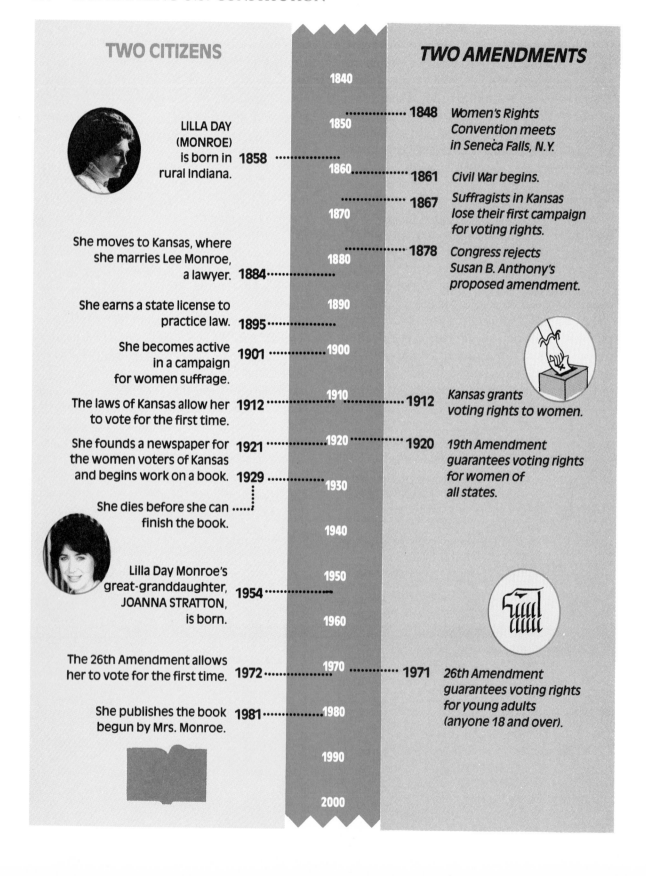

TWO AMENDMENTS

1848 *Women's Rights Convention meets in Seneca Falls, N.Y.*

1861 *Civil War begins.*

1867 *Suffragists in Kansas lose their first campaign for voting rights.*

1878 *Congress rejects Susan B. Anthony's proposed amendment.*

1912 *Kansas grants voting rights to women.*

1920 *19th Amendment guarantees voting rights for women of all states.*

1971 *26th Amendment guarantees voting rights for young adults (anyone 18 and over).*

REVIEW

A. Making Inferences

Four amendments gave the suffrage to different groups of Americans. They were adopted in the following years:

Fifteenth Amendment—1870
Nineteenth Amendment—1920
Twenty-third Amendment—1961
Twenty-sixth Amendment—1971

Refer to these dates and to information in the text to answer each of the following questions:

1. Which of the following groups could vote in the election of 1800? (*a*) 18-year-olds (*b*) women (*c*) blacks (*d*) male property owners.
2. Which of the following Americans could vote *for the first time* in the presidential election of 1872? (*a*) 18-year-olds (*b*) women (*c*) freed black men (*d*) male property owners.
3. Which group could *not* vote for Franklin D. Roosevelt in the election of 1932? (*a*) male residents of Colorado (*b*) female residents of Vermont (*c*) male residents of the District of Columbia (*d*) female residents of California.
4. In the election of 1976, which was the only group that still could *not* vote? (*a*) blacks who failed to pay a poll tax (*b*) citizens under 18 years old (*c*) women born before 1920 (*d*) 19-year-old college students.

B. Before and After

The first sentence of each activity below describes democratic issues **before** the Constitution was amended. Complete the second sentence by naming an amendment. Then describe the **effect** it had.

1. *Before* the Civil War, blacks were not considered to be citizens. But *after* the adoption of the ______ Amendment in 1868, what happened?
2. *Before* 1913, U.S. senators were elected by a vote of the state legislatures. But *after* the adoption of the ______ Amendment, what happened?
3. *Before* 1920, women could vote in some states but not in others. *After* the adoption of the ______ Amendment, what happened?

C. Projects

Do **one** of the following:

1. Make your own **time line** similar to the one on page 106. You might call it: A VOTER'S LIFE. Place the following dates on the time line.
   - 1971 (adoption of the Twenty-sixth Amendment)
   - The year of your birth
   - The year of the first election in which you will be eligible to vote
   - Election year of 2000 (and your age in that year)
   - Election year of 2004 (and your age in that year)
   - Election year of 2008 (and your age in that year)
2. Find out if your library has a copy of Joanna Stratton's *Pioneer Women*. If not, ask a librarian if the book can be obtained on an interlibrary loan. Select one chapter to read. **Summarize** it in a report to your class.
3. From library sources, find out about the political efforts of **one** of the following suffragists: Susan B. Anthony, Carrie Chapman Catt, Alice Paul, Elizabeth Cady Stanton, or Lucy Stone. In a **short essay,** (*a*) state what the person did and (*b*) explain why her work was significant for American democracy.

3. WHAT AMENDMENTS MADE OUR GOVERNMENT MORE EFFICIENT?

As a practical plan for governing a nation, the Constitution has worked wonderfully well. But it has not worked perfectly. Flaws are bound to appear in any system. In computer language, we speak of programs having "bugs" (mistakes or flaws) in them and needing to be "debugged" (corrected). In this section, we will see how "bugs" in the original Constitution were eliminated, as amendments were added one by one.

One flaw in the court system. The first flaw showed up very early during the presidency of George Washington. In the 1790s, a British citizen had sued the state of Georgia for failing to pay its debts. After hearing the case, judges on the Supreme Court said the Britisher was right: Georgia must pay. The Court's decision angered the people of Georgia and worried the citizens of other states as well.

So an amendment was proposed by Congress in 1794 and ratified in 1795. The **Eleventh Amendment** said that the Supreme Court had no power to settle disputes between a state and the citizen of either (*a*) some other state or (*b*) a foreign country. For example, suppose that the government of Maine ordered textbooks from a New York publisher but then failed to pay for the books. Because of the Eleventh Amendment, the publisher could *not* take its *suit* (or complaint) to the Supreme Court. The case would have to be settled in a state court.

One flaw concerning Congress. You know about the *income tax* that workers pay every year to the federal government. Today's government could not possibly get along without it. Yet, not so long ago, Congress was unable to collect an income tax.

Article I of the Constitution said that Congress could tax people directly only if the amount of taxes collected from each state was proportional to the state's population.

For example, suppose the population of State X is 4 million; the population of State Y is 1 million. Then, according to the Constitution (Article I, Section 9), the people of State X would have to pay four times as much in federal taxes as the people of State Y. That seems fair enough. *But* suppose the average household in State X earns only half as much income as the average household in State Y. The X-citizens, being relatively poor, would have a harder time than Y-citizens paying their state's share of the tax burden.

Collecting taxes by this means would not be fair to people of the poorer states. Therefore, for many years, no income tax was collected under the "unfair" rule of the original Constitution.

Finally, in 1913, the Constitution was amended to allow Congress to collect an income tax in any way that it saw fit. The **Sixteenth Amendment** stated: "Congress shall have power to lay and collect taxes on incomes from whatever source derived, without apportionment among the several states. . . ." Because of these 21 words, hundreds of billions of tax dollars flow yearly into the U.S. Treasury. The poor in every state pay proportionately *less* than the rich—just the opposite of what would have happened under the original rule.

Several flaws concerning the presidency. Most of the "bugs" in the Constitution concerned the office of the president. To correct them, four amendments were added.

1. "Bug" in the Electoral College. Article II said that the president and vice president would be chosen by an *Electoral College*. As explained in Chapter 11, this is a small group of people called electors whose only job is to cast ballots in a presidential election.

A "bug" was discovered in the Electoral College system in 1800. In that year, Amer-

CARTOON CORNER

icans voted for electors. The electors then voted for president and vice president. A majority of voters wanted Thomas Jefferson to be president and Aaron Burr to be vice president. But the system described in the Constitution did not allow electors to cast separate ballots for president and vice president. So, voting for two candidates, they gave exactly the same number of votes to both Jefferson and Burr. To break the tie, the House of Representatives had to choose a president. After much confusion and bitter argument, a majority of the House members voted for Jefferson.

An amendment was needed to prevent a crisis like this from happening at every election. The **Twelfth Amendment,** adopted in 1804, said that electors were to cast one set of ballots for president and another set of ballots for vice president.

2. "Bug" in the system for changing leaders. Franklin Roosevelt was elected president for the first time in November 1932. He was to replace Herbert Hoover in March 1933. But March was four months away. During this period, President Hoover had almost no power because his term of office was coming to an end. An almost powerless president like this was known as a "lame duck." Roosevelt could not lead the nation either, since the Constitution required him to wait until *Inauguration* Day in March.

Leadership was desperately needed. In 1932, the nation's economy was being shaken by the Great Depression. Yet Americans could do nothing but wring their hands, waiting for the long "lame duck" period to end.

The **Twentieth Amendment**, adopted in 1933, shortened the "lame duck" period of waiting by more than six weeks. Instead of a president's term beginning on March 4, the amendment set an earlier date: January 20.

3. Too many terms? After winning election in 1932, Franklin D. Roosevelt won again in 1936 . . . again in 1940 . . . and again in 1944. No other president—not even George Washington—had been elected to serve more than two terms. A few Americans worried that some future president might hold office permanently and thus become a kind of dictator. Others wanted the Constitution changed for reasons of party politics. They were Republican politicians who disliked seeing the White House occupied for so many years by a popular Democrat.

In 1947, two years after Roosevelt's death, the **Twenty-second Amendment** was adopted. It said that nobody could be elected president more than twice.

4. "Bug" of an injured or ailing president. In 1963, President John Kennedy was shot and killed almost instantly by an assassin. People wondered what might have happened if Kennedy had been severely wounded instead. Who would then have carried on the duties of president?

Under Kennedy's successor, Lyndon Johnson, the **Twenty-fifth Amendment** was ratified in 1967. It describes in detail a system for determining whether a disabled president can or cannot perform his or her duties. If not, then the vice president takes over for as long as the president is unfit.

SAD CEREMONY. Only an hour after President Kennedy was assassinated in Dallas in 1963, Vice President Lyndon Johnson took the oath of office aboard a plane at the Dallas airport. Which amendment was later adopted to serve in emergencies like this?

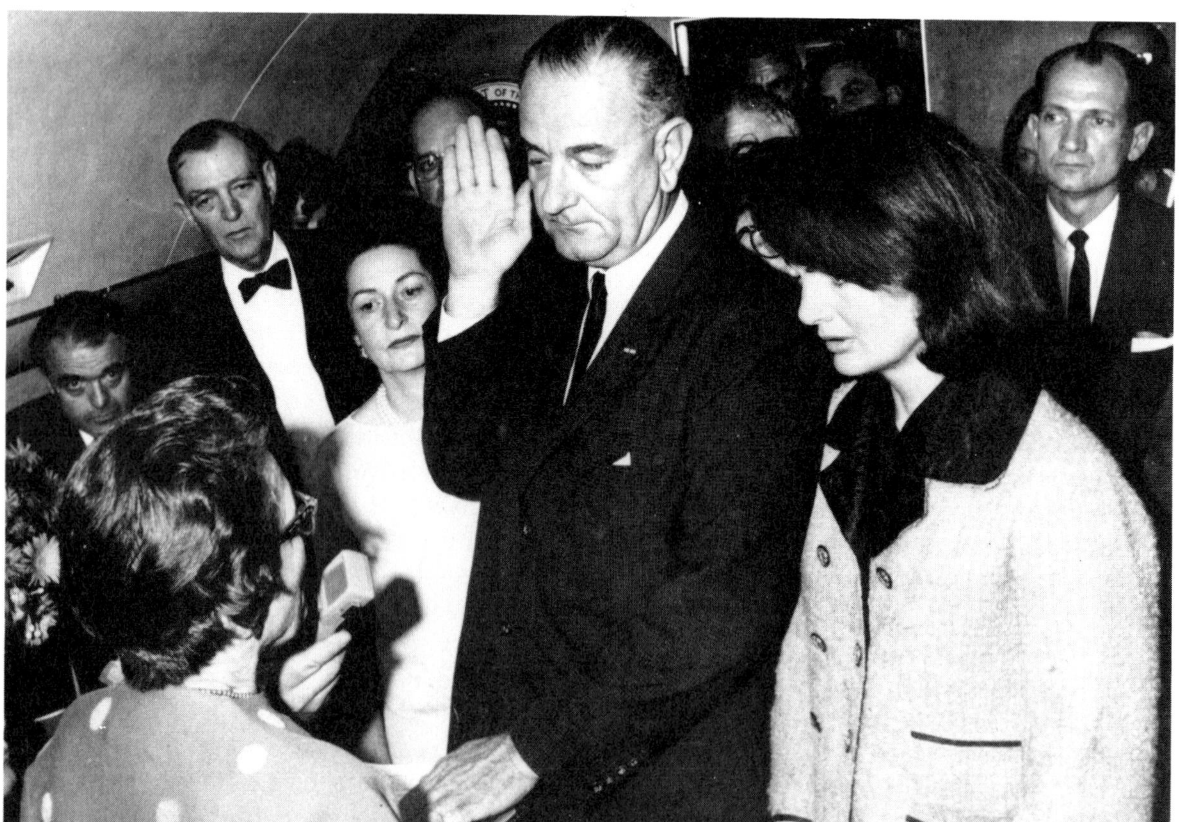

An amendment that was repealed. All amendments are made in the hope of strengthening our government. But one amendment may have had just the opposite effect. This was the **Eighteenth Amendment**, better known as the Prohibition Amendment. It prohibited "the manufacture, sale, or transportation" of wines, beers, liquors, and other alcoholic beverages. Adopted in 1919, it went into effect in 1920.

People who wanted prohibition thought it would prevent excessive drinking and drunkenness. But opponents of prohibition thought consumers had a right to buy alcohol, beer, and wine if they chose. They had no respect for a law that they regarded as wrong to begin with. Therefore, during the 1920s, gangsters made a fortune selling beer and liquor illegally to millions of customers.

By 1933, it was generally conceded that the Prohibition experiment had not worked. In that year, the Eighteenth Amendment was repealed—or cancelled—by the adoption of the **Twenty-first Amendment**. Today, the sale of alcohol is regulated by state laws—not prohibited by federal law.

An amendment proposed by James Madison. Oddly enough, the most recent amendment, the Twenty-seventh, is as old as the First Amendment. It was proposed by James Madison in the first Congress of 1789. Ten other amendments proposed by Madison were ratified by the states and became Amendments 1-10—the Bill of Rights. But another of Madison's proposed amendments was not ratified within his lifetime. In fact, it was not ratified by three-fourths of the states until 1992—more than two centuries after it was originally proposed!

The **Twenty-seventh Amendment** restricts Congress's ability to raise the salaries of its own members. It states:

> No law varying the compensation for the services of the senators and representatives shall take effect until an election of representatives shall have intervened.

Let us say that Senator X and Representative Y are elected to Congress in 1994. The Congress elected that year immediately votes to raise the lawmakers' salaries. The Twenty-seventh Amendment prevents Senator X and Representative Y from receiving the pay raise until after a new Congress is elected in 1996.

REVIEW

A. Problems and Solutions

Match the constitutional **"bug"** to the **amendment** that corrected it.

"BUGS"

1. Congress lacked the power to collect an income tax.
2. The electoral system caused two candidates for president to receive the same number of votes.
3. The president could be re-elected many times.
4. It was unclear what would happen if a president became disabled.
5. States could be sued by citizens of other states in the Supreme Court.
6. After an election, there was a four-month wait before a president-elect took office.

AMENDMENTS

a. Eleventh Amendment
b. Twelfth Amendment
c. Sixteenth Amendment
d. Twentieth Amendment
e. Twenty-second Amendment
f. Twenty-fifth Amendment

B. Facts, Errors, and Opinions

Tell whether each sentence below: (A) accurately states a **fact**, (B) contains a factual **error**, or (C) expresses an **opinion**.

1. The Prohibition Amendment should never have been adopted.
2. The first income tax was collected in 1803.
3. The Twenty-first Amendment repealed the Eighteenth Amendment.
4. Franklin Roosevelt was the only person to be elected president four times.
5. The Eleventh Amendment concerned one of the legislative powers of Congress.
6. After November 1932, Herbert Hoover was known as a "lame-duck" president.
7. Something should be done to reform the tax laws, especially the income tax.
8. The Constitution is now perfect because of the amendments added to it.

C. Cartoon Corner

Refer to the cartoon on page 109.

1. What seemed to be wrong with the presidency "car" before it was fixed by amendment?
2. Besides a change in the electoral system, name two other repairs that were made in the presidency.
3. The mechanics working on the car are not labeled. How would *you* identify them? (Several answers are possible.)

4. HOW MAY THE CONSTITUTION BE CHANGED IN INFORMAL WAYS?

Adding amendments to the Constitution is the only *formal* way of changing it. But there are also *informal* ways of changing it. These have been as important as the amendments in keeping the Constitution alive and well for 200 years.

Actions of Congress and the president. As the muscles stretch when exercised, so the Constitution may be stretched by those who use it. Constitutional powers are used by Congress whenever it passes new laws. They are also used daily by the president in carrying out executive duties.

Change of this informal type occurs naturally and easily as time passes. For example, one president may decide to act in a certain way and afterwards, other presidents may do the same. George Washington decided to meet regularly with a *Cabinet* of top officials. The presidents after him followed his example. Today, holding Cabinet meetings is just as much a habit as holding presidential elections every four years.

Here are other examples of informal change:

- Congress is now in the habit of using *committees* to consider different types of bills.
- Whenever there is a crisis, the president is expected to speak to the nation about it in a special address, usually on television.
- Every four years, political parties hold conventions to nominate candidates for president and vice president.

The Constitution says nothing about Cabinet meetings, Congressional committees, TV speeches, or political parties. Yet they are now a popular part of our system of government. They have become a habit. The Constitution does not forbid these or other habits of our political life. So they may continue to exist as long as they are needed.

Decisions of the Supreme Court. In the Fourteenth Amendment, we find the phrase "equal protection of the laws." What does this mean? Does it guarantee that black students can go to the same school as white students? Once the answer was "no" because, according to the Supreme Court, the words "equal protection" did not apply to black students in the 1890s. Now the answer is "yes" because, according to a later Supreme Court decision, the same words do ensure equal treatment for black students today.

How can the same phrase change its meaning? It is because the Constitution is interpreted by nine human beings. Being human, these nine have different points of view. They are the nine judges—or justices—who sit on the U.S. Supreme Court and review hundreds of cases of law every year.

Each case involves a question about a certain clause of the Constitution. How does a clause written in 1787 apply to a case involving TV broadcasting, for example? It is hard to know. Supreme Court justices listen to lawyers' arguments in a case and then reach a decision by majority vote. They do not always agree among themselves. Those who were in the majority 15 years ago may not be in the majority today. So the opinion of the Supreme Court shifts from time to time—and so does the meaning of the Constitution.

Congress, the president, and the Supreme Court keep making decisions day after day. As they do, the Constitution slowly changes its meaning. Thus, it grows as the nation grows. For 200 years, the Constitution has endured as the "supreme law of the land."

INTERPRETING THE CONSTITUTION. William Howard Taft (seated, center) was both a president (1909–1913) and a chief justice of the Supreme Court (1921–1930). How do the decisions of the Supreme Court allow the Constitution to change with the times?

REVIEW

A. Supporting the Main Idea

Below are **main ideas** of the reading. Illustrate what each means by giving an example or fact.

1. Informal methods of change are as important as the formal method of amendment.
2. Over a period of time, Congress has worked out standard ways of carrying out its lawmaking function.
3. The judges are aware that changing conditions sometimes call for new laws and new thinking.

B. Making Inferences

Tell whether you think each statement below describes either (*a*) a **rule** of the Constitution or (*b*) a **practice** of government established by informal habit and custom.

1. Every four years, a group of electors cast separate ballots for president and vice president.
2. January 20th is the date that a newly elected president takes office.
3. The wife of a president is often referred to as the "First Lady."
4. Women as well as men are allowed to vote on Election Day.
5. Congress has the power to collect an income tax.
6. The president's press conferences are broadcast on the major TV networks.
7. The president may veto an act of Congress.
8. Political parties nominate candidates for president in July or August.
9. Each weekday, the nine judges on the Supreme Court usually hear two cases of law.

CHAPTER REVIEW

A. Completing the Summary

Select terms from the word list to fill in the blanks in the summary below. Write your answers on a separate piece of paper.

amendment	flexibility
Bill of Rights	income tax
Cabinet	informal
citizenship	legislatures
Civil War	Prohibition
Congress	repealed
conventions	slavery
democratic	Supreme Court
District of Columbia	vote
equal protection	women

A formal means of changing the Constitution is by the process of __(1)__. Almost always this process begins as a proposal voted upon by __(2)__. The proposal then goes to the state __(3)__ for ratification. Only once has an amendment been ratified by state __(4)__.

The Constitution was first changed in 1791 when ten amendments were added all at once. Together, they are known as the __(5)__. After the __(6)__, three amendments were adopted that guaranteed the rights of black Americans. The Thirteenth Amendment abolished __(7)__. The Fourteenth Amendment defined the meaning of __(8)__ and guaranteed "__(9)__ of the laws." The Fifteenth Amendment said that states had to allow black men the right to __(10)__.

Later amendments also made our government more __(11)__. One of them, the Nineteenth Amendment, gave __(12)__ the right to vote. Another, the Twenty-third Amendment, gave residents of the __(13)__ an opportunity to vote in presidential elections.

The Constitution has also been amended several times to make our government more efficient. Probably the most important of these changes was the Sixteenth Amendment, which made it possible for Congress to collect an __(14)__. An amendment that many people later regretted was the __(15)__ Amendment of 1920. It failed to stop people from buying and selling alcoholic drinks and was __(16)__ in 1933 by the Twenty-first Amendment.

__(17)__ ways of changing the Constitution are as important as the formal method. Examples of such changes include the committee system of Congress and the meetings of the president's __(18)__. Also, nine judges of the __(19)__ are constantly interpreting the Constitution and giving it new meaning. The key reason that the Constitution has worked so well for so long is its great __(20)__.

B. Clues

Each phrase is closely linked with a constitutional amendment. Read it as a clue. Then identify the amendment by number and explain how the clue "gave it away."

1. final triumph for the suffragists
2. new method for electing U.S. senators
3. tax that Congress may now collect
4. tax that states may *not* collect
5. experiment that failed to change people's habits

6. what caused the experiment to end
7. a change in date from March to January
8. end of slavery
9. one result of the assassination of John F. Kennedy
10. result of a tied election
11. a new limit of two elected terms
12. a right made available on your eighteenth birthday

C. Applying What You Know

Imagine yourself to be a dedicated politician—a kind of James Madison for the 1990s. Here are three amendments that you might want to add to the Constitution.

AMENDMENT X would guarantee that women are treated exactly the same as men by their employers.

AMENDMENT Y would permit U.S. senators to be elected to only two terms—a total of 12 years. (There is currently no limit to the number of years they may serve.)

AMENDMENT Z would require that justices of the Supreme Court retire after the age of 75. (Currently, justices may continue in office until their death.)

Choose **one** of these amendments to support. Describe what you would have to do to get your amendment adopted.

HOW TO READ THE CONSTITUTION AND MASTER ITS VOCABULARY

On the pages that follow (116–142) is the "supreme law of the land"—the United States Constitution. Every American citizen should be familiar with the powers that it gives the U.S. government and the rights that it guarantees to "We the people."

Reading the Constitution is not easy. It was written by lawyers from a past century. For readers today, not trained in the law, many of its words and phrases need to be defined. That is why, in this text, you will find difficult terms defined in the margin near to where they appear in the Constitution.

Many of the defined terms are ones that you should add to your political vocabulary. You may come across these words in newspaper articles, on TV news, and in later chapters of this book. Therefore, to help you learn the vocabulary in the margins, five exercises are provided. Notice the "Vocabulary Review" feature on the following pages:

- for reviewing the Preamble and Article I . . . . page 123
- for reviewing Article II . . . . . page 126
- for reviewing Articles III–VII . . . . page 131
- for reviewing the Bill of Rights . . . . page 134
- for reviewing Amendments 11–27 . . . . page 143

What follows is an *edited* text of the Constitution. Its words are spelled and capitalized in the modern style, not in the style of Benjamin Franklin. Also, certain features were added to make the Constitution easier to understand for modern readers.

The Constitution of the United States

Preamble

We, the people of the United States, in order to form a more perfect union, establish justice, insure domestic tranquillity, provide for the common defense, promote the general welfare, and secure the blessings of liberty to ourselves and our posterity, do ordain and establish this Constitution for the United States of America.

domestic tranquillity: nation's ability to maintain law and order

posterity: people to be born in the future

ordain: to command something to happen; to give authority

Article I: The Congress

***Section 1.* Legislative power**

1. All legislative powers herein granted shall be vested in a Congress of the United States, which shall consist of a Senate and House of Representatives.

vested in: granted or given to

***Section 2.* The House of Representatives**

1. The House of Representatives shall be composed of members chosen every second year by the people of the several states, and the electors in each state shall have the qualifications requisite for electors of the most numerous branch of the state legislature.

requisite: required or necessary

most numerous branch: the larger house in a two-house legislature

2. No person shall be a representative who shall not have attained to the age of twenty-five years, and been seven years a citizen of the United States, and who shall not, when elected, be an inhabitant of that state in which he shall be chosen.

3. Representatives and direct taxes shall be apportioned among the several states which may be included within this union, according to their respective numbers, which shall be determined by adding to the whole number of free persons, including those bound to service for a term of years, and excluding Indians not taxed, three-fifths of all other persons. The actual enumeration shall be made within three years after the first meeting of the Congress of the United States, and within every subsequent term of ten years, in such manner as they shall by law direct. The number of representatives shall not exceed one for every thirty thousand, but each state shall have at least one representative; and until such enumerations shall be made, the state of New Hampshire shall be entitled to choose three, Massachusetts eight, Rhode Island and Providence Plantations one, Connecticut five, New York six, New Jersey four, Pennsylvania eight, Delaware one, Maryland six, Virginia ten, North Carolina five, South Carolina five, and Georgia three.

apportioned: distributed; divided up in proportion to something

all other persons: the Framers' indirect name for slaves

enumeration: counting

subsequent: following or coming after

4. When vacancies happen in the representation from any state, the executive authority thereof shall issue writs of election to fill such vacancies.

5. The House of Representatives shall choose their speaker and other officers and shall have the sole power of impeachment.

***Section 3.* The Senate**

1. The Senate of the United States shall be composed of two senators from each state, chosen by the legislature thereof, for six years, and each senator shall have one vote.

2. Immediately after they shall be assembled in consequence of the first election, they shall be divided as equally as may be into three classes. The seats of the senators of the first class shall be vacated at the expiration of the second year, of the second class at the expiration of the fourth year, and of the third class at the expiration of the sixth year, so that one-third may be chosen every second year; and if vacancies happen by resignation, or otherwise, during the recess of the legislature of any state, the executive thereof may make temporary appointments until the next meeting of the legislature, which shall then fill such vacancies.

3. No person shall be a senator who shall not have attained to the age of thirty years, and been nine years a citizen of the United States, and who shall not, when elected, be an inhabitant of that state for which he shall be chosen.

4. The vice president of the United States shall be president of the Senate, but shall have no vote, unless they be equally divided.

5. The Senate shall choose their other officers, and also a president pro tempore, in the absence of the vice president, or when he shall exercise the office of president of the United States.

6. The Senate shall have the sole power to try all impeachments. When sitting for that purpose, they shall be on oath or affirmation. When the president of the United States is tried, the chief justice shall preside. And no person shall be convicted without the concurrence of two-thirds of the members present. Judgment in cases of impeachment shall not extend further than to removal from office, and disqualification to hold and enjoy any office of honor, trust or profit under the United States. But the party convicted shall nevertheless be liable and subject to indictment, trial, judgment and punishment, according to law.

***Section 4.* Elections**

1. The times, places and manner of holding elections for senators and representatives, shall be prescribed in each state by the legislature thereof. But the Congress may at any time by law make or alter such regulations, except as to the places of choosing senators.

vacancy: an office not filled by anyone

executive authority: as used here, the phrase means the governor of a state

writ of election: orders to hold a special election to fill a vacancy in office

speaker: chief leader of the House of Representatives (also referred to as the speaker of the House)

impeachment: a formal accusation concerning some wrong or unlawful act

vacated: left empty

expiration: end

resignation: the decision to leave an office voluntarily

recess: a period when meetings are not held

appointment: assigning someone to fill an office

president pro tempore: a senator who directs meetings of the Senate when the vice president is absent

affirmation: a solemn vow or declaration of purpose

liable: held responsible

indictment: a formal accusation in a court of law

prescribed: announced as a rule

regulations: rules

2. The Congress shall assemble at least once in every year, and such meeting shall be on the first Monday in December, unless they shall by law appoint a different day.

***Section 5.* Membership and Rules**

1. Each house shall be the judge of the elections, returns and qualifications of its own members, and a majority of each shall constitute a quorum to do business; but a smaller number may adjourn from day to day, and may be authorized to compel the attendance of absent members, in such manner, and under such penalties as each house may provide.

2. Each house may determine the rules of its proceedings, punish its members for disorderly behavior, and, with the concurrence of two-thirds, expel a member.

3. Each house shall keep a journal of its proceedings, and from time to time publish the same, excepting such parts as may in their judgment require secrecy; and the yeas and nays of the members of either house on any question shall, at the desire of one-fifth of those present, be entered on the journal.

4. Neither house, during the session of Congress, shall, without the consent of the other, adjourn for more than three days, nor to any other place than that in which the two houses shall be sitting.

***Section 6.* Privileges and Restrictions**

1. The senators and representatives shall receive a compensation for their services, to be ascertained by law, and paid out of the treasury of the United States. They shall in all cases, except treason, felony and breach of the peace, be privileged from arrest during their attendance at the session of their respective houses, and in going to and returning from the same; and for any speech or debate in either house, they shall not be questioned in any other place.

2. No senator or representative shall, during the time for which he was elected, be appointed to any civil office under the authority of the United States, which shall have been created, or the emoluments whereof shall have been increased during such time; and no person holding any office under the United States, shall be a member of either house during his continuance in office.

quorum: the smallest number of members who must be present at a meeting. If this minimum is lacking, business may not be conducted.

adjourn: to close or bring a meeting to an end for a temporary period

proceedings: the speeches and decisions made at a meeting

concurrence: agreement; consent

journal: a daily record of speeches, votes, and other business. (The journal kept by Congress is known as the *Congressional Record*.)

yeas and nays: the way members of Congress vote yes or no

compensation: the payment of a salary

ascertain: to determine or find out definitely

treason: the crime of betraying your own country

felony: any serious crime

breach of the peace: disturbing your neighbors or refusing to obey law officers

civil office: any government job

emoluments: payments of money in the form of salaries or fees

Section 7. Making Laws

1. All bills for raising revenue shall originate in the House of Representatives; but the Senate may propose or concur with amendments as on other bills.

2. Every bill which shall have passed the House of Representatives and the Senate, shall, before it become a law, be presented to the president of the United States. If he approve he shall sign it, but if not he shall return it, with his objections to that house in which it shall have originated, who shall enter the objections at large on their journal, and proceed to reconsider it. If after such reconsideration two-thirds of that house shall agree to pass the bill, it shall be sent, together with the objections, to the other house, by which it shall likewise be reconsidered, and if approved by two-thirds of that house, it shall become a law. But in all such cases the votes of both houses shall be determined by yeas and nays, and the names of the persons voting for and against the bill shall be entered on the journal of each house respectively. If any bill shall not be returned by the president within ten days (Sundays excepted) after it shall have been presented to him, the same shall be a law, in like manner as if he had signed it, unless the Congress by their adjournment prevent its return, in which case it shall not be a law.

bill: a written proposal for a new law or a change in an existing law

revenue: taxes and other money received by the government

amendments: changes in a law or constitution

reconsideration: studying something a second time

3. Every order, resolution, or vote to which the concurrence of the Senate and House of Representatives may be necessary (except on a question of adjournment) shall be presented to the president of the United States; and before the same shall take effect, shall be approved by him, or being disapproved by him, shall be repassed by two-thirds of the Senate and House of Representatives, according to the rules and limitations prescribed in the case of a bill.

resolution: a statement declaring Congress's decision on an issue

Section 8. Powers of Congress

1. The Congress shall have power to lay and collect taxes, duties, imposts and excises, to pay the debts and provide for the common defense and general welfare of the United States; but all duties, imposts and excises shall be uniform throughout the United States;

2. To borrow money on the credit of the United States;

3. To regulate commerce with foreign nations, and among the several states, and with the Indian tribes;

4. To establish an uniform rule of naturalization, and uniform laws on the subject of bankruptcies throughout the United States;

duties, imposts, and excises: different kinds of taxes collected from the sale of goods

uniform: the same for all; not varying from one place to another

naturalization: the legal process through which an immigrant becomes a full citizen of his or her adopted country

bankruptcy: the condition of being unable to pay one's debts

5. To coin money, regulate the value thereof, and of foreign coin, and fix the standard of weights and measures;

6. To provide for the punishment of counterfeiting the securities and current coin of the United States;

7. To establish post offices and post roads;

8. To promote the progress of science and useful arts, by securing for limited times to authors and inventors exclusive right to their respective writings and discoveries;

9. To constitute tribunals inferior to the Supreme Court;

10. To define and punish piracies and felonies committed on the high seas, and offenses against the law of nations;

11. To declare war, grant letters of marque and reprisal, and make rules concerning captures on land and water;

12. To raise and support armies, but no appropriation of money to that use shall be for a longer term than two years;

13. To provide and maintain a navy;

14. To make rules for the government and regulation of the land and naval forces;

15. To provide for calling forth the militia to execute the laws of the union, suppress insurrections and repel invasions;

16. To provide for organizing, arming, and disciplining the militia, and for governing such part of them as may be employed in the service of the United States, reserving to the states respectively, the appointment of the officers, and the authority of training the militia according to the discipline prescribed by Congress;

17. To exercise exclusive legislation in all cases whatsoever, over such district (not exceeding ten miles square), as may, by cession of particular states, and the acceptance of Congress, become the seat of the government of the United States, and to exercise like authority over all places purchased by the consent of the legislature

weights and measures: standard units of measurement such as pounds and ounces, miles and yards, gallons and quarts

counterfeiting: illegal copying of money

securities: documents that give ownership and property rights to the person who holds them (for example, corporate stocks and government bonds)

tribunals: courts

inferior to: less powerful than; subject to the rule of some person or group that has greater power

piracy: robbery of a ship at sea

letters of marque and reprisal: documents issued to ship captains to permit them to attack enemy ships

appropriation: sum of money deliberately set aside for a specific purpose

militia: a part-time army of citizen volunteers instead of a permanent army of professional soldiers. (Today, the militia of each state is commonly called the National Guard.)

insurrection: an armed revolt against a government

cession: the giving away of a piece of land

seat of government: a capital city

of the state in which the same shall be for the erection of forts, magazines, arsenals, dock-yards, and other needful buildings;—and

18. To make all laws which shall be necessary and proper for carrying into execution the foregoing powers, and all other powers vested by this Constitution in the government of the United States, or in any department or officer thereof.

Section 9. **Powers Forbidden to Congress**

1. The migration or importation of such persons as any of the states now existing shall think proper to admit, shall not be prohibited by the Congress prior to the year one thousand eight hundred and eight, but a tax or duty may be imposed on such importation, not exceeding ten dollars for each person.

2. The privilege of the writ of habeas corpus shall not be suspended, unless when in cases of rebellion or invasion the public safety may require it.

3. No bill of attainder or ex post facto law shall be passed.

4. No capitation, or other direct, tax shall be laid, unless in proportion to the census or enumeration herein before directed to be taken.

5. No tax or duty shall be laid on articles exported from any state.

6. No preference shall be given by any regulation of commerce or revenue to the ports of one state over those of another. Nor shall vessels bound to, or from, one state, be obliged to enter, clear, or pay duties in another.

7. No money shall be drawn from the Treasury, but in consequence of appropriations made by law; and a regular statement and account of the receipts and expenditures of all public money shall be published from time to time.

8. No title of nobility shall be granted by the United States. And no person holding any office of profit or trust under them, shall, without the consent of the Congress, accept of any present, emolument, office, or title, of any kind whatever, from any king, prince, or foreign state.

magazine: a building or storage area for explosives

arsenal: building for storing weapons

foregoing: previous; mentioned earlier

migration: moving from one place to another

importation: purchasing and transporting something (in this case an enslaved person) into a different state

writ of habeas corpus: a court order demanding to know the reason why an arrested person is in jail. The court must set a deadline after which the person arrested must either be charged with an offense or be set free.

public safety: safety from violent acts such as rioting and invasion

bill of attainder: a law that declares someone guilty of a crime without a trial

ex post facto law: a law that punishes an action that already took place, before the law was passed

capitation or direct tax: a tax that takes the same amount from all citizens regardless of income

census: an official count of the population

receipts: money received

expenditures: money spent

public money: money that the government has available to spend

***Section 10.* Powers Forbidden to the States**

1. No state shall enter into any treaty, alliance, or confederation; grant letters of marque and reprisal; coin money; emit bills of credit; make anything but gold and silver coin a tender in payment of debts; pass any bill of attainder, ex post facto law, or law impairing the obligation of contracts, or grant any title of nobility.

2. No state shall, without the consent of the Congress, lay any imposts or duties on imports or exports, except what may be absolutely necessary for executing its inspection laws; and the net produce of all duties and imposts, laid by any state on imports or exports, shall be for the use of the treasury of the United States. And all such laws shall be subject to the revision and control of the Congress.

3. No state shall, without the consent of Congress, lay any duty of tonnage, keep troops, or ships of war in time of peace, enter into any agreement or compact with another state, or with a foreign power, or engage in war, unless actually invaded or in such imminent danger as will not admit of delay.

treaty: a written agreement between nations

alliance: an agreement between nations to come to each other's aid if attacked by a common enemy

confederation: a group of independent states that recognize a common government

bills of credit: a form of paper money

tender: something offered in payment (such as money)

impairing: interfering with

obligation of contract: the legal duty to obey the terms of a signed agreement

net produce: the sum of money left over after expenses have been subtracted

duty of tonnage: a tax on foreign cargo based on weight

compact: a formal understanding similar to a treaty (see above)

imminent danger: the likelihood that violent conflict or war will break out soon

VOCABULARY REVIEW

The Preamble and Article I

The phrases 1–14 below refer to the word list. On a separate piece of paper, write the word that either **matches** or **completes** each phrase. (Refer to definitions and constitutional clauses on pages 116–122.)

amend	facto	speaker
army	liable	war
census	militia	writ
cession	receipts	yeas
excise	Senate	

1. an officer of the House of Representatives
2. votes in favor of a bill
3. to change a law or constitution
4. a kind of tax
5. can be declared only by Congress
6. an official count of the population
7. a state's force of volunteer soldiers
8. a gift or grant of land
9. ex post __(?)__ laws prohibited by the Constitution
10. a legal document
11. the money that a government collects
12. the lawmaking body described by Article I, Section 3
13. obligated according to law
14. a group that Congress has the power to equip

Article II: The President and Vice President

Section 1. Executive Power

1. The executive power shall be vested in a president of the United States of America. He shall hold his office during the term of four years, and, together with the vice president, chosen for the same term, be elected, as follows:

executive power: the authority to see that laws are carried out

2. Each state shall appoint, in such manner as the legislature thereof may direct, a number of electors, equal to the whole number of senators and representatives to which the state may be entitled in the Congress: but no senator or representative, or person holding an office of trust or profit under the United States, shall be appointed an elector.

appoint: to name or select someone to fill an office

electors: a specially chosen group that has the responsibility of voting for president of the United States

3. The electors shall meet in their respective states, and vote by ballot for two persons, of whom one at least shall not be an inhabitant of the same state with themselves. And they shall make a list of all the persons voted for, and of the number of votes for each; which list they shall sign and certify, and transmit sealed to the seat of the government of the United States, directed to the president of the Senate. The president of the Senate shall, in the presence of the Senate and House of Representatives, open all the certificates, and the votes shall then be counted. The person having the greatest number of votes shall be the president, if such number be a majority of the whole number of electors appointed. And if

certify: to declare that something is correctly done

certificate: a document signed by a government official

there be more than one who have such majority, and have an equal number of votes, then the House of Representatives shall immediately choose by ballot one of them for president. And if no person have a majority, then from the five highest on the list the said house shall in like manner choose the president. But in choosing the president, the votes shall be taken by states, the representation from each state having one vote. A quorum for this purpose shall consist of a member or members from two-thirds of the states, and a majority of all the states shall be necessary to a choice. In every case, after the choice of the president, the person having the greatest number of votes of the electors shall be the vice president. But if there should remain two or more who have equal votes, the Senate shall choose from them by ballot the vice president.

4. The Congress may determine the time of choosing the electors, and the day on which they shall give their votes; which day shall be the same throughout the United States.

5. No person except a natural-born citizen, or a citizen of the United States, at the time of the adoption of this Constitution, shall be eligible to the office of president; neither shall any person be eligible to that office who shall not have attained to the age of thirty-five years, and been fourteen years a resident within the United States.

natural-born citizen: someone whose birth occurred in the United States

6. In case of the removal of the president from office, or his death, resignation, or inability to discharge the powers and duties of the said office, the same shall devolve on the vice president, and the Congress may by law provide for the case of removal, death, resignation or inability, both of the president and vice president, declaring what officer shall then act as president, and such officer shall act accordingly, until the disability be removed, or a president shall be elected.

discharge: to carry out

devolve on: to pass along to

7. The president shall, at stated times, receive for his services, a compensation, which shall neither be increased nor diminished during the period for which he shall have been elected, and he shall not receive within that period any other emolument from the United States, or any of them.

8. Before he enter on the execution of his office, he shall take the following oath or affirmation:—"I do solemnly swear (or affirm) that I will faithfully execute the office of president of the United States, and will to the best of my ability, preserve, protect and defend the Constitution of the United States."

***Section 2.* Powers of the President**

1. The president shall be commander in chief of the army and navy of the United States, and of the militia of the several states, when called into the actual service of the United States; he may

require the opinion, in writing, of the principal officer in each of the executive departments, upon any subject relating to the duties of their respective offices, and he shall have power to grant reprieves and pardons for offenses against the United States, except in cases of impeachment.

2. He shall have power, by and with the advice and consent of the Senate, to make treaties, provided two-thirds of the senators present concur; and he shall nominate, and by and with the advice and consent of the Senate, shall appoint ambassadors, other public ministers and consuls, judges of the Supreme Court, and all other officers of the United States, whose appointments are not herein otherwise provided for, and which shall be established by law. But the Congress may by law vest the appointment of such inferior officers, as they think proper, in the president alone, in the courts of law, or in the heads of departments.

3. The president shall have power to fill up all vacancies that may happen during the recess of the Senate, by granting commissions which shall expire at the end of their next session.

***Section 3.* Relations with Congress; Ambassadors**

He shall from time to time give to the Congress information of the state of the Union, and recommend to their consideration such measures as he shall judge necessary and expedient. He may, on extraordinary occasions, convene both houses, or either of them, and in case of disagreement between them, with respect to the time of adjournment, he may adjourn them to such time as he shall think proper. He shall receive ambassadors and other public ministers. He shall take care that the laws be faithfully executed, and shall commission all the officers of the United States.

***Section 4.* Impeachment**

The president, vice president and all civil officers of the United States shall be removed from office on impeachment for, and conviction of, treason, bribery, or other high crimes and misdemeanors.

reprieve: the postponing of a court-ordered sentence or punishment

pardon: an executive order stating that an accused person or prisoner may be forgiven and set free

advice and consent: debating and voting upon a policy suggested by the president

nominate: to name someone as a candidate for office

ambassador: an official who represents his or her government in the capital of a foreign nation

consul: an official who assists businesses and travelers in foreign countries

commission: a document giving someone the right to hold an office for a certain period of time

session: the period of time (between elections) when members of Congress meet and conduct business

state of the Union: the present condition of the country as well as the problems that it faces

expedient: practical and helpful

extraordinary occasion: a crisis or unusual challenge calling for immediate attention

high crimes and misdemeanors: actions that break the law

VOCABULARY REVIEW

Article II

Quoted below are statements from Article II. For each statement, (*a*) **define** the words in bold print and then (*b*) **tell** in your own words what the statement means.

1. "The **executive power** shall be **vested in** a president of the United States of America."
2. "The Congress may determine the time of choosing the **electors,** and the day on which they shall give their votes. . . ."
3. "In case of the removal of the president from office, or of his death, resignation, or inability to **discharge** the powers and duties of the said office, the same shall **devolve on** the vice president. . . ."
4. "The president shall, at stated times, receive for his services a **compensation,** which shall neither be increased nor diminished during the period for which he shall have been elected."
5. " . . . And he shall have power to grant **reprieves** and **pardons** for offenses against the United States."
6. "He shall from time to time give to the Congress information of the **state of the Union,** and recommend to their consideration such measures as he shall judge necessary and **expedient.**"

Article III: The Courts

***Section 1.* Supreme Court and Inferior Courts**

The judicial power of the United States shall be vested in one Supreme Court, and in such inferior courts as the Congress may from time to time ordain and establish. The judges, both of the supreme and inferior courts, shall hold their offices during good behavior, and shall, at stated times, receive for their services, a compensation, which shall not be diminished during their continuance in office.

judicial power: the authority to operate courts and judge cases of law

inferior courts: those courts whose judgments may be overruled by the Supreme Court

***Section 2.* Jurisdiction**

1. The judicial power shall extend to all cases, in law and equity, arising under this Constitution, the laws of the United States, and treaties made, or which shall be made, under their authority;—to all cases affecting ambassadors, other public ministers and consuls;—to all cases of admiralty and maritime jurisdiction;—to controversies to which the United States shall be a party;—to controversies between two or more states; between a state and citizens of another state;—between citizens of different states;—between citizens of the

admiralty and maritime jurisdiction: cases of law involving the navy and ships at sea

controversies: disputes or conflicts

same state claiming lands under grants of different states, and between a state, or the citizens thereof, and foreign states, citizens or subjects.

2. In all cases affecting ambassadors, other public ministers and consuls, and those in which a state shall be party, the Supreme Court shall have original jurisdiction. In all the other cases before mentioned, the Supreme Court shall have appellate jurisdiction, both as to law and fact, with such exceptions, and under such regulations as the Congress shall make.

3. The trial of all crimes, except in cases of impeachment, shall be by jury; and such trial shall be held in the state where the said crimes shall have been committed. But when not committed within any state, the trial shall be at such place or places as the Congress may by law have directed.

grants: gifts from the government (usually gifts of public land to private individuals)

original jurisdiction: the authority to be the first court to consider a certain case

appellate jurisdiction: the authority to hear and overrule the decisions of another court

Section 3. **Treason**

1. Treason against the United States shall consist only in levying war against them, or in adhering to their enemies, giving them aid and comfort. No person shall be convicted of treason unless on the testimony of two witnesses to the same overt act, or on confession in open court.

2. The Congress shall have power to declare the punishment of treason, but no attainder of treason shall work corruption of blood or forfeiture except during the life of the person attainted.

levying: carrying on or conducting

adhering: favoring

testimony: statements given in court in answer to a lawyer's questions

overt: obvious or outwardly visible

attainder of treason: the loss of civil rights by a convicted traitor

corruption of blood: making members of a traitor's family share in his or her punishment

forfeiture: the loss of one's property to government authorities

Article IV: The States

Section 1. **Recognition of Each Other's Acts**

Full faith and credit shall be given in each state to the public acts, records, and judicial proceedings of every other state. And the Congress may by general laws prescribe the manner in which such acts, records and proceedings shall be proved, and the effect thereof.

Section 2. **Citizens' Rights in Other States**

1. The citizens of each state shall be entitled to all privileges and immunities of citizens in the several states.

2. A person charged in any state with treason, felony, or other crime, who shall flee from justice, and be found in another state, shall on demand of the executive authority of the state from which he fled, be delivered up, to be removed to the state having jurisdiction of the crime.

3. No person held to service or labor in one state, under the laws thereof, escaping into another, shall, in consequence of any law or regulation therein, be discharged from such service or labor, but

full faith and credit: honoring and accepting the decisions made by another government

privileges and immunities: special freedoms and protections guaranteed by law

jurisdiction: area of responsibility

shall be delivered up on claim of the party to whom such service or labor may be due.

Section 3. **Admission of New States**

1. New states may be admitted by the Congress into this Union, but no new state shall be formed or erected within the jurisdiction of any other state; nor any state be formed by the junction of two or more states, or parts of states, without the consent of the legislatures of the states concerned as well as of the Congress.

junction: the joining together; the meeting point

2. The Congress shall have power to dispose of and make all needful rules and regulations respecting the territory or other property belonging to the United States; and nothing in this Constitution shall be so construed as to prejudice any claims of the United States, or of any particular state.

construed: interpreted

prejudice: to have a negative effect

Section 4. **U.S. Guarantees**

The United States shall guarantee to every state in this Union a republican form of government, and shall protect each of them against invasion; and on application of the legislature, or of the executive (when the legislature cannot be convened) against domestic violence.

domestic violence: rioting and rebellion against state authorities

Article V: Amending the Constitution

The Congress, whenever two-thirds of both houses shall deem it necessary, shall propose amendments to this Constitution, or, on the application of the legislatures of two-thirds of the several states, shall call a convention for proposing amendments, which, in either case, shall be valid to all intents and purposes, as part of this Constitution, when ratified by the legislatures of three-fourths of the several states, or by conventions in three-fourths thereof, as the one or the other mode of ratification may be proposed by the Congress. Provided that no amendment which may be made prior to the year one thousand eight hundred and eight [1808] shall in any manner affect the first and fourth clauses in the ninth section of the first article; and that no state, without its consent, shall be deprived of its equal suffrage in the Senate.

convention: meeting called for a special purpose and involving people from different towns or states

valid: acceptable

ratified: approved

suffrage: voting rights

Article VI: Supreme Law

1. All debts contracted and engagements entered into, before the adoption of this Constitution, shall be as valid against the United States under this Constitution, as under the Confederation.

engagement: a formal agreement or treaty with another nation

2. This Constitution, and the laws of the United States which shall be made in pursuance thereof, and all treaties made, or which shall be made, under the authority of the United States, shall be the supreme law of the land; and the judges in every state shall be bound thereby, anything in the Constitution or laws of any state to the contrary notwithstanding.

in pursuance thereof: in order to carry out the above (laws of the United States)

supreme law: law higher than any other (and therefore capable of canceling out local laws)

3. The senators and representatives before mentioned, and the members of the several state legislatures, and all executive and judicial officers, both of the United States and of the several states, shall be bound by oath or affirmation, to support this Constitution. But no religious test shall ever be required as a qualification to any office or public trust under the United States.

religious test: requirement that an officeholder belong to a specific church or hold certain beliefs

Article VII: Ratification

The ratification of the conventions of nine states shall be sufficient for the establishment of this Constitution between the states so ratifying the same.

Done in convention by the unanimous consent of the states present the seventeenth day of September in the year of our Lord one thousand seven hundred and eighty-seven and of the independence of the United States of America the twelfth. *In witness whereof we have hereunto subscribed our names,*

unanimous: agreed to by everyone voting

G^{o} Washington—Presid^{t}
and deputy from Virginia

New Hampshire	John Langdon Nicholas Gilman
Massachusetts	Nathaniel Gorham Rufus King
Connecticut	Wm Saml Johnson Roger Sherman
New York	Alexander Hamilton
New Jersey	Wil: Livingston David Brearley. Wm Paterson. Jona: Dayton
Pennsylvania	B Franklin Thomas Mifflin Robt Morris Geo. Clymer Thos FitzSimons Jared Ingersoll James Wilson Gouv Morris
Delaware	Geo: Read Gunning Bedford jun John Dickinson Richard Bassett Jaco: Broom
Maryland	James McHenry Dan of St Thos. Jenifer Danl Carroll
Virginia	John Blair— James Madison Jr.
North Carolina	Wm Blount Richd Dobbs Spaight. Hu Williamson
South Carolina	J. Rutledge Charles Cotesworth Pinckney Charles Pinckney Pierce Butler
Georgia	William Few Abr Baldwin

SIGNERS OF THE CONSTITUTION

THE SIGNERS OF THE CONSTITUTION OF THE UNITED STATES

1. George Washington
2. Daniel of St. Thomas Jenifer
3. James Wilson
4. Richard Bassett
5. George Read
6. Robert Morris
7. Richard D. Spaight
8. William Blount
9. David Brearley
10. John Dickinson
11. Jacob Broom
12. Gunning Bedford, Jr.
13. Hugh Williamson
14. James Madison, Jr.
15. William Jackson
16. Benjamin Franklin
17. Alexander Hamilton
18. William Paterson
19. John Blair
20. John Langdon
21. Gouverneur Morris
22. Thomas Mifflin
23. William Livingston
24. James McHenry
25. Roger Sherman
26. William S. Johnson
27. Jared Ingersoll
28. George Clymer
29. Nicholas Gilman
30. Thomas FitzSimons
31. Pierce Butler
32. Charles C. Pinckney
33. Charles Pinckney
34. John Rutledge
35. Rufus King
36. Jonathon Dayton
37. Nathaniel Gorham
38. William Few
39. Abraham Baldwin
40. Daniel Carroll

Numbers have been added to the signers' names to enable you to match each name to a figure in a painting that hangs in the U.S. Capitol. Number 15 in the scene is William Jackson, who acted as the convention's secretary (not as a state delegate).

VOCABULARY REVIEW

Articles III–VII

The phrases 1–10 refer to the words listed below. On a separate piece of paper, write the word that either **matches** or **completes** each phrase. (Refer to definitions and constitutional clauses on pages 126–129.)

controversy	laws
convention	overt
courts	supreme
felony	testimony
jurisdiction	valid

1. a serious crime
2. Constitution: the ______ law of the land
3. what the president enforces and the courts interpret
4. what judges preside over
5. witnesses' statements at a trial
6. obvious; in the open
7. conflict
8. an area of responsibility
9. proper or correct
10. an official meeting of many people

First Ten Amendments: THE BILL OF RIGHTS

(The first ten amendments were ratified December 15, 1791, and form what is known as the "Bill of Rights.")

Amendment 1. Freedom of Religion, Speech, Press, Assembly, and Petition

Congress shall make no law respecting an establishment of religion, or prohibiting the free exercise thereof; or abridging the freedom of speech, or of the press; or the right of the people peaceably to assemble, and to petition the government for a redress of grievances.

establishment of religion: the setting up of a church or creed by government decree

free exercise thereof: worshipping a divine being without restriction (so long as it does not injure others)

petition: a document expressing the opinions of citizens

redress of grievances: to obtain relief from practices that are thought to be harmful

Amendment 2. Right to Bear Arms

A well-regulated militia, being necessary to the security of a free state, the right of the people to keep and bear arms, shall not be infringed.

bear arms: carry weapons

infringed: disturbed or interfered with

Amendment 3. Quartering of Troops

No soldier shall, in time of peace be quartered in any house, without the consent of the owner, nor in time of war, but in a manner to be prescribed by law.

quartered: lodged; given a place to live

prescribed: presented or set forth as a rule

Amendment 4. Searches and Seizures

The right of the people to be secure in their persons, houses, papers, and effects, against unreasonable searches and seizures, shall not be violated, and no warrants shall issue, but upon probable cause, supported by oath or affirmation, and particularly describing the place to be searched, and the persons or things to be seized.

unreasonable searches and seizures: police officers' breaking into a person's home to take property or make arrests without good reason

warrants: documents signed by a judge authorizing a police officer to search property or make an arrest

Amendment 5. Rights of Accused Persons; Due Process of Law

No person shall be held to answer for a capital, or otherwise infamous crime, unless on a presentment or indictment of a grand jury, except in cases arising in the land or naval forces, or in the militia, when in actual service in time of war or public danger. Nor shall any person be subject for the same offense to be twice put in jeopardy of life or limb; nor shall be compelled in any criminal case

capital, or otherwise infamous, crime: murder or other very serious crime that can be penalized by death

presentment or indictment: a formal accusation against a person suspected of committing a crime

grand jury: a group of citizens who must determine in a court of law whether there is enough evidence to accuse a certain person of a crime

in jeopardy of life and limb: in danger of being executed or imprisoned for a crime to be a witness against himself, nor be deprived of life, liberty, or property, without due process of law, nor shall private property be taken for public use, without just compensation.

Amendment 6. Other Rights of Accused Persons at a Trial

In all criminal prosecutions, the accused shall enjoy the right to a speedy and public trial by an impartial jury of the state and district wherein the crime shall have been committed, which district shall have been previously ascertained by law, and to be informed of the nature and cause of the accusation; to be confronted with the witnesses against him; to have compulsory process for obtaining witnesses in his favor, and to have the assistance of counsel for his defense.

Amendment 7. Civil Trials

In suits at common law, where the value in controversy shall exceed twenty dollars, the right of trial by jury shall be preserved, and no fact tried by a jury shall be otherwise re-examined in any court of the United States, than according to the rules of the common law.

Amendment 8. Bails, Fines, and Punishments

Excessive bail shall not be required, nor excessive fines imposed, nor cruel and unusual punishments inflicted.

Amendment 9. Rights Not Enumerated

The enumeration in the Constitution of certain rights, shall not be construed to deny or disparage others retained by the people.

Amendment 10. Powers Reserved to the States

The powers not delegated to the United States by the Constitution, nor prohibited by it to the states, are reserved to the states respectively, or to the people.

due process of law: a standard set of procedures for deciding whether an accused person is guilty or innocent

criminal prosecutions: the process for bringing accused lawbreakers to trial

impartial jury: a group of citizens who, during a trial, may be trusted to decide a case fairly

compulsory process for obtaining witnesses in his favor: an accused person's right to have friendly witnesses appear at his or her trial

assistance of counsel: the help of a professional lawyer

common law: old rules of English and American law that guide the decisions of judges; body of laws that come from court decisions of the past rather than from written laws

bail: the sum of money that an accused person may pay to get out of jail while awaiting trial

cruel and unusual punishments: any penalty that may cause a convicted criminal to suffer in an unusual and painful way

disparage: to treat something with little or no respect

VOCABULARY REVIEW

The Bill of Rights

Quoted below are statements from the first ten amendments (the Bill of Rights). For each statement, (*a*) **define** the words in bold print and then (*b*) **tell** in your own words what the statement means.

1. "Congress shall make no law respecting an **establishment of religion**. . . ."
2. "No soldier shall, in time of peace, be **quartered** in any house, without the consent of the owner; nor in time of war, but in a manner to be **prescribed** by law."
3. "No person shall be held to answer for a **capital, or otherwise infamous crime,** unless on a presentment of **indictment** of a **grand jury**. . . ."
4. "In suits at **common law,** where the value in controversy shall exceed twenty dollars, the right of trial by jury shall be preserved. . . ."
5. "Excessive **bail** shall not be required, nor excessive fines imposed, nor **cruel and unusual punishments** inflicted."

Later Amendments

Amendment 11. Suits Against States

(Ratified February 7, 1795)

The judicial power of the United States shall not be construed to extend to any suit in law or equity, commenced or prosecuted against one of the United States by citizens of another state, or by citizens or subjects of any foreign state.

suit: the way that one person (or institution) takes a complaint to court about some injury or wrong

prosecute: to seek justice in a court of law

Amendment 12. Election of President and Vice President

(Ratified July 27, 1804)

The electors shall meet in their respective states and vote by ballot for president and vice president, one of whom, at least, shall not be an inhabitant of the same state with themselves. They shall name in their ballots the person voted for as president, and in distinct ballots the person voted for as vice president, and they shall make distinct lists of all persons voted for as president, and of all persons voted for as vice president, and of the number of votes for each, which lists they shall sign and certify, and transmit sealed to the seat of the government of the United States, directed to the president of the Senate.—The president of the Senate shall, in the presence of the Senate and House of Representatives, open all the certificates and the votes shall then be counted.—The person having the greatest number of votes for president, shall be the president, if such number be a majority of the whole number of electors appointed. And if no person have such majority, then from the persons having the highest numbers not exceeding three on the list of those voted for as president, the House of Representatives shall choose immediately, by ballot, the president. But in choosing the president, the votes shall be taken by states, the representation from each state having one vote. A quorum for this purpose shall consist of a member or members from two-thirds of the states, and a majority of all the states shall be necessary to a choice. And if the House of Representatives shall not choose a president whenever the right of choice shall devolve upon them, before the fourth day of March next following, then the vice president shall act as president, as in the case of the death or other constitutional disability of the president.—The person having the greatest number of votes as vice president, shall be vice president, if such number be a majority of the whole number of electors appointed, and if no person have a majority, then from the two highest numbers on the list, the Senate shall choose the vice president. A quorum for the purpose shall consist of two-thirds of the whole number of senators, and a majority of the whole number shall be necessary to a choice. But no person constitutionally ineligible to the office of president shall be eligible to that of vice president of the United States.

disability: an accident, injury, or illness that causes an official to be unable to perform his or her duties

Amendment 13. Abolition of Slavery

(Ratified December 6, 1865)

Section 1

Neither slavery nor involuntary servitude, except as a punishment for crime whereof the party shall have been duly convicted, shall exist within the United States, or any place subject to their jurisdiction

involuntary servitude: forcing someone to work against his or her will

Section 2

Congress shall have power to enforce this article by appropriate legislation.

Amendment 14. Rights of Citizens

(Ratified July 9, 1868)

Section 1

All persons born or naturalized in the United States, and subject to the jurisdiction thereof, are citizens of the United States and of the state wherein they reside. No state shall make or enforce any law which shall abridge the privileges or immunities of citizens of the United States; nor shall any state deprive any person of life, liberty, or property, without due process of law; nor deny to any person within its jurisdiction the equal protection of the laws.

abridge: limit or interfere with

equal protection of the laws: the government's guarantee that it will treat all individuals on the same basis whether they be rich or poor, black or white, male or female

Section 2

Representatives shall be apportioned among the several states according to their respective numbers, counting the whole number of persons in each state, excluding Indians not taxed. But when the right to vote at any election for the choice of electors for president and vice president of the United States, representatives in Congress, the executive and judicial officers of a state, or the members of the legislature thereof, is denied to any of the male inhabitants of such state, being twenty-one years of age, and citizens of the United States, or in any way abridged, except for participation in rebellion, or other crime, the basis of representation therein shall be reduced in the proportion which the number of such male citizens shall bear to the whole number of male citizens twenty-one years of age in such state.

Section 3

No person shall be a senator or representative in Congress, or elector of president and vice president, or hold any office, civil or military, under the United States, or under any state, who, having previously taken an oath, as a member of Congress, or as an officer of the United States, or as a member of any state legislature, or as an executive or judicial officer of any state, to support the Constitution of the United States, shall have engaged in insurrection or rebellion against the same, or given aid or comfort to the enemies thereof. But Congress may by a vote of two-thirds of each house remove such disability.

Section 4

The validity of the public debt of the United States, authorized by law, including debts incurred for payment of pensions and

pensions: sums of money awarded for service (in this case, service in the Union army or navy) bounties for services in suppressing insurrection or rebellion, shall not be questioned. But neither the United States nor any state shall assume or pay any debt or obligation incurred in aid of insurrection or rebellion against the United States, or any claim for the loss or emancipation of any slave; but all such debts, obligations and claims shall be held illegal and void.

bounties: government money awarded to citizens who perform certain acts

emancipation: setting free some person or group

void: stripped of any power; not to be obeyed or heeded

Section 5

The Congress shall have power to enforce, by appropriate legislation, the provisions of this article.

Amendment 15. Right of Male Blacks to Vote

(Ratified February 3, 1870)

Section 1

The right of citizens of the United States to vote shall not be denied or abridged by the United States or by any state on account of race, color, or previous condition of servitude.

previous condition of servitude: the fact of having been a slave at some time in the past

Section 2

The Congress shall have power to enforce this article by appropriate legislation.

Amendment 16. Income Tax

(Ratified February 3, 1913)

The Congress shall have power to lay and collect taxes on incomes, from whatever source derived, without apportionment among the several states, and without regard to any census or enumeration.

Amendment 17. Popular Election of U.S. Senators

(Ratified April 8, 1913)

Section 1

The Senate of the United States shall be composed of two senators from each state, elected by the people thereof for six years; and each senator shall have one vote. The electors in each state shall have the qualifications requisite for electors of the most numerous branch of the state legislatures.

Section 2

When vacancies happen in the representation of any state in the Senate, the executive authority of such state shall issue writs of election to fill such vacancies: *Provided,* That the legislature of any state may empower the executive thereof to make temporary appointments until the people fill the vacancies by election as the legislature may direct.

Section 3

This amendment shall not be so construed as to affect the election or term of any senator chosen before it becomes valid as part of the Constitution.

Amendment 18. Prohibition of Liquor

(Ratified January 16, 1919. Repealed December 5, 1933 by Amendment 21)

Section 1

After one year from the ratification of this article the manufacture, sale, or transportation of intoxicating liquors within, the importation thereof into, or the exportation thereof from the United States and all territory subject to the jurisdiction thereof for beverage purposes is hereby prohibited.

intoxicating liquors: alcoholic beverages that may cause drunkenness

Section 2

The Congress and the several states shall have concurrent power to enforce this article by appropriate legislation.

Section 3

This article shall be inoperative unless it shall have been ratified as an amendment to the Constitution by the legislatures of the several states as provided in the Constitution, within seven years from the date of the submission hereof to the states by the Congress.

inoperative: not valid

Amendment 19. Right of Women to Vote

(Ratified August 18, 1920)

The right of citizens of the United States to vote shall not be denied or abridged by the United States or by any state on account of sex.

Congress shall have power to enforce this article by appropriate legislation.

Amendment 20. Terms of Office; Succession to the Presidency

(Ratified January 23, 1933)

Section 1

The terms of the president and vice president shall end at noon on the 20th day of January, and the terms of senators and representatives at noon on the 3d day of January, of the years in which such terms would have ended if this article had not been ratified; and the terms of their successors shall then begin.

successor: an official who takes over a job after an earlier official has left it

Section 2

The Congress shall assemble at least once in every year, and such meeting shall begin at noon on the 3d day of January, unless they shall by law appoint a different day.

Section 3

If, at the time fixed for the beginning of the term of the president, the president-elect shall have died, the vice president-elect shall become president. If a president shall not have been chosen before the time fixed for the beginning of his term, or if the president-elect shall have failed to qualify, then the vice president-elect shall act as president until a president shall have qualified; and the Congress may by law provide for the case wherein neither a president-elect nor a vice president-elect shall have qualified, declaring who shall then act as president, or the manner in which one who is to act shall be selected, and such person shall act accordingly until a president or vice president shall have qualified.

president-elect: the person elected president but not yet in office

vice president-elect: the person elected vice president but not yet in office

Section 4

The Congress may by law provide for the case of the death of any of the persons from whom the House of Representatives may choose a president whenever the right of choice shall have devolved upon them, and for the case of the death of any of the persons from whom the Senate may choose a vice president whenever the right of choice shall have devolved upon them.

Section 5

Sections 1 and 2 shall take effect on the 15th day of October following the ratification of this article.

Section 6

This article shall be inoperative unless it shall have been ratified as an amendment to the Constitution by the legislatures of three-fourths of the several states within seven years from the date of its submission.

Amendment 21. Repeal of Liquor Prohibition

(Ratified December 5, 1933)

Section 1

The eighteenth article of amendment to the Constitution of the United States is hereby repealed.

repealed: withdrawn or canceled

Section 2

The transportation or importation into any state, territory, or possession of the United States for delivery or use therein of intoxicating liquors, in violation of the laws thereof, is hereby prohibited.

Section 3

This article shall be inoperative unless it shall have been ratified as an amendment to the Constitution by conventions in the several states, as provided in the Constitution, within seven years from the date of the submission hereof to the states by the Congress.

Amendment 22. Two Terms for the President

(Ratified February 27, 1951)

Section 1

No person shall be elected to the office of the president more than twice, and no person who has held the office of president, or acted as president, for more than two years of a term to which some other person was elected president shall be elected to the office of president more than once. But this article shall not apply to any person holding the office of president when this article was proposed by the Congress, and shall not prevent any person who may be holding the office of president, or acting as president, during the term within which this article becomes operative from holding the office of president or acting as president during the remainder of such term.

Section 2

This article shall be inoperative unless it shall have been ratified as an amendment to the Constitution by the legislatures of three-fourths of the several states within seven years from the date of its submission to the states by the Congress.

Amendment 23. Electors for District of Columbia

(Ratified March 29, 1961)

Section 1

The District constituting the seat of government of the United States shall appoint in such manner as the Congress may direct:

A number of electors of president and vice president equal to the whole number of senators and representatives in Congress to which the District would be entitled if it were a state, but in no event more than the least populous state. They shall be in addition to those appointed by the states, but they shall be considered, for the

the District: District of Columbia (Washington, D.C.)

purposes of the election of president and vice president, to be electors appointed by a state; and they shall meet in the District and perform such duties as provided by the twelfth article of amendment.

Section 2

The Congress shall have power to enforce this article by appropriate legislation.

Amendment 24. Prohibition of Poll Tax

(Ratified January 23, 1964)

Section 1

The right of citizens of the United States to vote in any primary or other election for president or vice president, for electors for president or vice president, or for senator or representative in Congress, shall not be denied or abridged by the United States or any state by reason of failure to pay any poll tax or other tax.

primary: an election to decide what candidates a political party shall nominate for office

poll tax: a tax collected from people who wish to vote in an election

Section 2

The Congress shall have power to enforce this article by appropriate legislation.

Amendment 25. Presidential Succession and Disability

(Ratified February 10, 1967)

Section 1

In case of the removal of the president from office or of his death or resignation, the vice president shall become president.

Section 2

Whenever there is a vacancy in the office of the vice president, the president shall nominate a vice president who shall take office upon confirmation by a majority vote of both Houses of Congress.

Section 3

Whenever the president transmits to the president pro tempore of the Senate and the speaker of the House of Representatives his written declaration that he is unable to discharge the powers and duties of his office, and until he transmits to them a written declaration to the contrary, such powers and duties shall be discharged by the vice president as acting president.

Section 4

Whenever the vice president and a majority of either the principal officers of the executive departments or of such other body as Congress may by law provide, transmit to the president pro tempore of the Senate and the speaker of the House of Representatives their written declaration that the president is unable to discharge the powers and duties of his office, the vice president shall immediately assume the powers and duties of the office as acting president.

Thereafter, when the president transmits to the president pro tempore of the Senate and the speaker of the House of Representatives his written declaration that no inability exists, he shall resume the powers and duties of his office unless the vice president and a majority of either the principal officers of the executive department or of such other body as Congress may by law provide, transmit within four days to the president pro tempore of the Senate and the speaker of the House of Representatives their written declaration that the president is unable to discharge the powers and duties of his office. Thereupon Congress shall decide the issue, assembling within forty-eight hours for that purpose if not in session. If the Congress, within twenty-one days after receipt of the latter written declaration, or, if Congress is not in session, within twenty-one days after Congress is required to assemble, determines by two-thirds vote of both houses that the president is unable to discharge the powers and duties of his office, the vice president shall continue to discharge the same as acting president; otherwise, the president shall resume the powers and duties of his office.

Amendment 26. Right to Vote (Age)

(Ratified July 1, 1971)

Section 1

The right of citizens of the United States, who are eighteen years of age or older, to vote shall not be denied or abridged by the United States or by any state on account of age.

Section 2

The Congress shall have the power to enforce this article by appropriate legislation.

Amendment 27. Congressional Pay Raises

(Ratified May 7, 1992)

No law varying the compensation for the services of the senators and representatives shall take effect until an election of representatives shall have intervened.

VOCABULARY REVIEW

Amendments 11–27

The phrases 1–13 refer to the words listed below. On a separate piece of paper, write the word that either **matches** or **completes** each phrase. (Refer to definitions and constitutional clauses on pages 134–142.)

age	repealed
bounty	servitude
civil	successor
equal	suit
intoxicating	void
poll	Washington, D.C.
primary	

1. subject of the Twenty-sixth Amendment: voting __(?)__
2. election of party candidates that precedes the final election
3. kind of beverages prohibited by the Eighteenth Amendment
4. government money awarded to citizens
5. not to be obeyed or heeded
6. kind of tax banned by the Twenty-fourth Amendment
7. The vice president is the __(?)__ of a president who dies in office.
8. not military
9. granted voting rights by the Twenty-third Amendment
10. The Twenty-first Amendment __(?)__ the Eighteenth Amendment.
11. banned by the Thirteenth Amendment: slavery and involuntary __(?)__
12. a complaint brought to court
13. guaranteed by the Fourteenth Amendment: __(?)__ protection of the laws

a.

b.

c.

a. *Voters*
b. *Delegates at a political convention*
c. *Members of a jury*
d. *Taxpayers (workers in an auto plant)*
e. *Naturalized citizens (taking oath)*

d.

e.

UNIT THREE

Your Role in American Government

Ours is a government of "We the people"—the citizens of the United States. It is not just a government of elected leaders. After all, who elects these leaders? The voters. Who has the final power to change—or not to change—the Constitution? Representatives elected by "We the people." In a court of law, who has the power to decide a person's innocence or guilt? A group of people meeting as a jury.

The unit that follows is the longest in this book.That is because your role and your decisions as a citizen are vital to the future of "We the people" government.

PICTURE PREVIEW

Five activities of a U.S. citizen are pictured on page 144. Below are statements about each activity. Tell whether you think each statement is true **(T)** or false **(F)**. By taking this quiz, you will begin to define your role in American government.

A. VOTERS

1. Voting is both a right and a duty of citizenship.
2. Most states require that you register before voting.

B. DELEGATES AT A POLITICAL CONVENTION

3. The platform agreed upon by these people expresses policies about many political issues.
4. Citizens are *not* required to join a political party.

C. MEMBERS OF A JURY

5. If these jurors are trying a civil case, they would decide whether the defendant is guilty or not guilty.

D. TAXPAYERS

6. A federal income tax is subtracted from these workers' paychecks.
7. January 30 is the deadline for filing tax returns.

E. NATURALIZED CITIZENS

8. These citizens have the same rights and obligations as the citizens in Pictures A–D.

Answers

1. t 2. t 3. t 4. t 5. f 6. t 7. f 8. t

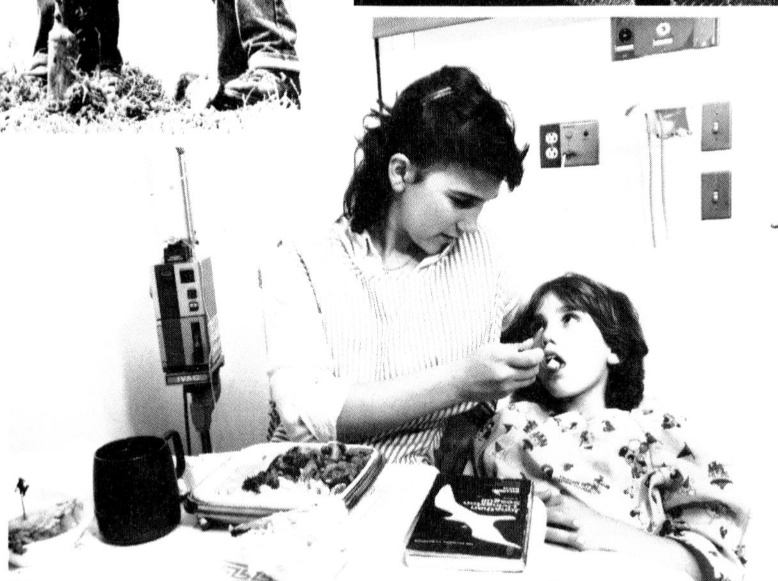

CITIZENS AT WORK. Top left: Forestry workers in the U.S. government's Youth Conservation Corps. Top right: The captain of a volunteer fire company. Bottom: Hospital volunteer with a patient. To what extent does a nation's strength depend upon the voluntary services of its citizens?

CHAPTER 7

Citizenship: You and the Law

OBJECTIVES

After reading this chapter, you will know

1. why you cannot have rights without obligations.
2. reasons for suing and being sued in court.
3. how to fulfill your obligation to serve on a jury.
4. how to fulfill your obligation to pay an income tax.
5. the process by which immigrants may become U.S. citizens.
6. how to use pie graphs as a source of information.

The scene: The delivery room of a U.S. hospital. A young mother and father watch the doctor hold up their squirming baby. A lusty cry sounds out. In that second, another citizen of the United States is born. The making of an American citizen is that simple, and it happens more than 4 million times a year. Babies born on American soil become U.S. citizens automatically.

In one sense, *citizenship* is as natural as breathing in and out. It seems so easy, in fact, that many Americans rarely think about it. Viewed in another way, however, citizenship is a lifetime of caring and hard work. Just as a good parent takes care of the family, a good citizen takes care of the country. Democratic government cannot survive for long without the active participation of millions of citizens.

One citizen who understood this idea was an Illinois lawyer and politician, Abraham Lincoln. "The price of democracy," he said, "is eternal vigilance." In other words, government by the people demands a lot of all of us. This chapter describes some of the chief obligations of U.S. citizenship.

You will be learning the answers to these questions:

1. What are your rights and obligations as a citizen?
2. How do citizens serve on juries and pay taxes?
3. How do immigrants become U.S. citizens?

1. WHAT ARE YOUR RIGHTS AND OBLIGATIONS AS A CITIZEN?

A coin has two sides: heads and tails. Citizenship also has two sides: rights on one side and obligations on the other side. The rights side is what the nation owes to every citizen. The obligations side is what every citizen owes to the nation. You cannot have one without the other (any more than you can have a coin with only one side).

An example of rights and obligations. Borrowing books at your local library is one example of the rights/obligations idea. You probably carry a library card. (If not, you should get one. You are entitled to it as a resident of the community.) Your parents pay taxes for the support of the library. It is their right—and yours—to borrow from its collection of books, magazines, tapes, and records.

But there are three rules to be followed in borrowing a book. The book must be returned by a certain date. You must avoid doodling on its pages or dropping it into a puddle. You discipline yourself to follow rules for the sake of other borrowers—not just for the sake of the library and its staff. Other citizens have rights to the book that it is your obligation to recognize. They are depending upon you to return a book on time and in good condition.

But suppose you forget your obligation. Then you may be penalized for it. The fine you pay—a nickel or dime each day for an unreturned book—should be small since your offense is small. There have been cases, however, of people who *never* return borrowed books. They protest angrily when their library card is taken from them. But have they been mistreated? They failed to meet one of their obligations to the public. Therefore, they should also recognize the fairness of losing one of their rights.

Here is the "golden rule" of citizenship:

Just as other people's actions help or harm you, your actions help or harm others.

The point is obvious. But it is strangely easy to forget it. It is the basis of mature citizenship and effective membership in any community (family, town, state, nation). If you care about the United States, you will try to remember this principle and live by it.

ONE OF THE "OWNERS" OF 11 MILLION BOOKS. The public library system in New York City has a collection of more than 11 million volumes. Why does the right to use public property also involve responsibilities?

What is public property? A library is just one example of property built and operated by the government for public use. Here are other properties that belong, in part, to you—*if* you are a U.S. citizen:

the Grand Canyon ***
the Washington Monument ***
the Pentagon (headquarters of the U.S. Department of Defense) ***
the courthouses in your state **
the parks and public beaches in your state **
the schools in your community *
the streets and public parking lots in your community *

Notice the symbols next to each example of public property. They indicate whether something is managed by the federal government (***), your state government (**), or the government of your local community (*). Governments only *manage* these properties. They are not the real owners of them. The owners are the American public—you and every other citizen.

The public monuments and museums in Washington, D.C., for example, belong to 245 million Americans. At the same time, citizens of different states share in the ownership of state lands and buildings. Missouri's citizens, for example, own the roads, schools, and parks maintained for them by Missouri's government. The Gateway Arch of St. Louis is one of their most famous possessions. In your state, what is the most famous public property? How many other citizens share in the ownership of it?

Citizenship gives you the right to enter government buildings, use public roads and sidewalks, borrow books from libraries, and enjoy public beaches, woods, and lakes. It gives you the right to attend classes in a public school free of charge. But balancing your rights are your obligations. DON'T BE A LITTERBUG, say the signs in your state parks. Treat public property with the same respect that you might treat the property of your best friend. Other citizens will benefit and—as one owner of public lands—so will you.

The responsible use of private property. In the United States, most property is privately owned by millions of citizens, including you. Owning property is every citizen's right. Once again, however, the right of ownership carries with it a burden of responsibility. As an owner of property (anything from a pencil to a house), you must be careful *how* you use it.

Why can't you do anything you wish with an object that belongs to you? It is because property is often used publicly in ways that affect other people. Think of the harm that might be done to others from these privately owned objects:

- a recklessly driven car
- an unleashed dog
- a baseball thrown too near a building.

If injury in fact results from the use (or misuse) of your own property, you can be sued in court by the injured person.

CARTOON CORNER

Being sued in court. To sue means that one person (or that person's lawyer) goes to court and complains in writing about the actions of a second person. Let us say that second person is **you**. The person filing the lawsuit against you is known as the *plaintiff*. As the person named in the *suit*, you are the *defendant*.

What could you have done to cause someone to sue you? Here are four possibilities:

- While playing golf, you sliced a ball toward a tree and out of sight. The plaintiff claims that the ball struck the tree, bounced off, and broke his elbow.
- One summer afternoon, you were using a power mower on your front yard. Suddenly a small dog yelped and fell to the sidewalk. The plaintiff argues that the stone that killed her dog had been flung by the whirling blade of your lawn mower.
- You invented a video game that features a pursuit by sharks and giant jellyfish. The plaintiff, also an inventor, sues you for "stealing" the idea behind his successful video game "Shark."
- Before moving into an apartment, you signed a contract in which you promised to pay the landlord a certain sum in rent on a certain date. The landlord sues you for failing to pay on time.

The summons. As the defendant in a case, what can you expect to happen? First, a court employee may visit you at your home or business to deliver two documents: (1) a copy of the complaint against you and (2) a *summons*. The summons directs you to appear in court at a certain date to defend yourself against the plaintiff's suit. If you fail to appear, the plaintiff will probably win the case by default. The judge will then order you to pay the plaintiff a certain sum of money in compensation for the injuries or damages you caused.

A lawyer's role. When "served" with a summons, you need the advice of an expert in the law. Call a lawyer promptly. The lawyer will take the necessary steps to defend your case in court. If you are legally to blame for the plaintiff's problems, the lawyer will meet with the plaintiff's lawyer. They will argue over what you should reasonably have to pay. The lawyers may reach an agreement and persuade their clients to accept it as a fair bargain. Such a procedure is known as "settling out of court."

But your lawyer may think that you are *not* legally to blame for the plaintiff's injured elbow or dead pet. He or she will then argue your side of the case in a courtroom. In a trial by jury, a small group of citizens (jurors) will listen to witnesses answer the questions put to them by your lawyer and the plaintiff's lawyer. After hearing the evidence, the jury will decide whether you owe any money to the plaintiff—and if so, how much.

Civil cases. Let us say that the plaintiff's name is Mickey Mulligan and that he is suing you for the golf accident that broke his elbow. The court refers to Mulligan's suit against you as the case of *Mulligan* v. *(your name)*.

This case—as well as the other cases listed above—are known as *civil cases*. They involve either accidental injury and property damage or failure to keep the terms of a contract. If you (the defendant) lose a civil case, the court may require you to pay money to the plaintiff. But you cannot be sentenced to a prison term because you did not commit a crime.

Criminal cases. Another type of court case is the *criminal case*. Suppose that the breaking of Mickey Mulligan's elbow was no accident. Instead, imagine that Mulligan was your golfing partner and that he insulted you on the 10th green. You lost your temper and hit him across the arm with your golf club. Under these circumstances, the case against you would be a criminal one.

CIVIL CASE/CRIMINAL CASE. Left: Mulligan sues for accidental injury. Right: Mulligan's injury is no accident. In this case, who is the plaintiff?

Whether or not you intended to commit a certain action makes all the difference in the eyes of a judge. Hurting Mulligan accidentally may result in a lawsuit against you but no jail sentence. Hurting him intentionally—"with malice aforethought"—may cause you to be arrested, charged with a crime, and held in jail.

Crimes are generally of two types. *Misdemeanors* are lesser crimes such as overparking or stealing tomatoes from a neighbor's garden. The penalty for committing a misdemeanor is to be fined a certain sum of money. More serious crimes may be penalized by imprisonment as well as by a fine. Such crimes (murder, burglary, manslaughter, fraud, kidnapping, etc.) are known as *felonies*.

You should know one other crucial difference between civil law and criminal law. If you have committed a crime, it is not your victim that brings you to a court of law. The plaintiff, or accuser, in a criminal case is the state itself. A police officer (an agent of the state) arrests you. Then a state official called a prosecuting attorney, or *prosecutor*, files charges against you. These two officers are supposed to be acting for all the people, or citizens, of the state. The people, after all, have an interest in seeing that laws are obeyed. Therefore, when a criminal case goes to trial, the "People of State Y" are named as the plaintiff.

For State Y, substitute the name of your own state. Write it on a piece of paper. Then, to represent the word *versus* (against), write *v*. Finally, write your own name. Thus, for the felony of assaulting Mickey Mulligan, you now stand accused in the case of *People of Y* v. (*your name*). How you may defend yourself before a jury of your fellow citizens will be explained in the next section.

REVIEW

A. Rights and Obligations

1. **Cartoon Corner.** Look at the cartoon on page 149. Would you say that each person has (*a*) the right idea or (*b*) the wrong idea of his or her "rights"? Explain.
2. Why do you have a **right** to hike the trails of the Grand Canyon? Why do you also have an **obligation** to heed the posted signs?
3. Give five examples of **public** property that are located within ten miles of your home. What makes such property public instead of private?
4. Tell why each statement below is **false:**
   a. The Washington Monument is the property of officials of the federal government.
   b. The law cannot touch you if you injure somebody by accident.
   c. Civil suits are always settled by a jury.
   d. Murder is an example of a class of crimes called misdemeanors.

B. Applying What You Know

Tell whether each of the following is a **civil** case or a **criminal** case. Explain your answers.

1. case entitled *The People of the State of Kansas* v. *Roger Sly*
2. case of an apartment owner who accuses a tenant of failing to pay his rent
3. case of a man accused of stealing a neighbor's watch
4. case of a driver who accidentally knocked over a homeowner's fence
5. case of a homeowner who brings suit against a plumber for damaging her bathroom
6. case of a man who finds a ticket on his car for overparking
7. case of a former prisoner who sues a neighbor for spreading false rumors about her
8. case in which the defendant is arrested for setting fire to his own restaurant

HOW DO CITIZENS SERVE ON JURIES AND PAY TAXES?

There is a price for living in a democratic society. "Government of the people, by the people, and for the people" involves effort and expense. At some time or other, most citizens are called upon to take time out from their jobs to serve on juries. Also, every year, wage-earning citizens must go to the trouble of mailing a tax form to the federal government—and probably to their state government as well.

You too will soon be carrying out these necessary chores of democratic government. What will be expected of you as both a jury member and a taxpayer?

Two kinds of juries. A jury is a small group of citizens who sit in a courtroom to hear a case of law. In criminal cases, juries must decide whether the defendant is guilty or not guilty of breaking a certain law. In civil cases, they decide whether the plaintiff is entitled to receive from the defendant a certain sum of money.

Both the state governments and the federal government make use of juries in their systems of justice. Both organize juries of two kinds: the *grand jury* and the *petit jury*.

The grand jury. The sole purpose of a grand jury is to decide whether there is enough evidence to *indict*, or charge, a certain person with a crime. The state's prosecuting attorney (or district attorney) presents the evidence. After listening to it, members of the grand jury vote on whether the suspect should be formally indicted and made to stand trial. Such a jury is called "grand" because of its large size—anywhere from 16 to 23 members.

The petit jury. The grand jury begins criminal proceedings; the petit jury ends them. This smaller jury of between 6 to 12 citizens is the type you see in televised dramas. Jurors are instructed by a judge who presides over the trial of a case. They listen to lawyers question witnesses. One lawyer represents the plaintiff, while the other represents the defendant. Finally, after all evidence has been presented, the jurors leave the courtroom. Behind a closed and guarded door, they discuss the case among themselves. When they reach a final decision—or *verdict*—they file into the courtroom to announce it.

Serving on a jury. Who is chosen to serve on either a grand jury or a petit jury? Usually, your name is selected at random from a long list of people who have registered to vote. If your name is drawn, you will receive in the mail a written notice, or summons. It informs you of the date, several weeks in the future, when you must appear in court. This call to service may come at an inconvenient time in your life. If so, you may reply to the court in writing that you wish to be excused from service. But your reason must be a good one.

Your employer is required by law to allow you time off to serve on a jury when called. You cannot be penalized by losing either your job or wages for the days of service on the jury. Only remember to give your employer fair notice about the day when your jury duty begins.

What happens when that day arrives? At the local courthouse, you will be seated in a waiting room with a large number of other citizens. This is the "pool" of people from which juries are selected. It may be several hours before you are finally assigned to a particular jury in a particular case.

Rules of evidence. Before a trial begins, the judge will lay down certain rules. Here are three important ones:

(1) Consider only the evidence presented

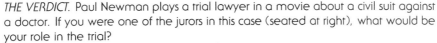

THE VERDICT. Paul Newman plays a trial lawyer in a movie about a civil suit against a doctor. If you were one of the jurors in this case (seated at right), what would be your role in the trial?

in the courtroom. Ignore everything about the case that may have been reported in the newspapers and television.

(2) Before the final verdict, do not discuss the trial with anyone outside the court—not even members of your own family.

(3) In criminal cases, remember this guiding principle of U.S. justice: a defendant is innocent until *proven* guilty beyond a reasonable doubt. In other words, if the evidence does not absolutely convince you of a person's guilt, you must judge that person "not guilty."

Many kinds of taxes. Your second regular obligation as a citizen is to pay taxes. Governments cannot function without money. Where can they collect the billions of dollars required each year to operate schools, patrol highways, and train armies? They cannot get it from voluntary contributions. People must be *made* to pay for government. The special system for doing this is called taxation.

Think of all the things that you have purchased from stores. For almost everything other than food, you may have paid a *sales tax.* Businesses collect this tax by adding a certain percentage to the price of a product or service. (The exact percentage is set by state law.) For example, a 5 percent sales tax on a $10 item would cost the buyer an extra 50 cents. Business owners are responsible for paying the state or local government the taxes they collect from their customers.

Your state and local governments may resort to other means to collect taxes from you. If you own a house, they may first assess, or determine, its value. They will then charge a certain percentage of the house's assessed value as a *property tax.*

Every day, on state highways and turnpikes, coins by the millions are tossed into toll baskets. They are an example of the user fees collected by most state governments. Only those citizens who actually use the toll roads have to pay this kind of tax.

A rich uncle may mention you in his will and leave you one of his mansions and two of his racing cars. But before you can take possession, the state and federal governments may collect a large estate tax. Not everyone pays an estate tax—only those who inherit money or property.

But one tax is paid by almost everyone. And you will pay it regularly for the rest of your working life. This is the federal government's most dependable source of money: the income tax.

Paying your federal income tax. The deadline is midnight April 15 of every year. Before the clock strikes 12 on that sometimes frantic night, every income-earning household is required to mail a standard tax form to a federal agency—the Internal Revenue Service (IRS). You may, if you wish, mail the tax form as early as January or February. But do not be late. The IRS may charge you a whopping fine if you send in your tax return after the April 15 deadline.

In your imagination, add a few years to your current age. Let us say you are 25 years old. You were married two years ago and have a child just four months old. You earn $22,000 a year as the assistant manager of a supermarket. A new year has just begun, and you are beginning to think about your obligations as a taxpayer. Here are the steps that you would take to file a tax return (or tax form) with the IRS.

1. The instruction booklet and enclosed forms. As early as January, you should have a copy of an IRS booklet telling you how to pay the previous year's taxes. Stapled inside the booklet are the tax forms you will need to fill out. The booklet will probably be mailed to you by the IRS. You can also pick up a copy at most banks and post offices and any IRS office in your local area.

The booklet contains: (*a*) detailed instructions for figuring your tax, (*b*) a form to be filled in, and (*c*) tax tables for finding the tax that you owe. (See the illustration on

INSTRUCTION BOOK AND TAX FORM 1040A: To make their yearly report to the IRS, taxpayers pick up an instruction book and tax form. In the third section of the form, how would you figure your exemptions? See page 156.

this page.) Some IRS forms are shorter and easier to complete than others. You can choose the one that applies best to your situation. The instructions in the IRS booklet tell you how to fill out each line of the form you select. First, after giving your name, address, and social security number, you are asked to check one of four boxes on the form:

☐ single ☐ married filing separately
☐ married filing jointly
☐ head of household

EXAMPLE: On the form, you check the box "married filing jointly." Besides describing your situation, the tax rate for this category is usually less than for any of the others.

2. Income: wages and interest. The next step is to record on the form the amount of income that you earned from January 1 to December 31 of last year. The income for most people comes from two sources: (*a*) wages from a job and (*b*) interest from savings.

Determining your total income from these sources is easy. The total wages for the year are recorded on a slip of paper called a W–2 form. This important document is mailed to you by your employer soon after the tax year ends—by January 31 at the latest. Just copy the income figure from the W–2 form onto the appropriate line of the tax form.

EXAMPLE: The W–2 form from your employer gives your total wages for the year:

$22,000. A separate W–2 form for your spouse, who also worked part of the year, gives this figure: $11,300. Combined wages: $33,300.

Interest is what a bank pays you if you deposit money in a savings account. It is a percentage (usually about 3 percent) of the sum deposited. If you have a savings account, you receive from your bank a record of the total interest earned for the year. Again, just copy the sum given onto the tax form.

EXAMPLE: The bank where you have $3,500 in savings earned $105 in interest. On the tax form, you record your total income for the year (wages + interest): $33,405.

3. Subtracting exemptions and deductions. You do *not* pay a tax on your total income. Instead, a certain amount of that income is completely exempt from taxes. Other sums may be deducted—or subtracted—for certain types of expenses you may have had during the year. The IRS instruction booklet explains how to subtract both exemptions and deductions from your total income. The sum that remains is known as your taxable income.

EXAMPLE: You find that you are entitled to subtract from your income a total of $13,250. (In 1993, *each* member of your family of three could claim $2,350 in exemptions. On top of that, a "standard deduction"—a fixed amount on the tax form—was allowed.) You are now left with a taxable income of $20,155.

4. Using the tax tables. Now comes the most interesting part of the process: figuring your tax. In the back of the instruction booklet are tax tables consisting of several columns of numbers. Listed in the lefthand column are different amounts of taxable income. You scan this column, looking for *your* taxable income. Then, in the columns to the right, you find the tax for your filing status ("married filing jointly").

EXAMPLE: Here is the section of the tax table that you would be looking at:

If Form 1040A, line 22, is—		And you are—			
At least	But less than	Single	Married filing jointly *	Married filing separately	Head of a household
		Your tax is—			
20,000					
20,000	**20,050**	3,004	3,004	3,209	3,004
20,050	**20,100**	3,011	3,011	3,223	3,011
20,100	**20,150**	3,019	3,019	3,237	3,019
20,150	**20,200**	3,026	3,026	3,251	3,026
20,200	**20,250**	3,034	3,034	3,265	3,034
20,250	**20,300**	3,041	3,041	3,279	3,041
20,300	**20,350**	3,049	3,049	3,293	3,049
20,350	**20,400**	3,056	3,056	3,307	3,056
20,400	**20,450**	3,064	3,064	3,321	3,064

5. The withholding tax. Do you now send off a check to the government for the tax you found in the tax table? No, not yet. You have *already* paid taxes to the IRS—perhaps more than enough to meet your obligation. Throughout the past year, taxes were automatically taken out—or withheld—from your weekly paychecks. The W-2 form gives the total amount already taken from your wages and paid to the government as a withholding tax. The government follows this system to prevent citizens from spending all their income and having nothing left on April 15 to pay the government.

EXAMPLE: On the tax form, you now record the amount of taxes already paid. The sum of your withholding tax and your spouse's withholding tax is $4,996.

6. Did you underpay or overpay? Do you owe the government more money in taxes? Or have you already paid too much so that the government now owes you? To find out, you subtract the total taxes withheld (W) from the total tax that you owe (X). If X is more than W, you must write a check to the Internal Revenue Service for the difference. If W is more than X, you record the difference on a line marked "refund." You can then look forward to receiving a check in the mail from the IRS—a tax refund.

7. Finishing touches. Check over the tax form to make sure your figures are correct. Sign the return. Make a photocopy of the completed form for your own records. Put the original form into an envelope, remembering to enclose your check (if required). Drop it in the nearest mailbox. Then congratulate yourself on fulfilling one of your obligations as a U.S. citizen.

REVIEW

A. Building Your Political Vocabulary

1. What is a grand jury? How does it differ from a petit jury?
2. What is a summons? If you receive one for jury service, how are you expected to respond to it?
3. What is a property tax? How does it differ from an estate tax?
4. What is a withholding tax? How does the IRS collect it?

B. Correcting the Sequence

The items in each set of events below are out of order. Copy them on another piece of paper, placing them in **correct order** and then numbering them.

1. Trial of a Criminal Case

Jury announces its verdict.
Judge instructs the jury before the trial begins.
Grand jury votes for an indictment.
Summons is mailed to each prospective member of a petit jury.
Members of a petit jury are selected.

2. Paying Your Income Tax

You look up your total tax in the IRS tax tables.
You count your exemptions.
You subtract taxes withheld from taxes due.
You mail the tax return to the IRS.
Your employer deducts a withholding tax from your wages.
You receive a W-2 form in the mail.

C. Applying What You Know

Consider all the facts about your imaginary life as a 25-year-old married taxpayer. Referring to these facts (under EXAMPLE, pages 154-156), determine your federal income tax for one year.

1. What is your taxable income?
2. What is the tax (from the tax table) that the government is entitled to collect from you?
3. Do you owe the government more money—or does the government owe you a refund? In either case, give the amount involved.

3. HOW DO IMMIGRANTS BECOME U.S. CITIZENS?

The United States has been called "a nation of immigrants." To find out why, just open your telephone book to any page. One city directory begins its "M" listings like this:

Ma, H Z Ming
Maag, Hans
Maas, Anthony
Macajoux, C
MacCallum, Douglas

We find family names that are Chinese, Swedish, Italian, English, Scottish, French, etc. In fact, every nationality in the world is now represented in the U.S. population. Foreign names have become the names of American citizens because of two facts: (1) the historic fact called *immigration* and (2) the legal fact called *naturalization*.

Immigration to "the land of opportunity." If you have ever moved from one part of the country to another part, then you have migrated. If you have moved out of the United States to settle permanently in a foreign land, then you have emigrated. If you were born in a foreign country and now live in the United States, you have immigrated.

You and everyone else listed in your local telephone book (except Native Americans) have ancestors who once left their home country (emigrated) and came to live in this country (immigrated). George Washington was born an American only because a British ancestor decided to leave England in the 1650s. John F. Kennedy's great-grandparents were among the many thousands of Irish who immigrated in the 1840s. Immigration caused the United States to grow strong and also caused you to be an American. It is a very important part of *our* identity as a nation and *your* identity as a person.

Who immigrates from what part of the world at what time? The answer keeps changing. From the beginning, American shores and inland woods attracted a mixed group, coming from many lands of Europe and Asia. This brief history identifies only some of the *major* immigrant groups from colonial times to our own times.

Immigrants to colonial America (1607-1776). Many thousands of British, Scottish, and German families sailed the Atlantic to take their chances settling England's colonies. At the same time, Spanish families brought their culture to the lands of Florida and California. These groups immigrated voluntarily. But also during these years, large numbers of enslaved Africans arrived in colonial ports in chains.

First century of independence (1776-1876). Officials of the U.S. government started counting immigrants only in 1820. The people counted most often in the 1840s and 1850s were Irish and Germans. Later, families of Swedes and Norwegians boarded immigrant ships bound for New York Harbor and immigrant trains bound for Chicago and Milwaukee.

New immigrants for a new century (1877-1921). New factories transformed America in these years. The immigrants who toiled in them came mostly from the southern and eastern part of Europe. They were Greeks and Italians, Armenians and Turks, Polish Jews and Russian Jews. Others from China and Japan settled mainly on the West Coast. After 1900, the newcomers—eager to become Americans—arrived in record numbers, often more than a million a year.

Closing the door (1921-1964). After World War I, immigrants were no longer as welcome as before. A quota (limit) was set by Congress on the number of people from

IMMIGRANTS AT ELLIS ISLAND, 1900. Perhaps thousands of Americans living today have ancestors pictured in this building in New York Harbor. Why did these people leave their own countries to seek citizenship in a foreign land?

any foreign country who would be allowed entry into the United States. The new laws of 1921 and 1924 favored immigrants from Great Britain, Canada, and Germany. The quotas discriminated against all other nationalities. Starting in 1929, the maximum number of foreigners who could legally immigrate in any year was only 150,000 (compared to the 1,285,000 admitted in 1907).

Our times (1965-present). Congress changed the immigration law in 1965. As a result, people from Asia and Latin America could enter the United States in greater numbers. Today, hundreds of thousands of Mexicans, Nicaraguans, Koreans, and Vietnamese are holding jobs and raising families in the United States. Further, in the late 1980s, many Soviet and other Eastern European peoples came to the United States.

These people are the "new immigrants" of our times.

SKILLS CHECK: Comparing pie graphs

Where did the American people come from? As you know, in the 1700s, the *free* population came mainly from England and other countries of Western Europe. The *slave* population came from Africa and the West Indies. In this early period, however, records of immigration were incomplete. Only in 1820 did the U.S. government begin to include a count of immigrants in its census reports.

Below are three **pie graphs** (A–C). They give us a visual idea of where new Americans came from after 1820. By interpreting the information in the graphs, we can see how immigration today compares with immigration a century ago.

First, study **Graph A** and answer questions 1–5.

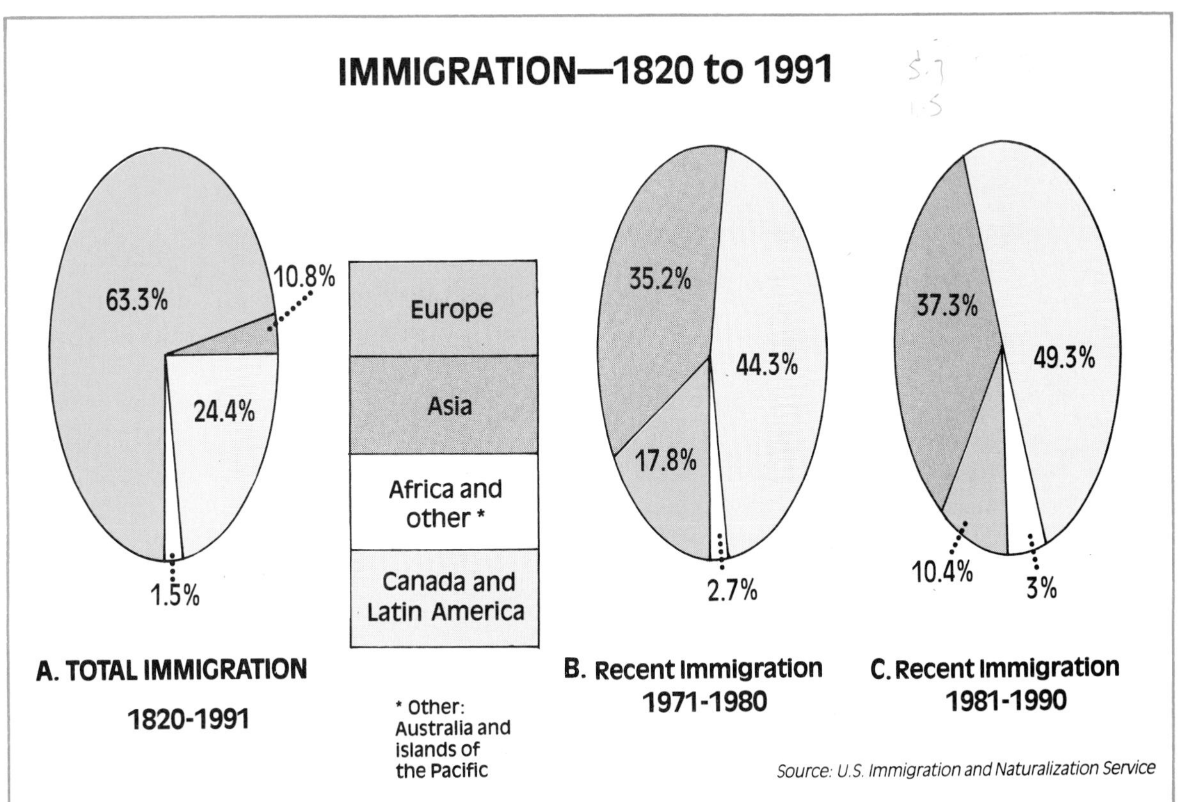

1. How many years of immigration are represented in Graph A?
2. From what continent did most immigrants come?
3. What percentage of the total immigrant population came from Asia? What percentage came from North and South America?
4. In the segment, AFRICA AND OTHER, what does "other" stand for?
5. The importation of slaves was forbidden by an act of Congress as of 1808. How does this fact help to explain the low percentage of immigrants from Africa?

Next, study **Graphs B** and **C** on page 159 and answer the remaining questions, 6–9.

6. What time period is represented by Graph B? By Graph C?
7. What changes do you notice in the percentage of immigrants coming from different regions of the world?
8. Do you think changes in the graphs (B and C) were due to changes in the immigration laws? Explain.
9. Imagine a fourth pie graph showing the years of immigration from 1820–1960. On this graph, do you think EUROPE would appear larger or smaller than in Graph A? Why?

Cause of immigration. What causes a family to leave their home and a culture that they have known since birth? Why do they journey half way around the world to settle in an unfamiliar American city? The reason is the same for all immigrants of any century. It is because they want a better chance in life than what their native country offered. Some want a chance to earn a good living, while others want a chance to be free from oppressive laws. Better than most native-born citizens, the foreign-born *know* the United States to be "a land of opportunity."

Becoming a naturalized citizen. In 1988, there were more than 15 million foreign-born people living in the United States. Nearly half of them had earned the right to call themselves U.S. citizens. The other half had either not yet applied for citizenship or had not yet met all the qualifications.

The process whereby immigrants may become U.S. citizens is called naturalization. Congress has the constitutional power to make laws concerning both immigration and naturalization. The agency that enforces Congress's laws is the Immigration and Naturalization Service (INS).

Let us say that your last name is Vong. You and your family fled for your lives when Laos, your country in Asia, fell under the control of a ruthless government. You have just arrived in California as an immigrant. You are eager to adjust to the American ways of life and eventually to become a U.S. citizen. A neighbor and friend from your native country—now an American citizen—tells you the steps for gaining citizenship:

1. You must live in the United States for at least five years. During this time you should make an effort to learn English so that you will be prepared for the government's test.

2. After five years of residence, if you are 18 or older, you may fill out a document issued by the INS. It is a petition—or request—to become a U.S. citizen.

3. The INS will now conduct an investigation concerning you. Agents will ask employers and neighbors about your character. They will want to determine whether you can be depended upon to respect the laws of your new country. You will be asked questions in a simple test about U.S. history and the Constitution. You may have to prepare for the test by attending classes and studying a book on U.S. government (given free by the INS).

4. The last step begins as you walk proudly up the steps of a federal courthouse. As

you stand with other immigrants in a judge's courtroom, you will take an oath of allegiance to the United States and its Constitution. The judge will then give you a certificate declaring that you are now a full citizen of the United States. You are as much a legal member of this nation as anyone born here. Like a wedding or a graduation, becoming a naturalized citizen is usually an occasion for family celebration.

Citizens from birth. Most Americans do not have to be naturalized. Instead, they are citizens from the moment of their birth. To be a native-born citizen, you must meet one or the other of these requirements:

(*a*) Born within the United States or one of its overseas territories;

(*b*) Having a mother or a father (or both) who is an American citizen. Thus, you can be born in a foreign country and still be an American citizen if one of your parents is American.

Most native-born Americans meet both tests of citizenship—place of birth *and* parenthood—even though only one is required.

How citizenship may be lost. Most Americans value their U.S. citizenship and wish to keep it as long as they live. It guarantees them the right to vote in any national election. It ensures them of the protection and support of the U.S. government when traveling abroad. Above all, they are proud to belong to one of the great countries of the modern world.

In rare cases, people have been known to lose their U.S. citizenship. They forfeit it if they emigrate abroad and become a citizen of a foreign country. They also lose it if a court convicts them of the crime of *treason*. (Spying for an enemy nation is an example of such a crime.) Special rules apply to immigrants who have become naturalized citizens. Their citizenship can be taken away if it is proven that they had once tried to deceive immigration officials.

REVIEW

A. Applying What You Know

Answer the following questions only if you are now a U.S. citizen:

1. On what date did you become a U.S. citizen? Did you achieve your status by birth or by naturalization?
2. Name at least one member of your family who was born abroad and immigrated to the United States. From what nation did this ancestor come? (If you do not know, ask a parent or grandparent.)
3. Why is your U.S. citizenship valuable to you? What rights and privileges does it give you?

B. Making Inferences

Imagine ships (or planes) transporting immigrants to the United States in different years. For each year, tell where the new arrivals most likely came from.

1. Ship arriving in 1705 probably brought immigrants from (*a*) Poland (*b*) Britain (*c*) South America (*d*) China.
2. Ship arriving in 1845 probably brought immigrants from (*a*) Italy (*b*) Ireland (*c*) Russia (*d*) Korea.
3. Ship arriving in 1905 probably brought immigrants from (*a*) Italy (*b*) Ireland (*c*) China (*d*) Germany.
4. Plane landing in 1985 probably brought immigrants from (*a*) Britain (*b*) Ireland (*c*) Italy (*d*) Korea.

C. Project

What should immigrants know about the U.S. government in order to qualify for American citizenship? Think of yourself as an INS agent. Write **eight** questions about government and the Constitution that you would expect a future citizen to answer correctly.

CHAPTER REVIEW

A. Completing the Summary

Select terms from the word list to fill in the blanks in the summary below. Write your answers on a piece of paper.

Asia	obligations
citizens	petit
civil	plaintiff
criminal	property
deductions	public
exemption	reasonable
Europe	refund
income	sales
indictment	taxable
IRS	verdict
naturalization	withholding

You are an American citizen if you were born in the United States or if one of your parents was an American citizen. Foreign-born persons can also become American citizens if they immigrate to the United States and go through the process of __(1)__.

Immigration laws determine the number of immigrants from different countries who may seek U.S. citizenship. In the 1800s, people of all nationalities were freely admitted. In these years, the largest number of immigrants came from the continent of __(2)__. But in the 1920s, changes in the law limited the number and type of immigrants who could come to the United States. Another change in the law in 1964 caused another shift in the immigrant population. Now the largest number of immigrants come from the Americas and from __(3)__.

Citizenship is a two-sided coin. Your rights (what the nation owes you) are balanced by your __(4)__ (what you owe the nation). Government buildings, parks, and highways are examples of __(5)__ property. They belong, not to the government, but to all __(6)__.

If you meet your obligations to others, it is unlikely that you will either be arrested for a crime or sued for damages. However, if others injure you in some way, it is your right to seek justice in a court of law. If someone causes injury intentionally, the suit is known as a __(7)__ case. If the injury or harm is accidental, judges treat it as a __(8)__ case.

In every civil suit, the __(9)__ (injured person) brings a complaint against the defendant. In criminal cases, it is the government that prosecutes the case against the defendant.

Serving on a jury is one of the obligations of U.S. citizenship. Juries are of two kinds: (*a*) the grand jury for bringing an accusation, or __(10)__, in criminal cases and (*b*) a __(11)__ jury for trying both criminal and civil cases. After jurors are selected for a certain trial, the judge instructs them on how they are to reach a __(12)__, or decision. In a criminal case, they must assume the defendant is innocent unless proven guilty "beyond a __(13)__ doubt."

Paying an __(14)__ tax is another obligation of citizenship. The deadline for mailing a tax return to the __(15)__ is April 15 of every year. How much tax you pay depends on several factors. You can claim an __(16)__ for each person in your family who depends on you for financial support. Also, if you decide to do so, you may fill out a two-page form (instead of the one-page EZ form), in which you itemize __(17)__ for certain expenses. By subtracting these sums from your total wage earnings and other income, you determine your __(18)__ income. You compare the tax on this income to the __(19)__ taxes you have already paid to the government. You can collect a __(20)__ from the government if you have already paid more taxes than you officially owe.

Other kinds of taxes are also collected by federal, state, and local governments. They include the __(21)__ tax on many consumer purchases and the __(22)__ tax on the ownership of houses, land, and buildings.

B. Applying What You Know

Choose the word that best completes each sentence.

1. The federal government __(?)__ public properties such as the White House and Capitol Building.
   (*a*) owns (*b*) manages (*c*) exempts (*d*) inaugurates
2. In the civil case of *Martha Myers* v. *José Gonzales*, Myers is the __(?)__.
   (*a*) defendant (*b*) prosecutor (*c*) plaintiff (*d*) attorney
3. After being convicted of a __(?)__, Joseph Granucci was sentenced to two years in prison.
   (*a*) naturalization (*b*) misdemeanor (*c*) criminal suit (*d*) felony
4. Though foreign-born, Jacob Weiss passed an INS test, took an oath of allegiance, and thus became a __(?)__ citizen.
   (*a*) deported (*b*) naturalized (*c*) migratory (*d*) temporary
5. By __(?)__ from the United States and becoming a German citizen, H. Hecht lost her U.S. citizenship.
   (*a*) traveling (*b*) emigrating (*c*) immigrating (*d*) naturalizing
6. News of the grand jury's __(?)__ brought tears to the eyes of the accused man.
   (*a*) prosecution (*b*) indictment (*c*) verdict (*d*) plea

C. Making Comparisons

1. Give two ways that a *petit jury* differs from a *grand jury*.
2. Explain the difference in function between the *INS* and the *IRS*.
3. Give two ways in which a *civil case* differs from a *criminal case*.
4. How were the *new immigrants of the 1980s* different from most *immigrants of the 1880s*?
5. What is the difference between an *income tax* and a *sales tax*?

D. Illustrating the Main Idea

Each sentence below expresses one of the main ideas of this chapter. Copy it on a piece of paper as the **topic sentence** of an original paragraph. Complete the paragraph by writing at least two sentences that illustrate the main idea.

1. Immigration caused the United States to grow strong and also caused you to be an American.
2. Like a coin, citizenship has two sides: rights on one side and obligations on the other.
3. Your right to own private property carries with it a burden of responsibility.
4. Judges classify cases of law into two main categories.
5. One of your obligations as a citizen is to pay state and federal taxes.

PRESENT AND FUTURE VOTERS. At a polling place in a New Jersey town, a citizen awaits her turn to vote in a national election. Her child will come of age in the 21st century. In what year will you be eligible to cast your first ballot?

CHAPTER 8

Your Right to Vote

OBJECTIVES

After reading this chapter, you will know

1. why committed citizens make a point of voting in elections.
2. the difference between liberals, conservatives, and moderates.
3. state laws that prevent certain groups from voting.
4. how to record your vote on official state ballots.
5. how to use statistical tables and line graphs to make inferences.

"Has anyone ever hung up on you?"

"Are you kidding? It happens all the time. You'll get used to it—maybe after your thousandth phone call."

"Ha! I'm quitting for the night in five minutes."

The two friends, Shirley Glass and Andrea Dawson, are calling voters on the night before Election Day. As volunteers at a candidate's headquarters, their job is to read a little speech to any adult who picks up the phone. This is the speech:

"Hello, Mrs. Jones. I'm a volunteer for Senator Jimenez. The senator has an outstanding record, having worked 12 years for the people of our state. Tomorrow is Election Day. Before you vote, do you have any questions about the senator that I can help you with?"

Most people respond politely to the caller's message. "No, my mind is already made up," they might say. "But thank you for calling." But a few express annoyance. They do not want to be bothered. They complain to Shirley Glass that politics does not interest them. They do not intend to vote for the senator or anyone else.

"Good-bye," they conclude. "And please don't bother to call again. We are not interested." Click!

Voting in elections is one of the great rights and obligations in a democracy. But unlike the obligation to pay your taxes every year, voting is not compulsory. In any election, you are free to vote—or not to vote.

CALLING ALL VOTERS. Phoning citizens at home is one way that campaign workers attempt to persuade people to vote. Why do you think some people are more concerned about politics than others?

Some citizens, like Shirley Glass and Andrea Dawson, like to become actively involved in elections. They think politics is both important and fun. But others take a negative view of the whole process. Rather than miss a favorite TV program, they stay home on Election Day, shrugging off their right to vote as unimportant.

Why do some Americans vote regularly while others almost never vote? Which type of citizen are you more likely to be? Will your right to vote be important to you? This chapter gives you the basis for making up your own mind. You will also be thinking about these questions:

1. How do candidates compete for your vote?
2. What are your choices as a voter?
3. Who can be stopped from voting?
4. Inside a voting booth, how do you indicate your choices?

ONE VOTE FOR JESSE JACKSON FOR PRESIDENT IN 1988. What reasons might this citizen have for participating in every election?

1. HOW DO CANDIDATES COMPETE FOR YOUR VOTE?

Campaign workers like Shirley Glass and Andrea Dawson stand for a certain type of citizen. They are the committed type. They care about democratic politics. The opposite type are those who almost never bother to vote. They are apathetic (apathy means an attitude of not caring).

Reasons for voting. Why do committed citizens feel it is important to vote in every election? These are three of their reasons:

1. Concern about public issues. The committed citizen is likely to have strong feelings about one or more issues in the news. Shirley Glass, for example, is concerned about endangered species of wildlife and their protection. She likes what Senator Jimenez is trying to do for the environment. That is her main reason for volunteering to take part in the senator's campaign.

On the other hand, many voters do not like what Senator Jimenez has said on the issues of national defense and women's rights. For that reason, they plan to be voting against him.

2. Feeling of civic duty. Committed citizens believe that the American system of government needs to be supported. They think that voting regularly is the least they can do to express their support. Andrea Dawson asks: "How can we call ourselves a democracy if only a small percentage of people bother to vote? Personally, I would feel that I would be letting my country down if I didn't vote."

3. Interest in politics. Some people are attracted to politics because they see the fun and excitement in it. For them, campaigns for election are like sporting contests. Who's going to win? Who's the best candidate? Interest in such questions motivate people like Andrea Dawson not only to vote but to get involved in political campaigns.

Citizens like Glass and Dawson enjoy the

colorful language of politics. By learning that language, you too will be able to follow political campaigns as reported in the news. You will then be prepared to vote and to choose between the "Ins" and the "Outs," between "liberals" and "conservatives."

Incumbents against challengers. Politicians who are currently *in* office are known as the incumbents (or the "Ins"). Rivals who lost to the incumbents in the last election are called the challengers (or the "Outs"). They are out of government office and want to get back in. Because of the election process, those who are in today may be out tomorrow. See the CARTOON CORNER below.

For example, in 1992, the incumbent Republican president, George Bush, ran for re-election against Bill Clinton, the Democratic challenger. The incumbent lost. Thus, the "In" candidate (Bush) was now out, and the "Out" candidate (Clinton) was in.

Why would voters want to remove the "Ins" and replace them with the "Outs"? Sometimes, it is because economic conditions are bad, and the voters hope that a change in government will help to improve conditions. Other times, a political scandal of some kind may cause voters to wonder whether officials at city hall or at the state or national capital are honestly serving the public. In a democracy, elections provide the people with a powerful means of "cleaning house" and ridding government of those who, in their opinion, are not properly fulfilling their duties.

Another reason for replacing one group of officials with another has to do with the voters' political values. At times, people may favor a liberal approach to public problems while at other times they favor a more conservative approach.

The liberals against the conservatives. Candidates for office are often described as either *liberal* or *conservative.* What is meant by these terms?

There are actually two ways of defining them. One way is to look at a person's

CARTOON CORNER

attitude toward change. Liberals are those who tend to like the idea of making major changes in the law. Conservatives are just the opposite. They would much rather keep things the way they are. For example, back in the 1770s, liberal Americans were more willing than conservatives to join the Revolution against Britain.

A liberal will say: "Our government is not working well. We must change it to make it better."

A conservative replies: "Not so fast. Our government is working fine. The changes you propose will only get us into worse trouble."

Liberals and conservatives also disagree about government's proper role. Liberals think the government should be very active in rebuilding the nation's cities, aiding the poor, and protecting the environment. Liberals say: "Government has a responsibility to try to solve society's problems. If government doesn't take action about these problems, who will?"

Conservatives, on the other hand, tend to view government social programs with suspicion. They fear that welfare checks for the poor may do more harm than good. The best way to help the poor, they say, is to allow business the freedom it needs to create jobs. Conservatives say: "Let's get rid of laws that regulate business too much. Business, not government, will find workable answers to society's problems."

Often in the course of a campaign, you will hear the words "left" and "right" to describe a politician's views on issues. Anyone with liberal ideas is said to be "on the *left*." Anyone with conservative ideas is "on the *right*."

As a voter, you can expect to hear candidates mock their opponents' ideas. Conservatives, for example, commonly accuse liberals of being "bleeding hearts." A liberal, they say, is always moaning insincerely about the poor and the downtrodden. At the same time, liberals accuse conservatives of being backward and insensitive to people's problems.

A liberal may joke: "Have you heard of the floo-floo bird? It is a bird that flies backward, being more interested where it's been than where it may be going. Such a bird is my fine-feathered conservative opponent."

Moderates "in the middle of the road." President Dwight Eisenhower once told voters that he was neither a liberal nor a conservative. Instead, he liked to stay "in the middle of the road." In other words, he followed policies that were neither left (liberal) nor right (conservative). His policies were somewhere in the middle.

Middle-of-the-roaders are also known as *moderates*. Most American politicians tend to like the middle, or moderate, path be-

WINNER BY A LANDSLIDE. A moderate Republican, Dwight Eisenhower, won the presidency by a landslide in 1952 and 1956. How would you define (*a*) moderate and (*b*) landslide?

cause that seems to win them the most votes. In the broad middle of the road, they can usually attract a larger following than in the narrower lanes to the left and right.

Front runners and dark horses. Which candidate stands the best chance of winning? Much of the fun of politics comes from trying to answer that question. In many ways, following an election *campaign* in the newspapers and on TV is like watching a horse race. The competing candidates are even described as if they were horses racing to beat each other to the finish line. We say that they are "in the race" for the presidency or for a seat in Congress.

The candidate who seems to be leading in the race is referred to as the *front runner.* But behind him or her are several others who might surprise everyone by catching up. Those who, in the beginning, are *not* expected to win are called *dark horses.* Occasionally, however, they do win. In 1975, few voters had ever heard of a candidate for president named Jimmy Carter. Other Democrats were much better known. But early in 1976, the dark horse candidate from Georgia received the TV attention and political support he needed to become the Democrats' front runner. From that point, Carter went on to win the election.

Hoopla and ballyhoo. In days gone by, riders would encourage their galloping horses by shouting: "Hoopla! Hoopla!" Today, hoopla is still part of the language of politics. The term refers to the colorful and noisy ways in which candidates stir the enthusiasm of campaign workers and voters. Hoopla is confetti and balloons, marching bands and straw hats, banners and buttons—anything at all that adds color and fun to voter gatherings.

A synonym for hoopla is ballyhoo. You can own a piece of a candidate's ballyhoo (or hoopla) by pinning a campaign button to your jacket or coat.

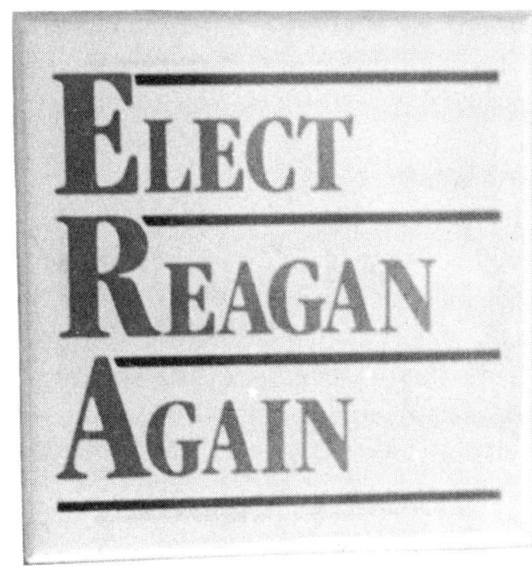

CAMPAIGN BUTTONS. Why are these buttons an example of political hoopla? What other examples of hoopla have you seen on television?

Buttons of the past are collector's items today. In 1928, Republicans gave out buttons saying: HOOVER AND HAPPINESS. Soon after Hoover was elected, the economy tumbled into a depression. Democratic buttons of 1932 said: IN HOOVER WE TRUSTED, NOW WE ARE BUSTED. Nobody knows what the campaign buttons of the next century will say. Just get ready to collect them when they are handed out. Wearing them is part of the fun of participating in American politics.

The mandate after a landslide. The excitement of a political campaign reaches a climax on Election Day in early November. Who will win: the incumbent or the challenger, the liberal or the conservative? Until now politicians and the press have given their "expert" opinions about who will win hundreds of times. But opinions are not facts. On Election Day, the great question of who will win is left finally to the voters to decide. The next morning, in bold headlines, newspapers proclaim the voters' answer. Said one headline of November 1964:

LBJ WINS IN A LANDSLIDE

To win by a landslide is to defeat your opponent by a great majority of votes. In 1964, the incumbent President Lyndon Baines Johnson (LBJ) received almost twice as many votes as his opponent, Senator Barry Goldwater.

Johnson was liberal; Goldwater was conservative. Because of his landslide victory in the election, Johnson said that he had a *mandate* to carry out his liberal programs. A mandate means great popular support to act in certain ways. It is like a green light or permission to move ahead with your ideas.

REVIEW

A. Building Your Political Vocabulary

Complete each sentence, using one of these words:

mandate — landslide
incumbent — hoopla
dark horse

1. Because she is a __(?)__ candidate, Jenny Winkler will surprise everyone if she comes from behind to defeat Senator Stebbins, the front runner.
2. In the race for Ohio governor, the popular __(?)__ Diane Altman easily defeated her little-known challenger.
3. The campaign rally seemed drab and lacking in the usual amount of __(?)__.
4. The mayor predicted this morning that he would be re-elected by a __(?)__ victory.
5. "The size of my election victory shows that the voters love my ideas. They have given me a __(?)__ to change government from top to bottom."

B. Making Inferences

Tell whether each statement expresses the view of a **liberal, conservative,** or **moderate** candidate.

1. "These bleeding-heart fakers make a lot of promises that only take money out of *your* pockets."
2. "I pledge to you tonight that, as your governor, I will stray neither to the left nor the right. Instead, I will steer our government straight down the middle of the road."
3. "To eliminate poverty, government should guarantee a certain minimum income for every American family."
4. "What is good for American business is good for all Americans."
5. "Our party is liberal—but not dangerously liberal. We are conservative—but not blindly conservative. On all issues, we stand solidly in the center."

2. WHO CAN BE STOPPED FROM VOTING?

Today, if you are younger than 18, you cannot vote for any government official. On Election Day in early November, what would happen if you tried to cast a vote for U.S. president? You might be allowed inside the *polling place* (a firehouse, school, or other public building where voting booths are temporarily installed). But you would be stopped from voting. None of the 50 states permits a person under 18 to vote.

It is your state government—not the U.S.

government—that makes the most important laws about voting. These laws must abide by what the Constitution says. For example, because of the Twenty-sixth Amendment, no state can require a voter to be older than 18. But within the bounds set by the Constitution, states may decide which of its citizens can and cannot vote.

Early barriers to voting. Think back to the 1790s when George Washington was president. At that time, which of the following groups were stopped from voting because of state laws?

a. anyone under 21 years old
b. adults who were female
c. adults who did not own much property
d. adults who were black

The answer is: *all* of the above could not vote. In fact, in George Washington's time, those who could not vote greatly outnumbered those who could. The ratio was perhaps as much as five or six to one.

But over time, in state after state, the laws changed. White males who owned no property were the first group to benefit. Most states permitted them to vote in the elections of the 1820s. (Earlier, state laws had said that voters had to own a certain amount of property.)

The next group who gained the right to vote were black males. Their status changed right after the Civil War as a result of the Thirteenth, Fourteenth, and Fifteenth Amendments. The Fifteenth Amendment said that no state could stop a person from voting because of his race. Therefore, in the 1860s, all states had to throw out their old laws that had made blacks ineligible to vote.

But some states still found ways of keeping blacks from voting. In the South, in the 1890s, voting laws commonly included something called a "grandfather clause." It guaranteed the vote to citizens whose

CHANGES IN THE ELECTORATE. Compare the voters of 1777 (left) with voters today (right). How did state requirements for voting change between these two dates?

grandfathers had voted before the Civil War. Southern blacks could not claim voting rights under this clause because their grandparents had been slaves. Only Southern whites were in a position to inherit the right to vote from their ancestors. Thus, the grandfather clause made it easy for whites to vote and very difficult for blacks to vote.

For many years, states defied the Fifteenth Amendment, and the federal government in Washington did nothing to stop them. But finally, in 1965, Congress stepped in to protect black voters in every state. In that year, it passed the Voting Rights Act. This law said that states could no longer require black people to pass a test in order to vote. In the 1960s, the literacy test and the poll tax were both abolished. So were other methods that white officials had sometimes used to stop blacks from voting. Today, by enforcing the Voting Rights Act, the federal government makes sure that blacks are given an equal opportunity to vote in all elections.

The third group to win the franchise (right to vote) were women. The story of the suffragists' struggle was told in Chapter 6. Recall that, in 1920, the Nineteenth Amendment was ratified. It said that a person's sex—whether male or female—could not be the reason for stopping a person from voting.

Current barriers to voting. The electorate is everyone in the population who is permitted to vote. Today, the American electorate is huge. Many more people are included in it than excluded.

EXERCISING THEIR RIGHTS. After the Voting Rights Act of 1965, blacks turned out to vote in record numbers. What barriers to voting were removed by the 1965 law?

Even so, there are millions who would be turned away at the polls (election places) if they tried to vote. Who are these Americans who are *disfranchised* (not allowed to vote)?

1. Children and teenagers. After your 18th birthday, all states *must* allow you to vote. The Twenty-sixth Amendment to the Constitution, adopted in 1971, guarantees this right. But before your 18th birthday, you cannot vote. Some day perhaps, there might be a state that lowers its age requirement for voting to 17 or even 16. But so far, no state has yet enfranchised any age group younger than 18.

2. Noncitizens (or aliens). All states require voters to be either native-born or naturalized citizens of the United States. Foreign-born immigrants to the United States cannot vote until after they gain their citizenship.

3. Mentally incompetent. Many states (but not all) have laws preventing people in mental hospitals from voting. Seriously retarded persons may also be kept from the polls.

4. Criminals. People who are convicted in court of committing felonies (serious crimes) may lose their right to vote. State laws differ. Some permit criminals to vote while others do not.

Why are the above groups stopped from voting? There is one main reason. State lawmakers have concluded that people in these groups cannot be trusted to vote responsibly. A five-year-old child obviously does not know enough about government to vote. A foreign-born noncitizen has not yet proven his or her loyalty to the United States. By breaking the law, criminals show that they lack respect for government and society. Someone who is retarded or mentally ill may not be capable of making decisions.

Residence requirement. Another requirement *temporarily* stops many thousands of people from voting each year. Many states require that you reside in a state for a certain number of days before you can vote. Suppose that, shortly before Election Day, your family moves from one state to another. Chances are that members of the family will not qualify to vote in that year's election. Most states have a residence requirement of 30 days. After living in the state that long, you can vote—but not before.

Even then, however, you can take steps to vote in your native state (the one you plan to be leaving). Special ballots for "absentees" (state residents who are either ill or away from home) are mailed to voters who request them and then mailed back to election officials. You must be sure to apply for an absentee ballot several weeks before the date of the election.

People who fail to register. You know that you cannot legally step into an unlicensed car and drive off. You must first register the car with the state and obtain a license plate for it. A similar step is required of qualified voters in almost every state. Before you can vote, you must fill out a simple *registration* form. You can call your local government and ask for the form to be mailed to you. Or you can visit your town hall or city hall and fill out the form there. If you meet the minimum requirements (age, citizenship, etc.), you will be allowed to vote in the next election.

In most states, you are required to register only once. So long as you do not change your address, you can vote year after year without bothering to register again. In a few states, your first registration must be renewed after a certain period.

Just remember that, before you can vote, you must register at least once. Failure to register disqualifies you from voting as surely as if you were a two-year-old noncitizen.

Young voters and old voters. In the past, it was state laws that stopped millions of

YOU MUST REGISTER TO VOTE. That was the message of the two registration drives pictured here. Right: Democrat Jesse Jackson leads a voter registration rally. Why do state laws require voters to register?

Americans from going to the neighborhood polling place to vote. Today, the laws make it easy for almost all adult citizens to participate in any election. And yet, millions of people neglect to exercise their right to vote. Year after year, these nonvoters do not bother to make the trip to their polling places on Election Day. Who are these nonvoters most likely to be?

✔✔ SKILLS CHECK 1: Making inferences from data

The table on page 175 shows the voting record of four groups from young to old. Some groups participated in the elections at a much higher rate than other groups. Make your own conclusions about the data by answering the questions:

1. In the five elections, which age group participated at the highest rate (percentage)?
2. In the five elections, which age group participated at the lowest rate (percentage)?
3. As a general rule, would you say that younger voters (ages 18–24) are (*a*) more likely or (*b*) less likely to vote in elections than older voters?
4. Does the record of the younger voters show an attitude of (*a*) political apathy or (*b*) political commitment? Why do you suppose this attitude exists among a majority of young citizens?
5. Do you think the data in the table pose a problem for American democracy? Why or why not?

There is one trait that many nonvoters of every age group have in common. They simply have no interest in politics. They are apathetic. Whenever they see a political show on TV, they quickly switch channels.

PERCENTAGE VOTING IN PRESIDENTIAL ELECTIONS

AGE GROUP	1976	1980	1984	1988	1992
18-24 *yrs. old*	**42.2**	**39.9**	**40.8**	**36.2**	**42.8**
25-44 *yrs. old*	**58.7**	**58.7**	**58.4**	**54.0**	**58.3**
45-64 *yrs. old*	**68.7**	**63.3**	**69.8**	**67.9**	**70.0**
65 yrs. *and over*	**62.2**	**65.1**	**67.7**	**68.8**	**70.1**

When flipping through a newspaper, they skip news about government.

Every American wonders: "What does politics have to do with me and my life?" Voters tend to be those who can answer this question in a positive way. Nonvoters have trouble answering. So, with a shrug, they turn away from elections.

Some nonvoters do care about elections and the democratic process. They choose not to vote because they dislike all the candidates on the ballot. Their argument goes like this: "By not voting, we're telling both major parties to do a better job of selecting candidates." Do you accept this argument for not voting? Why or why not?

SKILLS CHECK 2: Interpreting line graphs

In recent years, do you think there has been an increase or a decrease in the percentage of qualified voters taking part in elections? Before answering, study the line graph on page 176.

Now check your skill at interpreting **line graphs** by answering these questions:

1. How many election years are represented on the graph?
2. What does the line in color in the graph represent? What does the gray line represent?
3. In the elections shown, in which year did the highest percentage of voters vote for president? What was this percentage?
4. Would you say that the percentage vote for a U.S. representative is always MORE or LESS than the percentage vote for the president? Explain your answer.
5. From studying the graph, would you conclude that voter participation since 1968 has (*a*) increased or (*b*) decreased? Explain your answer.

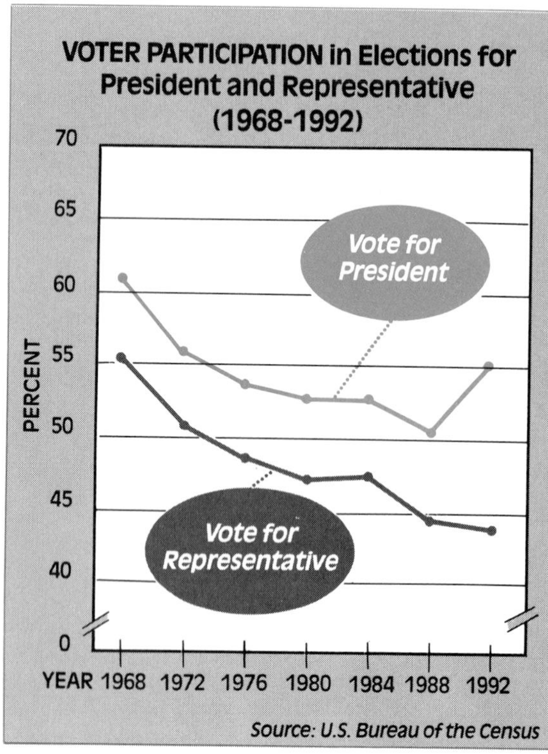

REVIEW

A. Applying What You Know

All questions refer to the chart on page 177. The five people in the chart are residents of the same state, Oregon.

1. Which persons are **not** eligible to vote in Oregon's next election in early November? (Assume that the date today is October 29.)
2. Tell why each of the individuals you named in question 1 will not be allowed to vote.
3. Suppose that there were no Twenty-sixth Amendment. In that case, which person might not be permitted to vote in this year's election? Explain why the Twenty-sixth Amendment is important to this person.
4. Suppose that the people in the chart, instead of living in the present, had lived in the 1850s. Which of them would then have been stopped from voting? Give the reasons for their being disfranchised.
5. Today, if state officials tried to stop Mary Howard from voting, what could she do about it? Name the law of Congress that currently protects her right to vote.
6. If you were a lawmaker in Oregon's legislature, would you change the law to permit Victoria Hubbs and others of her age group to vote? Explain.

B. Making Inferences

Each statement refers to the laws of a specific state. From what you know about state requirements in general, you can infer whether the statement is true or false. Answer either **true** or **false** and explain.

1. Oklahoma allows 18-year-old citizens to vote in all elections.
2. In New York State, voters are required to register before they can vote.
3. A literacy test prevents some black voters from participating in Kentucky's elections.
4. Immigrants who came to this country last year may vote in Massachusetts but not in Vermont.
5. In Virginia, the only qualification for voting is that female residents of the state register at the age of 30.
6. You do not have to own property in order to vote for the governor of Hawaii.
7. In 1790, you had to be a white male and own property in order to vote in a Maryland election.
8. In Oregon, a minimum annual income of $5,000 allows a citizen to vote.
9. Today, the federal government creates the most important laws about voting. State governments enforce these laws.

OREGON VOTING REQUIREMENTS

		RACE	AGE	CITIZENSHIP	ANNUAL INCOME	HOW LONG A RESIDENT OF OREGON *
ALVIN DONALD		black	32	U.S. citizen	$12,000	7 days
VICTORIA HUBBS		white	17	U.S. citizen	$2,500	11 days
CHARLES HUANG		Asian	67	Expects to become U.S. citizen in 18 months	$25,000	160 days
BARBARA O'CONNOR		white	19	Irish-born but now a naturalized U.S. citizen	$5,000	5 years
MARY HOWARD		black	51	U.S. citizen	$62,000	51 years

* *Oregon requires that a voter be a resident of the state for at least 20 days.*

3. INSIDE A VOTING BOOTH, HOW DO YOU INDICATE YOUR CHOICES?

When you enter a voting booth, nobody is allowed to look over your shoulder. All states require that you make your final choice of candidates in secret. Why do Americans cast ballots in secret instead of in the open? What does a ballot actually look like?

History of the American ballot. A ballot is anything that voters mark or manipulate in order to make their choices known on Election Day. Today, candidates' names are either printed on a piece of paper or displayed by a machine.

It is not completely necessary to use a ballot in elections. In colonial times, qualified voters would simply call out candidates' names in a practice known as voice voting. In colonial Virginia, for example, voters would walk up to a table where an election official sat with a book of blank pages. The candidates themselves might be sitting right next to the official. Looking one candidate in the eye, a voter would announce: "It is my privilege to vote for Mr. Madison." As Madison nodded, the official's book would be marked to record the vote.

After the year 1800, however, the most common practice was to drop paper ballots in a box—a ballot box. Some ballots were just blank slips of paper on which voters had written down the names of the candidates they preferred for different offices. At other election places, voters would be handed ballots that had candidates' names already printed on them. One ballot might be colored green and give the names of only the Republican candidates. A second ballot, colored blue, would list the Democrats running for different offices. As they lined up to vote, most people would ask either for the Democratic ballot or the Republican ballot and drop it in the box.

It was very easy to count ballots colored either blue or green. It was also all too easy to win elections by cheating. In the middle of the last century, politicians used to do personal favors for people in their neighborhood. Shortly before Election Day, they might pass out hundreds of turkeys and hams to "needy" families. They expected the favors to be repaid in the polling place. Politicians would be posted there to see that voters asked for ballots of the "right" color.

Another trick of those times was to teach voters how to hide one ballot inside another and then drop both into the box. Of course it was unlawful for anyone to vote twice. But the system made it easy to get around the law. In the 1860s and 1870s, stuffing ballot boxes with illegal votes was especially common.

How could all this cheating be stopped? Beginning in the 1880s, a few states experimented with a system that had originated in Australia. The system was known as the Australian ballot. It worked like this:

1. The state would print up thousands of copies of *one official ballot*. It would list the names of all candidates for two major parties (Democrats, Republicans) and perhaps some minor parties as well. Only

THE TECHNOLOGY OF VOTING. Left: Choosing a party ticket, 1872. Center: Sample ballot in Nevada, 1892. Right: Flicking the levers of a voting machine, 1948. What is the current method for voting in your community?

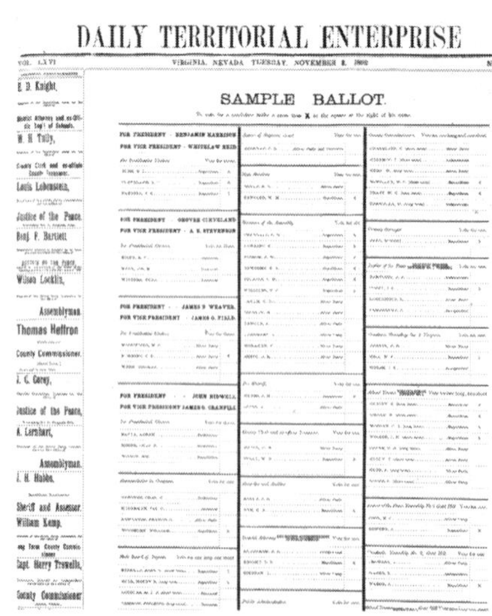

DAILY TERRITORIAL ENTERPRISE

SAMPLE BALLOT

this one ballot would be issued to qualified voters at the local polling place.

2. Voters would not be permitted to make their choices in public. Instead, they would be required to take state ballots behind a curtain. There they would secretly mark an X next to candidates' names.
3. Later, election officials would count all the ballots. Any ballot that was marked improperly would be thrown out or put aside as not valid.

The Australian ballot did not eliminate cheating altogether. But it was found to be a great improvement. Eventually all states adopted the basic idea of the Australian ballot. That is why, today, voting is done privately inside a curtained booth.

Voting machines. Before he invented either the phonograph or the light bulb, Thomas Edison worked on a machine for recording votes. But Edison's political invention of 1868 was ahead of its time. People actually started voting by machine for the first time in the 1890s. Today, the practice of using machines is even more common than marking paper ballots. Since voting machines display an official state ballot inside a curtained booth, they are just another form of the Australian ballot idea.

Voting by machine may seem complicated. In fact, it is about as simple as operating an electric toaster. All you do is push down little levers next to the names of the candidates you want. For example, suppose that Barbara Belcher and José Bolivar are running for the office of county prosecutor. On the flat surface of the machine, their names appear side by side next to the title PROSECUTOR. Do you prefer Belcher to Bolivar? Then push down the metal lever next to her name. Do the same for your choice of candidates for the several other offices listed on the ballot. You may take as much time as you need, but you will probably be finished in a minute.

OPERATING THE MACHINE. Throwing the handle to the right closes the curtain to the voting booth. Compared with paper ballots, what are the advantages and disadvantages of voting by machine?

A handle inside the voting booth opens and closes the curtain that gives you privacy. After you have made your final choice, pull the handle back to swing open the curtain. The movement of the handle automatically flips the levers beside your choices. By the same movement, your votes are registered and totaled by the machine.

In many communities, machines are preferred because they can quickly and automatically add up the votes. On the other hand, they have the disadvantage of sometimes jamming and breaking down.

Computers too are now being used to speed up the counting of votes. In some polling places, voters are handed several punch cards to insert in a small machine. Each card registers the person's vote for a particular office. When all the cards have been collected, they can be run through a computer at terrific speed.

Long ballots and short ballots. It is a challenge to vote intelligently in American elections. Inside the voting booth, you may face a ballot that lists more than a dozen offices. Some will be offices of the federal government (U.S. president, U.S. senator, and member of the House of Representatives). Others will be offices in your state government (governor, state lawmakers, and perhaps a few state judges). Still others will be offices of your county or local community (county executive, sheriff, mayor, member of the city council).

Usually, there will be two candidates listed for each office—a Democrat and a Republican. But for some of the more important offices (president, state governor), there may be two or three other candidates as well. Therefore, in a major election, you will probably see as many as 50 names or more on the ballot.

That is a lot of choices. "Too many!" say critics of the so-called long ballot. They object to ballots with a lot of minor offices on them. Such ballots, they say, only confuse most voters. Instead of a long ballot with a lot of elected offices, some favor a short ballot that lists only the major state and local offices.

Voting a "straight ticket" or "split ticket." One way that Americans simplify their choices is to vote for all the candidates of one party. This is known as voting a straight ticket. Suppose that you know almost nothing about the different names on the ballot. Suppose too that you generally like the Republican party better than the Democratic party. In that case, you may simply look for all the Republicans on the ballot and put a series of X's by their names.

Some states make it even easier for you to vote a straight party ticket. They list Democrats in one column, Republicans in another. At the top of each column is a box or circle. You would put an **X** there if you wished to vote for the party's entire list of candidates from top to bottom.

But what if you are the type of voter who likes to look at each candidate as an individual. You may like the Republican candidate for president but most of the Democrats for local offices. In that case, you would be voting a split ticket. Instead of going straight down the Republican row or Democratic row, you might switch back and forth. Your ballot might look like this:

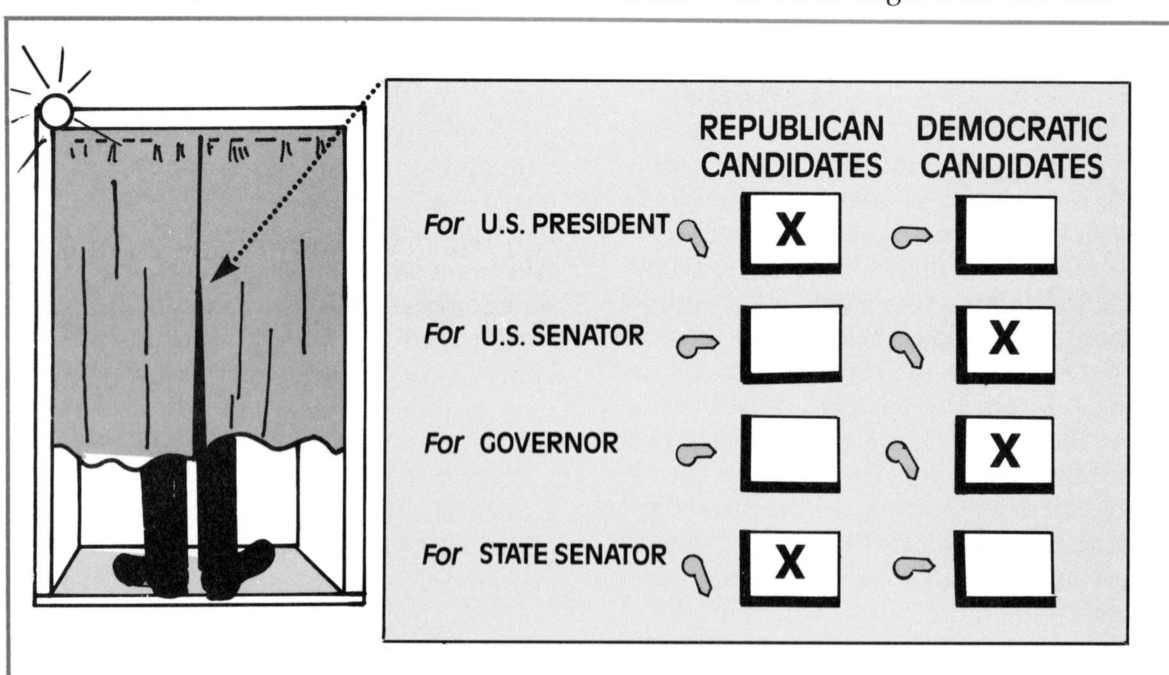

Voting on public questions. Often, on Election Day, electing candidates to office is only one part of a voter's job. The other part is deciding whether to vote **yes** or **no** on certain public questions. For example:

1. Should the state government be authorized (permitted) to borrow $500,000,000 in order to repair roads and highways? **(yes)** **(no)**
2. Should a new program be created so that the families of murder victims may receive government aid and counseling? **(yes)** **(no)**
3. Should the state constitution be amended to allow judges to be elected directly by qualified voters? **(yes)** **(no)**

Questions like this may be on the same ballot with the candidates' names. Or they may be printed on a separate ballot.

Initiative, referendum, and recall. When you vote on public questions, you are really acting as a lawmaker. You are participating in what is commonly called a *referendum.* This is a direct vote of the people themselves on a question of law.

A simple majority decides. Suppose that 1,100,000 voters say **yes** to question #2 (above). But 1,100,010 others vote **no**. Then the families of murder victims will receive no aid from the state government.

Who decides to put the proposed law on the ballot for vote by referendum? A state legislature may decide to do it. Or, in some states, a group of ordinary citizens may do it by a process known as the *initiative.* The group interested in changing the law write their proposal as a petition. They try to persuade thousands of qualified voters to sign the petition. If they get enough signatures, as required by state law, their proposal is either placed on the election ballot or voted upon by the state legislature.

Another type of special election is the *recall.* A group of citizens may be unhappy with the actions of a certain state official. They cannot wait for the next election to come around. They want him or her dismissed *now.* So they circulate a petition proposing that the "bad" official be voted out of office in a special recall election. If they collect enough signatures, the election is held.

Recall elections are not common. Only some of the states have such a practice. You cannot remove the president or any other federal official by recall.

Nevertheless, special elections can be as important as the regular election in November. In a democracy, after all, the people have the final responsibility for deciding how society shall be governed. Nothing shows this more clearly than the **yes** and **no** votes in a referendum.

REVIEW

A. Building Your Political Vocabulary

First **define** the terms in *italics.* Then, tell which of the two you prefer and why.

1. Which do you think is better: (*a*) voting a *straight ticket* (*b*) voting a *split ticket*? Why?
2. Which do you think is better: (*a*) *voice voting* (*b*) the *Australian ballot*? Why?
3. Which do you think is better: (*a*) a *long ballot* (*b*) a *short ballot*? Why?
4. Which do you think is better: (*a*) a *paper ballot* (*b*) a *voting machine*? Why?

B. Project

On a piece of paper, write the names of any eight adults whom you know. Assume that: (*a*) two of them are candidates for the U.S. Senate. (*b*) Another two are candidates for state governor. (*c*) Two others are candidates for county sheriff. (*d*) Two are running for a seat in the state assembly (lawmaking body). Also assume that, for each pair of rival candidates, one is a Democrat and the other is a Republican. Design a paper ballot for an election in your state. Make sure it lists the following:

- offices to be elected
- names of the candidates
- party of the candidates
- a place for voters to record their choices.

CHAPTER REVIEW

A. Completing the Summary

Select terms from the word list to fill in the blanks in the summary below. Write your answers on a piece of paper.

amendment	mandate
apathetic	moderates
Australian	recall
conservative	referendum
disfranchised	register
enfranchised	residence
incumbents	split
initiative	straight
landslide	suffragists
liberal	Voting Rights Act

Voting is both a right and a duty of American citizenship. It is essential to the democratic process. It is unfortunate, therefore, that many citizens have a(an) __(1)__ attitude and do not bother to vote on Election Day.

Those committed to the democratic process enjoy following news of political campaigns. The language of politics is familiar to them. They know the difference between (*a*) candidates "on the left" whose views are __(2)__ and (*b*) candidates "on the right" whose views are __(3)__. Most candidates present themselves as __(4)__ on most issues rather than as favoring either extreme on the political left or the political right.

In a contest between the "in" party and the "out" party, those candidates who currently hold office are known as __(5)__. If they are very popular, they will probably win by a __(6)__ and claim that their policies have received a __(7)__ from the people.

After reaching the age of 18, almost all American citizens have the right to vote in federal, state, and local elections. This was not the case 200 years ago when George Washington was president. At that time, only white, male property owners were __(8)__. The Fifteenth __(9)__, adopted in 1868, extended voting rights to black men. But until Congress passed the __(10)__ of 1964, blacks were often kept from voting because of state laws discriminating against them. The efforts of __(11)__ like Susan B. Anthony finally won equal voting rights for women. The Constitution was changed again in 1971 to guarantee voting rights for anyone 18 and older.

Not every citizen may vote. In some states, convicts and the "mentally incompetent" are ___(12)___. If you move from one state to another, a ___(13)___ requirement may temporarily stop you from voting. Each state requires that you ___(14)___ with local officials before you can participate in your first election in that state.

Like voting rights, the ballot box and the voting machine did not always exist. In the 1880s, the so-called ___(15)___ ballot, or secret ballot, began to replace the party tickets of the past. States differ in the number of offices that are elected. Therefore, some ballots are quite long while others are relatively short. Voters loyal to one party will vote a ___(16)___ ticket. Other voters who care more about individual candidates are more likely to vote a ___(17)___ ticket.

Besides voting for candidates, citizens are sometimes given an opportunity to vote directly on state laws. Voting **yes** or **no** on a public question is called a ___(18)___. In some states, the voters may use the ___(19)___ to put a certain proposal for a law on the ballot. Voting on whether or not to remove an elected official before the end of his or her term is known as the ___(20)___.

B. Making Inferences

For each question, answer either **all, most, few** (less than half), or **none**.

1. How many states now have the "grandfather clause" in their election law?
2. How many states allow 18-year-olds to vote?
3. How many states use a form of the Australian ballot?
4. In a landslide, the winning candidate receives how many votes?
5. How many states require voters to be U.S. citizens?
6. How many adult citizens of the United States are currently disfranchised for one reason or another?
7. How many states require voters to fill out a registration form?
8. How many states may, if they wish, give voting rights to 15-year-olds?
9. If a person votes a straight ticket, how many of the candidates selected belong to the same political party?

C. Applying What You Know

Imagine three candidates running for governor of your state.

Gary Gullickson: liberal; far behind in the race.

Fernando Velasquez: conservative; the front runner in the race.

Betty Brewster: middle of the road; only slightly behind the front runner.

In several articles on the campaign, your local newspaper has made the following statements. Tell which candidate is probably being described in each statement.

1. "The business community is solidly behind him/her because of his/her plan for reducing government rules for doing business."
2. "Though he/she is not well known in the northern part of the state, some experts think this dark horse has a chance of catching up."
3. "Most black voters like him/her because of his/her past record on civil rights."

4. "Critics say that his/her moderate stand on most issues makes him/her a safe but dull candidate."

5. "If he/she wins election, we are not likely to see much change in government—unless it is to the right."

D. Building Your Political Vocabulary

Make a copy of the crossword puzzle on page 185. Then use the 19 clues (across, down) to complete the puzzle. Do *not* write in the book.

Across

5. A candidate whose views are neither liberal nor conservative
8. Another term for the vote
11. How you would expect a lot of hoopla to sound
12. Something you had to own in order to vote in the 1790s
15. What is usually claimed after a landslide victory
16. A device for recording your choice of candidates
18. What qualified voters must do before they will be allowed to vote
19. Those who participate in elections

Down

1. The attitude of those who don't care enough to vote
2. A group enfranchised by the Nineteenth Amendment
3. If you are liberal, you lean to the __(?)__ on most issues.
4. A competition for election (similar to what horses do)
6. A synonym for hoopla
7. A device for showing increases and decreases from year to year
9. The candidate who is currently in office
10. If you have voted for every Democratic candidate on the ballot, you have voted a __(?)__ ticket.
13. An organization that helps its candidates win election is a political __(?)__.
14. An Australian ballot is a __(?)__ ballot.
17. The opposite of a *short* ballot

1
2
3
4
5
6
7
8
9
10
11
12
13
14
15
16
17
18
19

FIGHTING FOR THEIR LIVES. A health crisis in her community caused Lois Gibbs to organize her neighbors for political action. How did her efforts influence the federal government?

CHAPTER 9

How to Influence Government

OBJECTIVES

After reading this chapter, you will know

1. the ways that interest groups and lobbyists try to influence the decisions of lawmakers.
2. the ways that public opinion is expressed and measured.
3. how to recognize political propaganda.
4. how to write a letter expressing your opinion on a public issue.

Lois Gibbs and her neighbors feared for their lives. Their homes had been built near a mile-long canal into which a chemical company had once dumped toxic (poisonous) wastes. Their neighborhood in Niagara Falls, New York, was known as Love Canal.

Through the 1970s, residents of Love Canal noticed a black goo seep through the basement walls of their houses. Several children developed skin rashes and crippling illnesses. Expectant mothers gave birth to deformed babies. People in the community began to fear that the illnesses were all related to a common cause. They suspected that chemicals buried in the land were slowly poisoning them.

Why were the state and federal governments doing nothing to help the people of Love Canal? That was the question raised by a group of anxious citizens who called themselves the Love Canal Homeowners Association. Their president, Lois Gibbs, was a young mother who had never been much interested in politics or government. But now, because her family was threatened, she learned quickly how to organize her neighbors for political action.

Through the efforts of the Homeowners Association, the hazards of Love Canal received national publicity. At first, officials of New York State and the national government said they were doing their best to study the problem. But this did not satisfy Lois Gibbs and her neighbors. They insisted that the people of Love Canal could not wait. They needed help—now! Because of the hard work of Lois Gibbs and others, the hazards of Love Canal were publicized on TV news programs.

Finally, in 1980, President Jimmy Carter declared a state of emergency in the Love Canal area. The U.S. government, he said, would pay for 710 families to move into temporary homes, outside the danger zone. At the same time, the government would study the problem and take action to clean up the polluted land. The president's announcement was a triumph for the organization led by Lois Gibbs.

In a democratic nation, it is every citizens' right to try to influence government policy. Often, influence is exerted by groups of people who have a common interest. One example of such a group is the Love Canal Homeowners Association. Individuals can have an influence by writing letters to lawmakers and even by talking about public issues with friends.

Hou can *you* influence government? You will know several ways to do so after reading this chapter. Use these questions to guide your study:

1. How do interest groups influence policy?
2. How does public opinion influence policy?
3. What is political propaganda?

1. HOW DO INTEREST GROUPS INFLUENCE POLICY?

It is not easy to persuade the government to act as you wish it to act. To change the law may take many months and even years of work. Why would citizens go to such trouble to influence the government? There are two main reasons. The citizens may desire either (*a*) to gain some special benefit or (*b*) to prevent some benefit from being taken from them.

In other words, the people who try hardest to influence the government are those who have much to gain—or much to lose. They have special interests in seeing that the law reads one way or another. For example, corporations may want a reduction in taxes. Labor unions may want laws that give their members greater protection. Senior citizens may want increases in their Social Security benefits. The Girl Scouts of America may want laws to support their camping activities. The residents of a community like Love Canal may want emergency help. Such groups are called special-interest groups. Other names for them are pressure groups or interest groups.

Types of special-interest groups. How many special-interest groups exist in the United States? You would have to count all of the following:

- Every large corporation (IBM, NBC, Pepsico, etc.)
- Civic clubs and societies (Kiwanis Club, Rotary Club, American Legion, etc.)
- All labor unions
- Farmers' groups and associations
- Associations of professional people (teachers, doctors, dentists, lawyers, etc.)
- Organizations representing different religious groups (Protestants, Roman Catholics, Jews, etc.)
- Organizations speaking for special causes (rights for women, rights for blacks, rights for Hispanics, rights for veterans, etc.)
- Associations representing every kind of business you can think of (cosmetics, greeting cards, book publishing, professional baseball, imported cheese, etc.)

Nobody knows exactly how many special-interest groups there are. If they could be counted, the complete list would have to include almost *all* organized groups, large and small. The reason is that all groups and organizations are affected in some way by laws and government policies. To protect themselves, they must be alert to what the government is doing.

A lobbyist's job. Not long ago, an article about one powerful interest group appeared in the newsmagazine *U.S. News and World Report*. The title of the article read:

> GRAYING ARMIES MARCH TO DEFEND SOCIAL SECURITY
>
> Organized, strong and angry—lobbyists for the elderly are warning lawmakers not to tamper with their benefits.

The interest group described as "strong and angry" was made up of millions of senior citizens. They were alarmed by a proposed change in the laws of Congress concerning the Social Security system. If Congress passed this proposal, an upper limit would be set on the monthly payments they could receive from the Social Security office. Older Americans realized they had a great deal to lose if the new law went through. They also understood how to influence lawmakers to vote against any change.

The plan was to rally behind the associations that worked for them daily in the halls of Congress. One association was the National Council of Senior Citizens (NCSC). An even larger organization, the American Association of Retired Persons (AARP), had a membership in 1990 of over 20 million.

Each association employed full-time staffs of workers. Their main job was to keep in touch with lawmakers and government agencies. People employed in this way call themselves "Washington representatives" since they represent their employer in Washington, D.C. The general public and the news media, however, call them by a different name: *lobbyists*.

The term lobbyist comes from the hallways—or *lobbies*—outside the main chambers of Congress. For many years, such hallways have been good places to stand and wait if you want to talk briefly with some congressperson passing by. So the paid representatives (lobbyists) of different groups often gather there in the lobbies. The work they do—trying to influence laws—is known as lobbying.

There are thousands of lobbyists currently employed in the nation's capital. They represent labor unions, business groups, and every other kind of special-interest group—including the senior citizens associations.

Feel helpless about the high cost of health care?
There are some things you can do!
Your doctor shares your concerns. The latest Health Care Financing Administration figures based on the cost for National Health Expenditures in 1986 totaled 458.2 billion dollars. Physicians' services accounted for 92.0 billion dollars of the total expenditure (approximately 20%).
The rest was expended on other health services and supplies. While the cost of medical care has continued to escalate since 1986, physicians have had a freeze on their Medicare fees for the last three years. Doctors are doing their part to help control the upward spiral of medical costs.
You are the silent majority — now is the time to speak up. Bureaucratic constraints on the budgeting of funds for the delivery of health care may look good in an election year but they are devastating to the quality of health care.
Ask your legislators to review the DRG and Medicare payment programs.
You can help — write for a list of 10 Ways To Cut Your Medical Bills.
Your County Medical Society and
The Medical Society of New Jersey
2 PRINCESS RD., LAWRENCEVILLE, N.J. 08648

A SPECIAL INTEREST IN HEALTH CARE. This advertisement was placed in magazines by an association of doctors. Why would doctors want the public to understand their point of view about the rising costs of health care?

A lobbyist's methods. How do lobbyists attempt to influence a lawmaker's vote? They may use one of three general approaches:

1. *The "wine and dine" approach.* This method worked wonders for lobbyists about 100 years ago in the 1870s and 1880s. Almost every night, they would entertain leaders of the House and Senate. They would buy tickets for them to the theater and the race track. They would treat them to dinners at the finest Washington restaurants. One lobbyist at that time worked for several powerful railroad companies. He was not joking when he said, "The best way to a congressman's aye (yes vote) is through his stomach." (See the cartoon on page 190.)

The "wine and dine" approach gave lobbyists a bad reputation. People suspected that the favors given out by lobbyists came close to buying a lawmaker's vote. Fortunately, in our own times, lobbyists have changed their ways. Some may still throw late-night parties and give away tickets to the Kentucky Derby. Today's lobbyists, however, rely far more on two other approaches.

POLITICAL CARTOON, 1920. Why would a political cartoonist accuse lobbyists of the 1920s of gobbling up "the people's money"? Do you think the cartoon might also describe conditions in the 1980s?

2. *The informational approach.* Today, members of Congress consume facts almost as hungrily as they once consumed five-course meals. To vote intelligently on any law, they need information about the effect it is likely to have on different groups. Lobbyists are eager to provide them with all the information they need.

Of course, the information shows only one side of the picture—the side that the lobbyist represents. But lawmakers are usually careful to get information from many sources. They listen to lobbyists supporting a particular law. They also listen to lobbyists opposing it.

3. *The "grass-roots" approach.* A third approach rests on an important fact of life in American politics. *All lawmakers in the United States are elected to office by voters.* Lawmakers worry about whether they will win or lose the next election. They want to avoid doing anything that would be unpopular with a large group of voters.

Lobbyists know this fact of life well. They use it to their advantage when they "go to the grass roots." In political language, grass roots simply refers to the great mass of voters.

As an example, let us return to the case of the senior citizens' groups and their lobbying efforts. Recall that they wanted to defeat a proposed change in the Social Security laws. Their lobbyists in Washington sent out publicity about the proposed change and how it would hurt senior citizens. Millions of senior citizens received the same urgent message: "Write your congressperson. Write NOW!"

Many thousands of postcards tumbled into lawmakers' offices. A total of 800,000 were finally counted, all objecting to the one proposed law. Did any senator or rep-

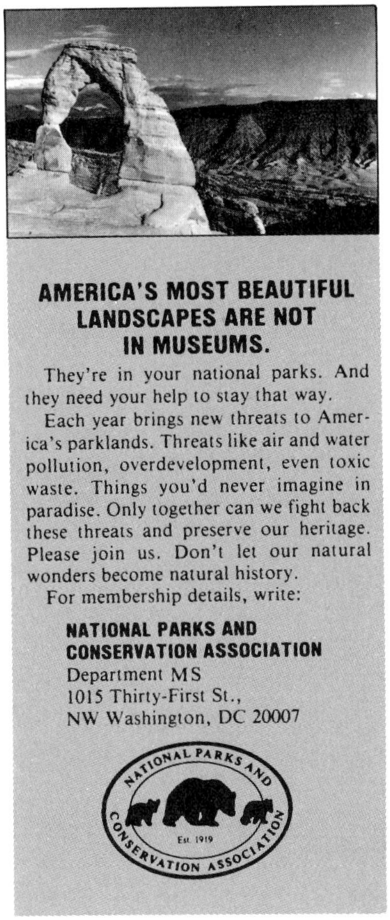

AMERICA'S MOST BEAUTIFUL LANDSCAPES ARE NOT IN MUSEUMS.
They're in your national parks. And they need your help to stay that way.
Each year brings new threats to America's parklands. Threats like air and water pollution, overdevelopment, even toxic waste. Things you'd never imagine in paradise. Only together can we fight back these threats and preserve our heritage. Please join us. Don't let our natural wonders become natural history.
For membership details, write:
NATIONAL PARKS AND CONSERVATION ASSOCIATION
Department MS
1015 Thirty-First St.,
NW Washington, DC 20007
NATIONAL PARKS AND CONSERVATION ASSOCIATION
Est. 1919

PROTECTING THE ARCHES. This advertisement (or public service announcement) was placed in many popular magazines in 1988. Would you call the organization that created it "a special-interest group"?

resentative dare to ignore the senior citizens' message? A lobbyist promised that the name of the uncooperative lawmaker would be "reported back to the grass roots." He warned, "We shall not forget if Congress behaves in an unfriendly fashion to the senior citizens of the United States. We shall remember [in the next election]!"

The influence of PACs. There is one other way that special-interest groups may gain the attention of lawmakers. That is by organizing something called a *Political Action Committee*—or PAC. The purpose of a PAC is to contribute money to candidates running for office.

Of course, a PAC will not give money to everybody. It usually gives the largest contributions to candidates who are most likely to win election. In effect, that means that most PAC money goes to incumbents, since they are more likely to win than their challengers. In the election of 1992, for example, 396 incumbents in the House campaigned for re-election. Although 47 lost their races, 349 others (86 percent) were returned to Congress.

Members of Congress have come to rely more and more on the money donated to their campaigns by PACs. After all, PACs help them pay the enormous costs of running for a seat in Congress. It is fairly common for a representative to spend more than $300,000 to get re-elected. A senator may spend as much as two million dollars or more. To meet such costs, candidates gladly accept contributions from any legal source.

From the public's point of view, however, there are dangers to be noted. What would happen, for example, if a certain member of Congress came to rely upon the contributions of one or two special-interest groups and their PACs? He or she might feel obliged to vote in the way being urged by lobbyists representing those groups. Lawmakers may think twice before voting in a way that offends a major contributor.

Laws regulating lobbying and PACs. It is proper and legal if lobbyists influence lawmakers by talk and argument. It is *not* proper if they try to influence them through contributions of money. What can be done to keep lobbying from getting out of hand?

First of all, a law passed by Congress in 1946 requires that every lobbyist and lobbying organization register with the federal government. The act of registration requires lobbyists to declare:

- their names
- the special-interest group or corporation that employs them
- the income they receive for their lobbying work.

Every year, thousands of people and organizations register under the lobbying law. However, it is suspected that thousands of other organization representatives occasionally lobby in Congress without bothering to register. They can easily excuse themselves by saying that lobbying is not their "principal activity."

Another law, the Federal Election Campaign Act of 1971, regulates PACs. The law states:

- no member of a corporation or interest group may contribute more than $500 to a PAC
- no PAC may contribute more than $5,000 to any one candidate.

There is no limit, however, to the total number of PACs that can be organized. Therefore, the combined impact of PACs is enormous. In 1992, they contributed a total of $161 million to all candidates for congressional seats. This sum represented 32 percent of the campaign money spent in that year.

Public-interest lobbies. Senior citizens and their lobbyists may look at lawmaking only from their special point of view. Farm groups, medical groups, and business groups do the same. What organization looks out for the welfare of *all* the American people? Who speaks for the general public, not just a special public with special interests?

Several organizations now exist that lobby for the average citizen. They may be called public-interest groups. For example, there is the League of Women Voters, a dedicated group of women (and some men) who study issues from all points of view. There is the Consumer Union, whose 200,000 members speak for the interests of consumers. Since

CARTOON CORNER

SHOOT-OUT. What is the cartoonist's point of view toward the "auto industry pollution lobby"?

all of us buy goods and services as consumers, the Consumer Union may be said to represent all Americans.

Another public-interest group, Common Cause, was started in 1970 by an educator, John Gardner. Anyone with an interest in improving government is welcome to join. Common Cause identifies ways that government may be made to work better. Then, using a "grass-roots" approach, it urges its thousands of members to write to their representatives to recommend any new law sponsored by Common Cause.

REVIEW

A. Building Your Political Vocabulary

Explain the meaning of each term by answering the questions.

1. What are **lobbyists?** How did they get their name?
2. What is a **special-interest group?** Why do such groups hire lobbyists and send them to Washington, D.C.?
3. What are **Political Action Committees** (PACs)? Why do some people think they pose a danger to democratic government?
4. What do lobbyists mean when they speak of a **"grass-roots" approach?** Give an example of this approach in practice.

B. Making Inferences

Identified in each numbered item below is an interest group and a proposal for changing the law. Tell whether you think the group would probably **favor** or **oppose** the bill (proposed law). Then explain your answer.

1. Farmers' group—A bill to reduce the amount of surplus grain purchased by the U.S. government.
2. Railroad company—A bill that would require railroads to install new safety devices.
3. Doctors' association—A bill that would give free medical care to families earning less than $10,000 a year.
4. Association of war veterans—A bill that would place an upper limit on the amount of aid given to disabled veterans of World War II.

C. Applying What You Know

Select one of the interest groups listed in B. Imagine that this group employs you as its lobbyist in Washington. Tell what **methods** you would use to influence several key members of Congress.

2. HOW DOES PUBLIC OPINION INFLUENCE POLICY?

Without even trying, people are constantly influencing one another's opinions and tastes. Surely you have already felt the force of *public opinion* in your own life. Have you ever. . .

- Refused to wear some piece of clothing, fearing that friends would laugh at you?
- Sensed that certain individuals in school were far more popular than others?
- Repeated what everyone else seemed to be saying about a certain rock group or celebrity?

If your answer is yes, you know how powerful the opinions of others can be. Public opinion influences the way you think and act. At the same time, you can influence others and thereby influence public opinion.

What is public opinion? The term public opinion is defined in different ways. Some scholars say that it is the dominant or main way of thinking of a particular group. For example, it may be the opinion of most students in school that Mrs. X is an excellent math teacher. There may be 15 students who criticize her, but their opinion will not count if we are concerned only with the dominant opinion.

A second definition of public opinion is the one we will be using in this text. It counts everyone's opinion on a question. For example, we could ask: *Should the school year begin a week later and end a week later?* If we asked 1,000 people this question, the results might be as follows:

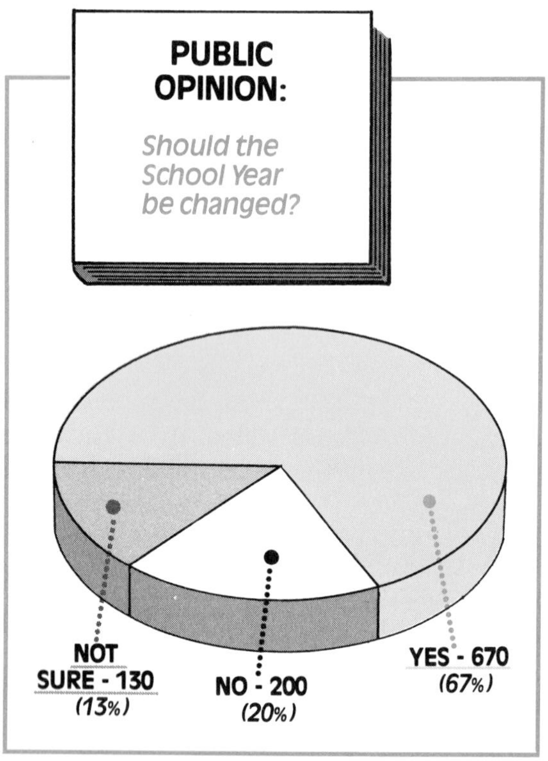

In this example, "public opinion" is the sum of the opinions of all who answered the question. It is not just the opinion of the dominant group. For example, public opinion on the school issue could be stated like this: "Although 67% of those surveyed favor a change, more than 20% oppose it."

Two other points must be added to our explanation. First, the size of a group represented in a public opinion poll varies. It may involve only a hundred people or fewer. It could also involve 100 million people or more. It depends on the issue. For example, estimate the size of the group that would likely have an opinion on the following:

a. whether to raise money for a class field trip
b. whether to build a new track for your high school
c. whether to elect Candidate A or Candidate B for governor of your state
d. whether to increase U.S. trade with Russia.
e. whether to begin a world-wide military effort to stop the drug trade.

A second point is that public opinion must be expressed in some way. You may have many opinions that you keep to yourself. They do not count as public opinion unless you make them public by communicating them to someone. Of course, it is your privilege to keep your opinions private; but then you are not part of *public* opinion.

How public opinion is created. Scholars who study public opinion admit that they do not fully understand it. They have two theories for explaining it: (*a*) the top-down theory and (*b*) the bottom-up theory.

The top-down theory stresses the role played by opinion leaders. Such people include college professors, newspaper editors, labor leaders, teachers, lawyers, writers, business executives, priests, rabbis, and ministers. These leaders frequently express opinions on public issues. It is assumed that their opinions are listened to and respected. Thus, public opinion moves downward in society from leaders to followers.

The bottom-up theory gives more importance to the average person. Let us say, for example, that the question is whether the president of the United States is doing a good job. There is general talk about the president in everyone's daily life (mixed with talk of sports and other topics). After a while, people may hear one another saying much the same thing. They either grumble about the president's actions or approve of them. Eventually, a large part of the public recognizes that the president is either liked or not liked.

How public opinion is measured. In the old days, before 1900, there was no scientific way of measuring public opinion. Politicians could only make reasonable guesses about it based on such signs as these:

- how many people attended political rallies for a candidate and how loudly they cheered
- what people said to reporters when interviewed about their opinions
- the opinions expressed on the editorial pages of newpapers.

Though useful, such signs of public opinion were often unreliable. Then, in the 1930s, two social scientists—George Gallup and Elmo Roper—developed techniques for polling opinion scientifically. Pollsters Gallup and Roper discovered a way to select a reliable sample of people to interview. Those participating in their survey had to be typical of the entire American population. It would be wrong, for example, to interview 800 women and 200 men since that group (or sample) would not be typical. If Gallup's or Roper's same group was really typical, he could safely predict how all other Americans would answer the same questions.

Gallup, Roper, and other researchers demonstrated that their polling techniques were reliable. Again and again, in presidential elections, their *opinion polls* usually predicted how Americans voted.

Today, newspapers regularly report the results of opinion polls. Usually the number of people interviewed in each poll is only about 1,500. And yet, because the sample group is typical, a poll can accurately represent public opinion for the whole country.

How to take a random sample. Suppose that you wanted to find out whether the American people today approve or disapprove of the president's leadership. What would you do to poll opinion in a scientific manner? First, you would divide the country into hundreds of areas of equal population and give each area a number. Tossed into a container, a few of the numbers would be picked out at random (completely by chance). For example, the areas you draw might be numbered 9, 112, 199, and 305.

Each of the areas drawn contains more than 100,000 people—far too many to be interviewed. So you now take a *random sample* of your first sample. You would divide, for example, area #9 into hundreds of mini-areas. Once again, these mini-areas are given numbers, dropped in a container, and scrambled. Picking out three or four mini-areas, you might need to subdivide them still further and repeat the process.

Finally, you arrive at a small enough number of people to participate in your poll. Because they were selected randomly, these people's opinions should fairly represent the opinions of the entire nation.

Questions in an opinion poll. Those who write questions for opinion polls may take many days doing it. Every question must be worded carefully so that it does not influence or bias a person's answer. Here are two examples of questions that pollsters have asked in past surveys on opinion.

A. Interview Date: Fall, 1991

QUESTION: Would you be willing to pay higher taxes if the money were used for:

	Yes
Feeding and providing medical care for very poor children?	86%
Fighting the war on drugs?	79%
Improving public schools in communities like yours?	72%

B. Interview Date: Spring, 1984

QUESTION ASKED OF TEENAGERS: What is the biggest problem facing teenagers today?

Drug abuse	42%
Alcohol abuse	14
Unemployment	10
Peer pressure	8
Fear of war	5
Growing up	5
Finding purpose in life	4
Getting along with parents	3
School problems	3
Other	6

The interview date is important because public opinion often changes from one year to the next. Today, for example, would most teenagers still think that drug abuse is their number-one problem? (See project B-2, page 198.)

Does your opinion count? Can your opinion on an issue influence other people's opinions? The answer is definitely yes—but only if you communicate your opinion in some manner. Consider some of the ways that your private thoughts can be brought into the light of public attention:

1. Conversation. Imagine two friends talking:

"Don't you think X is just awful!"

"I don't mind X so much. But Y is the worst!"

For X and Y, you could substitute the names of athletic teams, soft drinks, advertisements, TV shows, movies, or politicians. People spend their idle moments chatting about everything under the sun. Sometimes their conversations drift to political issues in the news. Someone might remark:

"Don't you think what's happening in Country X is terrible?"

You could contribute to public opinion by replying:

"I agree it's frightening but, so far, the president seems to be handling it all right."

2. Buttons and bumper stickers. Public opinions are now on sale. You can purchase them in the form of buttons that say: I LOVE NEW YORK or VIRGINIA IS FOR LOVERS. The same slogans may be displayed on T-shirts or on a car's rear bumper.

Do such slogans make an impression on strangers passing by? It is hard to know. At least you have the satisfaction of advertising your opinion.

THE INFLUENCE OF BUMPER STICKERS. This bumper sticker on a New Jersey car presented an opinion about a landfill law. What bumper stickers on public issues have you observed? Do you think a single bumper sticker could have an effect on public opinion?

3. Letters to the editor. Newspapers and magazines regularly print letters of opinion from their readers. The letters are usually brief—only two or three paragraphs. They may be about any subject of public interest. In your local newspaper, for example, you may read letters about:

- the need for the highway department to do something about the "disgraceful number of potholes" on Main Street
- the "brave and dedicated work" of the volunteer firefighters
- the lack of adequate parking spaces and the "urgent need to improve the situation for the sake of local merchants and their customers."

When writing such a letter, begin with this salutation: *"To the Editor."* Take care to express your ideas in a direct and sensible manner. An opinion carries greater weight if stated simply and supported with facts.

SKILLS CHECK: Writing a letter of opinion

The letter below is a student's first draft of a letter to the editor of a newspaper. It has not been mailed.

> To the Editor:
>
> I think the voters of this community are a bunch of cheap jerks because putting in a new track at the high school is an absolute MUST and they voted against it! Unbelievable! So what if it costs $350,000? We should have a track as good as any other in the state. I'm really upset about this because I'm not the only member of the track team who's now hurting from leg injuries on account of that thing they have the nerve to call a track.
>
> I thought I'd just write and let you know how everyone feels about this—not that it will do any good.
>
> Sincerely mad,
> "Ace" Greenley

Questions:

1. Do you think this letter of opinion is properly written? If not, how do you think the writer should improve it?
2. Write another draft of Greenley's letter, making whatever changes you think are necessary. Write your final draft on a piece of paper.

4. Letters to public officials. Lawmakers like to receive letters from their constituents (the people they represent). They want to know what voters think on different issues.

Suppose your congressperson receives 50 letters in favor of a certain bill (proposed law) and only seven letters against it. This fact will make an impression and may influence the way the congressperson votes. Yet, there may have been hundreds of people opposed to the bill who did not bother to write a letter. If they had written, letters against the bill would have outnumbered letters in favor of the bill.

In short, lawmakers cannot represent your opinion unless you take the trouble to write and tell them what you think.

5. Rallies and demonstrations. You have heard the expression "Actions speak louder than words." Probably the strongest way to express an opinion or belief is to act on it. In the United States, citizens have the right to gather in large crowds on the streets or in a public park for the purpose of promoting their ideas. Such gatherings are called demonstrations or mass rallies. Police are present to make sure that the demonstrators behave in an orderly and peaceful manner. If they do, they cannot be arrested.

In U.S. history, there have been peaceful demonstrations for many causes. In the early 1900s, women suffragists marched down the central avenues of Washington, D.C., campaigning for the right to vote. Also in Washington, in 1963, an immense crowd of blacks and whites applauded the powerful speech of the civil rights leader Martin Luther King, Jr.

MARCH ON WASHINGTON, 1963. About 200,000 people gathered in the nation's capital to demonstrate for laws to guarantee the civil rights of blacks and other minorities. How did this demonstration, led by Martin Luther King, Jr. (right), influence public opinion in the United States?

Demonstrations like these receive much publicity. They make an impression on public opinion. Eventually, changes in opinion may bring about changes in the laws.

REVIEW

A. Correcting the Statement

Tell why each statement is **not** correct.

1. Public opinion always refers to what 240,000,000 Americans think about an issue.
2. To be reliable, an opinion poll must survey the opinions of thousands of people on a certain issue.
3. You can be arrested for peacefully participating in a mass rally.
4. Before the 1930s, politicians had no way of knowing how the general public felt about an issue.

B. Projects

1. From your local newspaper, clip out and bring to class three letters to the editor. Which letter do you think is the best developed? Why?
2. Review the responses given in 1984 to this survey question: *What is the biggest problem facing teenagers today?* Ask 15 students in your school the same question. Combine your results with those of other members of your class. How does current opinion in your school compare with public opinion in 1984? If there is a difference, how would you explain it?

3. WHAT IS POLITICAL PROPAGANDA?

Recall the story of Lois Gibbs of Love Canal, New York. To make others aware of her cause, she had to try to influence public opinion. She needed to let thousands of Americans know about the situation in her community. The only way she could effectively reach many people was through the mass media (television, radio, newspapers, magazines). The messages that she kept sending out to the press were one example of something we call *propaganda*.

What is propaganda? Propaganda is any message whose main purpose is to influence the opinion of many people. Such propaganda messages are part of our everyday lives. They come to our eyes and ears in an amazing variety of forms. Look over this list, for example. In just one day, how often do you see forms of propaganda like these:

- Advertisements on highway billboards
- Mass-produced letters and brochures dropped in your mailbox
- Commercial messages on radio and television
- SALE signs posted on store windows ("Buy now and save! 30–50% off!")
- Bumper stickers on cars

Advertising is the kind of propaganda that most of us know best. There are other kinds as well. Politicians and special-interest groups may spread their information and ideas through (*a*) press releases, (*b*) media events, and (*c*) speeches.

The press release. Your local newspaper is probably filled with news items such as these:

- RED CROSS LAUNCHES BLOOD DRIVE
- CANDIDATES TO ADDRESS CHAMBER OF COMMERCE
- CHURCH GROUP HOLDS ANNUAL PICNIC

Each article is like a free advertisement for the organization named in it. In fact, the organization itself (Red Cross, Chamber of Commerce, church) probably wrote the article and sent it to the newspaper. An article of this kind is known as a press release. It was released (sent) to the press (newspapers, radio and TV stations) by an organization that wants publicity for its special programs.

CIVILIZATION AGAINST THE GERMAN "MONSTER." This political cartoon was printed in a New York City newspaper in January, 1917—shortly before the United States declared war on Germany. Why is it an example of propaganda?

The media event. Many politicians today think that the best publicity is the kind that shows them on TV news shows. They often depend on media experts to help them plan their campaigns. Such experts advise candidates to do things that will attract TV cameras.

Let us imagine, for example, a candidate named Ronald Rinaldo. In a letter mailed to local TV stations, he announces that he will be leading a three-mile "Run for Ron" along a strip of beach. Because it is active and lends itself to film, the event is likely to be covered by the TV news. Made for the TV cameras, such an event is known as a *media event*.

CAMPAIGN SPEECH. What unspoken message is suggested to an audience by (1) the large number of CLINTON signs and (2) the display of several American flags?

THE WHISTLE-STOP SPEECH. In 1948, President Harry Truman campaigned from the rear platform of a train, delivering short speeches at each train stop. Why do you think this campaign technique is no longer popular?

The speech. Before the days of television, a politician's chief form of propaganda was a stand-up speech. Newspapers would quote an important speech at length. The crowds that gathered to listen to a speech would feel cheated if it lasted for only a few minutes. Years ago, many people liked long speeches. They went to hear them as a form of entertainment.

Audiences today are different. Accustomed to fast-changing images on television, many people have trouble sitting through an hour-long speech. Even so, shorter speeches are still made, and they still make news.

Common techniques. Most political speeches are written to affect your emotions. One speech may arouse your anger against some foreign enemy or danger. Another speech may make you feel a warm glow of pride in your country. Some speeches do both at once, arousing anger and pride in turn.

When you hear such speeches on radio or television, be careful. Your mind can be swept away by the powerful force of the speaker's words. Be alert for four common techniques of propaganda. Each may be illustrated by a speaker whom we shall call P. R. Suade.

1. Appeal to tradition. At the microphone, P. R. tells us: "George Washington pointed the way. Abraham Lincoln followed in his path, and ever since, we Americans have been guided by their wisdom. My opponent in this election proposes to strike out in an entirely different direction. She presumes to know better than our greatest leaders, Washington and Lincoln. Do not be deceived, my friends. Do not abandon all that this nation has held dear through 200 years of greatness."

P. R.'s reasoning goes something like this: (*a*) Washington and Lincoln were great American leaders. (*b*) If we recognize their greatness, then we should *always* follow in their paths. Do you think the second idea follows logically from the first idea? What flaw can you find in P. R.'s "appeal to tradition"?

*2. **Glittering generalities.*** The speech of P. R. Suade continues with another propaganda technique. "This great nation of ours—land of the free, home of the brave—was built by men and women who dared to live free and, if necessary, to die in freedom's cause. If elected, I promise you today that we will fearlessly go forward—ever forward—in the spirit of the pioneers. I will preserve free enterprise, strengthen equal rights, maintain justice for all, and work for peace with honor."

P. R.'s phrases may sound wonderful and cause admirers to clap and cheer. But stop to think. Have we learned anything at all about P. R.'s policies? What does the speaker mean exactly by going "forward—ever forward—in the spirit of the pioneers"? In looking closely at the speaker's "glittering generalities," we find no ideas and no information.

*3. **Name-calling.*** A skillful propagandist like P. R. switches back and forth between positive words (glittering generalities) and negative ones (name-calling). Speaking negatively, P. R. tells us: "Do not listen, my friends, to the enemies of democracy who oppose my program. They are like wolves in sheep's clothing ready to pounce as soon as we turn our backs. Now there are well-meaning lambs in this country who say we can trust the wolf. Fortunately, most Americans are not lambs or fools. We will not be deceived by liars who hold out one hand in friendship while the other hand holds a dagger."

Notice P. R.'s choice of words: "wolves in sheep's clothing . . . well-meaning lambs . . . liars." We feel *compelled* to agree with P. R. because, if we disagree, we may be counted as "lambs" and "fools." It is an emotional trap that some speakers set for their audiences. Do not fall into it.

BRINGING AMERICA BACK! What propaganda technique is illustrated by this 1984 campaign slogan?

*4. **Card-stacking.*** Facts as well as emotions play a part in P. R.'s speeches. Pointing to brightly colored charts, he tells us that "business has never been better. Just look at these figures:

- Sales of U.S. autos have risen 10 percent in three years.
- Sales of home appliances have risen 28 percent in only two years.
- The production of computers has shot up almost 50 percent in just one year."

P. R.'s facts may be accurate. But there are many other facts that are left out of the speech. Perhaps stock market prices have declined three years in a row. Such a fact would harm P. R.'s argument. So it is omitted. In other words, the "cards" (facts) are "stacked" in the speaker's favor.

A candidate's "image" on TV. A propaganda message may be conveyed to us through pictures as well as words. Television is, of course, a medium of pictures and sound. The effect of such a medium upon our opinions can be quite powerful. The four propaganda techniques described above can be seen in TV advertisements for political candidates. Let us imagine one such ad:

- Appeal to tradition: We see an American flag flapping in the breeze before we see or hear the candidate. This symbol leaves us with the impression that the candidate's ideas are patriotic.
- Glittering generalities: We see crowds of smiling people shaking the candidate's hand. Next, we see the candidate talking with workers at a factory. The candidate is saying "full steam ahead." But we learn very little information about the candidate. Nevertheless, we get the idea that the candidate is popular, likable, and caring.
- Name-calling: Pictures can be used negatively to show a candidate's opponent in a bad light. For example, there might be a scene of heavy city traffic—honking horns, faces of frustrated drivers. "Did you know," says a voice, "that Amanda Emerson voted to cut back spending for new roads? What can she be thinking of?" The ad does not directly call Emerson any names. But the disgusted faces on the TV screen speak louder than words.
- Card-stacking: Several achievements may be quickly flashed on the screen to show a candidate's strong points. What are the candidate's weak points? They are not mentioned.

Television ads usually contain little information. Instead, after being repeated again and again, they leave viewers with an overall impression. Left in our minds is an image of someone who seems to be a strong leader and likeable person. We will perhaps vote for that candidate. If so, the ad writer's propaganda techniques have succeeded.

The value of propaganda. We need to know how to recognize techniques of propaganda so as not to be fooled by them. On the other hand, we should not reject all propaganda, thinking that it is merely an attempt to deceive us. Many messages of persuasion, after all, serve a useful purpose. They can be both informative and inspiring.

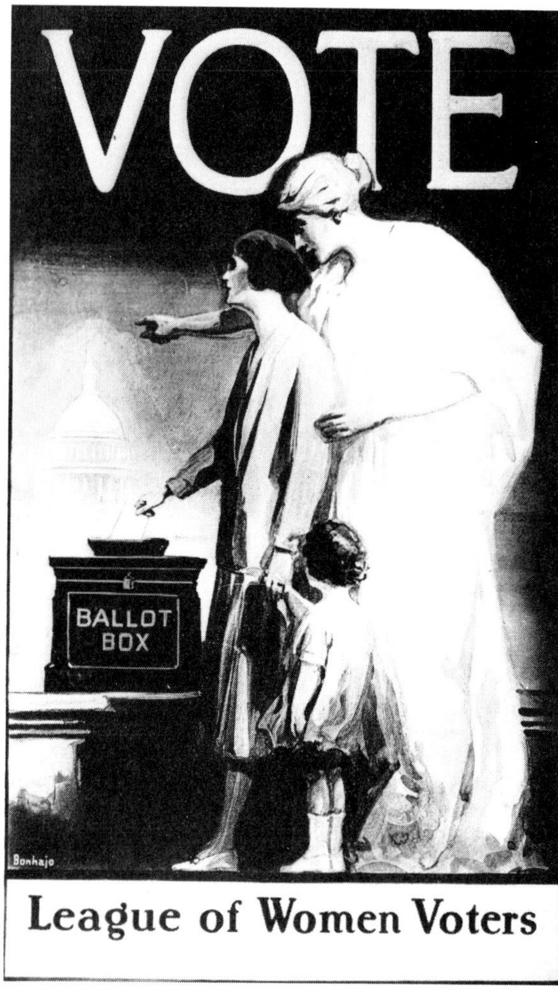

VOTE. How is this 1920s poster an example of both (*a*) the work of a public-interest group and (*b*) the use of propaganda to influence public opinion?

The Declaration of Independence is one example of this kind of propaganda. Thomas Jefferson's purpose in writing it was to influence public opinion in Europe and in the colonies. He wanted readers of the Declaration to think that Americans were right to fight for their independence. In accusing King George III of tyranny, Jefferson mentioned only those actions that put the king in a bad light. In other words, Jefferson "stacked the cards" against his opponent.

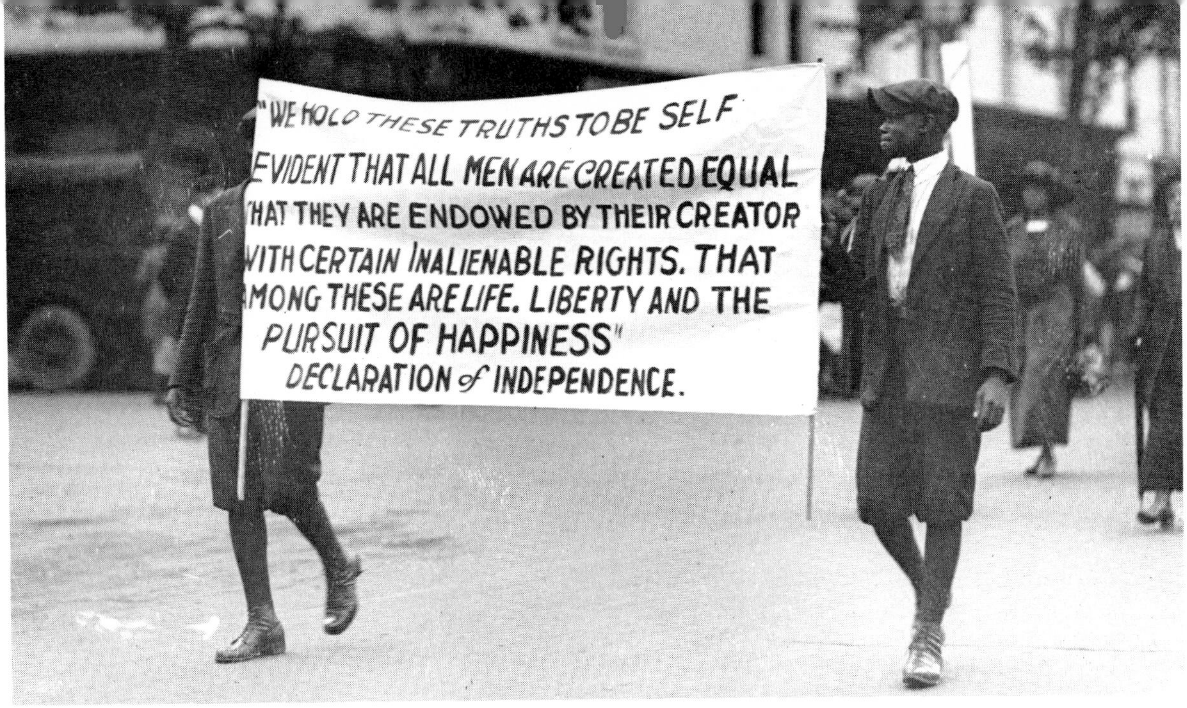

PROTEST MARCH, 1922. To protest racial injustice, these citizens quoted the Declaration of Independence. How is their banner an example of propaganda?

More important, the Declaration of Independence presented a valuable message. In its own time, it persuaded many people to believe in the American cause. In our time, it reminds us of the ideals of liberty and equality upon which our nation was founded. It is propaganda of a high order.

REVIEW

A. Applying What You Know

Each quotation below comes from a real speech or ad. Name the propaganda technique (or techniques) shown by each.

1. "We left America safe, we left America secure, we left America free, still a beacon of hope to mankind, still a light unto the nations."
—speech by Ronald Reagan, 1986

2. "The money changers have fled from their high seats in the temple of our civilization. We may now restore that temple to the ancient truths." (two techniques)
—speech by Franklin Roosevelt, 1933

3. "This is our hope. This is the faith that I will go back to the South with. With this faith we will be able to hew out of the mountain of despair a stone of hope."
—speech by Martin Luther King, Jr., 1963

B. Project

From a newspaper or a magazine, collect the following and attach them to separate sheets of paper. Analyze each as directed.

1. *Example of an advertisement that uses the technique of card-stacking.* Explain how the ad you selected illustrates the technique.
2. *Example of a newspaper editorial or a letter to the editor that uses name-calling.* Tell why you think it is an example of this technique.
3. *Example of a news article that probably started as a press release.* Identify the organization that probably wrote the press release.

CHAPTER REVIEW

A. Completing the Summary

Select terms from the word list to fill in the blanks in the summary below. Write your answers on a separate piece of paper.

campaigns	messages
card-stacking	name-calling
generalities	PACs
grass roots	polls
information	public
lobbyists	special-interest

You can influence the decisions of government either as a member of an organized group or as an individual. Organizations that try to influence government are known as __(1)__ groups. Those hired to persuade legislators to support or oppose certain bills are called __(2)__.

One hundred years ago, it was common for lawmakers to be "wined and dined" by those employed to influence them. Today, however, the __(3)__ provided by lobbyists is more likely to influence a lawmaker's decision than any other attempt at persuasion. Lobbyists may also organize a letter-writing campaign among members of an organization. In other words, lobbyists go to the __(4)__ to put pressure on legislators.

Making contributions of money to political __(5)__ is another method of gaining influence. Groups representing labor unions, business firms, and other interests organize committees for contributing money. Such committees, known as __(6)__, are regulated by law. Even so, people worry about the indirect influence that money may have on a congressperson's decisions.

Whether or not you belong to an interest group, you can still influence government as an individual. Your opinions become part of __(7)__ opinion when you express them in some way. Your thoughts influence others, just as the opinions of others influence you. You can communicate directly with your senator or representative by writing a letter about some issue that concerns you. Besides reading letters, lawmakers may also look at opinion __(8)__ to find out what their constituents are thinking.

Propaganda is a powerful force in shaping people's opinions. The term includes all the __(9)__ in the mass media that are designed to persuade the general public in some way. Candidates for office use different propaganda techniques in their speeches and TV ads. You cannot disagree with them if they use glittering __(10)__. The facts and opinions they present may sound convincing at first. But a cautious listener might suspect that the speaker is telling only part of the story. If so, the speaker is __(11)__. Another common technique is to refer to an opponent as a "bigot" . . . "a racist" . . . or worse. The propagandist hopes that you will accept this __(12)__ technique without stopping to think.

B. Examples of Main Ideas

The words in bold-face letters below are main ideas or concepts. Define each main idea, and then explain how each of the three terms following is an example of the idea.

1. **propaganda:** campaign button, media event, billboard advertisement
2. **special-interest group:** General Motors (a corporation), AFL-CIO (a labor union), Red Cross (a nonprofit organization)
3. **public opinion:** letter to the editor, mass demonstration, letter to a legislator

C. Organizing Information

Suppose that you are writing a short composition on the topic: **How people can influence the U.S. government.** You plan to organize your ideas under four main headings. Divide a piece of paper into four sections like this:

I.	II.
III.	IV.

After examining the list of phrases below, arrange them into four categories. Give a title to each category, and write it next to the roman numeral on your paper.

Finally, under each heading, list the phrases that you would include under that part of your essay.

LIST OF TOPICS

- organizing and contributing money to a PAC
- lobbyists' technique of appealing to the grass roots
- writing a letter to the editor
- writing a letter to your congressperson
- attaching a slogan to the bumper of your car
- sending press releases to TV stations and newspapers
- an informational strategy for influencing a lawmaker's vote
- political ad that consists of glittering generalities
- arguing with friends about the president's policies

D. Applying What You Know

Two readers of *Time* magazine wrote the following letters to the editor about the practice of lobbying. Read both letters and answer the questions that follow.

- To the Editors:

As a lobbyist, I find my job is one of educating busy legislators on matters that are minor to them but major to our industry. Protecting business interests is not always bad. I am continually amazed at how little lawmakers know about the effect a bill will have on the public.

- To the Editors:

I do not want a PAC or high-priced fat cat speaking for me. I am the lobbyist who should count. I vote.

1. Which of the letters was written by a lobbyist? Summarize this person's point of view about lobbying.
2. One of the letters includes an example of name-calling. Identify it and explain how it is an example of this technique.
3. Which letter comes closer to expressing your opinion of lobbying? Suppose that *you* had written that letter. Write an additional paragraph for the letter giving one more argument either for or against lobbying.

DEMOCRATIC CONVENTION, 1960. Adlai Stevenson and John Kennedy competed for their party's nomination in 1960. What is the role of political parties in the U.S. system?

CHAPTER 10

Choosing a Political Party

OBJECTIVES

After reading this chapter, you will know

1. the goals of an American political party.
2. why the United States is said to have a two-party system.
3. the differences and similarities between the Democratic and Republican parties.
4. how candidates are nominated by means of party primaries and conventions.
5. the role of minor parties in American politics.
6. how to research a selected topic in the library.

The auditorium in Los Angeles was packed with members of the Democratic party. Many in the crowd shouted: "We want Stevenson! We want Stevenson!" As trumpets blared and drums boomed, hundreds of men and women paraded up and down the aisles of the auditorium. The hats that they wore said STEVENSON. As the people marched, great bunches of golden balloons tumbled down from the ceiling.

Bobbing high over the Democrats' heads were tall signs that showed what states each group came from. There were signs for SOUTH CAROLINA . . . and VERMONT . . . and TEXAS . . . and Adlai Stevenson's home state, ILLINOIS.

Many times, the woman on the speaker's platform banged her gavel and shouted, "Order! Please clear the aisles." But Stevenson's supporters just kept on shouting, "We want Stevenson!" Finally, they settled back into their seats.

There were other demonstrations that night for other Democratic candidates. But the demonstration for Stevenson was the longest and the noisiest.

Finally, it was time for the thousands of Democrats in Los Angeles to vote for a candidate for president. They voted in groups, one state at a time, starting with the group from Alabama. Soon it became clear that Stevenson was *not* going to win—not this year. He had been the Democrats' candidate in 1952 and again in 1956. But this year, 1960, a young senator from Massachusetts was getting most of the Democrats' votes. His name was John F. Kennedy.

For many months, Kennedy had worked hard to make sure that more Democrats would vote for him than for Stevenson. And now, on this night in July, the votes were coming to him as expected.

The woman at the microphone was coming to the end of the list of states. "Wyoming," she said. Under the WYOMING sign, a Democratic politician stood up and announced: "Wyoming casts all fifteen votes for the next president of the United States, John Kennedy."

And so it happened that Kennedy, not Stevenson, became the candidate of the Democratic party in 1960. Later, Kennedy went on to defeat the Republican party's candidate, Richard M. Nixon, and thus became the 35th president of the United States.

THE DEMOCRATS' NOMINEE, JOHN KENNEDY. Many of the delegates who voted for Kennedy's nomination in 1960 were chosen at state primaries. What are primaries?

As you will see, Democrats have been nominating candidates for president—and for many other offices—ever since 1800. Republicans have done the same ever since 1856. Why do these parties exist? What functions do they perform in American government? After reading this chapter, you will know the answers to the following questions:

1. Why do we have political parties?
2. How do parties *nominate* candidates?
3. How do Democrats differ from Republicans?
4. Can minor parties succeed?

1. WHY DO WE HAVE POLITICAL PARTIES?

Nothing could be easier than joining an American political party. All you have to do is to say "I am a Republican," "I am a Democrat," or "I belong to Party X." Just identifying yourself with one party makes you a member of that party automatically. Leaders of the party will gladly accept you. They want your vote and support for the party's candidates.

Changing parties. Suppose that you call yourself a Democrat in January but change your mind a month later. Can you be a Republican on Valentine's Day after you had been a Democrat on New Year's Eve? The answer is yes. Do you have to notify party headquarters that you are leaving your old party and joining a new one? No. Belonging to an American political party just means that *you* have decided to belong.

There is also a formal and official way of announcing your choice of party. When registering to vote, you may be asked to write the party of your choice on the registration form. If you wish, you may write "none" or "independent," meaning that, at that moment, you choose not to be a member of any party. But if you name a party, then you become a "registered" member of that party.

Naming a party on the registration form does not commit you to much. In the general election in November, you can still vote for any candidate of any party. However, in some states, a "registered Democrat" cannot vote in Republican primaries and a "registered Republican" cannot vote in Democratic primaries. A primary is an election (before the main election in November) in which voters decide who will be their party's candidates for different offices. You will be learning more about primaries later in the chapter, pages 212–214.

Four kinds of party members. Some members of political parties are far more active than others. From the least active to the most active, these are the groups that make up an American political party:

1. Voters. In any party, this is the huge majority. They may be inactive members 364 days of the year. Only on the 365th day—Election Day—do they become active by going to the polls to vote for party candidates.

2. Occasional workers and contributors. From time to time, a few of the voters may decide to take an active part in an election campaign. They may take a special interest in a certain candidate and want to see that he or she wins. So they call up local leaders of the party and volunteer their time. They may be asked to address envelopes and mail out campaign letters. They may assist in calling up voters on the phone. Or they may donate a small sum of money to help pay some of their favorite candidate's campaign expenses.

3. Local leaders. These are members of a party who can be counted upon to work in *every* election. They hold party meetings at their homes. They collect donations and send out information. Above all, they keep in touch with other active members of the party. For them, politics is a major interest.

4. Professional politicians and candidates. The most active members of a party are those who devote full time to it. Included in this group are the party's candidates for different offices. Winning candidates receive salaries from the government for filling the offices to which they are elected. Then, if they want to continue in office, they must organize another campaign and win another election.

Also working full time at politics are party "bosses," who wield power behind the scenes. They work for the party as a whole, choosing candidates, raising funds, and organizing campaigns. Their goal is to build a party organization so strong that voters will turn out to vote a straight party ticket.

No rigid boundaries separate these four groups of party members. At any time, you can pass from a less active to a more active role—and vice versa. You may start out in party politics as a one-day-a-year voter. Then, just by volunteering to help in someone's campaign, you become an "occasional worker." Finally, you may become so interested in politics that you run for office yourself and turn into a "pro."

OHIO DELEGATES FOR KENNEDY. To become a delegate from their state, what kind of voluntary work did these Ohioans probably perform for their party?

The goal of winning elections. One purpose of American political parties is to win elections for their members. In fact, this may well be the *chief* reason that parties exist in the United States. The Republican and Democratic parties are little more than loose organizations for gaining votes at election time.

In other countries of the world, political parties exist for other reasons. In China, for example, the Communist party has no trouble winning elections. It cannot lose, because it is the only legal party. Its chief purpose is to decide how the government of China should be run.

American political parties also have a strong interest in running the government and making policy. But they can do so only if their candidates are voted into office. Therefore, parties in the United States concentrate their efforts on winning elections.

The rewards of victory. Why is it so important for parties to win elections? It is because of the political rewards that go to the winner. The main rewards are: (1) top jobs in government, (2) appointed jobs in government, and (3) power to make policy.

1. Top jobs in government. The most powerful jobs in the legislative and executive branches of government are usually reserved for winners of elections. In the national government, the president and all members of Congress are elected. In state government, the governor and all members of the state legislature are elected. In the government of cities and towns, the mayor and members of the local school board are elected.

Do you want to be a leader in government? If so, joining a party can help you win elections.

2. Appointed jobs in government. A president, a state governor, and a city mayor have the power to fill other jobs in government. The people they choose to assist them are almost always members of their own party. Instead of being elected, such people are *appointed* (named) to their offices. They are often the hardest-working members in the winning candidate's campaign. The reward for their political work is a government job with a good salary.

Those jobs that can be given out to party members are known as *patronage* jobs. Do not suppose, however, that all jobs in government are filled by politicians. In fact, the great majority are filled through a *civil service* system (described in Chapter 18). But the political, or patronage, jobs that do exist are among the highest-paying in government.

3. Power to make policy. Let us say that, in one election, the Republicans win more seats in Congress than the Democrats. The Republican candidate for president also wins. That means that the Republicans, as a party, have a chance to dominate the U.S. government. They may decide to raise taxes or to lower them. They may spend more on defense than on education, or vice versa. In other words, they are in a strong position to put into effect the laws and policies that they favor.

Because of the success of their candidates, they belong to the more powerful party—the IN party. But they realize that they must govern well. Otherwise, they may be blamed for governing badly by the voters. Then the OUT party is likely to take over after the next election as the IN party.

REVIEW

A. Who, How, and Why

Explain the special character of American parties by answering these questions.

1. Who can join an American political party?
2. If you wish to change from one political party to another, how do you go about doing it?

3. How does the Chinese political party system differ from the American party system?
4. How do candidates who win in an election often reward those who worked hardest for them?
5. Who are the least active and most numerous members of a political party? Why are they also the most important to the party's success?

B. Project

Answer the questions below. Use an almanac or other reference book.

1. Which party today has a majority of seats in the U.S. Senate? In the U.S. House of Representatives?
2. In your state, which party has the most seats in the legislature?
3. What is the political party of (*a*) the president and (*b*) your state governor?
4. Would you say the Republicans or the Democrats are currently the more powerful party in your state? Why?

2. HOW DO PARTIES NOMINATE CANDIDATES?

Just as an athletic team needs to recruit strong players, a political party needs to recruit strong candidates. Among the millions who belong to a party, who is best able to win the confidence of voters? A party's hope for success depends on how well it can answer this question.

Recall that only a small percentage of party members spend much time working at party business. Naturally, the most active members are the ones with the most influence when it comes to choosing the party's candidates. We call them the leadership group. The others—the voters and occasional volunteers—are sometimes referred to as the party's *rank and file*.

In the past, the members of the leadership group had much greater power than they do today. Let us see how they gradually lost some of their power to the rank and file.

The caucus and the convention. Turn the clock back to 1801. This was Thomas Jefferson's first year as president. At that time, the leaders of a party were usually members of the U.S. Congress or of their state legislature. After a day of lawmaking, they might meet together in a private room to discuss party business. Such a closed gathering was called a *caucus.*

As they sat around a candlelit table, the party leaders would draw up a list of candidates for different offices. Their choices then became the party's nominees for office. A nominee is any candidate who is officially named—or nominated—by a political party.

The caucus system for nominating candidates did not last long because people viewed it as undemocratic. In the 1820s and 1830s, it became common for parties to hold conventions. These were large gatherings that were open to some members of the rank and file as well as the party leadership. At state conventions, held every year or two, the chief business was to nominate candidates for different offices. Thus, the closed-door caucus of old was replaced by an open meeting of party members: the convention.

How "bosses" used to control parties. Not everybody could attend a party's convention. Those who did come were delegates (party representatives) from different counties and communities. Each delegate could cast one vote for a candidate. Often, however, delegates voted the way state "bosses" ordered them to vote. They did not have a free choice.

Why would delegates allow themselves to be bossed? To understand it, you must know how American parties are organized at the local level.

BOSS TWEED. The central "vulture" in the cartoon was William Tweed, the boss of the Democratic party in New York City in the 1860s. Tweed was jailed for using his power to enrich himself at the public's expense. Can there be such a thing as a "good" party boss?

Think of the political map of your home state as a kind of checkerboard. (See page 213.) The board (map) shows a local unit, a county, within the state. Counties in turn are divided into smaller units called cities, villages, towns, and townships. A major city may be divided again into sections called wards. Finally, each ward is subdivided into neighborhoods of only a few city blocks. Such neighborhood areas are called precincts.

Every political unit, large or small, has its own committee of party leaders to look after the politics of that area. Every county has a committee of party leaders. Every city ward has a committee, and so on. At the head of each committee is a chairperson.

One hundred years ago, before women could vote, the committee head was always a man. Often he was also very powerful and could "boss" other members of the committee. If you dared to challenge the *boss*, you would swiftly be fired from your job in city hall. Delegates picked by a boss to go to a convention could be counted upon to do as they were told.

In theory, the party conventions of old were supposed to speak and act for the rank and file. In fact, they often spoke only for the bosses.

Then, in the early 1900s, the bosses' grip on power began to weaken when large numbers of voters began protesting against "boss rule." In one state after another, a new system replaced the convention as the chief means for nominating party candidates. It was called the direct *primary*.

How the primary works. A primary is a special election among party members that precedes the general election in November. On a certain date early in the year, voters go to their local polling places and make their choice of candidates on a ballot. The day for this election is set by a state's law. When the ballots are counted, a party member receiving the most votes is declared the official nominee of his or her party. Since two or more political parties exist in every state, several candidates may be nominated for the same office—but *only one candidate per party*.

As an example, take the office of state governor. Let us say that three Republicans are competing in the Republican primary. Call them Alfred X, Barbara Y, and Charles Z. Barbara Y gets the most Republican votes and thus becomes the Republican nominee for governor.

At the same time, two Democrats—Samuel P and Theresa Q—are listed in the

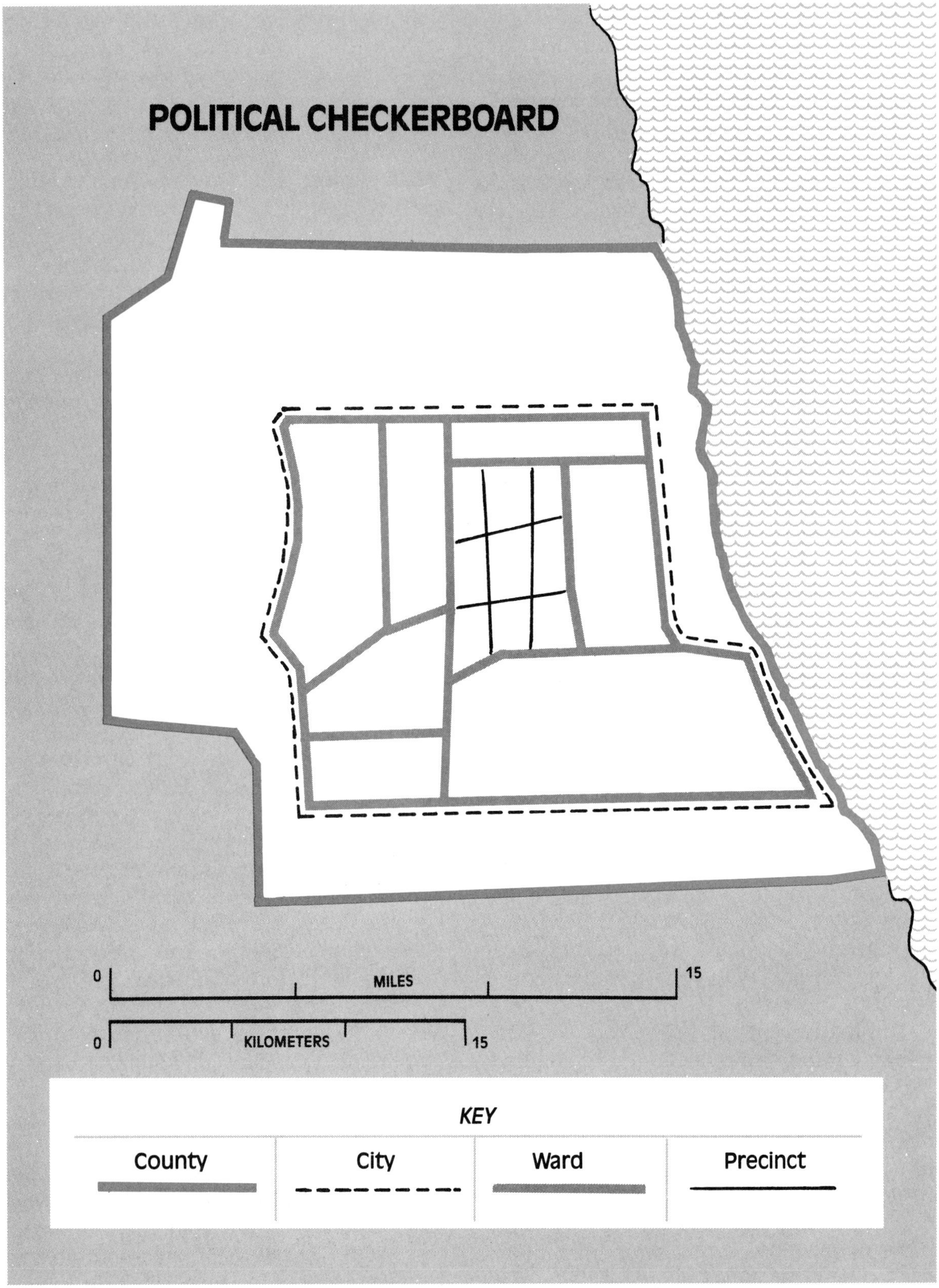
POLITICAL CHECKERBOARD
0
MILES
15
0
KILOMETERS
15
KEY
County
City
Ward
Precinct

primary on the Democratic ballot. Samuel P wins the most Democratic votes to become the Democratic nominee.

Finally, in the general election in November, the contest is between Samuel P (Democrat) and Barbara Y (Republican). Who wins? Since the race is imaginary, your guess is as good as anyone's!

Two kinds of primaries. Must you be registered as a member of a party before you can vote in that party's primary? In some states, yes; in other states, no.

The most common method for nominating party candidates is the closed primary. One ballot listing Democratic candidates is for voters who are registered as Democrats. A separate ballot listing Republican candidates is presented to registered Republicans. If you are Republican, you cannot cross over to mark the Democratic ballot. Nor can a Democratic voter mark the Republican ballot.

What if a person is independent and belongs to no party? The so-called independent cannot vote at all in the closed primary.

Other rules apply in those states that have open primaries. Republicans may, if they wish, make choices on the Democratic ballot. And Democrats have an opportunity to mark the Republican ballot. The ballots are kept separate. With the exception of two states, you cannot choose among the Republican candidates for governor and then switch parties to choose some Democrat for U.S. senator.

The two exceptions to this rule are the western states of Alaska and Washington. In their "wide open" primaries, you can switch back and forth between parties as often as you like. Voting in such a primary is just like voting in a general election. Instead of two party ballots, there is only one. It lists everyone who wants his or her party nomination. Let us say nominations are being made for five offices. You can vote for three Republicans and two Democrats or four Democrats and one Republican—any combination adding up to five.

The run-off. Often, in a primary election (whether open or closed), there may be a large number of candidates in the same party competing for nomination to the same office. Suppose that a candidate does not receive a majority (more than half) of the votes cast. In some states, the nominee is the person who receives a plurality (more votes than anyone else).

In other states, however, the law may require that there be a second primary following the first. In this run-off primary, the two candidates winning the most votes in the earlier election are placed on the ballot. Then a majority of voters decides between them.

Role of the party's committees. What ever happened to the party "bosses" mentioned earlier? Because of the primary system, their power has declined. Even so, parties still rely on committees to lead them at different levels of government. Heading each committee is a chairperson who devotes a lot of time to the business of party nominations.

Suppose you are thinking of running for sheriff of your county. One of the first persons you would want to see is the chairperson of your party's county committee. Let us call her Martha Powers. As an experienced politician, she knows people who can help you win the primary.

On the other hand, Powers may try to discourage you from getting into the race. "You're not experienced enough," she may tell you. "And besides, my committee thinks Don Watson deserves the nomination."

Even without the support of the party leadership, your name can be placed on the primary ballot along with Watson's and any other candidate's. But your chances of success would be better if the committee in your area is behind you.

CARTOON CORNER

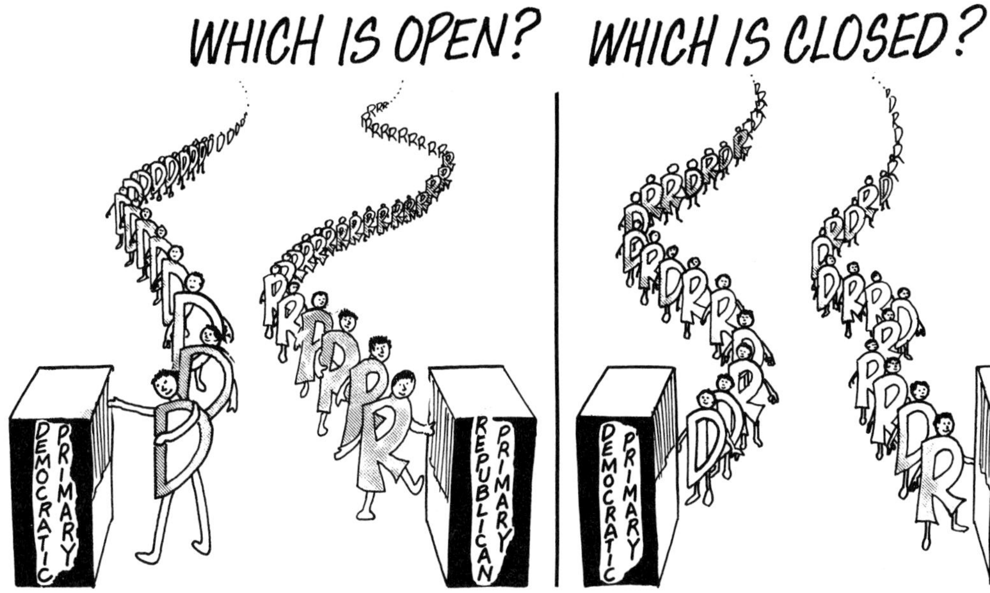

REVIEW

A. Building Your Political Vocabulary

Complete each sentence, using one of these terms:

caucus	closed primary
convention	run-off
open primary	rank and file
"boss"	precinct

1. A voter who is "independent" is not allowed to participate in a (n) __(1)__.
2. Meeting in __(2)__ in 1816, members of Congress decided that James Monroe should be their party's nominee for president.
3. If you are a registered Democrat, you are one of millions who belong to the __(3)__ of the Democratic party.
4. In some states, it is necessary to hold a (n) __(4)__ election if several candidates have competed for the same nomination.
5. Before 1900, the most powerful party leader in a state was known as that party's __(5)__.
6. A party's __(6)__ committee may be responsible for supervising the politics of only a few city blocks.
7. In a (n) __(7)__, you do not have to vote for a member of your party.
8. To nominate candidates for governor, party delegates from around the state would meet in a __(8)__.

B. Making Comparisons

1. If Arthur Jones wanted his party's nomination for mayor in 1890, how would he go about getting it?

2. If Maria Hayashida wanted her party's nomination for mayor next year, how would she go about getting it?
3. Which system do you think is better: (*a*) the system of 1890 or (*b*) the system of today? Why do you think so?

C. Cartoon Corner

In the cartoon on page 215, the **D** voters are Democrats, while the **R** voters are Republicans.

1. Which panel of the cartoon (left or right) illustrates a closed primary? Explain.
2. Which panel of the cartoon illustrates an open primary? Explain.
3. How does a "wide open" primary in Alaska differ from the open primary in the cartoon?

3. HOW DO DEMOCRATS DIFFER FROM REPUBLICANS?

So far in this chapter, only two parties have been mentioned: the Republican party and the Democratic party. That is because, for more than 100 years, almost all nationally elected officials in the United States have belonged to one of these parties. As we shall see, many other American parties have also existed—and continue to exist. But rarely do the nominees of the minor parties win election.

Therefore, Americans are said to have a two-party system.

Three stages in American political history. How and when did the two-party system originate? As time passed, how did the two major parties change? These questions can be answered briefly if we divide U.S. history into three periods of political development.

- The **first period** lasted about 70 years from the election of George Washington in 1788 to the election of Abraham Lincoln in 1860.
- The **second period** also lasted about 70 years. It began with the crisis of the Civil War (1861–65). It ended with another crisis: the collapse of the American economy in the Great Depression (1929–1933).
- The **third period** started with the presidency of Franklin D. Roosevelt in the 1930s and continued through the 1980s to the present.

Let us see how two major parties developed in each of these historic periods.

Parties before the Civil War. In 1796, at the end of his presidency, George Washington warned Americans about the dangers of organizing political parties. He said parties would tend to divide the country. And yet, during Washington's presidency, two major parties were already taking shape. The leaders of both had once been President Washington's closest friends and advisers. They were Thomas Jefferson of Virginia and Alexander Hamilton of New York.

Hamilton founded the Federalist party in the 1790s. Its main support came from bankers and merchants. To oppose Hamilton's policies and ambitions, Thomas Jefferson founded the Democratic-Republican party. Its main support came from farmers. In 1800, the Democratic-Republicans scored their first great victory by electing Jefferson president.

The Federalists did poorly in the next few elections. After 1820, their party ceased to exist. However, another party very similar to it came into being. Members of this new party called themselves Whigs. Their most famous candidate was a tall, tobacco-chewing senator from Kentucky, Henry Clay. But the Whigs too failed to elect enough candidates. They also died out as a major party. Their place was taken by a new party consisting mainly of Western farmers and Northerners opposed to slavery. They called themselves Republicans. Founded in 1854, the Republican party attracted to it a lanky lawyer from Illinois: Abraham Lincoln.

Through all these years (1800–1854) Jefferson's party—the Democratic-Republicans—grew in strength. In the 1830s, during the presidency of Andrew Jackson, it dropped the Republican part of its name. Ever since, it has been called the Democratic party.

What did members of the two major parties argue about in these years? A chief issue was states' rights. Democrats, particularly in the South, thought the different states should be permitted a great deal of freedom. Their opponents (Federalists, Whigs, and Republicans) were more interested in seeing the national government grow strong.

Between the Civil War and the Great Depression. The argument over states' rights was finally settled—not by party ballots—but by soldiers' bullets. Southern Democrats hated to see a Republican like Abraham Lincoln elected president in 1860. They feared that he meant to end their practice of slavery. War broke out between the North and the South when Southern states tried to leave the Union. The former Democrat who led the Southern states in these war years was Jefferson Davis of Mississippi.

As you know, the North won the war. Republican leaders of Congress accused Southern Democrats such as Davis of being traitors. For many years afterward, Republican politicians in the North won elections by reminding voters of the thousands of Northern soldiers killed in the Civil War.

In the South, voters remembered all too well the occupation of their lands by Northern troops during the post-war period called Reconstruction. They had bitter feeling about the Republican government of the North, and, therefore, Southerners almost always elected Democrats to office.

Another issue that challenged and changed the two parties was the rising power of big business. For a while, it seemed that railroad companies and other businesses could buy votes in a state legislature. Big business could use their money and influence to pass laws that gave them special privileges. When a politician accepts bribes from rich supporters, it is known as corruption.

In the early 1900s, a Republican president, Theodore Roosevelt, made himself popular with voters by trying to regulate big business. Later, a Democratic president, Woodrow Wilson, did much the same thing. Because of their leadership, the two major parties became less corrupt. Also, businesses came to be regulated by laws enforced by the national government.

The next major change in the two parties came about as a result of an economic disaster. The Republicans were in power in 1929 when the stock market collapsed and a terrible depression began. Millions of people were thrown out of work. They blamed the Republicans for their trouble and turned to new leadership from the Democratic party. In 1932, they elected as their new president a New York Democrat named Franklin D. Roosevelt.

Major parties in our own times. Roosevelt changed the character of his party and of American politics. Ever since his presidency, Democrats have been known for their programs of social welfare. They started the *Social Security system* for retired people. They gave help to labor unions. They helped poor people, farmers, and members of racial minorities. As a result, Democrats gained a reputation for championing liberal causes. Democratic presidents of the 1960s—John F. Kennedy and Lyndon B. Johnson—expanded the liberal programs that began under Roosevelt.

THREAT TO LIBERTY. What political issue of the 1880s and 1890s is the subject of this cartoon?

As the opposition party, Republicans fought the social programs of the Democrats. They objected to them as "giveaway" programs. Gradually, the Republicans gained a reputation of being more conservative than the Democrats. Republican presidents such as Richard Nixon and Ronald Reagan attempted to apply brakes to the liberal programs of the Democrats.

In brief, that is the story of how our two major parties have developed over the past 200 years. In the next century, the parties may change again. Whether they do or not, you will have a lifetime to observe what happens. In addition, by voting often, you will influence the future of American politics.

Party traditions. Democratic politicians tend to be proud of what their party has accomplished in its long history. They love to talk of their past heroes: Thomas Jefferson, "FDR" (Franklin D. Roosevelt), and "Jack" Kennedy.

Republicans are just as proud of their own party and its heroes: "Abe" Lincoln, "Teddy" Roosevelt, and "Ike" Eisenhower. They speak fondly of their party as the *GOP* (short for Grand Old Party).

One hundred years ago, a famous cartoonist named Thomas Nast poked fun at the two major parties. He portrayed the Republican party as a clumsy elephant and the Democratic party as a stubborn donkey. After a while, members of both parties took a liking to the animal symbols. Democrats adopted the donkey as their party symbol. The elephant represented the Republicans.

Party conventions. Each party has a huge membership, numbering in the millions. Each party consists of thousands of local groups. One group, for example, is made up of Republican leaders from Montpelier, Vermont. In another group are Democratic leaders from Little Rock, Arkansas. A Republican group in Hawaii may have little in common with a Republican group in Rhode Island. Nevertheless, once every four years, party delegates from all 50 states meet at a national convention.

SYMBOLS. The GOP elephant carries the Republican candidates (left). The donkey was an ornament on a Democrat's Christmas tree (right).

Recall how this chapter began with shouts of "We want Stevenson!" The people making all the noise were delegates to the national convention of the Democratic party in 1960. National conventions are held for two main reasons: (1) to nominate a candidate for president and (2) to draw up a party platform. How presidential candidates are nominated will be explained in Chapter 11.

Party platforms. What is a *platform?* As the word implies, it is something upon which a party can stand. But instead of a wooden stage, a party platform is a written statement of ideas and principles. It states the party's current positions on a number of issues. Specific parts of a platform are known as planks.

Imagine the job of writing a lengthy document that hundreds of convention delegates can agree upon. For example, how can city delegates understand the concerns of rural delegates? It is difficult. But after much argument, a platform gets written by a committee of delegates from various regions. It is then submitted to the whole convention for a vote.

Once written, a platform is almost always accepted by the delegates. They may not like everything in it. But they realize how necessary it is to compromise. After all, an American political party consists of a great variety of people from different regions of the country. If they are to win a national election, the different groups must find a way to unite behind one platform and one candidate. A unified platform helps the party to achieve its most important goal: victory on Election Day.

After a long week of platform-writing, speechmaking, and compromising, the delegates wearily depart. The national convention is over. Another four years will pass before they meet again in another convention in some other city.

SKILLS CHECK: Researching a topic

Below and on pages 221–222 is a feature entitled FAMOUS MATCHUPS. It shows six pairs of political opponents from past elections. The captions tell who won each election, or "matchup."

Suppose that you wanted to find out more about the last of the featured matchups: CARTER *v.* REAGAN. What library sources would you use to research the topic? Below is a list of books and reference tools that you might or might not use. For each source, say whether or not it would probably give information about your topic (Carter *v.* Reagan in the election of 1980). Answer **yes** or **no** and explain.

Would you use . . .

1. An article on "political parties" in the **P** volume of the *Encyclopaedia Britannica?*
2. A book by Jimmy Carter (copyright 1987) in the biography section of the library?
3. A book entitled *Presidential Elections, 1960–1984.*
4. *Webster's Dictionary* under "Election"?
5. In one of the **R** drawers of the card catalog, books listed under the subject heading: REAGAN, RONALD?
6. The 1979 edition of the *World Almanac and Book of Facts?*
7. The 1983 volume of the *Readers' Guide to Periodical Literature?*
8. A book entitled *American Political Parties From the Civil War to the Great Depression?*

FAMOUS MATCHUPS IN THE HISTORY OF U.S. POLITICAL PARTIES

Every election for president is a colorful episode in the history of American political parties. Here is a summary of six great "matchups" between **Democrats** (on the left) and **Federalists-Whigs-Republicans** (on the right).

1. THOMAS JEFFERSON *v.* JOHN ADAMS
Democratic-Republican Federalist

This great contest for the presidency occurred in 1800. Jefferson had the enthusiastic support of farmers in the South and West. Adams was the incumbent president. His chief support for re-election came from New England merchants. Each candidate warned that the country would go to ruin if his opponent won. Jefferson won the matchup—and the country did not go to ruin.

2. ANDREW JACKSON *v.* HENRY CLAY
Democrat Whig

Hero of the Western farmer, "Andy" Jackson founded the modern Democratic party. Also popular in the West, Clay was a Whig leader of the House of Representatives who opposed President Jackson's policies. Jackson proved the more popular of the two. In 1832, he was re-elected president, defeating Clay by a huge margin.

3. STEPHEN DOUGLAS *v.* ABRAHAM LINCOLN
Democrat Republican

Douglas was a famous U.S. senator from Illinois when he debated Lincoln (also from Illinois) on the slave issue in 1858. Lincoln, the Republican challenger for Douglas's Senate seat, was relatively unknown. Douglas won this election. But two years later, in 1860, there was a rematch. This time, running for president, Lincoln defeated Douglas. A unified Republican party won over a Democrat party split over the slavery issue.

4. WOODROW WILSON *v.* THEODORE ROOSEVELT
Democrat Progressive

"Teddy" Roosevelt had been a popular Republican president for eight years before retiring from politics. In 1912, he decided he wanted to be president again as the candidate of a new party—the Progressive party. The Democrats nominated a Southern-born professor, Woodrow Wilson. No Southerner had been elected president since before the Civil War. But Wilson defeated both Roosevelt and the Republican candidate, William Howard Taft.

5. HARRY TRUMAN *v.* THOMAS DEWEY
Democrat Republican

As president from 1945 to 1948, Harry S Truman had a lot of problems at home and abroad. His liberal position on civil rights offended many Southern Democrats. Therefore, in 1948, few people expected Truman to be elected. His Republican opponent, Thomas Dewey, was thought to be a sure winner. Hours after the election, a few newspapers in the East and Midwest declared that Dewey had won. But soon afterward, when *all* the votes had been counted, Truman had the last laugh, squeezing out a narrow victory.

6. JIMMY CARTER *v.* RONALD REAGAN
Democrat Republican

In 1980, a former movie star and governor of California, Ronald Reagan, challenged a former peanut farmer and governor of Georgia, Jimmy Carter, for the presidency. As the incumbent president, Carter was sometimes liberal, sometimes conservative. Reagan, a staunch conservative, promised to take the country to the right. After his landslide victory, he kept his promise.

ISSUES AND ANSWERS. Democrats Bill Clinton (top right) and Al Gore clashed on major issues with Republicans George Bush (bottom right) and Dan Quayle. Why did the Democrats win?

Clinton v. Bush, 1992. Elections of the past have made the Democratic and Republican parties what they are today. Each party contains a mixture of individuals who hold different beliefs on current issues. In both parties, you will find liberals, moderates, and conservatives. However, *most* Republicans are more conservative in their views than are *most* Democrats.

In national politics, how does the Democratic party differ from the Republican party on specific issues? One way to express the difference is to compare the views of the Democratic and Republican candidates for president in 1992. Their positions on key issues are summarized on page 223.

Use the information in the chart to help you decide a crucial question in your future life as a voter. When you vote, will you tend to support Democratic candidates or Republican candidates? Or will a candidate's party be of no importance?

CANDIDATES' POSITIONS ON ISSUES, 1992

	George Bush (Republican)	Bill Clinton (Democrat)	Ross Perot (Independent)
Economic policy	Proposed (1) cutting the tax on capital gains (profits from investments) to encourage businesses to expand; (2) supporting tax credits for businesses in poor urban neighborhoods.	Proposed (1) apprenticeship program for young workers; (2) spending billions of dollars a year on rebuilding U.S. highways, bridges, and other public structures needing repair.	Proposed (1) eliminating capital gains taxes for investment in new small businesses; (2) cutting spending by U.S. government by as much as 10 percent.
Tax policy	Suggested 1 percent cut in income tax rate for all taxpayers *if* Congress agreed to cut government spending by an equivalent amount.	Promised to cut taxes of middle class and raise tax rate of high-income persons (individuals earning more than $150,000 a year).	Proposed raising taxes on gasoline by 50 cents a gallon over a five-year period.
Education policy	Proposed allowing parents free choice in sending children to either private school or public school. Government would help pay for child's education at either type of school.	Opposed idea of government funds going to private schools. Supported free choice among public schools only.	Supported idea of choice among public schools and trying out idea of private school choice on a limited and experimental basis.
Health care and health insurance	Favored (1) setting upper limit on patients' claims in malpractice lawsuits against doctors; (2) allowing self-employed persons to deduct from their taxes the full cost of health insurance.	Favored (1) providing health insurance for all Americans (2) creating a national heath board to set budget limits on public spending for health care.	Proposed setting up a national board to oversee health care costs and to direct efforts at reforming health care industry.

REVIEW

A. Making Comparisons

Divide a piece of paper into two columns. Label one column **Republican** and the other column **Democratic.** Below is a scrambled set of names and terms. Unscramble them by listing all Democratic items in one column, all Republican items in another.

Ronald Reagan - donkey - elephant - GOP - Andrew Jackson - Abraham Lincoln - states' rights - Franklin D. Roosevelt - liberal - Thomas Jefferson - Theodore Roosevelt - founded in 1854

B. Cause and Effect

1. Why did the Civil War cause a major change in the Republican and Democratic parties?
2. Why did the Great Depression bring about an important change in the two major parties?

C. What's Wrong?

Each sentence below is inaccurate. On a piece of paper, **rewrite** the sentence to make it correct.

1. Each major party sends delegates to a national convention every two years.

2. After the Civil War in the 1860s, the Republican party was most popular in the South.
3. In our own time, politicians in the Republican party have been generally more liberal than politicians in the Democratic party.
4. A platform is one section of a party's plank.
5. George Washington favored the idea of a two-party system.
6. The Democratic-Republican party changed its name to become the Republican party.

4. CAN MINOR PARTIES SUCCEED?

There is no legal limit to the number of parties that may form in the United States. In fact, in 1988, more than 20 different parties nominated candidates for president. Yet you rarely hear about these other parties or their candidates. They are too small compared to the major parties. In 1992 an independent candidate received the highest percentage of votes for the presidency since 1912.

Smaller parties are known as either *third parties* or minor parties. Why do they have such a hard time competing with Republicans and Democrats?

"Winner take all." Let us imagine that candidates of four parties want to be elected to one seat in Congress. The votes are counted, and this is the result. (Party names are in parentheses.)

Lopez (Democratic)	110,322
Baldwin (Republican)	56,630
Lowenherz (Libertarian)	25,221
Blackman (Right to Life)	13,333

Who will be going to Congress? Some countries of the world would give three seats to the three candidates winning the most votes (Lopez, Baldwin, and Lowenherz). But in the United States, only one candidate (Lopez) can win the one available seat. The other candidates come away with nothing.

We have a "winner-take-all" system. Therefore, minor parties have a difficult time winning even a few seats in the legislature. Their candidates win votes, but seldom enough votes to beat their better-known Republican and Democratic rivals.

Parties with one candidate. Another weakness of some third parties is that they exist for just one candidate. Take, for example, the story of Governor George Wallace of Alabama. Wallace was a Democrat for most of his career. But in 1968, he decided to leave the Democratic party and run for president on his own. As expected, he came in third in the race behind the Republican, Richard Nixon, and the Democrat, Hubert Humphrey. After the election of 1968, George Wallace's party ceased to exist. It was not really a national party at all—just a local organization to support one candidate for one office in one race.

More recently, in the presidential election of 1992, H. Ross Perot was an independent candidate who posed a significant challenge to the candidates of the two major parties. (For a case study of this election and Perot's role in it, see pages 241–246.) The thousands of volunteers who campaigned for Perot were not a true political party. They represented a loose political movement that went by the name "United We Stand." Their one goal was to elect Ross Perot president and his running mate, James Stockdale, vice president. The Perot-Stockdale ticket won 19 percent of the popular vote—a strong showing when compared with most other independent or minor party candidates. Even so, the winner of the election, Bill Clinton, won more than twice as many votes as Perot. In a race for president, even when an independent gets a lot of votes, it has never been enough for victory.

Parties with one idea. Another type of third party can expect to last a little longer than the one-candidate party. It is the type that comes into being to campaign for a single idea. Here are two examples:

- After the Civil War, the Greenback party wanted the U.S. government to issue paper money (greenbacks) so that farmers could more easily pay their debts. Candidates of the Greenback party talked of nothing else except the need for greenback dollars. After losing elections from 1876 to 1884, the Greenback party stopped competing and eventually died out.

- Members of the Prohibition party were united in a single cause. They wanted to stop their fellow citizens from drinking liquor, beer, and wine. Their first candidate for president was nominated (and defeated) in 1872.

Failure to win elections did not stop the Prohibitionists from winning one great victory. In 1919, the Eighteenth Amendment for which they had worked was added to the U.S. Constitution. From then until the amendment was repealed in 1933, no alcoholic beverage could legally be sold in the United States.

Why do parties with just one idea have trouble electing candidates? It is because one idea never attracts a large enough number of voters. A small minority may be enthusiastic about a certain idea for a new law. But only majorities win elections, not minorities. To form a majority, a party needs to appeal to many different groups with many different ideas. Democrats and Republicans both understand this basic fact of political life. That is why they have been successful.

The influence of third parties. The candidates of third parties always start out as dark horses in a race. But sometime they *do* win. The city of Milwaukee, Wisconsin, once elected a candidate of the Socialist party. More recently, in the 1960s, New York City had a mayor named John Lindsay, who was a candidate of the Liberal party.

Probably the most famous third party in American history was the People's party,

AN INDEPENDENT. Thousands of volunteers helped Texas billionaire H. Ross Perot campaign for the presidency in 1992. Why did most news commentators assume that Perot could not win? Why were they surprised when he received 19 percent of the popular vote?

better known as the Populist party. It consisted mainly of Southern and Western farmers who were tired of being taken for granted by the two major parties. In their first national convention in 1892, the Populists adopted a platform presenting their ideas for reform:

1. The federal government should own and operate the railroads.
2. A great number of silver coins should be minted to help farmers pay their debts.
3. Rich people should pay an income tax.
4. U.S. senators should be elected directly by the people, instead of by state legislatures.
5. A president of the United States should serve only one term of office.
6. Immigration to the United States should be restricted.
7. Workers should have a shorter working day.

POPULIST LEADER, MARY LEASE. This reformer from Kansas wanted the rich to pay an income tax and railroads to be publicly owned. How did her third party (the People's party) both succeed and fail?

THE POPULIST-DEMOCRAT. In 1896 and 1900, William Jennings Bryan was the presidential candidate of both the Democratic party and the Populist party. What symbols are used to represent the two parties? Do you think the cartoonist was or was not a Populist?

The Populists won a few seats in their state legislatures, but that was all. Even so, their ideas had influence. Their loud cries for reform made the other parties pay attention to farmers' needs. About 25 years after they wrote their first platform, two of the Populists' ideas became part of the U.S. Constitution. Today, we pay an income tax and vote directly for U.S. senators largely because of the demands made by the Populists.

So we see that third parties can be important even if they rarely win elections. They put pressure on the two major parties to pay attention to different minorities. They come up with new ideas for reforming the political system. Sometimes, their ideas are adopted by the major parties and turned into laws.

REVIEW

A. Cause and Effect

For each pair of phrases below, tell which is the **cause** and which is the **effect.** Then explain how one causes (or caused) the other.

1. Direct election of U.S. senators—Platform of Populist party
2. "Winner take all"—Failure of most third party candidates
3. Founding of a third party—Failure of two major parties to pay attention to certain voters

B. Applying What You Know

Think of one public issue that concerns you. Then:

1. Write two or three sentences saying what you think should be done about this issue.
2. Write the name of a new political party that might be formed to campaign for your idea.
3. Tell whether you think such a party would be likely to have much influence. In your answer, refer to the success or failure of a third party from the past or present.

CHAPTER REVIEW

A. Completing the Summary

Select terms from the word list to fill in the blanks in the summary below. Write your answers on a piece of paper.

boss	Populist
committees	primary
conservative	rank and file
conventions	states' rights
corruption	third
elections	two-party
Federalist	voting
nominate	winner-take-all
open	

In the United States, a political party is a large group of citizens and office-seekers whose main goal is to help win __(1)__ for members of the party. Although a number of parties compete for votes, the United States is said to have a __(2)__ system dominated by Republicans and Democrats.

One of the main functions of a political party is to __(3)__ candidates for office. An early method for selecting party candidates was by caucus. But in the early 1800s, this method was replaced by party __(4)__. Not only the leaders but also the __(5)__ of the party took part in these large gatherings.

The most democratic method for choosing candidates is to hold __(6)__ elections before the general election in November. How such elections are held differs from state to state. For example, the choice of Democratic nominees may be either __(7)__ to all voters or limited to registered Democrats.

Each party is organized into different local committees, state __(8)__, and a national committee. At the local level, one powerful party leader may be referred to as the party __(9)__. In the past, such leaders often controlled the politics of big cities.

The history of the two major parties goes back to the 1790s when Alexander Hamilton led the __(10)__ party, while Thomas Jefferson led the Democratic-Republicans. In the early 1800s, the two parties debated the issues of slavery and __(11)__. Then, in the period after the Civil War, political __(12)__ became a major issue. The third major period in American political history was dominated by the liberal policies of Franklin Roosevelt and the __(13)__ policies of Richard Nixon and Ronald Reagan.

Minor parties, or __(14)__ parties, do not often win elections. One reason is the system of "__(15)__." Nevertheless, minor parties can have an important influence. For example, in the 1890s, the __(16)__ party proposed a series of reforms, including an income tax. Some of their ideas were later adopted by the major parties.

One of your freedoms as an American citizen is to support the political party of your choice. There are no membership requirements for joining a party. Simply by __(17)__ for the candidates of a certain party, you are contributing to the success of that party.

B. The Past and Present of Our Political Parties

In this multiple-choice exercise, give the **letter** of the phrase that correctly answers the question.

______ 1. What president thought Americans should *not* join political parties? (*a*) Thomas Jefferson (*b*) George Washington (*c*) Abraham Lincoln (*d*) Franklin Roosevelt

______ 2. Who was the first Republican candidate to be elected president? (*a*) Andrew Jackson (*b*) Abraham Lincoln (*c*) Theodore Roosevelt (*d*) Franklin Roosevelt

______ 3. What does *patronage* mean? (*a*) winning an election (*b*) campaigning for office (*c*) giving government jobs to loyal party workers (*d*) unfairly criticizing the candidate of a minor party

______ 4. How can you join a political party? (*a*) by saying that you are a member (*b*) by working in the party for a certain period of time (*c*) by becoming a candidate (*d*) by voting for a party's candidates in at least two elections

______ 5. Which of these statements describes *both* the Republican and Democratic parties? (*a*) They were founded at the same time. (*b*) They have always been most successful in the South. (*c*) Their platforms tend to be conservative. (*d*) Winning elections is a major goal.

______ 6. Which of these weakened the power of the old-time "bosses?" (*a*) the decline of the Whig party (*b*) the founding of the Republican party (*c*) the efforts of several minor parties (*d*) the use of the direct primary

______ 7. How did the Great Depression of the 1930s bring about change in the two major parties? (*a*) The Republicans became generally more liberal than the Democrats. (*b*) The Democrats became generally more liberal than the Republicans. (*c*) Both parties started to nominate candidates at conventions. (*d*) Both parties began to win the support of labor unions.

C. Applying What You Know

On a shelf of your school or local library, you may find a reference book entitled *Famous First Facts: A Record of First Happenings, Discoveries and Inventions in the United States*. Besides articles on the first "coast-to-coast bus" in 1928 and the first "perfect game pitched in baseball" (no player reaching base) in 1904, there are articles about American political parties and conventions. Three such articles are quoted below. After reading them, use your general knowledge of political parties to answer the questions.

I. *First nominating convention (state)* assembled at Utica, N.Y., in 1824 for the purpose of nominating candidates for governor and lieutenant governor. . . . DeWitt Clinton was nominated by the Democratic-Republican party and was elected November 3, 1824.

II. *First presidential convention (national) addressed by a woman* was the Republican National Convention in Cincinnati, Ohio, at which Sara Andrews Spencer spoke on June 15, 1876, against the disfranchisement of women. . . .

III. *Union Reform party* held its first convention in Baltimore, Md., September 3, 1900. Seth Hockett Ellis of Ohio was nominated for president and Samuel T. Nicholson of Pennsylvania for vice president. They received fewer than 6,000 votes, as compared with 7,200,000 votes cast for William McKinley of Ohio, the Republican candidate, in the election of November 6, 1900. The platform had been adopted March 1, 1899, in Cincinnati, Ohio.

1. For each statement, tell whether you think it is **true** or **false.** Then give the number of the passage that supports your answer.
   a. A party convention nominated the governor of Tennessee in 1816.
   True or **false.** Which passage supports your answer?
   b. DeWitt Clinton was the first governor to be nominated at a party convention.
   True or **false.** Which passage supports your answer?
   c. In 1860, Mary Lloyd Wilkins spoke at the Democratic convention that nominated Stephen Douglas.
   True or **false.** Which passage supports your answer?
   d. The only candidates for president in 1900 were the Democratic nominee and the Republican nominee.
   True or **false.** Which passage supports your answer?

2. Imagine that you are Seth Hockett Ellis, the Union Reform party's candidate. Two years after your defeat in the election, a newspaper reporter interviews you about your candidacy. **Explain** why it is difficult for a third-party candidate like yourself to win.

a.

b.

c.

d.

e.

f.

g.

h.

a. George Washington
b. Harry Truman
c. Andrew Johnson
d. Calvin Coolidge
e. Franklin Roosevelt speaking to Congress
f. Lyndon Johnson with U.S. troops
g. Jimmy Carter with Menachem Begin of Israel after signing a peace agreement with Anwar Sadat of Egypt
h. Ronald Reagan

UNIT FOUR

The President

At the top of the U.S. political system is the person we elect to be president. George Washington was the first to take the presidential oath of office in 1789. More than 200 years later, in 1993, the 42nd president, William Clinton, took the same oath.

How much do you know about the office of president and the famous Americans who once held that office? Washington and seven of his successors are pictured on page 230. Try to match them to the statements below. (Some answers may be given more than once.)

1. He was elected president four times.
2. They were vice presidents before becoming president.
3. These presidents acted as commander in chief of the armed forces.
4. He was president during the Vietnam War.
5. These presidents lived in the White House *after* World War II.
6. In this picture, the president is trying to influence the lawmaking process.
7. In this picture, the president is acting as chief of state and symbol of the American nation.
8. In this picture, the president is using his constitutional power to make treaties.
9. He was the only president to be impeached by the House and tried by the Senate.
10. This president was the first to hold Cabinet meetings.

Notice the sign on President Truman's desk: THE BUCK STOPS HERE! To Harry Truman, the sign was a reminder that he, as president, bore the final responsibility for making the toughest decisions in government. He could not "pass the buck" (pass responsibility to others). In this unit, you will be reading about the kinds of decisions that a president must make. You will also know how "We the people" make a crucial decision, every four years, when we decide by our ballots who will be president of the United States.

Answers

1. *e* 3. *a-h* 5. *b, f, g, h* 7. *d* 9. *c*
2. *b, c, d, f* 4. *f* 6. *e* 8. *g* 10. *a*

THE UNION.
LIBERTY
ABRAHAM LINCOLN,
REPUBLICAN CANDIDATE FOR PRESIDENT OF THE UNITED STATES.

THE REPUBLICAN CANDIDATE FOR PRESIDENT, 1860. Abraham Lincoln received only 39% of the people's votes in the election of 1860. How, then, did he win the election?

CHAPTER 11

Electing a President

OBJECTIVES

After reading this chapter, you will know

1. how the president and the vice president are elected.
2. whether or not *you* think the Electoral College system should be changed.
3. the personal and political qualifications of candidates for president.
4. how candidates for president conduct their campaigns.
5. the rules governing the succession to the presidency.
6. how to interpret a map of a presidential election.

On Election Day, in November 1860, the American people had a choice of four candidates for president. One of them was a lawyer from Illinois named Abraham Lincoln. The others were Stephen Douglas (also from Illinois), John Breckinridge from Kentucky, and John Bell from Tennessee.

Voters did not know a great deal about Lincoln. As a politician, he had much less experience than his opponents. The only national office he had ever held was as a member of the House of Representatives. And that was only for a single term of two years. Nevertheless, Lincoln was the nominee of the Republican party. He was popular among Westerners. But in the South, he was widely distrusted because of certain speeches that he had made on the slavery issue.

About 4.6 million votes were cast in the election of 1860. Lincoln received less than half of them—just 1,866,452. He received no votes at all in Texas, Florida, and eight other Southern states.

Nationally, the people gave Lincoln a plurality of their votes, not a majority. But the people's election in November was not the final one. In the second election in December, Lincoln received a majority of the votes cast by a group of people called electors. This fact enabled Lincoln to become president under the U.S. Constitution.

Four years later, in 1864, he was reelected. But then, early in his second term, President Lincoln was shot and killed by an assassin.

Everything about Lincoln's presidency was unusual. He entered office after winning only a plurality of votes (39%). He was the first president to be killed in office. Between those events, he gave such strong leadership that many historians judge him to be the strongest president in U.S. history.

Lincoln's unusual story helps us to focus on three questions for this chapter:

1. How do Americans elect a president?
2. How do candidates for president compete?
3. In case of the president's death or illness, who shall then be president?

1. HOW DO AMERICANS ELECT A PRESIDENT?

We can imagine a very simple method for electing a president. On a certain day in the year—Election Day—millions of eligible voters go to their local polling places to vote for the candidate of their choice. Their votes are then counted. The candidate who receives the most votes is declared the winner.

That may be the simplest and most democratic way to choose a president. But it is *not* the method used in the United States. Instead, the U.S. Constitution provides for a more complicated system known as the Electoral College system.

Basic rules. If you know just four basic rules of the Electoral College system, you can begin to understand how it works:

First rule: *The president is officially elected by a small group of individuals called electors.*

CANDIDATES FOR PRESIDENT AND VICE PRESIDENT. After campaigning in Tennessee, Bill Clinton (right) and Al Gore won all 11 of that state's electoral votes. What are electoral votes and how are they won?

This special group is known as the Electoral College. An elector's only task is to cast two separate ballots: one ballot for president and the other for vice president. Having done that, his or her official duties are over.

Second rule: *Every state is assigned a different number of electors, depending on the state's population.* For example, because it is a large state, Texas has more electors (32) than the smaller state of Vermont (3). The number of electors for each state is easily determined. Just add its number of U.S. senators (2) and its number of U.S. representatives. EXAMPLE: Because Texas has 2 U.S. senators and 30 U.S. representatives, it is entitled to 32 electors.

Third rule: *On Election Day in November, the voters of a state elect the number of electors to which that state is entitled.* They may think they are voting directly for a president and vice president. In fact, they are electing a college (group) of electors.

Fourth rule: *To be elected president, one candidate must receive a majority of the electors' ballots.* In recent elections, there have been a total of 538 electors assigned to the 50 states and the District of Columbia. The winning candidate had to receive the votes of at least 270 of them (a bare majority).

CASE STUDY: How Lincoln was elected

Let us see how these rules were applied in 1860 when Abraham Lincoln was running for president. At that time, there were only 33 states in the Union. Depending on its population, each state had a certain number of electors. The voters of Kentucky, for example, could choose 12 electors, while the voters of Ohio could choose 23 electors. In Kentucky, four sets of electoral candidates competed.

12 electors of the Republican party supported LINCOLN

12 electors of the Constitutional Union party supported BELL
12 electors of the Democratic party supported DOUGLAS
12 electors of the Southern Democratic party supported BRECKINRIDGE

Though Lincoln had been born in Kentucky, his set of electoral candidates were not chosen by Kentucky's voters. Instead, the winning group of 12 electors in Kentucky were all for John Bell.

Meanwhile, in Ohio, Lincoln's 23 supporters received more votes than the other groups. Thus, they became the winning electors in Ohio.

The results of a presidential election may be given in the form of a table like the one below. The popular vote means the votes that are cast in November by the voting public. The electoral vote means the number of electors who are expected to vote later for a certain presidential candidate. Below are the results of the election of 1860 in two states.

People in every other state also voted for electors for president. The group of electors winning a plurality (largest number) of votes won the right to cast *all* of the state's electoral ballots.

Counting the ballots. The next stage of a presidential election takes place in December (about a month after Election Day). Now the winning groups of electors in the different states fill out their ballots and send them to Congress. The following month, January, the electors' ballots are opened and counted.

In January 1861, the members of Congress witnessed the counting of electoral ballots. The sealed envelope from Kentucky was found to contain 12 presidential ballots—all for John Bell. The envelope from Ohio contained 23 ballots—all for Abraham Lincoln. There were no surprises. The different groups of electors chosen in November cast their ballots exactly as they were expected to do. When all the ballots from all the states were counted, Lincoln was found to have a majority of them.

Predicting an elector's vote. Although they are human beings, electors almost always act as automatically as robots. In theory, they may freely decide whether to vote for one presidential candidate or another. In fact, however, long before the actual election, they have already made up their minds. They will vote for the candidates of their

	KENTUCKY		OHIO	
	Popular vote	*Electoral vote*	Popular vote	*Electoral vote*
Lincoln	1,364	*0*	231,610	*23*
Bell	66,058	*12*	12,194	*0*
Douglas	25,651	*0*	187,232	*0*
Breckinridge	53,143	*0*	11,405	*0*

CARTOON CORNER

Why does the cartoon compare electors to windup toys? Do you think Uncle Sam's explanation of the Electoral College system is correct?

own political party. Republican electors will certainly vote for the Republican party's nominee for president. And Democratic electors will vote without fail for the Democratic nominee.

How can we be so sure? You might compare electors to the loyal fans of a baseball team. In a playoff game, it is a rare Red Sox fan who will suddenly start cheering for the Yankees. Just as rare is a Republican elector who suddenly decides to vote for a Democratic presidential candidate.

Since the first presidential election in 1788, thousands of people have served in the special role of elector. Only ten of them have marked their ballots for a "surprise" candidate (someone not nominated by their own party).

Lincoln was not officially elected president until the counting of electors' ballots in January 1861. But people started calling him the winner and president-elect right after Election Day in November 1860. That is because the popular vote in every state determines who the electors of that state will be. And we can safely predict how the winning electors are going to vote.

✔✔ SKILLS CHECK: Interpreting an election map

Maps like the one on page 237 show how different states voted in a certain election for president. The shading or patterns used to cover each state shows which candidate's electors received the most votes. What is the number within each state? It is the number of electors to which that state was entitled when the election was held.

For example, from the map key, we see that the states won by Lincoln are in color.

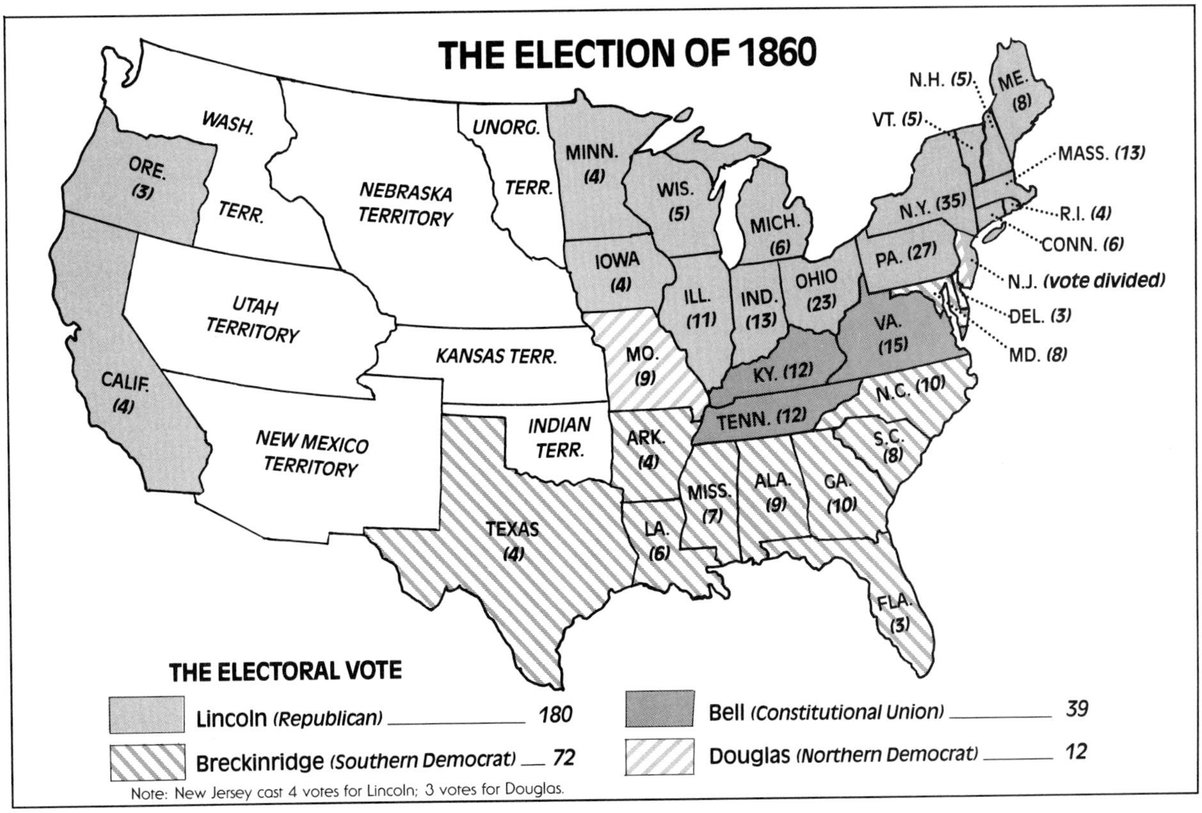

After studying the election map, answer the questions below.

1. Name the states that were won by electors of John Bell.
2. Name the states that were won by electors of John Breckinridge.
3. By simply looking at the map, is it possible to tell which candidate won the election of 1860? Explain.

What if there is no electoral majority? As you know, a majority means more than 50 percent of the total vote. Suppose that the electors cast 45 percent of their ballots for one candidate, 40 percent for a second, and 15 percent for a third. Then there is no majority—and no winner.

Fortunately, writers of the Constitution thought about this possibility. The job of settling an undecided election was given to the House of Representatives. The rules were these:

1. Each state represented in the House would be allowed to cast just one vote.
2. Only three candidates would be considered for election (those who had received the most electoral votes).
3. To be elected, one of the three candidates would have to receive a majority of the House's votes. If necessary, House members would have to vote again and again until a majority candidate finally emerges.

Has the House ever decided an election? Yes, it has happened twice. Thomas Jefferson was tied with Aaron Burr in the election of 1800. The House chose Jefferson after a long and bitter struggle. Then, in 1824, the electors divided their votes among four candidates. Though Andrew Jackson came closest to having an electoral majority, the House picked his rival, John Quincy Adams.

We can hope that the House never again has to choose a president. Such an event can be a nerve-wracking experience.

Electing the vice president. The electors who choose a president also have the job of choosing a vice president. Each elector casts two separate ballots—one for president, the other for vice president. To be elected, a candidate for vice president must receive a majority of the electors' ballots.

Is there a better way? Many Americans do not understand the U.S. system for electing a president and vice president. In the November election, they think they are voting directly for the two candidates they want. They have no idea that they are really voting for a group of people (electors) whose names they do not even know.

You too may be wondering about the Electoral College system. Why do we have such a system? Who created it and for what purpose?

The creators of the Constitution invented the Electoral College in 1787. At that time, political parties had not yet come into being. Democracy was not yet fully accepted as a good way to govern. Many of the creators did not trust the average person to use good judgment when choosing leaders. They expected that electors would be wiser and better informed than most citizens. Electors would therefore be able to vote for a president and a vice president with special care—more care than an average citizen would give.

That was the creators' thinking. Is it still valid for the world we live in? Critics of the Electoral College say, "No, it is not valid." These are a few of their criticisms:

- The system is undemocratic because people cannot vote directly for president and vice president.
- The system is so complicated that many Americans do not fully understand it.
- The system gives an unfair advantage to the more populous states, such as California, New York, and Texas. Since these states cast so many electoral votes, candidates may spend most of their time campaigning there while ignoring the less populous states.
- The system is as old-fashioned as quill pens and hoop skirts.

There have been dozens of proposals for either changing the Electoral College or abolishing it altogether. One proposal would divide a state's electoral vote in proportion to the popular vote. (For example, if a candidate won 60% of Ohio's popular vote, he or she would receive only 60% of that state's electoral vote—instead of 100%.) A second proposal would guarantee that the majority choice of the people would always be the majority choice of the electors. Again and again, ideas for reform have been considered by Congress—and then rejected.

"Leave well enough alone!" say defenders of the system. True, they say, the system is not foolproof. It has its quirks and dangers. But rarely in the past has there been any real trouble because of the system's weaknesses. People are generally satisfied after voting in a presidential election. They are confident that the more popular candidate will almost certainly win the election. In past elections, the electors have usually confirmed the people's choice. And they will probably continue to do so in the future. The argument for keeping the Electoral College unchanged can be summarized in one line: *If it's not broken, don't fix it.*

REVIEW

A. Applying What You Know

Let us imagine an election in which Jones was the Republican candidate for president and Kramer was the Democratic candidate. These are the results of the election.

	Popular votes	Electoral votes
JONES	55,520,000	251
KRAMER	48,790,000	287

The map below shows which candidate won the electoral votes of each state.

1. Who will probably be the next president, Jones or Kramer? Why do you think so?
2. When will it finally be decided whether Jones or Kramer is the official winner? Who will count the ballots?
3. In Minnesota, Jones received 1.5 million popular votes to Kramer's 1.2 million. Why will Jones probably receive all of Minnesota's electoral votes while Kramer gets none?
4. Judging from past presidential elections, is it likely that a few electors for Jones will change their minds in December and vote for Kramer instead? Why?
5. Jones has Jackson for a running mate. Kramer has Kasuri for a running mate. Who will probably win election as vice president? Why do you think so?
6. Suppose that a third pair of running mates (Rios for president, Rogers for vice president) had won popular majorities in three states: Florida, Virginia, and Ohio. The electoral totals would then be

   for Jones-Jackson: 251
   for Kramer-Kasuri: 228
   for Rios-Rogers: 59.

How would this election be decided?

B. Agree or Disagree

Tell whether you **agree** or **disagree** with each statement and explain.

1. The Electoral College system is undemocratic.
2. The Electoral College system is unfair to the less populous states.
3. The president and vice president should be elected by direct popular vote and not by a vote of electors.

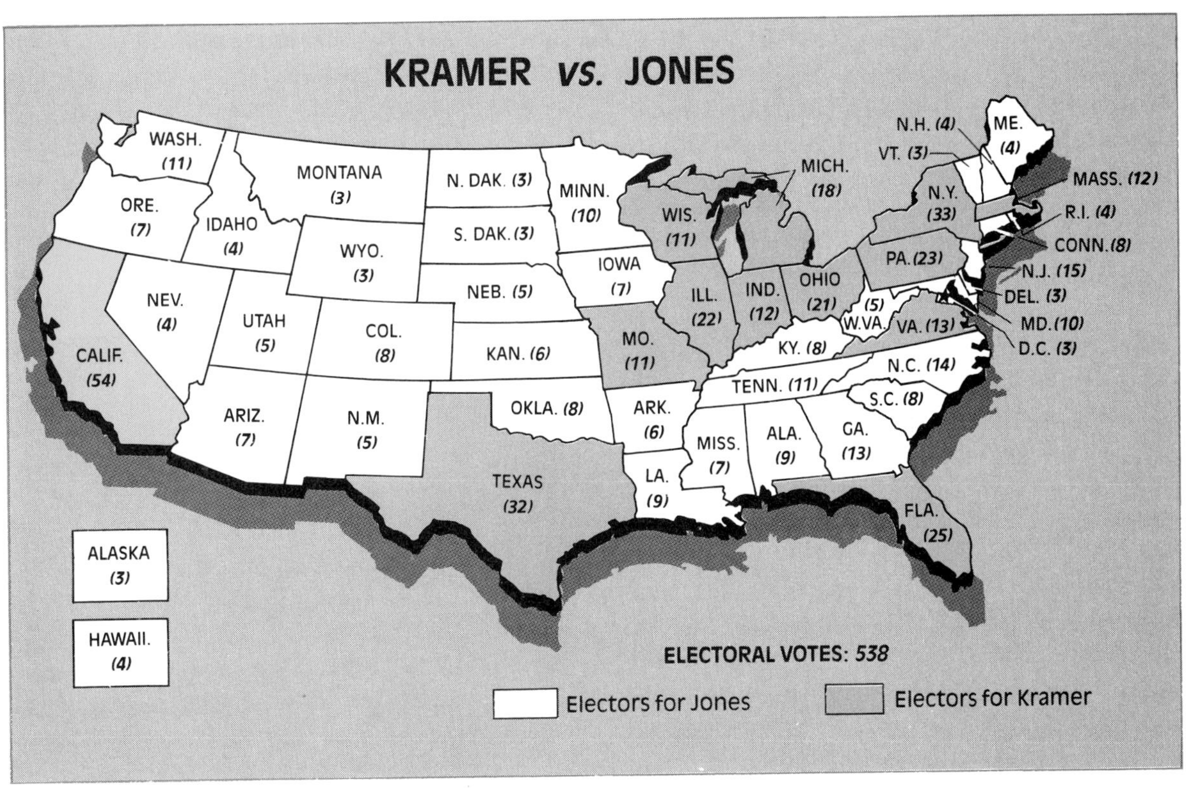

2. HOW DO CANDIDATES FOR PRESIDENT COMPETE?

Who will be the next president? American politicians, reporters, and citizens are constantly asking this question and offering their own guesses. The names mentioned by people as possible candidates for president keep changing. But the characteristics they look for in a serious candidate remain basically the same from one election to the next.

Characteristics of a successful candidate. Here is a basic list of the characteristics you would need if you ever wanted to run for president.

1. Name recognition. Millions of Americans would have to know your name. At the very least, people should be able to say something like this about you: "Oh, sure, she's that Westerner who is always speaking up for minorities." Or "He's the former vice president, isn't he?"

2. Experience in politics or a leadership role. Many rock stars and athletes are better known than politicians. But most voters expect a serious candidate for president to be either (*a*) an experienced politician or (*b*) a famous and successful leader. The great majority of presidential candidates have been either U.S. senators (John Kennedy, Lyndon Johnson), state governors (Franklin D. Roosevelt, Ronald Reagan), or vice presidents (Theodore Roosevelt, Richard Nixon).

The few who had little experience in politics rose to fame as either military or business leaders. For example, because General Dwight Eisenhower had led American armies to victory in World War II, many people thought he might also make a fine president. Other famous wartime generals who have become successful candidates are George Washington (Revolutionary War), Andrew Jackson (War of 1812), Zachary Taylor (Mexican War), and Ulysses S. Grant (Civil War).

3. A pleasing appearance on TV. Television is the most persuasive medium of our times. Voters now rely upon it to make judgments about candidates (just as they make judgments about entertainers). Does a certain candidate come across to them as exciting or boring, as confident or nervous? The answer may influence millions of voters one way or the other.

4. Money. It costs millions of dollars to

THE FIRST GREAT TV DEBATE. Most people who watched John Kennedy (left) debate Richard Nixon on television thought Kennedy had won. Those who heard the same debate on radio thought Nixon had won. What can you conclude from this about the medium of television?

run a successful campaign for president. Part of the campaign money may come from contributions of supporters. But having a private fortune of your own is also extremely useful. Other considerations being equal, a rich candidate has an important advantage.

5. No "skeletons in the closet." People expect candidates for president to be honest and moral in their private lives. Any hint of misconduct in your past may be used against you and prevent you from winning.

6. A strong desire to be president. Campaigning for the presidency is hard, grueling work. You must be willing to work at it several days a week, day and night, for months and even years. Your voice gets hoarse from all the talking and your hand becomes swollen from all the handshaking. It is an endurance test that only a few people have the ambition and desire to undertake.

7. The support of a major political party. Recall from Chapter 10 that the backing of a major political party is essential to a candidate's chances of success.

To stand a chance of winning the presidency, a candidate needs to meet most of the above requirements. The only one that is essential is the last. You *must* have the backing of a major political party.

CASE STUDY: Candidates for president, 1992

If you paid attention to political news in 1992, you were a witness to history. That was the year that a majority of electors cast their ballots for Bill Clinton for president and Albert Gore for vice president. In some ways, the campaigns of the leading candidates in the 1992 election resembled earlier presidential campaigns. In other ways, however, both Clinton's campaign and that of another candidate, H. Ross Perot, broke new ground. It was a remarkable election—truly one of the most interesting and important political contests of the twentieth century.

GREETING TROOPS. Bush (center) celebrated with U.S. troops home from the Persian Gulf in 1991. How did the war affect Bush's presidency?

The incumbent president, George Bush. In the spring of 1991 (a year and a half before Election Day, 1992), it seemed a sure bet that the Republican president, George Bush, would easily win re-election to a second term. Public opinion polls showed that 90 percent of the American people approved of the job Bush was doing as president. U.S. military forces had just won an overwhelming victory in the Persian Gulf against Iraq. For that victory, Americans gave President Bush much of the credit.

But the president's postwar popularity did not last. His chief problem was the gloomy economic news of 1991. Many U.S. businesses were either shutting down or cutting back their production of goods and services. Experts generally agreed that the U.S. economy was in the middle of a recession (a period of business decline). Americans became nervous about the economic situation. Many thought the president was out of touch with the needs and worries of the average person. From month to month, President Bush's ratings in the opinion polls slid downward. Even so, as 1992 began, most Republicans were still confident that Bush would be re-elected. After all, they reasoned, what Democrat was well enough known and liked by millions of people to stand a chance of defeating the president?

In January, there was no such candidate. At that time, few Americans knew much about the young governor of Arkansas named Bill Clinton.

Clinton and his Democratic opponents. William Jefferson Clinton was born in 1946 in the small town of Hope, Arkansas. His ambition, even as a teenager, was to enter politics and perhaps some day win election to his country's top office, the presidency. At the age of 32, he became the youngest person to be elected governor of Arkansas. After serving 12 years in this office, he decided that he had as much chance as any other Democrat to win his party's nomination for president. To achieve this goal, he knew that a long campaign lay ahead of him. For half a year, from January to June, he would have to travel to different states and persuade the Democratic voters in each state to vote for him in a primary election. Competing against him were five other Democrats. In February, Clinton and his opponents campaigned in New Hampshire, where the first of the primaries is held. Each candidate had the same two goals (1) to win a high percentage of the votes cast in the primary and (2) to win delegates to the Democratic party's national convention in July.

The quest for delegates. In campaigning for their party's nomination, candidates try to get a majority of delegates on their side even *before* the opening day of the convention. How do they accomplish such a feat?

It is difficult and complicated. One problem is that each of the 50 states has different rules for selecting delegates. In several states, active party members hold what is known as a party *caucus*. They meet in some hotel or convention center and cast their ballots for different lists of delegates.

In the great majority of states (40 of them in 1992), voters participate in party primaries. Delegates elected in a primary may be either committed or uncommitted. The committed ones are those who are required to vote for a certain candidate at the national convention. Uncommitted delegates may vote for anyone. Whether a delegate is one or the other again depends on the rules of a particular state.

Overcoming negative news. As Clinton was campaigning in the New Hampshire primary race, a bombshell hit. A woman told the press that Clinton had committed adultery with her. Clinton responded to the scandal by saying that the woman was lying. He and his wife, Hillary Rodham Clinton, went on television together and strongly affirmed their commitment to their marriage and family. Shortly afterward, Bill Clinton was rocked again by reports that, as a young man, he had taken steps to avoid being drafted into the armed services in the 1960s.

IN NEW HAMPSHIRE. On the eve of the primary vote, Clinton attended a rally. Why is it important to win early primaries?

The candidate admitted that he had opposed the Vietnam War but denied that there was anything wrong with his draft record.

Clinton's campaign was damaged—but not destroyed—by the negative news of February. In the New Hampshire primary, he received a respectable percentage of votes, coming in second behind a former senator from Massachusetts, Paul Tsongas. In later primaries, in Georgia, Florida, and Michigan, Clinton did much better. By April, he had won more primary votes and more delegates than any of his rivals. As Clinton became better known, Americans began to pay more attention to his views on various issues. How did he mean to solve the nation's economic problems? Did his ideas for putting people to work and reforming the health care system make sense? Day after day, the candidate explained his views and repeated his central theme that it was time for change in leadership.

Public opinion polls showed that Clinton's message was taking hold. In the spring, he was clearly the front runner in the race.

Gaining momentum. In politics, as in sports, momentum is extremely important. The candidate who is ahead in a race has an easier time getting campaign funds. At the same time, money runs out for those who are thought to be losing the race. After Clinton had won several primaries, the other candidates concluded that they could no longer hope to compete. One by one, they announced that they were withdrawing from the race. By May, Bill Clinton's momentum was unstoppable. Having won primary after primary, he now was assured that a majority of delegates would vote for his nomination at the Democratic party's national convention.

The Republican nomination of President George Bush was also certain. A president who wishes to run for a second term can almost always count on being nominated by his or her party. Even though Bush was opposed for the nomination by a conservative Republican, Pat Buchanan, the president won all the Republican primaries.

The Democratic and Republican conventions. The Democrats scheduled their convention for July, while the Republicans scheduled theirs for August. As thousands of Democratic delegates from the 50 states arrived in New York City, they understood that their party's decision was already made. Clinton would be their nominee. On the convention floor, the delegates would simply go through the motions of voting for Clinton. (At their convention in Houston, the Republican delegates would also vote predictably for Bush "by acclamation"—unanimously.)

A major purpose of national party conventions in the 1990s is simply to attract a large television audience. Party leaders think of the convention as a four-day TV spectacle for getting their chosen candidate's campaign off to a rousing and successful start.

Choice of a running mate. Just before the Democratic convention began, Bill Clinton announced his choice for the person to run with him as a candidate for vice president. Most presidential candidates of the past had made an effort to "balance the ticket." This meant that someone from a Southern state like Clinton's Arkansas would seek a running mate from a different region of the country—either a Northerner or a Westerner. It was thought that a Southerner on the ticket would appeal to Southern voters while the Northerner (or Westerner) would appeal to people in the other region.

To the surprise of many, Clinton broke with the balanced-ticket tradition by choosing a fellow Southerner, Senator Albert Gore from Tennessee. Clinton reasoned that in the new political era of the 1990s, regional differences were less important to voters than a candidate's ability to address important national issues. Senator Gore was widely respected nationally for taking a strong stand on the environment.

On the Republican side, there were no surprises. President George Bush praised the political efforts and conservative values of his vice president, Danforth Quayle. After nominating both men, the Republican delegates joined in chanting their hopes for victory. "Four more years! Four more years!" they shouted.

Independent candidate Ross Perot. As you know, the candidates of the two major parties expect to split between them almost all the popular votes cast in November. But 1992 was different from earlier election years. More than anything else, what made the election different was the candidacy of a Texas business leader and billionaire, H. Ross Perot. Unlike the other candidates, Perot did not compete in any party primaries because he did not belong to a political party. Many Americans admired Perot's success in business and liked his ideas for improving the economy and reforming U.S. government. They urged him to run for president as an independent. Appearing in February on a TV talk show, *Larry King Live*, Perot announced that he would run for the nation's highest office on one condition: citizen volunteers would have to do the hard work of placing Perot's name on the ballot of all 50 states.

TALK SHOW. Ross Perot (right) was a frequent guest of the talk show host, Larry King (left). In future elections, would you like to see candidates appear on talk shows?

Unhappy with politicians in general, millions of Americans liked the forceful, direct, and often witty statements of a man who had never in his life held political office. As measured by opinion polls in the spring of 1992, more people favored the independent candidate Perot than either of the other major candidates, Clinton and Bush. Amazed by Perot's sudden popularity, magazine and newspaper writers began to report possible flaws in his character. Perot was annoyed by these reports, which caused a drop in his popularity. In July, he shocked his dedicated team of volunteers by announcing that he was no longer a candidate. But in early October, he surprised everyone again by saying that he was back in the race.

An unusual fall campaign. The final stretch of a presidential campaign occurs in the months of September, October, and early November. Unlike their choices in previous elections, voters in 1992 had three major candidates to evaluate instead of the usual two. They also witnessed campaign techniques that were being tried for the first time. Among these innovative (new) techniques were:

- ***Cross-country bus tours.*** The very day after they were nominated, the Democratic running mates, Clinton and Gore, boarded a bus that would take them through the small towns and major cities of America from one end of the country to the other. Wherever they stopped to give short speeches and shake hands, they had a chance to talk with voters face to face—and also to win a lot of attention on the local TV station.
- ***Televised town meetings.*** At certain points on the bus route, Clinton and Gore would present their views on the issues in a televised event called a "town meeting." People in the audience were given the chance to stand up and ask the candidates questions about health care, education, foreign policy, taxes—anything at all that concerned them.

• ***Talk shows.*** The talk show host, Larry King, scheduled a series of informal, hour-long interviews with all three of the candidates. Far more than in any other election, viewers could get to know the candidates and compare them as they talked informally on a popular TV show.

• ***Perot's infomercials.*** In past elections, candidates' campaign ads on television and radio were just 15 to 30 seconds long—no longer than the usual toothpaste ad. But in 1992, Ross Perot spent millions of dollars of his own money to buy large chunks of time on prime-time television. His "infomercials" (ads presenting information instead of glitzy images) showed the candidate talking for half an hour or more on the issues that most concerned him. Perot's lectures, illustrated with fact-filled charts, were watched by millions.

The "character" issue. Behind in the opinion polls, President Bush hoped to persuade voters that his younger rival, Clinton, could not be trusted with the presidency. The president stressed that he had fought bravely in World War II, whereas Clinton had avoided military service in Vietnam. In a series of televised debates, Bush seized every opportunity to raise doubts about Clinton's character. Clinton counterattacked by saying that the candidates' positions on the economy and other issues were what really mattered to voters.

Voter interest and participation. Partly because of the new campaign techniques and partly because of Perot's challenge to the major parties, the American people took great interest in the outcome of the election. Most important of all, the issues debated in the campaign seemed vitally important to people's lives. People knew the economy was in trouble. Which candidate offered the best solutions? They knew that the costs of health care for the average family were getting out of hand. Which candidate could they trust to deal effectively with the problem?

THE WINNER! Celebrating news of victory in Little Rock, Hillary and Bill Clinton and Al Gore greeted supporters. What were the main reasons for Clinton's victory?

When Election Day finally came, on November 3, 1992, 55 percent of eligible voters cared enough about the issues and the candidates to vote. Even among the youngest voters, aged 18 to 24, the participation rate was well above the rate of previous elections.

Clinton's victory. Ever since the Democratic convention in July, Clinton had held a substantial lead over Bush and Perot in the opinion polls. But no candidate can be sure of victory until Election Day, when people finally cast their ballots. Before midnight of that day, the people's choice became known. Clinton and Gore were to be the new president and vice president of the United States. They had won by receiving just 43 percent of the popular vote, less than a majority. But they had scored victories in 32 states. The 370 electoral votes from these states and the District of Columbia were enough to guarantee victory in the all-important Electoral College.

The defeated president, George Bush, sent Clinton a gracious message of congratulations and good wishes. "The people have spoken," he said, "and we respect the majesty of the democratic system."

REVIEW

A. Distinguishing Details from Main Ideas

All of the following statements are true. Some present a main idea about campaigns for the presidency. Some present a factual detail. For each statement, tell whether it is a **main idea** or a **factual detail.**

1. Bill Clinton came in second in the Democratic primary in New Hampshire in 1992.
2. To be nominated for president, a candidate needs a majority of delegate votes at the party's national convention.
3. H. Ross Perot announced his willingness to become a presidential candidate on a TV talk show.
4. Though it helps to be nationally famous *before* running for president, it is not absolutely essential.
5. Most candidates for the president have previously been either state governors, U.S. senators, or vice presidents.

B. Supporting a Main Idea with Factual Details

For each **main idea** that you have identified in section **A** above, write a **detail** about the election of 1992 that supports and illustrates the idea. First, copy the general statement. Then, beneath it, write one detail supporting it. In all you should be giving factual support for *three* ideas.

C. Making Comparisons

In reviewing the election of 1992, **compare** the campaigns of *two* of the major candidates.

1. What was similar about the two campaigns?
2. What was different about the two campaigns?
3. What factors do you think were most important in explaining Bill Clinton's victory in the election?

D. Analyzing Causes and Effects

Imagine that you are a TV newscaster trying to explain the election results. In your brief analysis, mention how each of the following factors was involved in explaining Clinton's victory:

(1) the economy
(2) the candidates' positions on the issues (see page 223)
(3) the way the candidates conducted their campaigns.

3. IN CASE OF THE PRESIDENT'S DEATH OR ILLNESS, WHO SHALL THEN BE PRESIDENT?

Referring to the president, the Constitution states: "He shall hold his office during the term of four years."

After being elected, most presidents have served out a term of exactly four years. Jimmy Carter, for example, was sworn into office at noon on January 20, 1977, and left office at noon on January 20, 1981.

A few presidents, however, were not so fortunate. Several fell sick and died in the middle of their terms. Others like Abraham Lincoln and John F. Kennedy were killed by assassins. Such events put the entire nation in a state of temporary peril. The duties of the president are so important that somebody *must* perform them at all times. There must be no break in presidential leadership, not even for an hour. In case of emergency, we must have a system for deciding instantly who will be the new president.

Such a system is carefully spelled out in the Constitution. We call it a system of succession (an orderly procedure by which one person follows another in office). Let us describe the usual procedures first, the unusual ones next.

Inaugurating a president. The time line on page 248 shows the terms of seven presidents between 1961 and 1993 (projected). Notice that the bands are evenly spaced. Between the bands is the expected term of office for any elected president—exactly four years long.

Each term of office is preceded by a three-month period. The period starts in November of an even-numbered year (1960, 1964) and ends in January of an odd-numbered year (1961, 1965). November is the time of the popular election for president. By law, Election Day takes place on the Tuesday that follows the first Monday in November. The running mates who win the popular election are known for three months as the president-elect and vice president-elect. They have no official duties, however, until a later date: Inauguration Day, January 20 of the next year.

From November to January, the president remains the same as before the election. For example, though President Ford lost the election of 1976, he continued to be the president for another three months. To summarize, here is the order of events from Election Day to Inauguration Day.

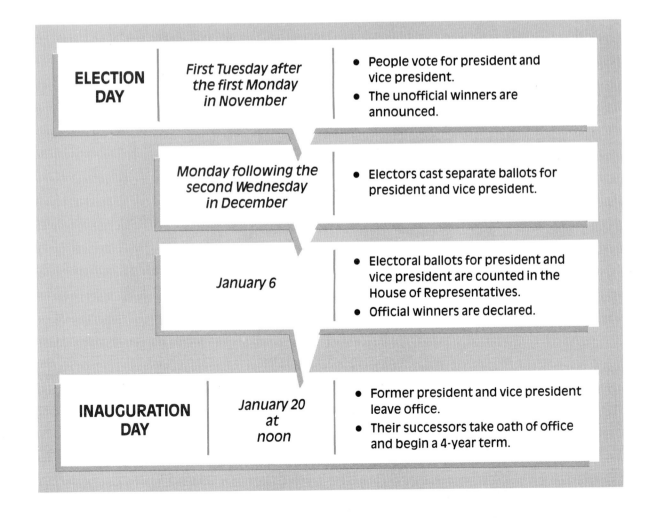

ELECTION DAY	*First Tuesday after the first Monday in November*	• People vote for president and vice president. • The unofficial winners are announced.
	Monday following the second Wednesday in December	• Electors cast separate ballots for president and vice president.
	January 6	• Electoral ballots for president and vice president are counted in the House of Representatives. • Official winners are declared.
INAUGURATION DAY	*January 20 at noon*	• Former president and vice president leave office. • Their successors take oath of office and begin a 4-year term.

PRESIDENTS • 1961 to 1997

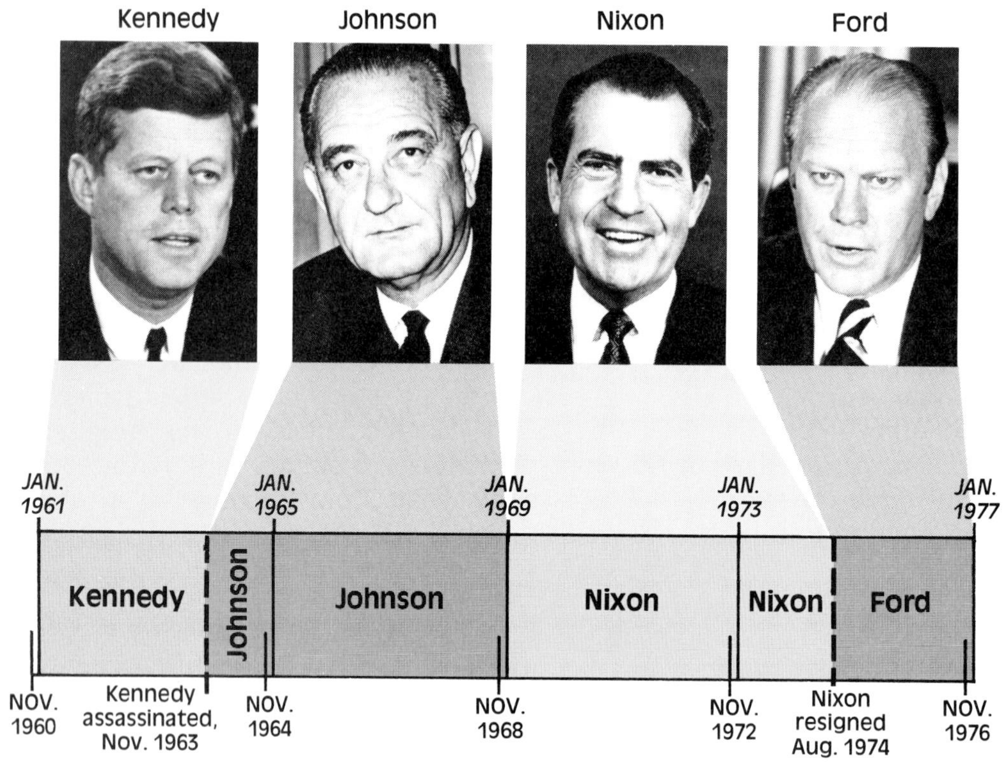
Kennedy
Johnson
Nixon
Ford
JAN. 1961
JAN. 1965
JAN. 1969
JAN. 1973
JAN. 1977
Kennedy
Johnson
Johnson
Nixon
Nixon
Ford
NOV. 1960
Kennedy assassinated, Nov. 1963
NOV. 1964
NOV. 1968
NOV. 1972
Nixon resigned Aug. 1974
NOV. 1976

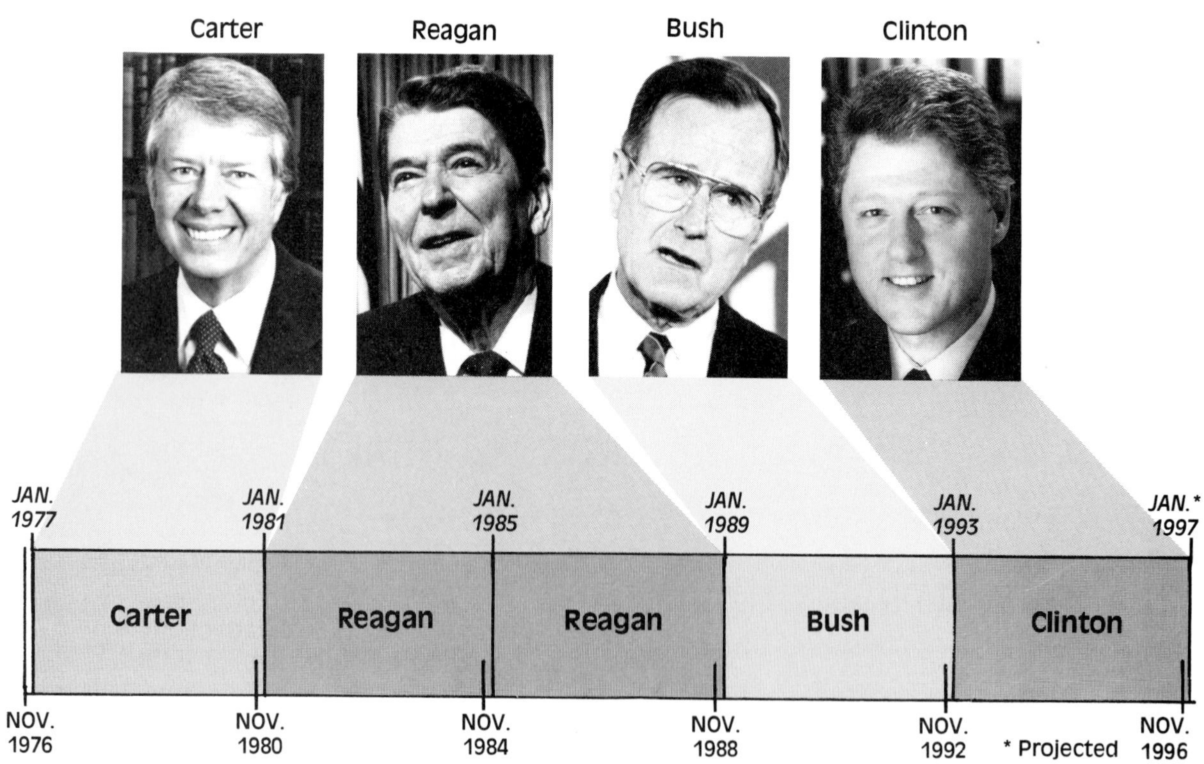
Carter
Reagan
Bush
Clinton
JAN. 1977
JAN. 1981
JAN. 1985
JAN. 1989
JAN. 1993
JAN.* 1997
Carter
Reagan
Reagan
Bush
Clinton
NOV. 1976
NOV. 1980
NOV. 1984
NOV. 1988
NOV. 1992
* Projected
NOV. 1996

The day of inaugurating a new president is filled with fanfare and ceremony. Immense crowds gather outside the Capitol. On a decorated platform, the chief justice of the Supreme Court stands and faces the president-elect. Microphones, TV cameras, and loudspeakers broadcast the new president's words to millions of Americans:

> I, ______, do solemnly swear that I will faithfully execute the office of president of the United States, and will, to the best of my ability preserve, protect, and defend the Constitution of the United States.

When the applause stops, the new president makes a speech to the nation known as the Inaugural Address. For the rest of the afternoon, marching bands and floats parade down the main street of Washington, D.C., in honor of the inaugurated president.

The two-term limit. The "new" president on Inauguration Day may or may not be different from the "old" one. You can see from the time line (page 248) that Ronald Reagan took over from himself on Inauguration Day in 1985. Every president is allowed to serve a second term, provided of course that he or she wins election.

Let us imagine someone with the initials M.A.Y. Assume that M.A.Y. begins a term of office as the vice president. The president dies midway into the four-year term. M.A.Y. becomes president for the remainder of the term—two years. Her party nominates her for president for the next four-year term. She wins. Toward the end of this term, she runs again and wins again. That entitles her to four more years in the White House. Thus: one-half term + two full terms = 10 years.

According to the Constitution, the above events *may* happen; but so far, they never have. The Twenty-second Amendment to the Constitution says that a president may be elected no more than two times. The amendment went into effect in 1951. Since then, two presidents—Dwight Eisenhower

INAUGURATING TWO PRESIDENTS NAMED GEORGE. Two hundred years after the inauguration of George Washington in 1789, George Bush was inaugurated as the 41st president in 1989. When will the next president be inaugurated?

and Ronald Reagan—have been in office for as much as two full terms (eight years). Franklin D. Roosevelt was elected to four terms; but that was before the Twenty-second Amendment was adopted.

Unusual circumstances: death. On the time line (page 248) notice the dashed line dated 1963. It marks the early end of John F. Kennedy's presidency. An assassin shot him as he rode in an open car through the city of Dallas. Vice President Lyndon Johnson was also in Dallas on the day of the killing. He was rushed to the airport. Aboard the plane carrying him back to Washington, Johnson took the oath of office as the next president.

The chief function of a vice president is to be on hand in case something happens to the president. He or she is like a substitute quarterback on a football team, sitting on the bench but ready to go into action if an accident happens. A vice president has one other constitutional duty: presiding over meetings of the Senate. Recent presidents have given their vice presidents other responsibilities as well. They may be sent abroad, for example, to meet with foreign leaders. Even so, the office of vice president exists mainly for emergencies.

FIRST PRESIDENT TO BE ASSASSINATED. This photograph of Abraham Lincoln was taken only four days before he was shot by an assassin on April 14, 1865. Why is the presidency one of the most dangerous jobs in politics?

FIRST PRESIDENT TO DIE IN OFFICE. Inaugurated on March 4, 1841, William Henry Harrison died of pneumonia only 30 days later. Who was president for the remainder of his term?

What would happen if *both* the president *and* vice president died at once? In 1947, Congress passed a law listing the government officials who could step into the president's job in an emergency. Backing up the vice president is the speaker of the House of Representatives. If the speaker too were dead, the next in line would be the Senate's leading officer—its president pro tempore. Next would come various heads of Cabinet departments, beginning with the secretary of state.

The 1947 law of succession exists as a precaution, but so far, it has never been used.

Unusual circumstances: impeachment. Look on the time line for a second dashed line marked 1974. This was the year that President Richard Nixon was *almost* impeached by the House of Representatives. To avoid the national crisis of being impeached, Nixon resigned from office. Vice President Gerald Ford then became president.

To impeach means to make a formal accusation against some official. The Constitution gives the power of impeachment to the House of Representatives. If a bill of impeachment passes the House by a majority vote, then the Senate meets as a trial court. The chief justice of the Supreme Court presides over the Senate's trial of the accused (impeached) official. A *yes* verdict by at least two-thirds of the states in the Senate means that the official must leave office immediately.

Thus, impeachment *may* lead to a president being forced out of office. In the case of Richard Nixon, a committee of the House recommended that he be impeached. They accused him of participating in an illegal scheme to cover up certain crimes. Rather than divide the country over the impeachment question, Nixon decided to resign.

No other president has ever left office for political reasons. Back in 1868, President Andrew Johnson was impeached by the House for defying a law of Congress. But the Senate voted to dismiss the charges against him.

Unusual circumstances: illness. Let us return to the story of M.A.Y., the imaginary president. Suppose that, during her sixth year in the White House, she is paralyzed by a stroke. In the hospital, she sinks into

A PRESIDENT ON TRIAL, 1868. By just one vote, the U.S. Senate decided not to remove President Andrew Johnson from office. What event in the House of Representatives preceded the Senate's trial?

a deep coma. She is unable to communicate with anyone. Would the nation then be leaderless?

No, it would not. In this emergency, the vice president would meet with M.A.Y.'s Cabinet. If a majority agrees that M.A.Y. is disabled (unfit to make decisions as president), they would inform Congress of this fact in writing. The vice president would immediately begin acting as president until M.A.Y. recovers from her illness. But the vice president would only be the *acting* president. He or she could not become the official president unless M.A.Y. dies.

Now suppose that M.A.Y. comes out of her coma and declares that she is fit to resume her duties. But the vice president and the Cabinet think that she is still unfit. In that case, Congress would have to settle the question by a two-thirds vote of each house.

Those are the rules we find in the Twenty-fifth Amendment for dealing with presidential illness. So far, the nation has been lucky. Since 1967, when the amendment was adopted, no president has become seriously ill. Earlier presidents, however, were the victims of strokes (Woodrow Wilson), heart attacks (Dwight Eisenhower), and major injuries (James Garfield, who lay dying for 80 days after an assassin had shot him). Serious illness or injury could strike again. If it does, the nation is now better prepared to deal with it because of the Twenty-fifth Amendment.

REVIEW

Creating a Time Line of the Future

1. Create a **time line** like the one on page 248. It should span the future time period, 2000 to 2021. Divide the period into five presidential terms. Use colored bands, and label them with dates to show when future elections and inaugurations will take place.
2. Why is it easy to predict when future presidential terms will start and end?

FIRST PRESIDENT TO BE SERIOUSLY ILL. After Woodrow Wilson was partly paralyzed by a stroke in 1919, his wife, Edith, acted for months as the most important decision-maker in the White House. Who would carry out the president's duties today if a similar misfortune occurred?

CHAPTER REVIEW

A. Completing the Summary

Select terms from the word list to fill in the blanks in the summary below. Write your answers on a piece of paper.

Amendment	popular
Cabinet	primary
College	running mate
Constitution	succession
convention	term
nomination	undemocratic
party	vice president

In 1860, Abraham Lincoln did *not* receive a majority of the __(1)__ votes. Yet he was elected president anyway because the electoral votes he received gave him a majority in the Electoral __(2)__.

The U.S. system for electing a president and a vice president is described in the __(3)__. Each state is allowed a certain number of electors. On Election Day, every four years, the voters of a state elect the number of electors to which their state is entitled. In December, electors mark separate ballots for president and vice president. In January, Congress counts the electoral ballots from all the states and announces the result.

But the winning candidates for president and vice president are known long before the electors cast their ballots. The reason is that the electors will surely support the two candidates of their own __(4)__.

This system for electing a president and a vice president has often been criticized. Some say that it is complicated and __(5)__. But the many proposals for changing the system have been rejected by Congress.

Candidates for president spend many months campaigning. At the start of an election year, there may be a dozen or more Democrats and Republicans trying to win their party's __(6)__. First, they compete for the support of delegates who will attend their party's national __(7)__. Delegates are chosen either at state conventions or at __(8)__ elections held by different states. Each state makes its own rules for choosing delegates. To win the nomination, a candidate must receive a majority of delegate votes. At the national convention, the party's nominee for president gets to choose his or her __(9)__ (the party's nominee for vice president).

The campaign in the fall is a contest between running mates of opposing political parties. The long campaign finally comes to an end on a Tuesday in early November—Election Day.

After winning election, the president expects to serve a four-year __(10)__ of office. But sometimes the unexpected happens. The president may either die or become too sick to carry out his or her duties. In that case, the Constitution and the laws of __(11)__ determine who shall take the president's place. In case of death, the __(12)__ automatically becomes the new president. In case of serious illness, the vice president and the __(13)__ inform Congress of the fact. The vice president may then make presidential decisions without actually being president. These rules of succession are found in the Twenty-fifth (14).

B. Applying What You Know

Below are eight events in a typical presidential election. They are out of order. Put them **in order** by copying them on a piece of paper and numbering them from 1 (for the first event) to 8 (for the last event).

- Ohio's electors cast their ballots for president and vice president.
- Democratic candidates for president compete against one another in New Hampshire's primary.
- A new president and vice president are inaugurated.
- Congress announces the official winner of the Electoral College vote.
- Texas voters go to the polls to vote for either the Republican or the Democratic candidate.
- The Republican candidate for president picks a running mate.
- Republican delegates meet in a convention hall to choose their party's nominee for president.
- The presidential campaign reaches its climax just as the baseball World Series is being played.

C. Making Inferences: The Next President Will Be . . .

You know enough to make some predictions about the next presidential election. Who will probably be a candidate in that election? Who cannot possibly be a candidate? Who might be the winner? Below are some predictions about the next election that might or might not happen. *You* decide whether each event is

a. **likely** to happen
b. **unlikely** to happen (but still possible)
c. **impossible**

Answer by letter on a separate piece of paper.

1. One of the leading candidates will be from the state of Hawaii.
2. The winner of the election will be the nominee of either the Republican party or the Democratic party.
3. The winner of the election will be a famous athlete who has not yet held political office.
4. Democratic candidates for president and vice president will come from different regions of the country.
5. The winner of the election will be inaugurated in November.
6. The winning candidate will have more popular votes *and* more electoral votes than the losing candidates.
7. The candidates will spend most of their time campaigning in the states of South Dakota, Montana, Utah, and Nevada. (See the map on page 239).
8. The incumbent president will be seeking election to a third term.
9. The Democrats will hold their national convention during the first week of May.
10. The winning candidates for president and vice president will come from the same political party.

11. The House of Representatives will determine who the next president shall be.
12. The winner of the Democratic nomination will be the candidate who has managed to win the greatest number of primaries.

D. Building Your Political Vocabulary

Which of the **terms** (*a-j*) are identified by each of the **phrases**? Write your answers on a piece of paper.

a. Electoral College
b. succession
c. popular vote
d. inauguration
e. impeachment
f. primary
g. national convention
h. name recognition
i. balanced ticket
j. committed delegates

1. method for replacing a president who dies in office
2. ceremony for beginning a president's term
3. an election in which members of the same party compete for votes
4. candidates for president and vice president who have different groups of supporters
5. an important characteristic in a serious candidate for president
6. group whose votes officially decide who will be the next president and vice president
7. the total number of votes cast on Election Day in November
8. those who must vote a certain way at their party's convention
9. a formal accusation against a public official
10. a party meeting for the purpose of nominating candidates

E. Rules of the Constitution

Answer each question in a **word** or **phrase.**

1. On what date does a new president take an oath to support the Constitution?
2. How many years make up a single presidential term of office?
3. How many times may a person be elected to the presidency?
4. Immediately after an election, what do you call the person who expects to become president?
5. If a president falls seriously ill, what part of the Constitution would apply to the situation?
6. Suppose that the president and vice president were both killed in an accident. Who would automatically become president?
7. Who decides whether a president should be impeached?
8. Who meets as a trial court to decide whether an impeached president should be removed from office?
9. What is the principal role of the vice president?

FRANKLIN ROOSEVELT ON THE AIR. To give strong leadership, a president must be able to communicate well with the American people. What other abilities and traits of character does a president need?

CHAPTER 12

The Many Jobs of the President

OBJECTIVES

After reading this chapter, you will know

1. the powers given to the president by the Constitution.
2. why the president is in a unique position to give leadership.
3. how the president is aided by Cabinet heads and a White House staff.
4. the ways that the president may influence Congress, party leaders, the American people, and foreign governments.
5. how to read an organization chart.

On a Sunday night in March 1933, a voice came over the radio. It was the voice of a man who had been president for just one week. His name was Franklin D. Roosevelt.

People were worried that night as they tuned their radio dials to the president's special talk. They had lived through almost four years of hard times. Businesses had failed. Millions of workers had lost their jobs. Many homeless people now roamed the streets. Many others feared that they too might lose everything—first their jobs, then their savings. What could they do then? How could they survive?

Americans in 1933 were struggling through the worst depression in recent history. Perhaps, they thought, government leaders might find a way to turn things around. That was why a huge majority of voters had elected a new president back in November 1932. They were encouraged by what this president, Franklin Roosevelt, had promised to do. "This nation," he had said, "asks for action, and for action now."

In his first days in office, Roosevelt had acted boldly and often. First, he ordered the closing of all the federal banks in the country for four days. He did this in an attempt to stop nervous depositors from crowding into banks and demanding all their money in hard cash. As he well knew, if people rushed to the banks in panic, the banks would fail and the depression would get even worse.

The American people needed to understand the president's bold effort to save the banks. That is why he decided to explain his actions on the radio. It was the first time any president used the radio for this purpose.

Americans huddled closer to their radios. The president began, "I want to talk for a few minutes with the people of the United States about banking." For 20 minutes, Roosevelt talked to his listeners in a friendly and confident tone. He explained the emergency banking law that Congress had passed just three days before. This law gave him power to determine which banks would be strong enough to reopen immediately. He told people that they could deposit their money in reopened banks without fear of loss. "I can assure you," said the president, "it is safer to keep your money in a reopened bank than under the mattress."

Roosevelt called his little speech on the radio a "fire-side chat." It was a great success. For many years afterward, President Roosevelt made other bold decisions and went on the radio to explain them. People were generally impressed and heartened by this president's vigorous style of leadership.

Today, though the Great Depression is over, the style of presidential leadership is much the same. Americans still expect their presidents to be strong leaders and to explain their policies on radio and television. What powers in the Constitution enable the president to give leadership? In this chapter, you will discover the answer to this question and others:

1. What powers does the Constitution give the president?
2. Why do Americans expect the president to give leadership?
3. Whose advice may guide a president in making policy?
4. How do presidents win support for their policies?

I. WHAT POWERS DOES THE CONSTITUTION GIVE THE PRESIDENT?

Written in 1787, the Constitution says nothing about presidents talking over the radio or appearing on TV. Nor does it say anything about a president's duty to give leadership.

What *does* the Constitution say about the president's job? It presents a brief list of

DEPRESSION BREADLINE, NEW YORK CITY. In an economic crisis, what can a president do to solve the problems of mass unemployment?

powers and duties in Article II, Section 2. The following powers are the most important:

1. Power to execute the laws. Congress's main job is to make the nation's laws. Once laws are made, the president has the duty of seeing that they are properly carried out. Another word for carrying out is "execute." Thus, the president is called the *chief executive.* As you know, the branch of government that the president directs is the Executive Branch.

According to the Constitution, the president "may require the opinion, in writing, of the principal officer in each of the executive *departments.*" The Constitution says nothing more about these departments or the officials in charge of them. It leaves to Congress and the president the question of how many executive departments to create.

As the first president, George Washington asked Congress to create three departments, each to be managed by a different "secretary." He appointed a secretary of the treasury, Alexander Hamilton, to head a department for collecting taxes and paying the expenses of the Executive Branch. He appointed Thomas Jefferson to be his secretary of state and a third official to manage the armed forces as secretary of war. These officials made up a group called the president's Cabinet.

THE FIRST CABINET. Henry Knox (seated) was George Washington's secretary of war. Others, from left to right, are Thomas Jefferson (secretary of state), Edmund Randolph (attorney general—back turned), Alexander Hamilton (secretary of the treasury), and Washington. How much larger is the current Cabinet?

Since Washington's time, the Executive Branch has grown tremendously. Today, it consists of 14 departments as well as many other separate agencies. Each of the major departments is headed by a different member of the president's Cabinet. The Cabinet members help the president to administer, or execute, thousands of U.S. laws. But the *final* responsibility for executing the laws rests with the president as chief executive.

2. Power to command the armed forces. The Constitution says, "The president shall be commander in chief of the army and navy." We still use the term *commander in chief* to describe the president. In this role, the president is responsible for the military defense of the United States. Generals and admirals in the army, navy, air force, and marines must obey the president's orders. Thus, military officers are always under the control of a civilian official—the president. Civilian control of the military protects our democracy from being taken over by a military dictator.

The Constitution says further that the president may call the state *militia* into the service of the United States. The militia consists of citizens who serve as part-time soldiers and may be called to duty in a time of emergency. Another name for the militia is the National Guard.

Congress too makes important decisions about the armed forces. For example, Congress can either grant or refuse the president's request for money to arm and equip U.S. troops. There are limits to what the president can do as commander in chief. Even so, the president's responsibility for the U.S. defense is awesome.

3. Power to appoint ambassadors. *Ambassadors* are officials who live abroad in the capitals of foreign nations. Their main job is to communicate the goals of their own government to the leaders of a foreign government. U.S. ambassadors to France, Mexico, Japan, and other countries are appointed by the president. The appointments, however, must have the *confirmation* (approval) of the Senate.

4. Power to make treaties. A *treaty* is an agreement signed by the heads of government of two or more nations. The Constitution gives the president the power to make and sign treaties. After a treaty is written, the Senate must vote on whether to accept it. For the treaty to be valid, at least two-thirds of the senators must approve, or ratify, it.

5. Power to inform Congress about the state of the Union. Every year, in January, it is the president's custom to present to Congress a special address, or speech. It usually begins by giving the president's opinion about the nation's welfare. Is business stronger or weaker than last year? Is employment up or down? Are there new dangers from abroad? The message ends by recommending laws that the president thinks are needed. This important speech is known as the president's state of the Union address. (As used here, "state" means a general condition of a thing—*not* a geographic state like Florida.) The speech is mentioned in the Constitution (Article II, Section 3).

Giving a speech is only the beginning of the president's attempt to lead Congress. Almost every day of the week, the president and White House aides talk with members of Congress to try to persuade them to vote for certain laws.

6. Power to veto acts of Congress. Congress is chiefly responsible for making federal laws. But the president is also involved in the lawmaking process. The president may choose either to sign or not to sign his or her name to an act of Congress. Not signing means that the president has rejected, or vetoed, Congress's action. Usually, the president sends the unsigned (vetoed) act back to Congress and gives reasons for not accepting it.

7. Power to grant pardons. The Constitution gives the president power to "grant *pardons* and reprieves for offenses against the United States." Examples from history show how this power may be used.

In the 1920s, a famous labor leader named Eugene Debs was in prison for breaking a federal law. During World War I, he had tried to persuade a crowd of people to resist the U.S. government's wartime laws. After the war, in 1923, President Warren Harding decided that Debs should be pardoned. Debs was then released from prison. Thus, to pardon is to set free a person convicted of a crime.

A president may also proclaim something called an amnesty. This means that a large number of law-breaking citizens are no longer subject to penalty. In 1979, for example, President Jimmy Carter granted an amnesty to thousands of young men who had illegally avoided military service during the war in Vietnam. After the president acted, none of the offenders faced either a trial or a jail sentence.

8. Power to nominate federal judges. Federal courts are located in cities all across the country. The judges who run these courts receive their appointments from the president. Among them are the nine judges who sit on the highest court—the U.S. Supreme Court in Washington, D.C.

TWO POWERS OF THE PRESIDENT. What clauses of the Constitution gave Ronald Reagan the power to (*a*) deliver a state of the Union message to Congress (left) and (*b*) sign a treaty with Soviet leader Mikhail Gorbachev?

The president's nominations to office must be submitted to the Senate for a vote. Usually the Senate confirms (approves) the president's choices. But there are times when a majority of senators vote against the president's nominee. Then the president must name another person for the job. The Senate must vote again on the second choice.

✔✔ SKILLS CHECK: Interpreting political cartoons

Political cartoons express a point of view toward events and people in the news. Study the cartoon below, and then answer the questions on page 262.

CARTOON CORNER

1. What does the "big wheel" represent?
2. What is the cartoon saying about the president's constitutional duties and powers? Choose the answer that you think best expresses the cartoonist's view.
   a. The president has too much power.
   b. The job of being president involves more than a single person can handle.
   c. Members of the Cabinet should take over most of a president's duties.
3. Do you **agree** or **disagree** with the cartoonist's point of view (your answer to question 2)? Why?

Formal qualifications for president. What person is strong enough and able enough to handle a job as big as the presidency? You might suppose that the Constitution would require a president to be unusually well qualified. But that is not the case. According to the Constitution, anyone can be president who is:

- a citizen born in the United States
- at least 35 years old
- a U.S. resident for at least 14 years.

Millions of Americans today meet these formal requirements for being president. However, only a few have the experience, the finances, the stamina, and the will to be a candidate for president.

Informal qualifications for president. In the preceding chapter, you read about several candidates for president in past elections. Some were successful (Abraham Lincoln, Jimmy Carter, Ronald Reagan). Others were not successful (Adlai Stevenson, Thomas Dewey). You also examined a list of eight characteristics needed by presidential candidates—political experience, no "skeletons in the closet," and so forth. Each is an example of an informal qualification.

Since George Washington's inauguration in 1789, 41 people have served as president. All of them were (*a*) of the male sex and (*b*) white. That fact shows us the importance

INFORMAL REQUIREMENTS FOR PRESIDENT AND VICE PRESIDENT. In 1984, Geraldine Ferraro (left) campaigned for vice president. In 1988, Jesse Jackson campaigned for the Democratic nomination for president. Both were defeated. Do you think successful candidates for president and vice president will continue to be white and male?

of informal qualifications. Until recently, it was assumed that neither a female American nor a black American could be elected president.

But the attitudes of voters and political parties are changing. In 1960, John F. Kennedy was the first Roman Catholic to be elected president. In 1984, the Democrats nominated a woman, Geraldine Ferraro, as their candidate for vice president. In 1988, a black preacher, Jesse Jackson, was one of the leading candidates for the Democratic nomination. Thus, informal qualifications in our times are different from what they were 100 years ago.

The Constitution uses the pronouns "he," "him," and "his" when referring to the president. But in this text, we are bearing in mind that a future president *could* be a woman. Therefore, when speaking about some unnamed president, this chapter uses the combined pronouns "he/she," "him/her," and "his/her."

REVIEW

A. Building Your Political Vocabulary

Select the word that correctly completes each statement.

Cabinet	state of the Union
commander	treaty
executive	veto
pardons	

1. The chief __(?)__ is responsible for carrying out, or executing, federal laws.
2. The president is the __(?)__ in chief of the armed forces.
3. The president acts as a judge when he/she grants __(?)__ to federal prisoners.
4. Officials who run different executive departments form the president's __(?)__.
5. A president uses his/her __(?)__ power by refusing to sign an act of Congress.
6. The president makes recommendations to Congress in a yearly __(?)__ address.
7. A __(?)__ is a formal agreement between two or more nations.

B. Making Inferences

In reviewing what you have read, you can infer whether or not each statement below is true. Answer either: (*a*) **probably true** or (*b*) **probably not true.**

1. The Constitution lists a number of informal qualifications for being president.
2. U.S. ambassadors to Spain, France, and Italy were appointed by the president.
3. As president from 1801–1809, Thomas Jefferson met with a Cabinet of 16 members.
4. Though born in the United States, 31-year-old Mary Peters is not yet qualified to be president.
5. For information about the president's veto power, you should refer to Article III of the Constitution.

2. WHY DO AMERICANS EXPECT THE PRESIDENT TO GIVE LEADERSHIP?

Is it the president's duty to provide leadership in a time of crisis? Almost all Americans would answer yes. But why do they look to the president for leadership instead of to Congress? Four reasons may be given.

1. The Constitution says that the president is "the chief." Twice the Constitution names the president as "the chief" (or leader) of the government. It says that the president is to act both as chief executive (leader of the Executive Branch) and as commander in chief (leader of the armed forces).

2. There is only one president. In the Senate, power is divided among 100 senators. In the House, power is divided among 435 representatives. In the Supreme Court, power is shared by nine justices. Disagreements are common in all three of these government groups. Decisions are slow and difficult.

Only one branch of government is under the control of a single person. Though advised by many, the president alone directs the Executive Branch. The president alone makes final decisions for the army, navy, Federal Bureau of Investigation (FBI), and hundreds of other units of government. When the nation is threatened by war or some other crisis, the president can take immediate action. Later there may be time for debate. Then Congress may challenge the president's decisions. But some leader in government must be able to act without delay in an emergency. In the United States, that leader can only be the president.

3. The president has great prestige as chief of state. In Great Britain, the main duty of the king or queen is to lead patriotic ceremonies. The royal family is looked upon as a symbol of the British nation.

Of course the United States has no royal family, because this would seem to us to be undemocratic. Nevertheless, the president is respected by Americans for much the same reasons that a king or queen is respected in other countries. We think of the president as a symbol of our nation. There are other symbols as well: the bald eagle, the Liberty Bell, the American flag. But the president is especially interesting to us as the only national symbol that lives, talks, and leads.

Why is the president regarded as a symbol, while members of Congress are not? It is because the president is the nation's one and only *chief of state.* This role is quite different from the more practical role of chief executive. A chief of state is like a master of ceremonies. In this role, the president conducts patriotic ceremonies and honors citizens for outstanding service. It is the president's custom, for example, to attend the first baseball game of the year. As chief of state, the president calls up astronauts to congratulate them on their achievements in space. At the White House, the president greets Eagle Scouts, artists, musicians, scholars, and Olympic athletes.

HONORING PEACE CORPS VOLUNTEERS. President Ronald Reagan is assisted by Vice President George Bush in honoring U.S. citizens at the White House. What role of the president is illustrated by this event?

None of these activities is listed in the Constitution. But a president devotes a lot of time to them anyway. Being chief of state adds to the prestige and dignity of the presidency. It also increases the president's power and ability to lead.

4. Modern presidents have given strong leadership. One hundred years ago, in the 1880s, presidents were not strong leaders. They performed their duties as defined by the Constitution—and not much more.

Then came the 20th century. One of the first presidents of this century was a man of great energy. Theodore Roosevelt, an older cousin of Franklin, thought it was his job to make America strong. A coal strike in 1903 made Americans shiver with fear as they looked ahead to a winter without heating fuel. "Teddy" Roosevelt used all of his powers as president to see that the strike was settled. In 1904, Roosevelt amazed Americans by moving to break up a powerful railroad company. He amazed them again in 1908 when he sent a fleet of U.S. battleships around the world. Members of Congress angrily objected. But this did not stop the president.

Scholars say that Theodore Roosevelt changed the office of president. He impressed Americans by the bold way that he faced problems. Many people admired this strong style of leadership and came to expect it of later presidents.

The next president to give strong leadership was Woodrow Wilson. In 1913, Wilson's first year as president, he proposed many major laws. He succeeded in persuading a majority in Congress to vote for his ideas. Wilson also took firm control of America's relations with foreign countries. As commander in chief, he sent U.S. troops to Europe to fight in World War I. He himself sailed to Paris after the war to make a peace treaty. No president before him had ever

"BULLY!" Theodore Roosevelt loved being president, calling his job a "bully pulpit" for speaking out on issues. Cartoonists often showed him swinging a big stick (right). Do Americans want every president to be as colorful and strong-willed as "Teddy"?

traveled abroad to make his leadership felt in person.

We have already met the third strong president of this century: Franklin Roosevelt. This Roosevelt came to office in the middle of the Great Depression. He was elected president in 1932, re-elected in 1936, re-elected again in 1940, and yet again in 1944. No other person was president this long—a total of 13 years. No other person used the powers of the presidency as Roosevelt used them.

We saw how he handled the banking crisis in 1933. Besides rescuing the banks, he also tried to help farmers, labor unions, retired people, unemployed youth, and the general public. He persuaded Congress to pass many laws to bring back prosperity. Some of his ideas worked. Others did not. But most people were glad just to see the government working hard to solve problems.

World War II was the second great challenge that Roosevelt had to face. At his request, more laws were passed to help fight the war. More workers were added to the government payroll. When the war ended, the Executive Branch was many

DEALING WITH FOREIGN LEADERS. In 1945, Franklin Roosevelt (center) traveled to the Soviet Union to meet with the British prime minister, Winston Churchill (left), and the Soviet dictator, Joseph Stalin (right). Why is influencing foreign leaders an especially difficult task for a president?

times larger than it had ever been. The president, as the head of this branch, had much greater power than ever.

When Roosevelt died in 1945, Vice President Harry Truman became president. Then came Dwight Eisenhower in 1953 and John Kennedy in 1961. All offered leadership to Congress, the nation, and the world at large. They followed in the footsteps of the other strong presidents of this century. Presidents were now expected to offer solutions to the nation's problems. Giving leadership was thought to be their main job.

REVIEW

A. Making Comparisons

1. What is the special role of the chief of state? How is it different from the role of the chief executive?
2. How did presidents of the 1880s think about their duties? What is different about the way modern presidents approach their job?

B. Examples of Main Ideas

Below are general statements about modern presidents. Illustrate each statement by telling how a specific president acted. The president might be either Theodore Roosevelt, Franklin Roosevelt, Woodrow Wilson, or Harry Truman.

1. To meet a sudden crisis, a president can take immediate action. For example, __(?)__
2. Strong presidents of the 20th century have given leadership to Congress. For example, __(?)__
3. A president's power usually increases in time of war. For example, __(?)__
4. Strong presidents sometimes act without getting the approval of Congress. For example, __(?)__
5. When business is bad, modern presidents take action to correct the problem. For example, __(?)__

C. Agree or Disagree

Tell whether you **agree** or **disagree** with each statement of opinion. Give your reasons.

1. A president's duties as chief of state are less important than his duties as chief executive.
2. A president cannot be truly "great" unless he/she governs during a time of national crisis.
3. The current president is an effective leader.

D. Project

WHAT IS TODAY'S NEWS ABOUT THE PRESIDENT? Turn on an evening news show on TV, and take notes on what is reported about the president. Also, look through a daily newspaper, reading and clipping all articles dealing with the president. Finally, describe the president's day in one or two paragraphs.

3. WHOSE ADVICE MAY GUIDE A PRESIDENT IN MAKING POLICY?

Americans expect a great deal of a president. They expect that he/she will

- make good decisions concerning national and international problems.
- take effective action on his/her decisions.
- convince others that the decisions are right and necessary.

For a president to accomplish all this is enormously difficult.

Selecting a team of advisers. Fortunately, modern presidents have plenty of help in dealing with problems and making decisions. In the White House, they surround themselves with special assistants and advisers. Outside the White House are the headquarters of the department heads. The secretary of defense, for example, has an office in the huge five-sided building known as the Pentagon. This adviser often calls the president on the telephone or visits the White House for special meetings. Other department heads also keep in close touch with their chief, the president.

Selecting a strong team of advisers is one of the president's most important tasks. Top advisers are chosen even before the president officially takes office. As you know, a president is elected in November but takes office in January of the following year. During this period, the president-elect is extremely busy trying to decide which men and women to appoint to different offices.

The president-elect has as many as 1,500 jobs to fill. The judges appointed to run federal courts are in the Judicial Branch. All other appointments are in the Executive Branch. The most important of the president's executive appointments are the following:

1. Cabinet members (department heads). As you know, the Executive Branch is divided into 14 major parts known as departments. Here they are, listed according to size.

Department	*Number of Employees (1993)*
Department of Defense	941,608*
Department of Veterans Affairs	265,014
Department of the Treasury	165,530
Department of Health and Human Services	132,406
Department of Agriculture	123,057
Department of Justice	98,022
Department of the Interior	84,736
Department of Transportation	69,922
Department of Commerce	38,651
Department of State	26,220
Department of Energy	20,637
Department of Labor	17,609
Department of Housing and Urban Development	13,208
Department of Education	5,001

* Figure represents only civilian employees, not the 1.8 million men and women in uniform.

Who heads each of these huge departments? The administrator (or director) in charge is usually called the department's secretary. The Department of State, for example, is headed by the secretary of state. The only department head with a different kind of title is the *attorney general,* who runs the Department of Justice.

The 14 department heads are regularly called to the White House to meet with the president. In this group, they are known as the Cabinet. Dwight Eisenhower treated Cabinet meetings very seriously. He relied upon them as a source of information and advice. Members of his Cabinet were required at every meeting to present a full report about their problems.

Other modern presidents have been more casual. Franklin Roosevelt liked to look across the table and say: "Well, Cordell, what's on your mind today?" Then Secretary of State Cordell Hull would talk informally about a problem in foreign affairs.

EXECUTIVES AT A CABINET MEETING, 1965. When seated at this table, President Lyndon Johnson (third from the right) acted as the chief executive. What parts of the Executive Branch are managed by members of the Cabinet?

2. Bureau chiefs. Each department of the Executive Branch consists of many smaller units. Some units are called bureaus. A famous example is the Federal Bureau of Investigation (FBI). Other units are called agencies (Environmental Protection Agency) and administrations (Social Security Administration). Administrators who direct these units have two bosses. Their day-to-day work is supervised by a department head (Cabinet member). But they may also receive orders from the person who appoints them to their jobs—the president.

3. Advisers in the Executive Office. One division of the Executive Branch reports directly to the president himself. It is *not* headed by any of the 14 Cabinet members. Many of the officials in this division have meeting rooms and offices right inside the White House itself. This special division of government is called the Executive Office of the President.

The Executive Office consists of several smaller divisions. One of them that serves the president directly is called the White House Office. Another draws up the yearly budget for the federal government. A *budget* is a plan for collecting and spending money. In 1991, the Office of Management and Budget (OMB) helped the president decide how to spend more than one *trillion* dollars! The director of the OMB can be as influential as any Cabinet member.

4. Members of the White House staff. One part of the White House is home for the president's family. Another part contains a large oval-shaped room, which is the president's office. Inside the famed Oval Office, the president is visited regularly by staff members. These special assistants carry out a number of vital tasks. They schedule the president's meetings, sort White House mail, make travel plans, and answer the questions of reporters. The reports that they write keep their chief informed about hundreds of problems.

Recent presidents have given a chief of staff the job of organizing and managing the White House staff. The chief of staff's power can be considerable, since he or she determines whom the president meets and how the president schedules the daily workload. A strong-willed chief of staff may seem to control the president, instead of the other way around. Critics of Ronald Reagan's presidency, for example, said that he allowed staff members to make policy without even consulting him.

At the opposite extreme was Lyndon Johnson. During his presidency (1963–1969), Johnson drove his staff to do his will. He worked 18 hours a day and expected his staff to do the same. They never knew when he would permit them to go home for the night. On one occasion, Johnson pushed them to keep working past midnight. They were too busy to eat. Finally, dinner was served to them at one in the morning.

5. The Vice President. The advisers mentioned so far are all appointed to their jobs by the president. Only one presidential adviser sits in Cabinet meetings and performs other duties as a result of being elected to office. That person is the vice president.

The U.S. Constitution says that the vice president shall preside over meetings of the Senate. The vice president may vote for or against a bill only when the Senators are deadlocked in a tie vote. Most vice presidents have found that presiding over the Senate is a routine chore that carries with it little real power or influence. On most days, a vice president will turn over the presiding officer's chair in the Senate to a senator of the majority party—the Senate's president *pro tempore.*

The vice president may or may not be given an active role to play in the executive branch. All depends on whether the president wishes to assign special tasks and duties to the vice president. President Eisenhower, for example, sent his vice president, Richard Nixon, on diplomatic missions to Latin America and the Soviet Union. President Bush sent his vice president, Dan Quayle, on speaking tours around the country to win support for the administration's conservative policies.

The vice president's most important role is to be available in case anything should happen to the president. As you learned in Chapter 11, the vice president may become president under special circumstances.

✔✔ SKILLS CHECK: Reading an organization chart

The organization headed by the president is huge. The chart on page 271 helps us to see its parts and how they relate to one another. Notice that this **organization chart** of the Executive Branch is divided into two main divisions: (*a*) Executive Office of the President and (*b*) Cabinet Departments. Because they connect with the president, we know that both divisions (and the boxes beneath them) are under the president's control. Study the organization chart, and then answer the questions below.

1. In this chapter, you read about a part of the Executive Office of the President whose name is *not* given in the chart. It is the box with a question mark (?). Write its name on a piece of paper.
2. Only 10 of the 14 Cabinet departments are named in the chart. On your piece of paper, write the four names that were omitted (marked by ?). Also give the titles of the advisers who head each of these four departments.

THE EXECUTIVE BRANCH

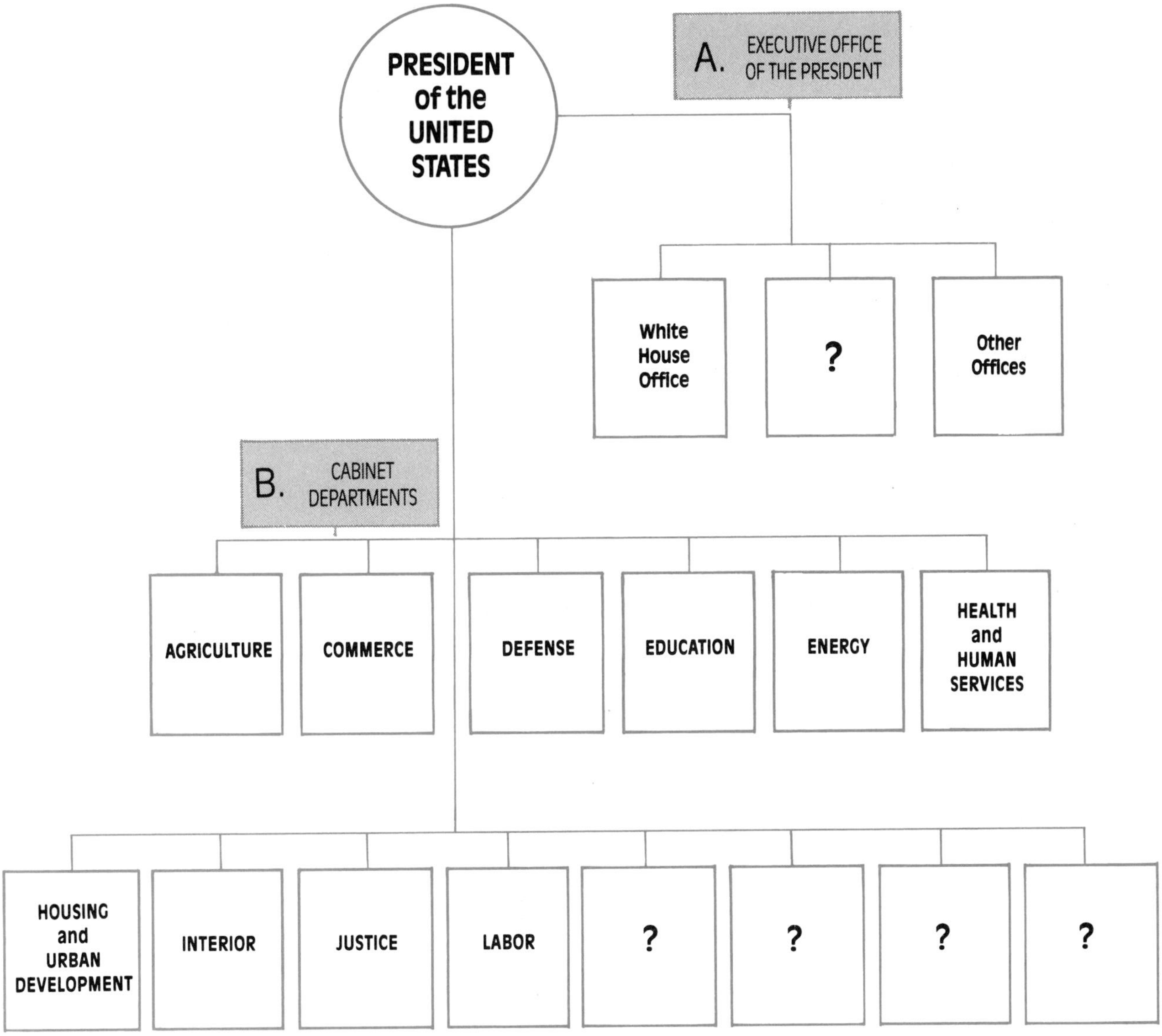

REVIEW

A. Applying What You Know

Assume that you are the president-elect. How would you choose members of your White House staff and Cabinet? Below are qualities, or traits of character, that may or may not be important to you as you pick your team of advisers. On a piece of paper, list the traits in order of their importance from **1** (most important) to **9** (least important).

- personal friend of yours for many years
- worked hard for you in your election campaign
- extremely intelligent
- excellent public speaker
- leading member of your own political party
- original thinker
- reputation for honesty
- opinions on public issues that agree with your own opinions
- much knowledge and experience in the assigned job

1. Explain why your first choice was most important to you.
2. Explain why your last choice was the least important to you.

B. Who's Who

Match each statement below with the official (or officials) that it describes. Some officials are described more than once.

1. works on assigned tasks in the White House
2. appoints to office as many as 1,500 people
3. meets regularly in the White House with thirteen other department heads
4. directs one of the major units within the department
5. manages the Social Security Administration
6. works for the Executive Branch
7. heads the Department of Commerce

a. the president
b. a Cabinet member
c. a member of the president's staff
d. a bureau chief
e. all of the above

4. HOW DO PRESIDENTS WIN SUPPORT FOR THEIR POLICIES?

A president counts upon the loyal support of the Cabinet members, the chief of staff, and other advisers. After all, they are members of the executive team. The president is their boss or chief.

Outside his/her own team, however, the president cannot be certain of anyone else's support. Many groups will surely oppose the president's policies. Ideas for new laws will meet resistance at home, while ideas for treaties will meet resistance abroad.

Even so, a president hopes to persuade four main groups to follow his/her leadership. They are: (1) members of Congress, (2) other politicians, (3) American voters, and (4) heads of foreign governments. What can a president do to influence each group?

Influencing Congress. Assisted by advisers, the president develops a legislative program. This is a set of bills that the president thinks Congress should enact into law. Usually, Congress passes *some* of the president's measures, while rejecting others. "You win some and lose some." That is a general rule of life—and also of politics.

One president was, very briefly, an exception to this rule. Franklin D. Roosevelt sent to Congress dozens of bills in early 1933. Without delay, majorities in both houses of Congress passed every one of Roosevelt's bills. There was an emergency bill to save the banks from failure and another bill to save the railroads. There was a bill to aid farmers and another to aid businesses. Every bill from the president's office was a major one. Roosevelt got almost all that he wanted from Congress in only 100 days of hectic lawmaking.

How did he do it? Three reasons explain this president's unusual success. First, Congress understood the need for action. The Great Depression was frightening. In times of crisis, Congress tends to follow wherever the president leads. Second, in 1933, large majorities in both the House and the Senate were Democrats. The president was also a Democrat. Membership in the same party makes it easier for a president to work with Congress. Third, Roosevelt understood politics as a chess master understands the game of chess. In small ways, he rewarded Democratic lawmakers who supported his program. For example, other Democrats who fought his program did not get special invitations to the White House.

A later president, John Kennedy, admired Roosevelt and wanted to be as effective. He too was a Democrat. He too was lucky that Democrats held majorities in both houses of Congress. He too was an experienced politician. Kennedy and his White House staff worked hard on their legislative program. They called their program the New Frontier. One bill after another was sent from the White House to Congress.

Kennedy called up members of Congress on the telephone. He knew many of them personally, having once served in both the House and the Senate. Like a good salesperson, he might joke and laugh with the congressperson before urging him or her to vote for a particular bill. He would explain why the bill was especially important to his presidency and to the nation. Sometimes he would suggest ways he might do political favors for a lawmaker in return for the lawmaker's support.

Despite these efforts, however, Kennedy was less successful than Roosevelt had been. In Congress, conservative Democrats joined Republicans in opposing the young president's liberal programs. Thus, more times than not, the majority in Congress refused to follow Kennedy's lead.

Leading Congress is never easy. All presidents, even Franklin Roosevelt, found this out.

Influencing a political party. A president's success depends in part on being able to lead his/her own political party. An American political party, as you know, is not tightly organized. Its members are not required to think alike or vote alike on any issue. It is very difficult to lead such a

PRESIDENT KENNEDY SIGNING A BILL. Although Kennedy had been a senator himself, he had trouble persuading Congress to pass laws that he recommended. How does this fact illustrate the U.S. system of checks and balances?

loosely organized group of voters and politicians.

But if a president is a skillful politician, he/she can have a strong influence on party members. Two methods of influence are most important. First, the president has hundreds of federal jobs to assign—Cabinet posts, judgeships, and so on. Jobs can be given in return for promises to support the president's programs.

Second, the president can do favors for politicians at election time. He/she can volunteer to travel to a candidate's home state and urge voters to elect that candidate. Politicians know how important it is to be seen with a popular president. In a close election, it can often mean the difference between victory and defeat.

Politicians speak of "riding the president's coattails" into office. This means that voters elect members of the president's party simply because they like the president. Popular presidents like Franklin Roosevelt, Dwight Eisenhower, and Ronald Reagan were well aware of the "coattail effect." They used it to give leadership to their parties.

Influencing the American people. A president's ability to lead depends partly on popularity. The more popular the president, the greater are his/her chances of influencing members of Congress and other politicians.

Woodrow Wilson knew this well. President Wilson was admired by many Americans because of his reputation for honesty and intelligence. In 1913, Wilson wanted Congress to reduce the tax on imported goods. He feared that lobbyists were spending a lot of money on behalf of powerful business interests to defeat his tax bill. At that time, there was widespread fear of big business controlling the votes of lawmakers. So President Wilson wrote an alarming message about what the lobbyists and "special interests" were doing. Newspapers all over the country printed the president's message on page one. People responded by sending angry letters to Congress urging them to stand behind the president. Wilson's tax bill then passed both houses.

President Wilson relied upon newspaper stories to win popular support for his ideas. Later presidents discovered ways of using the electronic media for this purpose. In the 1930s, Franklin Roosevelt's talks on radio made a hit with the American people.

Television came into widespread use in the 1950s. The first president to win popularity through this new medium was John Kennedy (president from 1961–1963). But the greatest master of TV for political purposes was the former movie actor Ronald Reagan (1981–1989).

Television is an especially powerful medium because the speaker's face and voice come directly into a person's home. Thus, a president who is camera-wise can have a powerful effect on the thinking of millions of people.

Influencing foreign governments. The more popular a president is, the greater tends to be his/her ability to influence leaders of other countries. It works the other way too. Presidents who show strength as world leaders tend to become more popular with voters. As examples of this, let us consider the leadership of two presidents, Dwight Eisenhower and John Kennedy.

In his first term as president, opinion polls showed that Eisenhower was popular with a large majority of Americans. He became even more popular in 1955 after traveling to Geneva, Switzerland, to meet with the heads of state of France, Great Britain, and the Soviet Union. Newspaper editorials praised the president for trying to bring about more peaceful relations with the Soviet leader Nikita Khrushchev.

Five years later, however, an event occurred that embarrassed Eisenhower. In May 1960, an American plane was shot

MOMENT OF DECISION, 1962. Members of the press photographed President Kennedy at his desk as he announced his decision to stop Soviet ships headed for Cuba. What constitutional powers did the president use in this crisis?

down over the Soviet Union. The Soviet leader Khrushchev accused the United States of using the plane to spy on Soviet military bases. At first Eisenhower denied the charge. But then he admitted that U-2 spy planes had been flying over the Soviet Union for some time. Eisenhower's popularity as well as his influence as a leader were hurt by this incident.

John Kennedy followed Eisenhower as president. At first, he blundered badly by giving half-hearted support to an invasion of Cuba—an invasion that failed. Then another crisis occurred involving Cuba. In October 1962, Kennedy found out that Soviet workers were preparing to place nuclear missiles in Cuba. This was a major threat to the United States. A worried Kennedy met with his team of advisers. He decided to blockade the island of Cuba with ships from the U.S. Navy. Commanders of the ships were instructed to stop Soviet vessels bound for Cuba and search them for nuclear weapons. The president explained his actions in a televised speech to the nation.

War between the United States and the Soviet Union seemed possible. But the Soviet leader Nikita Khrushchev wrote letters to Kennedy about the crisis. Kennedy sent carefully worded letters in reply. Finally, Khrushchev agreed to stop shipments of nuclear arms to Cuba and to remove the missile parts previously shipped. Kennedy then agreed to withdraw U.S. ships and call off the blockade.

President Kennedy had risked going to war over the Cuban missiles. The gamble worked and the crisis passed. Fortunately, threatening situations like the one in Cuba occur very seldom.

The Presidency in the 90s

How much can a president accomplish in one four-year term? Coming into office in January 1993, President Clinton pledged to take action on a large number of national and international problems. He promised to improve the education system, reform the health care system, overhaul the welfare system, strengthen law enforcement, and undertake dozens of other changes in American life.

Setting an agenda. Critics of Clinton's presidency said that he attempted to do too much. They said that his "agenda"—or list of goals for his presidency—was too long. Therefore, they argued, the American people became confused as the president skipped from one issue to another. One observer commented: "The president has a very long list of goals. Instead of having three big goals and taking lots of time to fight for them over many months, he has more. Managing such a long list of goals is his big challenge."

State of the Union, 1994. President Clinton announced his agenda for his second year in office, 1994, in his State of the Union address to Congress. He began his televised speech by congratulating the Congress for having passed several major laws in 1993 including a gun control law, a family leave act, and a free trade treaty with Mexico and Canada.

But he said that many more new laws and programs were needed. "And so tonight," Clinton declared, "let us resolve to continue the journey of renewal, to create more and better jobs, to guarantee health security for all, to reward welfare work over welfare, to promote democracy abroad, and to begin to reclaim our streets from violent crime and drugs and gangs, to renew our own American community."

The president then went down a long list of goals for the year. He wanted Congress to do all of the following:

1. Provide funds for building an "information superhighway" linking the nation's classrooms, libraries, and hospitals.
2. Enact a "school-to-work initiative" that would provide students with at least one year of job training before leaving school.
3. Change the welfare system so that people would receive welfare benefits for up to two years only. "After that, anyone who can work must work."
4. Reform the health care system to "provide health insurance that everybody can depend on."
5. Require stiffer penalties for those committing violent crimes, including imprisonment for life for those guilty of three such crimes. ("Three strikes and you are out.")
6. Help communities pay for the hiring of 100,000 more police officers.
7. Enact a law banning the sale of assault weapons.
8. Fight drug abuse by increasing federal funds for drug treatment and drug education.

Clinton's agenda also included goals in foreign policy. He wanted to:

9. Negotiate a treaty with other nations to stop all nuclear testing.
10. Help the struggling economies of Russia and Ukraine by giving more U.S. aid.
11. Do more to support "democratic renewal and human rights" in nations where citizens were mistreated.
12. Help to restore democracy in Haiti.
13. "Work for new progress toward peace in the Middle East."

When the president concluded his speech, members of Congress rose from their seats and applauded loudly. But news commentators raised doubts about the president's ability to carry out his ambitious agenda.

YOUR ADVICE: Imagine that you were the president's chief of staff in 1994. Would you have advised the president to (1) work equally hard on all items in his agenda or (2) concentrate his attention on just three or four goals and let the others go? Explain your choice.

President Bush and the Persian Gulf War. To be an effective leader, a president must try to win support for his policies from the American people *and* the press *and* the Congress—all at the same time. If the issue is foreign policy, lining up the support of allies and the United Nations is also crucial.

A recent example is President Bush's handling of a crisis in the Middle East. The crisis began in August 1990 when Iraq invaded its small neighbor Kuwait. Bush responded swiftly to this act of aggression. He went on television to condemn the attack and explain why it endangered the peace of the Middle East. He consulted with leaders of Congress and talked on the phone with the leaders of several foreign countries. Using his powers as commander in chief, the president ordered 200,000 U.S. troops to Saudi Arabia to hold back Iraq.

In the fall of 1990, Bush increased the pressure on the Iraqi dictator Saddam Hussein. Responding to U.S. leadership, the United Nations voted a number of economic sanctions (penalties) against Iraq and attempted to shut down Iraq's international trade. Opinion polls showed that a majority of Americans supported the president.

In December, the president and the news media made it clear that war with Iraq was a strong possibility. More troops were sent to Saudi Arabia. The United Nations voted for a U.S. resolution demanding that Iraq pull its troops out of Kuwait no later than January 15, 1991. Now Bush called up members of Congress. He urged them to vote for a resolution authorizing the use of U.S. troops in the Persian Gulf under certain conditions. Millions of Americans watched Congress debate the proposal. It passed.

In January 1991, Iraq's deadline for withdrawing from Kuwait came and went. The result was a war that took the United States and its allies just six weeks to win. It was the high point of George Bush's presidency—a fine example of what it takes to lead the United States and the world.

REVIEW

A. Making Inferences

Sometimes the information given in a reading is enough to enable us to make certain inferences from it. (*To infer* means to go beyond what is directly stated.) Other times, the information given is *not* enough to justify an inference. Tell whether each statement below (*a*) **can be inferred** or (*b*) **cannot be inferred** from what you have read.

1. President Franklin Roosevelt was more popular than President Woodrow Wilson.
2. President Roosevelt's popularity made it easier for members of his party to win election.
3. The presidents who followed Franklin Roosevelt had less success than he did influencing Congress in their first 100 days in office.
4. All presidents hope to influence members of their own political party.
5. All presidents travel abroad in an effort to influence the leaders of other countries.

B. Applying What You Know

The examples given in this chapter concern the actions of **past** presidents. Apply what you know to the **current** president by answering these questions about him/her.

1. Would you say the president is (*a*) very popular, (*b*) somewhat popular, or (*c*) not popular? Why do you think so?
2. Give an example of how the president has tried to influence the leader of a foreign country.
3. Give an example of how the president has tried to lead the Congress.
4. Give an example of how the president has tried to influence public opinion.

CHAPTER REVIEW

A. Completing the Summary

Select terms from the word list to fill in the blanks in the summary below. Write your answers on a separate piece of paper.

advisers	legislative program
ambassadors	natural-born
Cabinet	pardons
chief of state	press conferences
commander in chief	staff
department	state of the Union
Executive	treaties
informal	veto
leadership	

The American people expect the president to provide leadership for three reasons. First, he/she has sole power to direct the work of the __(1)__ Branch. Second, in addition to being chief executive, the president enjoys great prestige as the U.S. __(2)__. Third, in the 20th century, several strong presidents thought it was their job to lead the country through times of war and economic crisis.

The Constitution defines the president's powers and duties. These include:

- the power either to __(3)__ bills or sign them into law.
- the duty of reporting to Congress about the __(4)__.
- the power to give orders to the armed forces as their __(5)__.
- the power to make __(6)__ (agreements between nations)
- the power of appointing __(7)__ to foreign capitals.
- the power to grant __(8)__ to people accused or convicted of breaking federal laws.

According to the Constitution, anyone may be elected president who is at least 35 years old and a __(9)__ U.S. citizen. But there are also __(10)__ requirements for holding the office. As a result, until our own times, all presidents have been white and male.

In making decisions and leading the country, the president is daily aided by a team of __(11)__. Fourteen of them meet regularly as the __(12)__. Each is the head of a different __(13)__ in the Executive Branch. A separate group of advisers work in White House offices as the president's __(14)__.

A president's popularity affects his/her ability to give __(15)__. The __(16)__ of a popular president is more likely to pass Congress than the ideas of an unpopular one.

To explain their policies to the public, presidents answer questions on televised __(17)__. Many questions deal with foreign affairs, since one of the president's jobs is to talk with and influence other world leaders.

B. Applying What You Know

The following news article by The Associated Press (AP) appeared on page one of newspapers across the country on January 26, 1988. Read all six paragraphs (**A–F**). Then apply what you have learned from this chapter by answering the questions.

A WASHINGTON (AP)—President Reagan, declaring America is "strong, prosperous, at peace," asked Congress in his final state of the Union address last night to keep money flowing to Nicaragua's rebels and to ratify the newly signed arms treaty with the Soviet Union.

B Reagan, in a nationally broadcast speech before a joint session of the House and Senate, emphasized that he has a full agenda [group of proposals] for the next 12 months.

C "My thinking on the next year is quite simple: Let's make this the best of eight. And that means it's all out, right to the finish line. I don't buy the idea that this is the last of anything," said Reagan, who turns the White House over to a successor next January.

D Democrats and Republicans alike cheered and applauded when Reagan, urging reform of the congressional budget process, lifted three huge spending bills, each weighing upward of 15 pounds, and thumped them down, one by one, on a nearby desk. He said most lawmakers didn't even know what was in the bills.

E Reversing course from last year, Reagan called for increased spending for education and the war against drugs.

F He claimed for his administration "an untold success story"—an increase in the number of young people who are willing to turn away from drugs. He praised his wife Nancy for that development: "She has helped so many of our young people to say 'no' to drugs. Nancy, much credit belongs to you, and I want to express to you your husband's pride and your country's thanks."

Questions About the Article

1. What speech does the article summarize? In what paragraph (or paragraphs) do you find the answer?
2. Before 1988, how many times had President Reagan delivered a state of the Union message to Congress?
3. In different paragraphs, the article mentions *several* of the president's ideas for legislation (laws). Try to find and list four ideas.
4. From one of the paragraphs, you can infer that the president's proposal for 1988 differs in at least two ways from his proposal in 1987. Which paragraph mentions this change of mind? Summarize the change in your own words.
5. Speaking about his wife, Nancy Reagan, the president said: "I want to express to you your husband's pride and your country's thanks." When speaking like this, which of the following roles or functions was the president performing? (*a*) chief executive, (*b*) chief diplomat, (*c*) party leader, (*d*) commander in chief, or (*e*) chief of state. Explain.

UNIT FIVE

The Congress

Probably the best known building in the United States is the one pictured to the left. The Capitol in Washington, D.C., consists of three main sections: the domed rotunda, the House wing, and the Senate wing. Each year, about 10 million tourists climb the Capitol steps and sit in the galleries of the House and Senate.

Think of yourself as one of the tourists. Crossing from the House wing to the Senate wing, what differences would you observe? Do you think each sentence below (**1-11**) describes:

A. the House of Representatives?
B. the Senate?
C. both the House and the Senate?

1. It consists of 100 elected members.
2. Members serve for two-year terms.
3. Members meet with constituents.
4. All 50 states are represented equally.
5. Bills are considered by committees.
6. A speaker is the presiding officer.
7. It has the power either to approve or reject the president's treaties.
8. Its lawmaking powers are listed in Article I of the Constitution.
9. Members of the majority party hold positions of leadership.
10. It determines the amount of money that the federal government may spend for different purposes.
11. Every 10 years, there is a change in the number of seats assigned to each state.

After reading this unit on the Congress, you will know how laws are made inside the Capitol. You will also know why the lawmaking process neither begins in this building nor ends here. The Capitol is the official home and meeting place of Congress. But, as you shall see, a great deal happens elsewhere—in committee rooms, in the White House, and even in your own community. Everybody, including you, has opportunities to influence the laws of Congress. After all, those who make the laws are supposed to represent the voters who elected them. When you become 18 years old, one of the voters represented in Congress will be you.

Answers

1. *b* 4. *b* 7. *b* 10. *c*
2. *a* 5. *c* 8. *c* 11. *a*
3. *c* 6. *a* 9. *c*

A SENATOR FROM KANSAS. Nancy Landon Kassebaum was first elected to a Senate seat in 1978. Who currently represents your state in the Senate and your district in the House?

CHAPTER 13

The Two Houses of Congress

OBJECTIVES

After reading this chapter, you will know

1. how a member of Congress acts as a lawmaker.
2. how a member of Congress represents and serves constituents.
3. the method for apportioning seats among U.S. representatives from different states.
4. why political parties are important in organizing the House of Representatives and the Senate.
5. how the leaders of Congress are chosen.
6. how to organize information before writing an essay.

The U.S. Senate is known as an "exclusive club" because it consists of only 100 members. Further, in 1978, all of the senators were men. But then a woman from Kansas, Nancy Landon Kassebaum, won election to the Senate. That changed the count in the "club" to 99 men and one woman. She was only the fifth woman in history to be elected to a Senate seat.

How did Senator Kassebaum become interested in politics?

Back in the 1930s, her father, "Alf" Landon, had been a popular governor of Kansas. Landon had also been the Republican candidate for president in 1936, but lost to Franklin Roosevelt. Thus, Nancy Landon had grown up listening to talk of political issues. During her college years, she would sometimes dream about a career in politics. She recalls: "I enjoyed politics and public policy so much . . . . There were times in high school and college when I mused [dreamed] about becoming actively involved as a candidate. But it was a daydream, a fantasy."

It remained a fantasy for many years. After raising four children, Mrs. Kassebaum took a job working in Washington, D.C., for a Kansas senator. Her boss, an older man, told her that he intended to retire from the Senate in 1978. She decided that she was as well qualified as anyone to take his place. She campaigned for the Republican nomination and won. Her slogan was, "A Fresh Face, A Trusted Kansas Name." Then she defeated the Democratic candidate in the November election.

She had several advantages. First, being the daughter of Alf Landon gave her a name that Kansas voters recognized. Second, as a millionaire, she could spend a lot of money on her own campaign. Third, her conservative position on issues appealed to Kansas voters more than the liberal ideas of her Democratic opponent. Fourth, she had a winning personality. One reporter said, "She has a smile that explodes on her face."

You will learn more about Nancy Kassebaum and Congress in this chapter. The chapter will answer these questions:

1. How do members of Congress spend their time?
2. How does the Senate differ from the House?
3. Who are the leaders of Congress?

1. HOW DO MEMBERS OF CONGRESS SPEND THEIR TIME?

A good way to learn about the varied duties of a congressperson is to follow his or her activities for just one day of the work week. For example, whom did Senator Nancy Kassebaum meet and what did she do on Tuesday, March 15, 1988? One of her aides gave an hour-by-hour account of that day.

CASE STUDY: A day in the life of Senator Kassebaum

The day began, as it usually does, in the Senate Office Building a short distance from the Capitol.

A.M.

9:30 In her office, the senator met with several people from her state, Kansans who wanted to know her views on the farm problem.

10:00 Next to meet with her was the head of a federal agency. They discussed plans for improving the Washington, D.C., airport, a topic of concern to the senator since bills about aviation are one of her specialties.

10:30 Lights, action, camera! Into the office walked the movie actor Burt Lancaster and four movie directors. They wanted the senator's support for a bill to stop old black-and-white movies from being computer-colorized. TV crews taped Lancaster's comments for the evening news.

10:50 Suddenly a buzzer went off, a signal for senators to leave their offices and committee rooms and go to the Senate chamber to vote. The senator expressed her regret that she had to cut short her interview with the movie star. She took an elevator to the basement and to a subway that shuttles between the Office Building and the Capitol. Walking onto the Senate floor, she voted yes for a proposed change in the rules for debating a bill. The rule change passed.

11:30 Back in her office, the senator met with the head of the Federal Aviation Agency (FAA). Then, for her next meeting in the Capitol, the senator decided to walk there for the exercise.

P.M.

12:30 In one of the Capitol's meeting rooms, the senator ate lunch with other Republican lawmakers. During this "policy lunch," the Republicans reviewed their lawmaking strategy for the week. In a nearby room, Democrats also talked strategy as they ate.

2:00 The senator had planned to attend hearings in a Senate committee room but learned that they had been called off. Again, a buzzer sounded.

2:15 On the Senate floor, Senator Kassebaum answered "yes" as her name was called. She thereby voted in favor of an immigration bill. A majority of senators also voted yes, and the measure passed.

2:30 Waiting in the senator's office was a high school girl from Florida. The visitor was preparing to role play Senator Kassebaum in a student congress that her school had organized. The senator apologized that she could talk for only 10 minutes before her next appointment.

3:00 The senator was driven to a hotel where she joined a panel of guest speakers. Her audience was a Republican group that called itself the "Inner Circle." After presenting one of several speeches on U.S. foreign policy, she returned to the Senate Office Building.

4:30 She had 15 minutes to review letters at her desk when "Bzzz!" went the buzzer.

THE SENATOR AT WORK. Left: Riding in an open subway car from Senator Kassebaum's office to the Capitol takes less than a minute. On a typical day, why must a senator take this trip so often? Right: In the office of the senator's chief of staff, David Bartel, a TV monitor shows what business is being conducted on the Senate floor. What are the responsibilities of a chief of staff?

4:45 On the Senate floor, a bill was being debated. It proposed that the Executive Branch keep Congress better informed on matters affecting the national security. Again, Senator Kassebaum sided with the majority, and the bill passed. Next: another subway ride back to the Senate Office Building.

5:30 Down the hall from her office, a group of Jewish-Americans had gathered to discuss U.S. policy toward Israel. Senator Kassebaum dropped by to talk with them.

6:30 Time to leave the office for the day. But there was always homework to be done. The senator gathered up an armload of blue folders that her secretary had left for her. Several folders contained letters from constituents that demanded her attention. Other folders were stuffed with reports and bills that needed to be read for the next day's work.

10:30 At home, the senator signed the last letter and closed the last blue folder. So ended one day in her lawmaker's life.

The two functions of every congressperson. It takes a lot of stamina to serve in Congress as either a senator or a representative. The workday described above was actually shorter and less hectic than most days. On a typical day, members of Congress can expect to spend about 11 hours on the job.

Senator Kassebaum is one of 535 people who go to Washington to carry out a unique and demanding job. One hundred of them are senators; 435 are representatives. These members of Congress—or congresspersons—have two main functions to perform for American democracy. One function is to decide what laws to enact for the nation. For example, whenever the buzzer went off, Senator Kassebaum was reminded of the lawmaking part of her job. A second function of every senator and representative is to serve and represent "the people back home." Recall that Senator Kassebaum began her day by greeting a group of citizens from Kansas. During this hour, she acted partly as a lawmaker but even more as a representative of the people who elected her to office—her *constituents*.

Let us look closely now at both the lawmaking and representative functions of a congressperson.

The lawmaking function. Article I of the Constitution states: "All legislative powers herein granted shall be vested in a Congress

FOUR SENATORS. After winning election to the Senate in 1992, Carole Mosely Brown of Illinois (left), Patty Murray of Washington, and Barbara Boxer of California met with veteran Senator Barbara Mikulski of Maryland (right). In the 1990s, do you think women candidates for high office will stand as good a chance as men of being elected?

of the United States, which shall consist of a Senate and House of Representatives."

From a congressperson's viewpoint, what does it mean to have "legislative" power? It means that he or she may vote either "yea" (yes) or "nay" (no) on written proposals for new federal laws. Such written proposals are called bills.

Voting on a bill takes place in the Capitol in Washington in two immense rooms, or chambers. The House chamber is the main room in one wing of the Capitol. The smaller Senate chamber is in a second wing. Like students in a classroom, senators and representatives are assigned to seats of their own in their respective chambers.

Unlike a classroom, however, members of each house rarely sit in their seats for very long. They are free to come into the chamber and to leave it at any time. If bills that they care about are being debated, they will probably be there. If not, they may be in their offices or in one of the many committee rooms. Buzzers tell them when they are needed in the House or Senate to vote on a proposed law.

Voting by roll call. Voting in the Senate is not too much different from taking attendance in a classroom. A clerk reads down a list of senators' names. One by one, the senators call out their votes, either "yes" or "no." The method of collecting votes one person at a time is known as a roll-call method.

In the House, voting by roll call is speeded up by a push-button system. Entering the House chamber, representatives pull out plastic cards with their names on them. They insert the cards into voting slots located in 48 places around the chamber. Near each slot are three buttons, marked *yea*, *nay*, and *present*. As they push these buttons, their votes on a particular bill are instantly recorded beside their names on a huge electronic board hanging on one wall. (To push the *present* button means that a congressperson has decided *not* to vote either for or against the bill under consideration.)

Voting as a group. Group methods for counting votes may also be used in the Senate or House. There is, for example, the voice vote method:

"Those in favor signify by saying 'aye.' "

"Aye!" comes a general shout all at once from the mouths of many lawmakers.

"Those opposed signify by saying 'no.' "

"No!" comes another shout.

After judging which shout is louder, the presiding officer in the House or Senate announces that the bill is either passed or defeated.

A division, or standing, vote, is a second method by which everyone may vote at once. Members in favor of a bill will stand at their seats and wait for the presiding officer to "count heads." Members opposed to a bill will then stand as a group and be counted.

Having voted, certain lawmakers may decide to leave the "floor" (chamber) and rush back to a committee room in a different building. Committees consist of small groups of lawmakers who specialize in considering bills of one particular kind. Most of the work of making laws takes place in committee rooms. You will learn more about the work of congressional committees in the next chapter.

Senator Kassebaum's specialty. In the course of just one day, Senator Kassebaum had to deal with five public issues. She was called upon to decide what should be done about:

(1) a farm problem
(2) an airport in Washington, D.C.
(3) the colorization of black-and-white movies
(4) immigration
(5) national security.

On other days of the week, many other issues arose.

Lawmakers must work hard to keep informed about the dozens of issues that come their way. At the same time, most senators and representatives select two or three issues that particularly interest them. Much of their lawmaking time is devoted to the issues of their choice. Senator Kassebaum, for example, was especially concerned about U.S. policy toward South Africa. She disliked the racist laws of the South African government and wanted the United States to take a strong stand against them.

The representative function. Naturally, a lawmaker must spend a lot of time on the function of studying and making laws. But many hours of the day must also be reserved for a second function: keeping in touch with constituents back home.

Constituents generally fall into three groups. First, there are the organized pressure groups discussed in Chapter 10. They may send lobbyists to Washington to meet with a congressperson. Or the congressperson may be invited to travel home and make speeches to members of an organization such as a local Chamber of Commerce (a group of business leaders).

A second group of constituents are those who want a lawmaker's help with personal problems. Older constituents may have problems collecting their Social Security checks or veterans' benefits. Younger constituents may seek help in being admitted to a U.S. service academy, such as West Point. Middle-aged people may have run into problems with U.S. tax officials or the FBI. Their letters to a senator's or representative's office ask for assistance and information that will "clean up the mess." Other letters express constituents' views on public issues. They may be about such issues as foreign aid, women's rights, terrorism, taxes, pollution, the arms race, and so on.

The third and largest group of constituents are those who do *not* make their needs or opinions known. They are the "silent

CONSTITUENTS FROM KANSAS. While touring the nation's capital, this family from Topeka, Kansas, visited Senator Kassebaum's office and received tickets to the Senate dining room. Why is it essential for members of Congress to keep in touch with their constituents?

majority." And yet, these constituents cannot be ignored. At election time, their votes count as much as anyone's. So a congressperson must make an effort to find out what the "silent majority" may be thinking. For this purpose, questionnaires are mailed out from the congressperson's office. People are asked their opinions on a number of issues. Their answers are sorted, counted, and analyzed. The congressperson then takes action on the most important issues.

The will of the people. In a democracy, elected officials are supposed to serve the will of the people. But how are lawmakers to know what policies and laws are wanted by the people? They can know and serve "the people's will" only if they stay in close touch with their constituents. Thus, in Congress, the representative function (responding to constituents' problems) and the lawmaking function (voting on bills) go hand in hand.

Before voting on a bill, members of Congress are careful to consider public opinion in their home state or district. However, their vote *may or may not* agree with the opinion of the majority. Most lawmakers think it is their duty to form their own opinions on an issue. They are influenced by public opinion—but rarely controlled by it.

STAFF WORKERS IN THE HOUSE AND SENATE. The door to every congressperson's office displays the state seal. Among the thousands of staff members employed in Congress are Mary Detchmendy from California (left) and Angie Binder from Colorado (right). What tasks might they be assigned?

Staff support. Working 11 hours may seem like a long day. But it is not nearly enough to handle all that a congressperson must do. There are just too many bills to study, too many letters to answer, and too many committee meetings to attend. Members of Congress need a lot of help—and they get it. Those who assist a member of Congress are known as his or her personal staff.

Each representative in the House may hire as many as 18 full-time staff members. Rules in the Senate set an upper limit on the amount of money that each senator may spend on staff salaries. In 1993, Senator Kassebaum used her staff allowance of $1,054,000 to employ 22 people in her office in Washington and 10 people in her office in Kansas.

Staff members are assigned to various jobs. Some help out with lawmaking. They research bills, draft bills, write reports about bills, and even recommend how their boss should vote on certain bills.

Another group of assistants specialize in casework. When a constituent writes to a congressperson about a problem, it is usually a staff member who reads the letter and acts on it.

Suppose that you were a member of Senator Kassebaum's staff. You open a letter to the senator telling about the troubles of a farm family coping with the results of a bad harvest. The letter asks, "Is there any law or government program that can help us get through the winter?" As it happens, you do know of a law that might apply. You call the head of a federal agency that administers the law. Sure enough, the law does apply, and the Kansas family can be helped. You take the case to Senator Kassebaum. She is delighted to sign the letter you have written explaining what the family should do.

Instead of handling casework, Senator Kassebaum might employ you as one of her administrative assistants. In this job you help out with your boss's crowded schedule, making sure that every minute of her 11-hour day is wisely used. You also phone hotels and travel agents making the senator's travel arrangements. To keep in touch with their constituents, members of Congress fly home regularly. In her first year as a senator, Nancy Kassebaum flew from the nation's capital to Kansas almost every weekend.

Salary and other benefits. There are compensations for the long hours of making laws and helping constituents. Members of Congress have the power to determine what salaries they receive for their work. In 1991, members of the Senate voted to give themselves a nearly 50 percent increase in salary from $89,500 a year to $129,500. The American public reacted angrily to news of the salary increase and accused members of Congress of being greedy and self-serving. The general outcry led to the adoption of the Twenty-seventh Amendment in 1992 (see page 111). In effect, this amendment means that persons elected to Congress in one year must wait at least two years before receiving any pay increase.

In addition to their salaries, members of Congress enjoy special benefits and privileges, which include the following:

• ***Franking privilege.*** The U.S. government pays the cost of official letters and other kinds of mail sent out by members of Congress and their staffs. The free postage is known as Congress's franking privilege. This benefit is not small considering the amount of mail involved. In an average year, the U.S. Postal Service delivers more than 300 million pieces of franked (freely stamped) mail from Congress.

• ***Travel allowance.*** Representatives may travel to and from their home districts *free* as many as 26 times a year. Senators are allowed between 40 and 44 round-trips a year, all paid for by the U.S. government.

• ***Heath club.*** A third benefit is a special health club in Washington, D.C. Here senators and representatives may cool off in a swimming pool or warm up on a paddleball court. Use of the facilities is at a low cost to every member of Congress.

• ***Recording studios.*** Special studios exist in Washington where members of Congress may make videotapes of their activities for the voters back home.

House bank scandal. Congress had to give up one of its privileges in 1991 after the news media informed the public about it. It was learned that one bank in the nation's capital served only the 435 members of the House of Representatives. Unlike regular banks that charge fees if customers overdraw their accounts, users of the House bank could spend more money than they had on hand and do so without penalty. An investigation revealed that members of the House had overdrawn their accounts a total of 20,000 times in a three-year period. In response to the public outcry over the scandal, the House voted to shut down its special bank.

REVIEW

A. Building Your Political Vocabulary

Write six original sentences about the daily work of either (1) Senator Nancy Kassebaum or (2) a senator or representative from your own state. In each sentence, use a different word from the list below.

franked mail	silent majority
constituency	casework
roll-call vote	administrative assistant

B. Facts and Opinions

Facts can be turned into **opinions.** And opinions can be turned into facts. For example:

FACT: A senator is allowed to charge the U.S. government for as many as 44 trips a year to his or her home state.

OPINION: The U.S. government should pay for only 20 trips a year; anything more should be at the senator's own expense.

Change each fact below into an opinion. Change each opinion into a fact.

1. FACT: The average congressperson works more than 11 hours a day.
2. FACT: Representatives have two main functions: making laws and serving their constituents.
3. OPINION: Voting electronically is more practical than the voice-vote method.
4. OPINION: Members of Congress have too many special privileges and benefits.
5. FACT: Most people do not bother to write letters to their representatives in Congress.

✔✔ SKILLS CHECK: Organizing information

On a piece of paper, copy these MAIN TOPICS. Leave about five lines of space between topics.

1. MAKING LAWS
2. REPRESENTING CONSTITUENTS
3. STAFF JOBS

If you were writing an essay about Congress, you would want to give several **facts**—or supporting details—about each **main topic.** Under each main topic on your piece of paper, write those phrases from the list below that would support that topic.

- opening letters from the home district
- speaking at a Chamber of Commerce luncheon
- voting "aye" on a bill
- doing a lot of background research on a bill
- handling casework
- participating in a committee meeting
- making hotel reservations
- meeting with lobbyists
- making a speech in the Senate chamber
- talking with a class of students who are touring the Capitol

2. HOW DOES THE SENATE DIFFER FROM THE HOUSE?

In the last section, we talked about senators and representatives as if their jobs were the same. They are the same in some ways, but not in other ways. This section will tell what is *different* about senators on the one hand and representatives on the other.

A bicameral Congress. Look again at the floor plan of the Capitol on page 286. It shows the separation that exists between the Senate in one wing and the House of Representatives in the other wing. They are two separate lawmaking groups, or "bodies." Each considers different bills at different times.

Because of this separation into *two* lawmaking houses, we say that the U.S. Congress is bicameral. The earliest Congress under the Articles of Confederation (1781–1788) had been unicameral. It had only *one* house instead of two. What was the reason for changing to a bicameral (two-house) plan? If you do not remember, read again about the Great Compromise at Philadelphia in 1787 (pages 74–75).

Senators and representatives compared. Being a U.S. senator is different from being a U.S. representative in several ways:

1. Number of members. The House seats 435 members while the Senate seats just 100. Representatives outnumber senators by more than 4 to 1.

2. Length of term. A representative has a short term, only two years. A senator's term is three times as long—six years. However, both a representative and a senator may be re-elected again and again. Carl Hayden from Arizona was re-elected many times to Congress until he retired at the age of 91. By then, he had served 56 years in Congress, 15 of them in the House, and 41 in the Senate. Hayden holds the record for the longest service in Congress.

3. Constituencies. A senator serves *all* the people of a state. A representative serves just a fraction of the state's population—that fraction that lives in his or her congressional district.

4. Power and influence. The average senator has more power than the average representative. Why? First of all, senators derive power from being elected statewide and thus having a large constituency. Second, it is easier to influence a small group of people (100 senators) than a group four times as large (435 representatives).

5. Rules of debate. Because the Senate is smaller, its members are allowed more freedom to talk and debate. A senator may stand on the floor of the Senate and talk for hours about a bill. In the House, rules for debating a bill are much stricter. Opportunities to make a speech on the House floor are limited to only a few minutes per speaker.

Representation in the Senate. From Chapter 4, recall the dispute in 1787 between delegates to the Constitutional Convention at Philadelphia. One group of delegates wanted states to be represented equally in Congress. A second group wanted states to be represented according to the size of their populations. The two groups were finally satisfied by the "Great Compromise." According to this plan, states would be represented equally in one house (the Senate) but unequally in a second house (the House of Representatives).

The table below shows how this compromise is carried out in today's Congress:

STATE	POPULATION (1990)	NUMBER OF SENATORS	NUMBER OF REPRESENTATIVES
Alabama	4,089,232	2	7
Alaska	570,345	2	1
Arizona	3,749,693	2	6
Arkansas	2,371,950	2	4
California	30,379,872	2	52

We see from the table that California's population is more than 50 times the size of Alaska's. And yet, in the Senate, there are two seats for California and two for Alaska. Every state sends to the Senate exactly the same number of lawmakers: two.

Representation in the House. A state's population matters in the House even if it does not in the Senate. The populous state of California has 52 representatives in the House. Alaska, with its small population, has only one representative. To see how other states are represented in the House, study the chart on page 294. Remember this rule of the Constitution: *a state's representation in the House varies with the size of its population.*

The apportionment of House seats. The above rule does not change. But a state's population *does* change. For example, when California joined the Union in 1850, it was one of the least populous states. Today, it is the most populous.

How does representation in the House adjust to changes in the population? It does so by a system called *reapportionment.* Once every ten years, the U.S. government makes a count of the population of each state. Such a count is referred to as a *census.* The first census was completed in 1790, shortly after the Constitution was adopted. The most recent census was conducted in 1990.

The results of each census determine how seats in the House shall be distributed (or apportioned) among the states. Two rules

CHANGING PATTERNS OF CONGRESSIONAL REPRESENTATION:

Reapportionment Based on 1990 Census

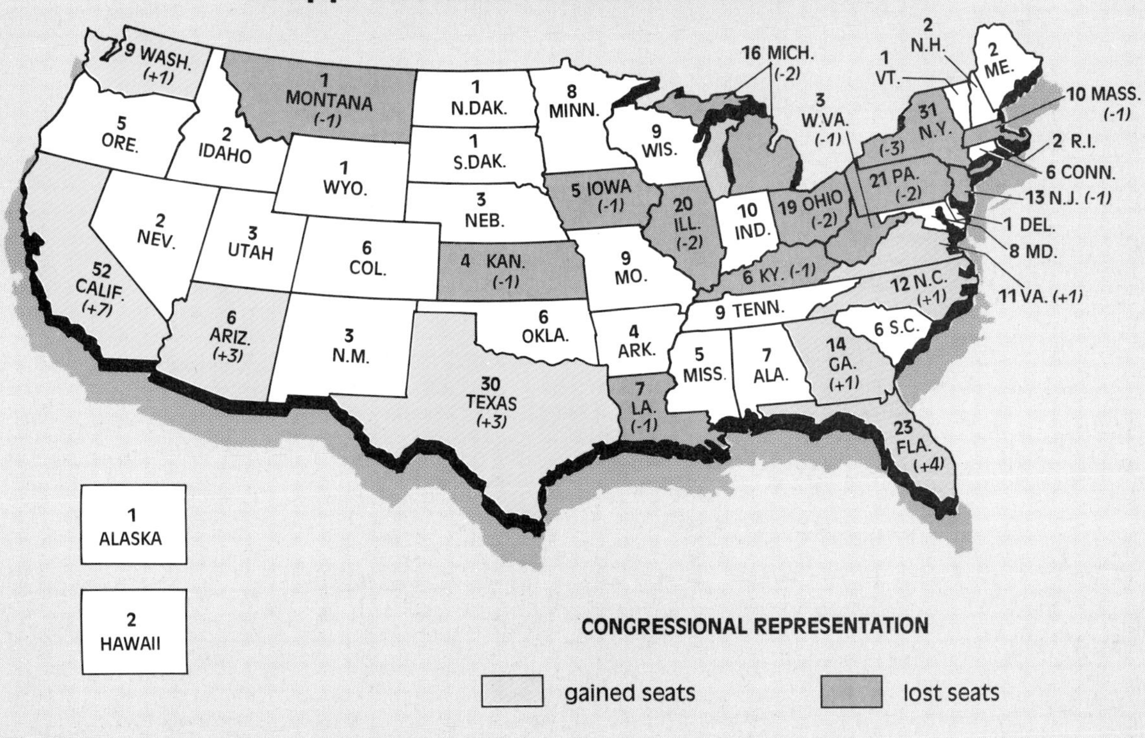

for apportionment must be taken into account:

1. Every state is entitled to a *minimum of one representative.*
2. The number of people served by a representative must be *at least 30,000.*

These rules are in the Constitution and cannot be changed except by amendment.

A law of Congress in 1929 added another rule. It provided that total membership in the House would always be the same number: 435. From the census every ten years, we know the relative sizes of the different states. By applying a mathematical formula, it is possible to distribute the 435 seats of the House fairly among the various states.

Of course, from one census to the next, a state may either gain House seats or lose them. The table below shows what has happened in some of the states since 1930.

Notice that there is only one representative from Wyoming. He or she serves all the people of that state. More populous states are divided into districts. Florida, for example, had 23 districts in the 1990s, each served by a different representative. Two representatives came from districts in the city of Jacksonville, the 4th and part of the 3rd. Three other representatives were elected from Miami's districts—Florida's 17th, 18th, and part of the 22nd.

Drawing district boundaries. The boundaries between districts are not permanent. In fact, they are subject to be redrawn after each census, once every ten years. Who redraws them? The answer is the legislature of each state. Let us suppose that Florida gains 7 seats in the House after the census year, 2000. Then Florida's state lawmakers must divide their state into 30 districts (instead of 23, the number in the 1990s).

Lawmakers are politicians who want to stay in office. They try to draw district boundaries so that candidates of their own

NUMBER OF REPRESENTATIVES

	After **1930** CENSUS	After **1990** CENSUS
California	20	52
Florida	5	23
Illinois	27	20
New York	45	31
North Dakota	3	1
Pennsylvania	34	21
Texas	21	30
Wyoming	1	1

party have an advantage on Election Day. In the past, politicians had two ways of doing this. One way was to create districts with unequal populations. Another way was to twist district boundaries into strange shapes.

"One man, one vote." The first method is no longer practiced because the Supreme Court ruled that it was unfair. An example will show you why. Suppose that District 1 has 800,000 people. District 2 right next to it has only 300,000 people. Each voter in District 2 would probably be better represented than a voter in District 1.

In 1964, in the case of *Wesberry* v. *Sanders*, the Supreme Court declared that districts with unequal populations were unconstitutional. In its decision, it proclaimed the principle of "one man, one vote." In other words, when voting for U.S. representatives, people in one district must not be better represented than people in another district.

Because of *Wesberry* v. *Sanders*, state lawmakers must take care to draw district boundaries so that districts are as nearly equal in population as possible. Today, the average population of a congressional district is about 500,000.

Gerrymandering. The second method for "playing tricks" with district boundaries is still in use (though less so than in the past). The practice is known as *"gerrymandering"* because of the shape of an old legislative district in Massachusetts. Back in 1812, Massachusetts politicians of the majority party drew an oddly shaped district that looked like the long, lizard-like body of a salamander. The Massachusetts governor who approved its shape was Elbridge Gerry. One writer jokingly referred to the district as a "gerrymander." Today, to gerrymander means to draw district boundaries to suit the political purposes of state lawmakers.

If you were a politician who wanted to gerrymander, how would you go about it? Imagine two cities in your state, City A and City B. As a politician, you know that a majority of voters in City A almost always supports Republican candidates. At the same time, certain neighborhoods in City B almost always vote for Democrats. (See Chart 1, page 296.)

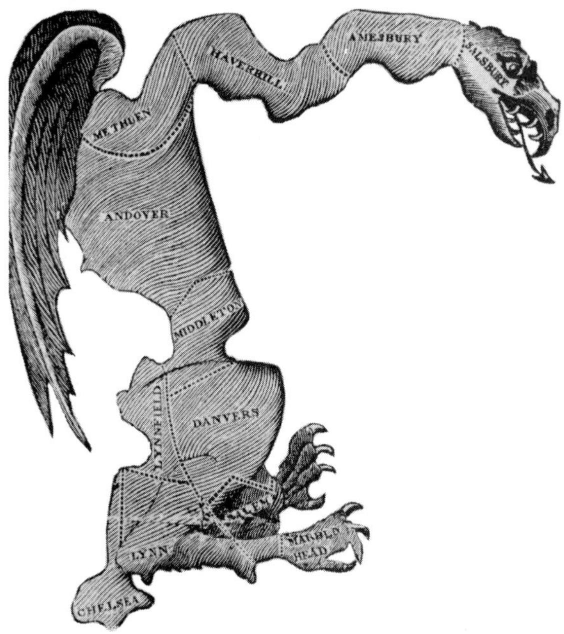

GERRYMANDER. The political district above was created by Massachusetts Governor Elbridge Gerry in 1812. Why do politicians create gerrymandered districts?

Suppose further that the Democrats hold a majority in the state legislature. When it comes time to redraw district boundaries, they would try to divide the voting strength of the Republicans. In Cities A and B, boundaries would be drawn so that "Republican" territories are split up. (See Chart 2.)

In District 1, notice that Democrats can outvote Republicans by a ratio of three to two. In District 2, Democrats have an advantage of four circles (neighborhoods) to three. Both districts then are likely to choose Democrats to go to the House of Representatives.

Now suppose that Republicians controlled the state legislature. Then different district boundaries would be drawn to give Republicans as much of an advantage as possible. (See Chart 3.)

With these boundaries, Republicans can usually count on winning one district: District 1. The second district would be conceded to the Democrats; but winning one out of two is better than none.

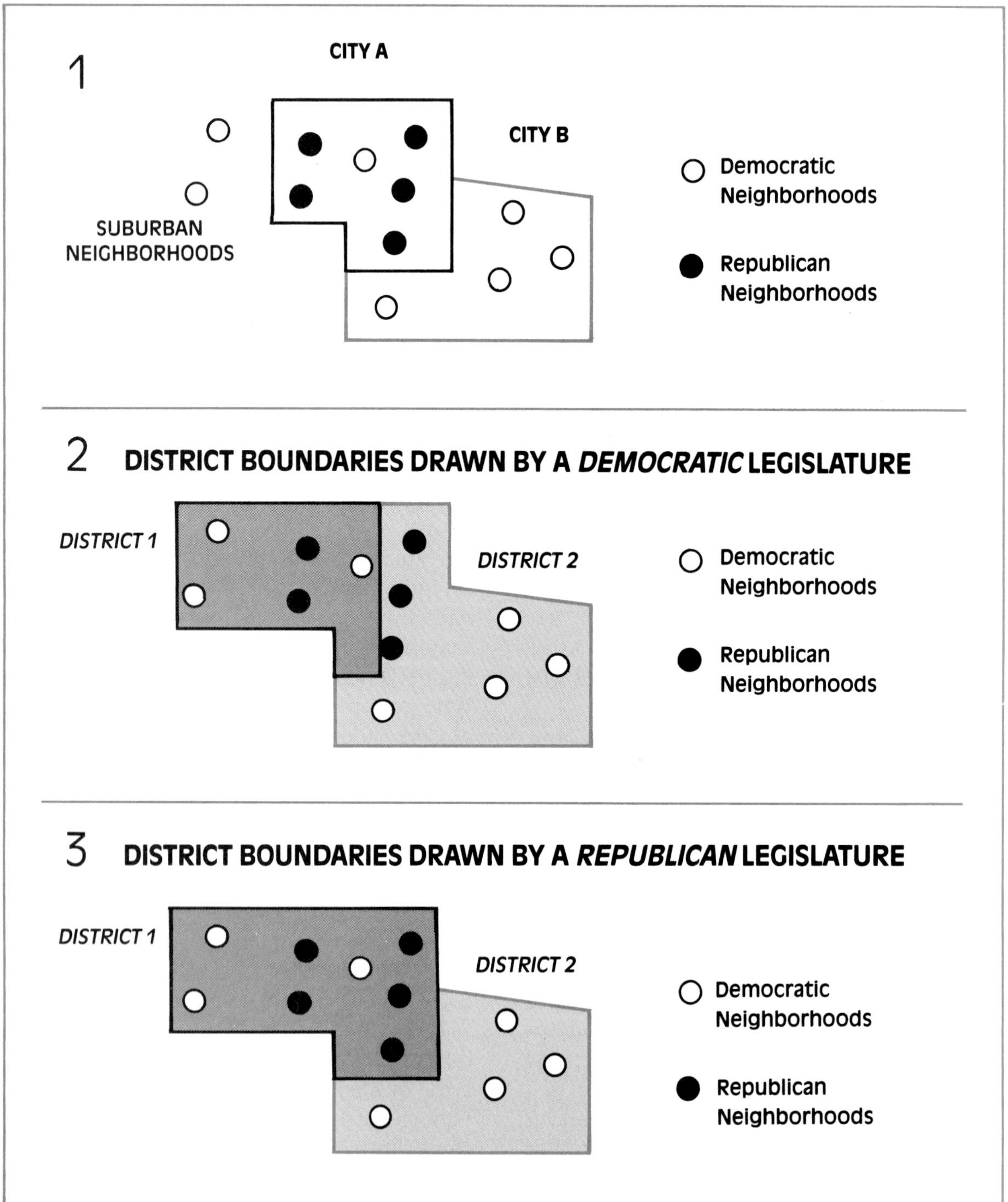

REVIEW

A. Making Inferences

Tell whether each statement below is probably **true** or **false.** Base your answers on what you can infer from the main ideas in the section.

1. Pennsylvania has more representatives than senators.
2. The boundaries of Texas's congressional districts are created by the Texas state legislature.
3. The number of senators from Rhode Island changes every ten years.
4. Congressional districts will be redrawn in the year 2006.
5. *No* congressional district has a population of only 25,000.
6. In North Carolina, the population of the 7th Congressional District is about equal to that of the 11th District.
7. If Democrats have a majority in the Iowa legislature, they will try to draw district boundaries to favor their party.
8. After the next census, the number of lawmakers in Congress will increase.

B. Making Comparisons

Create a chart that shows how the Senate is different from the House in terms of . . .

1. size
2. length of term
3. representation
4. power and influence
5. rules of debate.

3. WHO ARE THE LEADERS OF CONGRESS?

You know the basic differences between the Senate and the House. There are also differences *within* each house. Some members of the House and Senate are more powerful than other members. Also, some members are Republicans while others are Democrats. In Congress, such differences of power and party matter a great deal.

The majority party rules. The most important fact to know about a newly elected Congress is the number of members who belong to each party. Are there more Democrats than Republicans—or more Republicans than Democrats? Knowing just this one fact, you can predict which members of Congress will be the most powerful.

Take, for example, the Congress elected in 1984. Winning seats in the House were a total of 253 Democrats and 182 Republicans. The Democrats had a majority. Therefore, it was known immediately that *all* positions of official leadership in the House would go to Democrats. Not a single leadership post in the House would be assigned to a member of the minority party (the Republicans).

The Senate, however, was a different story. After the election of 1984, there were more Republicans in the Senate (53) than Democrats (47). As a result, all official positions of leadership in this chamber went to Republican senators.

In other words, in each house, the majority party rules. The minority party can only hope that it becomes the majority party in the next election.

Positions of leadership and power. What are the jobs of leadership that the majority party wins?

In the House of Representatives, the most powerful job is that of *speaker of the House.* Recall that laws are introduced, debated, and voted upon on the "floor" of the two separate chambers—the House chamber and the Senate chamber. The speaker presides over meetings of the House. Like a judge in a courtroom or a priest in a pulpit, the speaker sits on a raised platform in the front of the House chamber. Banging a gavel, he or she has the authority to direct all that happens on the House floor. The speaker's power includes:

- deciding what bills shall be sent to different committees
- enforcing rules of order
- deciding which representatives will be called upon to speak for or against a bill.

In the Senate, the presiding officer is *not* a senator. It is the vice president of the United States who presides over Senate meetings. Often, however, the vice president is absent from the floor. When that happens, a senator from the majority party presides. This official substitute for the vice president is known as the *president pro tempore* of the Senate. The main duty of the Senate's presiding officer is to carry out formal rules of order during a debate on a bill. Being little more than managers of debates, the vice president and the president pro tempore have much less power than the speaker of the House.

Recall that the business of Congress is conducted in two places: the two chambers of the Capitol and the many committee rooms. Those lawmakers who preside over meetings of the different committees are called *chairpersons.* The chairperson of a committee is far more powerful than any other committee member. He or she has the power to decide which bills the committee will consider seriously. A chairperson may kill a bill (prevent it from being passed) simply by filing it away—or pigeonholing it. *Every* chairperson of *every* committee in the House and Senate is a member of the majority party.

The custom of seniority. In addition to party membership, power in Congress depends on one other fact. It depends on how long a lawmaker has served in the House or Senate. Those who have served many terms are called senior members. Those who have served only one or two terms are called junior members. The greater your *seniority* (length of service), the greater is your chance of holding a position of power.

To illustrate, imagine a Senate committee consisting of seven members:

Republicans on the Committee

Senator Olds	30 years of service
Senator Long	18 years
Senator Shorter	12 years
Senator Young	6 years

Democrats on the Committee

Senator Wait	31 years of service
Senator Middleton	12 years
Senator Green	6 years

Notice that the four Republicans have a majority. Therefore, we know that a Republican will be the committee's chairperson. It will almost certainly be Senator Olds, since he is the most senior Republican member of the committee (served the longest). The most senior member of all, Senator Wait, cannot be the chairperson, since he belongs to the minority party. At the next election, if the Democrats win a majority of seats, Senator Wait will automatically become the committee's new chairperson.

Choosing committee heads on the basis of seniority is an old custom in Congress. In recent years, it has been challenged by young members impatient for power. Occasionally, a more junior member of a party will be selected chairperson over the most senior member. But exceptions to the seniority custom do not happen often.

CARTOON CORNER

From this cartoon, can we infer that there has been a change in leadership on other committees as well as this one? Why or why not?

Party caucuses. Why do members of the majority party always take the positions of leadership? Is it a rule of the Constitution? No, as you may recall, the Constitution says nothing at all about political parties.

The reason is that the majority party has the voting strength to elect officers. This party can outvote the minority party whenever it wishes. Before the election of officers takes place, members of the majority party get together in a party meeting—or caucus. The senators attending one caucus decide who among them shall be president pro tempore and who shall head the different Senate committees. In a separate caucus, members of the majority party of the House vote on their leaders.

The actual vote for leaders on the House and Senate floors is just a formality. Everyone knows in advance who will be chosen. The majority party nominates its list of leaders (those previously chosen in party caucus). Then every member of the party votes in favor of the list. Since it has a majority behind it, the list always win.

Majority and minority leaders. In addition to choosing official leaders of Congress, party caucuses choose leaders of a different kind. The majority party in each house chooses someone to act as its political leader. Thus, there is a *majority leader of the House* and a *majority leader of the Senate.*

In the Senate particularly, the majority leader wields a great deal of power and influence. By talking to party members and trying to rally support for certain bills, the majority leader often has a major influence

Congress in the 90s

In the 1990s, opinion polls show that most Americans have less respect for Congress than for either the president or the Supreme Court. They generally think that their own representative and senators are doing a reasonably good job. But they think that the other lawmakers in both houses are a bunch of windbags or scoundrels or both. Why is this? What, if anything, is wrong with the U.S. Congress?

Three problems. Critics of Congress point out a number of problems. Chief among them are these:

1. The pressure to get reelected. Like other workers in society, those elected to Congress are concerned about holding onto their jobs. A senator can count on staying in office for six years, a good stretch of time. In the House, however, a representative serves only two years before he or she must go to the voters again to seek reelection. As politicians are well aware, two years go by quickly. So members of the House spend as much as half their time campaigning for the next election. Little time remains for lawmaking duties that they were elected to perform.

2. The influence of special interests. Lobbyists for special interests have always had influence on Capitol Hill. But today their influence is probably greater than ever before. In part, that is because the number of interest groups with offices in Washington, D.C., is at a record high. Today's lobbyists do not normally make corrupt and illegal deals with lawmakers. But they do have great influence because, unlike average citizens, they talk with Congress members and their staffs every day. Above all, members of Congress rely upon the contributions of PACs for a large part of their campaign funds. Without a word being said, lawmakers and lobbyists understand that it pays both of them to be friendly toward one another.

3. Divided government. Another problem places both Congress and the president in a frustrating situation known as "gridlock." The two branches are at odds with one another because, more often than not, they belong to rival parties. Presidents Eisenhower, Nixon, Ford, Reagan, and Bush were Republicans. In all the years they were in the White House, only one Congress (1953–1955) had Republican majorities in both houses. The other Congresses had Democratic majorities in the House and usually in the Senate as well. The result was divided government and a lot of proposed laws and programs that went nowhere. President Bush, for example, would propose many measures that the Democratic Congress refused to pass. For his part, Bush vetoed 44 bills that the Democratic lawmakers had passed. The "gridlock" has been frustrating for politicians and citizens alike.

Three remedies. What can be done about Congress's problems? Here are three remedies proposed by scholars and journalists:

1. Change the term of office for a representative in the House from two years to four years. The benefit: perhaps the lawmakers would spend proportionally less time campaigning and more time doing their jobs.

2. Change campaign finance laws to reduce the influence of PACs and increase the influence of political parties. The benefit: special interests and lobbyists might lose some of their clout.

3. Change the U.S. Constitution to make the U.S. system more like that of Great Britain. The president would then be elected by the political party that has a majority in Congress. The people would vote every four years for a new Congress. Then, the majority party in Congress would choose the party's leader to be the head of the executive branch. The benefit: The problem of "gridlock" and divided government would be eliminated. The risk: There would be no more separation of powers between the executive and legislative branches.

YOU DECIDE: Turn your class into a house of Congress. Debate each of the three proposed remedies above. Then vote yes or no (yea or nay) on each proposal.

on the Senate's final voting. In the House, the majority leader is also powerful—but less so than the speaker of the House.

Meeting in caucuses of their own, members of the minority party in both houses also choose political leaders. There is a *minority leader of the House* and a *minority leader of the Senate.*

Also chosen in party caucuses are leaders called party *whips* (both majority whips and minority whips). The word "whip" comes from the British custom of using a "whipper-in" (man with a whip) to keep hounds from straying in a fox hunt. The job of a party whip is to assist the majority and minority leaders in the work of getting certain bills passed or defeated.

Though they belong to the same party, Democratic members of Congress often disagree about the laws they want passed. The same is true of Republican members of both houses. Party leaders and their whips try to overcome some of these disagreements. They talk to lawmakers of their own party and try to persuade them to vote in a certain way.

Terms and sessions of Congress. The Congress that was elected in November 1990 was known as the 102nd Congress. It met for the first time on January 3, 1991, and continued its existence until January 3, 1993. It was then followed by the 103rd Congress whose members were elected the previous November (1992).

Congresses have been numbered like this since the First Congress met in New York City from 1789 to 1791. The life, or term, of numbered Congresses is two years. It always begins at noon on January 3 of an odd-numbered year (1993, 1995, 1997 . . .).

Every Congress usually consists of two *sessions*—one session for each year of its existence. A session has no fixed length. Before World War II, Congress would be "in session" (conducting its business) for only about five months. Then both houses would vote to adjourn (stop work and go home) until the next year. In recent years, however, Congress has worked much harder and longer. A typical session now lasts as long as ten or eleven months.

On the first day of its term, January 3, Congress gets organized. New members are sworn in. Leaders are voted upon. Committee assignments are made. The organization and leadership of that first day continue for two years. Then a new Congress takes over for another two years.

Does the leadership of Congress also change every two years? Not usually. Senior members of Congress are those who win election in their districts time after time. These senior members keep returning to their House or Senate seats. If the majority party remains the same from one election to the next, so does the leadership.

A total change of leadership, however, *can* happen. The Senate, for example, went from a Democratic majority in 1979 to a Republican majority in 1981. Leadership then passed completely out of the hands of senior Democrats into the hands of senior Republicans.

REVIEW

A. Applying What You Know

Suppose that a new Congress has just been elected. It consists of the following members:

SENATE

Republicans	51
Democrats	49

HOUSE

Republicans	200
Democrats	235

1. Make predictions about how this Congress would be organized. Give the **political party** of its leaders (named below):
   a. speaker of the House
   b. majority leader of the Senate
   c. chairperson of the House Judiciary Committee
   d. minority whip in the House
   e. president pro tempore
   f. chairperson of the Senate Foreign Relations Committee
2. How long would the above officers serve?
3. On what day of the year would they begin their duties?
4. What presiding officer in the Senate is *not* listed above? What makes this officer different from all other congressional officers?

B. Explaining How the System Works

1. Why do all committee heads in Congress belong to the majority party?
2. Why do members of the minority party elect a minority leader and a minority whip?
3. Why is seniority important to a lawmaker's hopes for power? (In your answer, define *seniority*.)

CHAPTER REVIEW

A. Completing the Summary

Select terms from the word list to fill in the blanks in the summary below. Write your answers on a separate piece of paper.

bicameral	majority
casework	majority leader
caucuses	population
census	reapportionment
committees	roll call
constituents	Senate
floor	seniority
franking privilege	sessions
House of Representatives	speaker
	staffs

Because of its two chambers, the U.S. Congress is a __(1)__ type of legislature. Members of the smaller body, the __(2)__, are elected to a term of six years. Members of the __(3)__ are elected to a two-year term.

Members of Congress divide their time between two main functions. As lawmakers, they attend meetings of __(4)__ and also vote on bills on the House or Senate __(5)__. The method of voting is either by __(6)__, by voice vote, or by standing vote. As representatives of thousands of __(7)__ in their home districts, they write letters and take care of __(8)__. They are aided in these tasks by the dozen or more people on their __(9)__. Because of the __(10)__, it costs them nothing to mail a letter.

Every state has the same number of senators: two. Representation in the House, however, is based on the size of a state's __(11)__. Every ten years, a __(12)__ is taken. Then, in a process called __(13)__, a state may either gain or lose seats in the House. District boundaries must then be redrawn.

Power in Congress depends partly on how many terms a member has served. This fact of __(14)__ determines which members of the majority party become committee chairpersons. The choice of congressional leaders is made in party meetings called __(15)__. The most important leaders to be chosen are the __(16)__ of the House and the __(17)__ of the Senate.

The same leadership continues for the two __(18)__ that make up each Congress. Following an election, the leadership may change if the minority party wins more seats and becomes the new __(19)__ party.

B. Project: Who Represents You in Washington?

On a sheet of paper, make a chart of who represents you in Congress. At the top of the chart, list your two senators and representative. On the left side of the chart, list the following: name, political party, years of service, member of what committees, age, and address of Washington office. In the reference room of your library, you will find their names and other facts in these three sources: *The Congressional Record, The World Almanac and Book of Facts,* and *The United States Government Manual.* Use the information you find to fill in the chart.

C. Applying What You Know

An article about the 103rd Congress is excerpted below. It is from the weekly periodical, *Congressional Quarterly* (February 6, 1993). Read the excerpt and answer the questions based on it.

Senate Republican leader Bob Dole of Kansas has been preaching advice as old as the republic to his party's other 42 senators: United we stand, divided we fall.

"If we can be a cohesive force, then we'll have some influence around this place," Dole says. "If we become splintered and fractured, then there will be a tendency to ignore the Republican side."

As President Clinton prepares to send Congress his economic package, there is an urgency for the GOP [Republican party] in Dole's sermon. . . .

Losing the White House cost Republicans the veto, their most powerful legislative tool since Democrats captured complete control of Congress in 1986. Now Republicans must shape or stop legislation before it gets to the president. That is least likely to happen in the House, where Democrats field a decisive 255–175 advantage over Republicans.

But in the Senate . . . the Democrats need a supermajority of 60 votes to shut off Republican filibusters* and control the floor. Because there are only 57 Democrats, three shy of the magic number, any time 41 of the 43 Republicans stick together, they constitute a powerful minority.

1. In the 103rd Congress, which party had a majority (*a*) in the House? (*b*) in the Senate?
2. According to the article, did Senate Republicans or House Republicans have a better chance of defeating President Clinton's programs? Explain.
3. Explain this phrase: "Losing the White House cost Republicans the veto . . ." (Remember that in 1993, a Democratic president, Bill Clinton, replaced a Republican president, George Bush.)

* For a definition of filibuster, see Glossary.

A PROPOSED LAW TO PROTECT PET RABBITS. Laws can be about any subject, including the protection of animals. What bill might Congress consider concerning the care of rabbits?

CHAPTER 14

Lawmaking in Congress

OBJECTIVES

After reading this chapter, you will know

1. the powers given to Congress by the Constitution.
2. how bills are considered by committees and subcommittees.
3. how bills are debated and voted upon in Congress.
4. the role of the president in the lawmaking process.
5. some of the methods that lawmakers use to gain support for their bills.
6. how to think critically about clauses of the Constitution.

The 102nd Congress concluded its two-year life by adjourning in October 1992. It had considered thousands of proposals for new laws—called "bills." Most were rejected. But 589 of them were approved by majorities of both houses and signed into law by President George Bush. Among the bills considered by the 102nd Congress were:

- a bill to extend federal programs for the prevention of child abuse
- a bill to assure the people of Somalia the right to food and other basic necessities of life
- a bill to require businesses to give their employees temporary medical leave for family-related matters such as caring for a newborn child
- a bill to protect animal research facilities from illegal acts
- a bill to authorize a 1993 National Conference on Aging.

As you can see, bills can be about almost any subject. Think of the Congress that is currently in session. Among the bills it is considering, there *might* be one concerning the sale of rabbits as pets. The Rabbit Bill, as we shall call it, would require rabbit breeders and pet shop owners to meet certain standards of care.

In this chapter, you will learn the process of lawmaking in Congress by following the story of two bills. One bill—the Rabbit Bill—is imaginary. A second bill concerning river barges and waterways is real. Let these questions guide your study:

1. What kinds of bills may be considered by Congress?
2. What happens to a bill in committee?
3. What are the final steps for turning a bill into a law?
4. How do lawmakers win support for their bills?

1. WHAT KINDS OF BILLS MAY BE CONSIDERED BY CONGRESS?

You know that bills are formal proposals for new laws. The first page, or title page, of a bill looks like this:

105th Congress
1st Session H. R. 123

A BILL

To provide for the mandatory inspection of rabbits sold as pets in interstate commerce.

Bills are referred to either by a number (example: H. R. 123) or by a nickname (example: the Rabbit Bill). The Rabbit Bill's number is preceded by the letters **H. R.** because the bill was first considered in the House of Representatives. If the bill had been introduced in the Senate, the initial **S.** would have preceded the number.

Putting a bill into the hopper. Any citizen or lobbyist can write a bill and send it to his or her congressperson. If the congressperson approves the idea for the bill, it may be given to a staff member to be written in legal language. Then the congressperson, acting as the bill's sponsor, walks onto the House floor and drops the bill into a wooden box called the *hopper.* (Another hopper just like it is on a desk in the Senate.)

The bills pile up in the hopper until the clerk of the House (or Senate) takes them out and gives each a number. The bills are thus "introduced" for consideration.

Bills are much like the acorns dropped by an oak tree. Only a tiny percentage of acorns actually take root and grow. So, too, only a small percentage of bills are passed into law by the two houses of Congress. The thousands of bills dropped into the House and Senate hoppers every year may either "live" or "die." Most of them die. (Later sections of this chapter will explain what "kills" them.)

Public bills, private bills, and resolutions. Imagine pulling out of the hopper all the papers dropped into it on a typical day.

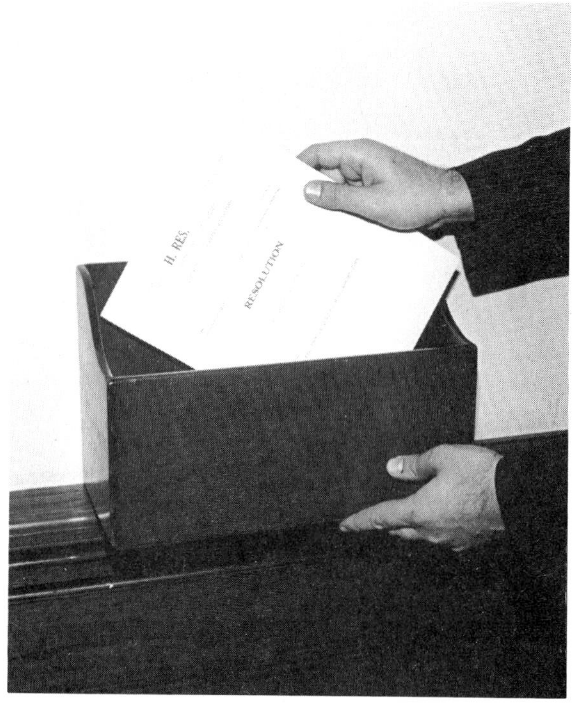

IN THE HOPPER. A resolution is introduced in the House. How does it differ from a public bill?

What would you find? After glancing through them, you would observe that the papers are of three kinds.

The most common kind deals with a variety of national problems. They are known as public bills because they affect the American public as a whole. The Rabbit Bill is one example of a public bill.

A small number of bills are *not* proposals for laws that would apply to everyone. They are known as private bills because they are written for the benefit of only a few people, or perhaps just one person. For example, a private bill might propose that a particular war veteran be granted special treatment in a navy hospital.

Finally, a third group of papers are marked either "H. Res." (in the House) or "S. Res." (in the Senate). The "Res." stands for resolution. A resolution of the House refers only to the business of that body. It might be a proposal for some change in the rules of the House. It might be a statement expressing either approval or disapproval of some action by the president. A resolution is usually the act of only one house. It goes no farther than that house and never becomes a law of the land. An exception is the joint resolution, which is passed jointly by both houses. If the president signs it, it is law.

From our imaginary stack of papers, let us put aside the resolutions and the private bills. In this chapter, we shall be talking about the majority of bills that become law—the public bills.

The lawmaking powers of Congress. Public bills may deal with almost any subject. However, a public bill must match up with at least one of the lawmaking powers given to Congress by the Constitution. In Article I, Section 8, there is a list of 18 such powers.

EIGHTEEN POWERS OF CONGRESS

Here is a summary of the 18 clauses of Article I, Section 8, that give Congress its lawmaking powers. The most important powers are explained on pages 309–311.

U.S. STAMPS AND COINS. What clauses of the Constitution permit Congress to provide for the creation of these objects?

Clause No.

1. ***Collecting taxes.*** (See page 309.)
2. ***Borrowing.*** Congress may borrow money to pay the debts of the U.S. government.
3. ***Regulating foreign and interstate commerce.*** (See page 310.)
4. ***Making rules for immigration and bankruptcy.*** Congress may determine (*a*) how an immigrant to this country may become a U.S. citizen and (*b*) how an individual or business company may be declared "bankrupt" (unable to pay debts).
5. ***Coining money.*** Congress may authorize the kinds and amounts of money that shall be issued to the public.
6. ***Punishing counterfeiters.*** Only the U.S. government may legally print and coin money. Private persons who attempt to manufacture money may be punished for the crime of counterfeiting.
7. ***Establishing post offices and post roads.*** Congress may set up a system for distributing the mail and building roads to be used as mail routes.
8. ***Protecting authors and inventors.*** Congress may grant copyrights and patents to people who invent or create original works.
9. ***Establishing federal courts.*** Congress may set up a number of courts to judge cases of federal law. Such courts are "inferior to" (less powerful than) the Supreme Court.
10. ***Punishing acts of piracy.*** Congress may determine how crimes committed at sea are to be defined and punished.
11. ***Declaring war.*** The United States is officially at war with another nation only if Congress votes to declare that a state of war exists. (As commander in chief, however,

the president may order troops and ships into battle whether or not war has been officially declared. The Civil War and the Vietnam War were both undeclared wars.)

12–14. Supporting and regulating the armed forces. Congress may decide how much money to set aside for maintaining an army and navy. It also has the final power to determine how the U.S. armed forces are organized.

15–16. Calling the state militia into federal service. Congress may draw up rules for organizing the militia (state troops) when they are called into federal service during an emergency.

17. Governing the nation's capital. All laws for governing the District of Columbia (Washington, D.C.) are made by Congress, not by any state government.

18. Making any other laws that are "necessary and proper." (See explanation, page 310.)

Other powers of Congress. Besides its powers for making laws, Congress has several other powers as well. It may:

1. Propose amendments. Congress may start the process for amending the Constitution. If each house passes a proposed amendment by a two-thirds vote, it goes to the states for ratification.

2. Ratify treaties (agreements between nations). The Senate alone has the power to review the treaties made by the president. For a treaty to go into effect, two-thirds of the membership must vote for it.

3. Investigate public issues. Is government doing enough to clean up the environment? To control the sale of illegal drugs? To protect the elderly in nursing homes? Any public issue could be the subject of a special investigation by a committee of the House or Senate. The results of the investigation might lead Congress to enact laws dealing with the problem.

THE POWER TO INVESTIGATE. In 1987, Lieutenant Colonel Oliver North (left) and other members of the White House staff were questioned by a special committee of Congress about the secret sale of American weapons to Iran. At right is Colonel North's lawyer. How do congressional investigations act as a check on the Executive Branch?

4. Confirm a president's nominees for office. The Constitution gives the president, as chief executive, the power to name (or nominate) ambassadors, members of the Cabinet, and other top officials in the Executive Branch. The president also nominates judges to fill vacant offices in the Judicial Branch. But a nominee cannot take office unless the Senate first confirms (accepts) his or her appointment by majority vote.

5. Impeach and remove officials. Congress may vote to remove, or "fire," a top official in the Executive or Judicial Branches if it finds the person guilty of wrongdoing. The process for doing this, known as impeachment, is explained in Chapter 11.

Three powers that are most important. Congress's power to impeach and its power to punish acts of piracy are rarely used. Other powers are used all the time. Of the 18 lawmaking powers, three may be viewed as "most important," because so many laws are based upon them. They are: (1) the power to tax, (2) the power to regulate commerce, and (3) the power to make laws that are "necessary and proper."

The power to tax. Perhaps most important of all is Congress's power to determine the kinds and amounts of taxes that may be collected from citizens and businesses. It is good for democracy that our elected lawmakers have the power to tax—a power also called the "power of the purse." Government by the people could not exist unless the people's representatives had the power either to approve or reject proposals for new taxes. To appreciate this idea, consider how people would feel if a dictator could force them to pay a certain tax against their will.

The Constitution makes one special rule about those bills that deal with taxes and public money. It says that such bills shall be introduced *first* in the House of Repre-

WELCOME TO CONNECTICUT. A truck crosses the New York-Connecticut border. What clause of Article I, Section 8, permits Congress to make laws regulating this truck and its cargo?

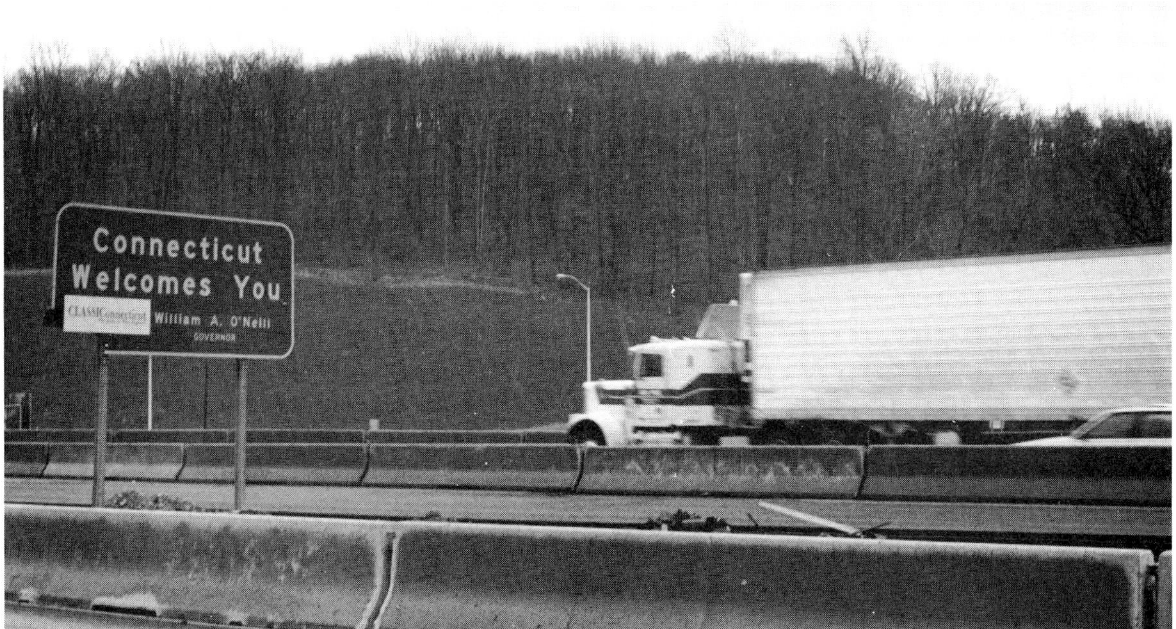

sentatives. But any bill passed by the House must also be passed by the Senate if it is to become law. Thus, the Senate too shares in the power of the purse.

The power to regulate foreign and interstate commerce. Foreign commerce involves the shipping of American-made goods to countries abroad and the receiving of foreign-made goods in U.S. cities. *Interstate commerce* is trade or business that crosses state lines. For example, a truck carrying rabbits from New Jersey into Pennsylvania is engaged in interstate commerce. It is therefore subject to laws made by Congress.

The title of the Rabbit Bill mentions "interstate commerce." That is to ensure that Congress is properly applying one of its powers under the Constitution. The bill would be invalid—or unconstitutional—if it said, "to regulate the sale of pet rabbits within the state of New Jersey."

The commerce clause gives Congress a great deal of power to regulate businesses of all kinds. That is because, in recent years, the clause has been interpreted loosely (or broadly) by the Supreme Court. Suppose that a pet shop owner in New Jersey gets all his rabbits and other pets from a New Jersey farm and sells them only to local customers. The business seems to involve only the people and products of one state. Even so, there is always the chance that someone from out of state may walk into the shop one day and buy a pet. Therefore, the shop may be called an "interstate" business subject to federal laws as well as state laws.

The power to make laws that are "necessary and proper." Where in the Constitution does it say that Congress may regulate pet shops and the sale of rabbits? The Constitution mentions interstate commerce in general but says nothing about specific businesses, such as the pet business. To justify

CARTOON CORNER

What do the stepping stones represent? Why are both needed to enable Congress to pass a rabbit bill?

a bill like the Rabbit Bill, Congress's 18th power is extremely helpful. According to the so-called "elastic clause" (the 18th clause of Article I, Section 8), Congress has the power:

> to make all laws which shall be necessary and proper for carrying into execution the foregoing powers.

In other words, Congress can deal with matters as specific as pet shops and rabbit sales and every public issue under the sun. If the Rabbit Bill, for example, is a "necessary and proper" means of regulating interstate commerce, then Congress may pass it. Congress's 18th power is "elastic" because it may be stretched to fit a wide variety of specific topics.

REVIEW

A. Wrong Word?

The *italicized* word or phrase in each sentence may be **correct** or **incorrect**. If it is correct, write "OK" on a piece of paper next to each number. If it is not correct, write the word that would make the sentence true.

1. Bills for raising taxes and spending federal money must originate in the *Senate*.
2. If something placed in the hopper has no chance at all of becoming a law, you know that it must be a *resolution*.
3. The power to *tax* is what gives Congress its power of the purse.
4. The *hopper* clause is what enables Congress to enact whatever laws are "necessary and proper" for carrying out its other powers.
5. Congress has the power to regulate *trade between states*.

B. Classifying Facts

The powers of Congress may be grouped, or **classified**, under four headings: FOREIGN AFFAIRS, DEFENSE, PUBLIC SERVICE, and MONEY. On a piece of paper, copy the boxes below and their headings. Fill in each box with two examples of powers belonging under the given heading.

FOREIGN AFFAIRS	**DEFENSE**
1. *Regulate foreign commerce*	1. ________
2. ________	2. ________
PUBLIC SERVICE	**MONEY**
1. ________	1. ________
2. ________	2. ________

2. WHAT HAPPENS TO A BILL IN COMMITTEE?

Let us assume that our Rabbit Bill leads a charmed life. Of the thousands of bills placed in the House hopper, it is only one of a few hundred to survive. It "hops" over all the dangers in its path, going from the House to the Senate to the White House until it is finally printed in a book of "public statutes" (laws).

Happy journey of the Rabbit Bill. On page 313, look at the diagram of the Rabbit Bill's route to final success. Briefly let us follow the bill's early progress from the House hopper (step 1) through steps 2, 3, and 4. The steps that follow (5-13) will be explained later in this chapter.

1. Lifted from the House hopper, the Rabbit Bill is given a number: H.R. 123. (The number means that the Rabbit Bill was the 123rd to be introduced in the House during the current session of Congress.) The bill is then assigned to one of the 22 standing committees of the House.

2. The committee's chairperson refers the bill to a smaller group called a subcommittee. Expert witnesses speak for and against the bill in subcommittee meetings called *hearings*.

3. Back in the main committee room, most committee members approve the bill and write a report explaining why they like it.

4. The Rabbit Bill goes to yet another committee: the House Rules Committee. This committee decides on what day the bill shall be taken up by the entire House.

Committees and subcommittees. Any bill that reaches step 4 is luckier than most. The great majority of bills take just one hop out of the hopper and die in committee. The fate of any bill, whether it lives or dies, is determined in meetings of committees and subcommittees.

Usually, if a committee likes a bill, so will a majority of the full House or Senate. But if it dislikes a bill, the full House or Senate will not even get a chance to consider it. A bill rejected by committee is almost always a dead bill.

A list of the standing committees of each house of Congress is on page 314. A *standing committee* is more or less permanent. It continues its life from one Congress to the next. Standing committees range in size from just 12 members (Senate Committee on Veterans' Affairs) to 63 members (House Committee on Public Works and Transportation).

Besides the standing committees, Congress also sets up temporary committees known as special committees. Their function is to investigate some current problem, such as drugs or organized crime. They do *not* consider and vote on bills. Special committees usually cease to exist when the two-year Congress that created them adjourns for the last time.

Large committees of the standing type cannot deal effectively with all the bills that come their way. So they rely more and more on subcommittees. A committee of 30 lawmakers, for example, could divide up the work among three subcommittees.

Again, we may take the work of Kansas's Senator Nancy Kassebaum as an example. In the 1980s and early 1990s, she was a member of the Senate Foreign Relations Committee. She also worked on three subcommittees of this main committee:

- the Subcommittee on International Economic Policy, Trade, Oceans and Environment
- the Subcommittee on European Affairs
- the Subcommittee on African Affairs.

Thus, Senator Kassebaum became an expert on U.S. policy toward Europe and Africa. Expert knowledge of other regions and topics was left to other senators on other subcommittees.

THE RABBIT BILL (H.R. 123) BECOMES *LAW*

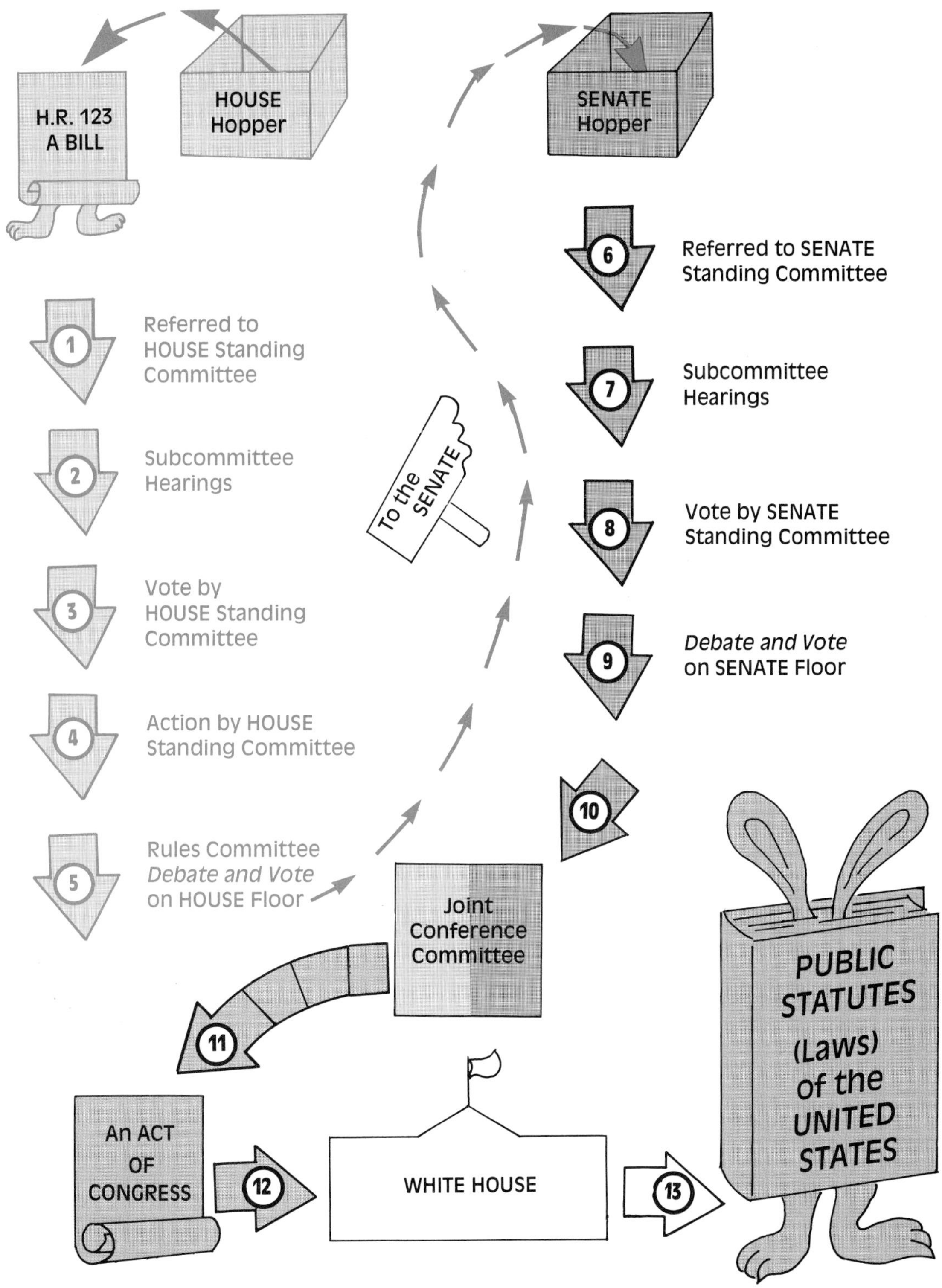

HOUSE COMMITTEE on	SENATE COMMITTEE on
AGRICULTURE	AGRICULTURE, NUTRITION, and FORESTRY
APPROPRIATIONS	APPROPRIATIONS
ARMED SERVICES	ARMED SERVICES
BANKING, FINANCE, and URBAN AFFAIRS	BANKING, HOUSING, and URBAN AFFAIRS
BUDGET	BUDGET
DISTRICT OF COLUMBIA	
EDUCATION and LABOR	LABOR and HUMAN RESOURCES
ENERGY and COMMERCE	COMMERCE, SCIENCE, and TRANSPORTATION ENERGY and NATURAL RESOURCES
FOREIGN AFFAIRS	FOREIGN RELATIONS
GOVERNMENT OPERATIONS	GOVERNMENTAL AFFAIRS
HOUSE ADMINISTRATION RULES	RULES and ADMINISTRATION
NATURAL RESOURCES PUBLIC WORKS and TRANSPORTATION	ENVIRONMENT and PUBLIC WORKS
JUDICIARY	JUDICIARY
MERCHANT MARINE and FISHERIES	
POST OFFICE and CIVIL SERVICE	
SCIENCE, SPACE, and TECHNOLOGY	
SMALL BUSINESS	SMALL BUSINESS
STANDARDS of OFFICIAL CONDUCT (ETHICS)	
VETERANS' AFFAIRS	VETERANS' AFFAIRS
WAYS and MEANS	FINANCE

Referring bills to committees. Neither the Senate Foreign Relations Committee nor the House Foreign Relations Committee would consider a bill like the Rabbit Bill. That is because the bill concerned only rabbits raised and sold on American soil. More appropriate would be the Agriculture Committee of either house.

Officers of the House and Senate decide which committee shall be given a certain bill. It should be an appropriate committee, one that specializes in the subject matter of the bill.

Killing a bill in committee. You know that most bills sent to committee die there. They may be "killed" (as the saying goes) by three types of committee action.

First, after just glancing at a bill, a committee's chairperson may decide that it is either foolish or unworthy of attention. The chairperson can then file the "unworthy" bill away. In the language of Congress, the bill has been *pigeonholed*—put aside, never to be seen again.

Second, a bill may be amended to death. A committee has the power to change the language of a bill. If it wishes, it can change every word. Thus, a wholly new bill may be substituted for the one dropped in the hopper. For example, the Rabbit Bill could end up as a bill about snakes, dogs—almost anything at all.

Third, the committee may decide to give a bill a negative or unfavorable report. The report explains why the committee thinks the bill is a poor one. Then it sends the bill to the House (or Senate) floor, giving to others the job of killing it with a negative vote. Can lawmakers ignore a committee's negative report and pass it anyway? Yes, it could happen; but it is not likely.

The House Rules Committee. In the House, any bill can be stopped dead in its tracks by one very powerful committee. The House Rules Committee looks at *every* bill that has been favorably reported on by all the other

TELEVISING A SUBCOMMITTEE HEARING. Why is a subcommittee better able to study a bill than a full committee?

standing committees. It decides when (if ever) the bill will reach the floor of the House for a final vote.

If the Rules Committee likes a bill, it can move it ahead of other bills. If it dislikes a bill, it can place it at the bottom of a long list. The bills at the bottom may never move up to be voted upon. Time may run out, and Congress may adjourn. After that, any bills that have not been voted upon die automatically.

The lists that the House Rules Committee prepares are known as calendars. There are five different calendars for different types of bills. Each calendar determines the order in which bills will be considered and voted upon.

The House Rules Committee decides not just when, but also *how* bills will be considered on the floor. How many minutes will representatives be permitted to speak for and against the bill? Will they or won't they be allowed to propose amendments to the bill? The answer given by the Rules Committee can make it either easier or harder for a bill to be passed.

The Senate also has a rules committee. But its powers are minor compared to those of the House rule-makers.

Bills introduced in the Senate. A bill concerning the sale of pet rabbits might have had a different journey through Congress. Instead of starting in the House, it could have been dropped into the Senate hopper and then moved to a Senate committee and subcommittee. In the diagram (page 313), steps 6, 7, and 8 would then have been steps 1, 2, and 3. Except for a number change (an S. number instead of an H.R. number), the Senate's Rabbit Bill could be identical to the one we have called H.R. 123.

The chances of a bill being passed in the Senate are no better than in the House. True enough, a rules committee is not the obstacle that it is in the House. But once a bill reaches the Senate floor, opponents can block it by a procedure called a *filibuster*. They can stand up and talk for hours at a time to prevent the Senate's presiding officer from calling for a vote. If no vote is called, the bill cannot be passed. A filibuster then is a means of talking a bill to death. It is a form of bill-killing practiced only in the Senate, not in the House.

A filibuster can be defeated in two ways. First, senators participating in it can give up from exhaustion. Second, those wanting a bill to pass can call for a *cloture*, a vote setting a time limit on debate. Cloture is not easy to get, since it requires a vote of three-fifths of the senators.

In the next section, other twists and turns of the lawmaking process will be described. Why is the process so complicated? Should it be made simpler? The SKILLS CHECK will help you to answer.

✓✓ SKILLS CHECK: Thinking critically about government

In the Constitution, the process of making laws in Congress is described in just two sentences:

> Every bill which shall have passed the House of Representatives and the Senate, shall, before it becomes a law, be presented to the President of the United States. If he approves, he shall sign it. . . .
>
> —Article I, Section 7, Clause 2

Another clause gives each house of Congress the power to make its own rules:

> Each house may determine the rules of its proceedings. . . .
>
> —Article I, Section 5, Clause 2

Obviously the process that Congress uses to make laws is far more complicated than the Constitution requires. Think about why that is true by answering these questions:

1. Referring to the Rabbit Bill diagram (page 313), identify those steps that are *not* required by the Constitution.
2. What gives Congress the right to add as many steps as it wishes to the lawmaking process?
3. Why do you suppose Congress uses so many different steps in making laws? Do you think all of them are necessary? If not, which would you eliminate?

REVIEW

Imagine a bill about handgun control that is numbered S.321. The questions that follow refer to this Handgun Bill.

A. Making Inferences

On a piece of paper, create a **diagram** of the first nine steps of the Senate bill's progress. Assume that it is not killed at any point. (CLUE: The ninth step leads to a debate and vote on the House floor.)

B. Applying What You Know

1. What do you think a bill on the control of handguns might provide?
2. Name two committees in the Senate that might consider the bill.
3. Name two committees in the House that might consider the bill.
4. For each house, select the committee that you think *should* consider the bill. Give a reason for each choice.

3. WHAT ARE THE FINAL STEPS FOR TURNING A BILL INTO A LAW?

Imagine that it is lunchtime in Washington, D.C. We are seated at a table in a Washington restaurant. At a nearby table are two adults and a young woman of college age. If we were politicians, we would instantly recognize the adults. The older woman is Representative Bonny O'Hare. The man is Senator John Hopwell. From their conversation, we understand that the younger woman is the senator's daughter, Linda Hopwell.

The two members of Congress are in a merry mood. Apparently, they have just come from the White House. There, in the president's office, they watched the president sign the Rabbit Bill into law. Because they had both sponsored the bill, the president had invited them to be present at the bill-signing ceremony.

As we sip our soup, we overhear the conversation at the next table.

LINDA: Was your bill ever in trouble?
SENATOR HOPWELL: Of course it was in trouble. Frankly, I never thought it would get out of committee. But once the committee cleared it, I was confident that our bill would go all the way.
REPRESENTATIVE O'HARE: Yes, the committees always pose the biggest threat to a bill's life. But after that, there's still plenty of work to be done.
LINDA: What kind of work?
REPRESENTATIVE O'HARE: Telling you the full story would take all afternoon.
LINDA: Just give me the highlights. You tell me your side of the Rabbit Bill story. Briefly, please. And then, Dad, you follow with what you did.

Public reading of a bill

REPRESENTATIVE O'HARE: Okay, I'll zip along, trying to finish before dessert. Let's skip over the committee stage of our bill's progress since you know all about that. We can then go right to the House floor where the Rabbit Bill (and all other bills) must be read aloud. I attended the public reading of the Rabbit Bill, since I was the bill's sponsor. But there were a lot of empty seats all around me. Those present were meeting as a Committee of the Whole and—

CELEBRATING PASSAGE OF H.R. 5015. In 1988, a bill to help farmers cope with a drought was sponsored by Texas Congressman Kika de la Garza. In his office, members of his staff celebrated the bill's passage. Why is passage of a bill difficult to achieve?

LINDA: Wait. I thought we weren't talking about committees.

House Committee of the Whole

REPRESENTATIVE O'HARE: Right, but the Committee of the Whole is a committee in name only. Real committees—the permanent, standing kind—meet in rooms *outside* the Capitol. The Committee of the Whole meets right in the House chamber. Think of it as the House itself—but in miniature.

LINDA: A mini-House. Okay, but what's the point of it?

REPRESENTATIVE O'HARE: The Committee of the Whole is a convenient way of getting work done. Do you have any idea how hard it is to get hundreds of lawmakers to come together in one place at one time? It's like herding mules. Fortunately, the rules of the House allow work to be done when only 100 or more members are present in their seats. That is the so-called Committee of the Whole. If the clerk counts just 100 people in the chamber, we can form a Committee of the Whole and get to work.

LINDA: Okay, back to your story of the Rabbit Bill.

REPRESENTATIVE O'HARE: As I said, every paragraph of the bill was read aloud. The reading was stopped only three times. Each time, a congressperson proposed that the bill be amended in small ways. I went along with one of the changes but fought the other two. The change that really annoyed me had to do with jack rabbits. One of Arizona's representatives wanted desert jack rabbits to be completely exempt from the terms of the bill. A majority went along with this silly amendment, and it was adopted.

THE READING OF A BILL. On the House floor, a bill is read aloud by the clerk of the House. Does this occur before or after a standing committee has considered the bill?

LINDA: Three cheers for the jack rabbits! What next?

Quorum and floor vote

REPRESENTATIVE O'HARE: The Committee of the Whole saves time. But it cannot vote on a bill. For that, you need a *quorum*. A quorum is—

LINDA: I know. It's the least number of members who must be present for an official meeting to take place.

REPRESENTATIVE O'HARE: Exactly right. Our quorum in the House is a majority of the total membership of 435. So at least 218 of us must be on the House floor for a vote to be taken. The Rabbit Bill was finally voted upon by the full House, not just once, not just twice, but *eight* different times. Some votes were on proposed amendments to the bill. Another vote was on whether to send the bill back to my committee for further work. You can be sure I fought that motion, and I won. In fact, every vote went my way.

SENATOR HOPWELL: Bravo! The final vote of course was on whether the bill, as amended, should be passed.

WAITER: Excuse me. Would you care for any dessert?

SENATOR HOPWELL: Yes, but give us a few more minutes, please. I guess it's my turn to talk.

REPRESENTATIVE O'HARE: Okay, if you promise not to filibuster.

Senate debate

SENATOR HOPWELL (*laughing*): Don't worry,

I'll be brief. On the Senate floor, there was very little debate about the Rabbit Bill. I talked for only 35 minutes. Opponents talked for 20 minutes. Then the bill came to a vote. Only three senators voted "nay" compared to 87 "yeas." It was wonderfully easy.

LINDA: Back up a minute. Did you start the debate by forming a Committee of the Whole?

SENATOR HOPWELL: No, that's done only in the House.

WAITER: How are we doing here?

SENATOR HOPWELL: I guess we're ready. Three pieces of your cheesecake and coffee all around.

WAITER: Very good, sir.

REPRESENTATIVE O'HARE: I have an appointment in 15 minutes. We must hurry. Having been acted upon by the House and the Senate, the Rabbit Bill became an *act* of Congress.

Conference committee

SENATOR HOPWELL: Correction. At this point, there were two acts on our hands.

REPRESENTATIVE O'HARE: True enough. There was the Rabbit Act passed by the House and a slightly different Rabbit Act passed by the Senate. A law cannot say two different things. So, a temporary committee had to be formed consisting of equal numbers of senators and representatives. The task of this joint *conference committee* was to turn two different acts into a single Rabbit Act acceptable to all.

SENATOR HOPWELL: The six senators and six representatives on the conference committee came to an agreement quickly. After only eight hours of argument, we had a new Rabbit Act.

REPRESENTATIVE O'HARE: Naturally, we liked our original bill better than the committee version. But in politics, getting 90 percent of what you want is pretty good. Copies of the committee's work went to the House and the Senate at the same time. In each chamber, the new version of the Rabbit Act was voted upon right away without debate.

SENATE PAGES. These pages are high school students who run errands for the senator to whom they are assigned. What kinds of papers might a senator need in preparing to give a speech on the Senate floor?

LINDA: Of course it passed.

REPRESENTATIVE O'HARE: Of course. When a conference committee returns a bill to Congress, it almost always goes through without trouble.

WAITER: Excuse me. Who wanted the pie?

REPRESENTATIVE O'HARE: Nobody. We ordered the cheesecake.

LINDA: I'll take it, thank you. Now let's finish the story.

Action by the president

SENATOR HOPWELL: As you know, the story came to a happy ending this morning in the White House when the president signed the Rabbit Act into law.

REPRESENTATIVE O'HARE (*taking a pen from her purse*): Here's one of the pens he used and gave me as a souvenir.

LINDA: And what if the president had *not* signed the Rabbit Act?

SENATOR HOPWELL: That's called vetoing a bill. And our Rabbit Act would not now be law.

REPRESENTATIVE O'HARE: No, but Congress would still have a chance to make it a law even without the president's signature.
SENATOR HOPWELL: The Constitution says that the president has *ten days* to study an act of Congress. If he decides to veto it, he returns copies of the act to the two houses. A veto message accompanies the returned act, telling Congress why the president rejected it.

Overriding a veto

LINDA: Then comes the override, right?
SENATOR HOPWELL: Then comes Congress's *attempt* at overriding the veto. It's not easy. You must get at least two-thirds of the Senate and two-thirds of the House to vote for a vetoed act. If you succeed, the act becomes law. It happens sometimes—but not often.
LINDA: You said the president has ten days to do something with an act. What if he does nothing with it, neither signing it nor returning it unsigned to Congress?
REPRESENTATIVE O'HARE: Time is all-important. Suppose that Congress has only nine days left before it adjourns for the year. Then there's no hope for a bill that the president wants to kill. He can *pocket veto* it. Just by keeping it in his office (or in his vest pocket) until Congress adjourns, the bill will die automatically.
LINDA: What happens if a bill is kept by a president for more than ten days and Congress is still meeting?
REPRESENTATIVE O'HARE: In that case, the act of Congress becomes law automatically without the president's signature.
SENATOR HOPWELL (*rising from the table*): That's the end of our story, Linda. And the end of our dessert at the same time. Now, back to work.
LINDA: Congratulations to both of you. You put a lot of effort into that Rabbit Act. I just hope the rabbits of America appreciate what you've done for their general welfare and *hoppiness*.

REVIEW

A. Applying What You Know

Refer to the diagram on page 313 of the Rabbit Bill's passage into law. Use the script you have just read to explain the final steps (10–13) of the lawmaking process.

1. *Step 10.* Why were the separate acts of the House and the Senate referred to a joint conference committee?
2. *Step 11.* Why does the diagram show movement in two directions at once?
3. *Step 12.* At this point, why is an act of Congress not yet a federal law?
4. *Step 12.* What are two ways that a president may reject an act of Congress?
5. *Step 13.* In the White House, how was the Rabbit Act suddenly changed into a public statute, or law?

B. Making Comparisons

Compare the terms or phrases in *italics*.

1. How does *debate in the Senate* differ from *debate in the House?*
2. How does a *joint conference committee* differ from (*a*) a *standing committee*, and (*b*) the *Committee of the Whole?*
3. How do the *procedures for overriding a veto* differ from the *procedures for passing a bill?*

4. HOW DO LAWMAKERS WIN SUPPORT FOR THEIR BILLS?

The imaginary Rabbit Bill moved through Congress with ease. In reality, however, important bills face a lot of opposition. Let us look now at the passage of a *real* bill and how it was changed again and again before becoming law.

CASE STUDY: The Bill That Worried the Barge Companies

This case study concerns a waterways bill sponsored by a Republican senator from New Mexico, Peter Domenici. Chiefly affected by the bill were two kinds of companies: railroad companies and river barge companies. For many years, these companies had competed for the business of hauling farmers' crops to market. The railroads were faster, but barge rates were cheaper.

Free passage on the nation's rivers. The railroads accused the barge companies of operating at an unfair advantage. How could the barge companies charge such low rates for hauling grain? According to the railroads, it was because the U.S. government saved barge owners the trouble and expense of keeping river channels open. The government paid the entire cost of dredging rivers, digging canals, and building dams. It spent as much as a billion dollars a year of taxpayers' money on the nation's waterways.

BARGE ON THE MISSISSIPPI. What gives Congress the power to regulate the movement of boats and barges on this river?

Barge owners benefited directly from the government's costly service. And yet they were not charged a toll of any kind. The privilege of motoring up and down the Mississippi River, for example, was completely free.

But in 1978, Senator Domenici introduced a bill proposing that a toll, or user fee, be collected from major users of the nation's waterways. Other senators snorted that Domenici's bill could not pass. They thought that powerful leaders of the Senate would stop the bill before it was even voted upon. Senator Domenici admitted that the odds were against him. He said to reporters: "Oh, I'd say the odds against me are 90 to 1. Of course, a lot of other guys around here will tell you it's more like 900 to 1."

Opponents of the river toll. Naturally, the interest group most opposed to Senator Domenici's bill were the barge companies. These companies had powerful friends in Congress. Chief among them was a senator from Louisiana, Russell Long. The Mississippi River passed right through Senator Long's state. The barge companies that operated in Louisiana were important to the state's economy. Senator Long therefore sided with the barge companies when their interests were under attack.

Senator Long had been in the Senate many years. He had far greater seniority than Senator Domenici. Also, as a Democrat, the Louisiana senator belonged to the majority party. Finally, he was the chairperson of one of the Senate's most powerful committees: the Senate Finance Committee. All bills concerning taxes had to pass through his committee.

Approval by the Public Works Committee. Senator Domenici's river tolls bill, S. 790, cleared the first hurdle without much trouble. As its sponsor, Domenici persuaded

FOR AND AGAINST A RIVER TOLL. Why did Senator Long (left) oppose the barge bill sponsored by Senator Domenici (right)?

the Senate's presiding officer to assign the bill to his committee (Public Works) rather than to Senator Long's Finance Committee. Subcommittee hearings on the bill went very smoothly. The full committee then changed a few words in the bill and sent it to the floor for a vote. So far, so good.

Senate vote on S. 790. But the fight for S. 790 had only just begun. Lobbyists hired by the barge companies were alert and active. Senator Long promised them that he would do all in his power to defeat S. 790.

He spoke with other senators about the bill. Many of them had no particular interest in the user fee one way or the other. But Senator Long knew other bills that interested them more. In effect, he told them: "You vote *against* this S. 790. In turn, you can count on my support for that other bill that your constituents want so badly."

Members of Congress often ask each other for political favors. They understand that the favors will probably be returned some day. The lawmakers' practice of trading favors is called *logrolling*. (The word comes from the days when pioneers would help one another in the heavy labor of rolling logs into one place to clear the land and then help build fences and cabins.)

Matching his opponent's efforts, Senator Domenici also did some logrolling. He approached one senator after another, asking for their help. Could he count on their support for S. 790? he asked. If so, he would be happy to vote later for some favorite bill of theirs.

Before a bill comes to a vote, lobbyists and lawmakers want to know in advance whether it is likely to pass. They make a count of which senators are for and against the bill. Senator Long made such a count. And the result worried him. He feared that he would probably lose.

Therefore Senator Long prepared to conduct a filibuster against S. 790. On his desk in the Senate chamber was a great pile of papers. He was ready to read from the pile very slowly hour after hour. But then the barge company lobbyists advised him not to filibuster after all. They too had made an informal count of the probable vote. And they were sure that Senator Domenici's user fee bill would *not* be passed.

Senator Long decided to trust the count

ON HIS WAY TO VOTE YEA OR NAY. As he leaves the Capitol subway to enter the Senate chamber, Senator Daniel Moynihan of New York already knows how he will vote on a certain bill. What influences a senator to vote either for a bill or against it?

of the lobbyists. He soon regretted it. By a vote of 51 to 44, the Senate sided with Senator Domenici. S. 790 was now halfway home.

Substitute bill from the House. But it never went any farther than half way. Leaders in the House learned about Senator Domenici's bill. They thought such a bill should have been introduced in the House first. After all, a waterways bill would raise millions of dollars in revenue for the U.S. government. *The Constitution said that all revenue bills should originate in the House (not the Senate).*

So the House refused even to consider S. 790. Instead, the speaker of the House arranged for an entirely new waterways bill to be created. It was given the number H. R. 8309 and referred to a House committee. S. 790 was dead.

To say the least, Senator Domenici was disappointed. He thought the House substitute for his bill was a poor one. It proposed collecting only a small tax on the fuel oil used by river barges. He was not enthusiastic when H. R. 8309 passed the House and came to the Senate. Senator Long, on the other hand, thought the bill was not too bad. He liked H. R. 8309 much better than S. 790. He tried to convince the barge companies to go along with it. The bill provided for only a very small tax, he said—just six cents a gallon. Lobbyists for the barge companies, however, objected even to a small tax. Fight it to the bitter end, they said.

Too much pork barrel. Another problem arose. One section of H. R. 8309 called for the building and repair of a dam near Alton, Illinois. In political language, the dam was an example of a *pork barrel project*. Pork barrel may be defined as costly government projects that benefit only one state or congressional district.

Lawmakers generally love pork barrel projects, such as the building of dams, bridges, and roads. After all, such public works bring millions of dollars of federal money into their home districts. Business is given a boost, and jobs are created. Voters tend to appreciate it, rewarding lawmakers responsible for bringing in pork barrel money. On the other hand, such projects are expensive and often wasteful.

The two senators from Illinois were delighted with the dam-building project included in H. R. 8309. But other senators from other states wanted their "fair" share of pork barrel projects. On the Senate floor, they added dozens of amendments to H. R. 8309. Each amendment provided for spending millions of dollars on construction projects in their home states.

Representatives in the House heard about what the Senate was doing with H. R. 8309. They instructed their staff aides to write more pork barrel bills for the people of their districts. They planned to have these bills added to H. R. 8309 when it reached the Joint Conference Committee.

But it never did reach that committee. President Jimmy Carter announced his intention of vetoing any bill that contained too much pork barrel. Four billion dollars was the staggering sum that members of both houses of Congress wanted to include in the waterways bill. Too much! said the president. Threatened with a veto, H. R. 8309 was dead.

The bingo rider. Time was running out. In the fall of 1979, Congress was coming to the end of its term. Could a brand-new waterways bill be written, introduced, and passed in less than 10 days?

Despite the opposition of his friends, the barge lobbyists, Senator Long was determined to get a waterways bill enacted—a bill just like H. R. 8309 but without any pork barrel projects. As a veteran lawmaker, the Louisiana senator knew a trick or two. There was a minor tax bill in his Finance Committee that he had saved for an occasion like this. The House had already passed it as H. R. 8533. It was about taxes on church-sponsored bingo games. Not one word in the original bill was about dams and waterways. But Senator Long suggested to his committee that the bingo bill be amended. One section of the bill, he said, should be about fuel taxes to help pay for dam construction.

His amendment was an example of something lawmakers call a *rider*. Riders are like the canoes you sometimes see on the tops of cars. They do not belong to the vehicle (original bill). But the vehicle is necessary for carrying them to final passage.

The bingo/fuel tax bill came to the floor of the Senate. It passed by a wide margin. One of those who voted for it was Senator Domenici. Naturally he thought his original bill, S. 790, would have been much better. But he also recognized that Senator Long's bingo/fuel tax bill was better than not having a fuel tax at all.

Meanwhile, in the House, the bingo bill had to be passed once more, this time with the Senate's rider attached. A special rule of the House Rules Committee rushed it to a final vote. It passed.

In the White House, President Carter studied the act of Congress. Though he had threatened to veto other bills like it, the president signed this one into law.

Senator Long said the chief credit for the law belonged to his Republican rival, Senator Domenici. After all, it was Domenici's fight for S. 790 that paved the way for the victory of H. R. 8533.

What is the final outcome of this congressional story? Today, taxpayers pay less for federal waterways projects because barge companies pay more.

THE FINAL STEP. President Carter signs an act of Congress as its sponsors look on. How can a bill become law without the president's signature?

THE FINAL RESULT. Did the legislative efforts of Senator Domenici and Senator Long make it more or less expensive for river barges to operate?

REVIEW

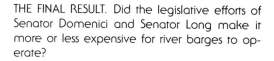

A. Building Your Political Vocabulary

Define each term. Then **explain** the role it played in helping either to pass or defeat the bill in parentheses.

1. Logrolling (S. 790)
2. Pork barrel (H. R. 8309)
3. Rider (H. R. 8533)

B. Agree or Disagree

Tell whether you **agree** or **disagree** with each statement of opinion. Give your reasons.

1. A toll, or user fee, charged to the barge companies was unfair.
2. The chief credit for passing a fuel tax bill in 1979 belongs to Senator Domenici, not to Senator Long.
3. The barge lobbyists had too much influence on the lawmaking process.
4. President Carter was right to threaten vetoing a bill containing $4 billion in "pork barrel."
5. The bingo/fuel tax bill was not worth all the trouble to get it passed.

CHAPTER REVIEW

A. Completing the Summary

Select terms from the word list to fill in the blanks in the summary below. Write your answers on a piece of paper.

act	override
committees	pigeonhole
elastic clause	pocket
filibuster	pork barrel
hearings	resolution
hopper	rider
interstate	Rules Committee
joint conference committee	taxes

The lawmaking process begins when a bill is placed in the __(1)__ of either the House or the Senate. A bill could be a private bill, a public bill, or a(n) __(2)__. For Congress to pass a public bill, it must be allowed to do so by one or more powers listed in the Constitution.

Among the 18 powers delegated to Congress, three are extremely important:

- the power to levy and collect __(3)__
- the power to regulate __(4)__ commerce
- the power to make all laws "necessary and proper" for carrying out Congress's other powers.

The "necessary and proper" clause is also known as the __(5)__ clause.

After a bill is introduced, it is referred to one of several standing __(6)__. Most bills do not go any farther than this. A chairperson who sees no merit in a bill may __(7)__ it and thus kill it. Bills that have the chairpersons' support may be sent to subcommittees where __(8)__ are held. The main committee then votes either for or against a bill's being sent to the full house. A positive vote and report means that the House or the Senate may eventually act on the bill. However, in the House, the powerful __(9)__ can block a bill's progress by listing it at the bottom of one of the House calendars.

The exact same bill must be approved on the floor of both houses. But if two versions of a bill are passed, members of each house meet in a(n) __(10)__ to iron out the differences. If they succeed, both houses vote again.

At this point, the bill becomes known as a(n) __(11)__ of Congress and goes to the president for his/her signature. If the president vetoes the measure, Congress may try to __(12)__ the veto. To do this, a two-thirds vote in each house is required. If less than 10 days remain to a term of Congress, the president may decide to __(13)__ veto the proposed law and thus kill it.

Senator Domenici's struggle to pass a waterways act in 1978 shows how tricky the lawmaking process can be. At first Senator Long opposed Senator Domenici's waterways bill. At one point, Long was prepared to lead a(n) __(14)__ against it. But the House then introduced a completely different idea for a waterways bill that Long could accept. President Carter objected to this bill because it seemed to be a costly __(15)__ scheme. But Long finally pushed another bill through his Senate Finance Committee by attaching a(n) __(16)__ to a bill concerning taxes on bingo games. Thus, in the final days of the 95th Congress, a tax bill was passed that made barge companies contribute payments for the use of American rivers.

B. House or Senate?

The following are common practices in the lawmaking process. Tell whether each is practiced by (*a*) **the House only,** (*b*) **the Senate only,** or (*c*) **both houses.**

1. filibustering
2. meeting as a Committee of the Whole
3. holding subcommittee hearings
4. logrolling
5. placing bills in a hopper
6. delaying bills in a rules committee
7. sending members to participate in a joint conference committee
8. introducing bills about taxes and government revenues
9. holding a vote on cloture
10. pigeonholing of bills in standing committees

C. Applying What You Know

You are serving your fourth term as a U.S. senator. You are sponsoring a bill that would give veterans of the armed forces help in starting small businesses of their own. You call it the Veteran Ventures Bill. Respond to the following questions and statements about your bill.

1. Name one power in the Constitution that would allow Congress to enact the bill.
2. Name two committees of the Senate that might consider the bill.
3. In subcommittee hearings on the bill, who might be called as expert witnesses?
4. What group would be likely to give you the greatest help in lobbying for the bill's passage?
5. Name a technique that you might use to persuade other senators to vote for the bill.
6. Suppose that a group of five senators plans to filibuster against your bill. What Senate rule would you try to use to stop them?
7. Suppose that your bill passes both the House and the Senate. But the president vetoes it 20 days before Congress is scheduled to adjourn. Can you still hope to enact the Veteran Ventures Bill? How?

a.

b.

c.

d.

a. *Supreme Court Chief Justice William Rehnquist*

b. *Police officers*

c. *A jury in a federal case*

d. *A demonstrator*

UNIT SIX

The Federal Courts

You now know about the president's job leading the Executive Branch. You also know about Congress's job making laws as the Legislative Branch. The third and final part of the U.S. government is the Judicial Branch, which consists of more than 100 courts. The most famous of them is the U.S. Supreme Court in the nation's capital. The two chapters in this unit describe the different courts, especially the highest court and its nine black-robed justices.

How much do you already know about the work of the U.S. courts? Find out by taking this multiple-choice quiz. Each set of questions (A–D) refers to the pictures on the facing page.

A. A SUPREME COURT JUSTICE

1. How long does a Supreme Court justice serve? (*a*) 4 years (*b*) 10 years (*c*) no time limit.
2. What is the Supreme Court's most important function? (*a*) interpreting the Constitution (*b*) conducting trials (*c*) executing the laws.
3. How does the Supreme Court make its decisions? (*a*) by a majority vote (*b*) by a two-thirds vote (*c*) by a unanimous vote.

B. POLICE OFFICERS

4. Which document sets limits on how a police officer may act? (*a*) the Declaration of Independence (*b*) the Constitution of 1787 (*c*) the Bill of Rights.
5. Police officers must show you a search warrant before searching your property because of (*a*) a law of Congress (*b*) the Fourth Amendment (*c*) the Twenty-sixth Amendment.

C. A JURY IN A FEDERAL CASE

6. At a trial in a federal court, what laws are involved? (*a*) the laws of Congress (*b*) the laws of a state (*c*) the laws of the Supreme Court.
7. Which document guarantees a fair trial to citizens accused of a crime? (*a*) the Declaration of Independence (*b*) the Constitution of 1787 (*c*) the Bill of Rights.

D. A DEMONSTRATOR

8. The First Amendment protects this person's rights to (*a*) freedom of speech (*b*) freedom of assembly (*c*) both freedom of speech and freedom of assembly.
9. Which of these has the last word in defining a demonstrator's rights? (*a*) a state court (*b*) any federal court (*c*) the U.S. Supreme Court.

Answers

1. *c* 3. *a* 5. *b* 7. *c* 9. *c*
2. *a* 4. *c* 6. *a* 8. *c*

THREE LAWYERS AT THE "MARBLE PALACE." Thurgood Marshall (center) worked with two other lawyers in 1952 in an attempt to persuade the Supreme Court that racially segregated schools were unconstitutional. What kinds of cases are brought to this courthouse for decision?

CHAPTER 15

The Supreme Court and the Lower Courts

OBJECTIVES

After reading this chapter, you will know

1. how the courts are organized at the federal level.
2. the difference between a trial court and an appeals court.
3. the kinds of cases that may be heard by the U.S. Supreme Court.
4. the meaning of the term "judicial review."
5. how the Supreme Court makes its decisions.
6. how to interpret a map of the U.S. court system.

One morning in 1952, a lawyer named Thurgood Marshall climbed the steps of the "Marble Palace" in Washington, D.C. The "Marble Palace" is a nickname for the Supreme Court Building, the most important courthouse in the United States. Within its white marble walls, nine Supreme Court justices decide cases involving the U.S. Constitution.

As he climbed the steps of the building, Marshall was well aware that the papers in his briefcase could change the future of his country. They concerned black students in different states who could not attend certain schools because of their race. Marshall represented these students as their lawyer. He believed that the *segregation* laws that made them attend racially separate schools violated a clause of the Constitution. The papers in his briefcase backed up the arguments he intended to use to prove his point.

Above the entrance to the Marble Palace, in large letters, are these words: EQUAL JUSTICE UNDER LAW. In Marshall's opinion, "equal justice" meant that members of different races should be treated as equals before the law.

Marshall strode into the building and took a front-row seat in the high-ceilinged courtroom. Facing him was a row of tall-backed chairs reserved for the nine Supreme Court justices. Behind the chairs was a purple velvet curtain.

That morning in 1952, the day in court began as it always begins. A court official called out: "Oyez, oyez, oyez! All persons having business before the Honorable, the Supreme Court of the United States, are admonished to draw near and give their attention, for the Court is now sitting. God save the United States and this Honorable Court."

Through the curtain, the justices entered and took their seats. Marshall stepped forward to argue the most important case in his career: the case of *Brown* v. *Board of Education of Topeka.*

In this chapter, you will learn how the *Brown* case was decided. But first, you must

THE BUILDING AND THE BENCH. The Supreme Court Building (above) was completed in 1935. Inside is the bench (right), a judicial term for the seat or seats used by judges in a courtroom. Who sits on the Supreme Court bench today?

know more about the Supreme Court and other courts in the U.S. system of justice. These are the questions discussed in this chapter:

1. What does the Constitution say about the Supreme Court?
2. How does the Supreme Court interpret the Constitution?
3. How does the Supreme Court make its decisions?
4. Case study: Why were segregated schools declared unconstitutional?

1. WHAT DOES THE CONSTITUTION SAY ABOUT THE SUPREME COURT?

You know that the U.S. government is separated into three branches. There is the lawmaking, or legislative, branch: Congress. There is the law-enforcing, or executive, branch headed by the president. You have studied these two branches in detail. Now we come to the third branch: the federal *judiciary*.

It truly is the third branch since it was the third article of the Constitution that created it. Article III is much shorter than the two articles that precede it. We can learn a great deal about the Judicial Branch and the Supreme Court just by quoting it.

The judicial power. Article III begins:

> The judicial power of the United States shall be vested in one Supreme Court, and in such inferior courts as the Congress may from time to time establish.

The judicial power means the power to say what U.S. laws mean in specific cases. Over the years, Congress has enacted many thousands of laws. Some of them define crimes. Others set up programs to help people. Still others regulate businesses and other organizations. Officials in the Executive Branch are supposed to make sure that the laws are properly carried out and obeyed.

If a federal law is broken, federal agents may arrest the suspected lawbreaker. Did the accused person in fact break the law? That is an example of a judicial question because it is about a specific act by a specific person under a specific law. Such questions can be settled only in court.

Under the Constitution, the Supreme Court and "inferior courts" may decide judicial questions. They have the power to decide both civil cases and criminal cases. (Review pages 150–151.)

Three levels of U.S. courts. What is an inferior court? It is any federal court that has less power than the Supreme Court. Think of the U.S. court system as a kind of pyramid consisting of three levels.

The Supreme Court is at the top of the system. Inferior to it are 12 courts of appeals. At the base of the pyramid (lowest in power) are 94 district courts where trials are held.

What is the chief difference between an *appeals court* and a *district, or trial, court*? An appeals court *never* holds trials; it reviews the decisions of other courts. Other differences between levels 2 and 3 will be explained later in the chapter.

Jurisdiction of federal and state courts. U.S. district courts are not the only ones that conduct trials. Each of the 50 states has its own system of courts. How does anyone know whether a certain case should be taken to a federal court for trial or to a state court? In other words, which kind of court—federal or state—has jurisdiction? (*Jurisdiction* means the authority and responsibility to handle matters of law.)

The Constitution gives this answer:

> The judicial power [of federal courts] shall extend to all cases . . . arising under this Constitution, the laws of the United States, and treaties made, or which shall be made under their authority. . . .

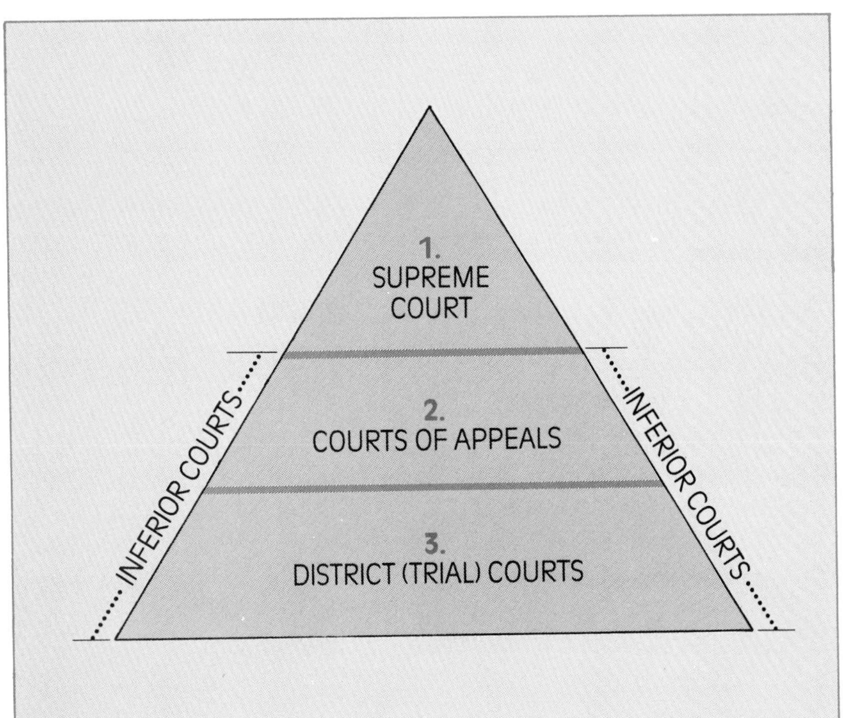

In other words, cases come to federal district courts for trial when a law or treaty of Congress is involved. When a state law is involved, the state courts usually have jurisdiction.

However, some cases involving the states must be tried in federal courts. They are:

- cases involving a dispute between one state and another (*example*: the government of Michigan bringing suit against the government of Wisconsin)
- cases involving a dispute between citizens of different states (*example*: a Floridian bringing suit against a Texan).

All of the above are federal cases, not state cases.

Original and appellate jurisdiction. There are two other kinds of jurisdiction. *Original jurisdiction* means the ability of a lower court to hold trials. Appellate jurisdiction means the power of certain courts to review the decisions of trial courts. In the *federal* judiciary, the district (trial) courts have original jurisdiction; courts of appeals have appellate jurisdiction. The court system of each *state* also has both trial courts and appeals courts.

CARTOON CORNER helps us to see the total picture. In the scene below, state courts are placed on one side of an "Avenue of Justice," federal courts on the other side. Notice that trials are held at a lower level (or "first floor") of each state or federal system, and appeals are heard at a higher level ("second floor").

Jurisdiction of the Supreme Court. The "Avenue of Justice" leads to the U.S. Supreme Court at the end of the road. This is the only court in the federal system that has both original jurisdiction and appellate jurisdiction. In other words, it can hold trials in certain cases while hearing appeals in other cases.

According to the Constitution, the Supreme Court's original jurisdiction applies to two kinds of cases:

CARTOON CORNER

- all cases affecting ambassadors
- most federal cases in which a state government is involved.

For example, suppose that a French diplomat, while living in Washington, is caught smuggling drugs. Suppose that Arizona brings suit against California for polluting its desert air. Both cases must come to trial in the Supreme Court.

Although it sometimes holds trials, the U.S. Supreme Court is best known as an appeals court. All cases brought to the highest court "on appeal" must first be tried in either a federal or a state court. They may then be appealed to one of the middle-level appeals courts. Finally, if a case is thought to be important enough, it may be heard by the "court of last resort," the Supreme Court.

In all cases that it hears, the Supreme Court's decision is final. Both the state courts and the lower federal courts must abide by it. You can understand then why the Supreme Court is called "supreme."

Life tenure. How long may a federal judge hold office? Here is the Constitution's answer:

> The judges, both of the Supreme and inferior courts, shall hold their offices during good behavior. . . .

"Good behavior" is the *only* requirement in the Constitution for serving as a federal judge. For a judge, "good behavior" means performing one's duties honestly and responsibly. You do *not* have to be a certain age to be a federal judge. You do *not* have to be a U.S. citizen. You are *not* required to graduate from law school—or, even from high school. Do you doubt it? Then search Article III yourself and see if you find an educational requirement.

So long as a judge's behavior is "good," he or she may stay in office for life. Take the case of a famous judge named Oliver Wendell Holmes. Holmes was 61 years old in 1902 when President Theodore Roosevelt appointed him to the Supreme Court. He was 90 when he finally resigned the office in 1932. The Constitution would have allowed him to serve even longer—until his death in 1934.

There is only one way to force federal judges to retire. They may be impeached (accused) by the House of Representatives and then tried by the Senate. If found "guilty" of the impeachment charges, a judge would be forced to leave office. In the history of the United States, only five federal judges were removed from office by means of impeachment. One Supreme Court judge, Samuel Chase, was impeached by the House in 1804. But Chase was acquitted by the Senate. So far, then, all Supreme Court judges and almost all lower court judges have behaved well enough to stay in office until they retired or died.

REVIEW

A. Rules of the Constitution

Tell whether Article III **does** or **does not** describe each of the following topics. (Check the full text of Article III on pages 126–127.)

1. Jurisdiction of the Supreme Court
2. Rules for selecting a Supreme Court judge
3. Powers of the state courts
4. Number of judges who may sit on the Supreme Court
5. Number of inferior courts in the federal system
6. Types of cases that may be tried in federal courts

B. Applying What You Know

Which court would have **original jurisdiction** for each of the following cases? Answer either *state court, lower federal court,* or *U.S. Supreme Court.*

1. Criminal case that violates the laws of Idaho
2. Case of drug smuggling that violates an act of Congress
3. Civil suit brought by the state of Maryland against the state of Delaware
4. Divorce case involving two citizens of Nevada
5. Divorce case involving a wife residing in Vermont and a husband residing in Maine
6. Case of an Egyptian ambassador who sues a Texas driver for damaging his car
7. Case of a U.S. fishing company that is accused of breaking a U.S. treaty with Japan
8. Case of a Michigan car dealer who sues the U.S. government

C. Making Comparisons

Make a chart that compares a Supreme Court **judge** with a U.S. **senator** in terms of the following:

1. Type of power
2. Length of term
3. Qualifications for office

(For information about senators, review pages 291–292.)

2. HOW DOES THE SUPREME COURT INTERPRET THE CONSTITUTION?

The Constitution is the supreme law of the land. But that law must be interpreted by some person or group of persons. As a document, it cannot think and speak for itself. Who then decides what the "supreme law" actually means in specific circumstances? That is the chief task of the U.S. Supreme Court.

John Marshall's contribution. Back in the 1790s, the first Supreme Court saw its role as modest and limited. It did not even try to interpret different clauses of the Constitution. The judges then sitting on the Court did not think interpreting the Constitution was within their power.

At that time, the Supreme Court consisted of five judges, one of whom acted as chief justice. When the first chief justice retired, President John Adams had an opportunity to appoint a successor. The person he chose for the job was a tough Virginia lawyer named John Marshall. Marshall proved to be a great leader. When he entered office in 1801, he found the Supreme Court lacking the power that he thought rightfully belonged to it. Marshall worked the rest of his life—34 years—to increase the Court's power. When he died in 1835, the power of the Supreme Court was about equal to that of Congress and the president.

CHIEF JUSTICE JOHN MARSHALL. Marshall served 34 years on the Supreme Court (1801–1835), longer than any other chief justice. How did he increase the Supreme Court's power?

Case of **Marbury** ***v.*** **Madison.** Legal scholars still marvel at the brilliant way that John Marshall handled a tricky case known as *Marbury* v. *Madison.* His cleverness in the case may be compared to the cleverness of the fictitious detective Sherlock Holmes.

The case has many complicated twists and turns. But we can reduce the story to seven essential facts:

1. William Marbury wanted to be a judge in a lower federal court. He said that President Adams had appointed him to the position. In fact, Adams had appointed more than 40 people including Marbury to judgeships. All belonged to Adams's own party, the Federalist party.

2. Appointing judges had been Adams's last act as president. The next day, Thomas Jefferson was sworn into office as the new president. He was a Democratic-Republican, not a Federalist.

3. Jefferson did not want Marbury and the other Federalists to take office. So he ordered Secretary of State James Madison *not* to give Marbury the commission (legal papers) that would authorize him to be a judge.

4. Marbury hoped the Supreme Court could force Jefferson and Madison to give him his commission. He said a law of Congress, enacted in 1789, had given the Supreme Court the power to issue *writs of mandamus.* Mandamus means the power of a court to order an executive official (like Madison) to carry out his or her duties. The *writ* (document) that Marbury wanted would have demanded that his judge's commission be given to him.

5. Listening to Marbury's arguments, Chief Justice Marshall agreed with most of them. He thought Marbury was entitled to receive his commission.

6. But, said Marshall, the Supreme Court could not help Marbury. Why not? As Marshall explained, Article III of the Constitution listed every type of case that properly belonged to the original jurisdiction of the Supreme Court. *Issuing writs of mandamus was not listed!* Congress's law of 1789 presumed to give the Supreme Court a power not mentioned in the Constitution. Therefore, the law itself was void (not to be obeyed).

7. Marbury lost the case. He never received the commission to be a federal judge.

The sixth fact in the case is the most important. In effect, John Marshall was telling Congress that it could not pass certain laws. The Supreme Court, he said, had the power of judicial review. The Court could review acts of Congress. If it found such acts went against the Constitution, then it could declare them void.

Judicial review. After his decision in *Marbury* v. *Madison* (1803), Marshall reviewed other laws of Congress. He judged some of them to be constitutional (allowed), while judging others to be unconstitutional (void). So began a practice of the Supreme Court known as *judicial review.*

Today, judicial review means that the Supreme Court and other federal courts may rule upon the acts of Congress, the president, and the governments of the 50 states. Through judicial review, the Court tries to act as a final interpreter and protector of the Constitution.

How does the nation benefit from the practice of judicial review? It is an important check against the misuse of government power. Sometimes, whether intentionally or not, a federal or state official may break the rules of the Constitution. Because of its power of judicial review, the Supreme Court can put a stop to the laws it judges to be "unconstitutional." It can also review acts of the president to determine whether or not the Constitution permits them.

The politics of Supreme Court justices. Judges are human beings dressed in black robes. Like other people, they have opinions about politics. Their opinions often influence how they think about the Constitution.

A good example is the politics of John Marshall. Before becoming a Supreme Court judge, Marshall belonged to the Federalist party. (See page 77.) He was appointed to the highest court by another Federalist, President John Adams. From Chapter 9, you may recall that Federalists wanted the federal government to become stronger than the state governments. The rival party led by Thomas Jefferson was more interested in protecting the rights of states.

Marshall did not abandon his Federalist ideas when he began to wear the chief justice's robe. Instead he used his position to strengthen the federal government. Many cases came to the Court involving conflict between states on the one hand, the federal government on the other. Usually Marshall decided in favor of the federal government.

Suppose the chief justice in those days had been from Jefferson's party. Would his opinion about a case have been different from Marshall's? It is very likely.

Another famous example of the influence of politics on the Supreme Court happened during Franklin Roosevelt's presidency. In the 1930s, most of the judges on the Court had conservative ideas. President Roosevelt was more liberal. Using their power of judicial review, the conservative judges declared certain liberal laws to be unconstitutional and void.

Feeling frustrated, Roosevelt asked Congress to pass a law that would have allowed him to appoint additional justices to the Court. The justices he wanted would surely have been liberal Democrats like himself. But Roosevelt did not get the law he so badly wanted.

Critics accused the president of trying to "pack the Court" with judges who thought a certain way. The critics were right. But then, given a chance, most presidents would want to "pack" the Supreme Court with judges whose political convictions agree with their own.

AN ATTEMPT TO "PACK" THE COURT. How are the three branches of the U.S. government represented in this cartoon? If you had been the "referee," would you have approved the "quarterback's" idea?

How justices are nominated and confirmed. Nobody can predict when one of the nine Supreme Court judges will either retire or die. When it happens, presidents are usually sorry for the loss, but glad for the opportunity it gives them to influence membership on the Supreme Court.

A vacancy on the Court is filled by a two-step process. First, the president nominates someone for the job. The nominee may or may not have previous experience as a judge. Usually, he or she has at least been trained as a lawyer. Usually too, the nominee belongs to the president's own political party. But as you know, none of these qualifications is mentioned in the Constitution.

The second step in the process is for the Senate to study the president's choice. The nominee is called to appear in person at a hearing of the Senate Judiciary Committee. It is called a confirmation hearing because its purpose is to decide whether to confirm (or approve) the president's choice.

Senators from the opposing party may be hard on the nominee and ask embarrassing questions. Sometimes, they put up a bitter and determined fight against the president's choice. In rare cases, the Senate opposition succeeds and the president must nominate someone else. Usually, however, the Senate votes to approve the president's choice. The newly appointed judge is then entitled to sit on the highest court (during "good behavior") for the rest of his or her life.

The independence of the justices. Once seated on the Court, justices are secure. They know that they can hold their jobs for life and do not have to worry about winning election or pleasing the president. In other words, they can make decisions independently without any political pressures.

CONFIRMED AND NOT CONFIRMED. To fill vacancies on the Supreme Court, President Reagan nominated Sandra Day O'Connor (left) in 1981 and Robert Bork in 1987. A Senate committee confirmed O'Connor's appointment but not Bork's. What might be a good reason for rejecting a president's nominee?

Because of their independence, justices may make decisions that surprise the president who appointed them. Someone expected to be a liberal judge sometimes makes conservative decisions. It happens the other way too. A conservative president is pleased to nominate a supposedly conservative judge. But then the president is dismayed when the new justice's decisions take a liberal turn.

For example, in 1953, President Eisenhower picked a Republican governor of California, Earl Warren, to be the new chief justice. Eisenhower expected Warren to live up to his conservative reputation. Instead, during his 16 years on the Court, Warren made decisions that delighted liberals while alarming conservatives.

Role of the chief justice. The Supreme Court consists of eight associate justices and one chief justice. The "chief" is the central figure on the Court. He or she has more administrative duties than the others and must see that the lower courts in the federal system are properly managed. The chief's annual salary is therefore slightly more than the salary of an associate justice.

In U.S. history, several chief justices were very influential. One was John Marshall in the early 1800s. Another was Earl Warren in the 1950s and 1960s. However, the eight associate justices do not take orders from the chief justice—far from it. They form their opinions independently. In the locked conference room, no chief justice can tell the others how to vote.

Activism or restraint? The Supreme Court consists of justices who were appointed at different times by different presidents. Often, the justices disagree among themselves about the role that the Supreme Court should play in American society.

Some are known as judicial activists because they think the highest court should use its judicial power actively and often to overturn "harmful" laws. Other justices think the Supreme Court should use its power with extreme caution, overturning laws only in rare cases. Such justices argue for a policy of judicial restraint.

In the past, when activists held a majority on the Court, they overturned many kinds of laws. For example, during the Great Depression of the 1930s, important laws were passed by Congress to help the economy recover. Two of its most important laws were ruled unconstitutional. In separate cases, activist judges said that the Constitution did not grant government the power to enact either the National Recovery Act (regulating business and labor) or the Agricultural Adjustment Act (regulating farm production). The activist justices said it was their duty to interpret the Constitution as the Framers of the 1780s meant it to be interpreted.

But a minority of judges on the Supreme Court in the 1930s disagreed. They thought the activists were wrong to impose their conservative views on the nation. Justice Louis Brandeis and other critics of the activist majority said that Congress should be given the benefit of the doubt. If its laws were at least loosely based on the Constitution, the Supreme Court had no business standing in the way. Brandeis, in other words, argued for judicial restraint.

The conflict between activism and restraint took a different turn in the 1950s and 1960s. At that time, Chief Justice Earl Warren and most of the associate justices were concerned about promoting equal rights for women and minorities. They were judicial activists who thought the Supreme Court had a responsibility to improve society. In case after case, they ruled that state laws discriminating against blacks and other minorities were unconstitutional. The Supreme Court in these years was praised by some and blamed by others for its "liberal" decisions.

JUSTICES WITH OPPOSING VIEWS. Louis Brandeis (left) argued for the idea of judicial restraint during his years on the Supreme Court (1916–1939). Earl Warren (right) was a judicial activist during his years as chief justice (1953–1969). How would you explain the differences in their ideas?

Notice that an activist judge can be *either* conservative (as in the 1930s) *or* liberal (as in the 1960s). What matters is a judge's view of whether or not the Supreme Court should make policy for the nation. Yes, say the activist judges, the Supreme Court can and should play a leading role in national affairs. No, say those who favor judicial restraint. Making laws and policies is the job of elected lawmakers, not the job of Supreme Court justices.

If *you* were a judge on the Supreme Court, which approach would you take: judicial activism or judicial restraint?

REVIEW

A. Building Your Political Vocabulary

Match the term in the word list to the phrase that describes it. Some answers may be given more than once.

confirmation hearing
judicial activism
judicial restraint
judicial review
writ of mandamus

1. any judge who thinks that Congress should abide strictly by rules in the Constitution
2. something that happens soon after a president nominates a judge for the Supreme Court
3. something that William Marbury wanted the Supreme Court to use
4. a power that John Marshall used in deciding the case of *Marbury* v. *Madison*
5. an event that takes place in a Senate committee room
6. the policy of giving Congress a great deal of flexibility in making laws
7. an important power that only the judicial branch may exercise

B. Applying What You Know

Imagine that you are living in the year 2011. The questions below are about the Supreme Court in that future year. Answer them according to the principles you have learned in this section. Explain your choice of answer.

1. The president in 2011 is a Republican with liberal policies. He is most likely to appoint which of the following to the Supreme Court? (*a*) a Democrat with liberal ideas (*b*) a Republican with liberal ideas (*c*) a Republican with conservative ideas.
2. In 2011, a majority of judges on the highest court take an activist approach to their duties. How often would you expect the Court to declare federal and state laws to be void? (*a*) often (*b*) seldom (*c*) never.
3. One Supreme Court judge having died, the president names Mary Lee to fill the vacancy. Who decides whether Ms. Lee will in fact get to sit on the Court? (*a*) the Senate (*b*) the House (*c*) both houses of Congress.

C. Agree or Disagree

Tell whether you **agree** or **disagree** with each statement, and give your reason.

1. John Marshall's decision in *Marbury* v. *Madison* was unfair to Marbury.
2. The Supreme Court would be wise to follow a policy of judicial restraint.
3. In the system of checks and balances, judicial review is the most powerful check of all.

3. HOW DOES THE SUPREME COURT MAKE ITS DECISIONS?

In the time of John Marshall, the judges of the Supreme Court would meet in Washington, D.C., for only two or three months a year. During the other months, they had to travel around the country. Each judge was assigned a different circuit, or territory, to cover. One judge, for example, might "ride circuit" in the South, while another traveled through New England.

The old judicial circuits. The purpose of the judges' circuit-riding was to hear cases appealed to them from the lower, trial courts. When a Supreme Court judge rode into town, he would be met by two trial judges. Together the visiting judge and the local judges formed an appeals, or *circuit*, court. Lawyers in the area whose clients had been disappointed by a jury's verdict would ask the appeals court to hear their arguments. Then, after the appeals in one place had been heard, the Supreme Court judge would pack up and ride on to the next town in the regular circuit.

As you might imagine, the workload was heavy and the travel wearying.

Year after year, the country expanded westward. The American population doubled and redoubled. The judicial circuits widened outward, across the Mississippi River and the Rocky Mountains to the Pacific Coast. Even with railroads to speed them on their way, the circuit-riding judges could not keep up with all the cases waiting for them.

Finally, in 1891, Congress voted to give the travel-weary judges some relief. An act was passed creating new judgeships in the federal system. Judges appointed to these offices would ride circuit within an assigned territory. They would have authority to hear appeals from the trial courts. In short, they would do much of the work previously done by the Supreme Court judges.

The new courts of appeals. Today, as you learned on page 333, the middle level of court in the federal system is known as a court of appeals. The country is served by 12 such courts. Each operates within a territory that is still called a "circuit."

A COURT ON THE FRONTIER, ABOUT 1840. In those times, how were the decisions of a federal judge in a lower court appealed to a higher court?

Look at the map on page 344. Notice that the 9th Circuit covers an immense area from Arizona all the way to Alaska and Hawaii. The 1st Circuit in New England is much smaller. The smallest is an unnumbered circuit serving only the people of Washington, D.C.

Cases brought to a court of appeals are usually reviewed and decided by three appellate judges. Occasionally, all the appellate judges of a circuit will hear a case together in one courthouse. To use their term, they are then judging a case *en banc.*

The appeals courts (also known as circuit courts of appeals) may either agree or disagree with the decisions made by the trial courts within their jurisdiction. If they agree, we say they uphold the verdict of a lower court. If they disagree, we say they overturn or reverse the lower court's judgment.

Appeals judges never conduct trials involving witnesses and juries. (Only trial courts do that.) Appeals judges want to know:

- Does the U.S. Constitution permit the government to act as it did in the case?
- Was a law of Congress correctly applied at the trial?
- Did the defendant in the case receive a fair trial?

If the appellate judges answer *no* to one of these questions, the trial court's decision is reversed.

Districts within circuits. Look at the key to the map. Note the lines that stand for judicial districts of the federal system. Iowa, for example, is divided into a North district and a South district. Missouri is split

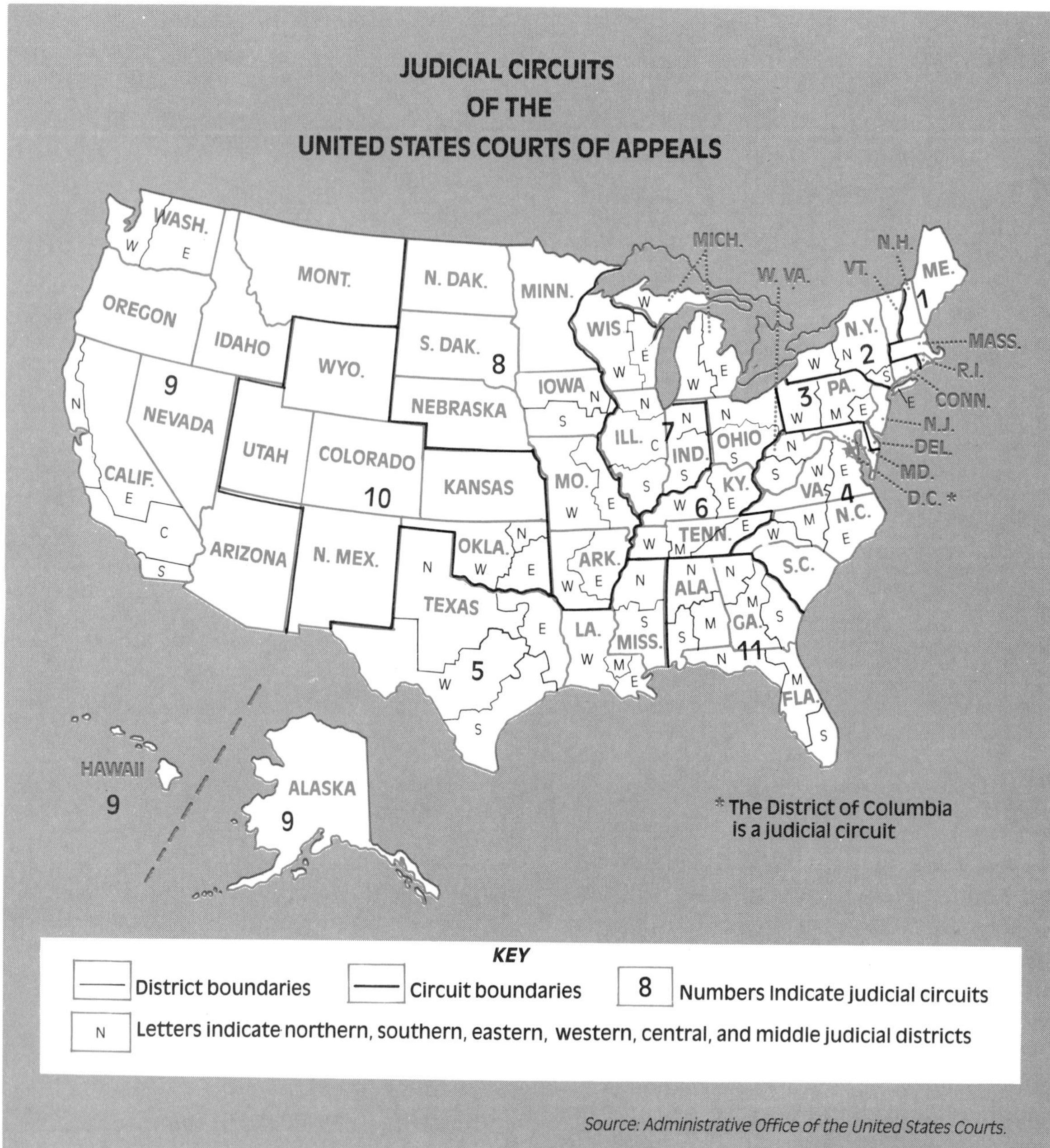

the other way into a West district and an East district. New York has four districts: North, South, East, West. A state like Utah, which is not divided, has just one district.

For every judicial district in the country, there is one trial court. Thus, trial courts in the federal judiciary are commonly known as district courts.

In 1990, there were a total of 90 district (or trial) courts serving the 50 states and the District of Columbia. The number of district judges, however, was much greater: 556. That is because several judges are often needed within a single populous district to handle the large number of cases. Otherwise, a backlog of cases would occur.

SKILLS CHECK: Interpreting maps

You can learn more facts about the federal judiciary by looking closely at the map on page 344. Use the following to guide your study:

1. Name any four states that have only one district court.
2. Name any three states that are divided into four districts each.
3. What is the federal circuit that serves your area?
4. How many district courts in all make up the circuit in which you live?

The final court of appeal. You recall that trial, or district, courts have original jurisdiction. Appeals, or circuit, courts have appellate jurisdiction. In other words, a case is originally tried in a district court. It may then be appealed to a higher court—the appropriate court of appeals.

Take, for example, a case involving the robbery of a U.S. post office in Cheyenne, Wyoming. Defendants in the case would stand trial in the district court of Wyoming. Let us suppose they are convicted and sentenced. An appeal could then be made to the court of appeals of the 10th Circuit. (See map.)

Now suppose the appeals judges uphold, or affirm, the lower court's decision. The lawyer for the convicted robbers could make one last appeal—to the U.S. Supreme Court. The lawyer could send to the highest court a paper arguing that the defendant's constitutional rights to a fair trial had been violated.

The Supreme Court now has a choice. It could either (*a*) hear the lawyer's appeal or (*b*) flatly refuse to consider it. The Supreme Court cannot possibly hear all the thousands of cases and petitions that yearly arrive in the mail. It can give careful consideration to an average of only 150–200 cases a year. Any case it selects for review must meet two tests:

1. The case must involve a question about one or more sections of the Constitution.
2. The case must have significance for American society as a whole (not just for the individual petitioner).

Now suppose that the Supreme Court refuses to hear the case of the Wyoming postal robbery. Then the decision of the court of appeals is final. The Supreme Court has the last word in a case *only if it wants the last word.*

The Supreme Court's schedule. Let us travel in our imagination to the Marble Palace (Supreme Court Building) in Washington, D.C. The best time to visit is in the fall, winter, or spring. The Supreme Court is not in session during the summer months. For the nine judges, summer is a time for traveling on judicial business. Each judge is assigned a different circuit where he or she meets with the judges of one of the courts of appeals.

By the first Monday in October, the Supreme Court justices must be back in Washington. On that date, they file into their famous courtroom with its purple curtains and high oak ceiling. For the next 36 weeks, until June 30, the highest court is in session.

Each week, the nine judges follow the same routine. Monday morning at 10 o'clock, they enter the courtroom and sit side-by-side in their high-backed chairs. (As members of the public, we could be there in the audience.) Two lawyers for opposing sides of a case stand and orally present their arguments. After an hour (sometimes longer) the judges dismiss the one case and take up the next. At noon, they adjourn. Then two more cases are heard between 2 and 4 o'clock in the afternoon.

Tuesday and Thursday are just like Monday: two cases in the morning, two more

ALL IN A DAY'S WORK. The clerk of the Supreme Court begins his day by distributing a stack of folders to the nine justices. Each folder contains a lawyer's appeal from a lower court. Is the Supreme Court obligated to accept every case appealed to it?

in the afternoon. On Wednesday afternoon and all day Friday, the judges retire to a private conference room. Nobody else can gain admission to this locked room. Not even the judges' own law clerks are permitted to enter. When meeting in conference, the judges make their decisions about the cases argued during the week. For each case, the chief justice is the first to express an opinion. The most junior judge (the one appointed most recently) speaks next, and the most senior judge speaks last.

As an example of Supreme Court decision-making, let us take the case of *Smith* v. *Jones.* Five judges are persuaded that Smith's legal position is stronger, while four side with Jones. The majority rules, and Smith wins the case.

Writing the opinion of the Court. Whether one person or another wins a case has little importance to American society as a whole. Far more important are the reasons that the Supreme Court gives for its decisions. The reasons are carefully presented in a formal essay written by one of the nine judges who voted with the majority. If the chief justice agreed with the majority, then it is usually his or her responsibility to write the majority opinion.

Other judges may, if they wish, write their own opinions in the case. One judge may have sided with Smith but for reasons different from those expressed in the majority opinion. Since this judge's essay generally concurs (agrees) with the majority's decision, the opinion is known as a *concurring opinion.*

Judges in the minority (siding with Jones) may choose to write their arguments in a *dissenting opinion.* (To dissent means to disagree with the majority.)

After the judges finish drafting and redrafting their opinions in a case, they send them down to the basement of the Marble Palace. There the Court's own print shop sets the judges' words into type. Usually on Monday morning ("decision Monday") the Court's decisions are passed out to members of the press.

Judges and lawyers throughout the country carefully study the latest opinions of the highest court. The arguments found there will guide the decisions in their own courtrooms for months and years to come. Again and again, in cases similar to *Smith* v. *Jones,* lawyers will remind trial judges of what the Supreme Court justices had decided. Both trial judges and lawyers place great importance on a precedent (a ruling by the Court on an earlier case) established by the Supreme Court.

THE SUPREME COURT IN EARLY 1994. Standing (from left): Clarence Thomas, Anthony Kennedy, David Souter, Ruth Bader Ginsburg. Seated (from left): Sandra Day O'Connor, Harry Blackmun, William Rehnquist (chief justice), John Paul Stevens, Antonin Scalia. Justice Blackmun resigned in mid-1994 and has been replaced by Stephen Breyer, a federal circuit court judge in Boston.

REVIEW

A. Making Inferences

For each statement, tell whether you think it is (*a*) **certainly true,** (*b*) **probably true,** (*c*) **probably false,** or (*d*) **certainly false.** Give your reasons.

1. Lawyers in the case of *Smith* v. *Jones* presented their arguments to the Supreme Court on a Friday afternoon.
2. Before appealing to the Supreme Court, lawyers for Smith argued their case in one of the 12 courts of appeals. (Assume that the case originated in a federal court.)
3. The Court's written opinion in the case of *Smith* v. *Jones* mentioned clauses in the U.S. Constitution.
4. If *Smith* v. *Jones* was originally tried in a district court in Iowa, it must have been appealed to the court of appeals of the 5th Circuit. (See the map on page 344.)
5. A reporter for *Time* magazine was present in the Supreme Court conference room when the case of *Smith* v. *Jones* was decided.

B. Applying What You Know

Invent a federal case that is eventually decided by the Supreme Court.

1. Give the case a name.
2. Describe the nature of the case.

3. Identify the district court where the case originated.
4. Identify a clause of the Constitution that permitted the case to be reviewed by the Supreme Court. (See, for example, Amendments 1–10 on pages 131–133.)
5. Tell what a majority of the Supreme Court decided in the case.

CASE STUDY: Why Were Segregated Schools Declared Unconstitutional?

Recall the civil rights lawyer, Thurgood Marshall, climbing the steps of the Marble Palace in Washington. (Review page 331.) In 1952, he represented black clients from four states. One of them, Linda Brown, was an 8-year-old student at an elementary school in Topeka, Kansas. It was a public school for blacks only. The Board of Education of Topeka had determined that certain schools in the city should be attended only by black students, while others should be attended only by whites. Such a policy was called school segregation.

The parents of Linda Brown wanted their daughter to attend one of Topeka's all-white schools. But the Board of Education refused to change its segregation policy. The Browns sued the board in a federal district court. The trial judge there decided in favor of the school board.

The Browns appealed their case. They were aided by Thurgood Marshall and by the National Association for the Advancement of Colored People (NAACP), a group working for the legal rights of blacks. The Supreme Court decided that the case of *Brown* v. *Board of Education of Topeka* was important enough to be heard. It also agreed to review three other cases involving school segregation in the states of Delaware, Virginia, and South Carolina.

In all four cases, the highest Court would either uphold school segregation everywhere or rule against it everywhere. After all, a constitutional principle was at issue, not just one child's desire to attend a certain school. By reading about the *Brown* case, you will see all that is involved in making a Supreme Court decision. First, however, you need to know the historic background to the case.

Segregation after the Civil War. In 1868, long before Thurgood Marshall was born, the Fourteenth Amendment was added to the Constitution. It said that no state could deny "any person within its jurisdiction the equal protection of the laws." The amendment was passed to protect the rights of blacks newly freed from slavery.

In the 1880s and 1890s, states of the South enacted laws to keep blacks and whites from mixing together in public places. In restaurants and hotels, separate washrooms

"WORSE THAN SLAVERY." This 1874 cartoon shows a Northerner's idea of conditions in the South. It shows "all-white" state governments failing to protect the rights of black citizens. How did the Fourteenth Amendment apply to these conditions?

were set aside for the exclusive use of whites. Railroad cars were also segregated by law.

***Case of* Plessy *v.* Ferguson.** Did such laws violate the meaning of the "equal protection" clause of the Constitution? Black citizens thought so. In 1892, a black citizen of Louisiana named Homer Plessy took a seat in a car reserved for whites. After being arrested for violating Louisiana's law, he sued a state judge named Ferguson. In 1896, the case of *Plessy* v. *Ferguson* came to the Supreme Court as a test of the equal protection clause.

Eight justices thought the segregation law in Louisiana was justified. In their majority opinion, they said that public facilities provided for whites and blacks could be "separate but equal." If they were indeed equal, they argued, then members of both races would receive equal protection of the laws. One judge, John Harlan, dissented. Harlan wrote: "Our Constitution is color-blind, and neither knows nor tolerates classes among its citizens."

Plessy lost his case. For many years afterward, judges in the federal courts ruled that segregation laws everywhere were constitutional. They cited (pointed to) the Supreme Court's "separate but equal" ruling in *Plessy* v. *Ferguson.*

***Case of* Brown *v.* Board of Education of Topeka.** Segregation continued for another 50 years. But the Browns of Topeka and others decided to challenge the old rules. Although the judges of the 1890s were now dead, their opinions were still influential. But the living judges who sat on the Supreme Court were willing to listen with open minds to Thurgood Marshall's arguments.

Marshall argued his case in 1952. The Supreme Court delayed making its decision for many months. Finally, in May 1954, the Court's opinion was released to reporters. By a unanimous vote, 9–0, the Court declared that segregated schools were *not* constitutional. They violated the equal protection clause of the Fourteenth Amendment.

Chief Justice Earl Warren wrote the historic opinion. These were his arguments:

- The *Plessy* v. *Ferguson* case was about railroad segregation, not school segregation. Therefore, the idea of "separate but equal" did not necessarily apply to schools.
- American society in the 1950s was different from the society of the 1890s. Public education had become far more important to all citizens.
- Black children attending segregated schools could not possibly receive an equal education. The very fact of attending such schools tended to make them think that they were inferior.

Therefore, Warren concluded, "in the field of public education, the doctrine of 'separate but equal' has no place."

ENFORCING THE SUPREME COURT'S DECISION, 1957. These were the first black students to attend a previously all-white high school in Little Rock, Arkansas. To prevent riots, units of the U.S. Army were called to the scene. Why was this event a result of the Supreme Court's decision in the *Brown* case?

JUSTICE THURGOOD MARSHALL. How can the written opinions of a Supreme Court justice have a major impact on U.S. society?

Many white citizens reacted angrily to the *Brown* decision. Segregation was a custom that was hard to change. But gradually, schools that had been all-white began opening their doors to black students. Across the country, racially integrated schools took the place of segregated ones.

A second Justice Marshall. Long after his triumph in the *Brown* case, Thurgood Marshall continued his visits to the courtroom in the Marble Palace. But starting in 1967, he viewed that room from a different angle. In that year, the president nominated Marshall to fill a vacant seat on the Supreme Court. When the Senate confirmed the nomination, Marshall became the first black to be a Supreme Court justice. Thus, he helped to integrate—not just the nation's schools—but the nation's highest court as well.

Marshall, who died in 1993, had a long and distinguished career as a Supreme Court justice. At first his liberal views on race relations and other issues were supported by other members of the Court. But as the years passed, justices with liberal views retired and Republican presidents replaced them with more conservative justices. In the 1980s, Justice Marshall was outvoted in many cases. Never afraid to disagree with his colleagues, he wrote a number of important dissenting opinions.

In 1991, after 24 years on the Supreme Court, Thurgood Marshall retired. Taking his place (after a bitterly contested confirmation hearing in the U.S. Senate) was Justice Clarence Thomas—the second African American to serve on the nation's highest court.

REVIEW

A. Making Comparisons

Compare the cases of *Plessy* v. *Ferguson* and *Brown* v. *Board of Education of Topeka*. In your comparison, mention (*a*) the issue involved in each case, (*b*) the Supreme Court's decision, and (*c*) the effect of the decision on American society.

B. Facts and Opinions

Tell whether each statement is a **fact** or an **opinion.** If it is an opinion, tell whether you agree or disagree with it and explain why.

1. "Our Constitution is color-blind."
2. The Supreme Court made the wrong decision in the case of *Plessy* v. *Ferguson*.
3. Segregated schools obviously violated the "equal protection of the laws" clause.
4. The Supreme Court's decision in the *Brown* case was unanimous.

C. Applying What You Know

Tell how the *Brown* case illustrates each of the following:

1. the idea of judicial review
2. the Supreme Court's appellate jurisdiction
3. the idea that the Constitution is "the supreme law of the land."

CHAPTER REVIEW

A. Completing the Summary

Select terms from the word list to fill in the blanks in the summary below. Write your answers on a piece of paper.

activism	majority
behavior	opinion
check	original
circuits	protection
confirmed	restraint
dissenting	retirement
final	review
Judicial	segregation
jurisdiction	void

The __(1)__ Branch of the federal government consists of three levels of courts. The lower, or district, courts have __(2)__ jurisdiction for holding trials that involve federal laws. Courts of appeals have appellate jurisdiction for reviewing the fairness of trials in the lower courts. These courts are organized into 12 __(3)__. At the top of the U.S. court system is the Supreme Court. It conducts trials for certain types of cases and acts as the __(4)__ court of appeals.

Each state has its own system of courts for handling cases involving state laws. But if a case involves two states or the citizens of different states, then the federal courts have __(5)__. State cases as well as federal cases may be appealed to the U.S. Supreme Court.

In 1803, the case of *Marbury* v. *Madison* established the Supreme Court's power of judicial __(6)__. Ever since, this power has served as an important __(7)__ on the powers of the president and Congress. It also is used to determine whether state laws are constitutional. If not, they are declared __(8)__.

How often should the Supreme Court be willing to overturn the laws of Congress and the states? Very rarely, answer those who favor judicial __(9)__. As often as may be needed, say those who favor judicial __(10)__.

Justices on the Supreme Court are nominated by the president and __(11)__ by the Senate. The nine justices serve so long as they demonstrate "good __(12)__." In effect, this means that their term ends only with their death or __(13)__.

The Supreme Court makes its decisions by __(14)__ vote. One of the justices writes the __(15)__ of the Court. Other justices who disagree with the decision may write their __(16)__ opinions.

A landmark case of 1954 was *Brown* v. *Board of Education of Topeka,* involving the issue of school __(17)__. It concerned the meaning of the Fourteenth Amendment and "equal __(18)__ of the laws." After hearing the arguments of a civil rights lawyer, Thurgood Marshall, the Court decided that all public schools had to be open to both blacks and whites.

B. Project: Updating Your Knowledge

In the reference room of your library, find out the following facts about judges on the **current** Supreme Court. Be sure to record the source of your information (its author, title, year published, and page numbers).

1. What are the names of the current justices?
2. Who is the chief justice, and when was he or she appointed?
3. Which justice has the most experience on the Supreme Court? Which justice has the least experience?
4. Were any of the justices appointed by the current president?
5. How many of the justices are women? How many are nonwhite?

C. Your Career As a Judge

Could you become a judge in a federal court? Think how you might serve in such a job by answering these questions:

1. What educational training do you think you would need?
2. Would you probably need to become active in a political party? (Why or why not?)
3. Who would be responsible for appointing you to the job?
4. What do you suppose your daily life would be like as a judge?
5. How could you find out whether your answer to question 4 is realistic?

D. Word Pyramid

Carry out the instructions in *italics* beneath each line of the "pyramid."

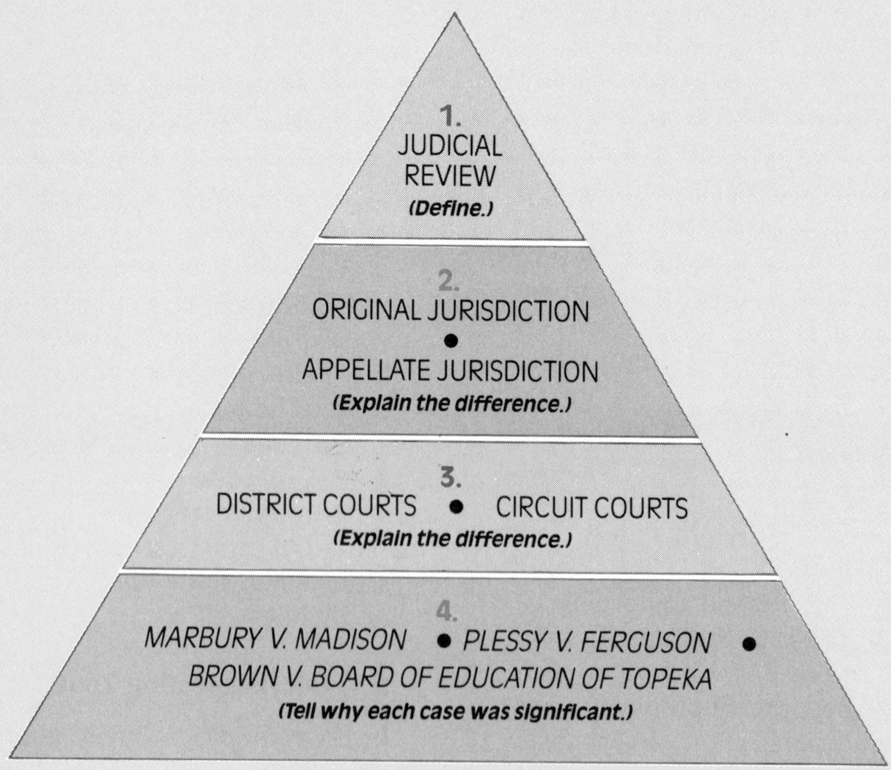

1.
JUDICIAL REVIEW
(Define.)
2.
ORIGINAL JURISDICTION • APPELLATE JURISDICTION
(Explain the difference.)
3.
DISTRICT COURTS • CIRCUIT COURTS
(Explain the difference.)
4.
MARBURY V. MADISON • PLESSY V. FERGUSON • BROWN V. BOARD OF EDUCATION OF TOPEKA
(Tell why each case was significant.)

E. Applying What You Know

Quoted below is part of a front-page news story that appeared in the *New York Times* in 1992. Read both the headline (*a*) and the first three paragraphs of the story (*b*, *c*, and *d*). Then answer the questions, applying what you have learned in this chapter.

(*a*) **COURT OPENS WAY FOR DAMAGE SUITS OVER CIGARETTES**

(*b*) WASHINGTON, June 24—The Supreme Court today opened the door wide to damage suits by smokers against the cigarette industry in a surprisingly broad decision rejecting many of the industry's arguments that such lawsuits were banned by Federal law.

(*c*) The decision, in its most significant aspects, overturned rulings by a Federal appeals court in a case brought against three cigarette manufacturers by the family of Rose Cipollone, a Little Ferry, N.J., woman who died of lung cancer in 1984 after smoking for 42 years. The vote in most parts of the decision was 7 to 2.

(*d*) The appeals court, the United States Court of Appeals for the Third Circuit in Philadelphia, had ruled that smokers could not sue cigarette companies for injuries that stemmed from their smoking after Jan. 1, 1966. On that day, the first Federal law requiring warning labels on cigarette packages and advertising took effect.

Questions about the reading:

1. What U.S. law was involved in this case?
2. (*a*) Who was the plaintiff in the case and (*b*) who was the defendant? (For definitions of "plaintiff" and "defendant" review pages 150–153.)
3. What kind of jurisdiction did the Supreme Court have in this case: (*a*) original jurisdiction or (*b*) appellate jurisdiction? Explain.
4. Did the Supreme Court's decision represent a victory or a defeat for the family of Rose Cipollone? Explain.
5. Did the Supreme Court's decision agree or disagree with that of the United States Court of Appeals for the Third Circuit?
6. How many of the Supreme Court Justices dissented from the majority opinion in the case?
7. According to the headline and news story, which of the following is the most likely result of the Supreme Court's ruling? (*a*) People will smoke fewer cigarettes. (*b*) Smokers will bring more lawsuits against cigarette companies. (*c*) Congress will pass a new anti-smoking law.

". . . WITH LIBERTY AND JUSTICE FOR ALL." In what ways is liberty protected and justice defined by the Bill of Rights?

CHAPTER 16

The Supreme Court and the Bill of Rights

OBJECTIVES

After reading this chapter, you will know

1. how the Fourteenth Amendment enlarged the meaning of the Bill of Rights.
2. the several freedoms guaranteed by the First Amendment.
3. why a person's right to freedom can never be absolute.
4. where *you* think the line should be drawn between freedom, on the one hand, and public order on the other.
5. how the courts define fairness and "due process of law" in dealing with criminal suspects.
6. how to interpret a political cartoon on a First Amendment freedom.

As you know, the U.S. Constitution guarantees "equal protection of the laws" to all citizens, whether they are rich or poor, black or white. It also guarantees that the police and the courts treat citizens fairly, *even if* they have committed crimes.

Imagine that you are one of nine justices on the U.S. Supreme Court. Read below the three summaries of criminal cases that have reached the highest court. In each case, would you say that the person's rights as guaranteed by the Constitution were or were not respected by government officials?

Case of the handcuffed suspect. Danny Escobedo admitted that he bitterly hated his sister's husband. But when that man was found murdered, Escobedo insisted that he was innocent. The police handcuffed him as a suspect and questioned him at the police station for 14 hours. Many times,

DANNY ESCOBEDO. Did the police treat him fairly?

Escobedo asked to see a lawyer. But the police would not allow it. Finally, under pressure, Escobedo told police that he had not actually pulled the trigger in the shooting of his brother-in-law. "My friend killed him," he said, "not me."

Escobedo did not realize that being an accomplice to murder was also a serious crime. (An accomplice is someone closely connected with another person's acts.) At his trial, he was convicted of first degree murder and sentenced to 20 years in prison. His friend was sentenced to imprisonment for life.

Case of the four-time loser. Nothing ever seemed to go right for Clarence Gideon. He had run away from home at the age of 14. He was jobless much of the time. Four times he had been in jail on burglary charges. Then, in 1961, he was accused of breaking into a poolroom to steal beer and money.

Gideon pleaded innocent to the charge and asked the judge to appoint a lawyer to defend him. He was too poor to pay the lawyer's fees himself. The judge refused Gideon's request, explaining that public defenders were appointed only for very serious crimes. At his trial, Gideon tried to act as his own lawyer but failed to convince the jury. The judge sentenced him to five years in a Florida state prison.

Case of the rich and famous doctor. On July 4, 1954, the murdered body of Marilyn Sheppard, wife of a wealthy doctor, was found in an upstairs bedroom of the Sheppards' home outside Cleveland, Ohio. Reporters treated the murder as a sensational news event. The doctor, Sam Sheppard, was accused by police of killing his wife. He protested that he was innocent.

But daily stories in the newspapers cast suspicion upon him. Jury members at his trial were probably influenced by what they had read in the papers and had seen on television. The judge permitted jury members to speak with reporters about the case.

DR. SAM SHEPPARD IN THE WITNESS CHAIR. Was he given a fair trial?

The much-publicized trial dragged on for several weeks. Finally, the jury brought in its verdict: guilty. Dr. Sam Sheppard was sentenced to life imprisonment.

QUESTION: *In each case, did the police and the courts respect the right to fair treatment guaranteed by the Constitution?* You may not know the constitutional clauses that apply to the three cases. But use your own sense of fairness to make your decisions. Write them on a piece of paper. Then, after reading the chapter, you will know what the Supreme Court ruled in each case—and why.

You will also know the answers to these questions:

1. How does the Bill of Rights protect every citizen?
2. What freedoms are protected by the First Amendment?
3. What rights may be claimed by a person accused of a crime?
4. What other rights are guaranteed by the Bill of Rights?

1. HOW DOES THE BILL OF RIGHTS PROTECT EVERY CITIZEN?

The Bill of Rights has a history that you learned in Chapter 2, pages 29–31. Recall the following facts about that history:

A. The English people created the first Bill of Rights after revolting against their king, James II, in 1688. The English legislature listed various actions that the new king and queen could not take. The document that presented these limits on the monarch's power was known as the English Bill of Rights.

B. Almost 100 years later, in the summer of 1787, George Washington, Benjamin Franklin, and other leaders of the United States met in Philadelphia. There they drafted the U.S. Constitution. But this document, as originally written, did not contain a bill of rights.

C. People in Massachusetts, Virginia, and other states objected to the lack of a bill of rights. Federalist supporters of the Constitution thought their opponents might be right. They promised to amend the Constitution by adding a bill of rights to it as soon as the first Congress met.

D. The Federalists elected to Congress in 1789 kept their promise. Ten of the amendments that they had proposed were ratified by the states in 1791. These first 10 amendments to the Constitution are popularly known as the American Bill of Rights.

The purpose of the Bill of Rights. Why did Americans of the past want a bill of rights so badly? Why do people today speak of it with such pride and respect?

The reason is that a government can do terrible things to people. It can pass laws that penalize you for speaking your mind. It can force citizens to practice just one religion, tolerating no other. It can jail you for criticizing a political leader. It can grant one group of citizens special privileges, while mistreating other groups. In short, government can abuse its powers and stifle freedom.

The purpose of the American Bill of Rights is to prevent government from acting in oppressive (cruel and unfair) ways. In effect, it says to government officials: "Stop! There are certain laws that you must never pass. There are certain unfair ways of enforcing the laws that you can never use."

State governments and citizens' rights. The First Amendment begins like this: "Congress shall make no law depriving any person of. . . . " Notice that this amendment (and others) refers only to *Congress*, the legislature of the national government. It says nothing about state legislatures. What is to protect the citizens of Kentucky, for example, from oppressive laws made by their state government?

The state of Kentucky has a written constitution all its own. Included in its constitution is a bill of rights for the people of Kentucky. It too protects citizens with a number of rights, including the right to a jury trial and the right to speak one's opinions freely. Other states also list the rights of citizens in their state constitutions. The list differs slightly from state to state.

The Fourteenth Amendment and the U.S. Bill of Rights. Between the years 1791 and 1868, the Bill of Rights was no protection at all against the laws and acts of state governments. During that early period, citizens had to rely on their state courts to honor the guarantees contained in their state constitutions.

After the Civil War, however, came a change. The Fourteenth Amendment was added to the Constitution in 1868. The first paragraph of that amendment is especially important. It says:

> No state shall make or enforce any law which shall abridge the privileges or immunities of citizens of the United

> States, nor shall any state deprive any person of life, liberty, or property, without *due process of law*, nor deny any person within its jurisdiction the equal protection of the laws. . . .

Notice that the paragraph is about state laws (not the laws of Congress). In italics are the most important words of this most important paragraph. You have already read about "equal protection of the laws" in the last chapter. Now let us consider the meaning of "due process of law." Even lawyers and judges have a hard time defining this phrase. But loosely speaking, due process is another way of saying "fair laws and procedures." Thus, according to the Fourteenth Amendment, governments must never deprive a person of "life, liberty, or property" by unfair means.

Answering one question only raises another. What laws shall be considered "unfair"? Over the years, the Supreme Court wrestled with the question. In case after case, it concluded that certain clauses of the Bill of Rights define what basic fairness (or due process) means. For example, it would be unfair for any government to execute an

EXECUTED WITHOUT TRIAL. This drawing by Francisco Goya shows Spanish victims of a French firing squad in the early 1800s. It shows what can happen when there is no due process of law. What does due process mean?

accused murderer without granting the person a jury trial. It would also be unfair for any person to be jailed for simply expressing an opinion.

Americans today are thus doubly protected against unfair acts by lawmakers and officials. The first 10 amendments (Bill of Rights) protect them against abuses of the national government. The Fourteenth Amendment protects them against abuses of the state governments. Of course, one of the citizens doubly protected in this way is you.

REVIEW

A. Making Inferences

Tell whether you think each statement is probably **true** or probably **not true.** Give your reasons.

1. In the 1850s, the Bill of Rights protected the citizens of North Carolina from unfair state laws.
2. The Eighth Amendment is one part of the Bill of Rights.
3. The Fourteenth Amendment guarantees a person's right to a fair trial in the state courts of Pennsylvania.
4. Both the First Amendment and the Fourteenth Amendment protect the rights of the citizens of Utah.

B. Applying What You Know

Think again about any **one** of the three cases on pages 355–356. How could the phrase "due process of law" be used by the defense lawyer in the case?

Write an argument defending the accused person (Escobedo, Gideon, or Sheppard), as if *you* were that person's lawyer.

2. WHAT FREEDOMS ARE PROTECTED BY THE FIRST AMENDMENT?

The First Amendment is a favorite of many Americans. In just one sentence, it guarantees our rights to six cherished freedoms:

- freedom from a state-sponsored religion
- freedom to practice the religion of your choice
- freedom of speech
- freedom of the press
- freedom of petition
- freedom of assembly

The amendment is worth framing:

> Congress shall make no law respecting an establishment of religion, or prohibiting the free exercise thereof; or abridging the freedom of speech, or of the press; or the right of the people peaceably to assemble and to petition the government for a redress of grievances.

Now let us try to understand every phrase in the frame.

Freedom from a state-sponsored religion. Supposing that you fail to attend a certain church or temple on Saturday or Sunday. Can the laws of your state or of Congress penalize you for it?

Certainly not. It is plainly prohibited by the First Amendment. The first words of the First Amendment are your protection against laws of a religious nature. "Congress shall make no law respecting an establishment of religion. . . ." That means that government must not support a particular religion. For example, it cannot name the Roman Catholic religion, the Jewish religion, or the Quaker religion as the one that the state officially favors. Neither can it tax citizens to pay the salaries of ministers, rabbis, or priests.

Freedom from a state-sponsored religion is often called "the separation of church and state." In other words, a religious organization is supposed to be completely self-supporting. According to the First Amendment, government has no business giving any religious group its official stamp of approval.

A case involving school prayer. One Supreme Court case of 1962 involved the use of prayer in the public schools of New York State. The prayer went like this: "Almighty God, we acknowledge our dependence upon Thee, and we beg Thy blessings upon us, our parents, our teachers, and our country." The prayer was written in 1951 by the board of officials who set standards for New York's schools. Saying the prayer in class every morning was only recommended by the board, not required.

But Steven Engel was one parent who objected to the regular use of the prayer in his child's school. He sued the school board of his local community. He lost his case in the lower courts but appealed to the Supreme Court.

Again, imagine yourself to be a Supreme Court judge. What is *your* opinion in the case of *Engel et al.* v. *Vitale?* Did school prayer in New York State violate the First Amendment? (After you have decided, read about the Supreme Court's decision on page 566.)

Freedom of religion. Government cannot compel you to practice a certain religion. Nor can it stop you from practicing a religion of your choice. This guarantee of worshipping freely may seem simple and clear-cut.

In fact, it is not simple at all. What happens if a group of people do things for the sake of their religion that violate the law? Is it their right to do so? "Thou shalt not kill," say the Jewish and the Christian bibles. If the government requires citizens to fight in a war, could someone refuse to fight in it on religious grounds? Could the government punish that person for defying its laws?

The Supreme Court has the last word in deciding difficult questions like this. The question of religious freedom can sometimes be so difficult that the Court may change its mind from one case to the next. That happened in the 1940s in two cases involving the religious beliefs of a group called the Jehovah's Witnesses.

Flag salute case 1. The first case to be decided was *Minersville School District* v. *Gobitis* (1940). In the schools of Minersville, Pennsylvania, children were required to begin the day by saluting the American flag. Two children, Lillian Gobitis and her brother William, wrote letters explaining why saluting the flag was against their religion as Jehovah's Witnesses. Lillian's letter stated:

SACRED BOOKS OF THREE RELIGIONS. Left to right: the Christian Bible, the Jewish Torah, the Moslem Koran. What part of the Bill of Rights guarantees the religious use of all three books?

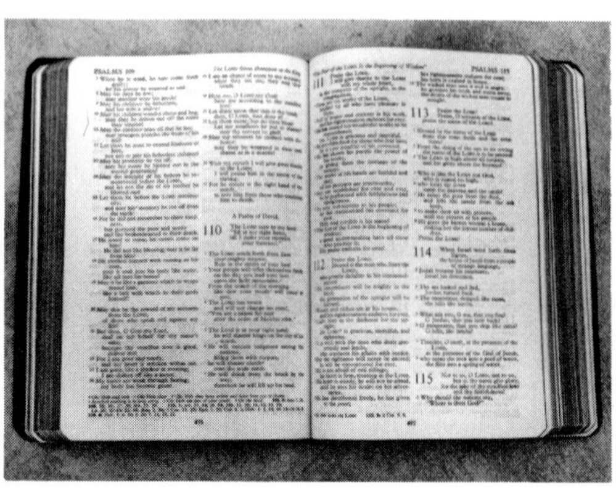

These are my reasons for not saluting the flag:

1. The Lord clearly says in Exodus 20: 3, 5 that you should have no gods besides Him and that we should serve Him.
2. The Constitution of [the] United States is based upon religious freedom. According to the dictates of my conscience, based on the Bible, I must give full allegiance to Jehovah God.

For failing to salute the flag, Lillian and William Gobitis were expelled from school. Their parents took the case to a federal district court, which ruled in their favor. But the Minersville School Board appealed to the Supreme Court. By a vote of 8 to 1, the Supreme Court ruled that the First Amendment's guarantee of freedom of religion had *not* been violated. The Gobitis children, it said, could be expelled.

Flag salute case 2. Three years later (1943), a similar case came to the highest Court concerning the rights of children in West Virginia schools. The title of the case was *West Virginia State Board of Education* v. *Barnette*. Several children had been expelled from public school in West Virginia because they had refused to obey the teacher's instructions to salute the American flag. The children were Jehovah's Witnesses. Pledging allegiance to a flag, they said, was forbidden by their religion. Their lawyer argued that the Supreme Court's earlier decision in the *Gobitis* case was wrong. He told the justices that, in this case, the children's rights to freedom of religion had been violated by school officials.

What do you think? Was the Jehovah's Witnesses' right to freedom of religion violated in the *Barnette* case? After answering, compare your decision with that of the Supreme Court. (See page 566.)

Freedom of speech. The next right to be guaranteed by the First Amendment is freedom of speech. It is your right under the Constitution to express your opinion on any issue. However, there are certain limits to free speech, just as there are limits to every other right.

For example, suppose you think a certain TV show is immoral. It bothers you so much that you go to the offices of the show's producer. On the side of the office building, you paint a message of protest in large orange letters.

Would other people call you a "nut" for expressing your ideas like this? Probably. That is *their* opinion, and they too have a right to express it. But the First Amendment does not judge your opinions. The free-speech clause of that amendment allows an idea to be expressed whether it is wise or foolish, sane or insane.

On the other hand, you could still be arrested for painting your opinion on the side of a building. After all, your actions would be damaging a company's private property. You cannot carry your First Amendment rights to the point of interfering with someone else's rights. In the privacy of your own home, you are absolutely free to say and write anything at all. In a public place, however, freedom of speech is limited by the public's need for order and safety.

Today, in cases involving free speech, the Supreme Court asks whether a speech or a piece of writing presents a "clear and present danger" to the public. If it does, then the speaker or writer may be punished for it. For example, as a joke, someone in a crowded theater shouts, "Fire! Fire!" There is a clear and immediate danger in that people may trample each other in panic. For such reckless use of speech, a person may be arrested.

Freedom of the press. Closely linked to freedom of speech is the idea of freedom of the press. Included in the modern press are

A CASE OF FREE SPEECH? In Hammond, Indiana, this person protested the burning of toxic materials at a chemical plant. Does the idea of freedom of speech include carrying signs as well as making speeches?

movies, computer software, and TV and radio programs as well as published writings of all kinds (books, magazines, newspapers, and pamphlets.) Government cannot punish a moviemaker, broadcaster, publisher, or writer for expressing any message *unless* that message:

(*a*) presents a "clear and present danger" to the public safety and morals.
(*b*) tells lies about a person that damages his or her reputation.
(*c*) offends public taste because it is blatantly obscene.

Sometimes the Supreme Court finds that a state or federal law wrongly restricts either the printing or broadcasting of ideas. Such violations of the freedom of the press are known as *censorship*.

Two more cases for YOU to decide. Once again, it is hard to know in specific cases where to draw the line between your right to express yourself freely and the community's right to protect itself from disorder. Where would you draw the line in the two cases that follow? The first case concerns free speech, while the second concerns a free press.

Case of the black armbands. In 1965, a war was being fought by American troops in Vietnam. In the United States, many thousands of civilians bitterly protested the war. Their antiwar demonstrations in public streets and parks brought them into conflict with the police. Many were arrested for disturbing the peace.

During this troubled time, John Tinker, 15, and his sister, Mary Beth Tinker, 13, attended school in Des Moines, Iowa. Saddened by news of the Vietnam War, they used a dramatic means for expressing their feelings. Each wore to class a black armband with a peace symbol on it. School officials warned the Tinkers that the armbands disrupted learning and could not be worn in

BURNING BOOKS IN NAZI GERMANY. In the 1930s, the German dictator Adolf Hitler (center) ordered the destruction of thousands of books written by critics of his regime. (If this artwork had been created inside Germany, it too would have been destroyed.) What stops the U.S. government from burning books by its critics?

school. But Mary Beth and John wore them just the same. They were promptly suspended.

Parents of the protesting students objected to the school's actions. They thought their children had a constitutional right to express their opinions freely. They sued the Des Moines school district. Eventually, after trial and appeal, the case came to the Supreme Court. Lawyers for the Des Moines schools argued that the armbands were just a piece of clothing. The First Amendment, they said, guarantees the right to free *speech*, not the right to wear any kind of clothing.

In the case of *Tinker* v. *Des Moines School District*, make your decision as if you were a Supreme Court justice. (See page 566.)

Case of the school newspaper. At Hazelwood East High School near St. Louis, Missouri, the principal disapproved of articles written by student reporters for the *Spectrum*, a school newspaper. One article was about teen pregnancies at the high school. A second article quoted students about the emotional effects of their parents' divorces. The principal thought such topics did not belong in a school newspaper. He feared that the reputations of the pregnant students might be harmed, even though they had agreed to be interviewed. Therefore, the principal stopped the student editors from printing the articles in the *Spectrum*.

The students thought their rights to freedom of the press had been violated. After trial and appeal, the case was heard by the Supreme Court in 1988. If you had been a justice on the Court, how would you have decided the case of *Hazelwood School District* v. *Kuhlmeier?* (For the actual decision, see page 566.)

Freedom of assembly and petition. We come now to the final clause of the First Amendment. It guarantees your right "peaceably to assemble and to petition the government for a redress of grievances." To assemble means to meet with others in a group. To petition means to ask government officials to change their laws or policies. Often a petition is signed by a group of citizens who have the same point of view about some political issue.

"Will you sign this petition for abolishing nuclear weapons?" You may be asked a question like this by a stranger on the street. If you are interested, you should read the petition carefully. It is your constitutional right to sign the paper—or not to sign it. Government officials may reject the petitioners' requests. But they may not punish you or others for making them.

DEMONSTRATION FOR EQUAL RIGHTS FOR WOMEN. Which of the First Amendment rights is illustrated by this picture? Does the First Amendment apply equally to both men and women?

May you also join, or assemble with, any group you wish without penalty? No, there are limits on assembly, just as there are limits on speech. You may not legally join a group who plot to steal. You may not go out on the streets of town to join others in a bloody riot. Assembling with others in a public place must be done peaceably.

✔✔ SKILLS CHECK: Interpreting a political cartoon

Interpret the political cartoon on page 365 by answering the following questions.

1. Describe what appears to be happening in the cartoon.
2. Which of the rights guaranteed by the First Amendment is the subject of the cartoon?
3. What are the black-robed figures demanding from the seated woman (who represents Joan of Arc)?
4. Joan of Arc was a French military leader in the 1400s. She said that her heroic actions were inspired by spiritual "voices" that spoke to her. She was put on trial by her enemies and burned at the stake. How does this information help you to interpret the cartoon?
5. With whom does the cartoonist sympathize: the press or the court? Explain.

HERBLOCK'S CARTOON

"Tell Us About The Voices That Speak To You"

Why would reporters sometimes refuse to tell judges about their sources of information (or "voices")?

The cartoon commented on a court case of 1972. The case involved a reporter who refused to tell the court where he had obtained his information for a news article that he had written. For a summary of the case, see page 567.

REVIEW

A. Agree or Disagree?

Tell whether you **agree** or **disagree** with each statement, and give your reasons.

1. A person has the constitutional right to do anything at all for the sake of his or her religion.
2. A person should not be arrested under any circumstances for expressing an opinion.
3. Private religious schools should be entitled to receive some financial support from government.
4. Criticizing the government in wartime is a disloyal act and should be prohibited by law.
5. A person's rights and freedoms under the First Amendment are more important than the public safety.

B. Applying What You Know

Each statement describes the imaginary actions of Citizen Q.

Tell whether you think each act **is** or **is not** protected by the First Amendment.

1. Citizen Q writes a letter to a newspaper accusing the mayor of "gross incompetence."
2. Late one night, Citizen Q glues a political slogan on the bumpers of 25 parked cars.
3. Citizen Q participates in a demonstration in front of the White House. She carries a sign that insults the president.
4. Citizen Q violates the laws of her community by painting a huge sign on the roof of her house. The sign reads: "BAN THE BOMB."

3. WHAT RIGHTS MAY BE CLAIMED BY A PERSON ACCUSED OF A CRIME?

In a free society, you should feel that you are at liberty to express your opinions. That is what the First Amendment guarantees. You should also feel that you will never be unfairly treated by the police or by the courts. Standards of fairness—or due process of law—are defined by three amendments in the Bill of Rights:

- *The Fourth Amendment* says that the police must observe strict rules when searching your property for evidence of a crime.
- *The Fifth Amendment* says that a person suspected of a crime may not be forced to confess.
- *The Sixth Amendment* describes a number of procedures that must be used in a criminal trial.

Recall the three cases at the beginning of this chapter (pages 355–356). The defendants in those cases were Danny Escobedo ("the handcuffed suspect"), Clarence Gideon ("the four-time loser"), and Sam Sheppard ("the rich and famous doctor"). In this section, we will be returning to those cases since they involve rights guaranteed by the Fourth, Fifth, and Sixth Amendments.

Your rights under the Fourth Amendment. Let us suppose that a police officer holds a personal grudge against one of his neighbors. Call the policeman Officer Scipio and the neighbor Ms. Lee. Scipio suspects that Lee may have committed a crime recently.

One Saturday morning, while Ms. Lee is away, Officer Scipio and his partner search the Lee house from attic to basement. They find some jewelry that was reported stolen. When Ms. Lee returns to the house, they arrest her.

At the police station, Lee calls her lawyer, Ms. Sharp, and tells her what happened. Within ten minutes, the lawyer arrives on the scene. "You have absolutely nothing to worry about," she tells her client. From her briefcase, Ms. Sharp pulls out a copy of the Constitution and reads aloud this phrase from the Fourth Amendment:

> "The right of the people to be secure in their persons, houses, papers, and effects, against unreasonable searches and seizures, shall not be violated. . . ."

The lawyer assures Ms. Lee that the search of her house was *not* reasonable. Therefore, Officer Scipio had acted unlawfully.

MS. LEE (nervously): How can I be sure that a judge will agree with us? The phrase "unreasonable searches and seizures" seems vague. Sure, *we* think Scipio's search was unreasonable. But it succeeded, didn't it? Criminal evidence was found in my home.

MS. SHARP: Wait, let me finish reading the Fourth Amendment. It says:

> . . . and no warrants shall issue but upon probable cause, supported by oath or affirmation, and particularly describing the place to be searched, and the persons or things to be seized.

Before they searched your house, did the police officers show you a *search warrant?*

MS. LEE: What's that?

MS. SHARP: It's a document signed by a judge authorizing a police officer to search for criminal evidence.

MS. LEE: No, I never saw anything like that.

MS. SHARP: The Fourth Amendment requires that a judge issue a search warrant *before* a search is made. Therefore, Officer Scipio's search must be considered unreasonable. He broke one of the rules. Furthermore, suppose for one minute that Officer Scipio had taken the trouble to apply to a judge for a search warrant. Do you think any judge would have given it to him?

MS. LEE (*shrugging*): Can't guess.

MS. SHARP: The answer is no. Before ransacking your house, Officer Scipio did not even know what he was looking for. He thought you *might* have committed a crime. What crime? To obtain a search warrant, he must know the exact crime that was committed and the exact piece of evidence for which he is looking. In your case, there was no "probable cause" for issuing a warrant, as required by the Constitution. Therefore, Officer Scipio could not have

UNDER ARREST. Even though these police officers have no search warrant, they may lawfully search an arrested person for concealed weapons. Why would the Supreme Court consider this to be a "reasonable" search? What would be unreasonable?

obtained the judge's warrant even if he had tried.

MS. LEE: The fact is that, by fair means or foul, the police have found criminal evidence against me.

MS. SHARP: But it is evidence that cannot hurt you because, in court, the judge and jury will not know that it exists.

MS. LEE: Why not?

MS. SHARP: The evidence *cannot* be introduced in court. It is a rule handed down by the Supreme Court—the so-called exclusionary rule. In the case of *Weeks* v. *United States* (1914), the Supreme Court ruled that evidence obtained in an illegal manner could not be used in court. For many years, the exclusionary rule applied only to *federal* cases, not state cases. But now it applies to state cases as well.

MS. LEE: Let me get this straight. The criminal evidence found in my house was obtained without a warrant. Therefore, it was an "unreasonable" search prohibited by the Fourth Amendment. Therefore, it cannot be used against me in court. Therefore, I will probably not go to jail. Correct?

The lawyer nods, ending the interview.

The imaginary Lee case is clear-cut. Real criminal cases are usually more difficult to judge. Under special circumstances, the police may legally seize or search for evidence without a search warrant issued by a judge. For example, if a police officer witnesses an armed robbery, the officer may seize the suspect's weapon and use it as evidence in court. Dozens of Supreme Court cases now define the rules concerning (*a*) police searches and (*b*) the use of evidence in court.

Your rights under the Fifth Amendment. The next amendment in the Bill of Rights—the Fifth—is the longest of the ten. It is also one of the most important. Appropriately, the number of rights granted by the Fifth Amendment is five.

1. Right to a grand jury. "No person shall be held to answer for a capital or otherwise infamous crime, unless on a presentment or indictment of a grand jury. . . ." You have read about grand juries in Chapter 7 (page 152). Recall that such juries do *not* determine the guilt or innocence of a suspect. They simply decide whether there is enough evidence against a person to require that the person stand trial. The criminal charges voted by a grand jury are known as an indictment.

A FEDERAL GRAND JURY. Filing into a federal courthouse in Cleveland, Ohio, these citizens were asked to decide whether there was enough evidence to indict eight men for shooting at college students. What does the Bill of Rights say about grand juries?

Kidnappers have a right to be indicted by a grand jury. But pickpockets do not. That is because kidnapping is both a federal crime and one that might be called "infamous" (extremely serious). But pickpocketing is a lesser crime that violates the laws of states. Although many states use grand juries, they are not required to use them by the U.S. Constitution.

2. Right not to be subject to double jeopardy. ". . . nor shall any person be subjected for the same offense to be twice put in jeopardy of life or limb. . . ."

Suppose that a federal grand jury indicts you for the crime of robbing a post office. At your trial, a petit (12-member) jury finds you "not guilty." A year later, the FBI turns up more evidence against you. Can you be indicted and put on trial a second time for the postal robbery? No, because that would put your life in *double jeopardy* and the Fifth Amendment does not allow it.

Supposing, however, that the petit jury originally found you "guilty." You appeal the decision to a higher court. You win the appeal. You must now stand trial again for the same crime. Only if you are found innocent in the first trial will you be free from a second one.

The right against double jeopardy applies only to the federal courts, not to the state courts.

3. Right to remain silent. ". . . nor shall [any person] be compelled in any criminal case to be a witness against himself. . . ." So important is this right that it deserves fuller discussion than the others. (See page 369.)

4. Right to due process. " . . . nor [shall any person] be deprived of life, liberty, or property without due process of law. . . ." Recall that "due process of law" means fair treatment. Two amendments guarantee it as a fundamental right. The Fifth Amendment says the *federal* government shall not imprison or punish someone without following fair procedures for doing so. The Fourteenth Amendment (page 136) makes the same requirement of state governments.

5. Right to be compensated for loss of property. ". . . nor shall private property be taken for public use, without just compensation." In certain situations the government has the power to seize the property owned by a citizen or business. It is called the power of eminent domain. According to the Fifth Amendment, government may seize property only for some public use, such as building a highway. The owner must be fairly compensated (paid a reasonable sum of money) for his or her loss.

WARNING AS TO YOUR RIGHTS

You are under arrest. Before we ask you any questions, you must understand what your rights are.

You have the right to remain silent. You are not required to say anything to us at any time or to answer any questions. Anything you say can be used against you in court.

You have the right to talk to a lawyer for advice before we question you and to have him with you during questioning.

If you cannot afford a lawyer and want one, a lawyer will be provided for you.

If you want to answer questions now without a lawyer present you will still have the right to stop answering at any time. You also have the right to stop answering at any time until you talk to a lawyer. P-4475

MIRANDA CARD. Why are the police required to read this card to an arrested person? Which amendment mentions "the right to remain silent"?

Escobedo, Miranda, and the Fifth Amendment. Of the five rights in the Fifth Amendment, the one that receives the most attention is the right to refuse to answer a police officer's questions. Danny Escobedo had either forgotten (or never known) this right when he submitted to 14 hours of questioning about the murder of his brother-in-law. As you recall from pages 355–356, the statements he made to the police were used in his trial to convict him.

The police did not allow Escobedo to see a lawyer. They knew very well what any lawyer would tell a suspect. "Don't talk," a lawyer would say. "You have a constitutional right under the Fifth Amendment to say nothing." Not hearing this advice, Escobedo talked and thereby gave evidence of guilt against himself.

On appeal, the case of *Escobedo* v. *Illinois* was decided by the Supreme Court in 1964. Escobedo had been unfairly treated, said the Court. First, he had been denied his right to see a lawyer. Second, he had been tricked or pressured into saying things that might be *self-incriminating*. Because Escobedo had been unfairly convicted, he was set free.

Two years later, in 1966, the Supreme Court heard another case involving self-incrimination. This was the case of *Miranda* v. *Arizona*. At a police station outside Phoenix, Arizona, Ernesto Miranda had confessed to the crime of rape. He was ignorant at the time of his Fifth Amendment rights. The Supreme Court ruled that Miranda should have been fully informed of these rights. Before any questioning took place, the police should have told Miranda

- of his right to see a lawyer
- of his right not to answer any questions because anything said could be used against him in court.

A suspect could still agree to answer questions. But first, he or she had to be warned of the consequences. Because Miranda had not been warned, his confession and the trial based on it were not valid. Miranda was set free.

After the *Miranda* decision, the police have had a hard time obtaining confessions from suspects. Before questioning anyone, a police officer must now read aloud a list of rights to the suspect. The card that officers read from is commonly known as a "Miranda card." (See above.)

CARTOON CORNER

What point is the cartoonist making about the rights of suspects? What title would you give to the cartoon?

An accused person's rights under the Sixth Amendment. Every person who is arrested and accused of a crime has certain rights guaranteed by the Sixth Amendment. They are:

- the person's right "to a speedy and public trial, by an impartial jury"
- the person's right to be informed of the criminal charges against him or her
- the right to expect two kinds of witnesses to appear at the person's trial: (*a*) witnesses for the prosecution and (*b*) witnesses for the defense
- if accused of a serious crime, the person's right to be defended by a trained lawyer.

At one time, these rights were guaranteed only in federal cases. But in recent years, the Supreme Court has ruled that state courts too must honor the list of rights found in the Sixth Amendment.

Two cases of "unfair" trials. At the beginning of this chapter, you read about the "unfair" trials of a poor person and a rich one. In the one case, Clarence Gideon was too poor to pay for a lawyer. In the other case, Dr. Sam Sheppard was rich, causing the press to make a sensational story of his murder trial. The Supreme Court's decisions in the two cases underline the idea that all accused persons have a right to fair treatment, whether they are rich or poor.

1. Gideon's trials. If Clarence Gideon was too poor to pay for a lawyer, how did his case finally come to the attention of the Supreme Court? From his prison cell, Gideon sent letters asking the Court to review his case. Six months later, the Supreme Court responded with a positive answer. It agreed not only to review the case but also to appoint one of the country's finest lawyers to represent him. Since Gideon was penniless, the lawyer's fees were paid by the U.S. government.

In 1963, the Supreme Court announced its decision in the case of *Gideon* v. *Wainwright*. It said that any person accused of a serious crime is entitled to be represented by a lawyer. If a person is too poor to pay a lawyer's fees, then the government must pay the fees.

Gideon's rights, said the Court, had been violated. Therefore, the state of Florida was ordered to give him a second trial. This time, with a lawyer in court to defend him, Gideon was found "not guilty" and set free.

2. Sheppard's trials. The rich doctor, Sam Sheppard, had no trouble paying for a lawyer. But he did have trouble with the press. The judge at his trial permitted jurors to talk freely with TV and newspaper reporters. Were the jurors' opinions of the doctor's guilt or innocence influenced by their contacts with the press? It is hard to know. In any case, Sheppard was found guilty of murdering his wife.

Sheppard's lawyers appealed. In the case of *Sheppard* v. *Maxwell* (1966), the Supreme Court decided that his trial had not been fair. It concluded that the judge at Sheppard's trial had done a poor job of dealing with the press. Therefore, it said, Dr. Sheppard deserved to be tried again.

The jury at the second trial announced its verdict: "not guilty." Sheppard was set free after having been imprisoned for almost ten years.

REVIEW

A. Applying What You Know

Imagine that you are the lawyer for a man named Perry Paine. For each event described below, tell what constitutional right was violated. Identify both the specific **right** and the **amendment** that guarantees the right.

1. Police officers in a patrol car stop Paine on a highway for speeding and demand to search the trunk of his car. Paine shouts at them: "Do you have a warrant? What's this all about?" But without showing a warrant, the police seize Paine's car keys, open the trunk, and find a box of stolen cash.
2. Placed under arrest, Paine submits to five hours of questioning. No lawyer is present. Finally, Paine confesses to the crime of stealing funds from his employer. A week later, he tells you, "Nobody told me that I could remain silent and refuse to answer the officers' questions."
3. At his trial, Paine tells the jury that he takes back his confession since it was forced out of him. The jury finds him "not guilty." But two years later, the police find new evidence against him, and a second trial is scheduled.
4. At the second trial, the prosecutor calls five people to the witness stand. But the judge does not allow any witnesses to testify for the defense.

B. Building Your Political Vocabulary

Match each term in the word list with its definition.

double jeopardy	indictment
due process of law	self-incrimination
eminent domain	unreasonable searches and seizures
grand jury	

1. a formal charge or accusation
2. the goverment's power to take over private property for a public use

3. a guarantee of fair treatment named in both the Fifth and Fourteenth Amendments
4. police actions that violate the Fourth Amendment
5. citizens who decide whether there is enough evidence to hold a person for trial
6. statements by a suspect or witness that might later be used as evidence against that person in a criminal case
7. being subject to trial more than once for the same crime

C. Agree or Disagree

For each case, tell what was decided by the Supreme Court. Then tell whether you **agree** or **disagree** with the decision and explain.

1. *Escobedo* v. *Illinois*
2. *Miranda* v. *Arizona*
3. *Gideon* v. *Wainwright*
4. *Sheppard* v. *Maxwell*

4. WHAT OTHER RIGHTS ARE GUARANTEED BY THE BILL OF RIGHTS?

So far, we have looked at only four of the ten amendments in the Bill of Rights. The ones that remain are:

- Second Amendment (the right of the militia to bear arms)
- Third Amendment (no quartering of troops in private homes)
- Seventh Amendment (the right to jury trial in civil cases)
- Eighth Amendment (no cruel and unusual punishment; no excessive bail)
- Ninth Amendment (other rights belonging to the people)
- Tenth Amendment (powers reserved to the states)

The right to "keep and bear arms." The Second Amendment states: " . . . the right of the people to keep and bear arms shall not be infringed." History helps us to interpret these words.

In the 1790s, when the Bill of Rights was written, people wanted to maintain the power and independence of their state governments. They relied upon citizens to keep muskets at home and be ready at a minute's notice to defend the community from Indian raids or other dangers. You may recall the "minute men" who grabbed their muskets one April morning in 1775 to fight the British.

States still maintain a militia of volunteer soldiers, known as the National Guard. These organized volunteers have a right to keep and bear arms under the Second Amendment. But an individual's ownership and use of weapons may be strictly regulated by law.

No quartering of troops in private homes. Before the American Revolution, some citizens of Boston were forced to make room in their homes for unwelcome guests. British soldiers were quartered (given living quarters) in the colonists' kitchens and bedrooms.

Today, the Third Amendment protects you from such annoyances. It clearly states:

> No soldier shall, in time of peace, be quartered in any house without the consent of the owner, nor in time of war, but in a manner to be prescribed by law.

Right to a jury trial in civil cases. Suppose that someone sues you in a federal court. You then would have a right to be tried by a jury. The Seventh Amendment guarantees this right for any suit amounting to more than $20.

This right does *not* apply to civil suits in state courts.

No excessive bail and no excessive fines. *Bail* is the sum of money that an arrested person is required to pay to be released from jail before the trial. The money is returned only if the person comes to the courthouse to stand trial. Thus, the purpose of bail is to ensure that an accused person will not flee the scene before the trial is held.

Bail can be any sum ordered by a judge. However, according to the Eighth Amendment, it must not be an "excessive" sum. In other words, a huge sum should not be required in a case involving some minor offense. The amount of bail must fit the nature of the alleged crime.

Excessive fines are also forbidden by the Eighth Amendment. Persons convicted of breaking federal laws may be fined—but only if the fine fits the crime. It would be excessive, for example, for someone to be fined $100,000 for dropping a candy wrapper in a national park.

No cruel and unusual punishments. The final words of the Eighth Amendment are puzzling. It says "cruel and unusual punishments" shall not be inflicted. Some people may think that hanging or electrocuting murderers is cruel. Does that mean that such a practice is also unconstitutional? The Supreme Court's answer is no. A punishment is illegal only if it can be judged to be both cruel *and* unusual.

The death penalty was a common form of punishment for centuries. Therefore, the Supreme Court allows state governments to execute murderers and others found guilty of violent crimes.

For a brief period, 1972 to 1976, the death penalty was not used in the United States. In a 1972 case, *Furman* v. *Georgia,* the Supreme Court had ruled that members of racial minorities tended to be executed more often than whites. Thus, their rights to equal protection of the laws were violated. The Court required states to adopt strict guidelines for using the death penalty fairly. Once the states complied with the Supreme Court's decision, they were once again allowed to carry out the death penalty.

Other rights belonging to the people. Protection from "cruel and unusual punishments" is the last *specific* right in the Bill of Rights. The next two amendments—the Ninth and Tenth—are quite general.

The Ninth Amendment says that people retain rights not specifically mentioned elsewhere in the Constitution. Privacy is one such right. The word is not mentioned in the Constitution. But it is implied in the Fourth Amendment as well as the Ninth. In a 1965 case, *Griswold* v. *Connecticut,* the Supreme Court decided that a Connecticut law violated people's basic rights to privacy. (The law had made it a crime to give out information to married couples about methods of birth control.)

Powers reserved to the states. In our federal system, the different states have rights to govern and make laws. The Tenth Amendment guarantees the governing powers of states. It says that a state's powers are limited only by two constitutional boundaries:

1. Powers specifically given to the federal government are one boundary of a state's power.
2. Powers specifically denied to the states by the Constitution are another boundary.

Outside these boundaries, all powers of government are "reserved to the states respectively, or to the people."

The Supreme Court in the 90s

The words of the Bill of Rights have not changed. They are the same in the 1990s as they were in the 1790s. But the interpretation of these words has changed.

Hate crimes. One controversial issue of our times concerns crimes that are committed for reasons of racial or religious hatred. In the 1980s, more than a dozen states, including New York, California, Texas, and Wisconsin, passed laws that tried to deal with hate crimes. But were these laws permitted by the U.S. Constitution? Or did they wrongly restrict a person's right to freedom of speech as guaranteed in the First Amendment? Two cases involving this question were decided by the Supreme Court in 1992 and 1993.

R.A.V. v. St. Paul, 1992. The city of St. Paul, Minnesota, had passed an ordinance in 1989 against "bias-motivated crimes." The ordinance made it a crime to speak or act in such a way as to arouse "anger or alarm" against a person because of the person's "race, color, creed, religion, or gender." The ordinance specifically prohibited the burning of a cross or the display of a swastika (Nazi symbol) because of the hatred that lay behind such symbols.

One June night in 1990, a 17-year old white teenager, Robert Viktora, taped together two pieces of a broken chair to form a crude cross. He placed the structure on the front lawn of a home recently purchased by a black family and set fire to it. The police arrested Viktora for violating St. Paul's hate crime ordinance. In court, the youth protested that his burning of the cross was an act of speech protected by the First Amendment. The case was appealed and eventually reached the U.S. Supreme Court.

The justices on the Court considered these questions: (1) Is cross-burning an act of speech? (2) Did St. Paul's ordinance wrongly single out certain kinds of hatred for punishment while letting alone other kinds of hatred?

Wisconsin v. Mitchell, 1993. A black youth, Todd Mitchell, was sentenced to two years in prison for assaulting a white youth and two additional years because the crime had been motivated by racial hatred. Here is the Supreme Court's summary of the crime:

"On the evening of Oct. 7, 1989, a group of young black men and boys, including Mitchell, gathered at an apartment complex in Kenosha, Wisconsin. Several members of the group discussed a scene from the motion picture *Mississippi Burning,* in which a white man beat a young black boy who was praying.

"The group moved outside and Mitchell asked them: 'Do you feel hyped up to move on some white people?' Shortly thereafter, a young white boy approached the group on the opposite side of the street . . .

"As the boy walked by, Mitchell said: 'There goes a white boy; go get him.' Mitchell counted to three and pointed in the boy's direction. The group ran toward the boy, beat him severely, and stole his tennis shoes. The boy was rendered unconscious and remained in a coma for four days."

Mitchell's lawyers challenged the Wisconsin law that lengthened Mitchell's prison sentence from two years to four years. They agreed that the first two-year sentence for assault was proper because it penalized Mitchell for criminal actions. But, they said, the extra two years in prison was wrong because it penalized Mitchell's racial attitude and way of thinking. The lawyers argued that it was unconstitutional to penalize someone just for thinking a certain way.

YOU DECIDE:

1. Do you think St. Paul's ordinance against cross-burning and other acts of hatred violated the First Amendment? Why or why not?
2. Do you think Wisconsin's law adding an extra penalty for racial hatred violated the First Amendment? Why or why not?

(The Supreme Court's decisions in the two cases are given on page 567.)

THE BOUNDARIES OF STATES' RIGHTS

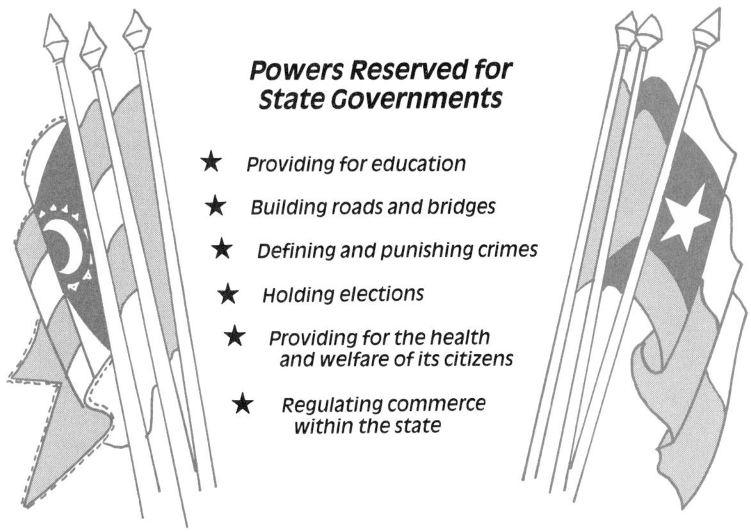

Powers Reserved for State Governments
★ Providing for education
★ Building roads and bridges
★ Defining and punishing crimes
★ Holding elections
★ Providing for the health and welfare of its citizens
★ Regulating commerce within the state

The right of habeas corpus. One right has not yet been mentioned because it is not found in the Bill of Rights. Instead, it is included in the original Constitution as drafted at Philadelphia in 1787. In a sense, it is Americans' *first* right because it was guaranteed before all the others. In Article I, Section 9, we read:

> The privilege of the writ of habeas corpus shall not be suspended, unless when in cases of rebellion or invasion the public safety may require it.

Habeas corpus is a Latin phrase that means literally "you have the body." The body in question is a living person who has been arrested and jailed. A writ of habeas corpus is a document telling the jailer to bring the arrested person before a judge immediately for a hearing. The judge may then determine whether there is good reason to hold the person as a criminal suspect. If not, then the person must promptly be set free. Only when public safety is threatened may the writ be suspended (as happened during the Civil War).

Habeas corpus is a cherished right of a free people. Without it, a tyrannical government might throw people in jail and keep them there indefinitely without giving a reason for their imprisonment.

REVIEW

A. Giving Examples

Give examples of laws or government actions that are **forbidden** by amendments treated in this section. Create the examples out of your own imagination.

1. An example of a law or action that would violate the Second Amendment.
2. An example of a law or action that would violate the Third Amendment.
3. An example of a law or action that would violate the Eighth Amendment.

B. Your "Most Important" Rights

Some rights may seem more important to you than others. On a sheet of paper, list the following rights in order of importance, putting the **most important** at the top, the **least important** at the bottom.

Right to keep and bear arms
Right to trial by jury in civil cases
Right not to be punished by "cruel and unusual" methods
Right not to have troops quartered in your home
Right to bail that is not excessive

Explain why the right at the top of your list was judged most important.

CHAPTER REVIEW

A. Completing the Summary

Select terms from the word list to fill in the blanks in the summary below. Write your answers on a piece of paper.

arms	lawyer
cruel	peaceable
danger	petition
due process of law	probable cause
excessive	quartered
exclusionary	seizure
federal	separation
incrimination	trial
jeopardy	

The Bill of Rights consists of the first 10 amendments to the Constitution. At first, it protected citizens from the unfair actions of the __(1)__ government only. But then the Fourteenth Amendment was adopted in 1868. It said that no state shall deprive any person of "life, liberty, or property without __(2)__." As a result, the Bill of Rights now applies to both federal laws and state laws.

The First Amendment guarantees a number of basic freedoms. It provides for the __(3)__ of church and state as well as for freedom of religion. It guarantees freedom of speech and the press, freedom of assembly, and freedom of __(4)__. However, there are limits to each of these freedoms. For example, if someone's speech presents a "clear and present __(5)__," it may be stopped by government officials. People have a right to demonstrate for a political cause, but the action must be done in a __(6)__ manner.

Several parts of the Bill of Rights define the rights of persons accused of committing crimes. The Fourth Amendment protects citizens from unreasonable searches and __(7)__ by the police. Only if there is __(8)__ can a judge issue a search warrant. According to the __(9)__ rule, evidence obtained by improper means cannot be used in court.

These are some of the rights guaranteed to an accused person by the Fifth and Sixth Amendments:

- the right to know the charges against him or her
- the right to remain silent when questioned by police officers, judges, or prosecutors. (This is a protection against self-__(10)__.)
- the right to a "speedy and public __(11)__" by an impartial jury
- the right to be represented in court by a trained __(12)__
- the right *not* to be subject to double __(13)__.

Because of the Eighth Amendment, the amount of bail charged by a court cannot be __(14)__. Nor can a convicted criminal be punished in a __(15)__ and unusual way.

Citizens also have the right to keep and bear __(16)__ for the defense of a state. Soldiers cannot be __(17)__ in people's homes against their will. Other rights, such as privacy, are not specifically mentioned in the Bill of Rights. But they too are protected by the Ninth and Tenth Amendments.

B. Applying What You Know

Imagine that you are a lawyer. The following people have asked you to defend them in court on the grounds that their rights have been violated. Identify **both the amendment and the clause** that would apply in each person's case. The answer to the first case is given as a model.

1. Convicted of shoplifting, J. Zabrisky was sentenced to be tarred and feathered at a shopping mall, as an example to others.
   ANSWER: *Violation of Eighth Amendment right: no cruel and unusual punishments.*
2. M. Rocco, the publisher of a magazine, is arrested for urging readers not to pay their taxes.
3. As a suspect in a bank robbery, P. Chang admitted to FBI agents that she had participated in the crime. Her rights had not been read to her at the time of the arrest.
4. R. Vitale found police officers searching his car for concealed weapons. They had no search warrant to show him.
5. In the civil case of *Johnson* v. *Jensen*, a federal judge ordered T. Jensen to pay $875 in damages to V. Johnson. No jury was present.
6. For leading a mass demonstration in front of the U.S. Capitol, J. Baker was found guilty of "treasonous acts" against the government.
7. C. Beniquez was twice put on trial for the same crime of counterfeiting. He was acquitted in the first trial but convicted in the second.
8. The prosecutor's key witness was absent at the murder trial of B. Stein. The prosecutor told the jury what this witness had said.
9. Accused of burglary, K. Bibbo's bail was set at $700,000.

C. Word Pyramid

Carry out the instructions in italics under each term or group of terms.

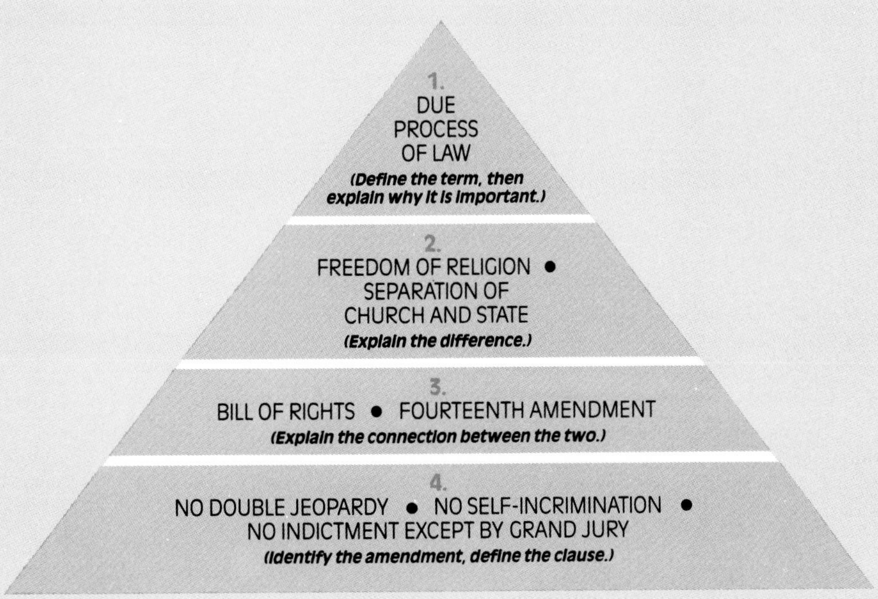

1.
DUE
PROCESS
OF LAW
(Define the term, then explain why it is important.)
2.
FREEDOM OF RELIGION •
SEPARATION OF
CHURCH AND STATE
(Explain the difference.)
3.
BILL OF RIGHTS • FOURTEENTH AMENDMENT
(Explain the connection between the two.)
4.
NO DOUBLE JEOPARDY • NO SELF-INCRIMINATION •
NO INDICTMENT EXCEPT BY GRAND JURY
(Identify the amendment, define the clause.)

A

B

UNIT SEVEN

Making Public Policy

Every year, the U.S. government spends more than one trillion dollars ($1,000,000,000,000) on national needs such as defense, parks and forests, highways, Social Security, and hundreds of other federal programs.

Every year, the president and Congress have a trillion-dollar question to answer. How much should be spent on "the common defense" (represented by Picture **A**), and how much should be spent on "the general welfare" (Picture **B**)? In this unit, you will find out (*a*) how the government leaders answer this question and (*b*) how *you* would answer it.

The quiz below identifies the 14 departments that spend most of the trillion dollars. Match the descriptions *a–n* with the functions 1–13.

Matching Quiz: U.S. Departments

a. Agriculture
b. Commerce
c. Defense
d. Education
e. Energy
f. Health and Human Services
g. Housing and Urban Development
h. Interior
i. Justice
j. Labor
k. State
l. Transportation
m. Treasury
n. Veterans Affairs

1. trains pilots to fly the Navy jets pictured in **A**
2. manages the use of forests and parks like the one pictured in **B**
3. sends out Social Security checks to retired workers
4. regulates nuclear power plants
5. finances the building of interstate highways
6. provides educational standards for U.S. schools
7. manages U.S. foreign policy
8. helps American cities to rebuild
9. collects taxes
10. provides services to Indian peoples living on reservations
11. counts the population every 10 years
12. includes the Federal Bureau of Investigation (FBI)
13. provides medical care for veterans
14. enforces safety laws for workers

Answers

1. *c* 3. *f* 5. *l* 7. *k* 9. *m* 11. *b* 13. *n*
2. *a* 4. *e* 6. *d* 8. *g* 10. *h* 12. *i* 14. *j*

PROTECTING THE CONSUMER. In a government office in New Jersey, Lillie Dortsch-Wright advises consumers on how to protect themselves from harmful or useless products. What other kinds of services would you expect the U.S. government to provide?

CHAPTER 17

Domestic Policy: The Cabinet Departments

OBJECTIVES

After reading this chapter, you will know

1. some of the services provided by the 14 Cabinet departments.
2. why the Executive Branch grew so much larger after World War II.
3. the difference between a Cabinet department and an independent agency.
4. some of the services provided by the independent agencies.
5. how to use information in a bar graph to draw conclusions.

Every day of the workweek, over 1,000 people call up the Newark, New Jersey, office of the Department of Veterans Affairs (VA). Many of them served in the U.S. armed forces during World War II, the Korean War, or the Vietnam War. As veterans, they are entitled by law to receive certain benefits. But first, they need to know what forms to fill out and what procedures to follow to apply for VA benefits.

Picking up the phone to answer veterans' questions is Tom Ruiz. As a VA employee, Mr. Ruiz must be able to explain every clause of every federal law concerning veteran benefits.

"Were you in the armed forces before January 1, 1977?" he asks one caller. "Okay, then the *old* GI bill applies and you're entitled to a maximum of $376 a month for up to 45 months to help pay for your college education. If you had been discharged from the Army after January 1, 1977, the new law would cover you."

Mr. Ruiz was himself a veteran of the Vietnam War. Naturally he wants to be able to help other veterans who call him. But he cannot change the law in their favor. He can only explain what the laws of Congress allow and do not allow in specific cases.

Meanwhile, in another New Jersey office building, Lillie Dortsch-Wright is also on the phone, talking with consumers about products that may be bad for their health. She works for a federal agency called the Food and Drug Administration (FDA). Her job as a consumer affairs officer is to inform people about problems like these:

- aids to digestion that have harmful side effects
- quack medicines that are said to cure everything but in fact cure nothing
- certain brands of eye makeup that contain chemicals strong enough to cause blindness
- drugs that are said to help a person lose weight but are really worthless.

Anyone who calls may request from Mrs. Dortsch-Wright and the FDA a government pamphlet about a specific problem. There is a pamphlet, for example, entitled, *How to Take Weight Off and Keep It Off Without Getting Ripped Off*. As a public service, many pamphlets like this are mailed out by FDA officers free of charge.

Hundreds of federal departments and agencies such as the VA and the FDA provide thousands of services for the American public. Daily, government officers like Tom Ruiz and Lillie Dortsch-Wright carry out U.S. laws. This chapter is about their work—how it is organized and who benefits from it. The chapter will provide answers to these questions:

1. What are the oldest departments of the Executive Branch?
2. Why were new departments added after World War II?
3. How do independent agencies serve the public?

1. WHAT ARE THE OLDEST DEPARTMENTS OF THE EXECUTIVE BRANCH?

In your imagination, turn the clock back about 200 years to 1789, the year that George Washington became president. The United States was then a nation of farmers with a population of less than 4 million. The nation's first capital, New York City, had a population of only 33,000.

Origins of the Cabinet. In 1789, one of the first acts of the first Congress was to create three executive departments to assist the president in enforcing the laws. Each department was to be headed by a "secretary." A secretary of state was put in charge of the Department of State for dealing with foreign countries. A secretary of war was put in charge of the Department of War for maintaining U.S. military defenses. A secretary of the treasury was put in charge of a Department of the Treasury for collecting taxes and paying the debts of the U.S. government.

To help the president handle court cases and other legal matters, Congress also created the office of attorney general. But this official worked alone. Only many years later was the attorney general given a department to manage—the Department of Justice.

At first, Washington met separately with his attorney general and three department heads. But in 1791 he decided to ask the advice of all four of them meeting in a group. The group was referred to as his Cabinet. Thereafter, Cabinet meetings became a standard part of U.S. government.

The Cabinet has grown, just as the nation has grown. Today, the president meets with 14 department heads, instead of the original three and the attorney general. Two of the 14 are mainly concerned with U.S. *foreign policy*. The departments led by the secretary of state and secretary of defense will be described in Chapter 19. This chapter deals only with the Cabinet officers in charge of *domestic policy*. Domestic means "at home" and refers to public matters within the United States. In this section, we will see how the early departments of the federal government were created, one by one, between 1789 and 1933.

Secretary of the treasury. In 1789, one of President Washington's major concerns was how to pay the bills of the federal government. Washington was not a financial genius. But he knew someone who was: a New Yorker named Alexander Hamilton. Nobody was surprised when Washington asked Hamilton to act as his secretary of the treasury.

Managing money successfully involves keeping track of two things. On the one hand, there are expenses to be recorded and bills to be paid. On the other hand, there are *revenues*, or income, to be collected. The secretary of the treasury must try to

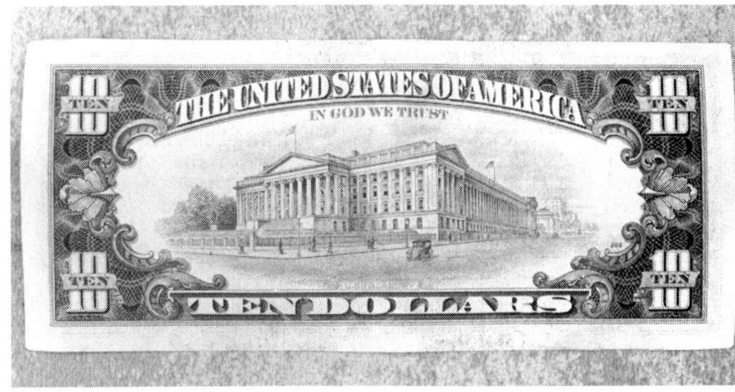

PRINTED BY THE TREASURY DEPARTMENT. The back of a $10 bill (right) shows the Treasury Department's building in Washington, D.C. Why do you think the front of the bill has a picture of Alexander Hamilton?

make sure that government money going out (expenses) is about equal to money coming in (revenues). How to achieve this goal was a major problem for Alexander Hamilton in 1789. It is *still* a problem today.

Hamilton's second problem concerned the coins and paper notes that Americans used as money. In 1789, most of the gold and silver coins that Americans carried had been minted in foreign countries. Spanish coins (*escudos*) were mixed with French coins (*écus*) and British coins (*shillings*). It was hard to know what an escudo was worth compared to a shilling. To end the confusion, Congress in 1792 created the American dollar as the standard unit of U.S. money. In the same year, a mint was established in Philadelphia for making gold coins and stamping them with their value in U.S. dollars.

The Treasury Department today. Today, the chief duties of the Department of the Treasury are much the same as Hamilton's original duties. It maintains a **Bureau of the Mint,** which manufactures millions of pennies, nickels, dimes, and quarters. Its **Bureau of Engraving and Printing** is responsible for printing the paper money that we carry in our wallets. One of the most common units of this money is the 10-dollar bill, which bears the portrait of Alexander Hamilton.

The Department of the Treasury keeps track of a staggering amount of government revenues and expenses. Most of the revenues are now collected by the department's most famous agency: the **Internal Revenue Service** (IRS).

At major U.S. airports and seaports, the Treasury Department posts other tax-collecting agents. They work for the **United States Customs Service** and collect taxes on goods imported from foreign countries. These taxes may also be called *tariffs,* duties, or customs. (See photo on page 384.)

As for expenses, more than half of the money spent by George Washington's government was for paying back old debts. Today, the government is still in debt. (See pages 429–430.) The department responsible for managing the debt and paying interest on it is the Department of the Treasury.

In making domestic policy, the secretary of the treasury can play an extremely important role. Usually the secretary is someone, like Alexander Hamilton, who knows a great deal about business and the economy. Therefore, at Cabinet meetings, the president may rely upon the secretary's opinions in deciding whether or not a proposed policy will be good for the economy.

Attorney general. Besides a financial expert to pay the bills, President Washington needed

CHECKING FOR PROHIBITED GOODS. Travelers entering the United States are required to open their luggage so that U.S. customs officials can check for foreign-made objects prohibited by law. In addition, what kind of tax is collected by customs officials?

a legal expert to help him enforce the laws. Therefore, in September 1789, Congress created the position of attorney general.

For many years, serving as attorney general was a hardship (as well as an honor). Congress authorized a small salary for the president's legal adviser but paid no expenses beyond that. So the cost of renting an office and hiring law clerks was paid for out of the attorney general's own pocket.

The situation improved in 1870 when Congress created the U.S. Department of Justice to be managed by the attorney general. The department's many clerks were now to receive salaries paid out of the U.S. Treasury.

The Justice Department today. The Justice Department and its leader, the attorney general, have three main responsibilities.

- *Giving legal advice to the president.* A staff of lawyers in the department advise the president about the legal and constitutional meaning of different bills.
- *Defending the U.S. government in court.* Like other organizations, the government can be sued for causing accidental harm. Lawyers who defend the U.S. government in such suits work for the Justice Department.
- *Investigating and punishing violators of federal laws.* It is a federal crime to sell narcotics across state lines, to kidnap a child, to evade federal tax laws, and to use the mails to swindle consumers. Officials who investigate and arrest persons suspected of breaking federal laws work for the **Federal Bureau of Investigation** (FBI).

TARGET PRACTICE. The FBI is training this civil servant to be one of its special agents. To what Cabinet department does the FBI belong?

Working closely with the FBI is one of the department's newest agencies, the **Drug Enforcement Administration** (DEA), created in 1973. Hundreds of DEA investigators work not only in the United States but in 40 foreign countries. They try to stop narcotics from being smuggled into the United States and arrest those in the United States suspected of dealing in illegal drugs. Local and state police forces are trained by the DEA to assist in the nationwide and worldwide "war against drugs."

Other agencies within the Justice Department enforce other kinds of laws. The **Antitrust Division** investigates businesses that may be guilty of unfair practices. The **Civil Rights Division** enforces federal laws designed to protect the voting rights of blacks and other minorities. The **Tax Division** helps the IRS to track down and prosecute violators of U.S. tax laws.

Secretary of the interior. The Cabinet post of secretary of the interior was created in 1849. In that year, most of the lands west of the Mississippi River were not yet states. They were divided into territories and governed by laws of the U.S. Congress. Hundreds of Indian tribes hunted on the Western plains as independent peoples.

But the situation changed rapidly, as the West was settled by farmers, miners, and ranchers. Defeated in war by U.S. troops, Indian peoples were made to live on mostly barren tracts called reservations. One state after another was formed out of the Western lands: Kansas in 1861, Nebraska in 1867, Colorado in 1876. But much of the lands in the new states, including the Indian reservations, were still under federal control.

The Interior Department today. The first main job of the Department of the Interior was to manage the vast Western territories. Its second job was to send agents onto reservations to work with the different Indian peoples. Today, two agencies in the department still perform these functions. They are: (*a*) the **Bureau of Land Management,** and (*b*) the **Bureau of Indian Affairs.**

The Bureau of Land Management. About 342 million acres of public lands—some in the East, but most in the West—are managed by the U.S. government. The agency that controls their use is the Bureau of Land Management. On the public lands, there is a huge amount of timber that could either be cut down or preserved. There are also oil and gas resources to be explored and minerals to be tapped. Should some of the public lands be sold to private mining, lumber, and oil companies? Within limits set by Congress, the bureau has the authority to decide.

The Bureau of Indian Affairs. Indian peoples never had an easy time adjusting to life on a reservation. To help them adjust, the Bureau of Indian Affairs operates schools for them and provides welfare services. Job-training programs are available to Indian youths who wish to leave the reservations. Nevertheless, many Indian people still have grievances against the U.S. government. Welfare and good intentions have not yet overcome the bitter experiences of the past.

New stress on conservation. Long ago, in the days of the "Wild West," the Interior Department would encourage pioneer families to make free use of land and water resources. After 1900, however, some people began to realize that "America the beautiful" could be ruined. Wildlife could be destroyed, mountain streams polluted, and forests laid low. *Conservation* (the careful use of land, water, and wildlife) became the major concern of the secretary of the interior.

The secretary's department is now the protector of the bald eagle, the whooping crane, the bison ("buffalo"), and every other form of American wildlife. Within the department is the ***United States Fish and Wildlife Service***. This organization oversees 434 National Wildlife Refuges, 150 Waterfowl Production Areas, and 73 National Fish Hatcheries.

Another agency, the ***National Park Service***, protects tourists from bears, and bears from tourists. This agency looks after the geysers in Yellowstone Park (Wyoming), the hiking trails in the Great Smoky Mountains (North Carolina), the sand dunes of Cape Cod (Massachusetts), and other natural wonders. For vacationers and nature lovers, it maintains hundreds of scenic park-

ENDANGERED SPECIES. The bald eagle is a symbol of our nation. It is also one of many species of birds and animals that environmentalists have placed on the endangered list. Birds are tagged to track their migrations. Which Cabinet department is the most active in protecting American wildlife?

ways, riverways, seashores, lakeshores, and historic buildings. The National Park Service is committed to conserving the natural beauty of the American wilderness. It too is under the authority of the secretary of the interior.

Secretary of agriculture. In the 1860s, people were just beginning to understand how important science could be to the progress of the nation. At this time, farming was still the occupation of the great majority of Americans. Using agricultural science and technology to increase farm production was the main idea behind the creation of the Department of Agriculture in 1862. Its secretary joined the president's Cabinet in 1889.

The first goal of the department was to teach farmers scientific ways of working the land. Its agents worked wonders. Farmers were taught advanced methods for growing crops and saving their livestock from various diseases. With the department's help, colleges were founded for the purpose of studying agriculture as a science. Within a 50-year period (1862–1912), American farmers used the new science and technology to triple their output of wheat and corn and double their output of cotton and tobacco.

The most prosperous years for farmers were those just before the outbreak of World War I in 1914. After that war, in the 1920s, farmers still produced huge crops. But they ran into economic problems as farm income often fell below farm costs. In other words, farming became, for many, a losing business.

The Agriculture Department today. Since the 1930s, the Department of Agriculture has tried to give farmers a helping hand. It runs programs that pay farmers subsidies of many kinds. (A *subsidy* is a sum of money given by government to pay part of a business's costs.) One program helps farmers find markets for their crops. Another program pays them to set aside part of their land for conservation and *not* to plant crops on it. A third program buys all the grain that farmers cannot sell at a reasonable price. It stores the grain in huge buildings and tries to sell it later, when the price is right.

INSPECTED BY USDA. A scientist in the Department of Agriculture inspects an ear of corn. In what ways does the USDA assist the American farmer?

Despite these subsidies, many American farmers are still in trouble. Every year, thousands of farms are sold. Instead of being in a majority, farmers today make up only 3 percent of the American labor force. Many of the family farms that remain may be forced to close down if crop prices do not improve. Should government stand by while thousands of farms go out of business? Or should the Department of Agriculture continue to provide subsidies and loans to farmers because of the importance of agriculture to a strong economy? For advice on this difficult issue, the president relies upon the expert knowledge of the secretary of agriculture.

Secretary of commerce. America's businesses were the next group to receive special government services and support. In 1903, Congress created the Department of Commerce and Labor. The secretary who ran the department gave most of his time to helping commerce (business) and much less time to helping labor (workers). Therefore, in 1913, the original department was split in two, Commerce becoming one department and Labor the other.

Gathering information about the economy is one of the chief functions of the department headed by the secretary of commerce. One of the fact-gathering bureaus within the department is the **U.S. Bureau of the Census.** Every ten years (1970, 1980, 1990, etc.), this bureau conducts a census, or count, of the U.S. population. On the basis of this census, each of the 50 states is assigned a proportionate number of seats in the U.S. House of Representatives. From the Census Bureau's work, we know the current population of every town, city, county, and state. We also know whether the U.S. population is becoming younger or older, whether the birth rate is rising or falling, and whether males outnumber females or vice versa.

COUNTING THE POPULATION. This is one of thousands of workers who interview citizens for the Census Bureau. Why does the Constitution require a census to be taken every ten years?

In addition, every four years, the Census Bureau determines the dollar value of all products manufactured and sold by U.S. businesses. Business managers of different companies take the government data and feed them into their computers for analysis. The plans they make for next year's production are based partly on the facts supplied by the U.S. Census Bureau.

Another bureau supervised by the secretary of commerce is the **Patent and Trademark Office** (PTO). Its main job is to protect inventors by granting government documents called *patents.* Suppose, for example, that you invent the world's first electric-powered carrot-masher. You file the necessary papers with the PTO. You are then granted a patent on your device. That means that nobody else can lawfully produce or sell a carrot-masher similar to yours without your permission.

Your patent gives you alone the right to produce and sell your invention for a certain number of years. Patent protection may last anywhere from 3½ years to 17 years, depending on the kind of invention. After that, others too can bring out carrot-mashers like yours. But by then, you may have made your fortune.

Other agencies in the Department of Commerce provide additional services for businesses. They include:

- advising businesses on opportunities for selling their goods in foreign markets
- charting the oceans for the benefit of shipping companies
- studying and reporting weather conditions
- promoting travel in the United States by foreign tourists.

Secretary of labor. Just as the Department of Commerce serves the interests of American business, the Department of Labor serves the interests of workers. The laws that it enforces assist everyone from shipping clerks to ship captains, from lifeguards to landscape gardeners. The department describes its purposes in these terms:

"to foster the welfare of the wage earners of the United States"
"to improve their working conditions"
"to advance their opportunities for profitable employment"

The secretary in charge of the department advises the president on policies for bringing about full employment.

One of the bureaus in the department, the **Bureau of Labor Statistics,** puts out a monthly magazine about current changes in the labor force. This *Monthly Labor Review* contains many statistical tables that may not interest the general reader. But they are extremely useful to labor unions in their dealings with employers.

Even if you are not yet employed, the Department of Labor tries to help you and other prospective workers to choose a suitable career. A book that it publishes, *Guide for Occupational Exploration,* helps young readers to identify their interests and match them to a satisfying occupation. Another of its books, *Occupational Outlook Handbook,* gives information about qualifications and salary levels for almost every kind of job.

Once you find a job, the Department of Labor tries to ensure that (*a*) you are paid at least a minimum wage and (*b*) you work in a safe and healthy environment. The minimum wage fixed by federal law was $4.25 per hour in 1994. The agency within the department that enforces minimum wage and other labor laws is the **Employment Standards Administration.**

Suppose that you find conditions at your place of business to be unsanitary or unsafe. You try to persuade your employer to correct the problem, but nothing is done. In this situation, a government bureau that might be able to help is the **Occupational Safety and Health Administration** (OSHA). Its main function is to see that employers provide safe and healthy working conditions for their workers.

The Cabinet before World War II. Until the 1930s, members of the president's Cabinet

ROOSEVELT'S CABINET, 1933. Surrounding the president (center) are the heads of the following departments:
Standing from left: Agriculture, Interior, Navy, Post Office, Commerce, and Labor (Frances Perkins, first woman Cabinet member)
Seated from left: War, State, President Franklin D. Roosevelt, Treasury, and Justice.
Which of these Cabinet posts no longer exist?

had always been men. In 1933, the first woman to be seated at the Cabinet table was a social worker from New York, Frances Perkins. For 12 years, she was Franklin Roosevelt's secretary of labor and trusted adviser on domestic policy.

The photo on page 389 shows that Roosevelt's Cabinet consisted of the different department heads mentioned so far: attorney general, secretary of the treasury, and so forth. (There was also a postmaster general and a secretary of war—Cabinet seats that no longer exist.) Roosevelt's Cabinet was more than twice the size of the first Cabinet under George Washington. Furthermore, each department in the 1930s had more people working for it than the entire federal government of 1790. As we shall see, the largest departments of all were added after World War II.

REVIEW

A. Making Inferences: Who's Responsible?

Name the Cabinet officer who is responsible for the job of:

1. finding new markets for a crop of cotton.
2. cleaning up litter in Yosemite National Park.
3. investigating a factory in which two workers are badly injured.
4. checking tax returns.
5. suing a state government for failing to protect the civil rights of voters.
6. reviewing an application for a trademark.
7. defending in a federal court the U.S. government's claims to 1,000 acres of desert land.
8. supplying schools with information about careers.
9. conducting experiments to find a safe way to kill weeds.
10. gathering facts about the number of garden hoses sold last year.

B. Project: Who's Who in Government

Select **one** of the Cabinet posts featured in this section. In the library, do the following:

1. Ask a librarian to point out the *United States Government Manual* (most current edition). Look up the name of the person who currently holds the Cabinet job.
2. Then, in the *Readers' Guide*, look up a magazine article about this person. Write a summary of the article.

C. If You Worked for the Government

Suppose you could apply for a job in any of the departments of the federal government . . .

1. Which department do you think would be most interesting to work for? Why?
2. Describe a job or function that you might be able to perform for the department mentioned in **1.**
3. Look up information about the job or occupation mentioned in **2.** Refer to one of the books published by the Department of Labor.

2. WHY WERE NEW DEPARTMENTS ADDED AFTER WORLD WAR II?

In the 1930s, the federal government was big—and growing bigger. President Franklin Roosevelt asked Congress for dozens of major new laws to help different groups struggle through the Depression. One agency after another was created to run the new programs.

Then in 1941, the United States entered World War II. To manage the war effort at home and abroad, government expanded even more. When the war ended in 1945, government eliminated some of its war bureaus. But most of the programs from the Depression were continued, while others were added.

A few statistics show what happened. First, we can measure the growth of the federal government by the amount of money it spent in different years.

1934 (Depression year) — $5.9 billion
1944 (war year) — $100.5 billion
1954 (after the war) — $77.9 billion

In other words, the government after the war (1954) was spending about *13 times* more money than before the war (1934).

SKILLS CHECK: Interpreting a bar graph

As another measure of growth, examine the number of people in the government. *Not* included in the bar graph below are either post office workers or people in the armed forces.

For each statement below, say whether it *(a)* **correctly interprets** or *(b)* **wrongly interprets** the data in the bar graph.

1. The greatest increase in employment occurred between 1954 and 1964.
2. The U.S. government employed more people after World War II (1954) than before the war (1934).
3. The federal government more than doubled in size between 1934 and 1954.
4. Almost 200,000 people were added to the payroll between 1954 and 1964.

CIVILIAN EMPLOYEES IN THE FEDERAL GOVERNMENT, 1934 - 1964

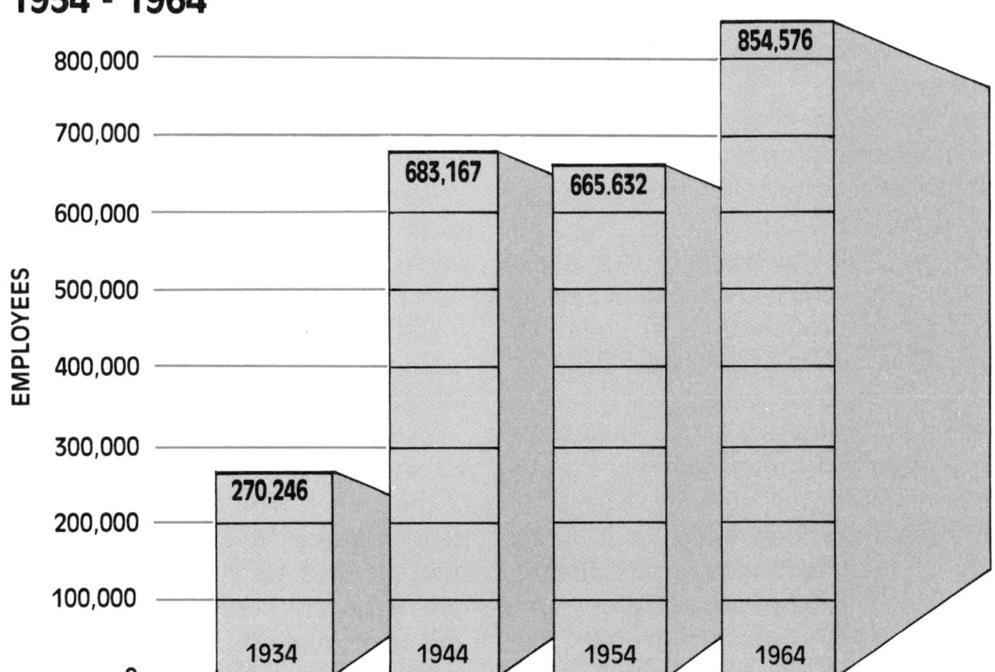

Reasons for growth. Why did the size of the federal government change as a result of the war? Think again of two of the government's goals stated in the Constitution:

- "to provide for the common defense"
- "to promote the general welfare"

Achieving the first goal, defense, became much more difficult in the years following World War II. After 1945, Americans felt threatened by the military might and political goals of a Communist power, the Soviet Union. To meet the Soviet challenge, the president and Congress thought it necessary to keep a huge army, navy, and air force in peacetime.

In 1950, about 1.5 million Americans were in uniform. In 1955, there were almost 3 million. Even more costly was the effort to equip each of the armed services (air force, army, and navy) with advanced weapons systems, both nuclear and non-nuclear. It often happened that a type of weapon would become obsolete (out-of-date) in a very short time. New weapons would then be planned and built until they too were made obsolete by Soviet advances. The *arms race* had begun.

To manage the vast expansion of U.S. defenses, a new department was created in 1947—the **Department of Defense.** Its work will be described in Chapter 19.

Serving the "general welfare" in ambitious new ways was the second major reason for the growth of the federal government after World War II. Retired workers liked the Social Security law enacted during the Depression. Younger workers liked the laws that guaranteed a minimum wage and bargaining rights for their unions. Farmers liked the security of knowing that, in bad years, the government would pay them subsidies to keep their farms going. As government moved to provide benefits, it grew larger.

New departments and their secretaries. For the sake of the common defense and the general welfare, several new departments were added to the Executive Branch. Directing each was a secretary who served in the president's Cabinet. The following seats were added to the Cabinet table in the postwar years:

Secretary of Defense (added in 1947)

Secretary of Housing and Urban Development (added in 1965)

Secretary of Transportation (added in 1967)

Secretary of Energy (added in 1977)

Secretary of Education (added in 1979)

Secretary of Health and Human Services (added in 1979)

Secretary of Veterans Affairs (added in 1989)

The largest of all the postwar departments were the last two: the DEPARTMENT OF HEALTH AND HUMAN SERVICES and the DEPARTMENT OF VETERANS AFFAIRS. Let us look at these "new" departments first, since they most directly affect the general welfare of everyone.

In the previous section, we looked at each Cabinet department from the point of view of the person who ran it. In this section, let us look at the "new" department from our own point of view. We the people are the ones who are served by the departments and their many bureaus. What benefits do we receive from their work?

Helping people who endanger their own health. Millions of Americans place their health at risk by smoking cigarettes or consuming too many alcoholic drinks. Many smokers die from ailments caused by their habit. People addicted to alcohol damage their own bodies. They also become difficult for family members to live with. Saddest of all perhaps are those who are "turned on" to illegal drugs like heroin and cocaine. The effects of a drug habit on a young person's life can be disastrous.

The federal government runs several programs that assist schools and communities in their efforts to combat drug abuse, alcoholism, and cigarette addiction. The programs are coordinated by the **Public Health Service** (PHS), an agency of the Department of Health and Human Services. Workers employed by this agency conduct research and give out information on the dangers of smoking, drinking alcohol, and taking drugs. Directing the agency is the surgeon general. On a pack of cigarettes, you may have seen this message:

> SURGEON GENERAL'S WARNING: Smoking Causes Lung Cancer, Heart Disease, Emphysema, and May Complicate Pregnancy.

Scientists employed by the Public Health Service work to discover the causes and cures of cancer, heart ailments, AIDS, and other diseases. Millions of federal dollars go to hospitals and medical schools every year to improve their services.

Helping to protect consumers from harmful foods and drugs. Another agency concerned with keeping Americans healthy is the **Food and Drug Administration** (FDA). It was founded by an act of Congress in 1906. Thus, like PHS, the FDA is older than the Cabinet department to which it belongs.

One of the workers in the FDA is Lillie Dortsch-Wright, the person introduced on page 380. She thinks consumers need to be much better informed about the pills they swallow and the foods they eat. The main job of the FDA is to ensure that *every* product on the market is safe to swallow (if it is a food or drug) or safe to rub onto your skin (if it is a lotion or cosmetic). Investigators for the FDA visit at least 125,000 factories each year to test the safety of everything from hot dogs and mustards to baby powders and shaving creams.

Even so, certain products are sold that do not meet FDA standards. Therefore, consumers must still use caution and common sense when buying medicines. That is the message that FDA educators and consumer advocates want people to receive. As part of their effort, they make available to

GOVERNMENT ADVERTISING. This magazine ad was created for the U.S. Department of Health and Human Services. Do you think the government should try to discourage people from smoking?

consumers a wallet-size card that can remind you of questions to ask in a doctor's office. The card says:

GET THE ANSWERS

Remember to ask your doctor, pharmacist, or other health care provider about your prescription medicines.

1. What is the name of the drug, and what is it supposed to do?
2. How and when do I take it—and for how long?
3. What foods, drinks, other medicines, or activities should I avoid while taking this drug?
4. Are there any side effects, and what do I do if they occur?
5. Is there any written information available about the drug?

DIETERS BEWARE. People fooled into buying the weight-control device held by Lillie Dortsch-Wright of the FDA will get nothing for their money. What kinds of products does the FDA inspect and regulate?

You can get this card for yourself (and many other publications of the FDA) by writing a brief letter to an FDA office in your area. Providing the card is just one of hundreds of the FDA's free services.

Helping senior citizens in retirement. We now come to the group that is most directly and regularly helped by a government agency. Your grandparents may be among them. They are people over the age of 65 who, every month, receive income from the **Social Security Administration** (SSA). (They can begin to collect smaller benefits as early as age 62, but not the full amount until after their 65th birthday.)

One fact about Social Security must be understood from the start. Retired citizens receiving government checks are merely getting back income that was deducted from their paychecks in the years that they worked. For them, Social Security is an insurance system for saving money in their earning years. When they were in the work force, a tax law forced them to save money and put it into a special fund banked by the government.

Let us take the case of Brenda Kolchak, born in 1916. She began her career in 1936 as an employee of the telephone company. She did not stop working until her 65th birthday in 1981. The first Social Security law (passed in 1935) went into effect the year that she started working, 1936. Every week of her working life, for 45 years, a small sum of money was subtracted from Brenda Kolchak's wages and paid into the Social Security fund. In addition, her employer contributed to the fund, every week, a sum equal to Kolchak's. That is one of the rules of the system: the employer matches the contribution of the employee.

The Social Security Administration kept a record of all the payments made by Kolchak and her employer over the course of her career. When she retired, the agency calculated how much money per month she was entitled to receive. The formula for determining each retiree's benefits takes into account the following:

- how much the person paid into the fund.
- whether the person continues to earn income after the age of 65. (If so, the amount of the monthly check may be reduced.)
- whether the cost of living has gone up because of inflation. (If so, benefits will go up proportionately.)

In 1981, Ms. Kolchak received the maximum amount allowed by law, $448 a month, the average benefit for retired workers. In 1994, she received a higher amount, $674 a month, because the cost of living had risen. The law allows for automatic increases in benefits if the cost of living goes up.

Besides paying monthly checks to Ms. Kolchak, the Social Security Administration mailed checks to some 41.8 million other people in 1993. Over half were retired workers. Others who received benefits were disabled workers, widowed spouses, and children under 18 of covered workers. The amount paid to these beneficiaries in 1993 came to a staggering $295.5 *billion*.

The Social Security system is currently so expensive that the government worries about finding enough money to keep it going. Why is this? Retired people are currently taking more money out of the system in benefits than younger people are putting into it in payroll taxes. This situation is a major problem.

In the future, this problem could become even more serious as the gap widens between two age groups. Older citizens are expected to become a larger part of the total U.S. population in the next century, while younger citizens of working age become a smaller part. Many economists predict that this trend will place a tremendous strain on the Social Security system.

Helping workers who are unemployed or injured. Without Social Security, most retired persons would have little income to live on. The same is true of a younger

CARTOON CORNER

In the future, would you want to see the "parade" of government services grow larger or smaller? Why?

person who has the misfortune of either losing a job or being disabled by some accident on the job. To make up for these workers' loss of income, the Social Security Administration uses two programs.

A program of unemployment insurance helps unemployed workers by issuing checks to them for a limited period of time. A program of workers' compensation issues checks to those who have been injured on the job. If a married person is killed in a factory accident or office fire, the wife or husband is entitled to receive survivor's benefits.

Both the federal government and the states finance these programs, but only the states operate them.

Helping elderly people with medical problems. Generally, after the age of 65, people will need more medical help than in their younger years. If they are retired, this is just the time in their lives when their incomes are too low to pay doctor's fees. That is why the Social Security system now includes a program for the elderly called Medicare. For retired people, it pays the major costs of hospital and nursing care.

Doctors' bills and medicines are covered under Medicare only if a senior citizen voluntarily enrolls in a public insurance program. Those who do decide to join the program must pay a small monthly fee. A visit to the doctor is then much less costly, since the government's insurance program pays for almost all of it.

The Social Security programs mentioned so far are *not* welfare programs. They are a form of insurance. During your income-earning years, you pay into the programs so that later you can collect benefits when you need them.

Helping people who are blind or disabled. Other programs run by the Social Security Administration are for the welfare and support of the poor. They help low-income people of all ages. A 21-year-old blind person, for example, may be unable to find work. Checks from the Social Security Administration help this person buy groceries and pay the rent. Millions of people are unable to work because of some physical or mental handicap. They too may be eligible to receive income supplements from the U.S. government.

Helping people living in poverty. Another welfare program sends checks to parents whose incomes are too low to support their children. The program is called Aid to Families With Dependent Children (AFDC). In most of these families, there is only one parent living at home with the children. The other parent (usually the father) is absent either because of death, divorce, or desertion.

The Food Stamp Program helps individuals or families with very low incomes. If you qualify for aid, you are allowed to purchase for a low price a book of coupons or stamps. When buying food in a grocery or supermarket, you present the coupons at the checkout counter as if they were money. Food stamps have kept millions of poor people from going hungry or living on unhealthy diets.

A second program, Medicaid, is sometimes confused with Medicare. But Medicaid is a welfare program for the poor—not an insurance program for middle-class retired workers. If you are sick and too poor to pay the expenses of a doctor or a hospital, you can apply for Medicaid. If you qualify, the U.S. government will pay part or all of your medical costs.

Helping veterans. People who served in the armed forces, either in a war or in peacetime, have made a special contribution. Therefore, the laws of the country treat veterans as a special group entitled to special benefits. For many years, these laws were administered by the Veterans Administration, an agency headed by a non-Cabinet officer. In 1985, the Veterans Administration employed a workforce of almost 250,000 people to serve the needs of about 30 million veterans. Partly because of the agency's great size, Congress decided to give it the status of a Cabinet department. The first secretary of veterans affairs was appointed by President Bush in 1989.

Providing health care is the VA's chief activity. For the benefit of veterans, it operates 172 medical centers, 225 clinics, and 99 nursing homes at locations around the country. It also works with private hospitals, doctors, and dentists to see that veterans receive good medical care at low cost.

The VA assists disabled veterans in finding jobs and pays them compensation for their injuries. It guarantees loans made to veterans for the purchase of housing. It assists them in getting a college education. And it provides life insurance for veterans and their families. Only two U.S. insurance companies operate a larger insurance system than the VA's.

Helping people who need low-cost housing. Building new houses and apartments is a huge expense. Construction companies and banks will not undertake a risky building project unless they are fairly certain of getting their money back. It is no problem if they build housing for rich people who can afford to pay high rents. But they have little incentive (reason) to build housing for families who earn small or modest incomes.

Agencies of the federal government were created to solve this problem. One of them, the **Federal Housing Administration** (FHA), no longer exists. But back in the 1940s and 1950s, millions of housing units in cities and suburbs were built with bank loans insured by the FHA. Because of FHA insurance, banks did not risk much when they lent money to families for the purchase of FHA-backed homes. If a family failed to make its monthly mortgage payments, then the bank could collect the money due from the government agency. Banks were happy because they were insured against loss. Young families were happy because new homes were available to them at reasonable rates.

The federal government continues to insure a bank's mortgages (lending contracts) to some buyers of new homes. This is so because the FHA's functions were taken over by a Cabinet department created in 1965, the DEPARTMENT OF HOUSING AND URBAN DEVELOPMENT (HUD).

Housing is one concern of HUD. Rebuilding cities is its second concern. Most Americans today live in cities and suburbs. Many of the cities they live in have old, rundown neighborhoods. Where will the money come from to restore abandoned buildings, repair streets and sewers, and provide decent housing for a city's poor and unemployed? The cities themselves are unable to collect enough taxes from their own citizens to do the job. Therefore, federal money is made available to them through various programs run by HUD.

One such program gives block grants to communities that qualify. A block grant is an outright gift of money that can be used for any purpose that a city government chooses. (The only condition is that the city's use of federal money be related in some way to the needs of low-income and middle-income people.) For example, Philadelphia may decide to create small parks with its HUD money. San Francisco may decide to use its grant to repair streetcars.

Do you live in a city or suburb? How might *you* spend a block grant from HUD of $10 million?

Another HUD program is an attempt to solve the problem of abandoned houses. Have you seen them—the smashed windows, the peeling paint, the gutted interiors? Someone with imagination and willpower could restore these ugly structures and make them livable again. That is the idea behind HUD's *homesteading* program. It gives an ambitious person the opportunity

FEDERAL AID FOR A CITY PARK. Money from the federal government helped pay these young workers to create and decorate a park in their New York City neighborhood. The money to paint this plane for the park probably came from which U.S. department?

to move into an abandoned building without paying any money for it. After living in and working on the building for five years, the person is given ownership of the property.

Helping travelers. Step into any vehicle: a car, a train, a subway, an airplane, a ship. Travel in that vehicle anywhere in the USA: Miami to Minneapolis, Detroit to Denver . . . you name it. You will probably have a safe journey, in part because of the work of the DEPARTMENT OF TRANSPORTATION (DOT). The act of Congress creating the department in 1966 said that it was to promote "fast, safe, efficient, and convenient transportation at the lowest cost." The agencies of DOT include:

• ***The United States Coast Guard.*** The Coast Guard patrols the rivers, lakes, and seaports of the country to ensure the safety of motorboats, rowboats, ferries—everything afloat. On frozen waters of the North, it operates icebreakers to clear paths for Navy vessels and commercial ships.

SUBWAY IN ATLANTA, GEORGIA. The Department of Transportation is one source of funds for modernizing city subway systems. What other Cabinet department is primarily concerned with aiding cities?

INTERCEPTING ILLEGAL DRUGS. In the duffel bags are drugs captured by the U.S. Coast Guard off the Florida coast. What are other duties of the Coast Guard?

In Atlantic and Pacific seaports, it is like a traffic cop of the seas, keeping boats and ships from colliding. Its rescue vessels are always on hand to save from drowning people whose boats have overturned in stormy seas.

Increasingly, Coast Guard cutters are being used to inspect ships suspected of carrying illegal drugs into the United States.

• ***Federal Aviation Administration (FAA).*** At busy airports across the country, employees of this agency direct air traffic, telling pilots when to land and take off. Before flying, all aircraft must meet FAA standards for safety. Their pilots must also pass demanding tests.

• ***Federal Highway Administration (FHA).*** Without the money distributed by this agency, travel by car would be slower and more frustrating. A total of 42,500 miles of highways have been built with federal tax dollars. About 800,000 miles of roads and streets have been improved with U.S. funds. State governments contribute to the road-building and road-improving effort, but most of the money comes from DOT. Running highway safety programs is another of the agency's important functions.

• ***Federal Railroad Administration (FRA).*** Traveling by train can be hazardous. To prevent trains from colliding and going off the tracks, the FRA makes sure that railroad companies meet strict standards of safety.

Helping consumers of energy. When you turn on a light switch, television, or toaster, you are using energy. Multiply such actions billions of times a day in the nation's homes, factories, and offices. Add the billions of gallons of gasoline (a source of energy) consumed each day by motor vehicles on the nation's roads. Day after day, the amount of consumed energy keeps growing. Some day soon, are we going to run out of the energy sources we rely upon for everything we do?

The answer is no *if* the DEPARTMENT OF ENERGY (DOE) succeeds in its work. DOE conducts and sponsors scientific research in three areas:

*1. **Old sources of energy*** (fossil fuels). Fuels such as coal, oil, and natural gas are burned to create energy. Once used, they cannot be renewed.

*2. **New sources of energy.*** If business and government can invent new technologies, Americans' reliance on fossil fuels may come to an end. In the future, we may be heating our homes and offices with energy from sources that will never be used up. Among such sources are winds, the sun's rays, and the intense heat from below the surface of the earth. (See photo on page 400.)

*3. **Nuclear energy.*** The splitting of a single atom releases vast amounts of energy. But can such energy be made available without major risks? DOE is looking for ways to increase the safety of nuclear power plants.

GIANT "EGGBEATER." Shaped like an eggbeater, the blade of this turbine spins in the Texas winds to generate electric power. Why do you think the Department of Energy paid for the invention of this modern windmill?

Helping students and teachers. The next group of people to be served by a Cabinet department is the youngest. You are one of those who could benefit from the work of the DEPARTMENT OF EDUCATION.

In our federal system, states and local communities have complete responsibility for hiring public school teachers and principals and saying what courses should be taught. But the federal government can help local schools by providing funds for certain purposes.

Laws of Congress have authorized money to be given to schools that operate certain types of programs. Some programs that receive federal aid are for the education of handicapped children. Others are for non-English-speaking children and teenagers who need special help with the English language. For educating these and other groups, the Department of Education grants money to public school systems that apply for aid.

In the 1980s, there was widespread concern about the quality of our nation's schools. Were schools doing enough to provide "excellence in education" for all? Special commissions were appointed to study the question. One of them said a decline in education standards put the nation "at risk." Secretary of Education Terrell Bell offered the opinion that many schools were *not* demanding excellence. His remarks focused a national debate on how to raise educational levels.

What's your opinion? Would you say "excellence in education" is mainly the responsibility of (*a*) teachers, (*b*) school administrators, or (*c*) you, the learner? If the U.S. Department of Education wants excellence, should it be willing to spend more federal money to achieve it?

REVIEW

A. Impact of Government on Your Life

Imagine that the U.S. government ran short of money. As a remedy, Congress abolished the agencies named below. Describe what you think the effect would be **if** . . .

1. the Social Security Administration was abolished.
2. the programs of HUD were abolished.
3. the Department of Education was abolished.
4. Which of the above losses (1–3) do you think would cause the most serious problem for the American nation? Why?

B. Project: Getting in Touch with Government

Select **one** of the government agencies whose addresses are given below. Send a letter to this agency asking for a free pamphlet or publication that it makes available to the public. Begin the letter, "Dear Sir or Madam." Explain that, as a student, you are interested in knowing more about the agency's services and programs.

For information about Medicare and Medicaid, write:

Administrator
Health Care Financing Administration
Department of Health and Human Services
200 Independence Ave., SW
Washington, D.C. 20201

For information about urban homesteading, write:

Office of Urban Rehabilitation
Department of Housing and Urban Development
451 Seventh St., SW
Washington, D.C. 20410

For information about the United States Coast Guard, write:

Information Office
United States Coast Guard
Department of Transportation
2100 Second St., SW
Washington, D.C. 20593

For information about the Food and Drug Administration, write:

Food and Drug Administration
5600 Fishers Lane
Rockville, MD 20857

C. Making Comparisons

Explain the **difference** between the terms in each pair.

1. Medicare - Medicaid
2. DOT - DOE
3. Social insurance benefits - Welfare payments
4. Federal bureaucracy before World War II - Federal bureaucracy after World War II.

3. HOW DO INDEPENDENT AGENCIES SERVE THE PUBLIC?

Around the Cabinet table in the White House are chairs for the heads of 14 departments. You have now studied 12 of the departments, leaving two others (State and Defense) for a later chapter.

You may think that the 14 Cabinet departments are all there is to the Executive Branch. But if that were so, Americans would sorely miss these services:

- the daily delivery of our mail
- the supplying of electric power to the people of Tennessee and other Southeastern states
- a system for regulating banks
- a means of ensuring that businesses compete fairly.

The above functions are performed by agencies that exist *outside* any Cabinet department. The president appoints the top leaders of these agencies and may speak to them directly or on the telephone. But they do not have the privilege of sitting around the Cabinet table.

There are more than 100 non-Cabinet agencies. You should know about some of the largest and most important ones.

U.S. Postal Service. Delivering mail to every home and business in the country is a huge task. In 1992, about 799,000 postal workers delivered about 170 *billion* letters, magazines, brochures, and other items. That amounted to about 680 items for every American citizen.

In the past, the Post Office was represented at the Cabinet table by its head officer, the postmaster general. Around 1900, its stamps were sold cheaply, only two or three cents for the average letter. At that time, the Post Office was expected to lose money every year—and it did. It was felt then that cheap postal rates helped businesses to grow and prosper.

But a major change came in 1970. Congress decided that the Post Office should not continue to lose money. Instead, it should sell its services at rates high enough to break even. The Post Office was therefore organized as a public corporation. It changed its name from Department of the Post Office to the U.S. Postal Service. As a corporation, it was supposed to operate in a businesslike manner and collect enough revenue to cover its costs. No longer could it pay for its operations using tax dollars.

You can understand then why the cost of a first-class postage stamp went from 12 cents in 1970 to 29 cents in 1991.

Tennessee Valley Authority (TVA). Another famous public corporation provides services for only one region of the country. It is a region of Southern farms and forests through which the Tennessee River flows. In the 1920s, before TVA was created, people in the Tennessee River Valley had a hard time making a living. The river often flooded, destroying homes and crops. No private company could take the risk of supplying electric power to the region, since

DAMS AND STAMPS. Left: Completed in 1936, the Norris Dam in Tennessee, 265 feet high, was the first of many dams created by TVA. Right: Workers for the U.S. Postal Service process billions of pieces of mail a year. What do TVA and the Postal Service have in common?

people were too poor to pay the electric bills.

Congress came to the rescue of the depressed region in 1933 by creating TVA. Its purpose was to control the river for the benefit of the farmers and other people living near its banks. TVA built a series of dams along the river's many branches. Soon the region sprang to life. TVA's dams and power plants brought electricity into people's homes. They tamed the Tennessee River, stopping it from flooding. Now boats for commerce and boats for pleasure could travel safely over its entire length.

The TVA today is a government-owned corporation. It sells electric power to the people of seven states: Tennessee, Kentucky, Virginia, North Carolina, Georgia, Alabama, and Mississippi. TVA's managers try to run the corporation as a business, charging just enough to pay expenses. In 1990, TVA collected $1 billion in electric bills from people served by its power plants. Next to the U.S. Postal Service, TVA is the federal government's most ambitious business.

Environmental Protection Agency (EPA). You probably know about pollution—but wish you didn't. It looks bad, smells bad, and endangers your health. The EPA was created by Congress in 1970 to bring pollution under control. Its chief functions are to:

- Check our drinking water to see that it meets standards of safety.
- Check the exhaust systems of automobiles to keep fumes to a minimum.
- Prevent factories from dumping harmful wastes into lakes and rivers.
- Help states and local governments with their efforts to stop pollution.

Federal Reserve Board (FRB). Right now, reach for your wallet and pull out a dollar bill. Notice what is printed at the top: FEDERAL RESERVE NOTE. The Federal Reserve is a system for regulating banks and the amount of money that banks issue.

CHECKING HAZARDOUS WASTES. The drums inspected by these EPA workers contain chemical wastes from the manufacture of paints. What other threats to the environment are subject to EPA regulations?

A small number of master banks (Federal Reserve banks) perform banking services for other banks. One master bank in Kansas City, for example, issues money (Federal Reserve notes or dollar bills) to member banks in Kansas and other Western states. A total of 12 master (or central) banks are located in different regions of the country. They get their currency (money) from the Treasury Department and then issue it to banks in their region. (See map on page 404.)

The small group of people that manage the Federal Reserve System is known as the Board of Governors of the Federal Reserve. The policies of the Federal Reserve Board (FRB) determine how much money banks are likely to lend to businesses. The FRB

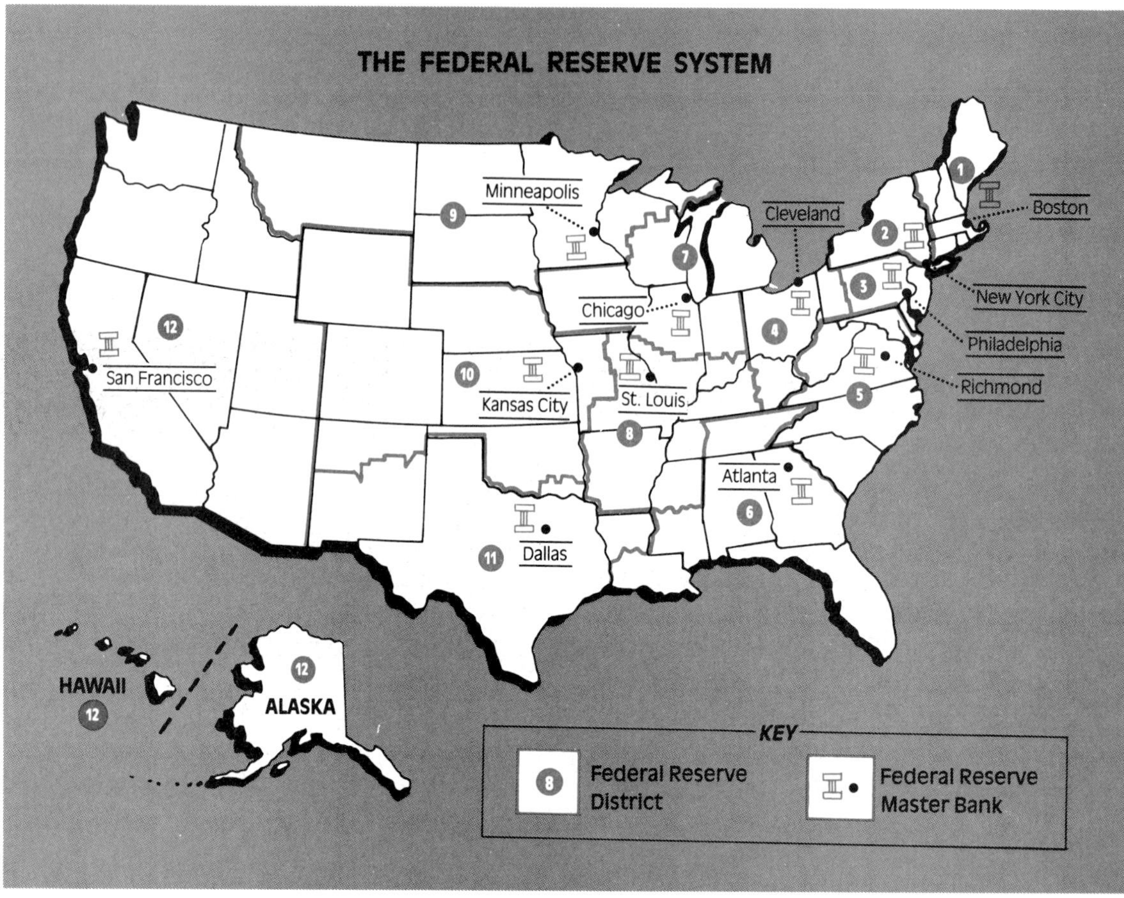

can either be "tight" or "loose" in its lending policy. Its decisions have a powerful effect on the nation's economy.

Federal Trade Commission (FTC). Suppose that a business tricks you into spending your money on a worthless or harmful product. For example, a salesperson fools you into believing that you will be getting something of value for very little. Or you order something from a magazine ad with a "money-back guarantee." Nothing comes to you—neither the product you ordered nor your money.

In situations like this, the Federal Trade Commission can help. It was created in 1914 to serve two purposes: (1) to stop businesses from using unfair methods of competition and (2) to help consumers who believe they have been cheated.

The FTC determines whether or not a complaint against a certain business is valid. If so, it may order the business owner to stop its unfair practice.

If you ever feel that a business has treated you unfairly, write a letter of complaint to the Federal Trade Commission in Washington, D.C. You can look up its address in the *United States Government Manual.*

Independent regulatory agencies. The FTC and the FRB are examples of a special kind of government agency. They are like free-floating islands that stand apart from the mainland of government. Neither the president nor a Cabinet head directs their work. Congress checks on them occasionally but rarely interferes. The Supreme Court can overrule certain decisions of an independent agency—but usually does not.

Agencies of this special kind are called *independent regulatory agencies.* They are "independent" because no outside authority sets policy for them. They are free to make policies and judgments as they see fit. They are "regulatory" because their chief function is to regulate, or make rules for, the operation of different kinds of businesses. For example:

- The **Federal Reserve Board** (FRB) regulates the banking business.
- The **Interstate Commerce Commission** (ICC) regulates railroad companies.
- The **Federal Communications Commission** (FCC) regulates the broadcasting privileges of radio and television stations.
- The **Securities and Exchange Commission** (SEC) regulates the buying and selling of stocks and bonds.

The laws that established these agencies gave them broad power both to make rules and to enforce them. The ICC, for example, determines how much railroad companies may charge for hauling freight. If a complaint is made against a certain railroad, the ICC may conduct a hearing that is very much like a trial. Other independent regulatory agencies also act like both a legislature (making rules) and like a court (deciding cases).

In each agency, power to make policy belongs to a small group of commissioners or board members. A commission or board may have anywhere from five to eleven members. Each member is appointed by the president and confirmed (approved) by a vote of the Senate.

Commissioners and board members serve for terms of at least seven years, sometimes longer. The long terms help an agency to be independent of outside influence and control.

REVIEW

A. Making Inferences

Imagine that you are president of an American corporation that makes and sells cars. How do you think your company's business might be affected by each of the following federal agencies?

1. the U.S. Postal Service
2. the Environmental Protection Agency
3. the Federal Trade Commission
4. the Federal Reserve Board

B. Agree or Disagree

Tell whether you **agree** or **disagree** with each statement, and explain why.

1. Delivery of the mail should be turned over to private companies.
2. The president should be given greater control over the independent regulatory agencies.
3. The federal government should create more agencies like TVA to supply electric power to other regions of the country.

CHAPTER REVIEW

A. Completing the Summary

Missing from this summary are names of the specific agencies and departments being described. As you read, write the missing names on a separate sheet of paper.

The Cabinet departments of the federal government were added one by one to meet different needs. When George Washington met with the first Cabinet in the 1790s, the most urgent need was for a reliable system of banking and money. Alexander Hamilton served brilliantly as the first secretary of the __(1)__.

Only one Cabinet officer has a title different from "secretary." The attorney general heads the Department of __(2)__ and helps the president enforce federal laws. The most famous law enforcement agency within the department is the __(3)__.

Two departments are chiefly responsible for the way American lands are used. The Department of __(4)__ manages national parks and oversees Indian reservations. The Department of __(5)__ aids farmers in a variety of ways through research and subsidies.

One department was split up to become the two departments in 1913. The Department of __(6)__ provides patent protection, statistics, and other assistance for businesses. The Department of __(7)__ enforces laws that promote safe working conditions and guarantee workers a minimum wage.

After World War II, the Executive Branch grew by leaps and bounds. Six Cabinet departments were created between 1960 and 1989. One of the largest of them is the Department of Health and __(8)__. Famous agencies within it are:

(*a*) the __(9)__ Administration, which protects consumers from products that may be unhealthy to eat or drink.

(*b*) the __(10)__ Administration, which operates both an insurance system and a welfare system, issuing checks to those who qualify.

The most recent addition to the Cabinet is the secretary who heads the Department of __(11)__.

The Cabinet department that helps to rebuild America's cities is the Department of __(12)__ (HUD). Whether traveling by land, air, or sea, Americans are safer because of the work of the Department of __(13)__ (DOT). New technologies for burning fuels and tapping energy from the sun are the specialty of the Department of __(14)__ (DOE). Schools benefit most from the programs of the Department of __(15)__.

Many bureaus and agencies are *not* directed by a Cabinet head. Among them are:

(*a*) The U.S. __(16)__, which delivers our mail. (It is an example of a public corporation.)

(*b*) The __(17)__ (TVA), which provides electric power and flood control for people living in seven Southern states. (It is another example of a public corporation.)

(*c*) The __(18)__, which attempts to reduce the pollution of America's land, air, and water.

(*d*) The __(19)__ (FTC), which protects businesses from unfair methods of competition and protects consumers from business frauds and advertising tricks.

(*e*) The __(20)__ (FRB), which regulates the banking industry and the money supply.

The last two of these agencies are largely free to carry out policies and make decisions of their own. Neither the president nor the Congress controls them directly. They are examples of independent regulatory agencies.

B. Applying What You Know

Below are a number of events that occurred in 1992. For each event, name one or more departments of the U.S. executive branch that would probably be most interested in the event.

1. *January:* A 3 percent increase in monthly Social Security benefits went into effect.
2. *February:* The U.S. Senate passed a bill on the elimination of chemicals that deplete the ozone layer in the atmosphere.
3. *February:* A study revealed that the United States had a higher percentage of its total population in prison than did any other nation.
4. *May:* A study concluded that by increasing their consumption of Vitamin C, people can lower their risk of death from heart disease.
5. *July:* Government economic figures showed that the U.S. economy grew by only 1.5 percent in the year's second quarter.
6. *July:* The United States announced that it would be joining other nations in financing the design of a nuclear fusion reactor for generating electric power.
7. *August:* About 2,400 workers participated in a strike against a General Motors plant in Lordstown, Ohio.
8. *November:* The U.S. government yielded to the demands of the Hopis (a Native American people) and agreed to give them almost 400,000 acres of public land in Arizona.

C. Projects for Research

Choose one of the following for making either an oral or a written report.

1. What were the first coins minted by the U.S. government? What were the first U.S. postal stamps, and when were they issued? Use the card catalog in the library to find books on early American coins and stamps. In class, report the results of your research. Illustrate your report with photocopies or drawings of the first American coins and stamps.
2. In your telephone book, look for listings of any U.S. department or agency that has offices in your area. Select an agency to call. Ask to interview someone in the agency about the job that he or she performs every day. Ask questions like these: What kinds of problems come to you? How do you deal with these problems?

   Take notes on what the person says. Then write a summary of the interview. To prepare yourself, read again about the work of Tom Ruiz and Lillie Dortsch-Wright.

THREE CIVIL SERVANTS. A mail carrier (above left), forester (above right), police officer. Among the three million jobs in the U.S. government, might there be an interesting one for you?

CHAPTER 18

Domestic Policy: The Bureaucracy and the Budget

OBJECTIVES

After reading this chapter, you will know

1. how today's civil service differs from the old "spoils system."
2. how to apply for a job in the civil service.
3. how a bureaucracy is organized.
4. the difference between a progressive tax and a regressive tax.
5. the policy questions involved in preparing the federal budget.
6. why it is difficult to balance the budget.
7. how to interpret an organization chart.

The title of this book is *Government for Everybody*. Are you convinced that government is indeed for everybody—including you? If you still have doubts, this chapter should eliminate them. The chapter is about money and how the money *you* earn helps to pay for government. It is also about government as an employer of human skills and talents.

In your adult career, who will be paying you for your work? It could well be the U.S. government, since it is by far the biggest single employer in the United States. In 1992, it employed over 3 million civil servants. (A civil servant is a government employee.)

You may suppose that most civil servants on the federal payroll live and work in Washington, D.C. The truth is, however, that only a fraction, 379,000, are employed in the nation's capital. The remainder, about 3 million people, report to work each morning in federal buildings located in every major city in America. Their job is to carry out the many programs and services described in the last chapter. In the future, you could be one of them.

What if you *never* work for government? Then your employer would probably be a private business. Or, if you are self-employed, you could even be writing paychecks to yourself. No matter who employs you, the U.S. government will regularly reach into your life. It will do so by subtracting taxes from every paycheck.

Suppose that you earn $300 a week at a department store. Then your paycheck would show two subtractions for federal taxes:

GROSS PAY	$300
less federal income tax	$45
less tax for Social Security	$23
NET PAY	$232

The check you receive each week would be for just $232. A good part of the money deducted from your gross pay would be used to pay the salaries of civil servants.

The money to pay for government involves *everybody* without exception. These questions then are important to everybody.

1. Who works for the federal government?
2. How is the federal bureaucracy organized?
3. What is a fair system for taxing people?
4. How much money should the government borrow?

1. WHO WORKS FOR THE FEDERAL GOVERNMENT?

In the 1870s, the requirements for becoming a civil servant were very different from today's requirements. What mattered then was the political party that a person belonged to. If you belonged to the "right" party (the one in power), you could hope to get a government job. If not, you had no chance at all (unless the "out" party became the "in" party at the next election).

TO THE VICTORS BELONG THE SPOILS. This cartoon of Andrew Jackson mocks his system for appointing people to government jobs. What was this system? Why was it associated with "plunder" and "fraud"?

End of the old spoils system. The old system for employing government workers was known as the spoils system. "To the victor belong the spoils," said a Democratic supporter of President Andrew Jackson in the 1830s. Spoils is another word for the loot seized by conquering armies. Applied to politics, the "spoils" to be seized after an election were hundreds of jobs in government. Under the spoils system begun by Jackson, a winning candidate for president would dismiss government workers from a rival party and replace them with workers from his own party.

Jackson and others thought the spoils system was fair and democratic. It was a good way, they thought, to reward party workers. Also, because of the rapid turnover of jobs, it gave many citizens an opportunity to be in government service.

However, there was one major question about the spoils system. Were party workers competent (able) to carry out their duties? Many were, but many others were not. After the Civil War, scandals connected with the civil service became a major issue. But nothing was done until a tragedy occurred. In a Washington railroad station in 1881, President James Garfield was shot by an assassin. The killer's motive was revenge for not having been appointed to a federal job after Garfield took office.

Soon after the murder—in 1883—Congress passed a law creating a new system. This system required applicants for certain federal jobs to take a test. Those who scored highest on the test would be hired. Thus, a person's competence (not his or her politics) became the chief requirement for being placed in a government job.

THE SHOOTING OF PRESIDENT GARFIELD, 1881. How did this event lead to a major reform in government?

The reform of 1883 affected only a few hundred jobs. Most jobs were still filled through party politics. Over time, however, the original civil service law was amended until, today, all low-level and middle-level jobs are covered by it. In other words, civil service jobs are filled strictly on the basis of merit.

Today, only the top jobs in government (Cabinet officers, agency directors) may be appointed by the president. The president's choices for these jobs are still guided by party politics. Republican presidents usually choose Republicans for their Cabinet, while Democratic presidents choose Democrats.

Kinds of jobs in the civil service. There is an amazing variety of jobs to be performed for the agencies of the U.S. government. To list them all would take many pages of this book. Below is a sample of just 20 jobs on the govenment payroll. The first ten are ones for which hourly wages are paid. The second ten are for jobs paying a weekly salary.

A. *Sample "blue-collar" jobs in government*
   Air-conditioning equipment mechanic
   Sandblaster
   Motor vehicle operator
   Fork-lift operator
   Laundry worker
   Store worker
   Animal caretaker
   Crane operator
   Locomotive engineer
   Gardener

B. Sample "white-collar" jobs in government
Park manager
Fingerprint identification specialist
Sports specialist
Labor relations specialist
Computer operator
Telephone operator
Soil scientist
Wildlife biologist
Dietitian
Dental hygienist

How much are civil servants paid? In any organization (whether a business or a government agency), some people are paid more than others. Usually, the more education and experience you need to perform a job, the higher will be your earnings. The U.S. government uses a complex system for determining the rate of pay of its workers. The system is like a series of 18 ladders, with each rung of each ladder representing a different salary. The first civil service ladder is known as GS-1. (GS stands for General Schedule.) You can be a GS-1 worker if you have a high school diploma and a few basic skills (typing and filing). In the early 1990s, the starting salary of federal workers at grade GS-1 was about $11,500, while the starting pay at GS-2 was around $13,000. The GS ladders from 3 to 15 are for workers and managers with higher and higher levels of training. Civil service managers at the highest rung of GS-17 and GS-18 received over $80,000.

A salary of more than $80,000 may seem high. In fact, however, it is far below salaries paid to most top managers in business. On the other hand, civil service jobs at the lower GS levels pay about as much as comparable jobs in private industry.

How to find out about job openings. Some day, you might be interested in applying for one of the 3 million jobs in the U.S. civil service. How would you find out whether a suitable job is open in your chosen field? Here are three job-hunting strategies. Which do you think is most likely to turn up a job opening?

1. Write a letter to the **Office of Personnel Management** (OPM). This is the agency that manages the civil service system from its offices in Washington, D.C.
2. Visit a **Federal Job Information Center**. Every state in the country has at least one office (called an "information center") for informing people about jobs in the civil service.
3. Visit the regional offices of different federal agencies. In Chapter 17, you read about dozens of government agencies. Every major agency has regional offices in at least ten cities around the country. A regional office closest to your home is probably the one where you would want to work.

Krandall Kraus, an experienced civil servant, is the author of a book entitled *How to Get a Federal Job*. Kraus recommends the third strategy, going directly to the federal agencies whose regional offices are in your area. Ask to see the office bulletin board where job openings are posted. If no opening is available on your first visit, don't give up. Keep calling and visiting. Persistence pays off.

Applying for a federal job. Once inside the government office building, the notice you would be looking for on the bulletin board is called a "Vacancy Announcement." Such an announcement tells you all you need to know about a job opening. It gives:

- the specific duties of the job
- civil service level (whether GS-1, GS-2, etc.)
- the kind of experience, education, and training required.

If you think a posted job is right for you, the next step is to fill out a standard civil

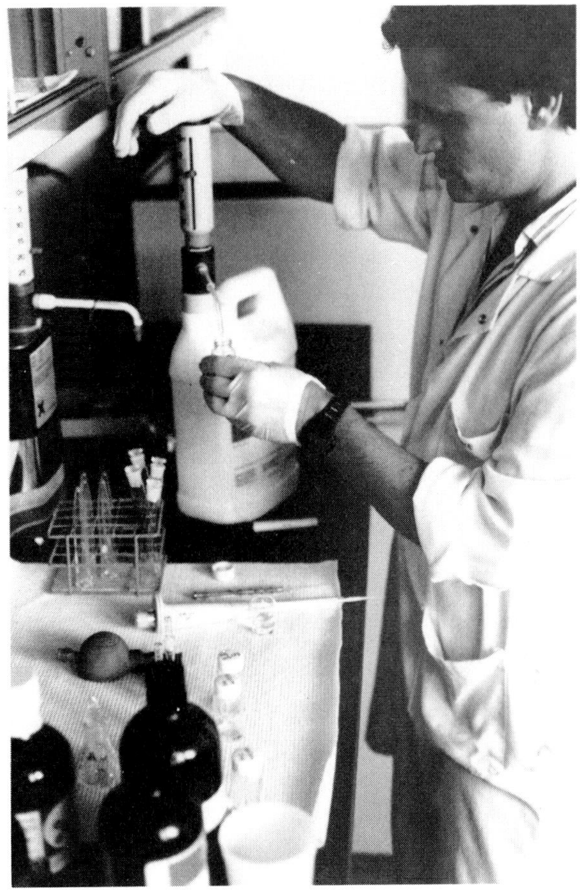

LAB TECHNICIANS IN THE FDA. If you wanted to work in a regional office of the FDA, how would you apply?

service form (known as SF-171). Take *great* care completing every section of the four-page form. Be neat. Be thorough. Be correct. Make sure that you mention everything that you have done that might qualify you for the position. You will be awarded points for each work experience and training course that relates to the job.

A committee of people in the agency will look over your application. If your qualifications fail to meet certain minimum standards, your application will be rejected. If it is acceptable, then you become one of several "eligibles" for the job. The committee members will review the applications that are still in the running. Points will be awarded according to what you say about your experience and other qualifications. If you score higher than the other "eligibles," the job will be yours. (For certain typing and clerical jobs, passing a skills test may also be required.)

That is the current system for ensuring that civil servants are competent to perform their duties. You should know that the system is weighted slightly to favor applicants who have served in the armed forces. Any veteran applying for a federal job is automatically awarded bonus points on the standard form. The head start for veterans amounts to a 10-point advantage over other applicants.

Why are veterans given this advantage? First, veterans have served their country in dangerous or possibly dangerous situations. Second, it is partly to make up for those years of military service during which their civilian careers were set back. Those who spent no time in uniform enjoyed a head start in civilian employment. Giving veterans a slight advantage in the civil service is thought to be a way of balancing things out.

REVIEW

Agree or Disagree

Tell whether you **agree** or **disagree** with each statement of opinion. Explain your answer.

1. The spoils system was more democratic than the current system.
2. Finding a job with a business firm would probably be easier than finding a job with the U.S. government.
3. Veterans should *not* be given an advantage in the competition for civil service jobs.
4. The rate of pay for employees of the U.S. government is generally too low.

2. HOW IS THE FEDERAL BUREAUCRACY ORGANIZED?

The Executive Branch of the U.S. government is one of the largest and most complex organizations in the world. It is an example of a bureaucracy. A *bureaucracy* is any large organization whose work is performed at different levels of responsibility. Workers at the "bottom" levels of the organization take orders from middle-level managers, who in turn take orders from top-level managers.

As you know, the Executive Branch consists of 14 departments. The top officials in charge of these departments are members of the president's Cabinet. In the previous chapter, you learned about their responsibilities. Now, in this section, you will see where *most* of the work of government is carried on—at the middle and lower levels of the bureaucracy. The over 3 million civil servants employed by the U.S. government work at these levels.

One department's agencies. The entire federal bureaucracy is too large to be described in one book. But we can learn about its overall structure by looking at just one department, the Department of Agriculture.

This department has about as many agencies as a classroom has desks: 29. The agencies are clustered into sets according to their function. A different "assistant secretary" is assigned the job of supervising the work of each set. For example, an assistant secretary for Natural Resources and Environment has two agencies to manage: (1) the Forest Service and (2) the Soil and Conservation Service. Seven assistant secretaries report to the department's top boss: the secretary of agriculture. They keep their chief informed about problems and progress in the agencies under their supervision.

Line and staff. Assistant secretaries are known as line officers because they direct orders and instructions to lower levels of the system. Other top-ranking officials in the department form the secretary of agriculture's staff. Staff members do *not* direct the work of agencies. Instead, they support the secretary by handling paperwork, legal problems, and other business.

SKILLS CHECK: Reading an organization chart

Offices of line and staff can be seen at a glance in an **organization chart.** In the chart on page 415, notice that only one of the department's agencies is identified by name. The others are indicated by a symbol only. Use the key to interpret the chart; then answer the questions on page 416.

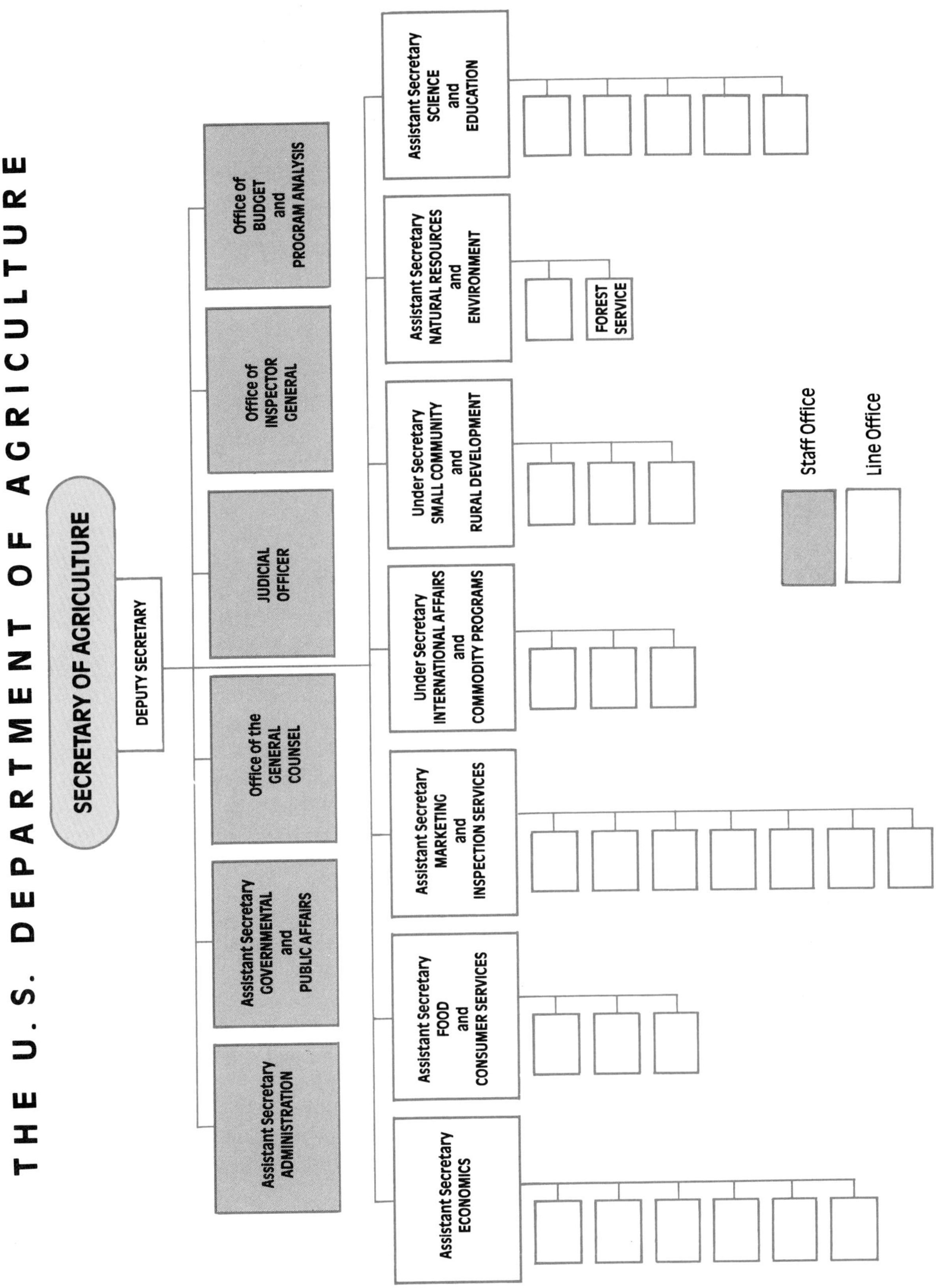
THE U.S. DEPARTMENT OF AGRICULTURE
SECRETARY OF AGRICULTURE
DEPUTY SECRETARY
Assistant Secretary ADMINISTRATION
Assistant Secretary GOVERNMENTAL and PUBLIC AFFAIRS
Office of the GENERAL COUNSEL
JUDICIAL OFFICER
Office of INSPECTOR GENERAL
Office of BUDGET and PROGRAM ANALYSIS
Assistant Secretary ECONOMICS
Assistant Secretary FOOD and CONSUMER SERVICES
Assistant Secretary MARKETING and INSPECTION SERVICES
Under Secretary INTERNATIONAL AFFAIRS and COMMODITY PROGRAMS
Under Secretary SMALL COMMUNITY and RURAL DEVELOPMENT
Assistant Secretary NATURAL RESOURCES and ENVIRONMENT
FOREST SERVICE
Assistant Secretary SCIENCE and EDUCATION
Staff Office
Line Office

1. Give the titles of three staff officers in the Department of Agriculture.
2. How many agencies are supervised by each of the following? (*a*) assistant secretary for Economics. (*b*) assistant secretary for Science and Education.
3. Which line officer is responsible for supervising the largest number of agencies?
4. One of the agencies in the department is called the Foreign Agricultural Service. Which line officer would you suppose directs the work of this agency? Why?
5. How did the key help you to interpret the organization chart?

CAROL DRESCHER DETERMINING THE AGE OF A MAPLE TREE IN PENNSYLVANIA.

CASE STUDY: Working for the Forest Service

The largest agency in the Department of Agriculture is the Forest Service. The 156 national forests and 19 grasslands managed by this agency are immensely important to vacationers, birdwatchers, loggers, lumber companies, cattle and sheep ranchers, and many others. Conserving forest resources is vital to our nation's economy as well as its environment.

The Forest Service is a bureaucracy in itself. How is it managed? What do its foresters and other employees do from day to day? To find out, four people in the Forest Service were interviewed: a forester (Carol Drescher), a public affairs officer (Ray Steiger), a scientist (Marilyn Buford), and a top manager (Jerry Sesko). Here are summaries of what they said about their careers in the Forest Service.

CAROL DRESCHER. She grew up amid the thickly forested hills of West Virginia. At West Virginia University, she studied the science of forestry, graduating in 1981. One summer, while still in college, she worked for the Forest Service. The experience helped to win her full-time employment with the agency.

The Forest Service sent her to the White Mountains of New Hampshire, where she joined other foresters to help manage the cutting and sale of timber. Almost daily, she would hike mountain trails in search of timber that needed to be cut. A few acres of the forest, for example, might show signs of disease or overcrowding. In that case, the area would be marked for cutting and careful replanting. Drescher and a crew of specialists would also evaluate *how* to do the cutting so that every user of the forest, including wildlife, would benefit. Trees whose berries were eaten by bear would be saved so as not to destroy the bear's habitat. Mountain slopes visible to hikers would never be cut in ways that would ruin the view.

In 1988, Drescher left the White Mountains to work as a forester at Grey Towers, a 100-acre wooded area in eastern Pennsylvania. She hopes to turn the area into a center for teaching visitors about the proper techniques for cutting trees and conserving forests.

RAY STEIGER. After 30 years in the Forest Service, this civil servant is approaching the end of his career. His work has

RAY STEIGER IN HIS OFFICE IN OREGON.

MARILYN BUFORD MEASURING A LOBLOLLY PINE IN SOUTH CAROLINA.

taken him to many parts of the country—the great forests of Washington State, the remote central wilderness of Alaska, the rolling woodlands of Pennsylvania.

Steiger thinks his agency in the federal bureaucracy is special. People who work for it naturally share an enthusiasm for trees, animals, and the outdoor life. In addition, according to Steiger, employees in the Forest Service have a sense of belonging to a kind of "family." Foresters keep in touch with each other as they travel from one assignment to the next. Over the years, bonds of friendship develop that are never broken.

Currently, Steiger works as a public affairs officer in an office in Portland, Oregon. Citizens seeking information about the Forest Service communicate with his office. Often he is still called to national forests on special assignments to share his expert knowledge with others.

MARILYN BUFORD. Computers are almost as important as trees in the daily work of this research scientist. Dr. Buford works with three other scientists in the Forestry Sciences Laboratory in Charleston, South Carolina. She says of her job: "I feel happy to get up and come to work every day. The work can be tiring at times, but exciting."

For many years, Dr. Buford has studied the southern loblolly pine, which grows in great abundance in the national forests of the Southeast. She and her assistants collect massive amounts of data about everything affecting the growth of the loblolly pine. Their goal is to create a computer model of the pine's habits under different conditions. When completed, Dr. Buford's computer program will respond to changing soil and weather conditions exactly as a real pine forest would respond.

Who stands to benefit from this computer study? Dr. Buford says that her project, if successful, will give foresters a better means of predicting forest growth—and therefore a better means of managing it.

JERRY SESCO. Dr. Buford's study is one of about 2,500 research studies conducted by the Forest Service in an average year. How many projects will continue for another year depends upon whether Congress will vote to spend more money for them. The person most aware of this fact occupies an important office in Washington, D.C. This deputy chief for research is Dr. Jerry Sesco. Across the hall from Dr. Sesco's office is the agency's top leader: the chief of the Forest Service, Dale Robertson.

Dr. Sesco wants to persuade both his chief and Congress that forest research needs and deserves more funding to solve impor-

JERRY SESCO IN THE FORESTRY SERVICE'S OFFICE IN WASHINGTON, D.C. How do decisions made in Washington affect the work of Carol Drescher, Ray Steiger, and Marilyn Buford?

tant problems. He does not think the current budget allows enough money to meet needs. But Dr. Sesco is an economist. He understands that there is really *never* enough money to do everything. So, as deputy chief, he must decide which projects should be supported with the most money and which should be cut back or eliminated.

Why, he wonders, have gypsy moths and other leaf-eating and tree-destroying insects been able to survive scientists' best efforts to control them? The chief agrees with his deputy chief that this problem should be given special emphasis. The word goes out from Dr. Sesco's office to the directors of research stations across the country: work harder on the insect and disease problems.

Bureaucratic "red tape." You have read about the work of just four civil servants in an agency that employs 33,000 people. These four expressed positive feelings about their jobs in the bureaucracy.

CARTOON CORNER

Outside the bureaucracy, however, people's views of it tend to be less positive. Businesses and citizens who deal with government agencies sometimes complain about "getting tangled up in a lot of bureaucratic red tape." The term "red tape" goes back to the 1700s when English officials used a red tape to bind up government papers. Today, the term refers to the many annoying delays that can occur in the operations of a government agency. Often, a decision by a lower-ranking official must be approved by several higher-ranking officials. Thus, it may take time for a simple matter to be passed up, down, and around the bureaucracy until action is finally taken.

A certain amount of red tape seems to be a fact of life in all large organizations (businesses as well as government agencies). Can at least some of it be reduced by simplifying an agency's paperwork and streamlining its management? Several presidents have tried to reform and simplify the federal bureaucracy—but with little success. Cutting red tape is a sticky matter.

What makes it sticky is the resistance of civil servants to having their jobs eliminated. Managers in a bureaucracy work hard to prevent their agencies from being taken apart or reorganized. For example, in 1979, President Carter thought it would make sense—and cut red tape—to place the Forest Service in the Department of the Interior. But the Department of Agriculture and the Forest Service resisted the proposed change with all their might. So the Forest Service remained where it was.

REVIEW

A. Facts and Opinions

Tell whether you think each statement is a **fact** or an **opinion.** If it is an opinion, say whether or not you agree with it.

1. Carol Drescher has an interesting job.
2. The chief of the Forestry Service has a higher-level job than anyone else in that agency.
3. The Forest Service is an example of a bureaucracy.
4. Dr. Buford's research project is worthy of financial support from Congress.
5. Foresters attempt to manage the cutting of timber so that it does not destroy the habitat of animals.
6. The public receives greater benefits from a forester's work than from a researcher's work.
7. How to control and eliminate leaf-eating pests is the Forest Service's most important goal.
8. There is no way that red tape can be reduced in the operations of a large government agency.

B. Making Inferences

Another agency in the Department of Agriculture is the **Agricultural Research Service** (ARS). Its main function is to serve farmers by carrying out research for the protection of plants and animals. What can you infer about the ARS from the information presented in this section? Tell whether you think each statement below is **probably true** or **probably not true.** Explain your answers.

1. The ARS is organized into bureaucratic levels headed by one top manager.
2. The ARS does not have as many employees as the Forest Service.
3. The animals studied by the ARS are bears, deer, and other wildlife.
4. Information about the ARS may be obtained from the public affairs office managed by Ray Steiger.
5. The ARS and the Forest Service are directed by the same assistant secretary.

C. Cartoon Corner

The following questions refer to the cartoon on page 418.

1. What symbols are used in the cartoon, and what does each stand for?
2. According to the cartoon, what is wrong with the federal bureaucracy?
3. What is *your* answer to the cartoon's question: "Can this machine be made more efficient?"

3. WHAT IS A FAIR SYSTEM FOR TAXING PEOPLE?

You know that the various agencies of the U.S. government employ more than 3 million civil servants. All of them must be paid regular wages and salaries. It is a huge sum, amounting to many *billions of dollars a month.* Additional billions must be spent on military weapons, government office buildings, dams, highways, welfare payments, farm subsidies, and so on.

The federal budget. To put it mildly, paying for government services costs a lot of money. How much *should* we pay for these services? The president and Congress share responsibility for answering the two main questions about government money:

1. The question of government expenditures. How many billions of dollars need to be spent for different purposes?

2. The question of government income (or receipts). Where is all the money going to come from?

Every year these questions are answered in a detailed, written plan outlining the spending and collecting of money. The plan is called a budget. Every institution uses a budget of some kind to manage its expenses. Business firms draw up budgets. So do schools, churches, clubs, and families. But by far the largest budget is the one for the U.S. government. By 1993, the list of expenditures in its budget came to about *1.5 trillion dollars!*

First, let's look at the expenditures side of the budget and then the income (taxes) side of it.

Policy choices in dollars and cents. Research in the Forest Service must be supported with money. So must every other program and activity of government. In next year's budget, should the Forest Service spend more money or less than the other agencies in the Department of Agriculture? In the Defense Department, should budget dollars be divided evenly among the Army, Navy, and Air Force? Or should one service receive more than the others? The same kind of question may be asked about every agency and department. How the president answers the budget question tells us what he/she believes to be most important, somewhat important, and least important.

Look at the chart on page 421. Compare the ideas of two presidents on the amounts that they think should be budgeted for three of the Cabinet departments.

From these numbers alone, we know something about the policies of the two presidents. For President A, building U.S. defenses is very important. President B, on the other hand, would spend a lot more than President A on domestic programs in agriculture and transportation.

In short, dollars in the budget are a clear sign of policies.

The president and the budget. Preparing the federal budget is a long and complicated process. First, a book-length proposal is put together in the White House by some of the president's top aides. The person chiefly responsible for creating this proposal is the director of the **Office of Management and Budget** (OMB).

Imagine that *you* have the job of putting together a budget as OMB's director. Do you think you would have the strength to

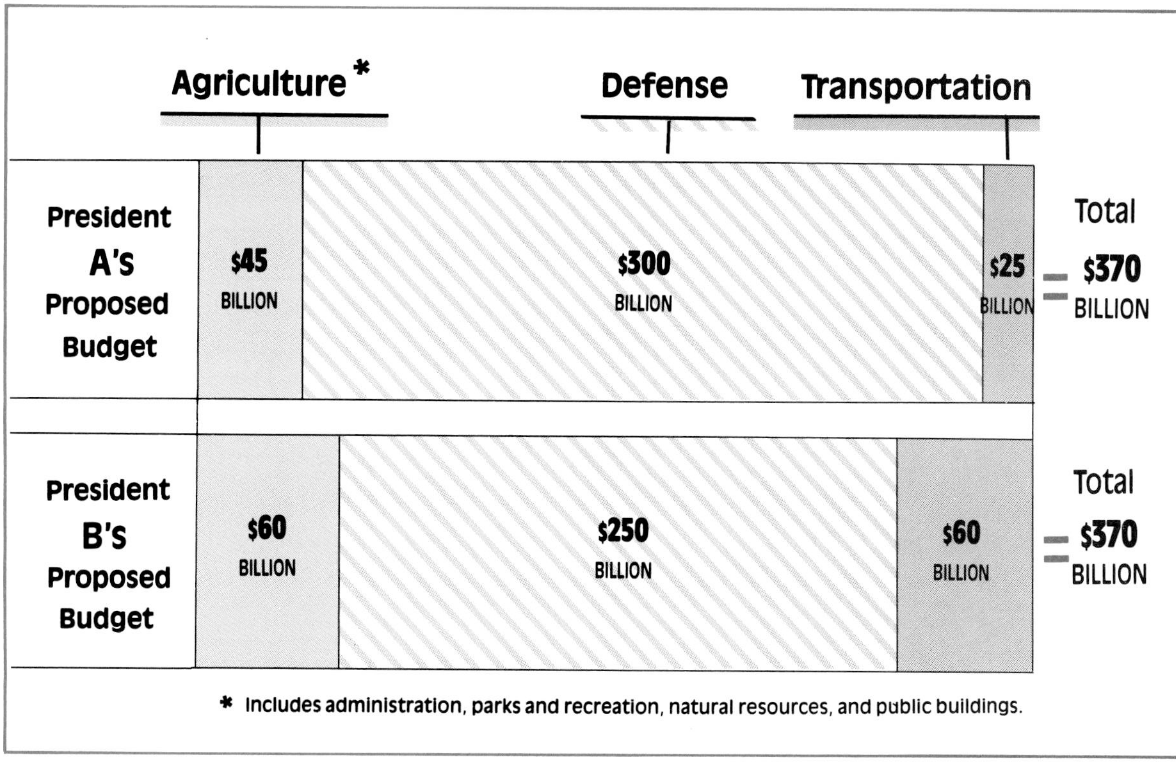

face the daily pressures? The demands made upon you would come from hundreds of directions at once. First, the president (your boss) wants you to prepare a budget proposal that is at least 5 percent less than the budget for the previous year. That may not seem like much. In fact, it involves cutting out billions of dollars.

Government agencies hate to think that any money at all might be cut from their expected share of the budget. The sum that they spent last year is the sum that they expect to spend this year—if not a little more. There are hundreds of federal agencies. Each is certain that its functions are vital and should not be cut back. What are you to do as the OMB's director? You *must* find ways to cut down the U.S. government's spending by 5 percent. But you can be sure that every agency will fight your attempt to trim even a little bit from last year's total.

At least you have a powerful ally at the White House. In messages to the agency heads, you can say that the president has *ordered* you to prepare a reduced budget. The agency heads must then cooperate. They submit to your office lengthy lists of future expenses and indicate certain items that might be cut. Even so, they urge you not to cut anything since their operations are "absolutely vital."

You try to shrug off the pressures. You understand that, in politics, you cannot expect to please everybody. Aided by computer printouts, you work on the budget day and night for months. The president regularly sits down with you to review your progress. Together you add millions of dollars to one department's total allowance, while subtracting millions from another department's.

Finally, in January, the deadline arrives for printing the full budget proposal. It comes to about a thousand pages. The book (budget proposal) begins with the president's message to Congress explaining what has been done.

OUT OF CONTROL? (1) What is the cartoonist's point of view toward government spending? (2) What evidence might he use to support that point of view? (3) Do you agree or disagree with the cartoon's point? Why?

Congress and the budget. At this point, Congress takes over the process of shaping the budget to its liking. Not a single dollar of federal money can be spent unless some act of Congress directs that it be spent for a certain purpose. That means that bills concerning the *appropriation* (spending) of money must now be introduced, debated, and passed in the House and the Senate. The thick book containing the president's spending plan is only the starting point for the lawmakers' work. They can reject parts of the plan and change other parts—in fact, do whatever they please.

Because the budget is both very complicated and very important, it takes Congress many months to decide what to do about it. The committees that work on it daily are the Senate Budget Committee and the House Budget Committee. They are assisted by financial experts who advise them on the likely effects of every proposed addition and subtraction. These experts work for the **Congressional Budget Office** (CBO). They do for Congress what the OMB does for the president—giving expert help in the budget-making process.

Members of Congress feel the pressure to spend money even more strongly than the OMB director. Pressure groups watch their every move. Labor unions, for example, oppose any budget cuts that would weaken the Department of Labor. Conservation groups fight any move to take money away from their favorite programs in the Department of the Interior. Veterans groups would protest strongly if any bill proposed cutting back their benefits. Farmers groups insist that certain programs in the Department of Agriculture receive *more* funds, not less.

And so it goes. Every item in the federal budget benefits one group or another. Therefore, to cut any item would cause unhappiness to someone. As you know, no congressperson wants to displease people.

September 30 is the absolute deadline for making a decision about the budget. It is the last day of the U.S. government's fiscal year. (Fiscal is a term accountants and bookkeepers use to refer to the spending of money.) The old budget—the one voted upon the previous year—is good for only one fiscal year. After the last day of that year (September 30), *no more money may be spent by any agency until a new budget is approved.* Usually, Congress is working feverishly on the budget through the last week of September. Finally, at the last minute, a budget bill of some kind is passed and sent to the White House for the president's signature.

October 1st begins the new fiscal year. If Congress does its work (as it always does, sooner or later), every federal agency will have sums of money to spend under the new budget.

There is one more detail to add about budget-making in Congress. Let us say that the FBI wants to spend $10 million on the training of its agents. One act of Congress must authorize the FBI to spend money for training. A second act must appropriate (set aside) a specific sum of money ($10 million in this case) for a specific use (training). The same rule applies to all money spent for any purpose by the U.S. government. First, the money must be authorized; then, it must be appropriated.

Components of the budget. Suppose you were to do nothing for the rest of your life but count: "1, 2, 3, 4," and so on. You would not come close to reaching the figure of $1,475,439,000,000 appropriated by Congress for the 1992 budget. (To round it off, let's call the sum $1.5 trillion.)

Where does all the money go? In other words, for what purposes is the money appropriated by Congress and then spent by the three branches of government? Think of the budget as if it were a huge money pie. One piece of that "pie" must be spent for military needs: defense. The rest of it is for domestic or civilian needs: nondefense.

People have different opinions on how big each of these two pieces should be. In past years, the defense piece was more than half the budget pie. Currently, it is only about one-quarter of the pie.

✔✔ SKILLS CHECK: Interpreting pie graphs

The **pie graphs** (or circle graphs) on page 424 show how federal budgets have changed between 1970 and 1992.

Notice that the four graphs represent total outlays (or expenditures) for four different years. Each is divided into defense and nondefense sections. The percentages indicate the exact proportion of the budget that was given to each purpose: defense or nondefense.

1. Why do you think the 1992 pie is drawn so much larger than the 1970 pie?
2. Would you conclude that the *total amount* spent for defense in 1992 was larger or smaller than the total amount spent for defense in 1980? Why?
3. Explain this statement: Viewed in one way, the defense budget has increased since 1970. But viewed in another way, it has decreased.
4. What are constant dollars? How does the use of constant dollars in the graphs help you read and interpret them?

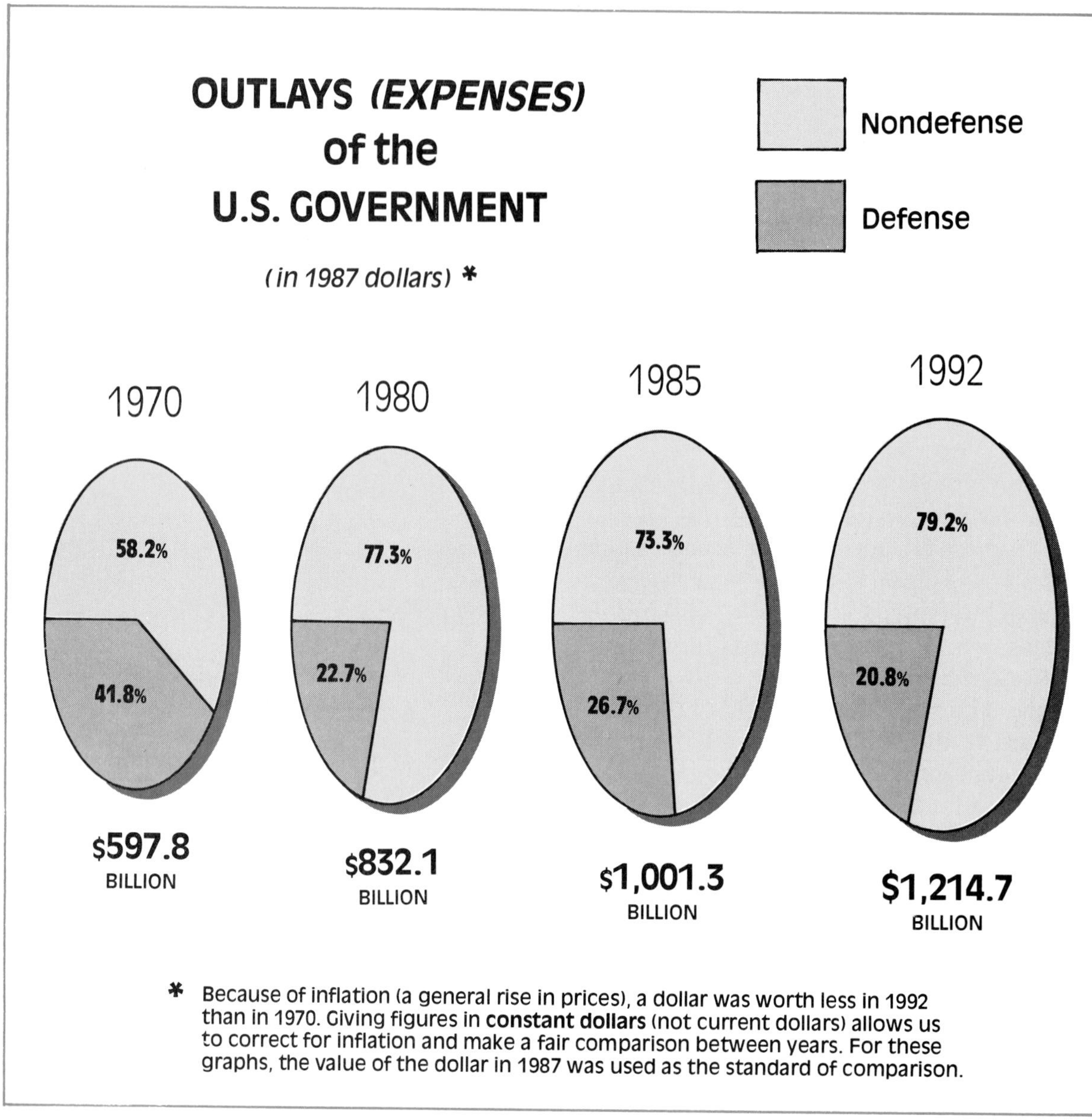
OUTLAYS (EXPENSES)
of the
U.S. GOVERNMENT
(in 1987 dollars) *
Nondefense
Defense
1970
58.2%
41.8%
$597.8
BILLION
1980
77.3%
22.7%
$832.1
BILLION
1985
73.3%
26.7%
$1,001.3
BILLION
1992
79.2%
20.8%
$1,214.7
BILLION
* Because of inflation (a general rise in prices), a dollar was worth less in 1992 than in 1970. Giving figures in constant dollars (not current dollars) allows us to correct for inflation and make a fair comparison between years. For these graphs, the value of the dollar in 1987 was used as the standard of comparison.

The domestic side of the budget. Let us look now at just the domestic (nondefense) part of the federal budget. In Chapter 17, you read about Cabinet departments and several independent agencies that carry out domestic programs. Which one of them do you think spends more billions than any other? (See the chart on page 425.)

The answer is: the Department of Health and Human Services. Recall that the Social Security Administration is included in this department. During the 1980s, payments for Social Security took more than one-fourth of each year's total budget. The government can do very little to trim back its Social Security expenses. After all, it owes the money to older Americans, since they had contributed taxes into the Social Security fund during their working years.

Another big slice of the budget (21.1 percent in 1992) goes for paying interest on borrowed money. As you will learn in the next section, the government has borrowed heavily from the American people and foreign investors. Like any debtor, it must pay interest (charges for the use of money) on past loans.

After subtracting for interest, Social Security, and defense, only a few hundred billion dollars remain to pay for everything else the government does. Most Cabinet departments must settle for extremely tiny slices of the budget pie. In 1992, for example, the Department of the Interior had to make do with a mere sliver—about half of 1 percent. As you can see from the list, the departments are not at all equal in terms of the money they spend.

Where the money comes from. Let us say that Congress one year votes to appropriate exactly 1.5 trillion dollars. At the same time, Congress must also find ways to collect 1.5 trillion dollars from the American people. If it succeeds, we say the budget is balanced because:

$1,500,000,000,000	=	$1,500,000,000,000
in government *income*		in government *expenses*

As you might imagine, collecting an income of 1.5 trillion dollars is not an easy task. Government has three ways of raising the money:

a. It can collect taxes from businesses and individuals.
b. It can charge fees for its services. (For example: users of the mails pay the postage, and inventors pay fees for obtaining government patents.)
c. It can borrow the money. (But borrowing usually means that the government is short of cash and cannot balance its budget.)

The first method—taxation—is the one the government counts upon to pay more

FEDERAL BUDGET: BILLIONS OF DOLLARS SPENT, 1992

Health and Human Services	$539.4
Defense	$314.9
Treasury *(includes interest payments)*	$293.4
Agriculture	$56.4
Labor	$47.2
Veterans Affairs	$33.7
Transportation	$32.6
Education	$26.0
Housing and Urban Development	$24.5
Energy	$15.4
Justice	$9.8
Interior	$6.6
State	$5.0
Commerce	$2.6

than 75 percent of its bills. We now come to the trillion-dollar question: What is a "fair tax"? To answer it, we need to know the difference between two kinds of taxes: the *regressive* kind and the *progressive* kind.

Taxes with a regressive effect. These are taxes that take a larger bite from a poor person's income than from a rich person's income. One example is the tax that the federal government collects on gallons of gasoline. Imagine you're at your neighborhood gas station. At the pump, a motorist named Max has an income of $8,000. The motorist right behind him—Martha—has an income of $80,000. After filling their tanks, both pay the 5 percent federal tax on a $20 purchase of gasoline. Five percent of $20 is one dollar. Max will have a harder time than Martha paying the dollar tax because it takes proportionately more out of his income.

A tax on the sale or manufacture of something is known as an *excise tax.* In addition to its tax on gasoline, the U.S. government collects other excise taxes on such things as liquors, tobacco products (cigars, cigarettes), automobiles, and cosmetics. They too are regressive.

Another tax of a regressive type is the tariff. It can be collected on any product imported from a foreign country. Congress writes the tariff laws that determine which goods shall be subject to a tariff and which may be brought in "free." The laws also fix the percentage rate that American merchants must pay for importing Irish sweaters, Canadian tires, Japanese cars, and so forth.

Tariffs have the effect of increasing the prices that consumers pay for store items. That is because the merchants who pay the taxes to the government push up their prices to include the added expense. Think again about Max (income of $8,000) and Martha (income of $80,000). Which do you think would have a harder time paying an added $200 in taxes for some imported motorcycle? Why?

Deducted weekly from Max's and Martha's paychecks is a third type of regressive tax. It is the Social Security tax that you read about in Chapter 17. The weekly deduction from Max's pay is $11.78. Martha

CARS READY FOR SHIPMENT. If Congress increased the tariff on imports to the United States, what effect would it have on American consumers?

pays about nine times as much, $102.47 a week, because her total pay is so much higher. Even so, proportional to total income, Martha has an easier time than Max paying the Social Security tax. Why? It is because her income is ten times Max's, while her Social Security tax is nine times his.

Taxes with a progressive effect. Progressive taxes are those that bite more deeply into higher incomes than lower ones. In other words, they have just the opposite effect of a regressive tax.

The best example of a progressive tax is the personal income tax. Again, let's look at the taxes paid by Max and Martha. Deducted from their paychecks is the withholding tax you read about in Chapter 7, page 156. The income tax withheld from Martha's check is about 17 times the income tax withheld from Max's check. In other words, this tax falls more heavily on her (the high-income person) than on him.

Before the April 15 deadline this year, Max and Martha filed their separate tax returns. The table below shows how their total income taxes compared. Martha's total tax for last year was about 60 times Max's tax.

Other progressive taxes are the estate tax and gift tax. The estate (or inheritance) tax is collected when a person dies. Before the person's property (house, car, savings, etc.) can be turned over to the children or other heirs, the government may tax a percentage of the money value of the property. In the past, wealthy people tried to avoid estate taxes by giving property to their children *before* their death. Today, however, the government may collect a gift tax on any transfer of property worth more than $10,000. Such taxes are progressive because they take much more out of a wealthy person's estate than from a smaller estate.

Corporation income taxes. Individuals are not the only ones who must pay income taxes to the federal government. Business corporations must also pay taxes on their yearly earnings. A *corporation* is an organization that has a legal existence—as if it were a person. It is "born" when a state charter (legal document) brings it into existence. It "dies" only when its owners apply to the state to dissolve (end) the corporation.

Like individuals, corporations must report their yearly income to the IRS. They may also deduct a number of expenses. The difference between income (sales) and deductions (business expenses) is the taxable income of a corporation. The corporate tax rate is progressive. The higher a company's profits, the higher will be its tax rate.

		INCOME	TAXABLE INCOME *(after exemptions)*	TAX RATE	TOTAL TAX
Max		**$8,000**	*$2,100*	15%	**$317**
Martha		**$80,000**	*$74,100*	31%	**$18,633**

Receipts: the grand total. At the end of its fiscal year, the government adds up all the taxes and fees that it has collected. Only then can it know whether or not its income is enough to pay all its expenses for the year.

It counts on the personal income tax to bring in a large share of the total (44.8 percent in 1994). The Social Security tax brings in almost as much (37.2 percent in 1994). All the other taxes combined (excise, customs, estate, corporation) represent a smaller amount—just 18.0 percent in 1994.

Do the percentages from all tax sources add up to 100 percent of expenditures? If so, then the federal budget is balanced. In fact, however, the combined taxes usually fall far short of expenses. The difference must then be made up with billions of dollars of borrowed money.

What are the consequences of borrowing? Let's leave that question for the next section.

What's a fair tax? Consider again the trillion-dollar question: What is a fair tax? Review six types of federal taxes: (*a*) personal income taxes, (*b*) corporation income taxes, (*c*) Social Security taxes, (*d*) customs taxes or tariffs, (*e*) estate taxes, (*f*) excise taxes. Suppose that the U.S. government decided to increase just *one* of these taxes. Considering fairness alone, which tax do you think should be increased? Why?

REVIEW

A. Applying What You Know

Tell whether each is an example of a **regressive tax** or a **progressive tax**. Give reasons for your answers.

1. collecting a duty of 15 percent on imported sofas and chairs
2. collecting an 8 percent tax on pipe tobacco
3. taxing a baseball player's million-dollar salary at a much higher rate than a bank teller's $20,000 salary
4. taxing the earnings of a small corporation at a lower rate than the billion-dollar earnings of a major corporation
5. collecting a large tax from a wealthy person's estate after that person's death

B. Agree or Disagree

Tell whether you **agree** or **disagree** with each statement, and explain.

1. A family living in poverty should not have to pay any income tax at all.
2. A progressive tax is fair, while a regressive tax is not fair.
3. It is unfair to make anyone pay 33 percent (one-third) of his or her income in taxes.
4. A trillion dollars a year is too much to spend for government services.
5. We should return to the days when about half of the budget went for defense.

C. Building Your Political Vocabulary

Define each term. Then explain how the term relates to the process of preparing the federal budget.

1. fiscal year
2. appropriations
3. Office of Management and Budget
4. interest
5. outlays and receipts

4. HOW MUCH MONEY SHOULD THE GOVERNMENT BORROW?

Year after year, the federal government has spent hundreds of billions of dollars more than it has raised in taxes. Year after year, it has made up the difference by borrowing the money. From whom does the government borrow? It could be from you or members of your family.

Government bonds. The government borrows the money it needs by selling bonds to the American public and even to foreign investors. A *bond* is a piece of paper issued by the government promising to repay the person who buys it. In other words, if you bought one of its bonds, you would actually be lending money to the government. The amount that the bond will be worth at the end of the loan period is printed on the face of the bond and is called the bond's face value. It could be for as little as $50 or as much as $10,000. The face value includes the selling price plus the interest that it will earn.

The government promises to pay back the face value of the bond after a certain period of time. At the end of that time, the bond is said to mature. The government sells several different types of paper for borrowing. Some mature (fall due) in a short period of only 30 days. Others are for a longer period—five, ten, even twenty years.

The government guarantees that holders of bonds will be repaid when their bonds reach maturity. Corporations too make promises like this when selling their corporate bonds. But the federal government is thought to be more reliable than anyone in paying its debts. Thus, buying government "saving bonds," as they are called, is a solid and practically risk-free investment.

Among the most commonly bought bonds are the "double E" (EE) bonds. When they come to maturity in 11 years, they pay exactly twice their selling price.

The national debt. The U.S. government is in debt to the millions of people who buy its bonds. Its debt is often referred to as the *national debt*. The size of the debt keeps getting bigger. In 1940, it was $50 billion. In 1950, after heavy borrowing to fight World War II, the debt climbed to more than $250 billion.

SKILLS CHECK: Interpreting a bar graph

The **bar graph** on page 430 shows how the national debt continued to grow in the period after World War II.

A U.S. SAVINGS BOND. Purchased in 1989 for $25, this bond will pay the owner $50 when it reaches maturity in 2001. Why does this bond represent one small part of the national debt?

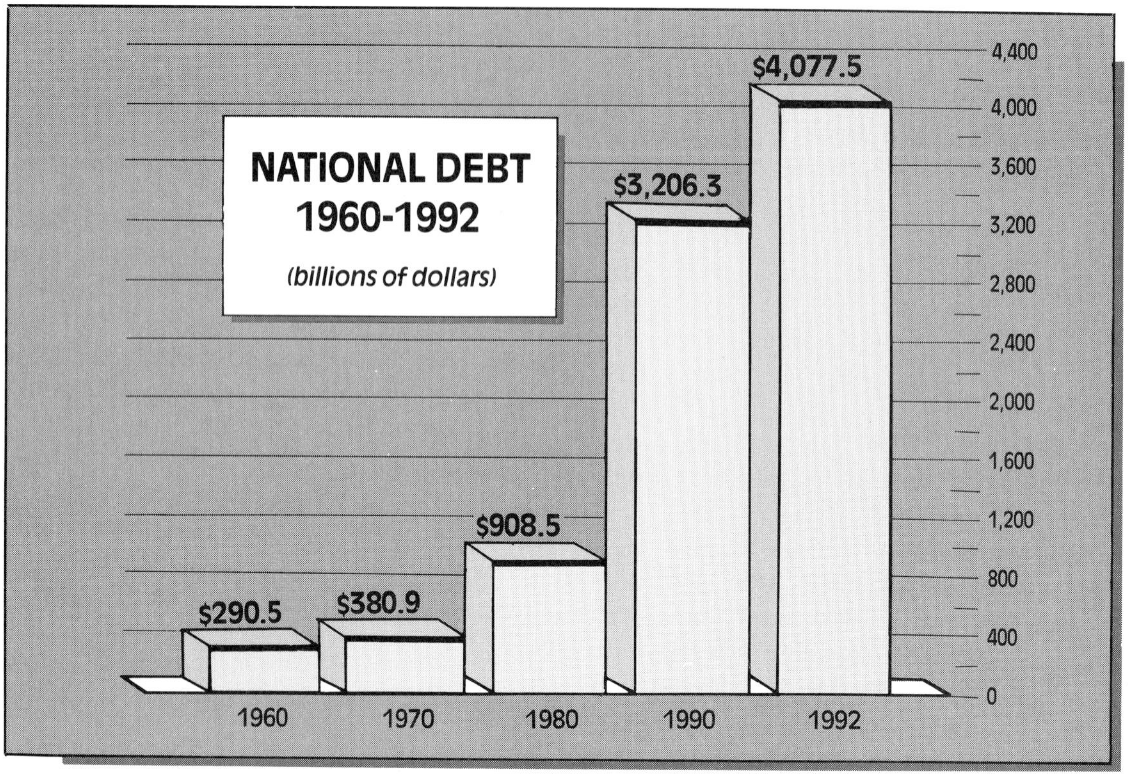

1. What was the size of the national debt in 1960? In 1980? In 1992?
2. In the period shown in the graph, did the national debt increase (*a*) almost three times, (*b*) about five times, or (*c*) more than ten times?
3. Between what years did the national debt increase the most?

In recent years, the national debt has become gigantic. Some look at it fearfully as if it were some all-devouring monster threatening our way of life. Others say: "Don't worry. It's not a problem, since we (the government) owe the debt to ourselves (the people)." Who is right?

Budget deficits. Before we can answer that question, we should know *why* the national debt keeps growing. The simple explanation is that government has great difficulty balancing its budget. Members of Congress hate to raise taxes, which are unpopular with voters. They much prefer spending money for popular government services and programs. Thus, the government finds that it must borrow more—and thus add to its total debt—because its total expenses exceed its total tax income. The budget gap between expenses and tax receipts is called the *deficit*.

✔✔ SKILLS CHECK: Interpreting a line graph

The graph on page 431 helps us to picture the deficit. The line graph consists of two heavy lines, both moving upward from 1980 to 1992. One line is for total outlays in the federal budget while the other is for total receipts. The gap between the lines represents the yearly deficit (the amount that must be made up through borrowing).

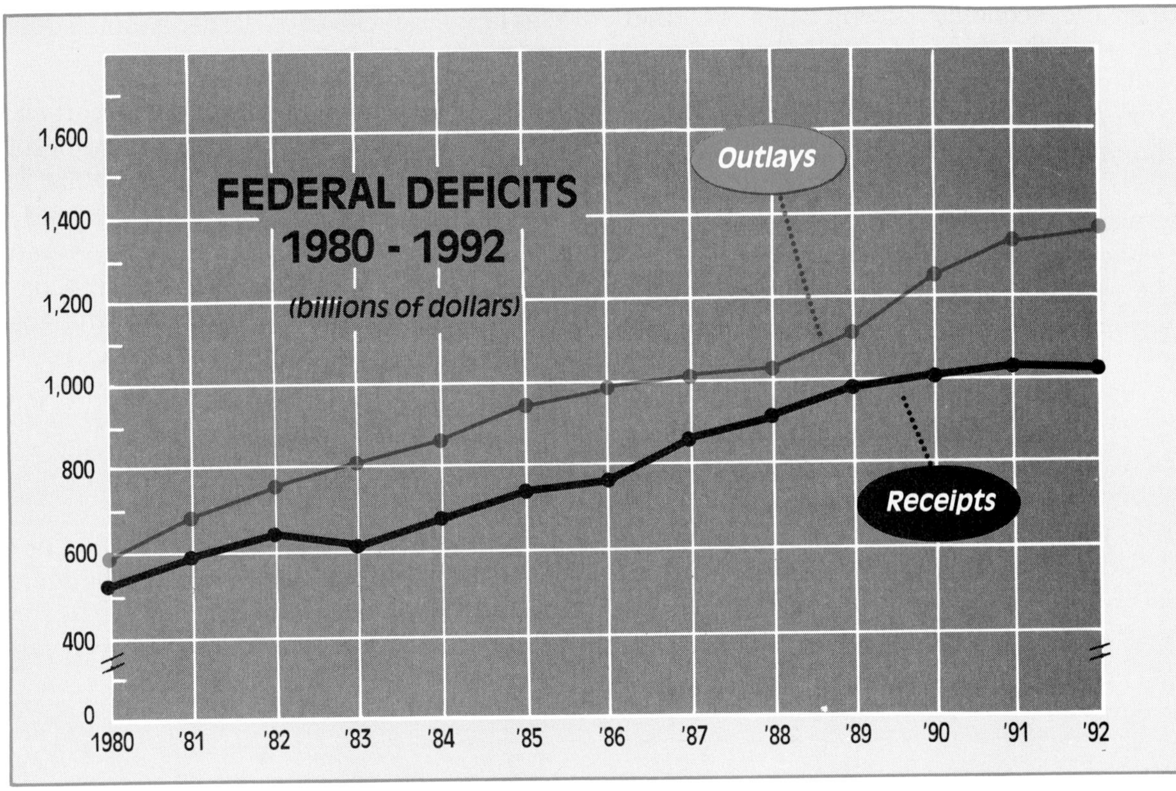

1. During what year was the deficit the smallest?
2. Approximately how large was the deficit in 1992?
3. How does the deficit of 1985 compare with the deficit of 1992? Is the deficit of 1992 (*a*) about the same, (*b*) about twice as great, or (*c*) about three times as great?

How deficits may affect the economy. A large deficit is neither good nor bad in itself. It must be judged in terms of the effect it has on the total economy. Does a federal deficit help the economy grow, or does it do just the opposite?

Economists make their living trying to answer such questions. But they do not agree themselves. Some are sure a deficit is good for the economy, while others think it is harmful. In a nutshell, these are their arguments:

1. "Good for the economy." Those who approve of deficits think back to the days of the Great Depression in the 1930s. A British economist named John Maynard Keynes proposed using deficits to cure a nation's economic troubles. By spending borrowed money, Keynes said, the government would be taking the lead in placing orders for goods and services. Businesses would then respond to government orders by expanding their operations. As they expanded, they would need to hire more workers. As workers were hired, the unemployment problem would be solved. President Franklin Roosevelt put Keynes's theory into practice, and it seemed to work. Business did get better as government spending (and deficits) increased.

Economists today who side with Keynes are known as Keynesians. They fear that the economy would go into a bad slump if the government suddenly succeeded in balancing its budget.

2. "Bad for the economy." Opposing the Keynesians are those who think deficits drag the economy down. They say that government produces a lot of paperwork rather than producing "real" goods (cars, computers, etc.). Therefore, a government should cut back its role in the economy and allow business greater freedom to produce more goods.

They say that two things should be done at once. (*a*) Reduce the tax rates people and corporations must pay. (*b*) Reduce government spending for domestic programs.

Economists who take this position are known as supply-siders because they stress increasing the total supply of goods. The politicians most likely to accept the supply-side theory are Republicans. Republican President Ronald Reagan tried to put the theory into practice during his two terms in office (1981–1989). But the final result was larger deficits and a larger national debt than ever.

Making fiscal policy. One thing is certain. The federal budget does have a profound effect on the nation's economy. What is uncertain is whether the effect of yearly deficits is for better or for worse. As you know, the president and members of Congress share responsibility for shaping the budget each year. Should they make taxes higher or lower? Should the government borrow more money this year or less? How they answer these questions is known as *fiscal policy*.

Can the federal budget be balanced? Conservative politicians say that future budgets *must* be balanced. If they are not, then the 300-billion-dollar deficit "monster" will only

CARTOON CORNER

ON THE ONE HAND, IT MAY BE GOOD FOR GROWTH.
DEFICITS
ON THE OTHER HAND, IT COULD RUIN US.
DEFICITS

In this cartoon, deficits are compared to a heavy rain drenching a farmer's fields. Whose economic point of view do you think is correct: that of the man or the woman?

get bigger and more dangerous. Laws must be passed, they say, to *force* the government to balance its budget.

One such law has already been enacted. In 1985, Congress passed and President Reagan signed the Budget Control Act—also known as the Gramm-Rudman Act after its two sponsors. This law requires that the budget deficit be reduced in stages until, in the 1990s, there would be no deficit at all.

Conservative politicians generally approve this measure as a first step in bringing the national debt under control. But they also would like to see an amendment added to the Constitution. This balanced-budget amendment would prohibit the U.S. government from spending more money than it collects in taxes.

Suppose the amendment is adopted. Even then, will the president and Congress be able to balance the budget? After all, about two-fifths of the budget goes for national defense and interest on the national debt. Defense needs and interest payments must be met regardless of changing economic conditions such as inflation or recession. These fixed payments leave little room for the executive and legislative branches to respond to these changing conditions. Can anyone guarantee that current tax receipts will be enough to pay not only for defense but also for other basic needs and services such as Social Security benefits? Critics of the balanced-budget amendment say no and that the amendment would put government in a straitjacket.

Which do you think is worse: (*a*) a government with a balanced budget that does not provide enough basic services for people, or (*b*) a government that keeps going more deeply into debt to provide basic services? Your answer represents *your* fiscal policy for the nation.

REVIEW

A. Building Your Political Vocabulary

On a separate piece of paper, copy and complete each statement.

1. The value of a savings bond at maturity is called its __(?)__.
2. The federal deficit is the sum left over when you subtract __(?)__ from __(?)__.
3. The total sum that the U.S. government owes to millions of lenders is known as the __(?)__.
4. How much the government spends and how much it borrows depends on __(?)__ policy.
5. Keynesians are economists who believe that __(?)__.
6. Supply-siders are economists who believe that __(?)__.

B. Making Inferences

State whether you think each statement is (*a*) **probably true** or (*b*) **probably not true.** Give your reasons.

1. The national debt was higher in 1992 than in 1980.
2. If you pay $50 for an EE savings bond, you will be entitled to collect $100 when it matures.
3. The Constitution does not yet contain an amendment requiring a balanced budget.
4. President Reagan agreed with the ideas of John Maynard Keynes.
5. Many Republican senators are in favor of the balanced budget amendment.

CHAPTER REVIEW

A. Completing the Summary

Select terms from the word list to fill in the blanks in the summary below. Write your answers on a piece of paper.

appropriations
budget
civil servants
corporation
customs duties
deficits
excise taxes
fiscal policy
fiscal year
merit
national debt
Office of Management and Budget
progressive
regressive
savings bonds
Social Security tax
spoils system
vacancy announcement
veterans

At some time in your career, you may be one of the 3 million __(1)__ employed by the federal government. In the past, these workers were selected on the basis of party loyalty and service—a system called the __(2)__. Today, government workers are selected through a competitive system on the basis of __(3)__.

Different agencies employ workers for a great variety of occupations. To find a government job for yourself, you might study a __(4)__ posted on some federal agency's bulletin board. You would then fill out a standard form presenting your work experience and training. Although __(5)__ are given bonus points, you still have a chance to score higher than anyone and thus win the job.

Paying for U.S. government workers and their services costs hundreds of billions of dollars a year. The yearly plan for paying these expenses is called the federal __(6)__. Assisting the president in creating a yearly financial plan is the director of the __(7)__.

Although the president proposes a spending plan, it is Congress that decides the specific __(8)__ of money that shall be made for different purposes. It must come to a vote on the spending plan before the new __(9)__ begins on October 1.

To raise all the money that it needs, the U.S. government relies upon collecting a number of taxes. There are __(10)__ on imports and __(11)__ on the sale of American goods such as gasoline, liquor, and cigarettes. These are examples of __(12)__ taxes because low-income people have a harder time paying them than high-income people. Taxes with just the opposite effect are called __(13)__. Two examples are the personal income tax and the __(14)__ income tax. Next to the personal income tax, the tax that brings in the most revenue each year is the __(15)__.

Because the government's expenses are usually greater than its income, it ends almost every fiscal year with large

(16) . Over the years, a huge (17) of more than four trillion dollars has built up. It is owed in part to citizens who have invested in (18) . Whether the U.S. government should borrow a lot of money—or none at all—has become a major political issue. How Congress and the president deal with the issue in their yearly budget is known as (19) .

B. The Federal Budget—Revenues

Study the table and answer the questions based on it.

Federal Receipts, 1980 and 1994

	Percent distribution	
	1980	1994 (est.)
Individual income taxes	47.2	44.8
Corporation income taxes	12.5	9.6
Social insurance taxes	30.5	37.2
Excise taxes*	4.2	4.1
Other	4.9	4.3

* Primarily on alcoholic beverages and tobacco

1. What was the largest source of federal revenue in 1980 and 1994?
2. Which source of federal revenue *increased* the most between 1980 and 1994?
3. Which source of federal revenue *decreased* the most between 1980 and 1994?
4. If the U.S. government needed to increase its revenues to balance the budget, which of the following would you recommend? (*a*) Increase every type of tax by a small amount. (*b*) Increase the tax rate on individual incomes. (*c*) Propose some other plan (if so, describe it). Explain your answer.

C. Making Comparisons

Compare and explain the following terms and concepts:

1. Explain the difference between the SPOILS SYSTEM for selecting employees and the CIVIL SERVICE SYSTEM.
2. Compare the GS-1 worker and the GS-5 worker in terms of the following: (*a*) QUALIFICATIONS, (*b*) SALARY.
3. Explain why a KEYNESIAN would favor an unbalanced budget while a SUPPLY-SIDER would favor a balanced budget.

D. Projects: Applying What You Know

Apply your knowledge by carrying out **one** of the following projects.

1. Data update. In the library, find out the income and expenses of the U.S. government for the *most current year*. The sources containing the information are: (*a*) *The World Almanac and Book of Facts*, (*b*) *The Statistical Abstract of the United States*, and (*c*) *The Budget of the United States.* Make a photocopy of the information, and post it on the class bulletin board.

2. Job search. In your telephone book, look for a listing of federal agencies in your area. (Look under the heading: UNITED STATES GOVERNMENT.) Visit one agency, and ask to see where civil service openings may be posted. If you find a "Vacancy Announcement," take notes on the job it describes. Report to the class about your experience.

U.S. TROOPS IN KOREA, 1950. Between 1950 and 1953, more than 54,000 Americans died in a war to defend South Korea. In sending troops to fight in Korea, did President Truman make the right decision?

CHAPTER 19

Foreign Policy: Defending Freedom

OBJECTIVES

After reading this chapter, you will know

1. the major goals of U.S. foreign policy.
2. how foreign policy is made by the president, Cabinet officers, the Congress, and others.
3. how nations communicate through diplomacy and the United Nations.
4. past policies of the United States toward different regions of the world.
5. what *you* think the United States should do regarding three issues.
6. how to find information on a political map of Europe.

A president's life is a little like a doctor's. At any time of the day or night, he can receive a phone call that plunges him into an emergency.

That is what happened to President Harry S Truman on a Saturday night in June 1950. He was vacationing with his family in the Truman home in Independence, Missouri. Years later, Truman talked about his memories of that night. He said:

> It was about ten-thirty on Saturday night, and I was sitting in the living room reading. The phone rang, and it was Dean Acheson calling from his home in Maryland. He said, "Mr. President, I have serious news. The North Koreans are attacking across the thirty-eighth parallel."
>
> I wanted to get on the plane and fly to Washington right that night, but he said that I shouldn't, that a night flight wasn't necessary. He said that I should stand by for another call from him when he'd have more details. And I agreed. . . .
>
> I went to bed, and that was one night I didn't get much sleep.

The caller, Dean Acheson, was Truman's secretary of state. Acheson was in Washington, D.C., when the news broke of an attack by North Korean troops against South Korea. After calling the president, Acheson was on the phone most of the night with other officials. These are Acheson's memories of the next morning:

> On Sunday morning I drove immediately to the State Department and found that my colleagues there had been working throughout the night with representatives in the Department of Defense. And they had brought together all the information available and necessary for decisions as to what should be done.

TRUMAN'S SECRETARY OF STATE, DEAN ACHESON. Who is the current president's secretary of state?

Acheson then placed another call to the president's home in Missouri. This is Truman speaking again:

> I went to the phone and said, "What is it, Dean?" And he said, "Mr. President, the news is bad. The attack is in force all along the parallel (the border between North and South Korea). . . ."
>
> I said I was returning to Washington immediately and we were on our way back in less than an hour. In fact we left in such a hurry that two of my aides were left behind.

Only four days later, American troops were dispatched to Korea to hold the line against the crushing North Korean advance. Commanding them was General Douglas MacArthur. The general had been ordered to defend South Korea by the commander in chief—President Truman.

In the end, the United States and its allies did not completely defeat North Korea and its ally, China. But the invading forces were stopped from winning any territory from their outright aggression. Years later, Truman said that his decision to send troops into Korea was the most important decision of his presidency.

This chapter will provide the background for understanding U.S. dealings with foreign countries. You will then know *why* President Truman made the decision to fight in Korea. You will review some of the highlights of our nation's history in peace and war. Next, you will look at the challenges from abroad that the United States faces today. As you read, think about these questions:

1. Who makes U.S. foreign policy?

GENERAL DOUGLAS MACARTHUR AND PRESIDENT TRUMAN, 1951. Shortly after this picture was taken, the general criticized the president's policies in Korea. Truman responded by firing MacArthur. Why is civilian control of the military an important principle of U.S. government?

2. How do nations use *diplomacy* to settle disputes?
3. What policies have guided the United States in the past?
4. What policies should guide the United States in the future?

1. WHO MAKES U.S. FOREIGN POLICY?

In its dealings with other countries, the United States has certain goals. Government leaders have a wide range of choices in deciding on actions to achieve those goals. The choices actually made by the president and others make up what we call U.S. foreign policy.

Long-term goals. Goals are like stars in the night sky. They are the same from one year to the next and even from one century to the next. These four goals have guided the making of U.S. foreign policy since the beginning of our history:

1. Peace. If it possibly can, the U.S. government will avoid going to war with other nations. By their nature, all wars are costly and destructive. Keeping the peace is therefore a goal of first importance.

2. Prosperity. Naturally, Americans want business to be good and jobs to be plentiful. In part, such prosperity depends on trading with other countries. The United States wants to make sure that it can buy all that it needs (oil, coffee, etc.) from foreign sources. It also wants businesses and farms to sell large quantities of American-produced goods in foreign markets.

3. Security. The United States has been fortunate. Only twice in its history did a foreign nation attack its territory. During the War of 1812, a British army marched through the nation's capital, burning government buildings. In 1941, Japanese planes attacked without warning a fleet of American ships anchored at Pearl Harbor in Hawaii. To prevent any such attacks in the future, the U.S. government tries to maintain a strong system of military defense.

4. Freedom. As you know, the U.S. government is committed to the freedom of its own citizens, the American people. But it is also concerned about the freedom of people outside its borders. It does what it can to see that other governments respect basic human rights.

It would be wonderful if American foreign policy could serve all four goals at once. But sometimes the United States must make a painful choice, temporarily sacrificing one goal for the others. Here are two examples:

- When Japan bombed Pearl Harbor, U.S. security was under direct attack.
- When North Korean forces attacked South Korea, President Truman believed that U.S. security (and the security of other free nations) was threatened.

In both cases, security was thought to be more important than peace. That is why the United States entered World War II in 1941 and the Korean War nine years later.

But going to war is only a temporary action. It is a short-term policy, not a long-term goal. War is a detour from the main road of American foreign policy. Even in wartime, the goals on the distant horizon remain the same: peace, prosperity, security, freedom.

Short-term strategies. Making foreign policy involves, first of all, knowing what your choices are in a certain situation. For example, consider President Truman's choices after being informed about the attack against South Korea.

A. Do nothing. Wait and see what happens.
B. Make a speech condemning North Korea for its aggression.

C. Send arms and supplies to the South Koreans—but no American troops.
D. Send American troops to Korea only if the United Nations (UN) Security Council votes to take action in the crisis.
E. Send American troops to Korea whether or not the UN approves.
F. Bomb North Korea and, if necessary, fight an all-out war against its supporters (China, the Soviet Union).

Truman chose Strategy D. If someone else had been president, a different choice might have been made. But no matter who decides, the procedure for making a decision is the same. It consists of these steps: (1) Obtain reliable information about the crisis. (2) List different ways of responding. (3) Think of the effect each choice is likely to have on your goals (peace, prosperity, etc.). (4) Choose. (5) Act on your decision.

Many advisers to the president. The president has the final responsibility for making decisions when the national security seems threatened. The president is, after all, the commander in chief of the armed forces. But before making a decision, the president consults with his/her top advisers.

Look at CARTOON CORNER below. Here we see the chief "cooks" that have a hand in preparing the president's foreign policy "sauce" (mix of decisions). Two of the assistant cooks (advisers) are members of the Cabinet: the secretary of state and the secretary of defense. Let us see how each contributes to the making of American foreign policy.

Secretary of state. Recall that the person who phoned Truman about the Korean crisis was Secretary of State Dean Acheson. Why was this adviser the one who informed

CARTOON CORNER

the president about a crisis abroad? The **secretary of state** is the member of the Cabinet who specializes in foreign affairs. He or she has a triple responsibility.

First, as a manager, the secretary of state directs the ambassadors and other foreign service officers who make up the Department of State.

Second, as a diplomat, the secretary of state meets with foreign ambassadors living in Washington, D.C. Also, the secretary composes diplomatic letters and notes. With the president's approval, these are sent to the foreign ministers and heads of state of other countries. When letters are not sufficient, the secretary may travel abroad to meet face-to-face with foreign leaders.

The secretary's third role is to advise the president about international problems that concern the United States. Such problems may arise in places that few Americans have ever heard of. Do you know what's happening, for example, in Szczecin, Poland? Or in Zagazig, Egypt? Suppose there is a riot or a bombing in either of these cities. Consulting with other experts, the secretary of state should be able to tell the president what's behind the trouble and how it may affect U.S. security. Meeting with the president, the secretary proposes different ways that the United States might respond to the crisis.

A strong secretary of state can have almost as great an impact on U.S. foreign policy as the president. The famed Monroe Doctrine bears the name of President James Monroe. In fact, however, it was chiefly the creation of Monroe's secretary of state, John

DIPLOMACY AT A HIGH LEVEL: U.S. Secretary of State Warren Christopher (right) met with Japan's foreign minister Michio Watanabe in 1993. If such a meeting were held today, what issues would the secretary of state probably discuss with the Japanese foreign minister?

Quincy Adams. (For an explanation of the Monroe Doctrine, see page 455.) In our own times, two secretaries of state were especially influential. Henry Kissinger was the mastermind behind President Nixon's attempts to bring about peace in the Middle East. George Shultz, as President Reagan's chief diplomat, constantly traveled to foreign capitals to negotiate important treaties.

Secretary of defense. Before World War II, two members of the Cabinet managed the armed forces. Directing and equipping the U.S. Army was the job of the secretary of war. Building American seapower was the job of the secretary of the navy. After World War II, a new Department of Defense was created to bring all the services together under one management. Each of three services was given its own secretary: a secretary of the air force, a secretary of the army, and a secretary of the navy. These three report to the department's top boss: the **secretary of defense.**

Today, the Department of Defense is gigantic. Its headquarters, the Pentagon, is the largest office building in the world. More than 25,000 people work in this five-sided building. About half are military officers while the other half are civilians. The secretary of defense does *not* wear a military uniform. The person chosen for this top job is required by law to be a civilian.

This fact underlines an important point about American government. Civilian leaders are supposed to be in charge of military leaders, not the other way around. The president (a civilian) and the secretary of defense (a civilian) outrank every five-star general. They set policy and give the orders. Our democracy (government of the people) is thus protected from being taken over by a military dictator.

The secretary of defense helps the president answer questions like these:

THE PENTAGON. About 25,000 people are employed in this building, one of the largest office buildings in the world. Which Cabinet secretary is responsible for directing everyone's work here?

- Where should American ground troops be stationed?
- Where should fleets of the U.S. Navy be positioned?
- How many nuclear missiles of different types are needed by the army, navy, and air force?
- What new weapons systems should be developed?
- How much will all of the above cost?

Army, Navy, and Air Force. The Department of Defense (DOD) is so huge that its three main divisions are called "departments" (not just agencies or bureaus). These departments-within-a-department are: (1) the **Department of the Army,** (2) the **Department of the Navy,** and (3) the **Department of the Air Force.** The three secretaries of these departments and their assistant secretaries are civilian officers who take orders from two other civilians: the president and the secretary of defense.

The mission, or chief purpose, of each military department is described in the *United States Government Manual* as follows:

Army—"The Army's mission focuses on land operation; its soldiers must be trained with modern arms and equipment and be ready to respond quickly."

Navy—"The primary mission of the Navy is to protect the United States, as directed by the president or the secretary of defense, by the effective prosecution of war at sea."

Air Force—"The Department of the Air Force is responsible for providing an Air Force that is capable, in conjunction with the armed forces, of preserving the peace and security of the United States."

A famous fighting force within the Department of the Navy is the **U.S. Marine Corps.** The Marines, though loosely tied to the Navy, guard their independence as a fourth and separate military service.

The three departments of DOD are supposed to cooperate with one another for the common defense. They do cooperate in a crisis, but there are also times when they compete. The four services (including the Marine Corps) are proud of their different traditions. Each thinks its own role in defending the country is the most important. Each demands that it be given a larger share of the defense budget than the others. Interservice rivalry is a powerful force, and the president is constantly aware of it when making defense policy.

" NOW THAT THE MISSILES ARE NO LONGER AIMED AT RUSSIAN CITIES AND MILITARY BASES, WHAT DO WE AIM THEM AT?"

THE MISSILE QUESTION: How would you answer the general's question? What is the use of nuclear weapons in the post-cold war era?

Joint Chiefs of Staff. The final decisions about troop movements and weapons systems are made by a civilian commander in chief (the president) as well as by Congress. But before making any major decision, the president always considers the advice of a group of military experts called the *Joint Chiefs of Staff.* This group of high-ranking officers in uniform are the "top brass" in the U.S. armed forces. These are their titles:

Chairman, Joint Chiefs of Staff

Chief of Staff, United States Army

Chief of Naval Operations

Chief of Staff, United States Air Force

Commandant of the Marine Corps

With offices in the Pentagon, the Joint Chiefs meet regularly with the civilian secretaries of the different defense departments. The chairman of the Joint Chiefs is called to the White House to advise the president directly whenever a crisis threatens the national security.

National Security Council. Certain advisers in the Department of State and the Department of Defense meet regularly with the president in the White House as the **National Security Council** (NSC). The chief purpose of the NSC meetings is to help the president make decisions in foreign policy that will best protect the national security. Meetings of the NSC are attended by the following: (1) the president, (2) the vice president, (3) the secretary of state, (4) the secretary of defense, (5) the chairman of the Joint Chiefs of Staff, and (6) the director of the Central Intelligence Agency.

Central Intelligence Agency (CIA). In political language, *"intelligence"* means the gathering of information about foreign governments (usually enemies or suspected enemies). "Counterintelligence" means blocking the efforts of foreign governments to gain top-secret information about the United States. The CIA works in both areas. It gathers useful information about foreign governments. At the same time, it tries to stop foreign governments from finding out

ADVISING THE COMMANDER IN CHIEF. Talking with President Clinton about U.S. policy in Bosnia in early 1994 are (from left): White House Chief of Staff Mike McLarty, Chairman of the Joint Chiefs of Staff General John Shalikashvili, Defense Secretary William Perry, Secretary of State Warren Christopher, and National Security Adviser Anthony Lake. Who makes the final decisions about foreign policy?

about U.S. weapons systems and other defense matters.

The CIA employs agents, reconnaissance planes, and electronic devices such as "bugs" (recording devices) for these purposes. But it also uses ordinary techniques, such as clipping articles from foreign newspapers. The information in the CIA's files helps the president and other members of the National Security Council to make foreign policy choices.

Policies of the president. The president gets advice from some of the brightest thinkers and experts in the country. But his advisers rarely agree with one another. In a certain situation, eight advisers might favor Strategy A while two others favor Strategy B. A strong president does not always side with the majority. He might choose Strategy B even though only two out of ten advisers think it's a good idea.

Even before taking office, the president should know what he wants to accomplish in foreign affairs. Then it becomes easier to give leadership and to know how to act in a crisis.

Here are some facts about three presidents whose goals guided the way they reacted to global challenges.

1. President Thomas Jefferson (1801–1809) wanted to keep the United States out of a war being fought between the French and the British. He therefore announced a policy of strict neutrality (not taking sides). The United States remained neutral and did not go to war during his presidency.

2. When a war broke out in Europe in 1914, President Woodrow Wilson (1913–1921) insisted on the principle of "freedom of the seas" for U.S. merchant ships. He wanted to avoid war if possible. But German submarine attacks on U.S. ships violated "freedom of the seas." In 1917, Wilson asked Congress for a declaration of war against Germany.

3. President Richard Nixon (1969–1975) and Secretary of State Henry Kissinger wanted to reduce tensions between the United States and the Soviet Union. With this goal in mind, Nixon traveled to Moscow to talk with the Soviet leader and negotiated a treaty on nuclear arms.

Policies of the Congress. The president bears most of the responsibility for making foreign policy. But Congress also has an important role to play. Recall our constitutional system of checks and balances. Congress has various ways of checking (defeating) the president's policies if a majority of its members oppose them.

Congress's chief check is its power over the use of federal money. It can, if it chooses, refuse to appropriate the sums of money that the president wants to spend on defense and foreign affairs. For example, in 1988 many members of Congress were not enthusiastic about President Reagan's request to give military aid to an anti-Communist group, the Contras, in Nicaragua. Because of Congress's opposition, the Contras received less U.S. aid than the sums recommended by the president.

A second check belongs to the Senate alone. It concerns the president's power to make treaties. As you know, a treaty is a formal agreement between the United States and a foreign government. Aided by diplomats in the State Department, the president draws up treaties on a great variety of subjects. For example, there are treaties about:

- borders between countries
- the testing of nuclear weapons
- the hunting of Arctic seals
- exploring Antarctica
- the use of international airports
- privileges and protections of travelers
- the giving and receiving of military aid.

The Constitution says that the Senate must give its "advice and consent" with regard to any treaty made by the president.

It requires that treaties be approved in the Senate by a two-thirds vote. Usually, they *are* approved. But there have been notable exceptions. The most important treaty *not* ratified was a treaty of peace ending World War I. President Woodrow Wilson had traveled to Paris in 1919 to arrange this treaty. It would have committed the United States to join the League of Nations, an international organization for keeping the peace. But many senators feared that the League would try to interfere with U.S. ability to make its own foreign policy. Wilson's treaty was never approved.

A third check on the president concerns his powers as commander in chief. This power enables the president to respond quickly to an enemy attack or foreign crisis. Within minutes, troops can be ordered overseas. Missiles can be launched against enemy targets. In an emergency, the president can take these actions without first getting Congress's approval. However, the Constitution gives to Congress alone the power to declare war. To stop a president from fighting a war without Congress's approval, Congress enacted the War Powers Act in 1973. It states that:

(*a*) The president must inform Congress of his actions and the reasons for them within 48 hours.

(*b*) Military operations must end after 60 days unless Congress votes to continue them.

Members of Congress argue that the War Powers Act is a proper check on the president. Richard Nixon and other presidents have said that it is *not* proper and not constitutional because it limits a president's power in ways not mentioned in the Constitution. So far, the issue has not yet come to the Supreme Court for decision.

The role of public opinion—and you. A final check on the president's foreign policies belongs to the American people. By

CURRENT CHALLENGES: This cartoon was created in January 1993, just before Bill Clinton was inaugurated president. (1) From whom did Clinton receive "the torch?" How does each country identified in the cartoon pose a challenge to U.S. foreign policy?

THE TORCH IS PASSED

expressing their opinions, citizens can either make it easier or harder for a president to do what he/she wants. As a rule, unpopular policies do not last long. Here are just two examples of how public opinion can influence foreign policy.

- In 1937, Japanese troops invaded northern China. President Franklin Roosevelt wanted to do something about it. But a speech that he made about Japan's acts seemed bold and alarming to many Americans. They did not want to get involved in a foreign war. Their negative reaction to the president's speech prevented him from using U.S. power to challenge Japan at that time.

- In the 1960s, President Lyndon Johnson kept sending large numbers of American troops and planes to Vietnam to fight Communist forces there. Public opinion polls showed that millions of Americans opposed President Johnson's war policies.

  The next president, Richard Nixon, began withdrawing troops from Vietnam partly because the war had become so unpopular.

In the future, other foreign problems and crises will be reported in the news. *You* will then have to decide whether the president's policies appear to be right or wrong. Combined with the opinions of others, your opinions may have an influence on American foreign policy.

REVIEW

A. Main Ideas and Supporting Details

Match each main idea with an example given at the right. Write your answers on a separate piece of paper.

MAIN IDEA	EXAMPLE
1. Treaties must be approved, or ratified, by a vote of the Senate.	*a.* President Truman gives orders to General Douglas MacArthur.
2. Top military leaders must follow the policies of civilian leaders.	*b.* President Wilson fails to win approval for the U.S. to join the League of Nations.
3. Sometimes a president may think the national security is more important than peace.	*c.* In 1988, the Contras fail to receive the aid requested by President Reagan.
4. Congress may use its power of the purse to oppose a president's policies.	*d.* President Truman decides that American troops should fight in Korea.

B. Applying What You Know

In October 1962, President John Kennedy was shocked to learn that nuclear missiles from the Soviet Union were secretly being shipped into Cuba. Kennedy thought these missiles—once installed—would pose a serious threat to U.S. security. The questions below ask you to apply what you know to the Cuban missile crisis of 1962.

1. In this crisis, what advisers would you expect the president to talk to? (Name at least four, and tell why each was probably consulted.)
2. Suggest at least three strategies for dealing with the crisis.
3. If you had been the president in 1962, what would you have decided to do? Why? (Compare your decision with that of President Kennedy by turning to pages 275–276.)

C. Agree or Disagree

Tell whether you **agree** or **disagree** with

each statement. Give a reason for your opinion.

1. When making foreign policy, the president should always consult the leaders of Congress.
2. The CIA should be allowed to use spies for its intelligence work.
3. The person best qualified to be secretary of defense would be a *retired* admiral or general.
4. Protecting the national security is more important than any other foreign policy goal.

2. HOW DO NATIONS USE DIPLOMACY TO SETTLE DISPUTES?

The war in Korea was just one of thousands of wars fought at some time in world history. The United States has fought in only ten of them:

- the Revolutionary War against Britain (1775-1783)
- the War of 1812 against Britain (1812-1815)
- a war against Mexico (1846-1848)
- a civil war against the Southern Confederacy (1861-1865)
- a war against Spain (1898)
- World War I against Germany and its allies (1917-1918)
- World War II against Germany, Italy, Japan, and their allies (1941-1945)
- Korean War (1950-1953)
- Vietnam War (1964-1973)
- Persian Gulf War against Iraq (1991)

(NOTE: U.S. troops also fought Indian peoples off and on until the end of the last century. But these violent episodes were not full-scale wars.)

Altogether, there were about 34 years of war out of 217 years of our national history (1776-1993). In roughly five years out of six, the United States was at peace.

All nations manage to get along peacefully with one another most of the time. Every day, citizens of different countries travel back and forth across international borders. Millions of tons of merchandise are shipped across the world's oceans in a typical day of trade. In other words, peaceful relations are normal. And the normal way to maintain such relations is through diplomacy.

REVOLUTIONARY WAR, 1775–1783

WAR OF 1812, 1812–1815

MEXICAN WAR, 1846–1848

WORLD WAR II, 1941–1945

CIVIL WAR, 1861–1865

KOREAN WAR, 1950–1953

SPANISH-AMERICAN WAR, 1898

VIETNAM WAR, 1963–1975

WORLD WAR I, 1917–1918

PERSIAN GULF WAR, 1991

Ambassadors abroad. Diplomacy is an orderly system by which the government of one nation communicates with the government of another nation. It is a system used by all nations of the world.

Some of the key players in diplomacy are known as ambassadors. These officials are appointed by the leaders (or heads of state) of their own countries. For example, the U.S. president appoints the American ambassador to Brazil. In turn, Brazil's president appoints his country's ambassador to the United States. The ambassadors travel to the capital cities of their assigned countries. The American ambassador to Brazil travels to Brasília. The Brazilian ambassador travels to Washington, D.C. They unpack their bags in diplomatic residences called embassies.

After moving in, an ambassador's main job is to be the representative for his or her own government. Telegrams from the home government give instructions about how to deal with certain problems. The ambassador carries out his or her instructions by meeting with officials in the foreign government. Carefully ("diplomatically"), the ambassador explains the concerns of the home government about some event or issue.

Take an example. Imagine that an American journalist in Brazil was arrested and jailed for "disturbing the peace." At the same time, Brazil's government is alarmed because the U.S. Congress is talking about raising its tariff (tax) on imports of Brazilian coffee. In Washington, the Brazilian ambassador discusses the tariff problem with the U.S. secretary of state. Meanwhile, in Brasília, the American ambassador tells a high official in Brazil's government that the jailing of the journalist was a violation of his rights as an American citizen.

Diplomatic messages go back and forth between the two countries. With luck, both problems are solved. In Brazil, the journalist is freed. In the United States, Congress does not pass a higher tariff after all. Relations between Brazil and the United States continue to be friendly.

Diplomacy at the highest levels. Every government has a special department, or "ministry," specializing in foreign affairs. Ambassadors and other diplomats of lower rank work under the direction of this home department. Brazil's embassies everywhere in the world are managed from Brasília. U.S. embassies receive their instructions

U.S. AMBASSADORS TO ITALY AND JAPAN. Clare Booth Luce (far left) was the U.S. ambassador to Italy from 1953 to 1956. Michael Armacost (right) was the U.S. ambassador to Japan in 1990. Here the ambassador is meeting with the Japanese prime minister. What is the primary role of an ambassador?

from the U.S. Department of State in Washington. Its leader, the secretary of state, is one of the most important members of the president's Cabinet.

Often problems between countries are too difficult for ambassadors to solve. It may then be necessary to hold a meeting among the highest officials of different nations. Let us say the problem this time involves Britain. The U.S. secretary of state might fly to London to meet with the British foreign minister. In turn, the British foreign minister could travel to Washington to meet with both the secretary of state and the president. Being a V.I.P. (very important person), the British diplomat would probably dine at the White House as the president's guest.

In the United States, the highest-ranking diplomat of all is the secretary of state's boss—the president. As you know, the president is the U.S. head of state. Heads of state of different countries spend much of their time as diplomats. They exchange letters and notes with one another. They even arrange to travel to other countries to try to solve international problems. (International means anything involving two or more nations.) When heads of state meet face to face, the event is known as a summit meeting.

Sometimes, little is accomplished at summit meetings. The leaders talk politely to each other, smile for the cameras, and that is all. But at other times, the leaders may reach agreements of great importance. Take, for example, a longstanding problem in the Middle East. In 1977, Egypt and Israel had been bitter enemies for 30 years. Then Egypt's leader, Anwar al-Sadat, visited with Israel's leader, Menachem Begin, in the Israeli cap-

ARRANGING A PEACE TREATY. In 1978, President Carter persuaded Menachem Begin of Israel (right) and Anwar al-Sadat of Egypt (left) to sign a peace treaty about disputed territories in the Middle East. Why is it in the interest of the United States to work for peace in the Middle East?

ital. Sadat's trip seemed to be a step toward peace. It was a bold diplomatic move that impressed the U.S. president, Jimmy Carter.

Carter invited Sadat and Begin to meet again, this time as his guests in the United States. In 1978, the three heads of state talked and argued for several days in the president's vacation cabin at Camp David in Maryland. Finally, they told reporters the good news. Egypt's president and Israel's prime minister agreed to a plan for settling their countries' differences. President Carter offered to back the plan with U.S. aid.

The agreement at Camp David was hailed as a diplomatic triumph. It probably could not have happened unless the three leaders had met together in face-to-face talks.

Goals of the United Nations. Another means for settling disputes was created during the last year of World War II. In 1945, diplomats from 46 countries met in San Francisco. There, they drew up the Charter (constitution or plan) of the United Nations (UN).

Today, nearly 200 nations belong to the UN. The United States is, of course, one of them. In fact, our country is the host nation, since UN headquarters is located in New York City. Here diplomats from around the world meet for four main purposes:

1. to ensure that governments around the world respect basic human rights
2. to promote better standards of living
3. to settle disputes between nations
4. to protect member nations from military aggression.

The UN's methods for dealing with a crisis. Most people judge the effectiveness of the United Nations according to how well it achieves its third goal: settling disputes. When a crisis breaks out anywhere in the world, the United Nations has various ways of dealing with it.

Imagine a crisis in South America. Suppose that a commercial plane from Brazil crashes in the mountains of Ecuador, killing the crew and passengers. Brazil's government accuses Ecuador's air force of shooting down the plane. It threatens war over the incident unless Ecuador agrees to pay a penalty of a billion dollars. Ecuador says the plane crash was an accident and refuses to pay. How might the UN try to settle this dispute? The matter could be brought to one or more of the three UN organizations that have peacekeeping authority.

1. Action by the General Assembly. First, the Brazil–Ecuador dispute could be debated in the UN General Assembly. Hundreds of diplomats make up this assembly. They represent every nation belonging to the UN. The delegation from Ecuador may ask the Assembly to condemn Brazil for its "warlike threats." It introduces a resolution for this purpose. (A resolution is a statement of a group's position on an issue.) To pass a resolution in the General Assembly, a majority of the member nations must vote for it. Resolutions on very serious issues can pass only if two-thirds vote "yes."

2. Action by the International Court of Justice. A second way to settle the dispute would be to take it to court. Both Brazil and Ecuador would have to take this step. Each nation would then send diplomats and lawyers to The Hague, a city in the Netherlands. An old palace at The Hague has been turned into the UN's International Court of Justice. Here a panel of judges would decide whether Brazil's plane had in fact been shot down by Ecuador. If so, Ecuador might be asked to pay for damages.

3. Action by the Security Council. Finally, the UN Security Council might attempt to deal with the dispute. Permanently represented on this council are five major nations of the world. They are: the United States, France, Great Britain, China, and Russia. Ten other nations also participate in debates and votes of the Security Council. But these "nonpermanent" members of the council only serve for two-year terms, after which they are replaced by other nations. For a resolution to be adopted by the Security Council, nine of the 15 member nations must vote for it. In addition, *all five of the permanent members* must vote for the resolution. Because of this requirement, any permanent member who disagrees with a resolution has the power to veto, or block, action by voting "no."

The Security Council has the power to recommend a certain course of action to all members of the United Nations. For example, if Brazil attacked Ecuador, the Security Council might pass a resolution declaring Brazil to be in the wrong and urging member nations of the UN to give military aid to Ecuador.

UN Peacekeeping during the Cold War. During the first 45 years of the UN's existence, its efforts to keep the peace were usually frustrated by one fact. Two permanent members of the Security Council, the United States and the Soviet Union, were locked in a global conflict known as the Cold War (see pages 457–458). The rivalry of these nations and their allies blocked the United Nations from taking action in a crisis. If the United States proposed a peacekeeping resolution in the Security Council, the Soviet Union would vote "no," thus vetoing the idea.

You read about President Truman's decision to obtain UN backing for sending U.S. troops to Korea in 1950. In this crisis, the Security Council did pass a resolution calling upon UN members to give military aid to South Korea. The resolution passed only because the Soviet representative happened to be absent when the vote was taken. Between 1945 and 1990, all other UN resolutions to take military action in a crisis were defeated.

UN Peacekeeping in the 1990s. The Cold War has ended. As a result, the United Nations is now in a much better position to live up to its original mission as a peacekeeping organization. The first major sign of change came in 1990, when Iraq invaded Kuwait. The UN Security Council voted to condemn the invasion. In this crisis, the United States and the Soviet Union were on the same side. Supporting U.S. troops in the Gulf War of 1991 were military units and supplies contributed by 31 other nations. Later that year, the Soviet Union broke up into 15 separate nations. The largest, Russia, was awarded a permanent seat on the Security Council.

After the Cold War, it became common for the United Nations to send peacekeeping forces to various parts of the world. In the early 1990s, UN forces were attempting to settle disputes in 12 troubled nations, including Cambodia in Asia, Angola in Africa, and Croatia in Europe.

Another type of UN action is becoming increasingly common in the post-Cold War era. When some nation violates human rights or invades a neighboring country, the UN Security Counil may vote for *sanctions*. A sanction is a penalty for wrongdoing. It can take various forms: banning trade with the offending nation, cutting off diplomatic relations, or suspending air travel.

The routines of trade and travel. Diplomacy can sometimes involve world-shaking matters of war and peace. More often, it involves simply smoothing the way for tourists and business people to travel safely abroad. The government officials who are most concerned with matters of travel and trade are called *consuls*. Their offices abroad are called consulates.

Let us suppose that you are planning a pleasure trip to Egypt. Before departing, you would be required to obtain a document proving that you are a U.S. citizen. Such a document (in the form of a small booklet) is known as a passport. Issuing passports is a function of the **Bureau of Consular Affairs** (part of the State Department). On receiving your passport, you are ready for your trip.

Upon landing at an airport in Cairo, you would be asked to show your passport to Egyptian officials. Later, suppose that you were to lose your passport while climbing one of Egypt's pyramids. You would then go directly to the U.S. consulate in Cairo for assistance.

Besides helping American tourists, consuls and their staffs help American businesses find foreign, or international, markets for their products. U.S. consulates are located in more than 100 major cities throughout the world. They form one of two major divisions of the **U.S. Foreign Service** (American diplomats serving abroad). The other division consists of ambassadors and their staffs at U.S. embassies.

U.S. PASSPORT. The U.S. citizen pictured below must present her passport to customs officials when traveling to foreign countries. How do passports provide protection to the persons named in them?

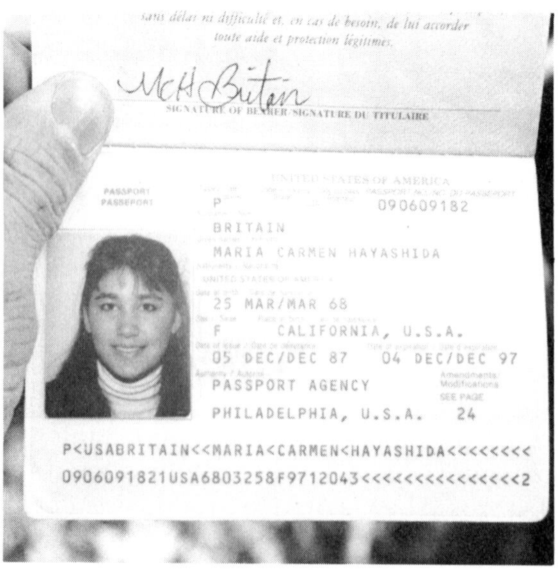

REVIEW

A. Building Your Political Vocabulary

Match each term (1–6) with its definition (*a–f*).

1. Department of State
2. General Assembly
3. passport
4. Security Council
5. diplomacy
6. consulate

a. a traveler's proof of citizenship

b. an office for helping U.S. citizens traveling abroad

c. an organization in which almost all nations of the world have equal voting power

d. an organization in which five countries have permanent seats

e. the part of the U.S. government that manages foreign affairs

f. a system by which nations communicate

B. Making Comparisons

As an organization for debating issues, the United Nations has sometimes been compared with the U.S. Congress. Make the comparison yourself by answering these questions.

1. Compare the organization of the United Nations with the organization of Congress.
2. Compare the powers of the United Nations with the powers of Congress.
3. Which do you think has greater power and influence in the world: the U.S. Congress or the United Nations? Why?

C. Making Inferences

This section used Brazil in an example of diplomatic relations. Select and name some other foreign country. Say whether or not you think the following statements would or would not describe that country's diplomacy. Give reasons for each answer.

1. This country currently has an ambassador living in Washington, D.C.
2. This country relies chiefly on the United Nations to settle its disputes with neighboring countries.
3. This country has one department of government that is very much like the U.S. Department of State.
4. Although it has fought wars in the past, this country is currently at peace with its neighbors.
5. If you fly to this country, you will be required to show an American passport.
6. An American consulate is located in a major city of this country.

3. WHAT POLICIES HAVE GUIDED THE UNITED STATES IN THE PAST?

Looking back at past policies will help us to see where current policies come from. In the history of U.S. foreign policy, World War II (1939–1945) forms a major dividing point. First, let us examine policies *before* that war toward three regions of the world: Europe, Latin America, and Asia.

U.S. policy toward Europe. In colonial times, the British, the French, and the Spanish were often at war. They would fight not only in Europe but also in the lands they claimed in North America. American colonists were dragged into these wars on the British side.

After revolting against British rule in 1776, Americans wanted to be free from European politics. As their first president, George Washington refused to take sides in the wars between France and Britain. President Thomas Jefferson continued this policy. Jefferson said the United States should avoid any "entangling *alliances*" with European powers.

The policy of not getting involved in Europe's struggles is known as *isolationism.* For many years, this policy seemed to work well, keeping the United States safely removed from the conflicts of others. There were no airplanes or missiles in the 19th century, so foreign armies could reach U.S. shores only on slow-moving ships. Vast oceans to east and west gave Americans a sense of security against sudden attack.

Isolationism, however, applied to politics only—not to business and trade. Presidents insisted on the U.S. right to "freedom of the seas" for U.S. ships trading in European ports. Germany did not respect this right when World War I broke out. Its submarines sank American ships without warning. Therefore, in 1917, President Woodrow Wilson asked Congress to declare war against Germany. American troops sailed to Europe to fight in the trenches alongside the British and the French. As soon as World War I ended, however, the American people turned their backs on Europe, never wanting to become involved again in a foreign war.

U.S. policy toward Latin America. Americans were far more willing to become involved in the politics of Mexico and the countries of Central and South America. They considered these lands to be in their own backyard. In 1823, President James Monroe sent a warning to the governments of Europe. He said the United States would firmly oppose any attempt by a European nation to interfere in the politics of Latin America. His diplomatic message became famous as the Monroe Doctrine.

Though Europeans were not supposed to interfere in Latin America, the United States often interfered there. In 1903, President Theodore Roosevelt used the U.S. Navy to support an uprising in Panama against the government of Colombia. His action enabled the United States to build

THE PANAMA CANAL. This canal connecting two oceans has been under U.S. control ever since it was completed in 1914. But in the year 2000, the nation of Panama will gain control. How is U.S. willingness to give up the canal an example of the Good Neighbor policy?

and operate the Panama Canal. Later, President Wilson sent the Marines into Nicaragua and Haiti to keep order. His use of military force to bring about political change is known as a policy of intervention.

In the 1930s, President Franklin Roosevelt changed U.S. policy toward Latin America. He recognized that the peoples of this region resented the interventionist policies of the past. In the future, Franklin Roosevelt said, the United States would follow a "Good Neighbor" policy and treat the countries to the south with respect.

U.S. policy toward Asia. When thinking about Asia, policy-makers were mainly concerned with promoting business. In the second half of the 19th century (1850–1900), U.S. factories turned out vast amounts of cloth, steel, machinery, and other goods. Manufacturers needed to find millions of buyers for their products. They hoped to sell them to the peoples of Asia—particularly to the Chinese.

But Europeans were trying to win exclusive control of the China trade. Therefore, in 1900, the United States announced its open-door policy. It declared that China's markets should be left open to everyone. Also, China's territory and independence should be respected.

When Japanese armies occupied part of China in the 1930s, a direct challenge was made to the open-door policy. In 1940, President Franklin Roosevelt began putting economic and diplomatic pressure on Japan to withdraw from China. But instead of withdrawing, the Japanese decided in 1941 to bomb the American naval base at Pearl Harbor. So began U.S. involvement in World War II against Japan and its allies, Germany and Italy.

Cold War policies after World War II. The United States and its allies (Britain, China, and the Soviet Union) won the war in Europe and Asia. But the great victory in 1945 also brought problems in foreign policy. These problems were unlike anything Americans had ever faced.

- *For the first time,* the United States had greater military power than any other nation in the world. This fact of superior power put the United States in a position of world leadership and responsibility.
- *For the first time,* a powerful nation and former ally now looked upon the United States as its enemy. This country, the Soviet Union, had the largest army in the world. Its power was second only to that of the United States. As a Communist country, the Soviet Union distrusted countries like the United States where private businesses operated freely. (For an explanation of communism, review pages 54–57.) The Soviet government was committed to a policy of aggressively promoting communism in other countries of the world.
- *For the first time,* there existed a weapon capable of destroying much of the world. The dropping of two atomic bombs over Japan in 1945 ended World War II. But ever since, people throughout the world have lived in fear that nuclear weapons might be used again in some future war.

The three conditions discussed above caused the United States to abandon its isolationist policies of the past. It was now a superpower confronting another superpower, the Soviet Union. U.S. leaders decided that they could not stand by and watch Soviet-sponsored communism spread to other countries. American diplomats and military leaders thought the United States should actively oppose—or "contain"—communism everywhere in the world. This policy came to be known as containment.

The first president to apply the policy of containment was Harry Truman. He persuaded Congress to give millions of dollars in aid to the democracies of Western Europe. The money helped strengthen France, Greece, and Italy so that the Communist parties in those countries would not take power. Also, as you know, Truman contained communism in Asia by sending U.S. troops to Korea.

The fighting in Korea was a "hot war" involving bombs and bullets. But the larger conflict between the two superpowers was a "cold war" involving angry words and threats. Through the 1950s and 1960s, Soviet and American leaders often expressed their distrust and fear of each other's governments. Therefore, this period in history is called the Cold War.

Defensive alliances around the world. Other countries besides the United States felt threatened by the Soviet Union. For their mutual protection, the anti-Communist countries signed a number of treaties of alliance. Such treaties are also called defense pacts. Nations agreeing to each pact promised to come to one another's defense if just one of them was ever attacked.

The pact for the defense of Western Europe and North America was signed in 1949. It set up a permanent system of defense called the **North Atlantic Treaty Organization** (NATO). NATO now maintains an army and air force staffed by personnel from every participating country, including the United States.

The map on page 458 shows what European nations belonged to NATO. (On the other side of the Atlantic, Canada and the United States were also NATO members.)

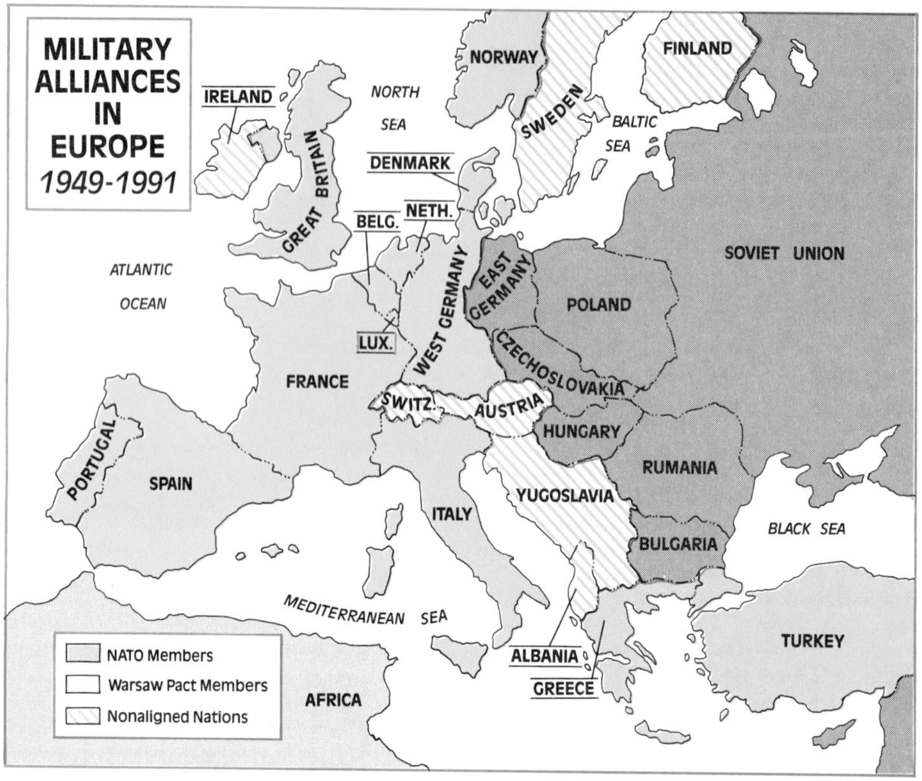

The map also shows the nations of Eastern Europe that were allied with the Soviet Union. This rival alliance, known as the Warsaw Pact, was created in 1955 as the Communist countries' system of mutual defense.

✔✔ SKILLS CHECK: Interpreting political maps

From the map above, you can learn a great deal about the alliances formed in the Cold War.

1. Do you think West Germany was one of the countries that originally signed the NATO treaty in 1949? Why or why not?
2. What European countries were part of NATO? Name them.
3. How many countries of Europe did not belong to the Communist alliance or to the anti-Communist alliance? Name them.
4. How many countries of the Warsaw Pact had borders that touch NATO countries? Name them.
5. In what country would you have expected to find the largest number of NATO troops? Why?

The United States is committed to the defense of nations around the world. In Asia, it has signed defense pacts with the Philippines, Japan, South Korea, Australia, and New Zealand. In our own part of the world, Latin America and the United States belong to a mutual defense system called the **Organization of American States** (OAS). Members of this organization are pledged to aid one another in fighting aggression. Almost all the countries of Central and South America belong to the OAS. One exception is Cuba, which dropped out of the alliance in 1960 after becoming a Communist nation.

End of the Cold War. Until as recently as 1989, it seemed that the Cold War between the United States and the Soviet Union would never end. Then, almost overnight, revolutionary changes occurred in both the Soviet Union and Eastern Europe. In the late 1980s, Soviet leader Mikhail Gorbachev began to make the politics of his country more open and democratic. For the first time, candidates who were not communists could run for election.

Reform in the Soviet Union led to revolution in the countries of Eastern Europe. Allowed to vote freely either for or against continued rule of the Communist party, the Polish people voted the communists out of office. So did the Hungarians, Czechs, Bulgarians, and Romanians. The people of these countries were at last free of domination by communists.

Because of these sudden changes of 1989 and 1990, the map of Europe today is not the same as the map on page 458. It is not sharply divided between one set of countries allied with the Soviet Union and another set of countries allied with the United States. One international border—the line separating East Germany from West Germany—has been totally eliminated. Ever since the end of World War II in 1945, these two territories had been governed as separate countries. They were kept apart by Cold War politics. Then in 1990 the World War II Allies signed a treaty permitting the two Germanys to become one nation.

At the same time, 12 nations of Western Europe looked forward to a major change in their economic life. These nations (including all European members of NATO *except* Norway and Turkey) belonged to a Common Market, or Economic Community (EC). The EC nations agreed that in 1992 they would place their economies under a single governing body.

Makers of U.S. foreign policy understood that the world of the 1990s would be radically different from what it had been. In this fast-changing world, how could the United States best achieve its four historic goals: freedom, peace, prosperity, and national security? In the next section, you will debate some of the alternatives.

REVIEW

A. Making Comparisons

This exercise will help you compare U.S. policies **before** World War II with policies **after** that war. Tell whether each statement below describes:

A. American foreign policy *before* World War II
B. American foreign policy *after* World War II
C. American foreign policy both *before* and *after* World War II.

1. Staying at peace was a major goal.
2. The United States formed alliances with anti-Communist countries.
3. The secretary of state played a role in making policy.
4. Japan became an enemy when it challenged the open-door policy.
5. The United States wanted to protect Latin America from foreign aggression.
6. The United States tried to avoid getting involved in European politics.
7. The risk of nuclear warfare was a constant worry.

B. Building Your Political Vocabulary

Complete each sentence by filling in the missing word __(?)__. Write your answers on a separate sheet of paper.

1. The purpose of the policy of __(?)__ was to stop the takeover of foreign governments by Communist forces.

2. The purpose of the __(?)__ was to prevent European powers from interfering in the politics of Latin America.
3. President Jefferson's attempt to avoid "entangling alliances" expressed the policy of __(?)__.
4. The policy of the __(?)__ in Asia was aimed at providing markets for American goods.
5. Harry Truman carried out a policy of __(?)__ when he sent troops to Korea in 1950.
6. The OAS and NATO are examples of __(?)__ pacts.

4. WHAT POLICIES SHOULD GUIDE THE UNITED STATES IN THE FUTURE?

We know about past events, since they have already happened. Future events cannot be known. Nevertheless, we can reasonably assume that important issues of the recent past will probably continue to be issues in the future.

This final section of the chapter consists of three debates on policy questions of the future. In one form or another, we can expect to see these questions argued in the newspapers and on TV news shows. They are problems that will be with us for a long time. Your opinions about them will be important to you—and also to those leaders who make foreign policy.

Terms that you should know. First, you should be familiar with a few terms that are often used in debates about defense policy and foreign policy. (You may refer back to this list when you come across a term in the debates that follow.)

Interdependence: the condition of nations depending on one another for their economic well-being. What happens in one region of the world is certain to have an effect on all other regions.

Third World: the poorer, less-developed nations of the world. These countries (mostly in Africa, Asia, and Latin America) have common economic problems. They want to catch up with the advanced economies of Europe, Japan, the Soviet Union, and the United States. But they are at a great disadvantage. Many nations of the Third World did not exist as independent states before World War II. Before winning their independence, they had been under the colonial rule of Europeans (Germans, British, Dutch, French, Spanish). Many people in the Third World have bitter memories of the colonial powers who had controlled them.

Intervention: the policy of sending troops to a foreign country in an effort to end a civil war, replace a hostile government, or solve some other political problem.

New world order: a term used by President Bush to describe what he hoped would be a more peaceful and stable world after the Cold War ended.

Arms race: a competition between two or more nations to have a more powerful stockpile of weapons than any rival. Weapons of all types from nuclear weapons to

A BUS IN BANGLADESH. Is it in the interest of the United States to aid the development of Third-World countries?

hand grenades may be involved in the competition.

Arms control: the diplomatic goal of putting limits on the arms race. When the Cold War ended, Russia and the United States agreed to a plan for eliminating thousands of their nuclear warheads.

Nuclear deterrence: a defense strategy for stopping another nation from attacking by threatening to retaliate with nuclear weapons.

Human rights: the political and legal rights of people everywhere in the world, as defined by the United Nations. Such rights include the right to a fair trial and the right not to be tortured. Many governments of the world do *not* respect the rights of their citizens.

Repression: the practice of using political power to deprive people of their freedom. Any government that fails to observe human rights may be called "repressive."

Foreign aid: lending or giving money to foreign governments to help them with their military or economic problems. Much of the aid voted by Congress goes to Third-World countries and to allies such as Israel.

Balance of trade: the difference in money value between a country's imports and exports. Usually, trade is *not* balanced. After one year of trade, a nation has either (*a*) exported more than it imported and has a trade surplus or (*b*) imported more than it exported and has a trade deficit.

Protectionism: the policy of putting a high tax (or tariff) on imported goods. The purpose of this policy is to lessen competition from cheaper foreign-made goods.

SUMMIT MEETING, 1990. The Soviet president Mikhail Gorbachev (left) came to the United States in June, 1990, to meet with President Bush. The two leaders signed an agreement on nuclear arms. To reduce the risk of nuclear war, do you think it is better to have more nuclear weapons or fewer?

DEBATE ONE: IF A CIVIL WAR CAUSES MASSIVE SUFFERING, SHOULD U.S. TROOPS INTERVENE?

Read the arguments on both sides of the question. Then make up your own mind.

YES. Of course U.S. troops should be used only after other means have been tried. But if diplomacy and economic sanctions fail, then the United States should rise to the challenge and take military action.

Just because the Cold War is over does not mean that the United States can neglect its responsibilities in the world. In fact, the challenges to U.S. foreign policy in the 1990s may be just as great as in the past. As we watch TV news reports of children starving in Somalia and people driven from their homes in Bosnia, we are shocked and horrified. As citizens of the most powerful nation on earth, we Americans have a moral duty to rescue the innocent victims of civil wars and ethnic hatreds.

We should intervene in other nations' civil wars not just for reasons of moral responsibility but also for reasons of national self-interest. The world today is completely interdependent. If one part of the world falls into chaos and ruin, the problem may well spread like a poison to surrounding areas. In such a world, the United States cannot be stable and secure unless other nations also have stable governments. True, a commitment of U.S. troops abroad involves great expense in both money and the potential loss of American lives. But we have a proud tradition to uphold as a nation that has sacrificed greatly to bring about peace. Continuing in that tradition, we can rescue other nations from the horrors of civil war. Eventually, if we persevere, we may see a stable world order emerge.

NO. History as well as common sense prove that it would be folly for U.S. troops to take part in another nation's civil war. Consider what happened in the 1960s when troops were sent by the hundreds of thousands to fight in a civil war in Vietnam. Americans believed at first that they were fighting in a good cause: preventing the fall of South Vietnam to Communist tyranny. But they soon discovered that Vietnam's civil war was a complicated and nasty struggle, in which both sides were guilty of brutal acts against civilians. U.S. involvement in Vietnam was a disaster not only for the United States but also for the people of Vietnam who had to endure a much longer and more destructive civil war because of U.S. intervention.

There are many other examples of military interventions that backfired. In 1983, U.S. Marines were stationed in Beirut, Lebanon—a city torn apart by civil war. Their mission was to put a stop to the killing. Instead, they became the target for a terrorist attack in which 241 marines were killed. The U.S. effort at peacekeeping, though well intentioned, could not and did not end the violence in Lebanon.

We should remember the bitter lessons of Vietnam and Lebanon. Sending troops to fight in another country's civil war can only have one result: failure of U.S. policy and increased suffering and violence for everybody involved.

DEBATE TWO: SHOULD THE UNITED STATES STOP GIVING AID TO MILITARY DICTATORS?

YES. Promoting freedom is supposed to be a major goal of U.S. foreign policy. During the Cold War, communism was one enemy of freedom—but it was by no means the only enemy. Today, in many countries of the world, people suffer from the cruel repression of military dictators. Anyone who criticizes these dictators may be arrested, jailed, and even tortured. Entire families may be punished simply because one member is suspected of being opposed to the government.

The United States should oppose *all* governments that suppress basic freedoms. But instead of this, both during and after the Cold War, millions of dollars of U.S. aid have gone to dictatorial regimes in Latin America, Asia, Africa, and the Middle East.

It looks bad for the United States to support dictatorships. It causes people to question whether the United States truly cares about freedom. Foreign aid is supposed to win friends in the world. Instead, it may have just the opposite result.

NO. It would be ideal if every nation was perfectly democratic. But we are not living in an ideal world. In the *real* world, we must recognize that our number-one goal at all times and in all circumstances is to preserve the freedom and security of our own nation, the United States. Promoting freedom and democracy elsewhere is important—but secondary.

True, a few of the governments that receive U.S. aid are guilty of violating human rights. This is an unfortunate fact that U.S. presidents cannot and do not ignore. Efforts are constantly being made to persuade offending governments to change their ways. We would have no influence at all on these governments if we suddenly cut off aid dollars.

DEBATE THREE: SHOULD WE PUT A HIGH TARIFF ON IMPORTS THAT COMPETE WITH AMERICAN GOODS?

YES. Every year, we hear the sad reports of U.S. plants and factories being closed. People thrown out of work by these closings have a hard time finding jobs. In Detroit, the decline of the automobile industry has depressed the economic life of the entire city. Many other cities have also felt the depressing effects of closed factories and lost jobs.

The main cause of these troubles is competition from abroad. American consumers naturally prefer low-priced, high-quality imports rather than the higher-priced products of U.S. factories. On our highways, therefore, we see almost as many imported cars as American cars. In our homes, we switch on radios, TV sets, and other appliances that are mainly foreign-made.

The best way to revive American industries is to shut down the flow of cheap imports. By passing high tariffs, we can raise the prices of foreign-made goods. Then, once again, we can look forward to a growing market at home for consumer goods marked MADE IN USA.

NO. By raising tariffs, we would only be hurting ourselves. This is true for two reasons. First, consumers would suffer from the higher prices they would have to pay. Second, other countries would almost surely fight back. Following our example, they would be inclined to raise their own tariffs on imports. American businesses would then have a harder time selling American-made goods abroad.

The results of this trade war would be disastrous. It could bring about a worldwide depression as bad as that of the 1930s.

Those who favor protectionism fail to understand the basic facts of economic life. The most important fact of our times is the interdependence of nations. Because of this fact, everyone in the world benefits from free trade. Everyone would lose—the United States perhaps worst of all—if that trade were cut back by protectionist tariffs.

Foreign Policy in the 90s

When the cold war ended and the Soviet Union collapsed, Americans and much of the world rejoiced. At last, they thought, there would be less danger of nuclear war and less need to spend billions of dollars a year on defense just to stay ahead of the Russians. Soon, however, people began to realize that the new era in world politics was also full of danger.

In 1993, President Clinton appointed James Woolsey to be the new director of the CIA. Woolsey said: "We have slain a large dragon [Soviet power] but we live now in a jungle filled with a bewildering variety of poisonous snakes. And in many ways, the dragon was easier to keep track of."

Identifying the "poisonous snakes." What are the various "snakes" that currently inhabit the international jungle and challenge U.S. interests? Chief among them are the following:

1. Nuclear proliferation. The United States and Russia are not the only nations that have nuclear weapons. When the Soviet Union broke up, its nuclear warheads were located in four different republics: Russia, Belarus, Ukraine, and Kazakhstan. In addition, several other countries including India, China, and France have tested nuclear weapons. The United States also worried that nuclear weapons might soon be developed by such nations as North Korea and Iraq. If that happened, what could stop an ambitious leader like Iraq's Saddam Hussein from resorting to nuclear warfare to achieve his aims?

2. Ethnic hatreds. Soviet power had suppressed freedom. But it had also stopped different ethnic groups from fighting one another. Early in the 1990s, violent conflicts erupted in more than a dozen nations of Eastern Europe and Central Asia. In Bosnia and Herzegovina, Serbs battled Muslims. In a small region between the Black and Caspian seas, seven different wars were being fought in 1993 involving Armenians, Azerbaijanis, Georgians, and others. At the same time, African nations such as Somalia, Rwanda, Angola, and Zaire were also torn apart by armed conflict among rival groups.

3. Terrorism. In February 1993, a terrorist's bomb exploded in the underground parking garage of the World Trade Center in New York City. In other nations, groups of terrorists have killed government officials, Olympic athletes, tourists, and even children. In the post-cold war era, the problem of terrorism is expected to become much worse.

4. Environmental damage. A fourth "poisonous snake" was more subtle but no less dangerous than the others. Daily pouring out of hundreds of millions of automobiles and factories were billions of tons of toxic chemicals. Daily the world's already poisoned atmosphere became more polluted. Daily the rain forests of Brazil, Central Africa, and Indonesia became smaller.

One nation among many. What should be the U.S. role—if any—in dealing with these international problems of the 1990s?

First, it is important to state the obvious. Today, as in the past, the United States is the world's most powerful nation. In 1992, the U.S. government spent $286 billion on defense, a sum greater than all the money spent for food, clothing, and housing in Mexico or Nigeria. Economic wealth is the basis of military power. In this respect, too, the United States is the number-one power. Its yearly production of goods and services surpasses that of any other nation, including Japan and Russia.

However, U.S. power is limited. The world today consists of more than 180 sovereign nations. Each is free to pursue its own interests in its own way. Therefore, the United States cannot dictate a solution to international problems, even if it wished to do so.

YOU DECIDE: Given this reality (great power but limited), how much responsibility does the United States have for dealing with the four "snakes" that threaten the world? Explain your position.

REVIEW

A. Agree or Disagree

For each debate question, tell how you would answer it and explain.

1. Should the United States intervene in the civil wars of other nations?
2. Should the United States stop giving aid to military dictators?
3. Should we put a high tariff on imports that compete with American goods?

B. Facts and Opinions

The arguments in the three debates presented both facts and opinions. Tell whether you think each statement below is a **fact** or an **opinion**. Explain your answers.

1. The challenges to U.S. foreign policy in the 1990s may be just as great as in the past.
2. TV news reports showed children starving in Somalia and people driven from their homes in Bosnia.
3. It would be folly for U.S. troops to take part in other nations' civil wars.
4. It looks bad for the United States to support dictatorships.
5. Millions of dollars of U.S. aid have gone to dictatorial regimes in Third World countries.
6. In the United States, factories have closed and workers have lost their jobs.
7. Imports from abroad are a major cause of the decline of U.S. industries.
8. If the United States adopted protectionist policies, other nations would do the same.

CHAPTER REVIEW

A. Completing the Summary

Select terms from the word list to fill in the blanks in the summary below. Write your answers on a piece of paper.

ambassadors	interdependent
Chiefs of Staff	international
CIA	intervention
Cold War	isolationism
consuls	open door
containment	protectionism
defense	secretary of state
diplomacy	Security Council
foreign aid	Third-World
General Assembly	treaties

Nations communicate with one another by means of a system called __(1)__. The U.S. __(2)__ assigned to different capitals of the world attempt to carry out the foreign policies of our government. Their boss is a member of the president's Cabinet and holds the title of __(3)__. It is the duty of __(4)__ to take care of passport problems and serve the interest of Americans traveling abroad.

The United Nations is a(n) __(5)__ organization whose chief goal is to settle disputes peacefully. For this purpose resolutions may be debated and adopted by both the __(6)__ (representing all nations) and the __(7)__. However, the UN lacks power to enforce its resolutions, and nations are free either to obey or ignore them.

In the making of U.S. foreign policy, the president works closely with the secretary of state, the secretary of

__(8)__, and the Joint __(9)__. Although the latter are military officers, they must carry out the defense policies of the president, a civilian. Another important adviser to the president in foreign affairs is the head of the __(10)__, an information-gathering agency.

Although the Constitution gives the president the power to make __(11)__, the "advice and consent" of the Senate is required for ratification. Three other checks on the president's foreign policies are (*a*) Congress's power to declare war, (*b*) Congress's power to appropriate money for defense, and (*c*) the pressure of public opinion.

World War II marked a major turning point in the history of U.S. foreign policy. Before that war, U.S. policy toward Europe was generally one of __(12)__. The policy of the __(13)__ in Asia protected U.S. trading interests. After World War II, conflict with the Soviet Union was referred to as the __(14)__. The policy of opposing Soviet expansion was called __(15)__.

One policy issue that is likely to cause heated debate in the future is whether to intervene in other nations' civil wars. One side says yes because we live in an __(16)__ world and must keep wars from spreading. Critics say no because our past experiences with military __(17)__ have backfired and caused increased suffering and violence.

Two other vital issues concern U.S. policy toward (*a*) trade and (*b*) human rights. Those arguing for a trade policy of __(18)__ are worried about the decline of American industries resulting from foreign competition. Those concerned about human rights say that the United States should stop giving __(19)__ to military dictatorships. People who suffer from human rights violations may also suffer economically from the poverty common in __(20)__ countries.

B. Applying What You Know

Every year, the *World Almanac and Book of Facts* summarizes the major news events of the year before. Below are five events of 1993 as reported in the 1994 almanac. After reading about the events, answer the questions that follow.

Events

(*a*) February: BOSNIA. President Clinton ordered supplies of food and medicine to be dropped from U.S. aircraft over Muslim areas in Bosnia and Herzegovina. He said the U.S. purpose was to give humanitarian aid.

(*b*) March: HAITI. In the White House, President Clinton met with the exiled leader of Haiti, Jean-Bertrand Aristide. Clinton promised to help Aristide return to Haiti as that country's democratically elected president.

(*c*) May: WEAPONS SYSTEM. Clinton's secretary of defense announced that research on the antimissile program called Star Wars, would not continue. A total of $30 billion had already been spent on research for this weapons system.

(*d*) June: UNITED NATIONS. The UN Security Council voted to impose a worldwide ban on oil shipments to Haiti.

(*e*) October: SOMALIA. President Clinton announced that thousands more U.S. troops would be sent to Somalia to help bring an end to that country's civil war. He said that all U.S. troops would be out of Somalia by April 1994.

Questions:

1. Select *three* events that you think were of the greatest concern to the Joint Chiefs of Staff. Explain your choices.
2. Which event is an example of international sanctions being applied to a situation?
3. Which five nations voted "yes" on the UN resolution to ban oil shipments to Haiti?
4. Before the president announced his decision concerning Somalia (event e), he probably conferred with which foreign policy leaders? Name at least three.
5. Which event most clearly shows a change in U.S. policy away from containment and deterrence?
6. Which *two* events most clearly illustrate the president's power as commander in chief?
7. If the United States declared war in Bosnia, which branch of government would make the official decision to do so?

C. Projects

Expand your knowledge of U.S. foreign policy by selecting **one** of these research projects:

1. The firing of a general. In the library, locate the book that was quoted at the beginning of this chapter: Merle Miller, *Plain Speaking: An Oral Biography of Harry S. Truman*, Berkley Publishers, 1984. Its author interviewed Harry Truman about major decisions of his presidency, including the decision to use troops in Korea. Read Truman's account of another decision: the firing of General Douglas MacArthur in 1951. Write a summary of the episode and the reasons for Truman's decision. Say whether or not you agree with the decision and explain why.

2. Current makers of U.S. foreign policy. Who are the chief foreign-policy advisers to the *current* president? Find out by going to the reference section of the library and looking for the names of top officials in the State Department and Defense Department. The best source of information is *The United States Government Manual* for the current year. Draw up a list of *ten officials* who help the president make foreign policy and defense policy. Post your list on the class bulletin board.

3. Serious TV. Look for regularly scheduled TV programs such as "Meet the Press" in which experts talk about current political and international issues. Watch one program dealing with a foreign policy issue, and take notes on the following: (*a*) names and titles of the participants, (*b*) nature of the issue, (*c*) arguments both supporting and opposing the president's policies. Write a summary of what you learned from the discussion.

AUGUSTA, MAINE: In the United States, the state capital located farthest to the east.

HONOLULU, HAWAII: The state capital located farthest to the south and west.

UNIT EIGHT

Your State and Community

Do you live within 250 miles of any of these places: Albany, New York . . . Columbus, Ohio . . . Springfield, Illinois . . . Nashville, Tennessee . . . Montgomery, Alabama . . . Flagstaff, Arizona . . . Portland, Oregon? Place names like these define what every American citizen calls "home." So far, in this text, you have studied a national government whose capital, Washington, D.C., may be hundreds and even thousands of miles from your home. Now, in this final unit, you will be studying the places that you know best—your own community and your own state.

The pictures to the left present two facts about the geography of the states. The quiz below gives STATEments that may be either true or false. Take the quiz in order to start thinking about your state and local governments. Answer either **true** (T) or **false** (F) on a piece of paper.

1. Of the 50 states, Hawaii was the last to win statehood.
2. Honolulu, Hawaii, and Augusta, Maine, are both examples of municipalities.
3. Your state government is not allowed to make treaties with the government of Canada or any other government.
4. Your state has its own written constitution.
5. The state capital located farthest to the north is Juneau, Alaska.
6. In every state, county government is far more important than town or city government.
7. The most important official in every U.S. city is the mayor.
8. Every state has a court system that is separate from the federal court system.
9. Every state has an elected governor.
10. The idea of separation of powers is carried out by all state governments.
11. The governor of your state has exactly the same powers as the governor of every other state.
12. Kentucky has the same number of U.S. senators as Ohio.
13. Every state must accept as valid the drivers' licenses issued to drivers from out of state.
14. Setting requirements for public schools is a major function of your state government.

Answers

1. *T*	5. *T*	9. *T*	13. *T*
2. *T*	6. *F*	10. *T*	14. *T*
3. *T*	7. *F*	11. *F*	
4. *T*	8. *T*	12. *T*	

THREE CAPITOLS. Top left: State capitol in Austin, Texas. Top right: State capitol in Sacramento, California. Bottom: U.S. Capitol in Washington, D.C. What similarities are there between the government of your state and the government of the United States?

CHAPTER 20

Comparing State Governments

OBJECTIVES

After reading this chapter, you will know

1. how state governments carry out the idea of separation of powers.
2. the titles and duties of state officials who are elected to office.
3. the types of services provided by your state government.
4. the ways that states both compete and cooperate.
5. how *your* state compares with other states.
6. how to make generalizations from a chart.

Imagine this: After boarding a plane, you fly to Austin, the state capital of Texas. The next day, you take off from the Austin airport and fly west and north to Sacramento, the capital of California. In each city, you visit the public buildings where laws are made for the state. Each building is called a capitol. (Note this distinction: A capi*tal* is a city; a capi*tol* is a building.)

Comparing capitols, you would see the similarities between them. Each is a massive stone structure crowned by a dome. Circling around the base of the dome are graceful, marble columns. Just above the columns are a series of windows, and above them rises the dome itself. In both Austin and Sacramento, you would be reminded of a third building: the U.S. Capitol in Washington, D.C.

Are the states of Texas and California as much alike as their capitols? The answer is a definite NO! Texans will tell you that they are not like Californians. People in both states are proud of their unique histories and traditions. In the 1840s, both Texas and California were not just separate states. They were completely independent nations. California called itself the Bear Flag Republic because its flag displayed a grizzly bear. Texas called itself the Lone Star Republic. For ten years (1836–1845), its national flag had just one star. Today, as states within the United States, the flags of California and Texas look like this:

Texas and California are alike in some ways, different in others. The same can be said of all 50 states, including your own. Throughout this chapter, we will be making comparisons among six selected states: **Texas, California, Florida, Missouri, New York,** and **Massachusetts.** These featured states are shaded gray on the map on page 473. All 50 states *should* be compared in detail. But the words needed to do that would fill a book much larger than this one. So it is necessary to be selective.

Your state may or may not be one of the six featured. If not, you will be looking up facts about your state in the final section of the chapter. You will then know enough about other states to see in what ways your state is like them—and not like them. Every section, including the last, involves the skill of making comparisons. By the end of the chapter, you should be a master of that skill. You will also know the answers to these questions:

1. In what ways are state governments similar to the U.S. government?
2. In what ways are state governments different from the U.S. government?
3. In what ways are the 50 states different from one another?
4. How does *your* state compare with other states?

1. IN WHAT WAYS ARE STATE GOVERNMENTS SIMILAR TO THE U.S. GOVERNMENT?

It is much easier to learn something if you can relate the new information to what you already know. Fortunately, you now know how the U.S. government is organized. State governments are organized very much like the U.S. government. By reviewing basic facts about the U.S. government, you will quickly become familiar with the general outline of state governments.

Look at the six states featured in gray on the map on page 473. To illustrate how *all* state governments are organized, these six will be used as examples.

All states have constitutions. In Chapter 5, you learned about the "four P's" of the U.S. Constitution. Found in that document are: (1) the **purposes** of the federal government, (2) the **powers** of the federal government, (3) the **procedures** for making federal laws and electing or appointing federal officials, and (4) the **protections** of your rights as a U.S. citizen.

Each of the 50 states has its own written constitution. Most state constitutions begin with a short paragraph—the "preamble"—similar to the Preamble of the U.S. Constitution. For example:

> We, the people of the State of Florida, being grateful to Almighty God for our constitutional liberty, in order to secure its benefits, perfect our government, insure domestic tranquility, maintain public order, and guarantee equal civil and political rights to all, do ordain and establish this constitution.
>
> —Florida Constitution

Protections (rights) are listed first. You recall the first ten amendments to the U.S. Constitution that make up our federal Bill of Rights. They prohibit the federal government from denying people their basic rights to freedom of speech, a fair trial, due process of law, and so on.

Every state government also lists the rights of its citizens. In Florida's constitution, this list is called a "Bill of Rights." In Missouri's constitution, it is called a "Declaration of Rights." In most state constitutions, the list of people's rights come *before* any mention of government powers.

Many of the rights in state constitutions are similar to those in the U.S. Constitution.

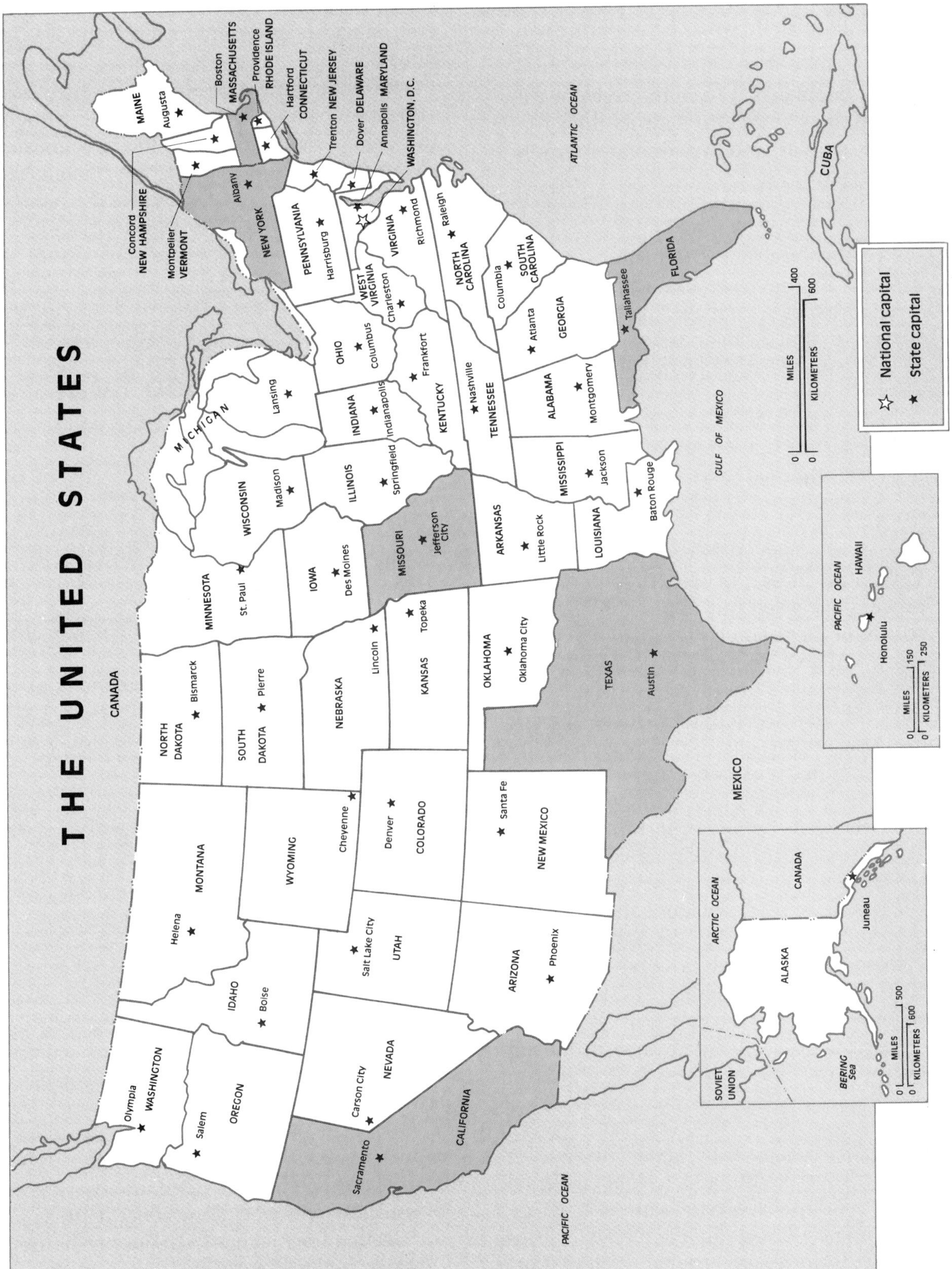
THE UNITED STATES
CANADA
MAINE
Augusta
Concord
NEW HAMPSHIRE
Montpelier
VERMONT
Boston
MASSACHUSETTS
Providence
RHODE ISLAND
Hartford
CONNECTICUT
Albany
NEW YORK
Trenton NEW JERSEY
Dover DELAWARE
Annapolis MARYLAND
WASHINGTON, D.C.
PENNSYLVANIA
Harrisburg
WEST VIRGINIA
Charleston
VIRGINIA
Richmond
NORTH CAROLINA
Raleigh
SOUTH CAROLINA
Columbia
GEORGIA
Atlanta
FLORIDA
Tallahassee
OHIO
Columbus
MICHIGAN
Lansing
INDIANA
Indianapolis
KENTUCKY
Frankfort
TENNESSEE
Nashville
ALABAMA
Montgomery
MISSISSIPPI
Jackson
LOUISIANA
Baton Rouge
ILLINOIS
Springfield
WISCONSIN
Madison
MINNESOTA
St. Paul
IOWA
Des Moines
MISSOURI
Jefferson City
ARKANSAS
Little Rock
NORTH DAKOTA
Bismarck
SOUTH DAKOTA
Pierre
NEBRASKA
Lincoln
KANSAS
Topeka
OKLAHOMA
Oklahoma City
TEXAS
Austin
MONTANA
Helena
WYOMING
Cheyenne
COLORADO
Denver
NEW MEXICO
Santa Fe
IDAHO
Boise
UTAH
Salt Lake City
ARIZONA
Phoenix
WASHINGTON
Olympia
OREGON
Salem
NEVADA
Carson City
CALIFORNIA
Sacramento
PACIFIC OCEAN
ATLANTIC OCEAN
GULF OF MEXICO
MEXICO
CUBA
MILES 0 400
KILOMETERS 0 600
National capital
State capital
PACIFIC OCEAN
HAWAII
Honolulu
MILES 0 150
KILOMETERS 0 250
ARCTIC OCEAN
CANADA
ALASKA
Juneau
SOVIET UNION
BERING Sea
MILES 0 500
KILOMETERS 0 600

The clauses below, for example, should sound familiar to you. (Compare them to clauses in the U.S. Bill of Rights.)

> The people shall have the right peaceably to assemble, to instruct their representatives, and to petition for redress of grievances.
> —Florida Constitution (Art. I, sect. 5)

> Every subject has a right to be secure from all unreasonable searches, and seizures, of his person, his houses, his papers, and all his possessions.
> —Massachusetts Constitution (Art. XIV)

> In all criminal prosecutions, the accused shall have a speedy public trial by an impartial jury.
> —Texas Constitution (Art. I, sect. 10)

Powers are separated among three branches. You know how the idea of separation of powers is carried out under the U.S. Constitution. Legislative (lawmaking) powers are given to Congress. Executive (law-enforcing) powers are given to a chief executive, the president. Judicial (law-interpreting) powers are given to a Supreme Court and inferior courts. In other words, there are three branches of government, each with its special set of powers and duties.

The same is true of all state governments, which divide powers as follows:

Legislative power belongs to elected representatives meeting in the state capitol.

Executive power belongs to several elected officials, chief of whom is the state's governor.

Judicial power belongs to a number of state courts, one of which is the final authority.

Two houses enact state laws. Just as Congress is divided into a House and a Senate, the legislatures of 49 states are also divided into an *upper house* and a *lower house.* These state legislatures are bicameral. Nebraska is the only exception. Its legislature is unicameral, since its laws are made by just one house.

The U.S. House of Representatives, as you know, has a larger membership than the U.S. Senate. Similarly, the two houses of a typical state legislature are unequal in size. The table on page 475 gives the names and relative sizes of the legislatures of six states.

SKILLS CHECK: Generalizing from data

Which of the statements below are supported by facts in the table? Which are not supported by them?

1. The lower house is always larger than the upper house.
2. The upper house is always called the state "senate."
3. States with the largest populations also have the largest legislatures. (CLUE: California, New York, and Texas are larger than the other three states.)
4. In Massachusetts, the lower house has four times as many members as the upper house.
5. The state senate in Texas is smaller than the state senates in the other states.

Lawmakers represent legislative districts. Recall how members of the U.S. House of Representatives are elected. Each state is divided into congressional districts. Voters from each district elect one U.S. representative.

A similar method is used for electing representatives to the *state* legislature. The map of most states is divided into two kinds of legislative districts. One set of districts is for electing lawmakers to the upper house, or state senate. Missouri, for example, is

COMPARING STATE LEGISLATURES

	NAME	NUMBER OF MEMBERS
CALIFORNIA		
Upper house	Senate	40
Lower house	Assembly	80
FLORIDA		
Upper house	Senate	40
Lower house	House of Representatives	120
MASSACHUSETTS		
Upper house	Senate	40
Lower house	House of Representatives	160
MISSOURI		
Upper house	Senate	34
Lower house	House of Representatives	163
NEW YORK		
Upper house	Senate	61
Lower house	Assembly	150
TEXAS		
Upper house	Senate	31
Lower house	House of Representatives	150

divided into 47 such districts. The other set of districts is for electing lawmakers to the lower house. How many districts would you expect to find for electing members of the Missouri House of Representatives? (Again, refer to the table on page 475.) To ensure that all citizens are represented equally, a state's legislative districts must be about equal in population.

Committees do most of the lawmaking work. In Chapter 14, you learned about the procedures in Congress for introducing, debating, and voting upon bills. Lawmaking procedures of the state legislature are much the same. A bill is given a number and assigned to a committee of either the upper or lower house. The committee may either (*a*) pigeonhole (put aside) the bill or (*b*) act upon it favorably. If the committee approves the bill, it goes to the floor of the full house for a vote. If a majority vote "aye," the other house must take up the bill. A committee in that second house reviews it. If approved there, another floor vote is taken.

If there are differences in two versions of a bill (an upper house version and a lower house version), a conference committee meets to draw up a compromise bill. The committee is made up of members from both houses. If passed by both houses, the bill goes to the governor, who either signs it or vetoes it.

Checks and balances are a feature of state constitutions. As you know, a chief executive's veto is a means of checking, or blocking, the actions of the legislature. A president's veto can check an act of Congress. Similarly, a governor's veto can check an act of the state legislature. Every state constitution except North Carolina's gives the governor the power to veto bills.

Most state constitutions also provide for a countercheck. A governor's veto can be defeated if two-thirds of the members of both lawmaking houses vote to override it. (In Nebraska with its one house, overriding is easier to achieve than in the two-house legislatures of other states.)

The governor has executive powers. The governor is to state government what the president is to the national government. He or she is the chief executive responsible for seeing that state laws are enforced. The governor is also the commander in chief of the state militia (National Guard), which may be called to active duty in time of emergency. For example, the governor may call upon the National Guard to control a riot or to rescue people from a disaster. In wartime, Guard units may be "federalized" and serve within the Army and Air Force.

People in state government look to the governor to provide leadership. At the beginning of each year, the legislature receives needed direction when the governor delivers a "state of the State" message. This message identifies issues that the governor thinks are important and includes recommendations for new laws. Then, like the president, the governor tries to persuade lawmakers to vote for his or her program.

A strong governor can do wonders for the economy of the state and the well-being of the state's citizens. "Being governor is the best job in politics right now," said a recent governor of New Jersey, Thomas Kean. "It's the job where you can get the most accomplished."

Cabinet officers advise the governor. The governor, like the U.S. president, needs a lot of help in executing state laws. He or she consults often with top state officials who run the executive departments (department of transportation, department of health, etc.). These officials who both administer state laws and advise the governor are known as the "cabinet."

The word "cabinet" does not appear in the U.S. Constitution. But it does appear in many state constitutions. For example:

TRAINING IN RIOT CONTROL. The National Guard of Connecticut receives training from the U.S. Navy in methods for controlling riots. What official in Connecticut is the commander in chief of these National Guardsmen?

There shall be a cabinet composed of a secretary of state, an attorney general, a comptroller, a treasurer, a commissioner of agriculture and a commissioner of education.
—Florida Constitution (Art. IV, sect. 4)

GOVERNOR OF VIRGINIA. In 1990, Douglas Wilder took the oath of office as the first African American to serve as the governor of a state. What document defines the Virginia governor's powers and duties?

The judicial branch consists of trial courts and appeals courts. Justice is an important goal of both state governments and the federal government. You learned in Chapter 15 that state courts and federal courts exist side by side. In the major cities of California, for example, there may be a state courthouse on one street and a federal courthouse only a few blocks away.

A system providing for appeals in the state courts is similar to the U.S. system of appeals described on pages 333–334. First, trials of both civil and criminal cases take place in lower, or trial, courts. Then, if a lawyer wants to challenge a trial court's decision, he or she may appeal it to a higher state court. One appeals court (like the U.S. Supreme Court) has greater power than all others in the state system. The building where this highest court meets is usually located in the state capital.

How many justices sit on a state's highest court of appeals? Compare the figures on page 478 for the states of California, Florida, Massachusetts, Missouri, New York, and Texas.

NAME OF HIGHEST COURT	NUMBER OF JUDGES
California Supreme Court	7
Florida Supreme Court	7
Massachusetts Supreme Judicial Court	7
Missouri Supreme Court	7
New York Court of Appeals	7
Texas Supreme Court	9

In the past, almost all of the higher court judges of all 50 states were men. But this fact is beginning to change. In Massachusetts in 1988, a woman judge sat on its supreme court and three women were among the 10 judges on its appeals court. This change at the state level is similar to what has happened at the federal level. Every justice on the U.S. Supreme Court had been a man until the appointment of Justice Sandra Day O'Connor in 1981.

REVIEW

A. Making Comparisons

AUSTIN: TEXAS = SACRAMENTO : CALIFORNIA

The above is an example of an **analogy.** It means: Austin is related to Texas in the same way Sacramento is related to California. Compare state governments to the federal government by completing each analogy.

1. GOVERNOR : STATE OF FLORIDA = PRESIDENT : __(?)__
2. STATE SENATE : LEGISLATIVE BRANCH = GOVERNOR'S CABINET : __(?)__
3. U.S. SUPREME COURT : U.S. CONSTITUTION = TEXAS SUPREME COURT : __(?)__
4. MISSOURI SENATE : MISSOURI HOUSE OF REPRESENTATIVES = U.S. SENATE : __(?)__
5. CAPITOL : BUILDING = CAPITAL : __(?)__

B. Building Your Political Vocabulary

First, define each term. Then explain how the term applies to the government of **your** state.

1. Constitution
2. Separation of powers
3. Cabinet
4. State bill of rights
5. Preamble
6. Checks and balances
7. Legislative districts

C. Making Inferences

Considering what you know about the six featured states, would you infer that each statement below is **probably true** or **probably not true** of your state? Give reasons for each answer. (NOTE: You will be checking your answers in the last section of the chapter.)

1. The number of judges sitting on your state's supreme court is more than 5 and less than 12.
2. One of the rights guaranteed in your state constitution is the right to be secure against unreasonable searches by police.
3. Your state's governor has the power to veto acts of the state legislature.
4. In your state legislature, there are more senators than members of the lower house.
5. The decisions of your state's trial courts are final and may not be appealed.
6. Bills that are approved by legislative committees in two houses stand a good chance of being enacted.

2. IN WHAT WAYS ARE STATE GOVERNMENTS DIFFERENT FROM THE U.S. GOVERNMENT?

In general terms, you now know how state governments are organized. You have seen that they have much in common with the U.S. government. Now let us see in what ways the two kinds of governments—state and national—are different.

States are not completely sovereign. The United States is a completely sovereign nation. But the states within it are not entirely sovereign, since they are prohibited from doing the following:

- issuing money
- declaring war
- negotiating treaties with foreign nations
- collecting taxes on trade with foreign nations
- collecting taxes on interstate trade.

A state's sovereign power to pass laws is limited by rules of a higher law—the U.S. Constitution. What happens, for example, when a state law contradicts either a rule in the Constitution or a law of Congress? Then the state law may be declared unconstitutional by a federal court. The state's governor may disagree with the U.S. court's ruling. But he or she must abide by and respect it because only the U.S. Constitution (not the state constitution) is supreme.

State constitutions may be long—or very long. The constitution of Georgia is almost *60 times* longer than the U.S. Constitution. Though Georgia's is the longest, other state constitutions are also much longer than the federal document.

State constitutions are long partly because they contain many details that the U.S. Constitution leaves out. For example, on page 480 are two details from the constitution of Texas.

CARTOON CORNER

Why is the constitution of your state longer than the U.S. Constitution? Do you agree with the governor in the cartoon?

> The Seal of the State shall be a star of five points encircled by olive and live oak branches and the words "The State of Texas."
>
> —Article 4

> The State tax on property . . . shall never exceed Thirty-five Cents ($.35) on the One Hundred Dollars ($100) valuation.
>
> —Article 8

Critics of state constitutions say that they contain too many details. They think the shorter U.S. Constitution is better because it gives only broad political principles. It gives Congress the power to collect taxes, but it does not fix the tax rate in dollars and cents.

The trouble with including a lot of details in a constitution is that they tend to go out of date quickly. Then the only way to change them is by formal amendment. Of course, amending a constitution dozens of times adds to its length. California's constitution, for example, has been amended more than 350 times!

In most states, the amendment process is relatively easy, involving just two steps:

1. An amendment is proposed in a bill adopted by the state legislature. (Passage could be by a majority vote as in Missouri, or by a two-thirds vote as in Texas.)
2. The proposed amendment is voted upon by the people of the state. If a majority vote "yes," the amendment is ratified and added to the constitution.

It is the second step, ratification, that is so much easier than the federal method of amendment. To ratify an amendment to the U.S. Constitution, recall that three-fourths of all of the state legislatures must approve it. As a general rule, legislators tend to vote "no" on proposed amendments, while voters tend to vote "yes." (One reason for this is that politicians must be careful not to offend special-interest groups. Voters, on the other hand, don't face the same negative pressures.)

State constitutions may be old or new. Besides being longer, many state constitutions are also newer. Florida's basic document, for example, was created in 1968 (compared to 1787 for the U.S. Constitution). Before 1968, Floridians had been governed under four earlier constitutions, the first one going back to 1839.

The people who create state constitutions meet in special conventions for the purpose. Each state has its own procedures for calling such constitutional conventions. Take New York as an example. First, majorities in the New York legislature must pass a proposal for holding a constitutional convention. A majority of voters must then approve the idea.

The oldest state constitution is that of Massachusetts. Created in 1780 (even before the U.S. Constitution), it has been amended more than 100 times.

State judges and cabinet officers may be elected by popular vote. Another major difference between the state and the federal governments shows up most clearly on Election Day. Recall that, in the Judicial Branch of the U.S. government, all federal judges are appointed to office, not elected. In the Executive Branch, only the president and vice president are elected. All members of the president's Cabinet are appointed.

State constitutions allow the voters many more opportunities to elect state officials in both the executive and judicial branches. New Yorkers, for example, vote for the following:

- 280 judges in the middle-level courts (what New York calls its "supreme courts")
- 7 judges on the highest court (New York Court of Appeals)
- a governor

- a lieutenant governor (a substitute for the governor in case of the latter's illness or death)
- an attorney general (an expert on the state's legal problems and an enforcer of state laws)
- a comptroller (an expert on state finances)

In most states, several top jobs in a state's executive branch are filled on Election Day. In Florida, for example, all six members of the governor's cabinet are elected. In many states, including Florida, Missouri, and California, voters may elect a secretary of state. Unlike the U.S. secretary of state, this official has nothing to do with foreign affairs. His or her main function is to keep state records and administer elections.

Most states also provide for the election of judges. Massachusetts is one of the few exceptions. Its judges are all appointed by the governor.

Should judges be elected? In a democracy such as ours, is it better for state judges to be (*a*) elected by popular vote or (*b*) appointed by the governor? Consider these arguments for both points of view:

a. Elect them. The governor is elected. All members of the state legislature are elected. Why then shouldn't top officials in the third branch, the judiciary, also be elected? Democratic government means that all top officials are responsible to the people. Judges will be careful to serve the people only if their jobs depend on winning election.

b. Appoint them. Judges should be highly trained specialists in the law. Their only concern should be conducting trials that are fair and just. They should not be politicians trying to win popularity by their courtroom decisions. If judges are appointed to office, they can concentrate on justice rather than on the next election.

Which argument do *you* think is the stronger?

Serving the general welfare is the main function of state governments. We now come to what is probably the most important difference between state governments and the federal government. It is a difference, not of organization, but of function.

- One of the FEDERAL government's main functions is to deal with *foreign* governments and "provide for the common defense" against *foreign* dangers.
- The STATE government's main function is to promote and protect the gen-

NORTH CAROLINA STATE BOARD OF EDUCATION. These officials were appointed by North Carolina's governor to make policy for all public schools in the state. What questions would you expect them to be discussing?

eral welfare of citizens living *within the state.*

State governments try to promote the general welfare of citizens in the following ways:

1. Educating. Because of state laws, all citizens have the opportunity to learn to read, write, and calculate with numbers. State laws, not federal laws, are responsible for operating public schools and determining what courses must be taken by students from kindergarten through high school.

2. Licensing. The public needs to be assured that motorists on the roads know how to drive and that doctors and other professionals know what they are doing. The state protects the public from quacks and incompetents by issuing *licenses* only to qualified individuals.

A driver's license is the most obvious example of the state licensing function. Other examples include: (1) issuing marriage licenses to those who meet state requirements, (2) issuing liquor licenses to owners of stores and restaurants, and (3) issuing licenses to doctors, lawyers, dentists, and nurses if they meet minimum standards for practicing their profession in the state. The standards for either granting or not granting such licenses are determined by state law.

FLORIDA BRIDGE AND FLORIDA LICENSE. At right is the construction stage of a seven-mile-long bridge in the Florida Keys. Most of the cars that cross it have Florida license plates. How do the two pictures show functions performed by every state government?

3. Incorporating businesses. Businesses wishing to operate as corporations within a state must apply to the state government for permission to *incorporate.* The document, or charter, granted by the state is like a birth certificate, giving the corporation its legal existence.

4. Regulating businesses. Whether a business is incorporated or not, it must comply with laws enacted by the state legislature. All states have laws designed to prevent businesses from polluting the environment, operating unsafe factories, and dealing unfairly or dishonestly with customers.

5. Giving aid to citizens. No society can be indifferent to the special needs of certain groups: the sick, the elderly, the disabled, and the poor. Many families either cannot or do not provide for the basic needs of family members. And private charities can do only so much for those in need. Recognizing this fact, states have laws for giving public assistance ("welfare") to people who

need it. Before the Great Depression in the 1930s, the states alone bore the responsibility for helping the homeless and the unemployed. Today, funds from the U.S. government support the states' efforts.

*6. **Policing.*** Most crimes that you hear about (murder, rape, theft, burglary, fraud, etc.) are defined by *state* laws, not federal laws. Highways are patrolled by state police, not federal police. Most criminal cases are tried in state courts, and most prisoners are confined in state prisons.

*7. **Holding elections.*** On Election Day, the officials who operate polling places and count ballots are employed by your state government, not the U.S. government. State legislatures make the rules for determining who is eligible to vote and how candidates may have their names included on the official, state-printed ballot.

*8. **Building public works.*** New York State boasts the longest suspension bridge in the world: the Verrazano Narrows Bridge. California's Golden Gate Bridge may be even more famous. These and the thousands of other bridges in the country were erected as public works of state governments. Other public works authorized by state laws are tunnels, subway systems, reservoirs, roads, highways, and airports.

Sales taxes and federal grants are the chief source of state revenue. How do states pay for their many services? In 1991, the money collected from *all* sources by all 50 state governments came to about $661.4 billion. Funds from the federal government accounted for a significant part of the total. Consider these figures:

STATE REVENUES, 1991 (figures rounded to nearest billion)

Total revenues	$661.4 billion
From federal government	$134.9 billion
From state sources (taxes, fees, other)	$526.6 billion

In other words, roughly one dollar out of every six was contributed by the U.S. government to the treasuries of the different states. Federal funds given to the states for specific purposes are known as *grants-in-aid*. Different departments of the state government apply for grants to finance various projects. For example, Missouri's Department of Highways and Transportation could apply for a federal grant-in-aid to build or repair Missouri's road system.

The states receive financial aid from the U.S. government, but they do not aid the U.S. government in return. This is one crucial difference between state and federal finances.

A second difference concerns the kind of tax that brings in the most revenue. As you know, the federal government gets most of its revenue from the personal income tax. The kind of tax that contributes the largest sum to most state treasuries is the state sales tax. This tax is collected from consumers whenever they make a purchase of a taxable item. State laws determine which consumer items are subject to tax. They also determine the percentage to be charged. In 1990, the

TAX STICKERS ON A TRUCK DOOR. Maryland, Mississippi, Illinois, and other states require trucks of a certain weight to display decals showing that they have paid road and fuel taxes to the state. What other kinds of taxes do states collect from businesses and individuals?

percentage varied from a low of .04 percent (Louisiana) to a high of 8.0 percent (Connecticut). For example, if you bought a $100 camera in a Connecticut store, you would have to pay an additional $8.00 in state sales tax. But if you bought a $100 camera in Louisiana, the state tax would be only $0.40.

REVIEW

A. Making Comparisons

Create a chart with two vertical columns. Label one column FEDERAL and the other STATE. Down the left side of the chart, copy this list of categories:

	FEDERAL	STATE
1. branches of government		
2. constitution		
3. armed forces		
4. elected offices		
5. appointed offices		
6. sources of revenue		

Complete your chart, giving information in each category about the federal government (column 1) and state governments (column 2). The completed chart will show at a glance how the two kinds of governments are alike and different.

B. Making Inferences

From what you have read, which of the following statements would you infer to be **true**? Which would you think is probably **not true**? Explain each answer.

1. Your state's constitution has many more clauses than the U.S. Constitution.
2. Amendments to the Tennessee Constitution must be ratified by a vote of the Tennessee legislature.
3. If an earthquake occurs in California, the governor may order units of the National Guard to the scene.
4. Texas collects a sales tax.
5. Policing the highways of Arkansas is a function of the federal government.
6. The high schools of New York State are required by law to teach certain subjects.

3. IN WHAT WAYS ARE THE 50 STATES DIFFERENT FROM ONE ANOTHER?

No state in the Union is exactly like any other. This section of the chapter will point out major differences among the states—particularly among the six featured states.

Terms of office differ from state to state. Every state constitution gives the number of years or terms that an elected official may serve. The table on page 485 summarizes the differences for six states.

SKILLS CHECK: Drawing conclusions from data

Would you say each statement below is **supported**—or **not supported**—by the data in the table?

1. The governors of all six states are elected for a term of four years.
2. A judge on the highest court in Massachusetts may stay in office for as long as he or she wishes.
3. In all six states, the term of a judge is longer than the terms of either a governor or a state legislator.
4. State senators always serve a longer term than state representatives.
5. The length of a state judge's term of office is never more than 12 years.

TERMS OF OFFICE IN SELECTED STATES

	TERM OF GOVERNOR		TERM OF LEGISLATORS		TERM OF JUDGES ON HIGHEST COURT
	Length of term	Limit on succession	Upper house	Lower house	
CALIFORNIA	4 years	No limit	4 years	2 years	12 years
FLORIDA	4 years	May serve no more than two consecutive terms	4 years	2 years	6 years
MASSACHUSETTS	4 years	No limit	2 years	2 years	"good behavior" (life)
MISSOURI	4 years	May serve no more than two consecutive terms	4 years	2 years	12 years
NEW YORK	4 years	No limit	2 years	2 years	14 years
TEXAS	4 years	No limit	4 years	2 years	6 years

Source: Adapted from Book of the States, 1987.

From the Terms of Office table, you might suppose that every governor serves a four-year term. This is true of most states, but not all. In four states (Arkansas, New Hampshire, Rhode Island, and Vermont), the governor's term is only two years.

Five states impose even stricter limits on a governor than the two-term limit shown in the table. Governors of Kentucky, Mississippi, New Mexico, South Carolina, and Virginia are allowed to serve only one term. Their state constitutions prohibit them from being re-elected.

"New" states differ from the original 13 states. New York and Massachusetts are among the 13 oldest states in the nation. The 13 states existed *before* the U.S. Constitution was drafted and ratified. The other 37 states (including Texas, California, Florida, and Missouri) joined the Union *after* the Constitution became law. Today these "new" states are equal in status to the original states. But their history is different.

Take Missouri as an example of the process for creating a "new" state. The land that is now Missouri was once part of a vast Western wilderness called the Louisiana Territory. The U.S. government purchased the territory from France in 1803 and divided it into two parts: Upper Louisiana and Lower Louisiana.

In the next few years, thousands of pioneers crossed the Mississippi River and cleared the wooded country for settlement. By 1812, enough people had settled in Upper Louisiana to divide it into smaller U.S. territories. One such territory was called the Missouri Territory. Its boundaries and a territorial government were established by an act of Congress. Then, in 1818, the settlers of the Missouri Territory petitioned Congress for the privilege of turning part of the Territory into a state. They drew up a state constitution and submitted it for Congress's approval.

For two years, members of Congress considered whether or not to make Missouri a state. Northerners tended to oppose the idea since many of Missouri's settlers owned slaves. But finally, in 1820, a majority of both houses of Congress voted to admit Missouri into the Union. On August 10, 1821, it became the 24th state.

Every other "new" state went through a similar process for gaining admission to the Union. First, it was a territory with a governor appointed by Congress. Next, after enough people moved into the territory, a state constitution was created and submitted to Congress. Finally, Congress approved the constitution and the former territory became a full-fledged, self-governing state. The last two states to go through this process were Alaska and Hawaii, both admitted to statehood in 1959.

Puerto Rico has a special status. U.S. territory extends far into the Caribbean Sea. The island of Puerto Rico lies about 1,000 miles east and south of Miami, Florida. Puerto Ricans speak Spanish since their island had been ruled by Spain for almost 400 years. In 1898, the United States acquired the island after its victory in the Spanish-American War.

Because they are born on U.S. territory, Puerto Ricans are U.S. citizens. But their island is not a state. It is a "commonwealth" with a governor and a two-house legislature elected by the people. It has its own constitution. It is represented in the U.S. House of Representatives by a nonvoting member. This "resident commissioner" participates in floor debates but cannot vote on bills. Puerto Rico is *not* represented either in the U.S. Senate or the Electoral College.

If its people vote to do so, Puerto Rico could apply for admission to the United States and become the 51st state. Its population of more than three million is greater than that of several states. At the moment, however, most Puerto Ricans prefer to keep their status as a self-governing commonwealth.

THE ORIGIN OF A STATE: MISSOURI

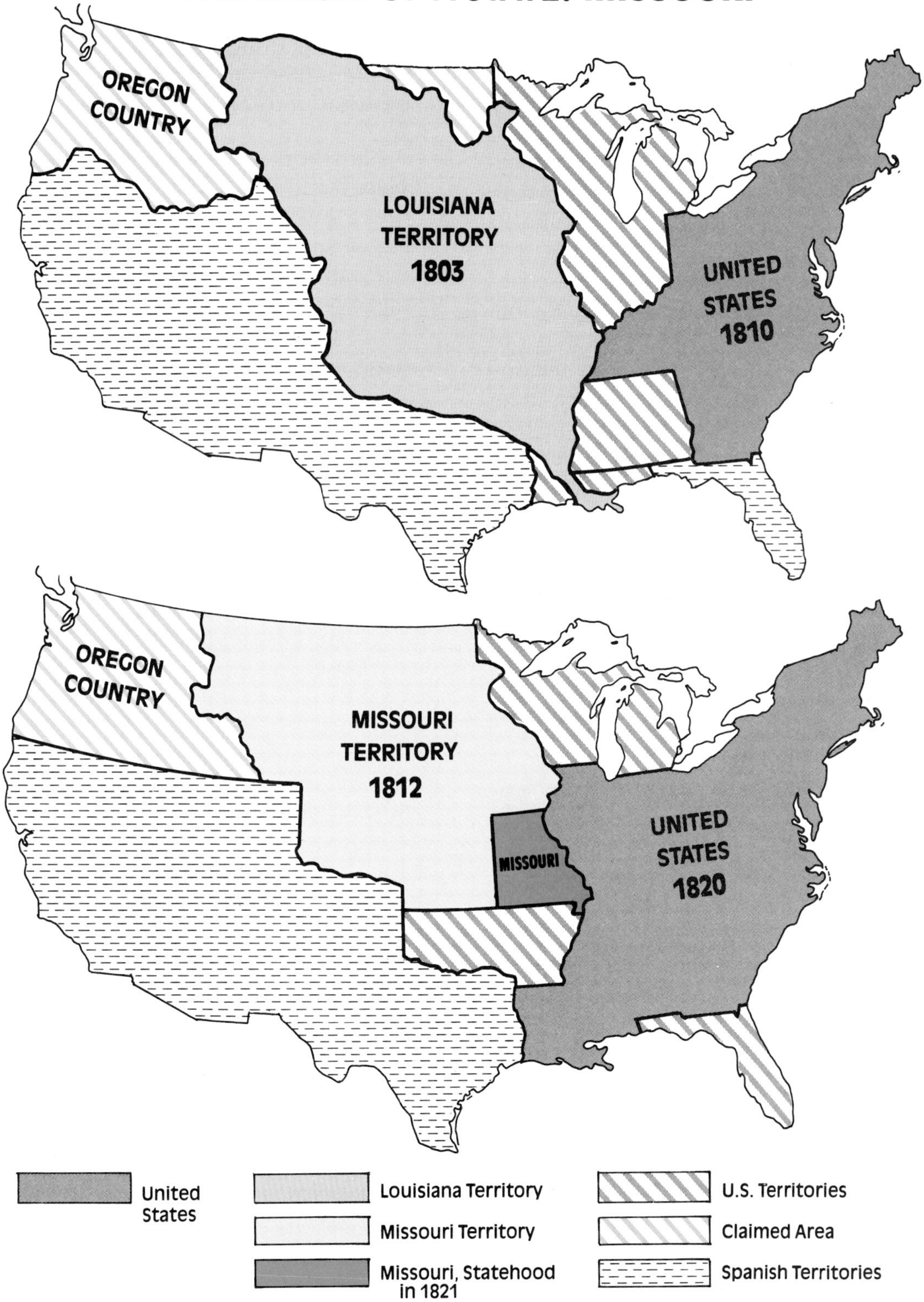

States compete with one another. Each of the 50 states takes pride in the special resources that make it unique. California has its redwood forests, Hollywood stars, and San Francisco cable cars. Florida has its citrus groves, sandy beaches, and Disney World characters. Texas has its oil wells, rodeos, and Houston Astrodome. Massachusetts has its historic sites at Bunker Hill, Lexington and Concord, and Plymouth Rock.

Besides giving a lift to state pride, the unique resources of a state boost its economy. Tourism is a major industry. People who travel out of state to snap pictures of the Alamo or Niagara Falls spend billions of dollars a year. Therefore, every state government has an office of tourism that prints and distributes colorful brochures about the state's unique charms.

Here, for example, is what one brochure says about the varied delights of visiting New York State.

SEE THE TWELVE "CALIFORNIAS." These brochures, posters, and maps encourage people to tour twelve different regions that make up California. Why does the California Office of Tourism mail these materials free to anyone who asks for them?

Dear Traveler:

New York welcomes you to a State full of fascinating places to see and interesting things to do; where you can spend a lifetime and still be surprised by what you can discover!

New York is a celebration of people, places, and things to do. Join us. Enjoy the I LOVE NEW YORK festivals, the seasons, the sports, the arts, and the natural beauty. Experience it all and make New York your own!

Besides competing for tourist dollars, states also compete to attract businesses. Take Massachusetts as a case in point. A computer company can decide to locate its office headquarters and assembly plants in Massachusetts—or any other state. Massachusetts's economy would gain if the company decided to locate there. It would give employment to hundreds of Massachusetts citizens and also pay millions of dollars in taxes for the support of state and local governments. On the other hand, if a company chooses to locate in California or some other state, Massachusetts misses an opportunity.

In the 1960s and 1970s, the older industrial states of the Northeast (including Massachusetts and New York) lost ground economically. Companies discovered that the costs of doing business were lower in the South and West than in the Northeast. Therefore, one corporation after another moved its operations out of New York City and Boston to the "Sunbelt" cities of Miami, Houston, Denver, and Los Angeles. Thus, the sunnier states tended to prosper at the expense of Northern states whose factories closed down.

In the 1980s, however, many of the Northeast states made a dramatic comeback as new industries replaced old ones. New office and manufacturing plants in Massachusetts turned that state into a leading producer of microcomputers, cameras, jet engines, and missile parts. At the same time, New York State's economy underwent a similar turnaround. In 1986, Connecticut, New Jersey, Massachusetts, and New York reported higher incomes per capita (per person) than any other state except Alaska.

Think now of your own state. Its laws and special resources give it both advantages and disadvantages in the competition with other states. These are some of the conditions in your state that a business would want to evaluate:

- whether or not the work force is skilled and well-educated
- whether state tax rates are high or low
- whether quality housing is available at reasonable rates
- whether energy costs in the state are high or low.

The U.S. Constitution sets limits on interstate competition. Competition among the states can go only so far. As you know, certain types of state laws are prohibited by the supreme law of the land, the U.S. Constitution. New York State, for example, cannot prevent motorists with Florida license plates from using New York highways. Also, a Texas family that moves to California cannot be kept out of California's public schools.

Two clauses of the Constitution guarantee that no state discriminates against the citizens of other states. Here they are:

> Full faith and credit shall be given in each state to the public acts, records, and judicial proceedings of every other state.
>
> —Article IV, Section 1

> The citizens of each state shall be entitled to all privileges and immunities of citizens in the several states.
>
> —Article IV, Section 2

The "full faith and credit" rule means that every state must accept as valid the court decisions and official records of other states. The "privileges and immunities" rule means that visitors from other states are entitled to the same services and protection as residents of that state.

States help one another to solve common problems. The states compete—but they also cooperate. Neighboring states cooperate by helping each other to govern a shared resource. For example, the Hudson River flows between New York and New Jersey. At its mouth is a busy harbor shared by New York City on one side and Jersey City on the other. To govern the heavy traffic (ships, trucks, cars) crossing between states, New York and New Jersey created an independent governing board called the Port Authority of New York and New Jersey. This interstate organization operates the bridges, tunnels, airports, and heliports used daily by millions of New Yorkers and New Jerseyans. The agreement creating the Port Authority is an example of an interstate compact.

Another way that states cooperate is through friendly meetings of their governors. There are only 50 governors in the country, a group half the size of the U.S. Senate. As shared problems such as unskilled labor and pollution grow, governors meet and exchange ideas about improving schools, rebuilding cities, cleaning up the environment, and other shared goals.

Right now, as you read this, 50 state governments are experimenting with different laws and programs for solving problems. If a certain program succeeds in one state, other states can benefit by adopting a similar program. Progress in government comes about from learning both what works and what doesn't. More than ever, state governors today are applying this important principle as they seek solutions to tough problems.

GOVERNORS WHO BECAME NATIONALLY FAMOUS. Attending a governors' conference in 1986 were governors Richard Riley of South Carolina (second from left), Bill Clinton of Arkansas, and Lamar Alexander of Tennessee. All three men later served in high positions in the U.S. government: Governors Alexander and Riley as secretary of education, Governor Clinton as president. In a future election year, might the governor of your state be considered a possible candidate for president?

REVIEW

A. Making Comparisons

For each pair of labels, explain how *a* is **different** from *b*.

1. *a*. How Massachusetts became a state
   b. How Missouri became a state
2. *a*. New York's tourist attractions
   b. Some other state's tourist attractions
3. *a*. Terms of office for elected officials in Florida
   b. Terms of office for elected officials in Massachusetts

B. Agree or Disagree

Tell whether you **agree** or **disagree** with each statement, and explain.

1. There should be no limit to the number of terms a governor may serve.
2. In the interstate competition for business and tourism, your state has many advantages.
3. In your lifetime, no new states will be admitted to the Union.

4. HOW DOES YOUR STATE COMPARE WITH OTHER STATES?

This section of the chapter will focus on just one state—your own. It does not give any facts about your state. Instead, it challenges you to research the facts in your library.

Profile of a typical state. You live in a state that is typical in some ways, not typical in others. Here is a list of 12 characteristics shared by more than half the states. Let's call this perfectly typical state "Wyobama."

PROFILE OF WYOBAMA, A TYPICAL STATE

1. Capital: The state capital is *not* the state's largest city.

2. Population: The state's population is between 2 and 5 million.

3. Admission: The state was admitted to the Union sometime during the 19th century (between 1801 and 1900).

4. Governor: The governor is elected for a term of four years.

5. Lower house: Legislators in the lower house are elected for a term of two years.

6. Upper house: Legislators in the upper house are elected for a term of four years.

7. Cabinet: Voters elect an attorney general, a state treasurer or auditor, and a secretary of state.

8. Veto: The governor has the power to veto specific parts of a bill instead of having to approve or reject all of it. This power is called the item veto.

9. Highest court: Seven judges sit on the highest court of appeals.

10. Sessions of legislature: The state legislature is in session for less than six months of every year.

11. Elections: Judges are elected by a majority vote of the people.

12. Taxes: The state collects an income tax.

How many of these "typical" characteristics describe *your* state? It will be your job to find out.

Researching facts about your state. In the reference section of your library are four books that contain the information you need:

A volume of any encyclopedia. In an article about your state, look for the heading: "Government and Politics." Read what this section of the article says about the executive, legislative, and judicial branches of your state government. Take notes.

World Almanac* and *Book of Facts (the current edition). This is your best source for finding up-to-date statistics. It contains hundreds of tables on a great variety of topics (population, taxes, elections, budgets, etc.). For this research project, look in the index under "States of the U.S." The index is found in the front of the *World Almanac* (unlike other books, whose indexes are in the back).

Book of the States (the current edition). Every year, an organization in Lexington, Kentucky, gathers detailed information about the governments of all 50 states. The book it publishes presents dozens of tables about governors, legislators, judges, laws, and finances.

Legislative manual. Printed by your state government, this handbook gives the names of current cabinet members, lawmakers, administrators, and judges of your state. It also contains a map showing how the state is divided into legislative districts.

How typical is your state? In your notebook, number from 1 to 12. From the "Profile of Wyobama" on pages 491–492, copy just the headings: Governor, Cabinet, etc. From the reference books in your library, find out whether or not each characteristic of a "typical" state also describes your state. If it does, write *typical*. If not, write the fact or facts about your state that make it different from most.

REVIEW

Making Comparisons

Summarize your research findings. Write one paragraph stating in what ways your state is **typical**. Then write a second paragraph stating in what ways it is **not typical**.

CHAPTER REVIEW

A. Completing the Summary

Select terms from the word list to fill in the blanks in the summary below. Write your answers on a piece of paper.

amend	grants-in-aid
appeals	legislature
bill of rights	licenses
Congress	militia
constitution	public works
conventions	sales
corporations	separation of powers
general welfare	tourist
governor	veto

In many ways, state governments are like smaller versions of the U.S. government. The powers of each state government are described in a __(1)__. Included in this document is a __(2)__, which sets limits on a state government's powers.

All states carry out the principle of __(3)__ by dividing power among three branches. The executive branch is headed by a __(4)__. In every state except Nebraska, a two-house __(5)__ enacts laws by majority vote. A state's judicial branch of government consists of both trial courts and __(6)__ courts. One example of checks and balances in state government is the governor's power to __(7)__ acts of the legislature.

There are some important differences between the state and federal governments. For one thing, states have longer constitutions in part because it is easier to __(8)__ them. Several states have constitutions that were adopted only recently, after the calling of constitutional __(9)__.

Unlike the U.S. government, states may not become involved in foreign affairs. Their volunteer armies, called the __(10)__ (or National Guard), are for emergency use and may be called into local service by the governor.

The main goal of state governments is to promote the __(11)__ of their citizens. Toward this end, states issue __(12)__ to qualified people who wish to drive, marry, or conduct a profession within the state. Businesses can become __(13)__ only by applying to the state government for legal papers. The states are chiefly responsible for seeing that students are properly educated, crime is controlled, and bridges, highways, and other __(14)__ are built and maintained. To pay for their services, states rely upon both federal __(15)__ and a __(16)__ tax on consumer purchases.

States are alike in some ways, different in others. Historically, the oldest 13 states did not go through the process of applying to __(17)__ for admission. Economically, the states compete with each other for __(18)__ dollars and other business.

By making comparisons throughout this chapter, you discovered to what extent your own state is unique.

B. Applying What You Know

The national newspaper *USA Today* features news from all 50 states. Quoted on pages 494–495 are news items from

THE NATION'S NEWSPAPER

50 CENTS

USA TODAY

NO. 1 IN THE USA . . . FIRST IN DAILY READERS

TUESDAY

DAVID BOWIE CH-CH-CH CHANGES INTO BOWIE

ROCK CHAMELEON COMES FULL CIRCLE ON NEW ALBUM 'BLACK TIE WHITE NOISE,' 1D

10,000 MANIACS: ROCK 'N' WRITING

SINGER MERCHANT LEADS SCHOLASTIC CONTEST, 6D

USA TODAY

NATALIE MERCHANT: Sharing tips, 6D

a single issue of that newspaper (January 28, 1993). The questions following each item ask you to apply what you know about state government and also about the federal government.

FLORIDA

MILTON: The state legislature will have the final OK on whether a vote to keep hard liquor sales illegal in Santa Rosa County will stand. The Circuit Court clerk's office erred by advertising the referendum 28 days before voters went to the polls Tuesday instead of 30 days.

1. How does this news item illustrate the idea that local governments are subject to control by the state?
2. What is a referendum?
3. How does the state legislature make its decisions?

LOUISIANA

NEW ORLEANS: A special election to replace a civil district judge and vote on changes to the City Charter has been canceled by Gov. Edwards. April 3 would be too soon to fill judgeship vacancies, officials said.

1. In what month are elections usually held?
2. In the executive branch of state government, what department would be responsible for supervising a special election?
3. What document gives Louisiana's governor the power to cancel elections? (*a*) the U.S. Constitution (*b*) the state constitution (*c*) the City Charter (*d*) the Bill of Rights

NEW JERSEY

TRENTON: Drug kingpins who commit murder when leading a trafficking network could face the death penalty under a new law. The previous law said capital punishment could only be imposed on someone who committed murder, was an accomplice, or hired someone to murder.

1. What function of state government is illustrated by this news item?
2. Which branch of New Jersey's government made the decision to change the law on the death penalty?
3. Which branch of New Jersey's government is responsible for deciding whether someone convicted of murder shall receive the death penalty?

SOUTH DAKOTA

PIERRE: A bill that would allow those who will be 18 at the time of each general election in November to vote in any earlier election that year breezed through a House committee. The idea came from West Central High students at Hartford-Humboldt.

1. If this bill is to become a state law, what steps would it go through after passing the House committee?
2. If you wanted the election laws in your state to change, what official would you contact either by letter or phone?

UTAH

SALT LAKE CITY: Gov. Leavitt issued an executive order restricting the taping or monitoring of government phone calls. The ban stems from a FBI probe into the illegal taping of personal phone calls within the state Dept. of Transportation.

1. The FBI is part of which of these governments? (*a*) the state government of Utah (*b*) the U.S. government (*c*) both Utah's government and the U.S. government
2. How does this news item illustrate the workings of the federalist system?

WEST VIRGINIA

ERBACON: Officials from the Miners Health Safety and Training Office are investigating a hillside dirt slide on a crew clearing timber for a road.

1. What function of state government is illustrated by the news item?
2. Besides the agency investigating the problem, what other agencies of state government might also be concerned about "a crew clearing timber for a road"?

CHICAGO. The skyline of the nation's third largest city is dominated by the Hancock Building, 100 stories high. How does the city government of Chicago compare with local governments in other parts of the country?

CHAPTER 21

Comparing Local Governments

OBJECTIVES

After reading this chapter, you will know

1. the differences between various types of local governments (counties, municipalities, townships, and districts).
2. how the idea of separation of powers is carried out by counties and municipalities.
3. the difference between a mayor, a city manager, and a commissioner.
4. what *you* think is the best way to organize the government of a town or small city.
5. some of the problems of governing a big city like Chicago.
6. how to use information from a map and one other source to make generalizations.

Chicago is like a magnet. As the third-largest U.S. city, it draws travelers to it from many nations and all 50 states. More airplanes fly into Chicago's international airport than into any other airport in the United States. Every year, thousands of workers come to Chicago seeking jobs. Graduates of American high schools come to Chicago's universities seeking an education. Tourists flock to Chicago's theaters, stadiums, and museums seeking excitement and culture.

Now suppose that you were to drive from Chicago across the length of Illinois to the southern part of the state. After leaving the main highway, you would eventually come to a town that seems completely different from the big city. The city of Jonesboro has a population of slightly over 2,000. The county in which it is located—Union County, Illinois—has a population of only 17,000. Chicago (population: 2,784,000) is about 1,400 times the size of Jonesboro. Chicago's population is greater than that of 21 states.

Besides being communities in the same state, do Chicago and Jonesboro have anything else in common? In this chapter, you will be looking for the answer. The chapter compares the governments of big cities, small towns, and counties. Let Chicago serve as one example of big cities. Let Jonesboro serve as an example of smaller communities. At the end of the chapter, you will know enough to compare your own local government with those governments selected as examples.

Use these questions to guide your study:

1. What are the different types of local governments?
2. How are municipalities governed?
3. How are counties governed?
4. What are some of the problems of metropolitan areas?

1. WHAT ARE THE DIFFERENT TYPES OF LOCAL GOVERNMENTS?

Imagine two families: the Garcia family of Chicago and the Jones family of Jonesboro. The Garcias and their three cats live in a two-bedroom apartment on the fifth floor of one of Chicago's high-rise buildings. The Jones family and their dog live in a three-bedroom, two-story house with an attached garage.

Though they live in very different communities, the Garcias and the Joneses have the same public needs. These needs include:

- good schools for their children
- safe, well-maintained roads
- police protection
- fire protection
- protection against environmental hazards
- a reliable, sanitary supply of drinking water
- opportunities for public recreation (playgrounds, parks)
- a means of deciding whether new businesses and construction projects should be permitted in certain neighborhoods.

In Chicago, Jonesboro, and all other communities (including yours), the above services are provided by some form of local government. Services delivered at the local level may be even more vital to people's way of life than services of the state or federal governments.

The types of local governments are many. And they vary greatly from one state to another. Furthermore, every citizen is served by at least two or three local goverments at the same time! Thus, it is easy to be confused unless you know: (*a*) the different kinds of local governments, (*b*) how they relate to one another, and (*c*) how they relate to the state governments.

Counties and municipalities. We can learn about the different kinds of local governments by studying a map of one small area of the country. On page 499 is a map of the counties of southern Illinois. This is the region that the Jones family of Jonesboro call home. Notice that Union County is shaded to make it stand out. Also, notice that Jonesboro, as a county seat, is located near the center of the county. As shown by the map, the star (★) stands for the county seat. What is a county, and what is a county seat?

> COUNTY: the largest division of the state for administering state laws. In most states, a county's chief functions are keeping records, building and maintaining roads, providing welfare services, holding elections, and conducting courtroom trials.
> COUNTY SEAT: a city where the county has its court and chief offices. (It is like the county's capital.)

Each county seat on the map is also an example of a type of community known as a *municipality*. What is a municipality?

> MUNICIPALITY: a city or town of any size that is incorporated by state law and has certain powers of self-government.

When Illinois became a state in 1818, one of the first acts of the state legislature was to incorporate settled communities. Incorporated in that year, 1818, Jonesboro was one of the first towns in Illinois to win corporate (or municipal) status. Chicago did not become incorporated until 1838.

What does it mean to be "incorporated" as a muncipality? The town or city receives from the state a legal paper called a charter. The charter is like a constitution. It states the kinds of powers that city officials have. It tells the local government how it is to be organized, what taxes it may collect, and what services it may provide.

Illinois has issued charters to 1,200 cities—more than any other state.

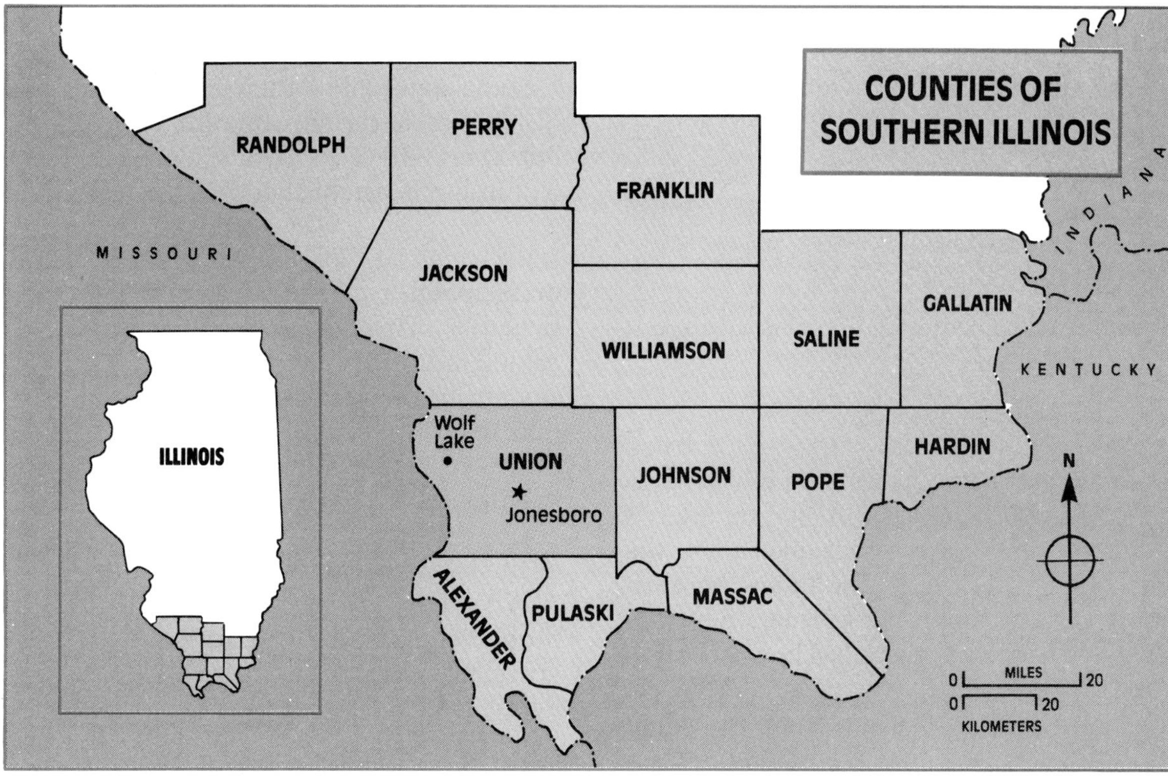

Small, unincorporated communities. On the map, look for Wolf Lake in Union County. Since it has a population of only 250 people, Wolf Lake has not yet been issued a municipal charter. It is an example of an unincorporated village or town. It has no government of its own. Services for Wolf Lake and other unincorporated places in Union County are provided by the county government.

Townships, boroughs, and parishes. Communities call themselves by different names. Probably the most confusing name is "township" because it is defined differently in different parts of the country. In Illinois, a township is a municipality. In Maine, New Hampshire, and Vermont, a township is an unincorporated part of a county. In states of the South, a township is a district of the county set up for collecting county taxes and holding local elections.

"Borough" is another term with more than one meaning. In some states, it is just another name for a township or small, incorporated community. In Alaska, however, a borough is a huge division of the state. It is exactly like a county except for its name. "Borough" has yet another meaning in New York City. The nation's largest city is divided into five huge sections or communities including the borough of Brooklyn and the borough of Manhattan.

Instead of counties, Louisiana's main subdivisions are called "parishes." No other state calls its counties by this name.

School districts and other special districts. Besides being divided into counties (boroughs or parishes), states are also divided into districts for carrying out special services. Public education, for example, is a service *not* provided by the municipal government. Instead, a board of education, elected by the voters, runs the schools for a certain local area. The area is known as a school district.

Besides school districts, state laws may

also create other districts for special purposes. Depending on the state you live in, special districts may provide services like these:

- garbage collection
- hospital care
- sewage disposal
- library services
- mosquito control

In charge of each special district is a different board of officials.

Problems of overlapping functions. Are you unsure which local government in your area performs which services? If so, you are not alone. Several local governments in the same area may have a hand in law enforcement, garbage removal, or some other service. Their functions overlap. Thus, it is often hard to know who is supposed to do what.

One criticism of local governments is that there may be too many of them. Illinois alone has 6,350 units of local government of every kind. They often get in one another's way. Citizens then become confused, not knowing which local government to go to for help.

On the other hand, many people like the idea of having several units of local government, each with a different function. The more units there are, the greater is the average citizen's opportunity to take part in democratic government at the local level. For example, parents who are concerned about the education of their children can speak up at meetings of the local school board. If educational decisions were all made in the state capital, parents' influence on local schools would be greatly reduced.

Relations with the state government. Local governments are *not* free to do whatever they please. They must obey and carry out laws made by the state legislature. For example, the state directs county governments to keep records of births and deaths. It also instructs them to administer elections.

Some states allow their counties and municipalities a certain amount of freedom. But everywhere local officials must work within limits established by state laws.

Home rule charters. In 40 of the 50 states, municipalities are given something called *home rule.* This means that the state does *not* tell municipalities how to organize their city governments. Instead, at a special election, voters decide to accept or reject a proposed *charter*. The charter may give the mayor a lot of power—or none at all. Home rule simply means that voters have a choice of the local government they want.

What happens in states where there is no home rule? Here communities are governed according to charters handed to them by the state.

Metropolitan areas. One local area may be the most important of all—and also the most complicated. It is known as a Standard Metropolitan Statistical Area, or SMSA. An SMSA is a large urban area consisting of two kinds of communities:

- a central city of at least 50,000 people
- a cluster of suburbs outside the central city. (A suburb is a small city located near the larger central city.)

Chicago is at the center of one of the largest metropolitan areas in the United States. The map on page 501 shows the six counties that make up the Chicago SMSA. Notice that the city of Chicago occupies most, but not all, of Cook County. Many suburbs are strung out along the shore of Lake Michigan. Still other suburbs fan out to the south and west. About half the population of this metropolitan area lives in the central city. The other half lives in the suburbs.

Find out more about the Chicago metropolitan area by working on the map exercise on page 501.

SKILLS CHECK: Interpreting maps

To find the answer to each question, refer to the map, map key, and scale of miles/kilometers.

1. What are the county seats of (*a*) Cook County, (*b*) Du Page County, and (*c*) Will County?
2. Name two counties that lie *outside* the Chicago SMSA.
3. If you drove due west from Chicago, what suburbs would you come to?
4. Name two suburbs in Cook County.
5. What is the distance *in miles* between the northern and southern boundaries of the SMSA?
6. What is the distance *in kilometers* from Chicago Heights to Arlington Heights?
7. Name two counties that are on the state border between Illinois and Indiana.
8. In terms of geographical location, why might Chicago be the political and economic hub of its SMSA?

The map shows only a small sample of the communities that actually exist in the northeast corner of Illinois. Chicago's SMSA has a total of more than 400 municipalities and more than 700 special districts. Sometimes the many local governments try to cooperate with one another in solving common problems. More often they do not cooperate.

The SMSA has no government of its own. Would Chicago and its suburbs be better off if a metropolitan government did exist? You will answer this question in a later section, page 523.

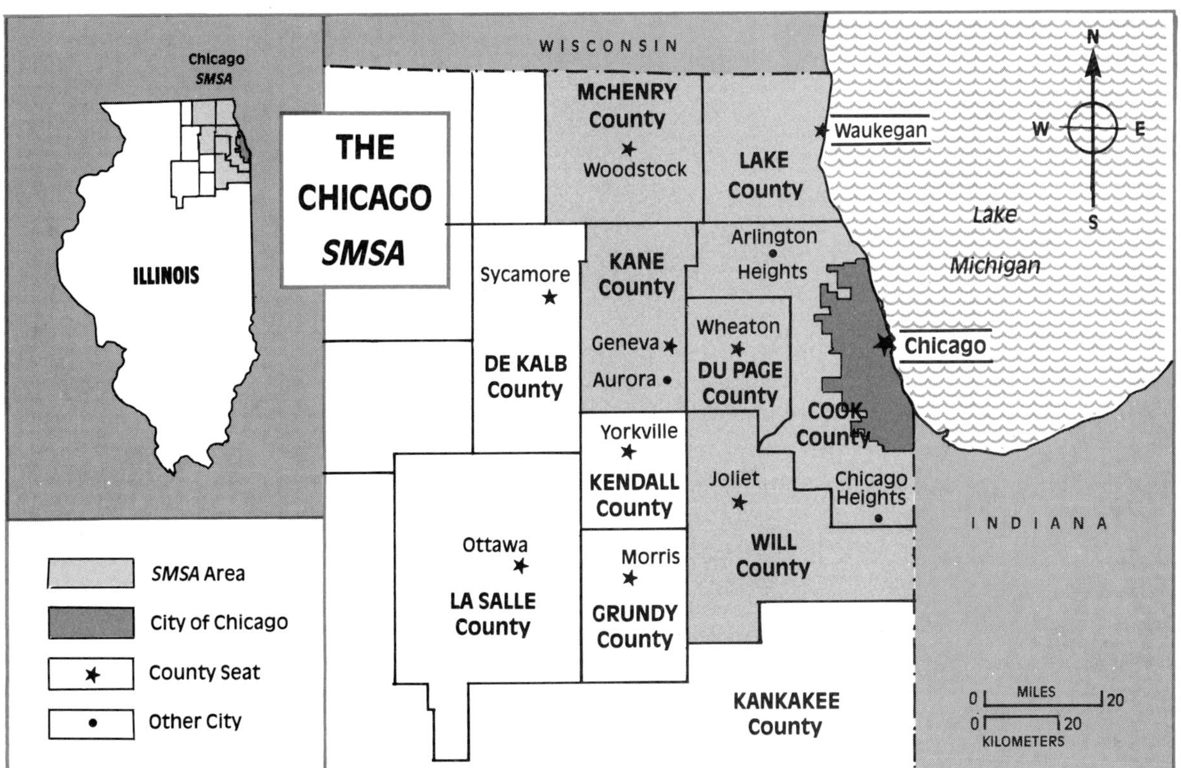

HIGH SCHOOL STUDENTS. Which local government decides how money shall be spent for running a city's public schools?

REVIEW

A. Building Your Political Vocabulary

Explain what is meant by each of the following terms:

1. home rule
2. metropolitan area
3. county
4. special district
5. municipality

B. Making Inferences

A municipality is usually (but not always) a smaller place than a county. Jonesboro, for example, is a small place that fits inside Union County. Paired below are the names of places within a certain state. For each pair, ask yourself: *Which place fits inside the boundaries of the other?* You can **infer** the answers from the information presented on pages 498–499.

1. The city of New York—the borough of Brooklyn
2. A township in South Carolina—a county in South Carolina
3. A parish in Louisiana—a small city in Louisiana
4. Cook County, Illinois—Chicago's SMSA
5. A borough in Alaska—the city of Anchorage, Alaska

C. Applying What You Know

Tell whether you think each statement below **does** or **does not** describe your own community. Tell why.

1. Your community is part of an SMSA.
2. Your community is a municipality.
3. You live in a county that maintains a county courthouse and a county jail.
4. Some of the communities in your state are called townships.
5. Several local governments provide services for you and your neighbors.
6. The government of your county is limited to state laws and the state constitution.

2. HOW ARE MUNICIPALITIES GOVERNED?

Recall the idea of separation of powers. In the federal government, the legislative branch is Congress, and the executive branch is headed by the president. In state government, a legislature has the lawmaking power, and a governor has the executive power to enforce state laws. At both the state and federal levels, courts form a third, judicial branch of government.

At the local level, most municipalities also carry out the idea of separation of powers. They give judicial power to magistrates (judges) who preside over traffic, police, and small claims courts. These courts hear cases involving (1) traffic violations, (2) lesser crimes and misdemeanors, and (3) civil suits for small sums of money.

Methods of separating legislative and executive powers differ from one city to the next. The most common method is to give legislative power to an elected group called a council and executive power to an elected official called a mayor. Jonesboro and Chicago are two examples of the *mayor-council* system of city government.

An interview with the mayor of Jonesboro. The mayor of Jonesboro, John Gardner, was interviewed about his duties. Here is a summary of what he said.

QUESTION: Why did you want to be mayor?

MAYOR: Well, I've always had a personal interest in the town. My family has been in the area since the 1880s, and I was born only a mile from city hall. Before being elected mayor in 1981, I had served 12 years on the city council. So I guess I'm a public-spirited person.

QUESTION: Do you work full-time at being mayor?

MAYOR: No, my regular job is with the county highway department. I'm at my desk at city hall only from 4:15 to about 5:00 every weekday afternoon.

JOHN GARDNER, MAYOR OF JONESBORO. To be an effective mayor of a small city, what abilities and experience do you think are needed?

QUESTION: Are you paid a salary?

MAYOR: A thousand dollars a year.

QUESTION: How would you describe your powers and duties as mayor?

MAYOR: Jonesboro's city charter does not give the mayor a great deal of power. I'm in charge of administration at city hall. A city clerk, who is also an elected official in Jonesboro, keeps track of city business and records. As mayor, I'm responsible for directing the city clerk's work. I also have some powers of appointment. For example, I appointed the police chief, and the council approved my appointment.

QUESTION: How many people are on the council?

MAYOR: Six. Jonesboro is divided into three wards, and two council members are elected from each ward.

QUESTION: Are council meetings open to the public?

MAYOR: Oh, yes. But not many people come to them. It's unusual to have as many as five or six in the audience. I guess the people trust us to make sensible decisions.

QUESTION: How often does the council meet?

MAYOR: Twice a month.

QUESTION: What kinds of issues are discussed at the council meetings?

MAYOR: Recently, there was the question of whether to permit a woman to keep 20 to 30 rabbits in a pen on her property. It's against city ordinances to be raising animals in a residential area. (An *ordinance* is a local law or rule.) Another issue involved taxidermy—the stuffing of birds and animals for sale. The council decided that a resident had to be stopped from using his trailer as a place for stuffing geese and ducks.

QUESTION: As the mayor, you attend council meetings. But do you also cast a vote on proposed ordinances?

THE MAYOR AT CITY HALL. Jonesboro's mayor supervises the spending of a yearly budget of about $6 million. Would you expect the municipal budget of your community to be larger or smaller than Jonesboro's budget?

MAYOR: Not normally. If the council members are divided, three to three, I vote to break the tie. Otherwise I have no vote. I can veto the council's decision, but since they can override my veto, they have the last word.

QUESTION: How about the city budget? Is that a problem?

MAYOR: Not really. We need to raise about $6 million a year. The chief expense is paying for public utilities: gas and water. And that's not a big problem because Jonesboro's gas department and water department are self-supporting. People who buy gas and water from the city are charged enough to cover all costs. Besides that, we have only a three-man police department. The fire department is an all-volunteer force.

QUESTION: How are street repairs paid for?

MAYOR: The city pays for minor repairs but contracts with the county to do major construction and maintenance. So we manage to keep expenses to a minimum. We haven't had to increase the local tax rate in nine years.

The "weak mayor" system of small cities. The mayor of Jonesboro admitted that, in some ways, he had fewer powers than the council. He could not appoint many officials. The few he did appoint had to win the approval of the council. Furthermore, he could neither hire nor fire the city clerk, since this official was elected by the voters.

Jonesboro has what is sometimes called a "weak mayor" system. In such a system, the council makes most of the major decisions of local government. It passes ordinances of its own making. Also, in many cities, the council—not the mayor—may appoint the heads of city departments (the fire chief, the police chief, and others). In some cities like Jonesboro, the council has the power either to accept or reject appointments made by the mayor. A system like this (strong council, weak mayor) is com-

AN ORDINANCE AGAINST JAYWALKING? Some cities have ordinances fining people who jaywalk (cross a street in the middle of a block instead of at a traffic light). Do you think a jaywalking ordinance is needed in your community?

mon in small cities of fewer than 5,000 people.

The "strong mayor" system of the largest cities. The four largest cities in the United States are: New York, Los Angeles, Chicago, and Houston. All four have a system of local government known as the "strong mayor" system. In this system, the city charter gives the mayor several important powers. Chief among them are:

- the power to draw up a budget for the city
- the power to hire and fire the heads of city departments
- the power to veto acts of the council.

These powers enable a big-city mayor to provide leadership in solving the city's problems. But sometimes the problems get worse instead of better. In that case, it is usually the mayor who is blamed by the press and the voters.

Unlike the part-time mayors of small cities, big-city mayors devote all their time to governing. They are paid a salary in keeping with their responsibilities. Mayors of the nation's largest cities generally receive the largest salaries. For example, New York City's mayor is paid about $110,000.

Mayor Daley and Mayor Washington of Chicago. The mayor of Chicago in the 1960s was one of the most powerful mayors in U.S. history. His name was Richard J. Daley. Chicagoans referred to Daley as "the Boss" because little could be done in the city without his support. All building projects—new highways, new housing, new office buildings, new schools—had to be approved by Mayor Daley.

Daley's power was based on his control of the Democratic party both in Chicago and in Cook County. Democratic voters in Chicago greatly outnumbered Republicans. So Democratic candidates almost always won local elections. The mayor (always a Democrat) had the power to pick all party nominees to other city offices. Thus, to have

MAYOR DALEY OF CHICAGO. Daley's power came from: (*a*) his leadership of the Democratic party and (*b*) Chicago's city charter. Which was more important in making him Chicago's "boss"?

MAYOR WASHINGTON OF CHICAGO. After being reelected in 1987, Harold Washington died suddenly in 1988. What did he attempt to accomplish during his five years as mayor?

a career in Chicago's government, you needed to be (*a*) a Democrat and (*b*) a loyal supporter of the mayor. When Daley was first elected mayor in 1955, he made sure that other Democratic politicians took orders from his office. If they refused, they knew they would not be nominated again.

Daley was elected mayor for six consecutive terms of four years each. Only his death in 1976 put an end to his amazing 21-year career as Chicago's mayor and "Boss." Chicago politics has not been the same since. After Daley, nobody has wielded the same degree of power.

In 1983, black citizens of Chicago voted in overwhelming numbers for a Democratic candidate for mayor named Harold Washington. In his youth, Washington had been a loyal supporter of Mayor Daley. But in the election of 1983, he promised that major changes would be made in Chicago's government. Thousands of white Chicagoans joined the black community in electing Washington to the mayor's office.

In his first term as Chicago's mayor (1983–1987), Washington had problems. Most members of the city council opposed his leadership. Even so, his powers of appointment enabled him to make important changes. More women and blacks were appointed to city jobs than under any previous mayor in Chicago's history. For the first time in many years, the poorest neighborhoods in Chicago were not neglected. Washington made sure that they received city services and funds for development equal to what was given to middle-class neighborhoods.

The examples of Mayor Daley and Mayor Washington show how a "strong mayor" can use executive power to lead a city.

The council-manager form of government. Most cities, large and small, elect a mayor and council as their chief officers. But there are also hundreds of cities that use a different system—the *council-manager system*. These cities may have no mayor at all. Or they have a powerless mayor whose only duties are to greet visitors to the city and speak at local ceremonies. The real executive power in such cities belongs to a city manager who

THE MANAGER AND THE MAYOR. In the township of Millburn, New Jersey, the city manager (center) attends meetings of the city legislature but has no vote. Although the mayor votes on public questions, he has less responsibility than the manager for running the city. Which would you think has greater power: the manager or the mayor?

is *not* elected. Instead, this official is appointed by the city council.

Since they are not elected, city managers do not have to worry about winning votes and can concentrate on the job of managing city business. Most of them have learned about the needs and problems of city government by taking university courses and then gaining experience as public servants. Government is their specialty just as medicine is a doctor's specialty.

The city council has the power both to hire and to fire a city manager. Once hired, the city manager acts as a strong mayor might. He or she decides how the city government should be run and directs the work of other city employees. The council retains the power either to approve or reject the city manager's policies.

The council-manager form of government is common among both large and medium-sized cities. Here are just a few cities where city managers administer city laws:

CALIFORNIA: Palo Alto, Pasadena, San Diego
COLORADO: Boulder
FLORIDA: Miami Beach, Sarasota
GEORGIA: Savannah
ILLINOIS: Evanston, Peoria
MICHIGAN: Grand Rapids, Kalamazoo
OHIO: Cincinnati, Dayton, Toledo
TEXAS: Austin, Dallas

Some communities have neither an elected mayor nor an appointed city manager. Nor is legislative power given to a city council. Instead, certain cities have a *commission* form of government. In other communities, lawmaking power is given to a town meeting. First, let's look at the commission.

The commission form of city government. The diagram on page 508 shows how a typical city commission is organized. Notice that there are five officials, each known as a commissioner. All five are elected by the

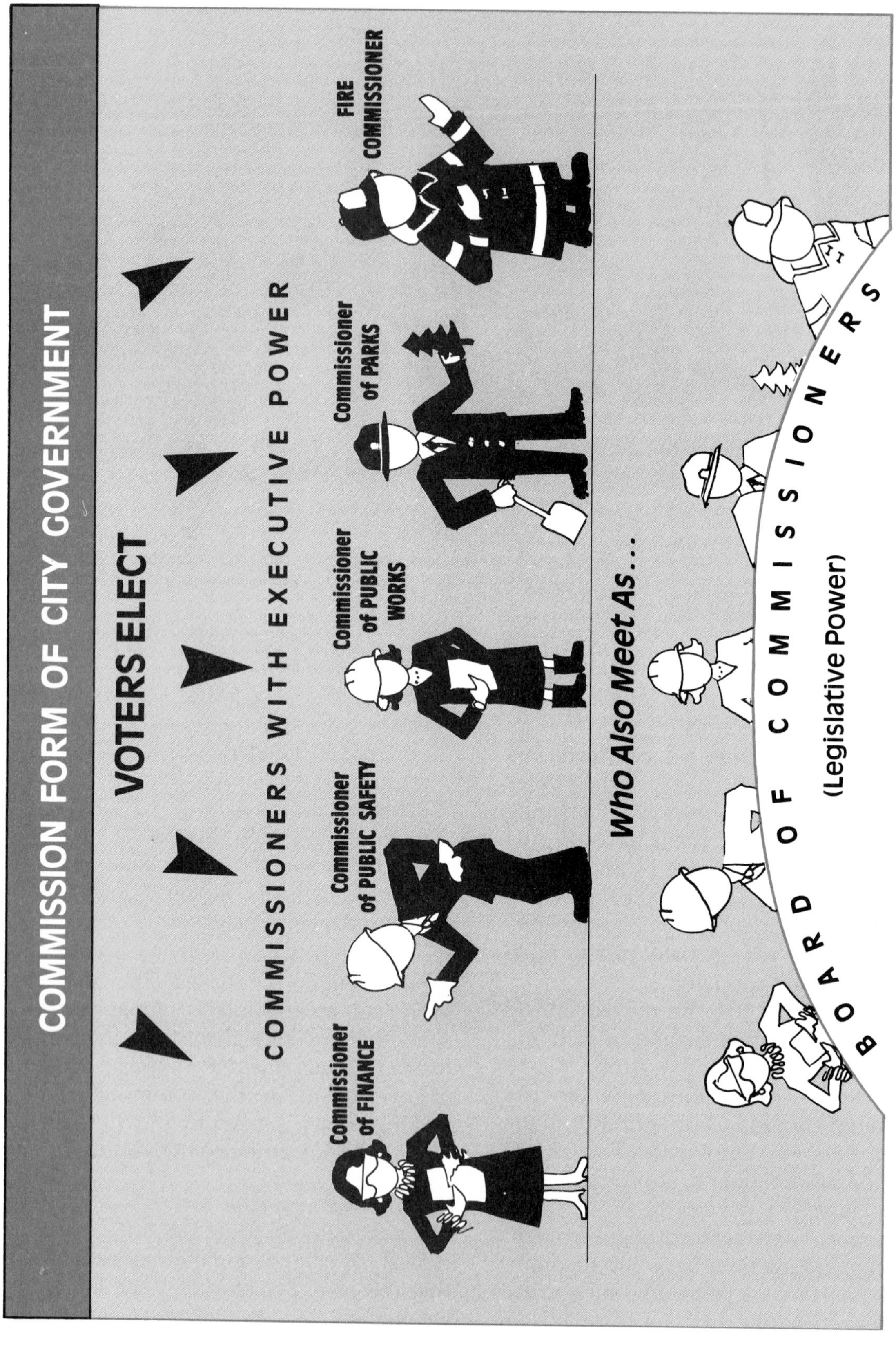

COMMISSION FORM OF CITY GOVERNMENT
VOTERS ELECT
COMMISSIONERS WITH EXECUTIVE POWER
Commissioner of FINANCE
Commissioner of PUBLIC SAFETY
Commissioner of PUBLIC WORKS
Commissioner of PARKS
FIRE COMMISSIONER
Who Also Meet As...
BOARD OF COMMISSIONERS
(Legislative Power)

voters. A commissioner of finance sees that taxes are collected and bills are paid. A commissioner of public safety heads the police. A commissioner of public works is in charge of streets and sewers. A fourth commissioner is in charge of parks and recreation. A fifth is in charge of fire protection. Working as individuals at city hall, the commissioners run their separate departments.

They also hold regular meetings as a "Board of Commissioners." In this group, their powers are similar to those of a city council. They propose and enact ordinances. And they vote upon the city budget. In other words, the commissioners combine two kinds of powers. They have legislative power when meeting as a board, executive power when working as department heads. Under the commission form of government, there is no separation of powers.

The diagram shows five commissioners, because this is the most common number in many cities. Some cities have three commissioners. Others have as many as seven.

The town meeting. A final type of local government is one of the oldest. The town meeting dates back to early colonial times. Today, in small communities of New England, it is still a common form of government.

The town meeting allows the voters of a community to make laws directly. It is thus a form of direct democracy, unlike the indirect form in which laws are made by elected representatives. Once a year, adult citizens of the town are invited to gather in a meeting hall to discuss town business. Everyone attending may vote directly on any public issue affecting the town. Citizens argue about how much tax money should be spent for different purposes. The town's budget for the year is proposed and voted upon right there in the meeting hall.

At the same meeting, townspeople also elect officials to carry out their decisions. Usually, they choose three people to meet regularly as a board of selectmen. The selectmen's job is to see that town business is properly administered during the year.

NEW ENGLAND TOWN MEETING. These citizens are assembled in a school auditorium for their annual town meeting. Why is this assembly an example of direct democracy?

A town clerk and a town treasurer may also be elected for a one-year term between meetings.

Deciding which system is best. You have read about four ways of organizing a local government:

- the town meeting system
- the commission system
- the council-manager system
- the mayor-council system

Imagine some city in your state that has a population of about 10,000. Let us say that the city has home rule and may choose one of the four systems listed above. Which of the four do you think would be best for the imagined city?

Before deciding, consider both the strengths and weaknesses of the four systems. Scholars have studied how each system works in different cities and towns. They have observed the following:

1. The *town meeting* is the most democratic form of local government. But it is practical only for small communities.

2. The *commission system* is also democratic. It gives voters the power to elect all the department heads of city government. However, commission government lacks overall leadership. Being equal in power, the several commissioners seldom agree on a common policy. In general, the commission system does not deliver services as efficiently as other systems. (To be efficient means getting work done properly and at a minimum cost.)

3. Most efficient of the four systems is the *council-manager system*. After all, the professional manager is trained to take expert care of a city's business. On the other hand, though the council is elected by voters, the city manager is *not* elected. So the council-manager system may be considered less democratic than the others.

CITIZEN PARTICIPATION. City residents are welcome to attend meetings of the city council and to present their views on public questions. What is the difference between the town meeting (pictured on page 509) and the city council meeting below?

4. A *mayor-council government* may be both democratic and efficient. Or it may be just the opposite. All depends on the ability and honesty of the elected officials. In big cities like Chicago, strong mayors may be so powerful that they may sometimes act like dictators. On the other hand, if a mayor gives weak leadership, city business will be poorly managed. Such problems, however, can be corrected by democratic means. If a mayor is thought to be too weak or too strong, voters can always turn him/her out of office.

Considering the above points, which system do you think would be best for a city of 10,000 people? Why?

REVIEW

A. Agree or Disagree

For each statement, tell why it is an opinion—not a fact. Then tell whether or not you agree with it, and explain.

1. Every big city needs the kind of leadership that Mayor Daley gave Chicago.
2. Even in small cities like Jonesboro, the mayor should have the power to veto decisions of the city council.
3. A city manager should be allowed to cast one vote at city council meetings.
4. New York City's mayor deserves to be paid 110 times more than Jonesboro's mayor.
5. Cities with a "strong mayor" are always more efficiently run than cities with a "weak mayor."

B. Making Inferences

Tell whether you think each statement is **probably true** or **probably not true**. Give your reasons.

1. Before being elected mayor, John Gardner lived in Jonesboro all his life.
2. Harold Washington was elected mayor of Chicago in 1983 mainly because of the support of black voters.
3. Houston's chief of police is appointed by the mayor of Houston.
4. The town of Norwich, Vermont (population 1,966) holds an annual town meeting.
5. In Dayton, Ohio, voters elect all members of the city council.
6. In Sarasota, Florida, voters elect a city manager.
7. In Wolf Lake, Illinois, voters elect a mayor.

C. Applying What You Know

Do you live in an **incorporated** city or town? If so, find out how it is governed. In the card catalog of your library, look for cards headed by the name of your community. Then, in the sources you locate, seek answers to these questions:

1. Which type of local government does your community have?
2. What are the terms of office of the elected officials?
3. What are the main departments of government?
4. What were the sources of your information?

3. HOW ARE COUNTIES GOVERNED?

Do you happen to live either in Hawaii, Rhode Island, or Connecticut? If so, the counties in which you live are extremely unusual. They are either far *more* important or far *less* important than the counties of other states. Why?

The counties of Hawaii. County government in Hawaii is the only local government that matters. Hawaii has hundreds of towns and villages, but they are unincorporated. The only governments that deliver services and collect taxes at the local level are Hawaii's four counties. One of the four is the county that governs Hawaii's largest city, Honolulu.

Voters of each Hawaii county elect a county executive called a "mayor." They also elect a county legislature called a "county council." In other words, county government in Hawaii is much like city government in other states.

The counties of Connecticut and Rhode Island. At the other extreme are counties of two New England states: Connecticut and Rhode Island. On a map of these states, you will see boundaries dividing Connecticut into eight counties and Rhode Island into five counties. But no county officials are elected. That is because, in these two states, county government does not exist. Here township governments and town meetings are very important. But counties are little more than areas on a map.

Government of a "typical" county. In the other 47 states, county governments play an important role. In states of the South, they are especially important. Each state organizes its counties differently and gives them different functions. Even so, the great majority of counties are similar in many ways.

In Chapter 20, you studied the profile of a typical state ("Wyobama"). In this chapter, let us imagine a typical county, giving it the name "Typicounty." It has these characteristics:

- ***Population:*** fewer than 25,000 people
- ***Elected officials:*** sheriff, coroner, tax assessor, superintendent of schools, prosecuting attorney, recorder of deeds, board of commissioners
- ***Most costly service:*** welfare
- ***Other services:*** keeping records, maintaining roads, enforcing state laws, judging civil and criminal cases, issuing licenses, overseeing elections
- ***Chief source of revenue:*** property tax.

The elected officials of Typicounty. As an adult citizen, you will vote for county officials and evaluate the quality of county services. Therefore, you need to know about the typical duties of Typicounty's elected officials.

You are familiar with three kinds of powers: legislative, executive, and judicial. At the county level, let's see what officeholders exercise each kind of power. First, consider Typicounty's legislature—the board of commissioners.

Board of commissioners. The board of commissioners is a group of elected officials who have *both* legislative *and* executive powers. Typically, it is a group of five commissioners, each elected to a four-year term.

As county legislators, the commissioners meet regularly to set the county tax rate and adopt a county budget. They may also pass ordinances about such matters as speed limits on county roads and book fines at a county library. All county ordinances must comply with the constitution and laws of the state.

As county administrators, each commissioner looks after a different service. One sees that elections are properly held. Another sees that welfare assistance is provided. A third sees that roads are maintained.

Typicounty's board of commissioners is much like the city commission you read about on pages 507–509. Meeting as a group, board members have legislative power. Working in their separate offices, they have executive power. Note one other similarity. In the county as well as the city, commissioners are equal in power. None is officially in charge as the top executive. So county business may suffer from lack of leadership.

In some states, counties are governed by a much larger group than five commissioners. Their top officials are called supervisors. Each supervisor may represent a different city or township in the county. Thus, if a county has 50 municipalities, there may be 50 people on the county's board of supervisors. This governing group has the same functions of Typicounty's board of commissioners. It administers services, adopts a yearly budget, and passes local ordinances.

Judges at the Typicounty courthouse. The busiest and most important government building in Typicounty is its courthouse. It is the place where the county's citizens come to seek justice in both civil cases and criminal cases. Here you see lawyers walking the halls as they file damage suits against those who caused injury to their clients. In this building are held most of the criminal trials that are reported on TV and in the newspapers. Here the county's prosecuting attorney attempts to convict those accused of murder, robbery, and other felonies. Here citizens are called by the hundreds to serve on different juries in different courtrooms.

The judges who preside in the courtrooms may be either elected or appointed to office, depending on the state constitution. Their task is to conduct trials in a fair

PRESIDIO COUNTY COURTHOUSE, TEXAS. The trials conducted in a county courthouse involve the laws of the state government. In what city is the county courthouse that serves *your* county?

manner and to sentence those convicted of crimes. The laws that they interpret are state laws and the state constitution. Thus, they are key officials in the judicial branch of state government.

Officials who maintain law and order. Executive powers in Typicounty are divided among other elected officials besides the commissioners. Three of them—a sheriff, a prosecuting attorney, and a coroner—share responsibility for law enforcement.

The sheriff heads the county's department of law enforcement. He or she serves warrants for the arrest of suspected lawbreakers. The sheriff also supervises conditions in the county jail.

The prosecuting attorney (also called a district attorney) is active in every criminal case tried in the county courthouse. First, the prosecuting attorney tries to convince a grand jury that a certain person should be indicted (accused). Then he or she tries to convince a petit jury that the indicted person is guilty of the crime.

If someone dies suddenly or mysteriously, the county coroner investigates the cause of death. In a murder trial, the coroner's testimony is often crucial.

Officials who keep records. Keeping complete and accurate records is an important function of local government. The clerk of Typicounty keeps a file of the county's legal papers and business records. He or she also supervises elections and issues licenses for marriage, hunting, and fishing. Another official, the recorder (or registrar of deeds), keeps track of property ownership in the

ENFORCING THE SPEED LIMIT. A deputy sheriff of Travis County, Texas, issues a ticket to a speeding driver. In your community, which of these is most active in enforcing the law: (*a*) a municipal police force, (*b*) a county sheriff, or (*c*) the state police?

county. Filed away in the recorder's office are records of land and house sales.

Officials who collect and spend tax money. Most of Typicounty's revenue comes from a property tax on privately owned houses, farms, and businesses. The county's tax assessor visits the taxable properties in the county to assess, or determine, the value of each.

Some day, if you become a homeowner, you may have to pay a tax on your property. You should know how the tax on your house or other property would be determined. First, the assessor estimates the likely price of the property if you were to sell it. Let us say that figure—the appraised value of your property—is $100,000. In Typicounty, a homeowner has to pay taxes on only a certain percentage of the appraised value—perhaps 35 percent. The assessed value of the house is then $35,000 (.35 × $100,000). If the county's tax rate is $1.50 for every hundred dollars of assessed value, then the owner would pay $525 in county taxes.

Once taxes are collected, another official makes sure that they are spent in a lawful and correct manner. The county auditor should be skilled at checking financial records to see that all payments for county services are promptly and properly processed.

Officials who administer services. Typicounty's roads must be kept in good repair. Its schools must maintain the educational standards required by state law. The health and welfare of its citizens must be safeguarded.

An elected superintendent of schools administers Typicounty's educational services. The other county services (roads, health, welfare) are supervised by Typicounty's most powerful group of officials: the board of commissioners.

EXPENSES OF COUNTY GOVERNMENTS, 1991

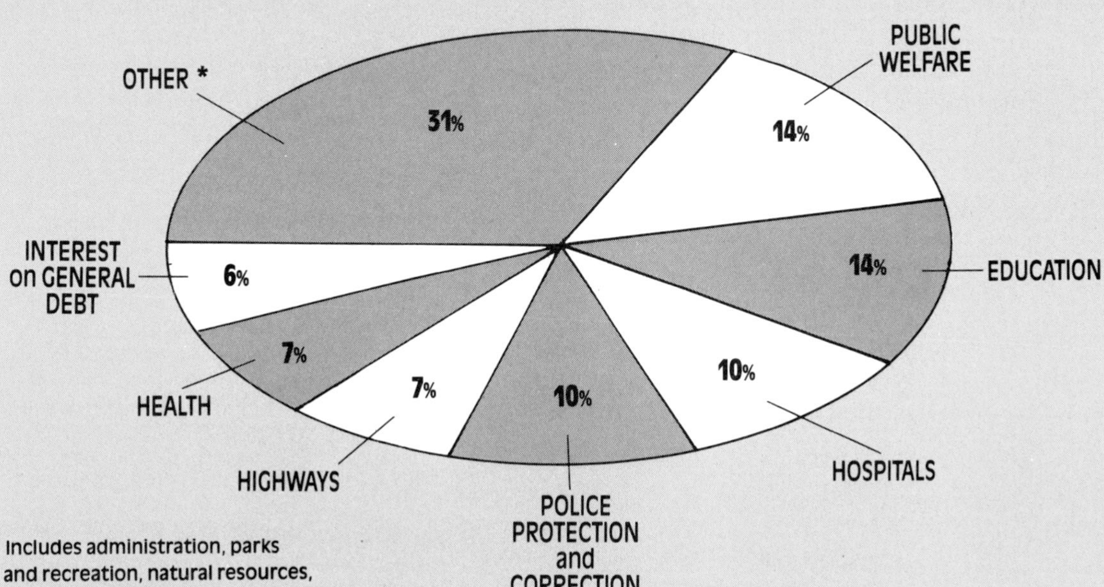

* Includes administration, parks and recreation, natural resources, and public buildings.

Taking care of the homeless. Welfare (assisting the poor) is the most costly of county services. Let us look now at the welfare services provided by a real county: Westchester County in New York State. Several of the suburbs in Westchester County are known for their great wealth. Even so, a few thousand people in the county are too poor to pay rent for even low-cost housing. They are among the nation's homeless.

To shelter the homeless, Westchester County's officials reserved rooms in hotels and motels. Half of the people housed in this way were school-age children. Besides paying for motel rooms, the county also paid to transport children of the poor to and from school. Special arrangements for this service were made with private bus companies and taxi companies.

The children generally disliked riding the "welfare taxis," as they called them. Sometimes they had to wait after school for more than an hour before a taxi finally came. Back at their motel rooms after a long day, they could not concentrate on homework. In school, children of the homeless were difficult to teach. As one school principal said, "Some of these kids are in families living in one room, eating off a hot plate."

In every county, more could be done to help the homeless. But always, in making the county budget, officials must answer two questions: (1) What will it cost to expand a service? (2) Are taxpayers willing to bear that cost? Often the answer to the second question is "No."

REVIEW

A. Building Your Political Vocabulary

What are the **duties** of each county official named below?

1. coroner
2. sheriff
3. prosecuting attorney
4. commissioner (or supervisor)
5. recorder (or registrar of deeds)
6. clerk
7. assessor
8. auditor

B. Making Comparisons

1. In what ways is a county's board of commissioners (or supervisors) similar to the commission form of city government?
2. How are Hawaii's counties different from the counties in other states?
3. Which approach to county government do you think is better? (*a*) Hawaii's approach or (*b*) the more typical approach of other states? Why?

C. Applying What You Know

1. From sources in the library, find out how the government of your county is organized. Write one paragraph telling in what ways it is **like** the government of Typicounty. Write a second paragraph telling in what ways it is **unlike** Typicounty.
2. Imagine that you own a single-story house in Typicounty. After looking over your property, the county assessor writes down the following figures:

(*a*) appraised value of your house	$60,000
(*b*) assessment percentage	30%
(*c*) assessed value	?
(*d*) tax rate	$2 for each $100 of assessed value
(*e*) property tax due	?

What property tax would you have to pay? First, determine the assessed value of your home (*c*) and then the property tax on it (*e*).

4. WHAT ARE SOME OF THE PROBLEMS OF METROPOLITAN AREAS?

Which large city in the United States has the least crime, best schools, purest air, lowest unemployment, least humidity, and highest average income? If such a city exists, we could call it "the best city to live in." Its "quality of life" (those things that most people desire in their public life—healthful environment, good schools, safe streets, and so on) would be higher than any other city. But is there in fact an ideal city better than others? Find out by completing the Skills Check.

✔✔ SKILLS CHECK: Making generalizations from two sources

This exercise challenges you to work with two sources of information at once. First is a map of the 100 most populous cities in the United States. Second is a list of categories that may be used to measure the "quality of life" in cities. Closely examine both sources of information before answering the questions on page 518.

Note: The map is based on the 1990 census. The nine categories (A–I) in the rankings were selected from categories studied by John Tepper Marlin in *The Book of American City Rankings* (published by Facts on File).

I. The 100 Largest U.S. Cities (map)

II. City Rankings

A. Best overall air quality
  1. Tampa-St. Petersburg, Florida
  2. Richmond, Virginia
  3. Columbus, Ohio

B. Least humid
  1. Las Vegas, Nevada
  2. Tucson, Arizona
  3. El Paso, Texas

C. Lowest crime rate (per 1,000 population)*
  1. Columbus, Georgia
  2. Huntington Beach, California
  3. Yonkers, New York
  4. Chicago, Illinois

D. Fewest deaths per 1,000 population
  1. Anchorage, Alaska
  2. Aurora, Colorado
  3. Arlington, Texas

E. Lowest high-school dropout rates
  1. Baton Rouge, Louisiana
  2. Honolulu, Hawaii
  3. Yonkers, New York

F. Highest percentage of college-educated adults
  1. Washington, D.C.
  2. San Francisco, California
  3. Denver, Colorado

G. Most money (per capita) spent for parks and recreation
  1. Detroit, Michigan
  2. Anaheim, California
  3. Honolulu, Hawaii

H. Highest circulation (per capita) of metropolitan newspapers
  1. Spokane, Washington
  2. Omaha, Nebraska
  3. Richmond, Virginia

I. Lowest population density (or least-crowded population)
  1. Anchorage, Alaska
  2. Oklahoma City, Oklahoma
  3. Jacksonville, Florida

* Based on FBI index of seven crimes: homicide, rape, robbery, assault, burglary, larceny, and motor vehicle theft.

Questions about the map and rankings

Tell whether each statement below is **correct** or **incorrect**. Explain your answer by saying whether it was based upon (*a*) the map only, (*b*) the ranking only, or (*c*) both the map and the ranking.

1. The only city ranking "number one" in two categories is Anchorage, Alaska.
2. The least-crowded cities are among the largest cities (more than 1 million people).
3. From the data, we may infer that Washington, D.C., has the best public school system.
4. The highest-ranking cities in all categories tend to be those with *fewer than* 1 million people.
5. The state with the largest number of top-ranking cities (in the nine categories) is California.
6. California's cities generally offer a better quality of life than the cities of any other state.
7. In terms of crime, the safest place to live is Columbus, Ohio.
8. In the nine categories, Yonkers, New York, is the only city in the Northeast to be ranked at or near the top.
9. We can assume that every city on the map has a population of at least 100,000.
10. There is no such thing as an ideal city that is superior to all other cities in every respect.

▶ CASE STUDY: Chicago

Rankings based on numbers (census data) are helpful only up to a point. One problem with numbers is that they keep changing from year to year—and so do the rankings based upon them. For example, after the 1980 census, Chicago was the second-largest

CHICAGO AT NIGHT. More people live in Chicago than in Montana, Idaho, North Dakota, and Wyoming combined. What urban problems come about as a result of size alone?

city in the United States. But by 1982, a growing Los Angeles had caught up and gone ahead to become "number two" in population. Nothing remains the same—least of all a city's statistics.

Cities and their governments are constantly coping with change. How can they solve the serious problems that change always creates? Let us take Chicago as one example of a big city coping with change. Chicago's problems are not unique. To a greater or lesser degree, its problems are similar to the ones faced by every one of the 100 large cities on the map. Therefore, as you read about Chicago, think about the metropolitan area closest to you.

Three-pronged problem: poverty, crime, housing. One of Chicago's neighborhoods stretches for several blocks along Division Street. It consists of 23 high-rise buildings. The tenants of these buildings are mainly black families living below the poverty line. They are only some of the more than 600,000 Chicagoans (whites, blacks, Asians, Hispanics) who, in 1985, were counted as "poor." (NOTE: The U.S. government defines the "poor" as those whose yearly income falls below a certain figure.)

Parents in the Division Street housing projects worry about their children's safety. One incident, reported in a Chicago newspaper, explains their fear:

> Dorothy awaited her turn in a jump-rope game on the walkway to her building. Suddenly, gunfire broke out between rival gangs. A bullet pierced Dorothy's chest, and she fell to the pavement. She died on the hospital operating table. Dorothy was nine years old.

Violent crimes occur in every neighborhood of every city. Middle-class people are afraid of being stopped on the street, robbed, and beaten. But statistics prove that the city's poor are the most common victims of crime. In poorer neighborhoods, property is "trashed." Stores are broken into. The elderly are attacked. Children are in danger of being shot in street wars between teenage gangs.

A third problem—the rising cost of city housing—makes the other two problems (poverty and crime) even worse. As apartment rents go up, people with low incomes cannot find any housing that they can afford. Thus, they are forced to join the ranks of the homeless. In Chicago, in the early 1990s, the lowest rent for a one-room apartment was about $300 a month. This was well above the monthly earnings of an estimated 60,000 homeless Chicagoans.

The problem of "white flight." Racial prejudice is a fourth problem that is difficult to overcome. As blacks move into a white neighborhood, many whites tend to seek housing elsewhere, usually in the suburbs. The whites' abandonment of the center city is sometimes called "white flight."

Those who leave the center city usually have higher incomes than those who stay. Thus, the average income level in the city declines. As the city's population becomes poorer, the need for government services becomes greater. More police protection is needed to control crime. More welfare money is needed to help the poor and homeless. But how is the city government going to pay for increased services? Its chief source of revenue is the local property tax. If it

CARTOON CORNER

'PARDON ME, SIR! WE'RE DOING A SURVEY ON FEAR IN AMERICA ...'

Would you suppose that there is greater fear of violent crimes in large cities than in smaller ones? Is the fear justified?

raises the tax rate, landlords who pay the taxes would have to raise their rents. If they do that, thousands more of the city's poor would be homeless. Further, expensive city housing would give the middle class one more reason to move to the suburbs.

"Council Wars" at city hall. How does a mayor deal with all the problems of a city like Chicago? How can he or she raise enough money in taxes to pay the salaries of a huge police force (11,000 officers in 1987) and thousands of other city workers (firefighters, welfare workers, sanitation workers). In 1986, the city of Chicago's expenses came to more than $2 billion.

Solving a big city's problems is never easy. It is even harder if the mayor is opposed by the city council. That was the situation in 1983 when Harold Washington was elected the first black mayor of Chicago. Also elected were 50 aldermen (council members) from Chicago's different wards. Only 21 of these aldermen supported the mayor. The other 29 were his political opponents. They voted against almost everything he proposed.

The bitter quarrels between Mayor Washington and the city council were compared with space battles in the movie *Star Wars*. The press referred to them as the "Council Wars." It was like Luke Skywalker (the mayor) battling Darth Vader (head of the city council). For almost four years, Chicago's government was in a state of deadlock.

Zoning in the suburbs. Around Chicago (and other major cities) are a great number of suburban cities and towns. Citizens of the suburbs are mainly middle-class whites. The typical suburban home in the Chicago area sits on a small grassy plot and sells for more than $100,000. It is not the kind of housing that a poor family from Chicago can afford.

Many suburbanites want to prevent the poor from moving into their communities. That is one of the reasons for a suburb's *zoning ordinances.* The map of a suburb is divided into zones. The land in each zone is reserved for a different use. One zone may be for house lots of a certain minimum size (for example, quarter-acre lots or half-acre lots). Another zone is set aside for downtown shops and a third zone for office buildings and light industry. In many suburbs, none of the zones allows the building of low-cost housing. Because such zoning often excludes the poor, it is called exclusionary zoning.

The zoning issue. Should the suburbs be forced to make room for low-income families? Or is it their right of self-government to forbid certain kinds of construction? The question has often been raised by low-income black families seeking homes in the suburbs. They have challenged zoning ordinances in both state courts and federal courts.

One court case of 1977 involved the Chicago suburb of Arlington Heights. Zoning in this suburb did not permit the construction of multi-family housing. The builder brought suit against the Arlington Height's government. He was joined in the case by two blacks who hoped to move into the new housing. They argued that the zoning ordinance discriminated against blacks and was therefore unconstitutional. But the courts ruled in favor of the ordinance because racial discrimination could not be proved.

The tax issue. Another major issue in metropolitan areas concerns money. Naturally, people want their local taxes to be low. Also, they want their taxes to pay only for services actually received from their own local government. For example, suburban homeowners may object to paying taxes to fund welfare programs in the center city.

Mayors of big cities like Chicago look at taxes from a different point of view. They think middle-class suburbanites should be made to pay taxes for the center city. After all, the suburbanites enjoy coming into Chicago to shop, see a show, or cheer for the Chicago Bears. Office workers daily commute into the business district, leaving at night for their suburban homes.

Do suburbanites benefit from being near a big city? Yes. Do they have a responsibility then to help pay for the city's upkeep? Yes, say the big city mayors. No, say the suburban homeowners.

Funding from the state and federal governments. Indirectly, suburbanites do contribute taxes for the center city. As you know, both the state and the federal governments collect income taxes and sales taxes from everyone. They then use part of their tax income to aid cities.

Suburbs as well as center cities receive funds from the state and federal governments. But because the center city has greater needs, it receives a greater share of outside funds. In *all* U.S. metropolitan areas, local governments get almost 45 percent of their revenue from state and federal grants. City mayors think even more aid is needed.

The bond issue. Tax rates are determined by a vote of elected officials at city hall. Voters are rarely given a chance either to accept or reject their local government's decision about taxes.

One kind of issue, however, is often decided by the voters. That is the question of whether or not the city should borrow a large sum of money to pay for some major building project. For example, Chicago's school district may need a new high school costing $3 million. The building of a school, highway, airport, jail, or library is known as a capital project. Because of their huge cost, such projects can be paid for only with borrowed money.

A city borrows money by selling municipal bonds to investors. A bond is a contract between the investor who buys it and the government that sells it. The city promises to repay the sum printed on the bond after a certain number of months or years. Since interest is added, borrowed money often costs more in the long run than money raised through taxes.

Does Chicago really need a new high school badly enough to borrow $3 million

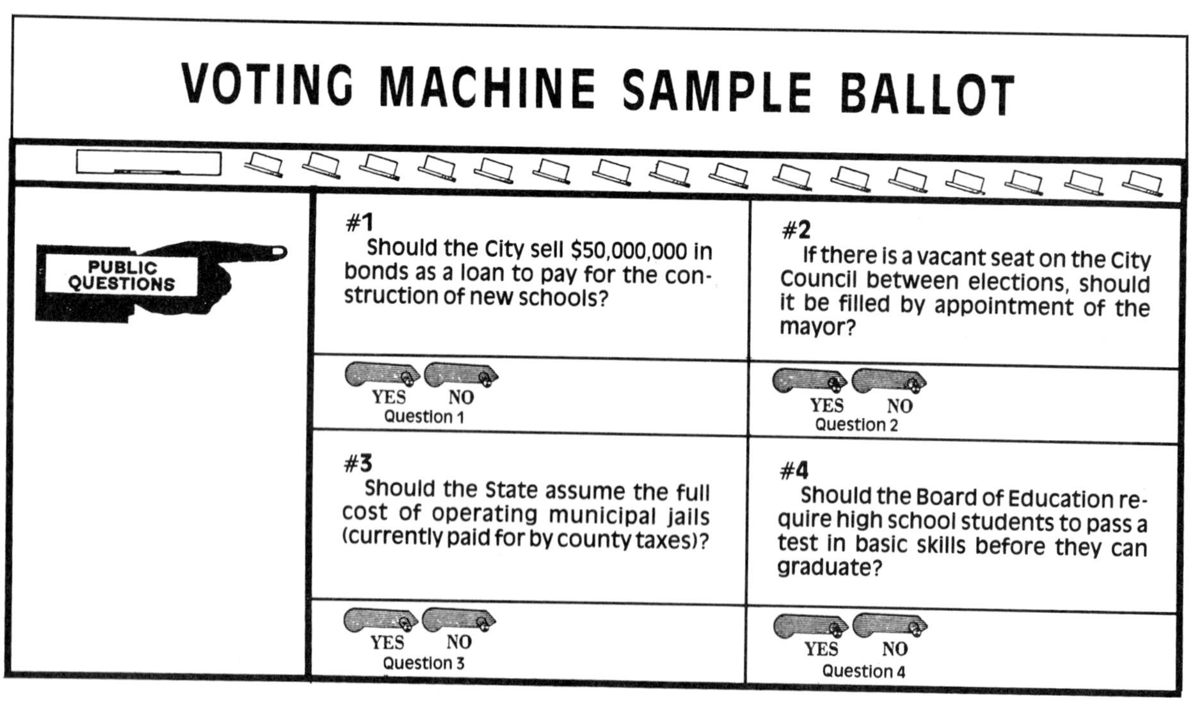
VOTING MACHINE SAMPLE BALLOT
PUBLIC QUESTIONS
#1
Should the City sell $50,000,000 in bonds as a loan to pay for the construction of new schools?
YES NO
Question 1
#2
If there is a vacant seat on the City Council between elections, should it be filled by appointment of the mayor?
YES NO
Question 2
#3
Should the State assume the full cost of operating municipal jails (currently paid for by county taxes)?
YES NO
Question 3
#4
Should the Board of Education require high school students to pass a test in basic skills before they can graduate?
YES NO
Question 4

to build it? The voters decide. A question about the proposed bond issue is placed on the ballot. If a majority vote YES, the city may sell enough bonds to build the school. If a majority vote NO, the bond issue is defeated, and the school cannot be built.

Should cities and suburbs be consolidated? One solution for a city's financial problems is often proposed. It is the idea of consolidating—or bringing together—the many units of local government in a metropolitan area. Instead of hundreds of separate governments, there would then be just one metropolitan government.

For example, in the Chicago area, suburbs would lose their municipal charters. Their names would continue to exist as post office addresses, but there would be only one city hall serving the entire metropolitan area.

Like all suggestions for reform, consolidation would probably have both good effects and bad effects.

Good effect 1. One local government would be easier to manage and easier for voters to understand. Services could be delivered more efficiently if bureaucrats did not have to worry about district lines, county lines, and city lines.

Good effect 2. A consolidated government would make it much easier to plan for the future growth of the entire metropolitan area.

Good effect 3. The center city would benefit because property taxes could be collected directly from the richer suburbs.

But opponents of consolidation fear these bad effects:

Bad effect 1. In the suburbs, people might be forced to change their zoning laws.

Bad effect 2. In the center city, blacks and other minorities might lose the political power they now have. After all, in a metropolitan election, white voters would be in the majority.

Bad effect 3. A metropolitan government would be very large, employing thousands of bureaucrats. Citizens might have a hard time dealing with such a government.

Examples of metropolitan government. Though not common, metropolitan governments do exist. The first to be formed in North America was for the Canadian city of Toronto. In 1954, the people of Toronto and 12 suburbs thought that common problems called for common solutions. The metropolitan area was divided into six areas of about equal size. Around the center city of Toronto, boundaries were drawn for five outlying cities. Each city elected its own mayor. But the metropolitan area as a whole also had a government. Mayors from all six cities sat on a metropolitan council and

THE "METROMOVER" OF MIAMI-DADE COUNTY. In Miami, Florida, the cars on the elevated track are operated by Metro, the first metropolitan government in the United States (created in 1957). In a large city, should public transportation be managed by (*a*) a city government, (*b*) a county government, or (*c*) a metropolitan government?

made decisions about police, fire, and welfare services for metropolitan Toronto. Today, about four million Canadians are governed by this six-city council.

Nashville, Tennessee, is another city that has taken a metropolitan approach to local government. The voters of Nashville, a city famed for its country music, are also proud of their decision of 1962 to merge two governments into one. Davidson County joined with the city of Nashville to form a single government. Thus, there is no longer any conflict between city services and county services. They are one and the same.

Chicago in the year 2010. The next census year is 2000. The next after that is 2010. Officials in city government (mayors, city managers, city planners) are looking to the future even as they deal with problems day to day. They ask themselves: What is our most important goal? Which city services should be expanded and which, if any, should be trimmed back? In what areas can we make the most progress for the least cost over the next 5 to 10 years?

Imagine that you are the mayor of Chicago planning your city's future. You are determined that Chicago rank among the top three cities in the nation in at least two "quality-of-life" categories. You think your goal can be accomplished by the time the census is taken in 2010. Given the list of top rankings below, which **two** would you choose as the most important for a big city like Chicago? Why?

a. lowest high-school dropout rate
b. lowest crime rate
c. best overall air quality
d. lowest unemployment rate
e. highest teacher salaries
f. most money (per pupil) spent for public schools
g. lowest housing costs
h. least number of homeless per 1,000
i. most money (per capita) spent for parks and recreation
j. most money (per capita) spent for police and fire protection

PLANNING CHICAGO'S FUTURE. In the distance is the Chicago skyline. If you were hired by the city of Chicago to plan its future, what goals would you consider the most important?

REVIEW

A. Agree or Disagree

Tell whether you **agree** or **disagree** with each statement of opinion. Explain your answer.

1. The bad effects of metropolitan government outweigh the good effects.
2. Suburban communities should *not* be taxed to finance services in the inner city.
3. Crime is every big city's most serious problem.
4. The city of Chicago would probably be better off under a metropolitan government.

5. Every community has a right to have a local government of its own.

B. Making Inferences

Name a large U.S. city other than Chicago. Tell whether each statement below **does** or **does not** describe the city you have named. Give your reasons.

1. In this city, people who are rich are more often the victims of violent crime than are the poor.
2. In this city, revenue from the local property tax is never enough to pay for city services.
3. This city receives millions of dollars in financial aid from the federal government.
4. If this city needs money to build a public skating rink, it might ask the voters to approve a bond issue.
5. The suburbs around this city have zoning ordinances that limit the amount of low-income housing.

CHAPTER REVIEW

A. Completing the Summary

Select terms from the word list to fill in the blanks in the summary below. Write your answers on a piece of paper.

board of education	municipalities
capital projects	ordinances
charters	property tax
city managers	selectmen
commission	sheriff
consolidation	town meetings
counties	unincorporated
home rule	veto
mayor-council	welfare
metropolitan area	zoning

In the United States, there are many thousands of local governments. The largest areas governed at the local level are usually called __(1)__. Different places in a county may be either incorporated or __(2)__. Incorporated places are usually called __(3)__. Their governments have __(4)__ granted to them by the state.

The larger cities of a state are usually granted __(5)__. In these cities, the voters may decide what kind of local government to adopt.

Most of the larger cities have a __(6)__ form of local government.

Members of the city council are elected to office. Meeting regularly, they have the legislative power to enact __(7)__ (local rules or laws).

In some smaller cities like Jonesboro, Illinois, the mayor usually has less power than the council. But in Chicago and other major cities, a "strong mayor" has power to appoint department heads, propose a budget, and __(8)__ the council's acts.

The charters of many cities do not give executive power to an elected mayor. Instead, the chief executive is hired by the city council. This person is known as a __(9)__. He or she is professionally trained to administer the city's business and manage its departments.

In a third type of government, all department heads are elected by the voters. There is no chief executive and no separation of powers. It is called the __(10)__ type of local government.

The most democratic of small local governments are the __(11)__ of the New England states. Voters of a town meet together once a year to vote on a budget, enact ordinances, and elect officials called __(12)__.

County government varies from one state to the next. Usually, a board of commissioners is elected to administer county services. In addition, the voters elect a __(13)__, a coroner, a prosecuting attorney, and a recorder of deeds. A typical county's largest expense is providing __(14)__. Its main source of revenue is the __(15)__.

Another type of local government is the special district. It delivers one kind of service to people within its borders. There are water districts, sewer districts, mosquito control districts, and many others. The most common type of special district is the school district managed by an elected __(16)__.

Chicago and its suburbs are an example of a __(17)__. Big cities like Chicago have a hard time paying for public services. Their income from the property tax needs to be supplemented by state and federal funds. If approved by the voters, municipal bonds raise money for __(18)__, such as building a new library.

The suburbs are generally more prosperous than the inner city. They use __(19)__ laws both to control growth and to protect their middle-class way of life.

Should there be one metropolitan government making laws for all cities and towns in a local area? Those who think so favor a plan called __(20)__. They argue that it would eliminate confusion and solve the center city's tax problem. Opponents of the plan fear that they would lose control of their communities.

B. Projects: Applying What You Know

Select **one** of the following projects.

1. ***Local issue in the news.*** In a recent issue of a local newspaper, read the following: (*a*) news stories on the front page, (*b*) editorials on the editorial page. Clip an article (either news item or editorial) that you think raises an important local issue. Attach the clipping to a piece of paper. Then write a letter to the editor expressing your thoughts on the issue you selected. Keep a copy to present to the class.

2. ***Map of five counties.*** In an atlas, find a map of your state. Carefully copy the boundaries of your county and four neighboring counties. Then do the following:

(*a*) Give the locations and names of all county seats.

(*b*) Shade those counties that may be part of a standard metropolitan statistical area (SMSA). You can find out which counties, if any, make up an SMSA by consulting the *World Almanac and Book of Facts*. In the index of that book, look under "Cities, U.S.—Metropolitan areas."

3. Interviewing a local official. Your telephone directory has a listing of all the government offices and departments in both your county and municipality (or township). You might find, for example, a listing like this:

BOARD OF HEALTH.... (number)
  Dog Warden........... (number)
  Environmental Health . (number)
  Tuberculosis Control... (number)
  Vital Statistics.......... (number)
CITY CLERK'S OFFICE .. (number)
COMPLAINTS
  HOTLINE .... (number)
DRUG ABUSE
  PROGRAM............ (number)

Select one office that you would like to investigate. In your notebook, write five questions that you would want to ask. For example, if you were interested in the dog warden's office, you might ask: Who is the dog warden? What local ordinances are enforced by the warden? Who supervises the warden's work?

Call the selected office, and explain that you would like to interview the person in charge. Explain that you are finding out about your local government for a school project. Write down the person's answers to your questions. Report your findings in class.

PAST AND FUTURE ISSUES. Eleven of these magazine covers show public issues and major events of the early 1990s. What issues are likely to be featured on magazine covers between now and 1999?

CHAPTER 22

Your Decisions on Three Public Issues

Applying What You Know

OBJECTIVES

By applying your knowledge of American government in this chapter, you will make informed decisions about

1. an election campaign.
2. a public policy issue.
3. a Supreme Court case.

Think of all that you have learned about government since Chapter One. By reading *Government for Everybody*, you have learned how local, state, and federal governments interact with one another.

By carefully examining the photos, maps, charts, and cartoons, you have strengthened your skill of analyzing issues in government.

By working on the Review exercises in this book, you have steadily built your political vocabulary. For example, the political terms in the pyramid below are among hundreds that you mastered:

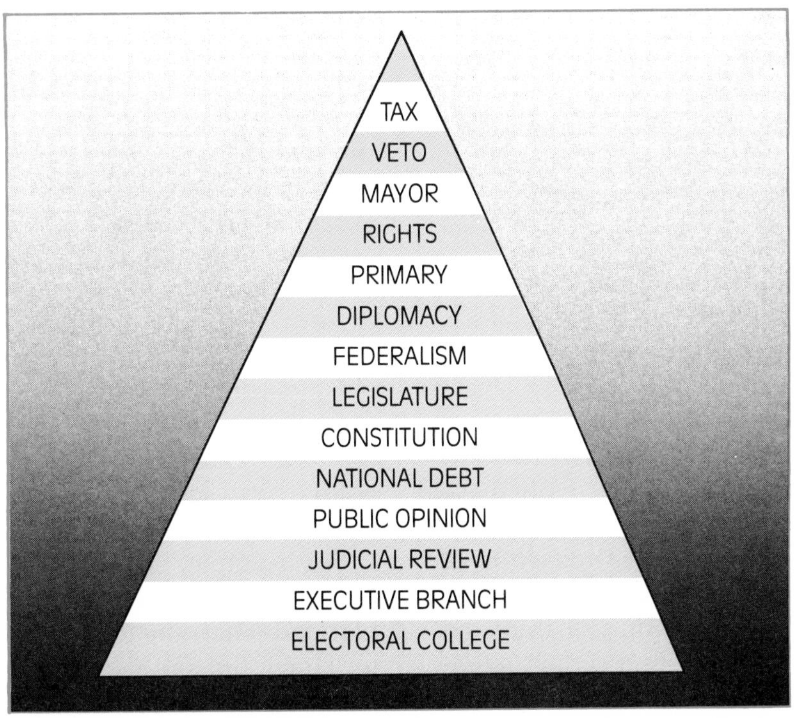

In addition, you were challenged to make many comparisons. You have learned:

- How DEMOCRACY compares with OTHER SYSTEMS OF GOVERNMENT
- How the REPUBLICAN PARTY compares with the DEMOCRATIC PARTY
- How the POWERS OF CONGRESS compare with the POWERS OF THE PRESIDENT
- How the SENATE compares with the HOUSE OF REPRESENTATIVES
- How the SUPREME COURT compares with the LOWER COURTS
- How STATE GOVERNMENTS compare with the U.S. GOVERNMENT
- How a MAYOR-COUNCIL form of local government compares with the COUNCIL-MANAGER form.

You now know how the American political system works. But your knowledge becomes important to others only when you put it to use. This last chapter challenges you to apply your knowledge to three issues of public policy:

1. In an election for U.S. senator, for whom would you vote?
2. What should be done about drug abuse?
3. Do you think the Supreme Court made the right decision in a case involving civil rights?

The decision that you make on each question will depend on two things: (*a*) **facts** that are the same for everyone and (*b*) **civic values** that are yours alone.

Facts, as you know, are statements about the real world that can be proven true. For example, nobody will disagree with these facts: Ronald Reagan was elected president in 1980 and again in 1984. Thousands of other facts can be given about Reagan's actions as president. But do *you* think he acted rightly or wrongly in a certain situation?

To answer questions like this, you need to draw upon the civic values that slowly have formed within your own mind. Civic values are those standards of good and bad, right policy and wrong policy that citizens apply to public questions. Without such values, a citizen would not be able to vote or to make a political judgment of any kind.

For each question in this final chapter, you will be presented with a set of facts. Then you will draw on your civic values to decide what those facts mean to you as a voter and citizen.

ISSUE 1: IN AN ELECTION FOR U.S. SENATOR, FOR WHOM WOULD YOU VOTE?

Your first decision is between a Republican and a Democrat who once competed as their parties' candidates for U.S. senator. Although the election was real, the candidates' names as given below are fictitious. This allows you to think about them as candidates from *your* state who are competing for *your* vote.

Imagine that it is a Tuesday early in November: Election Day. Imagine too that you are a registered voter. Before going to the polls to vote, you review the following facts about the candidates: Mildred Fenton and Hank Arlenberg.

MILDRED FENTON, the Republican candidate. Fenton is well known in the state for her colorful character. She is a 72-year-old grandmother who is often seen on TV news shows smoking a pipe as she answers reporters' questions. She speaks her mind boldly, not seeming to care whether her audience agrees with her.

For example, she once spoke to a group of Jewish-American war veterans. They applauded when she told them of her support for Israel. But she also said that she thought American Nazis (enemies of democracy)

had a right to march peacefully on the streets of any town. "We must defend the rights of everyone," said Fenton, "even those with whom we disagree."

Fenton was born in the state and has never moved away. She has vivid memories of growing up in a 50-room house as the daughter of a millionaire. She still lives in the same house.

Fenton has been active in the politics of the state for the last 20 years. She served one term in the lower house of the state legislature. The governor then appointed her to head the state's Department of Consumer Affairs. At the age of 64, she won election to a seat in the U.S. House of Representatives. She was re-elected three times. In her own district, she is thought to be unbeatable. She is also very popular among Republican voters in every county of the state.

However, registered Democrats in the state greatly outnumber registered Republicans. To win election to the Senate, Fenton must try to appeal to people who normally vote for Democrats.

Fenton's voting record in the House has been conservative on some issues, moderately liberal on others. She has voted for certain cuts in social programs as a way of trimming the federal budget. Critics accuse her of "balancing the budget on the backs of the poor." This charge angers her because she has also supported bills on behalf of the poor.

Fenton is not a college graduate. In fact, she never finished high school. However, on her own, she has read hundreds of books and has learned to speak three foreign languages. Her mind is quick and witty.

HANK ARLENBERG, the Democratic candidate. The business career of Hank Arlenberg is an American success story. He started life as the son of immigrants who worked long hours in a textile factory for low wages. His father died of cancer when Arlenberg was still in school, an event that deepened the family's poverty. After graduating from high school, Arlenberg spent four years in the U.S. Army fighting in World War II. Home from the war, he continued his education, eventually earning a college degree.

He was an insurance salesman for a few years, before a big opportunity came his way to invest in a computer company. At that time, in the early 1950s, the computer

industry was just beginning. Arlenberg's investment made him a part-owner of a tiny company consisting of only five employees. Under his direction, the company expanded at an amazing rate. Now, 30 years later, the company is a giant, employing 20,000 workers. As the chief owner of the business, Arlenberg is many times a millionaire.

Arlenberg wants to use part of his fortune to launch a career in politics. Until now, he has not held any elective office. However, in recent years, he has contributed both time and money to several causes. The center for cancer research that he financed is one of the largest in the world. He sits on the board of an art museum. And he was appointed by the governor to serve on a commission to study the state's transportation needs.

Arlenberg is not well known among the voters of the state. But his campaign ads on radio and television have been extremely effective in making him better known. Again and again, his campaign ads make this argument: "As a successful businessman, I'll be a senator with practical experience in solving economic problems."

The Democratic candidate is 58-years-old. He is married and has four children.

You now know about the candidates' careers. But before deciding how to vote, you should also consider (*a*) the state of the nation and (*b*) the candidates' views on at least one vital issue.

STATE OF THE NATION: A sagging economy. During this election year, the president is a Republican. Arlenberg and other Democrats are blaming Republican leadership for a serious business slump (or recession) that has thrown thousands of people out of work. Republicans reply that the economy is stronger than it was two years ago when a Democrat was president.

CANDIDATES' VIEWS. Question for the candidates: **If elected to the Senate, what policies would you favor to get over the business slump?** The League of Women Voters asked Fenton and Arlenberg to write their replies to this question. Here is what they said:

Fenton's Answer. From the point of view of the economy, high interest rates are the prime problem. From a human point of view, the loss of jobs must be our chief concern. The president, most businessmen, and economists agree that the basic cause of high interest rates is the federal budget deficit projected for this year and the next two. Business confidence is shaken by the deficits, and loss of jobs follows.

To cut the deficit, Congress has limited spending in many educational and social programs. We must now turn to an examination of other parts of the budget. My proposals for budget cuts follow: (1) B-1 bomber cost estimated up to $40 billion, (2) MX missile, a $4 billion cost, (3) two nuclear aircraft carriers with escorts, $28 billion. In nondefense areas, $7 billion in subsidies to agriculture could be cut in half. Public works projects could also be cut.

Arlenberg's Answer. We can promote a growing economy. Government must again invest in what counts: people. We must invest in education, training, and retraining of our workers. Our economy will grow only if people are equipped to make it grow. Government must again finance transportation, communications, and public works systems that are vital to economic growth. Our crumbling roads, rails, and waterways stymie [interfere with] productivity.

I don't believe environmental protection is too costly. Pollution is too costly—in terms of health costs, damaged farmland, and fouled water and air.

We can halt wasteful spending on obsolete weapons, nuclear overkill, and pork barrel projects. By closing tax loopholes and reordering our budget, we can have growth, jobs, and low interest rates.

REVIEW

A. Reviewing the Facts

Tell which candidate (Fenton or Arlenberg) is described by each of these phrases:

1. The winner of the Republican primary.
2. The more liberal of the candidates.
3. The person who has already served as a legislator.
4. The person who became wealthy after growing up in poverty.
5. The person who, if elected, would probably cut the defense budget.
6. The more experienced politician.
7. The candidate with the better record in school.
8. The candidate who blames the president for the business slump.
9. The candidate who would probably support greater federal efforts to fight pollution.

B. Identifying Your Civic Values

By answering these questions, you will have a clearer idea of your own civic values. (NOTE: This exercise is for your own benefit and self-knowledge. Do not compare your answers with others unless you wish to do so.)

1. Does it matter to you whether a candidate is a Republican or a Democrat? If so, which do you prefer?
2. Does it matter to you whether or not a candidate has a lot of previous experience in politics?
3. Does it matter to you whether a candidate is a man or a woman? If so, which do you prefer? Why?
4. Does it matter to you whether a candidate has liberal views or conservative views on most issues? If so, which do you prefer?
5. What do you like (if anything) about Mildred Fenton as a candidate?
6. What do you like (if anything) about Hank Arlenberg as a candidate?

C. Making Your Decision

You have now compared the candidates in two ways. First, you compared their careers and views on the economy. Next, you considered what matters to you personally when evaluating candidates.

Match your **civic values** (B) with the **facts** (A). Then decide for whom you would vote: Fenton or Arlenberg. Write one paragraph explaining your choice.

(NOTE: Are you curious to know the real names of the two candidates? Turn to page 566.)

ISSUE 2: WHAT SHOULD BE DONE ABOUT DRUG ABUSE?

Stories of the destructive effects of drugs are all too common. Two citizens whose lives were almost ruined had this to say about their involvement with cocaine:

> I was a nationally known sports hero. And then I got busted. As a result of my lust for cocaine, I bypassed high and went straight to messed up. Some of you know exactly what I'm talking about because you're taking the exact same ride.
>
> —MERCURY MORRIS, professional football player

> I had a beautiful family, a big house in the suburbs, everything I wanted. Then I got into cocaine and I almost lost it all. It's a lie that cocaine's not addictive. I didn't choose to be an addict. Quitting cocaine was the only thing I couldn't do by myself. I'll be a recovering addict day by day for the rest of my life.
>
> —WILLIAM, a former user

Selling cocaine, heroin, and other drugs for nonmedical use has been illegal since 1914, when Congress passed the Harrison Narcotics Act. Yet, in spite of the law, increasing numbers of Americans have been "hooked" into taking addictive drugs gotten from criminal sources. What should be done about the problem?

The problem. Before you can propose a solution, you need to examine some of the basic facts that define the problem. The following facts were reported by a federal agency, the National Institute on Drug Abuse (NIDA).

Number of people using illegal drugs.

1. In a 1992 study, it was estimated that 75 percent of young adults aged 19 to 28 had tried an illegal drug at least once.
2. In the same study, it was found that about 30 percent of young adults had tried cocaine.
3. About one out of every four high school seniors reported smoking marijuana within the past year.
4. Only 3.5 percent of the high school seniors surveyed in 1991 said that they had ever used cocaine. This percentage was well below what it had been in 1989 when 10.3 percent of high school seniors reported having used cocaine. Officials at NIDA believe that the decline was due largely to the anti-drug campaign and education efforts of the late 1980s.

How the most commonly used drugs affect mind and body.

1. The repeated use of *marijuana* impairs a person's ability to remember, to concentrate on a task, and to drive a car. Women who smoke marijuana during pregnancy may give birth to babies with serious defects.
2. *Cocaine* is a powerfully addictive drug. In laboratory studies, animals given free access to cocaine ingested it to the point of death, selecting cocaine in preference to food and water. Thus, anyone experimenting with cocaine cannot predict or control the extent to which he or she will be affected by it.
3. *Crack* is a form of cocaine that comes in small chunks or "rocks," which are smoked. It does as much damage to the nervous system as other forms of cocaine.
4. *Heroin* is a highly addictive narcotic. It weakens the body's ability to resist infection. Injected with an unsterile needle, it is a factor in transmitting AIDS, a deadly disease. Heroin overdose may result in death.

The costs to society of drug abuse.

1. Every year, the economic losses due to drug abuse in the United States are staggering. Billions of dollars are spent or lost annually as a result of: (*a*) crimes committed for the purpose of obtaining illegal drugs, (*b*) the increased cost of law enforcement, (*c*) government programs for treating drug addiction, and (*d*) reduced productivity of the work force.
2. In addition to the above, the health costs of drug abuse are estimated to be more than $60 billion annually.
3. Costs to society in the form of human grief and social stress are beyond measure. In a family where someone is hooked on drugs, everyone's life is affected. If the drug-user is an adult, he or she stops caring about family responsibilities. The mortgage or rent goes unpaid. Other bills stack up. Even grocery money goes for drugs. Serious arguments or physical abuse may begin.

Alternatives for dealing with the problem. What's to be done? Proposed solutions to the problem of drug abuse are many. In general, however, there are two main approaches to control:

(a) The supply approach. Cut off the supply of drugs by intercepting those who smuggle foreign-made drugs across our borders and by cracking down on criminal drug rings and pushers.

(b) The demand approach. Reduce the demand for illegal drugs through educational and treatment programs that persuade people to stay away from drugs.

Will tougher law enforcement (the supply approach) solve the problem? The opinion of Joseph McNamara, police chief in San Jose, California, is not encouraging. In a magazine article (*Time,* May 30, 1988) he was quoted as saying: "The fight against drugs for the past 70 years has been one long, glorious failure. The courts are overflowing, there is violence in the streets, and the problem seems to be getting worse."

DRUG FREE. Anyone who carries drugs into a school zone is subject to a mandatory jail sentence. Do you think harsh penalties can reduce drug violations?

Agreeing with San Jose's police chief was the mayor of Minneapolis, Donald Fraser. He said: "We've spent over $300,000 in the past few months in police overtime alone raiding crack houses. We've brought in front-end loaders to knock down walls to get into some of these places, but as soon as we put one out of business, another springs up. We need to direct more attention to educating the user to reject drugs."

Is education the answer? A high-school principal in Detroit is not so sure. He told *Time* magazine: "We almost have programs running out of our ears. We've got churches, youth foundations and charity organizations working with us. Everybody is just pounding the kids all day long." Some heed the message while others ignore it.

Civic values: Whose responsibility is it? Start thinking about the approach to drug abuse that *you* favor. For each question, choose the answer that best expresses your opinion. (Recognize that your civic values, more than the facts, will be the basis of each answer.)

1. Imagine a household in which nobody has any interest in taking an illegal drug. To what extent is drug abuse a problem for the members of this household?
   (*a*) It's not a problem.
   (*b*) It's certainly a problem for others—but it's not a problem that the drug-free household can do anything about.
   (*c*) Because it is a problem for society, it is bound to have some effect on the drug-free household.
2. Which of these should be *most* concerned about drug abuse?
   (*a*) The police
   (*b*) Public welfare agencies
   (*c*) School authorities
   (*d*) State legislators
   (*e*) Agencies of the federal government
   (*f*) Every citizen
   (*g*) All of the above should be equally concerned.

3. If you know someone who has either bought or sold an illegal drug, is it your responsibility to do something about it?
   (*a*) Yes, and I know exactly what I'd do.
   (*b*) Yes, but I doubt that I'd do anything.
   (*c*) No, it's the other person's business.
   (*d*) Not sure.

Your advice to the president. Imagine that you work in the White House as one of the president's advisers on domestic policy. On your desk is a memo from the president asking for your help in preparing part of this year's State of the Union message to Congress. In his speech, the president wants to launch a national campaign against drug abuse, which he has often called "public enemy number one." The memo asks for your advice on four questions. Read the questions carefully, and then draw up a reply addressed to the president.

1. *How much should be budgeted for the anti-drug campaign?* As I recall, in 1987, about $8 billion was spent by all levels of government on the drug problem. An additional $500 million was spent that year on drug education programs. I'm willing to spend more *if* we come up with a workable and promising plan. However, I insist that the U.S. budget this year cannot exceed $1 trillion. How much of the budget do you think should be set aside for the anti-drug campaign?

2. *How should the anti-drug money be spent?* Please indicate whether you think most of the anti-drug money should be spent for (*a*) law enforcement in the cities, (*b*) intercepting smuggled goods at our borders, (*c*) drug education, and (*d*) treatment centers.

3. *Who should be in charge of spending the money?* Should the anti-drug dollars be given as grants-in-aid to the states and the cities to be spent as they see fit? Or should most of the money be spent by the FBI, the Drug Enforcement Agency, and other federal agencies?

4. *What is your idea for solving the problem?* Please suggest an original and workable plan for dealing with the drug abuse problem. Give arguments for your proposal that I might use in my speech to Congress.

ISSUE 3: DO YOU THINK THE SUPREME COURT MADE THE RIGHT DECISION IN A CASE INVOLVING CIVIL RIGHTS?

The final issue for you to decide is a question of justice. It concerns the decision of a county government to hire a woman instead of a man. The woman was Diane Joyce. The man was Paul Johnson. In the 1970s, both were employed as road maintenance workers by the Transportation Agency of Santa Clara County in California. Joyce was the first woman ever to be employed by the agency on a road crew.

In 1979, a high-paying county job opened up for a road dispatcher. Both Joyce and Johnson were among 12 people who applied for the job. Agency officials interviewed the applicants and gave each a score, depending on his or her qualifications. Johnson received the top score, 75. Joyce's score of 73 was a close second.

Affirmative action in Santa Clara County. The choice of Johnson might have been automatic except for one thing. An affirmative action plan had recently been adopted by the county's Transportation Agency. (*Affirmative action* means that an employer seeks to balance its work force so that women and members of racial minorities are well represented in every kind of job.) In the case of Santa Clara County, no women had ever held any of its 238 skilled crafts jobs. Hiring a woman for road dispatcher would serve the county's affirmative action goals.

In 1980, the county's Transportation Agency gave the job of road dispatcher to

Diane Joyce. Paul Johnson was disappointed. He thought his high score proved that he was better qualified than Joyce. He brought suit against the Transportation Agency in a federal district court. His lawyer argued that he failed to get the job only because he was male. It was a case, he said, of sexual *discrimination* prohibited by the Civil Rights Act of 1964.

Congress had passed the Civil Rights Act in order to end discrimination against women and minorities. Then employers adopted affirmative action plans. Male job seekers like Johnson complained that such plans unfairly discriminated against them.

A verdict appealed. After a two-day trial, the district court reached a verdict in the Johnson case. It concluded that Paul Johnson had been discriminated against and that the county's affirmative action plan was not valid. The county appealed to a higher court. The U.S. Court of Appeals for the Ninth Circuit agreed with the county. It reversed the lower court's decision. Diane Joyce kept her job. But Johnson still would not give up. He appealed to the U.S. Supreme Court, which agreed to review the case.

The case was settled once and for all in March 1987—seven years after it began. The Supreme Court's decision made the front pages of big city newspapers around the country. It was a split decision, six judges voting one way and three the other. The majority opinion of the Court was written by Justice William Brennan. See if you agree with it.

Johnson v. *Transportation Agency, Santa Clara County, California*

Here is a point-by-point summary of Justice Brennan's arguments:

1. In previous cases decided by this Court, we have said that some affirmative action plans are valid while others are not. To be valid, an employer's plan must meet three tests. **First test:** Is the plan an attempt to correct a "manifest imbalance" in the workforce? In other words, do male workers greatly outnumber female workers in a certain job category? Clearly such an imbalance did exist in the Transportation Agency in Santa Clara County.

JUSTICE WILLIAM BRENNAN

2. **Second test:** Does the county's affirmative action plan require women to be hired, even if they are less skilled than male applicants? If so, the plan would violate the Civil Rights Act. But the Santa Clara plan calls for many factors to be considered when hiring a person—not just that person's sex. The director of the Transportation Agency said that he did not choose Joyce only because she was a woman. Her background and experience definitely qualified her for the position.

3. **Third test:** Does an employer's affirmative action plan mean that female applicants for a job will always be preferred over male applicants? Such a plan would be invalid. But in this case, the agency's plan does not set aside a certain job category for women only. Men can still be hired and promoted in the Transportation Agency. Its plan for recruiting women is gradual and moderate.
4. **Conclusion:** This Court finds that Santa Clara County's affirmative action plan is proper. It does not violate the Civil Rights Act of 1964. Therefore, the judgment of the Court of Appeals is affirmed.

Voting with the minority, Justice Antonin Scalia wrote a dissenting opinion. His main points were these:

1. The Civil Rights Act of 1964 made it unlawful for an employer to discriminate against any person because of that person's race, color, religion, sex, or national origin. The majority's opinion in this case reverses the meaning of the law. It was supposed to guarantee that a person's sex would *not* be considered in an employer's hiring plan. But now the Court's decision guarantees that sex will often be considered.
2. Paul Johnson had worked in the Transportation Agency for 12 years while Diane Joyce had worked there for only 4 years. Johnson was clearly the leading candidate for promotion to the job of road dispatcher. He was passed over for one reason only: he was male.

JUSTICE ANTONIN SCALIA

REVIEW

A. Reviewing the Facts

By answering the questions below, you will better understand the facts in the case of *Johnson* v. *Transportation Agency*.

1. What did the Civil Rights Act of 1964 prohibit?
2. What is an affirmative action plan?
3. Why did Johnson think he was better qualified than Joyce for the job of road dispatcher?
4. Why did Johnson sue his employer, the Transportation Agency, instead of suing Joyce?
5. In the *Johnson* case, what was the verdict of the federal district court? What was the decision of the Court of Appeals?
6. Justice Brennan did not state directly whether Paul Johnson won or lost the case. But you can infer what happened. After the Supreme Court's decision, did Johnson replace Joyce as Santa Clara County's road dispatcher? Explain your answer.

B. Separating Fact from Opinion

Tell whether you think each statement below is a **fact** or an **opinion**. Explain your answers.

1. Agency officials who interviewed Diane Joyce in 1979 gave her a score of 73.
2. Johnson was better qualified than Joyce because of his longer record of employment.
3. The selection of Joyce was a case of unfair discrimination.
4. Three Supreme Court justices disagreed with the majority opinion of the Court.
5. The Transportation Agency's affirmative action plan was a good one.

C. Identifying Values

What *you* consider to be fair or unfair depends largely on your personal values. Do you think anyone was treated unfairly in the *Johnson* case? If so, who? If not, why not?

D. Explaining Your Decision

Imagine that you are a newspaper editor. The Supreme Court has just announced its decision in the *Johnson* case. Write an editorial explaining whether or not you think the Supreme Court made the "right" decision. Take into account Justice Scalia's dissenting opinion.

GOVERNMENT FOR EVERYBODY. Magazine covers like these show some of the problems that government is expected to solve. To what extent is it government's job to solve social problems? To what extent is it everybody's job?

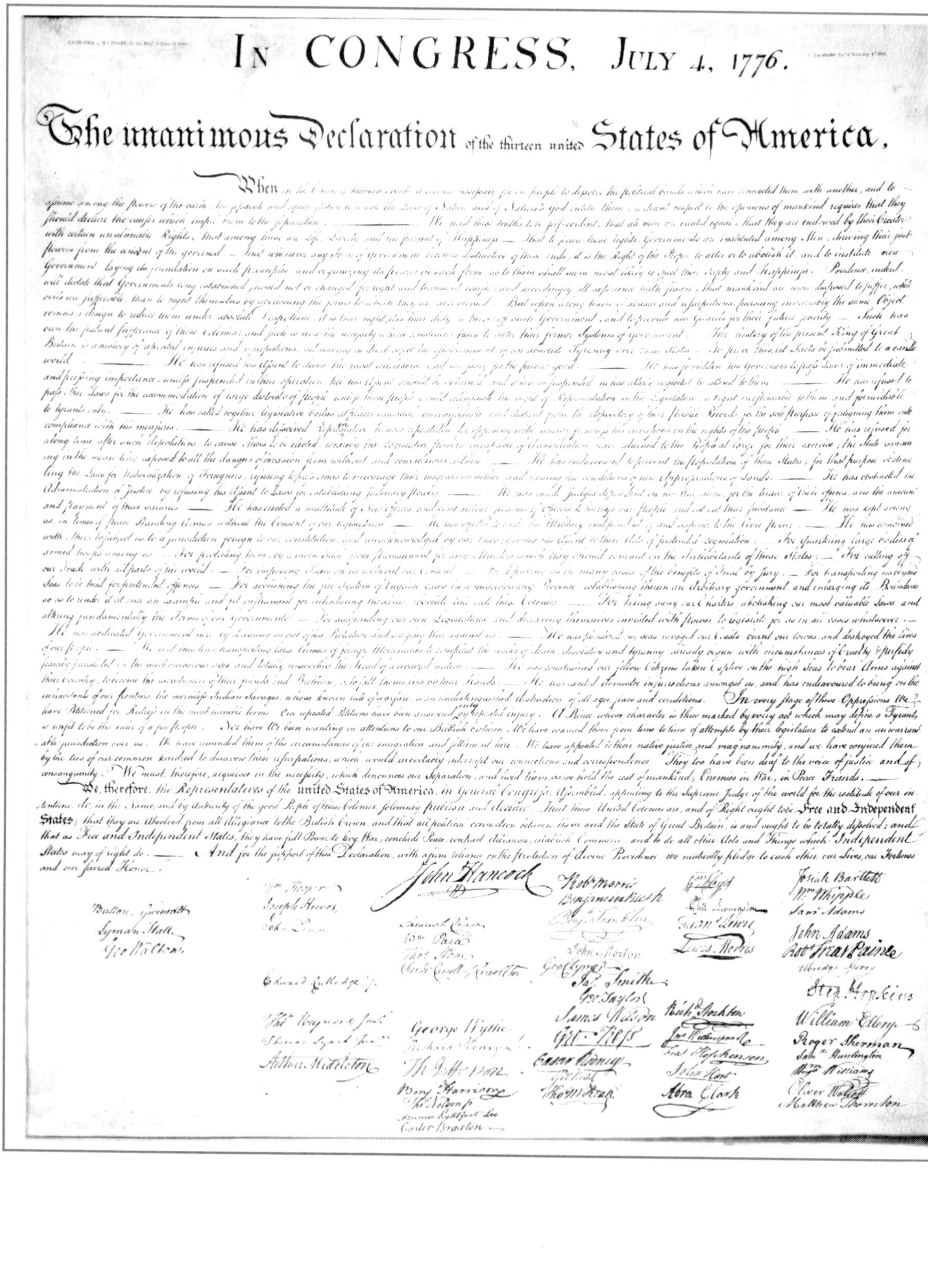

IN CONGRESS, JULY 4, 1776.

The unanimous Declaration of the thirteen united States of America,

When in the Course of human events, it becomes necessary for one people to dissolve the political bands which have connected them with another, and to assume among the powers of the earth, the separate and equal station to which the Laws of Nature and of Nature's God entitle them, a decent respect to the opinions of mankind requires that they should declare the causes which impel them to the separation. —— We hold these truths to be self-evident, that all men are created equal, that they are endowed by their Creator with certain unalienable Rights, that among these are Life, Liberty and the pursuit of Happiness. — That to secure these rights, Governments are instituted among Men, deriving their just powers from the consent of the governed, — That whenever any Form of Government becomes destructive of these ends, it is the Right of the People to alter or to abolish it, and to institute new Government, laying its foundation on such principles and organizing its powers in such form, as to them shall seem most likely to effect their Safety and Happiness. Prudence, indeed, will dictate that Governments long established should not be changed for light and transient causes; and accordingly all experience hath shewn, that mankind are more disposed to suffer, while evils are sufferable, than to right themselves by abolishing the forms to which they are accustomed. But when a long train of abuses and usurpations, pursuing invariably the same Object evinces a design to reduce them under absolute Despotism, it is their right, it is their duty, to throw off such Government, and to provide new Guards for their future security. — Such has been the patient sufferance of these Colonies; and such is now the necessity which constrains them to alter their former Systems of Government. The history of the present King of Great Britain is a history of repeated injuries and usurpations, all having in direct object the establishment of an absolute Tyranny over these States. To prove this, let Facts be submitted to a candid world. —— He has refused his Assent to Laws, the most wholesome and necessary for the public good. —— He has forbidden his Governors to pass Laws of immediate and pressing importance, unless suspended in their operation till his Assent should be obtained; and when so suspended, he has utterly neglected to attend to them. —— He has refused to pass other Laws for the accommodation of large districts of people, unless those people would relinquish the right of Representation in the Legislature, a right inestimable to them and formidable to tyrants only. —— He has called together legislative bodies at places unusual, uncomfortable, and distant from the depository of their public Records, for the sole purpose of fatiguing them into compliance with his measures. —— He has dissolved Representative Houses repeatedly, for opposing with manly firmness his invasions on the rights of the people. —— He has refused for a long time, after such dissolutions, to cause others to be elected; whereby the Legislative powers, incapable of Annihilation, have returned to the People at large for their exercise; the State remaining in the mean time exposed to all the dangers of invasion from without, and convulsions within. —— He has endeavoured to prevent the population of these States; for that purpose obstructing the Laws for Naturalization of Foreigners; refusing to pass others to encourage their migrations hither, and raising the conditions of new Appropriations of Lands. —— He has obstructed the Administration of Justice, by refusing his Assent to Laws for establishing Judiciary powers. —— He has made Judges dependent on his Will alone, for the tenure of their offices, and the amount and payment of their salaries. —— He has erected a multitude of New Offices, and sent hither swarms of Officers to harrass our people, and eat out their substance. —— He has kept among us, in times of peace, Standing Armies without the Consent of our legislatures. —— He has affected to render the Military independent of and superior to the Civil power. —— He has combined with others to subject us to a jurisdiction foreign to our constitution, and unacknowledged by our laws; giving his Assent to their Acts of pretended Legislation: —— For Quartering large bodies of armed troops among us: —— For protecting them, by a mock Trial, from punishment for any Murders which they should commit on the Inhabitants of these States: —— For cutting off our Trade with all parts of the world: —— For imposing Taxes on us without our Consent: —— For depriving us in many cases, of the benefits of Trial by Jury: —— For transporting us beyond Seas to be tried for pretended offences —— For abolishing the free System of English Laws in a neighbouring Province, establishing therein an Arbitrary government, and enlarging its Boundaries so as to render it at once an example and fit instrument for introducing the same absolute rule into these Colonies: —— For taking away our Charters, abolishing our most valuable Laws, and altering fundamentally the Forms of our Governments: —— For suspending our own Legislatures, and declaring themselves invested with power to legislate for us in all cases whatsoever. —— He has abdicated Government here, by declaring us out of his Protection and waging War against us. —— He has plundered our seas, ravaged our Coasts, burnt our towns, and destroyed the lives of our people. —— He is at this time transporting large Armies of foreign Mercenaries to compleat the works of death, desolation and tyranny, already begun with circumstances of Cruelty & perfidy scarcely paralleled in the most barbarous ages, and totally unworthy the Head of a civilized nation. —— He has constrained our fellow Citizens taken Captive on the high Seas to bear Arms against their Country, to become the executioners of their friends and Brethren, or to fall themselves by their Hands. —— He has excited domestic insurrections amongst us, and has endeavoured to bring on the inhabitants of our frontiers, the merciless Indian Savages, whose known rule of warfare, is an undistinguished destruction of all ages, sexes and conditions. In every stage of these Oppressions We have Petitioned for Redress in the most humble terms: Our repeated Petitions have been answered only by repeated injury. A Prince whose character is thus marked by every act which may define a Tyrant, is unfit to be the ruler of a free people. Nor have We been wanting in attentions to our Brittish brethren. We have warned them from time to time of attempts by their legislature to extend an unwarrantable jurisdiction over us. We have reminded them of the circumstances of our emigration and settlement here. We have appealed to their native justice and magnanimity, and we have conjured them by the ties of our common kindred to disavow these usurpations, which would inevitably interrupt our connections and correspondence. They too have been deaf to the voice of justice and of consanguinity. We must, therefore, acquiesce in the necessity, which denounces our Separation, and hold them, as we hold the rest of mankind, Enemies in War, in Peace Friends.

We, therefore, the Representatives of the united States of America, in General Congress, Assembled, appealing to the Supreme Judge of the world for the rectitude of our intentions, do, in the Name, and by Authority of the good People of these Colonies, solemnly publish and declare, That these United Colonies are, and of Right ought to be Free and Independent States; that they are Absolved from all Allegiance to the British Crown, and that all political connection between them and the State of Great Britain, is and ought to be totally dissolved; and that as Free and Independent States, they have full Power to levy War, conclude Peace, contract Alliances, establish Commerce, and to do all other Acts and Things which Independent States may of right do. —— And for the support of this Declaration, with a firm reliance on the protection of divine Providence, we mutually pledge to each other our Lives, our Fortunes and our sacred Honor.

John Hancock

Button Gwinnett
Lyman Hall
Geo Walton

Wm Hooper
Joseph Hewes
John Penn

Edward Rutledge

Thos Heyward Junr
Thomas Lynch Junr
Arthur Middleton

Samuel Chase
Wm Paca
Thos Stone
Charles Carroll of Carrollton

George Wythe
Richard Henry Lee
Th Jefferson
Benja Harrison
Thos Nelson jr
Francis Lightfoot Lee
Carter Braxton

Robt Morris
Benjamin Rush
Benja Franklin
John Morton
Geo Clymer
Jas Smith
Geo Taylor
James Wilson
Geo Ross

Caesar Rodney
Geo Read
Thos M:Kean

Wm Floyd
Phil Livingston
Frans Lewis
Lewis Morris

Richd Stockton
Jno Witherspoon
Fras Hopkinson
John Hart
Abra Clark

Josiah Bartlett
Wm Whipple
Saml Adams
John Adams
Robt Treat Paine
Elbridge Gerry
Step Hopkins
William Ellery
Roger Sherman
Samel Huntington
Wm Williams
Oliver Wolcott
Matthew Thornton

★ The Declaration of Independence ★

If you visit the National Archives Building in Washington, D.C., you can see the document pictured at the left. Displayed in a glass case, the Declaration of Independence is written in a beautiful script on a single piece of parchment. At the bottom are the signatures of 56 men who attended meetings of the Second Continental Congress in Philadelphia and voted for American independence from Great Britain.

The full text of the famous document is given below. If you compare this text with the original, you will notice these differences:

- ★ The modern text is presented in paragraph form, rather than the block form of the original.
- ★ Only a few words of the modern text are capitalized. For example, the original phrase, "Life, Liberty, and the pursuit of Happiness" appears here as "life, liberty, and the pursuit of happiness."
- ★ Next to the names of the signers, the states that they represent are listed in parentheses.

These editorial changes were made so that you can more easily read the document that serves as the birth certificate for our nation.

For an explanation of the main ideas in the Declaration of Independence, see Chapter 2, pages 33–34.

When, in the course of human events, it becomes necessary for one people to dissolve the political bands which have connected them with another, and to assume, among the powers of the earth, the separate and equal station to which the laws of nature and of nature's God entitle them, a decent respect to the opinions of mankind requires that they should declare the causes which impel them to the separation.

We hold these truths to be self-evident: That all men are created equal; that they are endowed by their Creator with certain unalienable rights; that among these are life, liberty, and the pursuit of happiness.

That to secure these rights, governments are instituted among men, deriving their just powers from the consent of the governed.

That whenever any form of government becomes destructive of these ends, it is the right of the people to alter or to abolish it, and to institute new government, laying its foundation on such principles and organizing its powers in such form as to them shall seem most likely to effect their safety and happiness. Prudence, indeed, will dictate that governments long established

should not be changed for light and transient causes; and, accordingly, all experience hath shown that mankind are more disposed to suffer, while evils are sufferable, than to right themselves by abolishing the forms to which they are accustomed. But when a long train of abuses and usurpations, pursuing invariably the same object, evinces a design to reduce them under absolute despotism, it is their right, it is their duty, to throw off such government, and to provide new guards for their future security.

Such has been the patient sufferance of these colonies; and such is now the necessity which constrains them to alter their former systems of government. The history of the present king of Great Britain is a history of repeated injuries and usurpations, all having in direct object the establishment of an absolute tyranny over these states. To prove this, let facts be submitted to a candid world:

He has refused to assent to laws the most wholesome and necessary for the public good.

He has forbidden his governors to pass laws of immediate and pressing importance unless suspended in their operation till his assent should be obtained; and, when so suspended, he has utterly neglected to attend to them.

He has refused to pass other laws for the accommodation of large districts of people unless those people would relinquish the right of representation in the legislature, a right inestimable to them and formidable to tyrants only.

He has called together legislative bodies at places unusual, uncomfortable, and distant from the depository of their public records, for the sole purpose of fatiguing them into compliance with his measures.

He has dissolved representative houses repeatedly for opposing with manly firmness his invasions on the rights of the people.

He has refused for a long time, after such dissolutions, to cause others to be elected; whereby the legislative powers, incapable of annihilation, have returned to the people at large for their exercise; the state remaining, in the meantime, exposed to all the dangers of invasion from without and convulsions within.

He has endeavoured to prevent the population of these states; for that purpose obstructing the laws for naturalization of foreigners, refusing to pass others to encourage their migrations hither, and raising the conditions of new appropriations of lands.

He has obstructed the administration of justice by refusing his assent to laws for establishing judiciary powers.

He has made judges dependent on his will alone for the tenure of their offices and the amount and payment of their salaries.

He has erected a multitude of new offices, and sent hither swarms of officers to harass our people and eat out their substance.

He has kept among us, in times of peace, standing armies, without the consent of our legislatures.

He has affected to render the military independent of and superior to the civil power.

He has combined with others to subject us to a jurisdiction foreign to our constitution and unacknowledged by our laws; giving his assent to their acts of pretended legislation:

For quartering large bodies of armed troops among us;

For protecting them, by a mock trial, from punishment for any murders which they should commit on the inhabitants of these states;

For cutting off our trade with all parts of the world;

For imposing taxes on us without our consent;

For depriving us in many cases of the benefits of trial by jury;

For transporting us beyond seas to be tried for pretended offences;

For abolishing the free system of English laws in a neighbouring province, establishing therein an arbitrary government and enlarging its boundaries so as to render it at once an example and fit instrument for introducing the same absolute rule in these colonies;

For taking away our charters, abolishing our most valuable laws, and altering fundamentally the forms of our governments;

For suspending our own legislatures, and declaring themselves invested with power to legislate for us in all cases whatsoever.

He has abdicated government here by declaring us out of his protection and waging war against us.

He has plundered our seas, ravaged our coasts, burnt our towns, and destroyed the lives of our people.

He is, at this time, transporting large armies of foreign mercenaries to complete the works of death, desolation, and tyranny already begun with circumstances of cruelty and perfidy scarcely paralleled in the most barbarous ages, and totally unworthy the head of a civilized nation.

He has constrained our fellow citizens, taken captive on the high seas, to bear arms against their country, to become the executioners of their friends and brethren, or to fall themselves by their hands.

He has excited domestic insurrections among us, and has endeavoured to bring on the inhabitants of our frontiers the merciless Indian savages, whose known rule of warfare is an undistinguished destruction of all ages, sexes, and conditions.

In every stage of these oppressions we have petitioned for redress in the most humble terms. Our repeated petitions have been answered only by repeated injury. A prince whose character is thus marked by every act which may define a tyrant is unfit to be the ruler of a free people.

Nor have we been wanting in attentions to our British brethren.

We have warned them from time to time of attempts by their legislature to extend an unwarrantable jurisdiction over us. We have reminded them of the circumstances of our emigration and settlement here. We have appealed to their native justice and magnanimity, and we have conjured them by the ties of our common kindred to disavow these usurpations, which would inevitably interrupt our connections and correspondence. They too have been deaf to the voice of justice and of consanguinity. We must therefore acquiesce in the necessity which denounces our separation, and hold them, as we hold the rest of mankind, enemies in war, in peace friends.

We, therefore, the representatives of the United States of America, in General Congress assembled, appealing to the Supreme Judge of the world for the rectitude of our intentions, do, in the name and by authority of the good people of these colonies, solemnly publish and declare; that these united colonies are, and of right ought to be, free and independent states; that they are absolved from all allegiance to the British crown, and that all political connection between them and the state of Great Britain is, and ought to be, totally dissolved; and that, as free and independent states, they have full power to levy war, conclude peace, contract alliances, establish commerce, and to do all other acts and things which independent states may of right do.

And for the support of this Declaration, with a firm reliance on the protection of divine Providence, we mutually pledge to each other our lives, our fortunes, and our sacred honor.

John Hancock (Mass.)

Button Gwinnett (Ga.)
Lyman Hall (Ga.)
George Walton (Ga.)
William Hooper (N.C.)
Joseph Hewes (N.C.)
John Penn (N.C.)
Edward Rutledge (S.C.)
Thomas Heyward, Junior (S.C.)
Thomas Lynch, Junior (S.C.)
Arthur Middleton (S.C.)
Samuel Chase (Md.)
William Paca (Md.)
Thomas Stone (Md.)
Charles Carroll of Carrollton (Md.)
George Wythe (Va.)
Richard Henry Lee (Va.)
Thomas Jefferson (Va.)
Benjamin Harrison (Va.)
Thomas Nelson, Junior (Va.)
Francis Lightfoot Lee (Va.)
Carter Braxton (Va.)
Robert Morris (Pa.)
Benjamin Rush (Pa.)
Benjamin Franklin (Pa.)
John Morton (Pa.)
George Clymer (Pa.)
James Smith (Pa.)
George Taylor (Pa.)
James Wilson (Pa.)
George Ross (Pa.)
Caesar Rodney (Del.)
George Read (Del.)
Thomas McKean (Del.)
William Floyd (N.Y.)
Philip Livingston (N.Y.)
Francis Lewis (N.Y.)
Lewis Morris (N.Y.)
Richard Stockton (N.J.)
John Witherspoon (N.J.)
Francis Hopkinson (N.J.)
John Hart (N.J.)
Abraham Clark (N.J.)
Josiah Bartlett (N.H.)
William Whipple (N.H.)
Samuel Adams (Mass.)
John Adams (Mass.)
Robert Treat Payne (Mass.)
Elbridge Gerry (Mass.)
Stephen Hopkins (R.I.)
William Ellery (R.I.)
Roger Sherman (Conn.)
Samuel Huntington (Conn.)
William Williams (Conn.)
Oliver Wolcott (Conn.)
Matthew Thornton (N.H.)

AN AMERICAN CALENDAR

Notable events in the history of American government and society

As a nation, we the people have much to celebrate. Going back into our history, we find that significant events occurred on almost every day of the calendar. As you scan each month of the AMERICAN CALENDAR below, you will find:

- days on which the U.S. Constitution was ratified by the 13 original states
- admission of states into the Union after 1789
- birthdays of U.S. presidents
- birthdays of famous Americans
- civic and political holidays
- battles won
- treaties signed
- the founding of major American institutions
- "firsts" in American history
- achievements in business, science, entertainment, and the arts

The calendar presents only a sampling of memorable events. By doing some research, you can easily discover others.

NOTE: Capital letters are used for (*a*) the names of states in entries related to ratification of the Constitution or admission to the Union, and (*b*) the names of presidents whose birthdays are given.

..sident Lincoln issues Emancipation Proclamation, 1863

2 GEORGIA ratifies Constitution, 1788

3 ALASKA is admitted to Union as 49th state, 1959

4 UTAH is admitted to Union as 45th state, 1896

5 Nellie Tayloe Ross becomes first woman governor (Wyoming), 1925

6 NEW MEXICO is admitted to Union as 47th state, 1912

7 MILLARD FILLMORE (13th president) is born, 1800

8 Americans defeat British at Battle of New Orleans, 1815

9 CONNECTICUT ratifies Constitution, 1788
RICHARD M. NIXON (37th president) is born, 1913

10 First great oil strike in Texas, 1901

11 Alexander Hamilton (first secretary of the treasury) is born, 1755

12 John Hancock (signer of Declaration of Independence) is born, 1737

13 Census Bureau reports that U.S. is more urban than rural, 1921

14

15 Martin Luther King, Jr., Day (born 1929)

16

17 Benjamin Franklin (author, inventor, patriot) is born, 1706

18 Captain James Cook becomes first European to visit Hawaiian Island, 1778

19 Robert E. Lee (Confederate general) is born, 1807

20 Inauguration Day (every 4th year)

21 Founding of Kiwanis International (community service organization), 1915

22

23 Congress establishes a Tuesday in early November as day for electing a president, 1845

24 Gold discovered in California, 1848

25

26 MICHIGAN is admitted to Union as 26th state, 1837

27 Samuel Gompers (labor leader) is born, 1850

28 Congress establishes the U.S. Coast Guard, 1915

29 KANSAS is admitted to Union as 34th state, 1861
WILLIAM McKINLEY (25th president) is born, 1834

30 FRANKLIN D. ROOSEVELT (32nd president) is born, 1882

31 Jackie Robinson (baseball player) is born, 1919
U.S. launches its first earth satellite, *Explorer 1*, 1958

FEBRUARY

1 National Freedom Day (to celebrate abolition of slavery by 13th Amendment, 1865)
2 Treaty of Guadalupe-Hidalgo ends Mexican War, 1848
3 First paper money is issued in colonies (Massachusetts), 1690
4
5 Roger Wiliams Day (to commemorate the arrival of Rhode Island's founder in America, 1631)
6 MASSACHUSETTS ratifies Constitution, 1788
RONALD REAGAN (40th president) is born, 1911
7 General Douglas MacArthur liberates Manila from Japanese occupation, 1945
Beatles begin first musical tour of U.S., 1964
8 Seven Southern states proclaim Confederate States of America, 1861
Boy Scouts of America is incorporated, 1910
9 WILLIAM HENRY HARRISON (9th president) is born, 1773
10
11 Thomas Edison (inventor) is born, 1847
12 ABRAHAM LINCOLN (16th president) is born, 1809
George Gershwin first performs *Rhapsody in Blue*, 1924
13 University of North Carolina is established as first state university in U.S., 1795
14 OREGON is admitted to Union as 33rd state, 1859
ARIZONA is admitted to Union as 48th state, 1912
15 Susan B. Anthony Day (to commemorate her birthday, 1820)
U.S.S. *Maine* is blown up in Havana Harbor, 1898
16 Founding of Elks Society (fraternal order), 1868
17 National Congress of Parents and Teachers is organized, 1897
18 Jefferson Davis is inaugurated as president of Confederacy, 1861
19 U.S. Marines land on Iwo Jima, 1945
20 John Glenn becomes first U.S. astronaut in orbit, 1962
21 Richard Nixon is first president to visit China, 1972
22 GEORGE WASHINGTON (general and 1st president) is born, 1732
23 W.E.B. Du Bois (black author and leader) is born, 1868
24 Winslow Homer (painter) is born, 1836
25 First U.S. aircraft carrier is launched, 1933
26 Segregation laws in transportation facilities are ruled unconstitutional by Supreme Court, 1962
27 Henry Wadsworth Longfellow (poet) is born, 1807
28 Republican party is formed at Ripon, Wisconsin, 1854
29 *Gone With the Wind* wins best movie award, 1939

ASKA is admitted to Union as 37th state, 1867
OHIO is admitted to Union as 17th state, 1803
2 Texas Independence Day (to celebrate Texas declaration of independence from Mexico, 1836)
3 FLORIDA is admitted to Union as 27th state, 1829
4 VERMONT is admitted to Union as 14th state, 1791
Thomas Jefferson is first president to be inaugurated in Washington, D.C., 1801
5 "Massacre" in Boston angers colonists, 1770
6 Alamo Day. Last Texas defender of the Alamo is killed, 1836
7
8 Oliver Wendell Holmes (Supreme Court justice) is born, 1841
9 *Monitor* and *Merrimac* (*Virginia*) fight first battle between ironclad ships, 1862
10 Daniel Boone begins blazing the Wilderness Road, 1775
11
12 Founding of Girl Scouts of America, 1912
13
14 Casey Jones (railroad engineer of legend) is born, 1864
15 MAINE is admitted to Union as 23rd state, 1820
ANDREW JACKSON (7th president) is born, 1767
16 JAMES MADISON (4th president) is born, 1751
Congress authorizes new coin—the nickel, 1866
17 St. Patrick's Day (first celebrated in Boston, 1737)
18 GROVER CLEVELAND (22nd and 24th president) is born, 1837
19 Earl Warren (14th chief justice) is born, 1891
20
21 Bird Day in the state of Iowa
22
23 Patrick Henry delivers speech ending "Give me liberty or give me death," 1775
24 Agriculture Day (a day of tribute to farmers and ranchers)
25 Maryland Day (to commemorate landing of first colonists in Maryland, 1634)
26 Robert Frost (poet) is born, 1874
27 U.S. Navy is established, 1794
28
29 JOHN TYLER (10th president) is born, 1790
Last U.S. troops leave Vietnam, 1973
30 Seward's Day in Alaska (to commemorate purchase of Alaska from Russia, 1867)
31 Commodore Matthew Perry negotiates treaty opening Japan to U.S. trade, 1854

APRIL

1 U.S. launches first weather satellite, *Tiros 1*, 1960
2 Juan Ponce de Léon discovers Florida, 1513
Congress establishes first U.S. mint, 1792
3 Pony Express is begun, 1860
4 Congress approves a U.S. flag with 13 stripes, 1819
NATO is established, 1949
5 Booker T. Washington (educator and author) is born, 1856
6 Admiral Robert Peary reaches North Pole, 1909
Congress declares war on Germany, 1917
7 Walter Camp (organizer of game of modern football) is born, 1859
8
9 Robert E. Lee surrenders to Ulysses S. Grant, 1865
10 Congress passes first patent law, 1790
11 Jackie Robinson (first black to play major league baseball) plays first game for Brooklyn Dodgers, 1947
12 First shots of Civil War fired at Fort Sumter, South Carolina, 1861
13 THOMAS JEFFERSON (3rd president) is born, 1743
14 President Lincoln is shot at Ford's Theater, 1865
Thomas Edison demonstrates his kinetoscope (movie machine), 1894
15 About 1,500 die as passenger ship, *Titanic*, sinks in Atlantic, 1912
16 Wilbur Wright (aviator and inventor) is born, 1867
17 Giovanni da Verrazano discovers New York Harbor, 1524
18 Paul Revere rides to warn of British attack, 1775
Hundreds perish in San Francisco earthquake and fire, 1906
19 First shots of Revolutionary War fired at Lexington, 1775
Running of the first Boston Marathon, 1897
20 Daniel Chester French (sculptor) is born, 1850
21 John Muir (naturalist) is born, 1838
22 Oklahoma Day (to commemorate opening of Oklahoma Territory to settlement, 1889)
Millions participate in first Earth Day, 1970
23 JAMES BUCHANAN (15th president) is born, 1791
24 Library of Congress is established, 1800
25 Opening day of San Francisco Conference that established the UN, 1945
26
27 ULYSSES S. GRANT (18th president) is born, 1822
28 MARYLAND ratifies Constitution, 1788
JAMES MONROE (5th president) is born, 1758
29
30 George Washington is inaugurated as first president under Constitution, 1789
LOUISIANA is admitted to Union as 18th state, 1812

549

cago, construction begins on rld's first skyscraper, 1884

in New York City, Empire State Building opens, 1931

2

3

4 Horace Mann (educator) is born, 1796

Rhode Island declares its independence from British rule, 1776

5 Alan Shepard is first U.S. astronaut in space, 1961

6 Peter Minuit buys Manhattan Island from Indians, 1626

7 German submarine sinks the *Lusitania*, 1915

Germany surrenders to end World War II in Europe, 1945

8 HARRY S TRUMAN (33rd president) is born, 1884

9

10 Transcontinental railroad is completed at Promontory Point, Utah, 1869

11 MINNESOTA is admitted to Union as 32nd state, 1858

12

13 Jamestown founded, 1607

U.S. declares war against Mexico, 1846

14 *Skylab 1* is first U.S.-manned space station, 1973

15 National Woman Suffrage Association is organized, 1869

16 Elizabeth Palmer Peabody (educator) is born, 1804

17 Running of first Kentucky Derby, 1875

Supreme Court declares school segregation to be unconstitutional in *Brown* decision, 1954

18

19 Boys Club of America is organized, 1906

20 Charles Lindbergh begins transatlantic flight to Paris, 1927

21 American Red Cross is organized by Clara Barton, 1881

22 Steamship leaves Savannah, Georgia, on first successful transatlantic voyage by steam, 1819

23 SOUTH CAROLINA ratifies Constitution, 1788

24 First message is sent over first telegraph line, 1844

Brooklyn Bridge is opened to traffic, 1883

25 Constitutional Convention opens in Philadelphia, 1787

26

27 Julia Ward Howe (author of "Battle Hymn of the Republic") is born, 1819

28

29 RHODE ISLAND ratifies Constitution, 1790

WISCONSIN is admitted to Union as 30th state, 1848

JOHN F. KENNEDY (35th president) is born, 1917

30 First daily newspaper is published in Philadelphia, 1783

National Association for the Advancement of Colored People (NAACP) is founded, 1909

31 Walt Whitman (poet) is born, 1819

Flood destroys much of Johnstown, Pennsylvania, 1889

JUNE

1 KENTUCKY is admitted to Union as 15th state, 1792
TENNESSEE is admitted to Union as 16th state, 1796
2
3 Japanese navy suffers first defeat of Pacific war at the Battle of Midway, 1942
4 Assembly of first Ford automobile is completed, 1896
5
6 D-Day: Allied forces land on beaches in Normandy to begin liberation of France, 1944
7
8 Frank Lloyd Wright (architect) is born, 1867
9
10 Founding of Alcoholics Anonymous, 1935
11 Jeannette Rankin (first woman member of Congress) is born, 1880
12 GEORGE BUSH (41st president) is born, 1924
13
14 Group of Californians proclaim California's independence from Mexico, 1846
15 ARKANSAS is admitted to Union as 25th state, 1836
Law of Congress makes all Indians U.S. citizens, 1924
16
17 American revolutionaries fight Battle of Bunker Hill, 1775
18 Sally Ride becomes first U.S. woman astronaut in space, 1983
19 First recorded baseball game in history is played at Hoboken, New Jersey, 1847
20 WEST VIRGINIA is admitted to Union as 35th state, 1863
21 NEW HAMPSHIRE ratifies Constitution, 1788
22 Congress establishes U.S. Department of Justice, 1870
23
24 Americans defeat Spaniards in battle for San Juan, Puerto Rico, 1898
25 VIRGINIA ratifies Constitution, 1788
George Custer and his men die at Little Big Horn, 1876
26 First presidential wedding takes place, as John Tyler marries Julia Gardiner, 1845
27 President Truman orders U.S. forces to Korea, 1950
28
29 Signing of Federal Highway Act inaugurates interstate highway system, 1956
30 Margaret Mitchell publishes *Gone With the Wind*, 1936

JULY

1 First adhesive U.S. postage stamps are placed on sale, 1847
2 President Garfield is shot by assassin, 1881
3 IDAHO is admitted to Union as 43rd state, 1890
4 Independence Day (to celebrate adoption of Declaration of Independence, 1776)
CALVIN COOLIDGE (30th president) is born, 1872
5 David Glasgow Farragut (naval hero of Civil War) is born, 1801
6 John Paul Jones (naval hero of Revolutionary War) is born, 1747
7
8 John D. Rockefeller (business leader) is born, 1839
9 Elias Howe (inventor of sewing machine) is born, 1819
10 WYOMING is admitted to Union as 44th state, 1890
11 JOHN QUINCY ADAMS (6th president) is born, 1767
Alexander Hamilton is fatally wounded in duel with Aaron Burr, 1804
12 Henry David Thoreau (author) is born, 1817
13 Congress enacts Northwest Ordinance, 1787
14 GERALD FORD (38th president) is born, 1913
15
16 Mary Baker Eddy (founder of Christian Science religion) is born, 1821
17
18
19 Women's Rights Convention meets at Seneca Falls, New York, 1848
20 U.S. astronaut Neil Armstrong is first to walk on moon, 1969
21 In Civil War, Union forces are defeated at first Battle of Bull Run, 1861
22 Emma Lazarus (poet) is born, 1849
23
24 Mormons enter Great Salt Lake Valley, Utah, 1847
25 Puerto Rico Constitution Day (to honor proclamation of Puerto Rico's constitution, 1952)
26 NEW YORK ratifies Constitution, 1788
27 U.S. Department of State is established by act of Congress, 1789
28
29
30 Settlers of Virginia elect first House of Burgesses, 1619
Henry Ford (auto maker) is born, 1863
31

AUGUST

1 COLORADO is admitted to Union as 38th state, 1876
2 Declaration of Independence is signed by members of Continental Congress, 1776
3
4
5 Mary Beard (historian) is born, 1876
6 First atomic bomb is dropped on Hiroshima, Japan, 1945
7 Congress passes Tonkin Resolution, authorizing presidential action in Vietnam, 1964
8
9 Richard Nixon is first president to resign from office, 1974
10 MISSOURI is admitted to Union as 24th state, 1821
HERBERT HOOVER (31st president) is born, 1874
11
12 Isaac Singer manufactures first continuous-stitch sewing machine, 1851
13 Annie Oakley (markswoman of legend) is born, 1860
14 Social Security Act is signed by President Franklin Roosevelt, 1935
V-J Day (signaling end of fighting in World War II, 1945)
15
16 First cable message is sent across Atlantic, 1858
17 Gold discovered in Yukon, beginning Alaska gold rush, 1896
18 Virginia Dare is first English child born in North America, 1587
19 Orville Wright (aviator and inventor) is born, 1871
WILLIAM CLINTON (42nd president) is born, 1946
20 BENJAMIN HARRISON (23rd president) is born, 1833
First regular radio broadcasting begins, 1920
21 HAWAII is admitted to Union as 50th state, 1959
22 Protestant church for Indians is founded in Massachusetts, 1670
23
24 Ratification of Nineteenth Amendment gives women the right to vote, 1920
NATO alliance is established, 1949
25
26 Woman's Equality Day (to commemorate final approval of Nineteenth Amendment, 1920)
27 LYNDON JOHNSON (36th president) is born, 1908
28 Edwin Drake strikes oil in Titusville, Pennsylvania, 1859
Martin Luther King, Jr., leads civil rights demonstration in Washington, D.C., 1963
29 John Locke (British philosopher) is born, 1632
30
31

SEPTEMBER

1
2 Japanese officials sign surrender on U.S. battleship *Missouri*, 1945
3 Signing of Treaty of Paris ends Revolutionary War, 1783
4 Coast-to-coast TV broadcasting is begun, 1951
5 Harriet Wilson is first black writer to publish a novel in U.S., 1859
6 President McKinley is shot by an assassin, 1901
7 Dutch surrender Manhattan to British naval force, 1664
8 Spaniards settle St. Augustine, Florida, 1565
9 CALIFORNIA is admitted to Union as 31st state, 1850
10 U.S. fleet defeats British in Battle of Lake Erie, 1813
11 William Sidney Porter (writer of "O. Henry" short stories) is born, 1862
12
13
14 National Anthem Day (to honor writing of the verses of "The Star Spangled Banner," 1814)
15 WILLIAM HOWARD TAFT (27th president) is born, 1857
16 Cherokee Strip Day (to commemorate great land rush in Oklahoma, 1893)
17 Citizenship Day (to celebrate signing of Constitution in Philadelphia, 1787)
18 First edition of *New York Times* is printed, 1851
19 George Washington's Farewell Address is published in a Philadelphia newspaper, 1796
20 Slave trade in U.S. is abolished in Washington, D.C., 1850
21
22 American patriot Nathan Hale is executed by British, 1776
23
24 John Marshall (4th chief justice of Supreme Court) is born, 1755
25 William Faulkner (novelist) is born, 1897
26
27 Samuel Adams (patriot and revolutionary) is born, 1722
28 A woman is arrested in New York City for smoking a cigarette in public, 1904
29
30

OCTOBER

1 JIMMY CARTER (39th president) is born, 1924
2
3
4 RUTHERFORD B. HAYES (19th president) is born, 1822
5 CHESTER A. ARTHUR (21st president) is born, 1829
6 First talking motion picture premieres in New York movie theater, 1927
7
8 In Chicago, fire destroys much of the city, 1871
9 Leif Ericson Day (to commemorate landing of Norsemen in New England, 1000)
10
11 Eleanor Roosevelt (humanitarian) is born, 1884
12 Columbus Day (to celebrate sighting of American land on Christopher Columbus's first voyage, 1492)
13 First World Series is won by Boston Red Sox, 1903
14 DWIGHT EISENHOWER (34th president) is born, 1890
15 British general John Burgoyne surrenders at Saratoga, 1777
16 Use of anesthesia is demonstrated for first time, 1847
17
18
19 British general Cornwallis surrenders at Yorktown, Virginia, 1781
20
21
22
23
24 United Nations Day (to commemorate founding of United Nations, 1945)
25 Thanksgiving Day in Virgin Islands (to celebrate end of hurricane season)
26
27 THEODORE ROOSEVELT (26th president) is born, 1858
28 Eli Whitney applies for patent on cotton gin, 1793
29 National Organization for Women (NOW) is organized, 1966
30 JOHN ADAMS (2nd president) is born, 1735
31 NEVADA is admitted to Union as 36th state, 1864

NOVEMBER

1 JAMES POLK (11th president) is born, 1795
WARREN G. HARDING (29th president) is born, 1865
2 NORTH DAKOTA and SOUTH DAKOTA are both admitted to Union as 39th and 40th states, 1889
3 Stephen Austin (Texas pioneer) is born, 1793
4 Will Rogers (humorist and author) is born, 1879
5
6 Rutgers beats Princeton at first intercollegiate football game, 1869
7
8 MONTANA is admitted to Union as 41st state, 1889
9
10 Founding of U.S. Marine Corps, 1775
11 Veterans Day (to celebrate signing of armistice ending World War I, 1918; and to honor men and women who have served in the armed forces).
WASHINGTON is admitted to Union as 42nd state, 1889
12 Elizabeth Cady Stanton (woman's suffrage leader) is born, 1815
13 Louis Brandeis (Supreme Court justice) is born, 1856
14 Robert Fulton (inventor) is born, 1765
15 Congress adopts Articles of Confederation, 1777
16 OKLAHOMA is admitted to Union as 46th state, 1907
17
18
19 JAMES GARFIELD (20th president) is born, 1831
President Lincoln reads Gettysburg Address, 1863
20
21 NORTH CAROLINA ratifies Constitution, 1789
Pilgrims draft Mayflower Compact, 1620
22 President Kennedy is assassinated, 1963
23 FRANKLIN PIERCE (14th president) is born, 1804
24 ZACHARY TAYLOR (12th president) is born, 1784
25 Andrew Carnegie (steel manufacturer) is born, 1835
26 World's first streetcar begins operation in New York City, 1833
27
28
29 Louisa May Alcott (author) is born, 1832
30 Samuel Clemens (author "Mark Twain") is born, 1835

DECEMBER

1 Civil rights movement begins as Rosa Parks refuses to give up bus seat to a white man, 1955

2 Monroe Doctrine is made public, 1823

John Brown is hanged for treason, 1859

3 ILLINOIS is admitted to Union as 21st state, 1818

4

5 MARTIN VAN BUREN (8th president) is born, 1782

6

7 DELAWARE is first state to ratify Constitution, 1787

Japan attacks U.S. naval base at Pearl Harbor, Hawaii, 1941

8 U.S. declares war on Japan, 1941

9 Founding of John Birch Society, 1958

10 MISSISSIPPI is admitted to Union as 20th state, 1817

Wyoming Territory is first to grant woman suffrage, 1869

11 INDIANA is admitted to Union as 19th state, 1816

12 PENNSYLVANIA ratifies Constitution, 1787

World's first motel opens in San Luis Obispo, California, 1925

13 First savings bank in U.S. is organized in Boston, 1816

14 ALABAMA is admitted to Union as 22nd state, 1819

15 Bill of Rights Day (to celebrate date that Bill of Rights went into effect, 1791)

16 Colonists protest tax on tea with Boston Tea Party, 1773

17 Wright Brothers Day (to celebrate first successful flight, 1903)

18 NEW JERSEY ratifies Constitution, 1787

Thirteenth Amendment abolishing slavery is ratified, 1865

19

20 South Carolina is first state to announce secession from Union, 1860

21 Pilgrims land at Plymouth, 1620

First crossword puzzle appears in *New York World*, 1913

22

23 Joseph Smith (Mormon leader) is born, 1805

24

25 Clara Barton (organizer of American Red Cross) is born, 1821

26 George Washington wins surprise victory at Battle of Trenton, 1776

27

28 IOWA is admitted to Union as 29th state, 1846

WOODROW WILSON (28th president) is born, 1856

29 ANDREW JOHNSON (17th president) is born, 1808

TEXAS is admitted to Union as 28th state, 1845

30

31 Ellis Island is opened as immigration center, 1890

Landmark Cases of the U.S. Supreme Court (1967–present)

A landmark is an event that marks a turning point. In our system of justice, a landmark case is one that has a particularly important effect on later cases decided by the courts. For example, you can understand why *Marbury* v. *Madison*, decided in 1803, is considered a landmark case. (Review page 337.) Within the last 20 years, other landmark cases have been decided involving such issues as abortion, capital punishment, discrimination, police methods, and public education. Twelve landmark cases from 1967 to the present are summarized below.

Ake v. *Oklahoma*, 1985

The facts: Glen Ake murdered two people in Oklahoma. Doctors examining him after his arrest found him to be mentally ill. But after six weeks of treatment, he was diagnosed to be of sound mind. He then stood trial and was convicted. During the time of the trial, Ake's request for psychiatric help was denied, and he was too poor to pay for such help himself.

The constitutional question: Does an indigent (poor) defendant with a history of mental illness have the right to receive psychiatric help (paid for by the state) while standing trial?

The decision: Yes, the trial of such a person cannot be fair unless psychiatric help is provided by the state.

Edmund v. *Florida*, 1982

The facts: At Earl Edmund's trial for murder, it was determined that Edmund had waited in a getaway car while his partner committed armed robbery. In the process, Edmund's partner killed two persons. Since Edmund had assisted in the killer's crime, he as well as the co-defendant were sentenced to death.

The constitutional question: Is it cruel and unusual for the death penalty to be imposed on a person who is only an accomplice to murder?

The decision: Yes, this is a case of cruel and unusual punishment prohibited by the Eighth Amendment. Therefore, Edmund's sentence was reduced to a long prison term.

In Re Gault, 1967

The facts: Gerald Gault, age 15, was a juvenile with a record of delinquency (actions that would have been considered criminal if he had been an adult). For one offense, he was detained by police, questioned in a juvenile court, and committed to an Arizona state industrial school (or reform school). In court, he had not been represented by a lawyer or formally notified of the charges against him.

The constitutional question: Does the right to due process of law, as guaranteed by the Fourteenth Amendment, apply to juveniles as well as adults?

The decision: Yes, juveniles are entitled to many of the same due process rights as adults. Gault's rights under the Fourteenth Amendment were violated.

Mississippi University for Women v. *Hogan*, 1982

The facts: Joseph Hogan was a man who wanted a degree in nursing. He sought admission to the Mississippi University for Women School of Nursing where the students were all female. His application was turned down. Hogan filed suit against the university, complaining that his sex was the chief reason for being rejected.

The constitutional question: Can a state-supported university maintain an institution strictly for women?

The decision: No, a school of nursing must be open to men as well as women because of the equal protection clause of the Fourteenth Amendment.

Plyer v. *Doe*, 1982

The facts: A Texas law denied free public education to children of illegal aliens (immigrants who enter the United States unlawfully). Lawyers brought suit on behalf of children excluded from Texas schools.

The constitutional question: Are children of illegal immigrants protected by the equal protection clause of the Fourteenth Amendment?

The decision: Yes, they are entitled to equal protection. Therefore, the Texas law is unconstitutional.

Roe v. *Wade*, 1973

The facts: A Texas law prohibited pregnant women from having abortions unless giving birth would place the woman's life in danger. A young woman prevented by the Texas law from having an abortion claimed that the law violated her constitutional rights.

The constitutional question: Do pregnant women have a right to protect their privacy under the U.S. Constitution?

The decision: Yes, the Fourteenth Amendment's guarantee of due process implies a right to privacy, which was infringed by the anti-abortion law of Texas. Therefore, no state can prohibit an abortion during the first three months of pregnancy.

Trammel v. *United States*, 1980

The facts: Otis Trammel was convicted of conspiring to import heroin into the United States. As one of the witnesses at his trial, his wife gave testimony that helped to convict him of the crime. Trammel argued that his trial was unfair because a husband and wife should not be allowed to testify against each other in a criminal trial.

The constitutional question: Is a trial unfair and therefore unconstitutional if one spouse testifies against the other?

The decision: No, it is not unfair. Trammel's conviction based upon his wife's testimony was proper.

United States v. *Nixon*, 1974

The facts: In connection with a burglary at the Watergate Apartments, seven White House officials were indicted by a federal court. The prosecutor in the case learned that President Nixon had taped his conversations with staff members. The prosecutor requested that the tapes be turned over to him as evidence. Nixon refused, claiming that as president he had "executive privilege" to prevent White House documents from being used in court.

The constitutional question: Does the president have the executive privilege to decide whether or not to cooperate with the Judicial Branch?

The decision: No, the executive privilege claimed by the president was not absolute. The tapes had to be handed over to the prosecutor.

United States v. Washington Post, 1971

The facts: The federal government had classified as "top secret" a military study of the Vietnam War. The *Washington Post* obtained a copy of the study and published large portions of it. The government filed suit against the newspaper to prevent it from publishing any more of the so-called Pentagon Papers.

The constitutional question: Does freedom of the press, as guaranteed in the First Amendment, apply to a newspaper that publishes "top secret" documents?

The decision: Yes, the *Washington Post* was acting within its constitutional rights in publishing the government study.

Walz v. *Tax Commission,* 1970

The facts: As a taxpayer in New York City, Frederick Walz insisted that religious organizations in the city should pay taxes on their property just as he did. He brought suit against the city's tax commission because it exempted churches and synagogues from paying taxes. In Walz's view, this was a violation of the idea of separation of church and state.

The constitutional question: Does a tax-exempt status for religious organizations violate the First Amendment guarantee of separation of church and state?

The decision: No, tax exemption for churches and synagogues is a means of ensuring the free exercise of religion.

Wyman v. *James,* 1971

The facts: Barbara James had received welfare payments from the state of New York. But she refused to permit a caseworker to visit her home, as required by the state's welfare laws. The state then cut off welfare payments. James sued, claiming that her rights under the Fourth and Fourteenth Amendments had been violated.

The constitutional question: Can a state law require home visits to be part of its procedure for administering welfare services?

The decision: Yes, New York's law was reasonable. Under the Fourth Amendment, James had a right to refuse the home visits. But the state was also entitled to cut off welfare payments as a result.

Morrison v. *Olson*, 1988

The facts: Alexia Morrison was a special prosecutor appointed under federal law to investigate possible acts of wrongdoing by officials in the Executive Branch. As a *special* prosecutor, she was independent of the authority of the attorney general and the U.S. Justice Department. The law providing for the appointment of special prosecutors had been enacted by Congress in 1978. President Reagan wanted Morrison to stop her investigation. He argued that the Ethics in Government Act of 1978 was unconstitutional because it gave Congress the power of interfering with the business of the Executive Branch.

The constitutional question: Can a special prosecutor investigate officials and programs of the Executive Branch as provided by the Ethics in Government Act?

The decision: Yes, Congress's law is constitutional. As a result of the decision, Morrison and other prosecutors continued to investigate reports of misconduct involving members of Reagan's administration.

Planned Parenthood v. *Casey*, 1992

The facts: A Pennsylvania law required women seeking an abortion to be provided with certain information at least 24 hours before the abortion is performed. It also required teenagers seeking an abortion to have the consent of either one parent or a judge. Five abortion clinics in Pennsylvania challenged the state's abortion law. They argued that the law was an unconstitutional infringement of a woman's right to privacy.

The constitutional question: Was the landmark case of *Roe* v. *Wade* (see page 561) still a valid interpretation of the Constitution—or should it be overturned?

The decision: According to the majority opinion, "the essential holding of *Roe* v. *Wade* should be retained and once again reaffirmed." On the other hand, the Pennsylvania law restricting abortions was also declared to be valid.

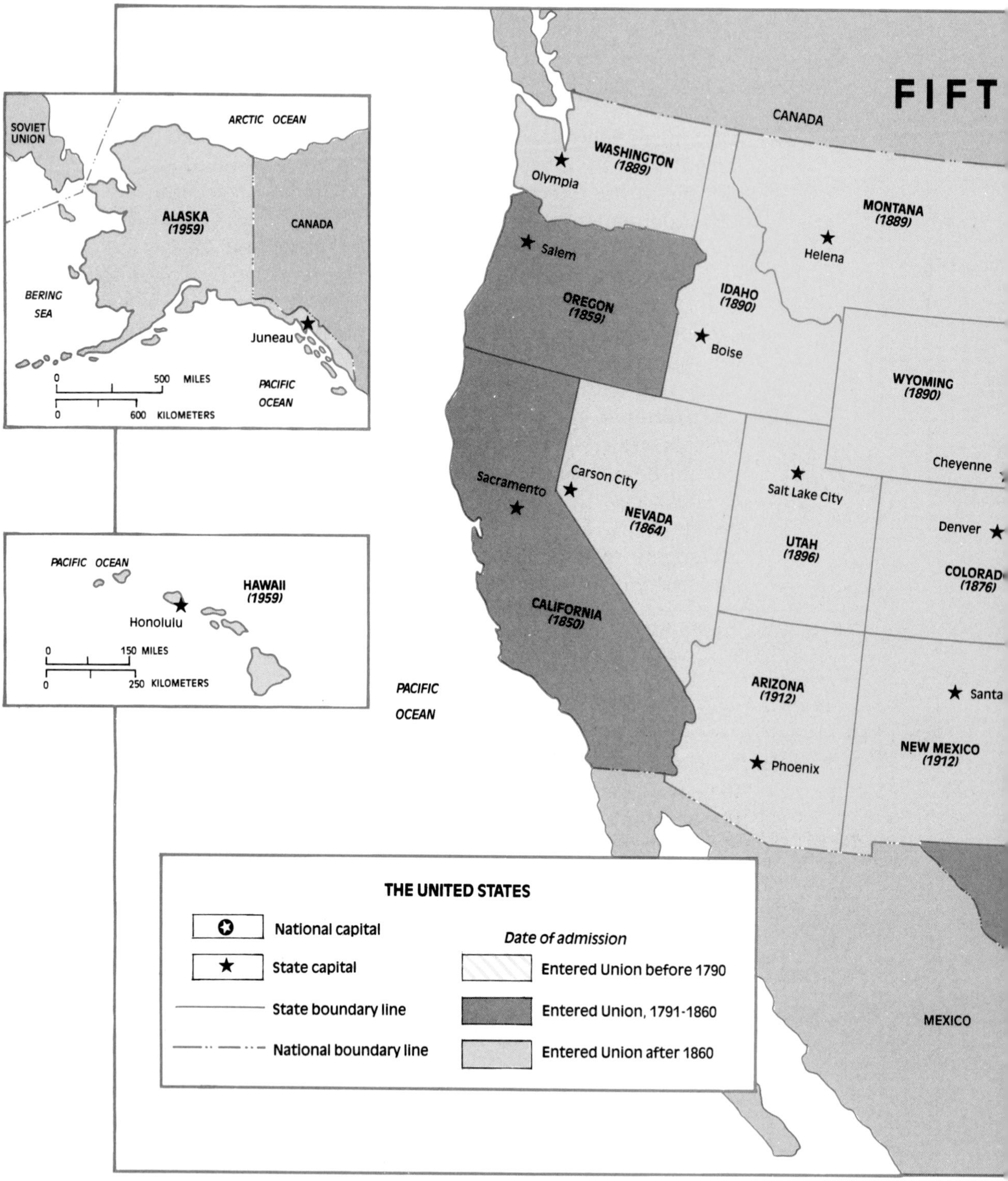
FIFT
CANADA
WASHINGTON (1889)
Olympia
MONTANA (1889)
Helena
Salem
OREGON (1859)
IDAHO (1890)
Boise
WYOMING (1890)
Cheyenne
Carson City
Sacramento
NEVADA (1864)
Salt Lake City
UTAH (1896)
Denver
COLORAD
(1876)
CALIFORNIA (1850)
ARIZONA (1912)
Phoenix
Santa
NEW MEXICO (1912)
PACIFIC OCEAN
MEXICO
SOVIET UNION
ARCTIC OCEAN
ALASKA (1959)
CANADA
BERING SEA
Juneau
PACIFIC OCEAN
0 500 MILES
0 600 KILOMETERS
PACIFIC OCEAN
HAWAII (1959)
Honolulu
0 150 MILES
0 250 KILOMETERS
THE UNITED STATES
National capital
State capital
State boundary line
National boundary line
Date of admission
Entered Union before 1790
Entered Union, 1791-1860
Entered Union after 1860

ATES OF THE UNION

DAKOTA
889)
Bismarck
DAKOTA
1889)
Pierre
RASKA
867)
Lincoln
KANSAS
(1861)
Topeka
OKLAHOMA
(1907)
Oklahoma City
EXAS
845)
Austin
MINNESOTA
(1858)
St. Paul
WISCONSIN
(1848)
Madison
MICHIGAN (1837)
Lansing
IOWA
(1846)
Des Moines
ILLINOIS
(1818)
Springfield
INDIANA
(1816)
Indianapolis
OHIO
(1803)
Columbus
MISSOURI
(1821)
Jefferson City
ARKANSAS
(1836)
Little Rock
LOUISIANA
(1812)
Baton Rouge
MISSISSIPPI
(1817)
Jackson
ALABAMA
(1819)
Montgomery
TENNESSEE
(1796)
Nashville
KENTUCKY
(1792)
Frankfort
WEST VIRGINIA
(1863)
Charleston
VIRGINIA
(1788)
Richmond
NORTH CAROLINA
(1789)
Raleigh
SOUTH CAROLINA
(1788)
Columbia
GEORGIA
(1788)
Atlanta
FLORIDA
(1845)
Tallahassee
PENNSYLVANIA
(1787)
Harrisburg
NEW YORK
(1788)
Albany
NEW HAMPSHIRE
(1788)
Concord
VERMONT
(1791)
Montpelier
MAINE
(1820)
Augusta
MASSACHUSETTS
(1788)
Boston
RHODE ISLAND
(1790)
Providence
CONNECTICUT
(1788)
Hartford
NEW JERSEY
(1787)
Trenton
DELAWARE
(1787)
Dover
MARYLAND
(1788)
Annapolis
WASHINGTON, D.C.
ATLANTIC
OCEAN
GULF OF MEXICO
0
MILES
400
0
KILOMETERS
600
13—STAR FLAG, 1777
20—STAR FLAG, 1818
48—STAR FLAG, 1912
50—STAR FLAG, TODAY

Cases and Candidates

Checking Your Decisions

Chapter 16: Interpreting the Bill of Rights

These were the Supreme Court's decisions in five cases.

1. *Engel et al.* v. *Vitale* (1962). By writing an official prayer for the public schools, the New York Board of Regents had violated the First Amendment guarantee of separation of church and state. Writing for the Court majority (7 of the 9 justices), Justice Hugo Black argued: "It is no part of the business of government to compose official prayers to be recited as a part of a religious program carried on by government."
   Review your decision, page 360.

2. *West Virginia State Board of Education* v. *Barnette* (1943). By a vote of 6 to 3, the Court decided that it had been mistaken in the *Gobitis* case. The Jehovah's Witnesses had a right to choose not to salute the flag. Freedom of worship, wrote Justice Robert Jackson , could be restricted "only to prevent grave and immediate danger" to the public. There was obviously no such danger either in the *Gobitis* case or the *Barnette* case.
   Review your decision, page 361.

3. *Tinker* v. *Des Moines School District* (1969). It was the Tinkers' right under the First Amendment to wear armbands to school. Writing for the Court majority, Justice Abe Fortas argued that the armbands had been used as a symbolic form of speech. Des Moines's school officials had wrongly suspended the students, violating their right to free speech.
   Two justices wrote dissenting opinions in the case (decided by a 7 to 2 vote).
   Review your decision, page 363.

4. *Hazelwood School District* v. *Kuhlmeier* (1988). By a 5 to 3 vote, the Court ruled in favor of the high school principal who had censored the student newspaper. Justice Byron White argued that school officials could control the style and content of student publications if, in doing so, an educational purpose was served. Teachers and principals could prevent publication of material that was "poorly written" or "unsuitable for immature audiences."
   Review your decision, page 363.

5. SKILLS CHECK: Interpreting a political cartoon, pages 364–365
The Supreme Court case to which the Herblock cartoon refers was *Branzburg* v. *Hayes* (1972). An investigative reporter for the Louisville *Courier-Journal* had refused to tell a grand jury the names of drug users whom he had interviewed for his story. The Supreme Court ruled, 5 to 4, that the First Amendment guarantee of freedom of the press did not apply in this case. Writing the majority opinion, Justice Byron White argued that to rule otherwise would be giving reporters special privileges in court that other citizens did not enjoy. In a dissenting opinion, Justice Stewart Potter said that the Court's decision would tend to "undermine the historic independence of the press."

6. *R.A.V.* v *St. Paul* (1992). By a vote of 5 to 4, the Supreme Court decided that St. Paul's ordinance was unconstitutional. Writing the majority opinion, Justice Antonin Scalia argued that the ordinance made religion, race, and gender the only grounds for punishing acts of hatred. Other types of hatred (political hatreds, for example) were ignored. Therefore, the majority concluded that St. Paul's law was discriminatory and improper.
Review your decision, page 374.

7. *Wisconsin* v. *Mitchell* (1993). By a unanimous vote, the Supreme Court ruled that Wisconsin's law for punishing hate crimes did *not* violate the First Amendment. Chief Justice William Rehnquist wrote the opinion of the Court. He accepted Wisconsin's argument that "bias-motivated crimes are more likely to provoke retaliatory crimes, inflict distinct emotional harms on their victims, and incite community unrest." Therefore, punishing hate crimes more severely than other crimes was justified.

Chapter 22: Your Decisions on Three Public Issues: Applying What You Know

The Senate contest described in pages 530–532 took place in New Jersey in 1982. Early in the race, MILLICENT FENWICK ("Mildred Fenton") was expected to win easily against her lesser-known opponent, FRANK R. LAUTENBERG ("Hank Arlenberg"). But Lautenberg's wealth enabled him to spend huge sums for political advertising. He won the election by a close vote: 1,005,000 to 943,000. After serving one term in the Senate, he was re-elected in 1988. Millicent Fenwick meanwhile had retired from politics.

GLOSSARY

The glossary words below are defined to help clarify their meaning and use in the text. Page numbers in *italics* following the definitions refer to the places in the text where the words first appear. Occasionally, a second page number refers to an expanded explanation of the term.

abolition doing away with something; used in U.S. history especially with doing away with slavery. *22*

act a bill, or proposal for a law, passed by a majority of lawmakers. *319*

affirmative action an effort to insure that qualified women and members of minority groups are given employment and promotion. *536*

alliance two or more nations that pledge to assist one another in defending against a common enemy. *455*

ambassador an official who represents his or her government in its dealings with another nation. *260*

amendments changes in a bill, a law, or a constitution. *73, 98*

appeals court a federal court that reviews the decision of a lower (trial) court. *333*

appoint to name someone to fill an office. *210*

appropriation money set aside for a specific use by an act of the legislature. *422*

arms race competition among nations to achieve military superiority by acquiring more and better weapons. *392*

assembly a public meeting or gathering; also the name commonly given to the larger house in a state legislature. *20*

attorney general the head of the executive department who is chiefly responsible for enforcing U.S. laws or state laws. *268*

autocracy a type of government in which one person (a monarch or a dictator) has all the power. *41*

autonomy the freedom of a political unit such as a city or a state to make important decisions of its own. *53*

bail the sum of money that an accused person may deposit with a court as security to get out of jail while awaiting trial. *373*

bicameral legislature a lawmaking body with two houses. *75, 291*

bill a proposal for a law to be considered by Congress or a state legislature. *92*

bill of attainder a law naming a person guilty of a crime without a trial. (Such laws are not allowed by the U.S. Constitution.) *89*

Bill of Rights the first ten amendments of the U.S. Constitution. (Their common purpose is to protect the American people from abuses of government power.) *78*

bond a document sold by the government as a means of borrowing money from citizens and investors. *429*

boss a powerful leader of a political party. *212*

budget a plan for spending money over a certain period of time, usually a year. *269, 420*

bureaucracy any large organization, such as a government department or agency, that has subdivisions, a chain of authority, and fixed rules. *414*

cabinet a group of department heads who meet regularly with the president or with a state's governor. *112*

campaign an organized effort carried out over a period of months or years; specifically, the efforts of a candidate and his/her supporters to win election. *169*

capitalism an economic system in which factories, businesses, and stores are run for profit by private owners. *54*

caucus a meeting of party members to decide policy or nominate candidates. *211*

censorship a government's practice of stopping certain ideas from being published or expressed. *362*

census an official count of the U.S. population conducted every ten years. *293*
chairperson the leading member of a committee who runs the committee's meetings. *298*
charter a document granting powers of self-government to a city or municipality; also a document giving legal status to a business organization. *500*
checks and balances a system by which each branch of government has the power to block or overrule the decisions of the other branches. *88*
chief executive the elected official who is chiefly responsible for enforcing the laws of a state (the governor) or a nation (the president). *259*
chief of state a national leader such as a king or a president who carries out ceremonial duties and acts as a living symbol of the country. *264*
circuit court a court in the federal system that has the power to hear appeals from trial courts. *342*
citizen anyone who is officially counted as a member of a nation or a state. *7, 147*
citizenship the status of being a citizen. *147*
civil case a dispute brought to court for settlement. *150*
civil service a government system whereby workers are hired because of their job qualifications, not on the basis of political party loyalty. *210*
cloture a means of preventing a filibuster (unlimited debate) on a bill. *316*
commander in chief the supreme commander of a nation's armed forces. (In the United States, it is the president.) *259*
commission a plan of local government in which legislative and executive powers are shared by a group of elected officials known as "commissioners." *507*
committee a small group of lawmakers assigned to consider bills of a special type. *112*
communism an economic system in which the government owns the factories, stores, and other resources in a nation and decides what each shall produce and sell. *54*
compromise to give up a part of one's original demands or desires in order to reach agreement on an issue. *74*
concurring opinion the written arguments of a Supreme Court justice who agrees with the decision of the Court's majority. *346*
confederate government a group of states or nations loosely held together by a central government that has only a few powers. *51*
conference committee a group of lawmakers drawn from both houses of Congress (or a state legislature). (Their goal is to resolve the differences between two versions of a bill passed by the two houses.) *319*
confirmation process by which the U.S. Senate approves a president's appointments to office. *260*
consent of the governed acceptance by the people in a democracy of the government ruling them. *33*
conservation the policy of carefully planning and controlling the use of natural resources so that they are not permanently lost or damaged. *386*
conservative someone who wants government's role in society and the economy to be strictly limited; also, someone who prefers that changes in policy be gradual, not rapid. *167*
constituents the residents of a district or state who are represented by a legislator from that same district or state. *285, 287*
constitution the set of basic laws and rules defining a nation's or state's system of government. *30*
consul an official sent to a foreign country to serve the interests of travelers and businesses from his or her own country. *453*
convention a large meeting of delegates from different states or districts. *65*
corporation a private business or other organization with a special legal status conferred by state law. *427*
council-manager system a system of local government in which legislative power belongs to an elected group (the council), which hires a professional manager to conduct city business. *506*
criminal case a matter involving the violation of a state or federal law. *150*

dark horse a candidate for election who, in the beginning, is little known and far behind the other candidates. *169*

debate a formal process for presenting arguments for and against a bill or a public issue. *77*

defendant the person at a trial who has been accused of some offense, injury, or crime. *150*

deficit the sum of money that government must borrow if its expenses for the year are greater than its income. *430*

delegated powers those rights that the federal government is free to exercise because they are specifically mentioned in the Constitution. *88*

delegates persons chosen to represent others at a special meeting. *32*

democracy a system of government in which the people (citizens and voters) have the final power. *41*

department a major division of the executive branch of government. *259, 268*

deterrence a nation's attempt to prevent nuclear attack by threatening to retaliate with nuclear weapons of its own. *462*

dictator a ruler who has total control over the military forces and the government of a nation. *39*

diplomacy the means by which nations communicate with one another and try to settle their differences peacefully. *439*

direct democracy a form of government in which the laws are made by the voters, not by their elected representatives. *48*

discrimination the practice of favoring one person or one group over another. *537*

disfranchised not permitted to vote. *173*

dissenting opinion the argument of a Supreme Court judge who disagrees with the Court's decision in a case. *346*

district courts federal courts that hold trials. *333*

domestic policy government's decisions about issues *within* the nation. *382*

domestic tranquillity the maintaining of law and order (one of the goals of the Constitution). *14*

double jeopardy the putting of an accused person on trial a second time after that person had been found innocent in the first trial. (This practice is prohibited by the Constitution.) *368*

due process of law a constitutional guarantee that persons under legal investigation receive fair treatment from government officials. *358, 365*

elastic clause a statement in the Constitution giving Congress the power to do what is "necessary and proper" for carrying out its other powers. *89*

Electoral College the group of politicians (several from each state) who are authorized by the Constitution to cast official ballots for president and vice president. *108*

electors a group elected for the sole purpose of casting official ballots for president and vice president. *92, 108*

empire a large territory made up of different lands and peoples and controlled by a single government. *10*

equal protection of the laws a guarantee in the Constitution entitling all citizens to the same treatment by government. *102*

excise tax a tax on the sale of specific items, such as gasoline, liquor, and cigarettes. *426*

Executive Branch the part of the U.S. government headed by the president and responsible for carrying out federal laws. *86*

executive power the ability of an official or group of officials to enforce and carry out the laws. *10*

***ex post facto* law** a law that would punish acts committed in the past, though they had been legal at the time. (Such laws are prohibited by the Constitution.) *90*

federal government the United States government. *54*

federalist or **federalism** a political system that gives significant powers to both a national government and state governments. *51*

felony a serious crime usually punished by a long jail sentence. *151*

filibuster a tactic of making long speeches on the Senate floor as a means of defeating a bill. *316*

fiscal policy the ways in which a government uses its spending and taxing powers to influence the economy. *432*

foreign policy one government's goals and methods in dealing with foreign governments. *382, 437*

free enterprise a system by which privately owned businesses compete for profits in the marketplace; another term for capitalism. *55*

front runner a candidate for election who appears to be ahead of the other candidates. *169*

gerrymandering drawing the boundaries of a voting district so that the political party in power has an advantage over rival parties. *295*

government a system for managing a community or nation and the leaders or lawmakers who control that system. *5, 6*

grand jury a group of citizens who decide whether there is enough evidence to indict (accuse) a certain person of a crime. *152*

grants-in-aid funds given to the states by the federal government. *483*

grievance a cause of complaint. *34*

habeas corpus an arrested person's right to appear before a judge. (If the judge finds no legal reason to detain the person, he or she must be released.) *375*

hearings meetings held for the purpose of obtaining evidence from different witnesses or experts. *312*

home rule the privilege granted to some communities to decide how their local governments will be organized. *500*

homesteading the policy of giving citizens the ownership of a previously unused property if they inhabit it for a certain period of time. *397*

hopper a box in which bills introduced in one house of a legislature are deposited. *306*

immigration the movement of people of foreign birth from their own country to an adopted country. *157*

impeachment to accuse an official of wrongdoing. (This step precedes trial and removal from office.) *87, 251*

inauguration a ceremony for beginning the term of office of a president, a vice president, or some other official. *109, 247*

income tax a tax collected on wages, salaries, tips, and other forms of personal earnings. *108, 427*

incorporate to form legally a business or community that has received a special charter from the state. *482*

independent regulatory agencies those agencies for regulating business that are *not* part of any Cabinet department. *405*

indict to formally accuse a person suspected of committing a crime. *152*

indirect democracy a system in which a small group of representatives make laws on behalf of the voters who elect them. *48*

initiative a procedure by which voters may propose a law without going through the legislature. *181*

intelligence the gathering of information. *444*

interest group people with a common political goal who try to persuade government to pass laws implementing their ideas. *70*

interstate commerce trade that is carried on across state lines. *310*

isolationism the policy of keeping the United States from involvement in the political conflicts of other nations. *455*

Joint Chiefs of Staff the top-ranking military officers who command the U.S. Army, Air Force, Navy, and Marines. *443*

Judicial Branch the part of government made up of courts. (Its function is to interpret laws in specific cases.) *86*

judicial power the ability of judges to decide court cases based upon their interpretation of the laws and the Constitution. *10*

judicial review the power of a federal court—and especially the Supreme Court—to determine whether the acts of Congress and the president are allowed by the Constitution. *337*

judiciary the court system. *332*

jurisdiction a court's authority to decide certain kinds of cases and not others. *333*

justice the ideal of settling disputes and determining responsibility for crime in a fair manner. *14*

left a reference to people who have liberal ideas. (See *liberal*.) *168*

Legislative Branch the part of government that has responsibility for making the laws. *86*

legislative power the ability of certain officials to make laws for a city, a state, or a nation. *10*

legislature a group of elected officials who make the laws. *69*

liberal someone who thinks government should take an active role in promoting social and economic progress. Also, someone who favors rapid change. *167*

liberty the right to make free choices and to express opinions without fear of being arrested and punished. *15*

licenses privileges granted by the state to those who qualify to engage in a certain activity or profession. *482*

lobbies organized efforts by interest groups to influence the opinion and votes of lawmakers. *189*

lobbyist a person hired by an interest group to speak to legislators about bills that concern the group. *189*

logrolling an informal agreement between lawmakers that they will vote for the bill that each is most interested in. *322*

lower house the chamber in a two-house legislature that has more members than the other. *474*

majority part of a group that is more than half the total. *44*

majority leader someone chosen by members of the majority party to lead their lawmaking efforts. (The majority party is the one holding the most seats in the legislature.) *300*

mandate the overwhelming support of voters for a certain policy. *170*

mayor-council system a plan of city government in which the executive is an elected mayor and the legislature is an elected body of councillors or aldermen. *503*

media event an event staged by an interest group or candidate for the purpose of attracting publicity and news coverage. *199*

militia citizen-volunteers trained by the state to take up arms in an emergency. *259*

minority leader someone chosen by members of the minority party to lead their lawmaking efforts. (The minority party is the one that holds fewer than half the seats in the legislature.) *301*

misdemeanor a minor violation of the law that is punishable by a fine or a short jail sentence. *151*

moderate someone whose political opinions fall in between those of a liberal on the one hand and a conservative on the other. *168*

monarchy a system of government in which members of one family inherit the power to make and enforce the nation's laws. *10*

municipality any city or town that the state permits to be self-governing. *498*

nation a people with common customs whose government has sovereign control over a certain territory. *7*

national debt the total sum of money owed by the federal government. *429*

naturalization the process by which an immigrant to the United States may become a U.S. citizen. *157*

nominate to name someone as a candidate for office; to select a party member to be that party's candidate for election. *208*

oligarchy a form of government in which power is held by a small, privileged group. *45*

opinion poll a survey consisting of carefully worded questions used to find out what people think on selected issues. *195*

ordinance a law passed by a local government. *504*

original jurisdiction the authority possessed by a court to hear and decide a case first, not an appeal from another court. *334*

override the ability of Congress or a state legislature to pass a bill a second time after the executive vetoes (or rejects) it. *87*

pardon a decision of the governor or the president to stop criminal proceedings against an accused person or to free a prisoner. *260*

Parliament the group of officials who make laws for Great Britain and also elect the British prime minister. *26*

parliamentary government a government in which the legislature (parliament) chooses the chief executive (prime minister). *48*

patent a document that grants an inventor exclusive rights to his or her invention for a certain number of years. *388*

patronage the government jobs that a winning candidate may give to supporters and other party members. *210*
petit jury a group citizens, usually 12 in number, who reach a verdict (decision) at a trial after listening to evidence. *152*
pigeonhole to kill a bill in committee by laying it aside and never considering it. *315*
plaintiff the person at a trial who claims to have been injured in some way. *150*
platform a political party's declaration of what it stands for on a number of issues. *220*
plurality a higher number of votes given to one candidate than to any other. *44*
pocket veto a president's way of defeating an act of Congress by taking no action on it until after Congress adjourns. (This method can be used only within the last ten days that Congress is in session.) *320*
political action committee (PAC) an organization formed by a group of citizens to raise money for a candidate's campaign. *191*
political party an organization whose members help one another to win elections and shape government policy. *44*
politics the process of deciding who gets to run the government and make its laws. *7*
polling place a building where people come to vote on Election Day. *170*
pork barrel projects construction projects authorized by Congress that involve spending federal money in local areas. *323*
power of the purse the supremely important power of a legislature to decide the kinds and amounts of taxes to be collected. *26*
Preamble the first paragraph of the Constitution. *13, 14*
presidential government a government in which the head of state is elected by popular vote (or electors representing the voters). *48*
president pro tempore an officer of the Senate who presides when the vice president is absent. *298*
primary an election by party members to determine (1) who will be the candidates of the party and (2) what delegates will be sent to the party's state or national convention. *212*
progressive tax any tax that takes more from high-income people than from low-income people. *426*
propaganda messages that are intended to influence people's opinions. *199*
property tax a tax collected on the value of lands, buildings, and major articles of property. *154*
prosecutor an attorney employed by the state to prove in court that an accused person is guilty of a certain crime; a district attorney. *151*
public opinion what people think about candidates, political issues, and other matters. *193*
public policy a government's decisions on important issues of the day. *40*

quorum the number of legislators who must be present in a chamber in order to conduct official business. *318*

random sample a small group of people selected in such a way that their views on an issue accurately represent the views of a much larger group. *195*
rank and file the voters who belong to a political party. *211*
ratify to vote in favor of an amendment or a treaty. *77*
reapportionment the changing of the boundaries of voting districts in order to allow for changes in population. *293*
recall a special election to decide whether or not a state official is to be removed from office. *181*
referendum a special election on a proposed law so that voters (not legislators) can either adopt or reject it. *181*
registration the process of signing up to vote and thus qualifying to participate in an election. *173*
regressive tax any tax that takes proportionately more from low-income people than from high-income people. *426*
regulation a rule enforced by a government agency. *10*
republic a nation whose laws are made by representatives elected by a popular vote. *44*
reserved powers the powers belonging to a state government. *89*

revenues taxes and other money received by government as income. *382*

rider an amendment to a bill that has little to do with the main subject of the bill. *324*

right a reference to people who have conservative ideas on political issues. (See *conservative.*) *168*

rights powers guaranteed to all citizens that cannot legally be taken away by government. *28, 147*

sales tax a tax paid by consumers when purchasing certain products. (The government then collects the tax from the merchant or seller.) *154, 483*

search warrant a document signed by a judge authorizing the police to search someone's property for evidence of a crime. *366*

segregation a practice (now illegal) of providing separate schools and other public facilities for whites and blacks. *331*

self-incrimination the making of any statement by an arrested or accused person that makes the person appear to be guilty of a crime. *369*

seniority a system for awarding positions of leadership to members of Congress who have served the greatest number of terms. *299*

separation of powers the division of a government into three main parts or branches: a legislative branch, an executive branch, and a judicial branch. *86*

session the period of time during which a legislature is meeting or a court is sitting. *301*

socialism an economic and political system in which certain industries are managed by the government while others are run for profit by competing businesses. *54*

Social Security system a federal program that pays benefits (monthly checks) to retired and disabled workers. *218*

sovereign the power of a completely independent nation to run its own affairs. *8*

speaker of the House the presiding officer of the U.S. House of Representatives or of the lower house of a state legislature. *297*

standing committee a committee (group of lawmakers) that continues its work from one term of the legislature to the next. *312*

subsidy money or special services given by government to assist farms and businesses in carrying out some public purpose. *387*

suffrage voting rights. *102*

suffragists citizens who, years ago, campaigned for the right of women to vote. *103*

suit a court case. *108, 150*

summons an order to appear in court. *150*

tariff a tax on imports (foreign goods) as they enter a country. *383*

tax any sum of money that citizens are required by law to pay to the government. *20, 154*

third party a U.S. political party that is smaller than the two major parties. *224*

toleration willingness to accept others who have different beliefs. *27*

treason the crime of betraying one's country. *161*

treaty a written agreement between the governments of two or more nations. *260*

tyrants government leaders who misuse their power for their own ends. *19*

unconstitutional not allowed by the constitution. *30*

unicameral legislature a lawmaking body with only one house. *75*

union a nation that is united under one government. *14*

unitary government a political system in which state and local governments are tightly controlled by a strong national government. *51*

upper house the chamber in a two-house legislature that has fewer members than the other. *474*

verdict a jury's decision at the end of a trial. *153*

veto a chief executive's decision to reject an act of the legislature. *87*

welfare whatever is good for society as a whole. *12, 13*

whip a legislative leader who tries to persuade members of his or her party to vote a certain way on a bill. *301*

writ any court document ordering that a certain action be taken. *337*

zoning ordinances the practice by local governments of setting aside parts of a city or township for special uses. *521*

INDEX

Key to words in italics

Const. text of the U.S. Constitution
illus. all illustrations except maps (charts, graphs, tables, cartoons, picture captions)
map maps

Note: A topic that includes a reference to the Constitution (*Const.*) enables you to find information about that topic in two places: (a) the regular chapters of this book and (b) the Constitution itself. For example, here is the index entry for the U.S. Army:

Army, U.S., 442, 443; *Const.* 120, 124

In other words, a chapter of the text discusses the U.S. Army on pages 442 and 443. Clauses of the Constitution concerning the U.S. Army are on pages 120 and 124.

ACKNOWLEDGMENTS

Art and Design

Cover design: Lee Rosenberg • Cover photograph: © 1989 Jay Maisel • Maps, graphs, and charts: Corinne Hekker Graphics • Cartoon Corners: Erikson/Dillon Art Service • Photo researcher: Anne Hobart

Photographs and Prints

Billy E. Barnes Photos: 146 (bottom), 165, 481 • The Bettmann Archive: 2 (b, c, e), 21 (right), 27, 29, 31 (left, center), 33 (left), 34, 40, 41 (top), 43 (left), 62 (a, c), 71 (left, right), 73, 77, 84, 92, 96, 104, 113, 158, 171 (left), 178 (center, right), 198 (right), 212, 218, 221 (Jefferson, Adams, Jackson, Lincoln, T. Roosevelt), 222 (Truman), 226 (top), 230 (c), 249 (right), 250 (bottom), 251, 252, 258, 259, 265 (right), 269, 304, 338, 343, 402 (left), 410, 411, 449 (World War II), 468 (bottom), 540 • California State Capitol, Museum Volunteer Association: 470 (top right) • Bob Daemmrich Photos: 513, 514 • Jay Dorin/Southern Stock Photos: 523 • Federal Bureau of Investigation: 385 • Food and Drug Administration: 413 • Herblock Cartoons: — from HERBLOCK ON ALL FRONTS (New American Library, 1980): 192, 365 • Jerry Howard/Positive Images: 509 • Steven L. Jantzen: 14, 55, 70, 81, 90, 144 (a), 146 (top right), 148, 155, 164, 169, 196, 201, 219, 262 (right), 280, 285, 288, 289, 295, 307, 309, 317, 323, 360, 380, 383, 394, 408 (top right, bottom), 416, 417 (right), 429, 454, 482 (left), 483, 488, 503, 504, 505, 507, 510, 528, 535, 539 • K. Jewell: 306 • Kansas State Historical Society, Topeka: 103 (right) • Tony Kelly (Photo Researchers, Inc.): 386 • King Features Syndicate (Jim Borgman cartoon): 446, reprinted with special permission • Library of Congress: 2 (a, f, g), 4, 6 (both), 11, 13, 20, 21, 22, 24, 31 (right), 33 (right), 38, 43 (right), 62, (d, e, f, g), 64, 66, 68, 71 (center), 89, 93, 102, 103 (left), 130, 146 (top left), 168, 171 (right), 172, 174 (left), 178 (left), 190, 198 (left), 199, 200 (right), 202, 206, 208, 221 (Clay, Douglas, Wilson), 222 (Carter) 226 (bottom), 230 (a, b, d, e, h), 232, 240, 248 (Carter), 250 (top), 256, 265 (left), 266, 273, 315, 318, 319, 321, 325 (right), 328 (b), 332, 336, 341, 346, 348, 349, 350, 358, 363, 367, 384, 398 (bottom), 436, 438, 448, 449 (Mexican War, Civil War, Spanish-American War, World War I), 450 (left), 451, 470 (bottom), 502, 538 • Maine Office of Tourism: 468 (top) • John P. G. McKenzie (Photo Researchers, Inc.): 470 (top left) • The Medical Society of New Jersey: 189 • Movie Star News: 144 (c), 153 • National Geographic Society: 347 • National Parks and Conservation Association: 191 • Princeton University: 67 • Reuters/Bettmann Newsphotos: 2 (h), 41 (bottom), 56, 88, 200 (left), 222 (top right), 225, 242, 244, 245, 248 (Clinton), 261 (right), 286, 441, 449 (Persian Gulf War), 450 (right), 458 • Rothco Syndication: 422 (Schwadron cartoon), 443 (Leed cartoon) • Joanna L. Stratton: 105 (right) • Swedish Information Service. Photo: Ulf Lodin: 2 (i) • Tribune Media Service (Jeff MacNelly cartoon): 520, reprinted by permission • UPI/Bettmann Newsphotos: 2 (a), 18, 23, 49, 62 (b), 80, 82, 105 (left), 110, 144 (b, d, e), 166, 174 (right), 179, 186, 203, 209, 222 (Dewey, Reagan; top right), 230 (f, g), 234, 249 (left), 261 (left), 262 (left), 264, 270, 275, 282, 308, 322, 325, 328 (a), 330, 339, 354, 355, 356, 362, 368, 389, 398 (top), 399, 402 (right), 403, 408 (top left), 426, 442, 449 (Korean War, Vietnam War), 456, 461, 477, 490, 496, 506, 519, 524, 537, 558 • U.S. Bureau of the Census: 388 • USDA-Forest Service: 15 (left), 378 (bottom), 417, 418 • USDA Photo: 387 • U.S. Department of Energy: 400 • U.S. Department of Health and Human Services: 393 • U.S. Department of Housing and Urban Development: 328 (c), 364 • U.S. Department of Transportation: 482 (right) • U.S. Navy Photo: 15 (right), 378 (top) • D. Wallmeyer, *Press-Telegram*, Long Beach, California: 370 • WIDE WORLD PHOTOS: 50, 241, 248 (Kennedy, Nixon, Ford, Johnson, Reagan, Bush), 347, 444 • World Bank: 51 (Kay Chernush), 460

Printed Material

Definitions of political terms. By permission. From *Webster's Ninth New Collegiate Dictionary* © 1988 by Merriam-Webster Inc., publisher of the Merriam-Webster ® dictionaries. Page 9. • Excerpt from Lilla Day Monroe, "An Autobiography of Lilla Day Monroe," unpublished manuscript. By permission of Joanna L. Stratton. Pages 103–104. • Excerpt from an article titled "Graying Armies March to Defend Social Security," April 29, 1985. By permission of *U.S. News & World Report*. Page 188. • Excerpts of two letters to *Time* magazine. Copyright 1986 Time Inc. All rights reserved. Reprinted by permission. Page 205. • Three excerpts reprinted from *Famous First Facts*, 4th edition. Copyright © 1933, 1935, 1950, 1964, 1981 by Joseph Nathan Kane. Copyright renewed © 1961, 1963, 1978 by Joseph Nathan Kane. Reprinted by permission of The H. W. Wilson Company, New York. Page 229. • Article from The Associated Press, January 26, 1988. By permission of The Associated Press. Pages 278–279. • Excerpt from "Republicans Face Long Odds in Protecting Senate Clout" by Chuck Alston, *Congressional Quarterly Weekly Report*, Feb. 6, 1993. Reprinted with permission of Congressional Quarterly, Inc., Page 303. • Excerpt from "Court Opens Way for Damage Suits Over Cigarettes," June 25, 1992. Copyright © 1992 by The New York Times Company. Reprinted by permission. Page 353. • Excerpts from *Plain Speaking: An Oral Biography of Harry S. Truman* by Merle Miller (Berkley Publishing Company, 1984). By permission of the Putnam Publishing Group. Pages 437–438. • Excerpts reprinted from THE WORLD ALMANAC AND BOOK OF FACTS, 1993 edition, copyright © Pharos Books, 1992, New York, N.Y. 10166. Page 466. • Excerpts from "Across the USA: News From Every State" column, Jan. 28, 1993. Copyright 1993, USA TODAY. Reprinted with permission. Pages 494–495.